DATE DUE

PRINTED IN U.S.A.

WITHDRAWN

Archaeology in America

Archaeology in America
An Encyclopedia

Volume 3
Southwest and Great Basin/Plateau

Francis P. McManamon, General Editor
Linda S. Cordell, Kent G. Lightfoot,
and George R. Milner, Editorial Board

GREENWOOD PRESS
Westport, Connecticut • London

Library of Congress Cataloging-in-Publication Data

Archaeology in America : an encyclopedia / Francis P. McManamon, general editor ; Linda S. Cordell, Kent
G. Lightfoot, and George R. Milner, editorial board.
    v. cm.
  Includes bibliographical references and index.
  Contents: v. 1. Northeast and Southeast — v. 2. Midwest and Great Plains/Rocky Mountains — v. 3.
Southwest and Great Basin/Plateau — v. 4. West Coast and Arctic/Subarctic.
   ISBN 978–0–313–33184–8 (set : alk. paper) — ISBN 978–0–313–33185–5 (v. 1 : alk. paper) — ISBN
978–0–313–33186–2 (v. 2 : alk. paper) — ISBN 978–0–313–33187–9 (v. 3 : alk. paper) — ISBN
978–0–313–35021–4 (v. 4 : alk. paper)
   1. United States—Antiquities—Encyclopedias. 2. Excavations (Archaeology)—United States—
Encyclopedias. 3. Historic sites—United States—Encyclopedias. 4. Archaeology—United States—
Encyclopedias. 5. Canada—Antiquities—Encyclopedias. 6. Excavations
(Archaeology)—Canada—Encyclopedias. 7. Historic sites—Canada—Encyclopedias. 8. Archaeology—
Canada—Encyclopedias. I. McManamon, Francis P. II. Cordell, Linda S. III. Lightfoot, Kent G., 1953– IV.
Milner, George R., 1953–
  E159.5.A68   2009
  973.03—dc22   2008020844

British Library Cataloguing in Publication Data is available.

Library of Congress Catalog Card Number: 2008020844
ISBN: 978–0–313–33184–8 (set)
        978–0–313–33185–5 (vol. 1)
        978–0–313–33186–2 (vol. 2)
        978–0–313–33187–9 (vol. 3)
        978–0–313–35021–4 (vol. 4)

First published in 2009

Greenwood Press, 88 Post Road West, Westport, CT 06881
An imprint of Greenwood Publishing Group, Inc.
www.greenwood.com

Printed in the United States of America

The paper used in this book complies with the
Permanent Paper Standard issued by the National
Information Standards Organization (Z39.48–1984).

10 9 8 7 6 5 4 3 2 1

Cover: Hikers climbing the ladder to Alcove House, Frijoles Canyon, at Bandelier National Monument. For a
related essay, see Tim Kohler, "Bandelier National Monument: The Development of Puebloan Agriculture
and Towns."

CONTENTS

About the Editorial Board and *About the Contributors* can be found in volume 4.

VOLUME 3: SOUTHWEST AND GREAT BASIN/PLATEAU

ENTRIES FOR THE GREAT BASIN/PLATEAU

Southwest Region

KEY FOR SOUTHWEST REGIONAL MAP

1. Apache Pass Battlefield
2. Agua Fria National Monument
3. Arroyo Cuervo sites
4. Bandelier National Monument
5. Betatakin
6. Canyons of the Ancients National Monument
7. Casa Grande Ruins National Monument
8. Cerro Juanaqueña
9. Aztec Ruins National Monument
10. Cienega Phase sites
11. Cline Terrace Platform Mound
12. Ventana Cave
13. El Camino Real National Historical Trail
14. Elden Pueblo
15. Galisteo Basin Pueblo sites
16. Gault
17. Homol'ovi Ruins State Park
18. Hovenweep National Monument
19. Kuaua Ruin, Coronado State Monument
20. Mesa Verde National Park
21. Three Rivers Petroglyph Site
22. Old Town
23. Palace of the Governors, Santa Fe
24. Palo Alto Battlefield National Historic Site
25. Pecos National Historical Park
26. Petroglyph National Monument
27. Lowery Ruins, National Historical Landmark
28. Pueblo Alto, Chaco Canyon, Chaco Culture National Historical Park
29. Pueblo Bonito, Chaco Canyon, Chaco Culture National Historical Park
30. Pueblo Grande Museum and Archaeological Park
31. Salinas Pueblo Missions National Monument
32. Second Canyon, Davis Ranch and Reeve Ruin
33. Sand Canyon Pueblo
34. Sunset Crater National Monument
35. Schoolhouse Point Mesa sites
36. Shabik'eschee Village, Chaco Canyon, Chaco CultureNational Historical Park
37. Snaketown
38. San Antonio Missions National Historical Park
39. Grasshopper Pueblo
40. Houghton Road
41. Marana Mound
42. Point of Pines
43. Paquimé (Casas Grandes)
44. Tumacacori National Historical Park
45. Tusayan Village site
46. Montezuma Castle National Monument
47. Wupatki National Monument
48. Walnut Canyon National Monument
49. Bat Cave
50. SU site
51. Gila Cliff Dwellings National Monument
52. Galaz, Swartz, and NAN Ranch Ruins
53. Lower Pecos River canyonlands and Amistad National Recreation Area
54. Bluff Great House
55. Salmon Ruin
56. Jemez Cave
57. Hawikuh
58. Awatovi
59. Cieneguilla battlefield
60. Fort Stanton
61. Pine Springs "Buffalo Soldiers" camp site
62. Lime Ridge
63. El Bajío
64. Keet Seel
65. Inscription House
66. Tonto National Monument
67. Tuzigoot National Monument
68. Naco
69. Lehner
70. Murray Springs
71. Tres Alamos

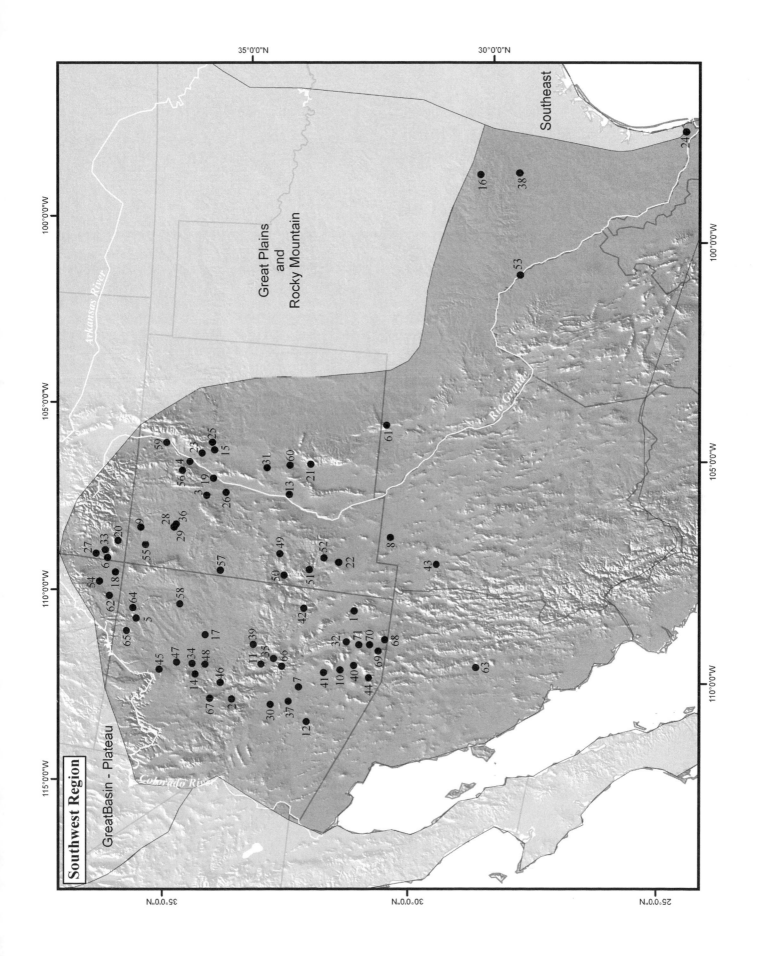

INTRODUCTION

This section of *Archaeology in America* includes essays about archaeological sites in the Southwest region of North America. The archaeological sites in the Southwest region are the best known among Americans. The first archaeological site set aside for preservation and protection by the federal government, Casa Grande Ruins near Coolidge, Arizona, and the first national park created for its archaeological value, Mesa Verde National Park in southwestern Colorado, both lie in this region. The Southwest is probably the area most associated with American archaeology by the general public.

For this encyclopedia, the Southwest region includes most of Arizona and New Mexico, plus portions of southern Utah and Colorado, and the northern portions of the Mexican states that border the United States—Sonora, Chihuahua, Coahuila, Nuevo Leon, and Tamaulipas. As with most of the regional boundaries used in *Archaeology in America*, the borders delimited here are not hard-and-fast. The eastern sliver of New Mexico and eastern third of Colorado, for example, are included in the Great Plains region, and much of western Utah falls within the Great Basin region. We have included in the Southwest region south Texas and sites related to the Spanish and Mexican colonization and settlement of that area during historic times. This arrangement keeps essays covering events and sites of the historic period in Arizona and New Mexico (e.g., Pecos, El Camino Real, Salinas Pueblo Missions, and Tumacacori) together with those of the same time and with related events in Texas (e.g., essays about the Spanish period missions of Texas and the nineteenth-century U.S.-Mexican war).

Physiographically, much of the Southwest consists of the high mountains and river valleys of the Colorado Plateau and, in the southern part of the region, the arid plains of the Sonoran Desert. Generally, the region is dry and mountainous, but local environments vary considerably, as described in an essay on the Southwest environment by Nash and Sheppard. In the Southwest rivers and streams (even some that run with water only seasonally) often were the focus of human settlement and activities. Examples include essays about ancient and historic sites along the San Pedro River in southern Arizona; in portions of the San Juan River drainage in New Mexico, Colorado, and Utah (e.g., sites along and related to Chaco Wash and the Aztec, Lowery, and Bluff sites); and the northern Rio Grande drainage in New Mexico (e.g., sites at Bandelier National Monument, Kuaua Pueblo, and Petroglyph National Monument).

Essays for this region cover the earliest recognized sites and time periods, dating from as early as 12,000 to 13,000 years ago onward (e.g., the earliest inhabitants and the Arroyo Cuervo sites, Ventana Cave, and Bat Cave). Of particular note are essays describing investigations and sites related to the earliest development of agriculture and village settlements in the region (e.g., early agriculture and related cultural developments, as well as the Cerro Juanaqueña site in northwest Mexico, Cienega phase sites near Tucson, and the Shabik'eschee Village and SU sites, both in New Mexico). Recent studies have pushed the evidence of early uses of domesticated plants and related changes in social and settlement patterns back hundreds of years.

Even more complex economic systems and cultural traditions developed later (from about AD 1000 onward) in the Southwest (e.g., the essay introducing the archaeology of the Southwest). Studies of a very wide range of archaeological data on architecture, pottery, burials, settlement patterns, and subsistence remains (often better preserved in the arid climate of the Southwest than in other regions) provide a rich array of information for describing, analyzing, and debating interpretations about these cultures and their histories. In central Arizona, different cultural traditions in the Phoenix Basin (e.g., the essays on Pueblo Grande, Snaketown, Casa Grande, and Hohokam Platform Mounds) and, to its north, the Verde River valley (e.g., the essays on Verde Valley sites and the Agua Fria National Monument and Perry Mesa sites) developed and existed in a wary relationship toward one another.

During this period, in the northern Southwest, the regional cultural system centered on Chaco Canyon initially expanded, but then contracted and collapsed, resulting in a series of migrations outward to the Hopi mesas, Zuni, and beyond (e.g., the essays on Chaco Canyon, Pueblo Bonito, Pueblo Alto, Chacoan Great Houses, and Chaco Outlier sites). In the Mesa Verde region in the far northern Southwest, related cultural developments also led to an out-migration of people eastward onto the Pajarito Plateau and beyond into the upper Rio Grande region (e.g., the essays on the Mesa Verde region and sites, Sand Canyon Pueblo, Hovenweep, Bandelier National Monument sites, and Galisteo Basin sites).

Spanish exploration and colonization of the Southwest is also an important part of the story and one with a rich archaeological record. There were two Spanish movements into the region, initially along the Rio Grande and more generally within New Mexico and Arizona (e.g., the essays on the colonial period and mission period archaeology, as well as those on Pecos, Salinas Pueblo Missions, El Camino Real, and Tumacacori), and later along the southern Texas coastal plain (see the essay on San Antonio Missions and other sites). More recent historical events and related Southwest archaeological sites also are covered in essays about subsequent Euro-American settlements, the U.S.-Mexican war of 1846–48, and battles during the Indian wars of the later nineteenth century.

We have focused these essays on the most important and interesting archaeological sites and topics in the Southwest region. Readers can learn more about these sites, and others as well, by using the additional sources of information and references listed at the end of each essay. Additional articles, books, Web sites, museum information, and other sources are available to those who want to learn even more about these fascinating places and subjects. In many cases, the sites can be visited as parts of national, state, local, or other public parts.

The articles in the Southwest section of *Archaeology in America* include eleven general essays on topics that cover ancient or historic time periods. The general essays are followed by fifty-one essays on specific archaeological sites or about archaeological sites in a particular region. These more specific essays are arranged in roughly chronological order.

ENTRIES FOR THE SOUTHWEST REGION

INTRODUCTION TO THE ARCHAEOLOGY
OF THE SOUTHWEST

When agents of the Spanish empire in the sixteenth century entered the region later known as the American Southwest, they encountered a multitude of cultural groups who spoke languages that represent at least six distinct linguistic families: Uto-Aztecan, Zunian, Keresan, Tanoan, Yuman, and Na-Dene. Zunian is a linguistic isolate (i.e., no other language is known to be related to it), whereas Uto-Aztecan speakers are spread from the northern Great Basin to central Mexico and beyond, and they speak many languages that are now mutually unintelligible. Na-Dene is also a language family that was widely spread from far northern Canada to northern Mexico, but the language of Southern Athapaskan spoken by Apache and Navajo groups in the Southwest is so close to Northern Athapaskan spoken by Dogrib, Beaver, and other groups in northern Canada as to be still nearly mutually intelligible. Race, language, and culture are largely independent variables that differentiate and unite southwestern populations into groupings called Hopi, Zuni, and Rio Grande Pueblos, who live in large masonry/adobe "apartment buildings," and non-Puebloan peoples, whose domestic arrangements vary from dispersed rancherías to seasonal camps. What explains the co-occurrence of this fascinating array of cultural diversity, and how did it evolve? How did these groups come to be as they are? How have these people adapted to the Southwest's arid landscapes, why do those adaptations vary, and how have they endured for so long, both competing and cooperating with one another? What explains the ecological successes and failures of their adaptations? Anthropological questions like these have long been at the heart of archaeological inquiry in this region.

To take stock of the current archaeological understanding of the American Southwest after over 160 years of sustained inquiry is a daunting task. Archaeologists now know so much; and yet there is still so little known about what they would like to know. The questions have changed; so, too, have they varied among investigators at any given moment, although in some periods there was greater consensus than in others. The discovery that time relations (chronology) could be known by documenting the facts of stratigraphy, constructing artifact classifications, and linking tree ring dates to target events revolutionized Southwestern archaeology in the early twentieth century. The comparisons facilitated by this approach led

to the finding that during the period that ceramics were being made (the last 1,800 years), the Southwest was not a culturally homogeneous place, but it could be divided into five geographically discrete cultural traditions: the Hohokam, Mogollon, Anasazi, Patayan, and Fremont "cultures." A phase concept was invoked to divide each of these "cultural traditions" into temporal sequences that sometimes were also partitioned by stages, such as the Pioneer, Colonial, Sedentary, and Classic periods in the Hohokam sequence. Toward the end of his long career, Emil W. Haury in 1976 published a magnum opus, *The Hohokam: Desert Farmers and Craftsmen*, which elegantly defended and elaborated his understanding of the Hohokam cultural sequence. By then, however, a new generation of Southwestern archaeologists were asking different questions and had begun to fashion a fundamentally new conception of what Southwestern archaeology should be about.

Whereas Haury's generation had been primarily preoccupied by interests in the things that could be found in the archaeological record (artifacts and architecture) and their classification, the new archaeologists of the 1960s, in many cases, were primarily interested in human behavior and its expression by a multitude of social groups (populations). Relationships rather than artifacts became the primary objects of study, and interaction rather than categorization became the objective of measurement. The study of settlements and their internal structure, patterns in their distributions on multiple spatial scales, and the patterns of artifact distributions on multiple spatial scales led to methodologically new ways of defining archaeological constructs of households, supra-households, regional and macro-regional systems, hinterlands, and exchange structures. The Hohokam ball-court regional system, the Chacoan regional and macro-regional systems of great houses and great kivas, the Casas Grandes world, and the Plains-Pueblo macro-economy thus became the centers of much discussion and debate. Patterns in the clustering of settlements or the nature of their deployment on the landscape, and the voids among the clusters have resulted in concepts of political organization, warfare, and economic divisions of labor. New technologies, especially those allowing the "sourcing" of ceramic or lithic artifacts to their loci of manufacture or geological context, and the development of sophisticated computer software for geographic information systems (GIS) and agent-based modeling have made it practicable to map the distributions of very large data sets and to define significant new relationships among networks of social groups on many spatial scales of interaction. Every day, it seems, the synthesis of GIS data is producing fresh insights; the pace of Southwestern archaeology is thus accelerating.

Coincident with the growth of archaeological knowledge has been the creation and development of institutions that have structured and driven that growth and have acted as repositories where the knowledge gained can be maintained in perpetuity and made accessible to educate the general public. Emil Haury, for example, as part of a new generation of professional archaeologists, became the director of the Arizona State Museum and the head of the anthropology department at the University of Arizona. Museums and university departments similarly emerged and grew in many other southwestern communities or, like the Amerind Foundation near Dragoon, Arizona, were located on private estates.

Beginning in 1906 with passage of the federal Antiquities Act and the law establishing Mesa Verde National Park, another kind of institutional framework became established to preserve the archaeological record and to make it accessible to the public. The National Park Service was created in 1916 to administer many of these places; in the 1990s the U.S. Bureau of Land Management was also entrusted with the stewardship of a new kind of national monument that was designed to protect not only archaeological sites but also whole cultural landscapes and the ecology of whole regions. All of these institutions to one extent or another seek to interpret the meaning of the resources entrusted to them to the general public.

A measure of the success in the dissemination of archaeological knowledge about the Southwest (and all of America) is the passage of new federal, state, and local legislation to protect the archaeological record. To name only one example, the National Historic Preservation Act of 1966 established a new framework for the conduct of archaeology using the federal procurement system, created state historic preservation offices nationwide, and required a process of consultation with numerous parties, especially with Native American tribes. One of the unforeseen consequences of this law in the Southwest was the rapid emergence of private archaeological companies that soon wrested what was now a market for archaeological research from the older academic and museum institutions. Thus, what is thought to be important to the study of history or prehistory has increasingly become a matter of complex negotiations among many parties, professional archaeologists being only one of many players in this conversation. Enactment of the Native American Graves Protection and Repatriation Act (NAGPRA) as a federal law in 1990 further enhanced the weight of Native American opinion concerning their own history, whose oral traditions had long been rejected and largely ignored by professional archaeologists.

How, then, can archaeologists summarize what is known or suspected about Southwestern archaeology at this time in the twenty-first century? Despite the diversity of approaches and the cacophony of voices, there has been a cumulative process that could result in a consensus, a baseline from which to proceed with the inquiry. Many of the classificatory schemes devised by Haury, Harold Colton, Lyndon Hargrave, Paul S. Martin, H. P. Mera, and Anna Shepard, among others, have held up as sound scientific bases for measuring temporal change and spatial variability, and refinements to them have proven possible. It is also now well established that before the ceramic period, the peopling of the Americas occurred relatively recently, at the end of the Pleistocene period, a little over 13,000 years ago. During what Bruce Huckell has called the first 10,000 years of Southwestern archaeology, the Paleoindian period gave way successively to the Early, Middle, and Late Archaic periods; by the latter part of the Archaic, about 4,000 years ago, maize and other cultigens were introduced from Mexico to some southwestern populations. Huckell calls this the "early agricultural period," noting that it may be that some hunter-gatherers did not adopt agriculture as quickly as others. Whether the cultigens diffused from the south or were introduced directly by migrating groups remains a matter of debate.

One of the most exciting discoveries over the last twenty-five years has been a series of sites, especially in the Tucson Basin of southern Arizona, documenting a 2,000-year sequence of early (pre-ceramic) agricultural settlements. In the more recent of these sites, the remains of maize and nondomesticated plant foods are found very commonly, associated both with numerous storage pits and with small pit houses numbering as many as 600–800 in sites that were occupied for only a few centuries. Close study of these pit houses by David Gregory and others has found, however, that they were built using slender withes and probably only existed for a couple of years each. At any one time, the population living in one of these early agricultural settlements may have been no larger than about twenty-five people, the size of a typical hunting and gathering band. By about 1,800 years ago, ceramics were being made, the pit houses had become much more substantial, and the ubiquity of the nondomesticated plants was no longer high. Fully sedentary lifeways then began to evolve. A few centuries later, true villages of 100 people or more emerged, further transforming the social dynamics of these agricultural settlements.

The general adoption of some form of maize agriculture and ceramic production by about 2,000 years ago defines the Southwestern culture area, differentiating it from the adjacent culture areas of hunter-gatherers in California, the Great Basin, the southern Rockies, and, in a different way, the high plains. Pacific shell and a scattering of other exotic artifacts found in southwestern sites show that interactions across the hunter-gatherer/agriculturalist boundary continued, although much more remains to be learned about them.

Within the Southwest, by the Late Archaic/early agricultural period, a cultural boundary between the western and eastern Basketmaker populations is well demonstrated by means of rock art and multiple classes of material culture. Most parsimoniously, this boundary can be interpreted as marking the difference between the language families of Uto-Aztecan (proto-Hopic) and Tanoan populations. The similarities of the western Basketmaker to cultural assemblages in southern Arizona probably indicate connectivity with other Uto-Aztecan (proto-Tepiman) peoples. If the early Mogollon populations spoke Zunian, as Gregory and Wilcox argue, that leaves us to infer that Keresan populations should be sought in the southern San Juan basin of northwestern New Mexico, an idea that has been long postulated, if not well demonstrated.

Linguist Jane Hill, having confirmed that Zunian is a linguistic isolate, argues that it must have differentiated from some other language at least 7,000–8,000 years ago—thus, probably during Paleoindian times. This finding probably also applies to other small, compact language families, such as Keresan and Tanoan. These linguistic groups may have been areal neighbors of one another for many millennia, throughout the long Archaic period and on into the present day. During that time they must have played off of one another, influencing one another, and evolving a kind of co-adaptation of Puebloan lifeways that survived many extreme environmental and cultural perturbations, including the dry, warm Altithermal period and the clash of civilizations brought about by Spanish and later American political and economic dominance. The resilience of these cultures is truly impressive.

From this perspective, it seems unlikely that environmental variability alone in the arid Southwest is sufficient to explain such resilience. Beginning in the second decade of the twentieth century, however, the friendship and collaboration among geographer Ellsworth Huntington, zoologist Harold Colton, and astronomer A. E. Douglass, scientists all, produced an essentially environmental-determinist theory that relegated southwestern peoples to the domain of nature and minimized their creativity in the domain of culture. Today, the most elegant and comprehensive theory to explain the trajectories of Southwestern archaeology is a direct descendent of this environmentalist tradition. Tree ring dating (developed by Douglass) affords a precision for measuring paleo-environmental variability in rainfall, temperature, and stream flow year by year that will never be matched by archaeologists seeking to measure the messy variables of economics, religion, warfare, or political organization. Although archaeologists do stand in awe of the knowledge of southwestern paleo-environments that has now been achieved (better than anywhere else in the world) and respect the scientific rigor of the theories designed to bring that knowledge to bear on questions of human action, it must be admitted that these theories are reductionist in their conception of the potentials of human culture and depend, in the end, on correlations to infer causality, which is always a weak position. Alternative explanations are in order that take into account the challenges the southwestern environments created for its human populations, but that postulate that the solutions found involved human agency, which does require attention to economic, political, and religious relationships.

Now that it has been shown how to discriminate household domains in pueblo and pit-house sites, the way is open to investigate network relationships among households. Ceramic and lithic sourcing studies multiply this potential. A remarkable pattern is already apparent: by the beginning of the Hohokam Colonial period, around AD 750, supra-household groupings that buried their dead in their own cemeteries first appeared in villages of several hundred people. At that same moment, the emergence of a distinct Hohokam religion is also apparent in their cremation death ritual and associated artifacts and symbols, the Gila style of rock art, and the construction of public architecture. These public constructions, arguably a form of ball court, consist of deliberately excavated holes in the ground with the dirt piled up to form a vulva-like earthen embankments. Like the sipapu holes found in the pit structures of the northern Southwest, these features may be interpreted as portals to the underworld, points of communication between humans and deities. Like Mesoamerican ball courts, their purpose may have been to encourage fertility. Be that as it may, they probably were places where supra-household groups could mark their identities vis-à-vis one another through ceremonial exchanges; it is likely that these groups were descent groups who owned rights to irrigation land or water and cooperated with one another in the management of large, multi-village irrigation systems. Distributional patterns of Hohokam ball-court villages indicate the operation of a regional system in which villages as civic-territorial groupings also used the context of the ball courts to mark their identities or adjudicate their relationships.

In the Mimbres area of west central New Mexico, by AD 750 its villagers, too, began to form supra-household groupings and to develop a distinct religious ideology best known from the iconography of later Mimbres pottery. In the northern Southwest, also by the middle 700s, villages of over 100 people began to form, and by the middle 800s they were arrayed in regional networks that had circular great kivas as public architecture and supra-household groups. But the historical trajectories in these three areas varied. In the Phoenix Basin, the Hohokam land-use pattern endured for centuries. In the northern Southwest, the villages and village networks shattered after three generations, and a diaspora occurred out of which emerged the more stable Chacoan Great House/Great Kiva system, which was centered at the middle of the San Juan basin in Chaco Canyon. The emergence of the Chacoan religious ideology, as in the cases of both the Hohokam and Mimbres, accounts for their relative stability—although in all three cases intense organizational dynamics internally and externally caused each regional social system to evolve.

Surrounding the Chacoan, Hohokam, and Mimbres regional systems of the villages directly participating in their respective religious ideologies were other populations that either emulated or rejected those ideologies. The former often established villages or village clusters and interacted in several ways with the regional systems, thus forming macro-regional systems. The latter usually remained hinterland of rural populations, living in dispersed farmsteads and small hamlets where they practiced their own religious beliefs, although there is some evidence of outside ideological influence affecting them. The nature of the civic-territorial political organizations that integrated or differentiated these multi-level systems remains a matter of vigorous debate. Crosscutting these systems, however, were long-distance exchange structures that brought rare copper bells and scarlet macaws from western Mexico to the Mimbres and Chacoan villages and sent turquoise south into Mesoamerica.

By about AD 1100, the Hohokam religious ideology was transformed, and the regional system was fundamentally reorganized: demographic dominance shifted within the Phoenix Basin from the middle Gila to the lower Salt valley, and platform mounds began to complement and then displace ball courts as public architecture. New forms of civic-territorial organizations emerged that arguably integrated the Phoenix Basin into a single political organization surrounded on three sides by a 30-mile buffer zone that by AD 1300 widened to 50 miles on the north. In the north, the dispersed hinterland populations of the Central Arizona tradition gave up their hilltop lookouts and defensive refuges around AD 1275 to coalesce into a tight network of large hamlets and small villages smartly deployed to form a "Verde Confederacy" against the Phoenix Basin Hohokam.

In the northern Southwest, the Chacoan regional system in the late 1000s expanded northward into the well-watered Animas, La Plata, and San Juan valleys, but by the early 1100s it was surrounded by comparably organized, but smaller, polities that constrained its further growth and eventually brought down its economy. Collapse of the Chacoan system resulted in a diaspora outward to the Hopi Mesas, Zuni/El Morro, and to the Rio Puerco of the East and beyond. The Mesa Verde region in the far north tried to reorganize using a modified version of the Chaco culture, but this experiment soon failed. Its populations appear to have "voted with their feet" and migrated eastward onto the Pajarito Plateau and on into the upper Rio Grande region.

The Mimbres regional system also collapsed in the twelfth century, its people shifting eastward and southward. Soon the Casas Grandes regional and macro-regional systems emerged, centered on the "primate" center of Paquimé, that is, a settlement much larger than any other in its region, where a population of 3,000–4,000 people were sustained by the functioning of a differentiated economic system that brought goods to this center from far and wide. Yet another distinct religious ideology evolved that legitimated and stimulated this economic activity. I-shaped ball courts were one of the many types of public architecture built at Paquimé. Debate continues over whether the Paquimé ideology resulted from a process of Mesoamericanization of the Southwest or was an expression of religious beliefs locally conceived out of a heritage of religious thought dating back to Paleoindian times and widely shared by all American Indians.

Construction of a "coalescent-communities database" of all known sites with thirteen or more rooms in the whole North American Southwest from AD 1200 to 1700 has resulted in the discovery of new patterns and the clarification of others. In the early 1200s, about 75 percent of all extant rooms were in either large hamlets of 13–99 rooms or small villages of 100–250 rooms. Together they formed nearly a single network in which a path could be charted throughout the whole region, neighbor-to-neighbor, with no segment over a day's travel apart. Nevertheless, the Southwest is clearly divisible into a northern (Puebloan) and southern Southwest whose spatial discreteness increased with time. By AD 1450, the remnants of the southern Southwest were organized into the Opata and Pima Bajo village clusters in central Sonora, while the northern Southwest was concentrated into discrete Hopi, Zuni, and Rio Grande village clusters. Over 50 percent of the extant rooms in the northern Southwest, by 1450, were in large villages of 1,000 or more rooms. Net demography, however, was declining from a high of over 180,000 rooms/people in the early 1300s to about 120,000 rooms/people by AD 1600, half in the northern, Puebloan world and half in the Sonoran world.

Movement of Na-Dene speakers into the southern plains around AD 1450 also involved the beginning of regular exchanges of bison products for maize, cotton textiles, and other goods between these Plains hunter-gatherers and the easternmost Pueblos. A Pueblo-wide macro-economy involving a multi-ethnic division of labor in which no party controlled its politics thus arose that continued to operate into the time of the Spanish colony established in New Mexico and northern Arizona in 1598. By at least 1540, coincident with the *entrada* of Vasquez de Coronado into the Southwest, Na-Dene (pre-Navajo) were already living in the area of the upper San Juan drainage, later to become the Dinetah of the Navajo. Similarly, in the western and northern sectors of the Southwest, Yuman speakers and Uto-Aztecan Numic (Paiute and Ute) speakers reclaimed territories formerly occupied by Puebloan populations, and they, too, developed exchange relationships with Pueblos. In between central Sonora and the Puebloan world, other hunter-gatherers or small-time farmers moved in, including Mansos, Sumas, Janos, Jocome, and Sobaipuri, many of whom in the eighteenth century were absorbed or driven out by expanding Apache populations.

European diseases had begun to devastate the Sonoran villages by the end of the 1500s and the Puebloans by the 1630s, cutting the latter populations in half by 1700. Many Puebloan villages were depopulated, yet most of the Pueblo polities (site clusters) endured, maintaining their distinct languages and religious systems even in the face of oppression by the Spanish state. In Sonora the story is sadder, with descendents of the Opata and Pima Bajo becoming largely invisible in the Mexican population. In Arizona, however, the O'otam (Piman) populations, which probably are descendants of southwestern populations—if not directly from the Hohokam, then from hinterland populations—also endure today.

The study of the social landscapes of the American Southwest has just begun. GIS technology is only now being implemented, and archaeologists can look forward to many new analyses of the data of site and artifact distributions that have been recorded over the last 160 years. Many parts of the southwestern landscape have yet to be intensively surveyed. The summary offered here of the current state of Southwestern archaeology is thus suggestive at best. If it provokes new inquiry, and better explanations, it hopefully may be judged useful.

Further Reading: Abbott, David R., "Hohokam Social Structure and Irrigation Management: The Ceramic Evidence from the Central Phoenix Basin," Ph.D. diss. (Tempe: Arizona State University, 1994); Cordell, Linda, *Archaeology of the Southwest*, 2nd ed. (San Diego, CA: Academic Press, 1997); Dean, Jeffrey S., *Chronological Analysis of Tsegi Phase Sites in Northeastern Arizona*, Papers of the Laboratory of Tree-Ring Research, No. 3 (Tucson: University of Arizona, 1969); Dean, Jeffrey S., Robert C. Euler, George J. Gumerman, Fred Plog, Richard H. Hevly, and Thor N. V. Karlstrom, "Human Behavior, Demography, and Paleoenvironment on the Colorado Plateaus," *American Antiquity* 50 (1985): 537–554; Fish, Suzanne K., and Paul R. Fish, "Civic-Territorial Organization and the Roots of Hohokam Complexity," in *The Hohokam Village Revisited*, edited by David E. Doyel, Suzanne K. Fish, and Paul R. Fish (Fort Collins, CO: Southwestern and Rocky Mountain Division of the American Association for the Advancement of Science, 2000), 373–390; Ford, Richard I., Albert H. Schroeder, and Stewart L. Peckham, "Three Perspectives on Puebloan Prehistory," in *New Perspectives on the Pueblos*, edited by Alfonso Ortiz (Albuquerque: University of New Mexico Press, 1972), 19–39; Gregory, David A., "Perspectives on Early Agricultural Period Population Size and Sedentism," *Archaeology Southwest* 13(1) (1999): 14–15; Gregory, David A., and David R. Wilcox, eds., *Zuni Origins, Toward a New Synthesis of Southwestern Archaeology* (Tucson, University of Arizona Press, 2007); Gumerman, George J., ed., *The Anasazi in a Changing Environment* (Santa Fe, NM: School of American Research, 1988); Haury, Emil W., *The Hohokam: Desert Farmers and Craftsmen* (Tucson: University of Arizona Press, 1976); Hill, Jane H., "The Zuni Language in Southwestern Areal Context," in *Zuni Origins, Toward a New Synthesis of Southwestern Archaeology*, edited by David A. Gregory and David R. Wilcox (Tucson: University of Arizona Press, 2007), 37–58; Huckell, Bruce B., "The First 10,000 Years in the Southwest," in *Southwest Archaeology in the Twentieth Century*, edited by Linda S. Cordell and Don D. Fowler (Salt Lake City: University of Utah Press, 2005), 142–156; Kohler, Timothy A., George Gumerman, and Robert Reynolds, "Simulating Ancient Societies: Computer Modeling Is Helping to Unravel the Archaeological Mysteries of the American Southwest," *Scientific American* 293(1) (2005): 76–83; Matson, R. G., *The Origins of Southwestern Agriculture* (Tucson: University of Arizona Press, 1991); Reff, Daniel T., *Disease, Depopulation, and Culture Change in Northwestern New Spain, 1518–1764* (Salt Lake City: University of Utah Press, 1991); Riley, Carroll L., *Becoming Aztlan: Mesoamerican Influence in the Greater Southwest, AD 1200–1500* (Salt Lake City: University of Utah Press, 2005); Rohn, Arthur, "Postulation of Socio-Economic Groups from Archeological Evidence," in *Contributions of the Wetherill Mesa Archeological Project*, assembled by Douglas Osborne, *Memoirs of the Society for American Archaeology* 19 (1965): 65–69; Sullivan, Alan P., III, and James M. Bayman, eds., *Hinterlands and Regional Dynamics in the Ancient Southwest* (Tucson: University of Arizona Press, 2007); Wilcox, David R., "A Strategy for Perceiving Social Groups in Puebloan Sites," *Fieldiana: Anthropology* 65 (1975): 120–159; Wilcox, David R., "Big Issues, New Syntheses, *Plateau* 2(1) (2005): 8–21; Wilcox, David R., and James Holmlund, *The Archaeology of Perry Mesa and Its World*, Bilby Research Center Occasional Paper No. 3 (Flagstaff: Northern Arizona University, 2007); Wilcox, David R., Thomas R. McGuire, and Charles Sternberg, *Snaketown Revisited*, Arizona State Museum Archaeological Series, No. 155 (Tucson: University of Arizona, 1981); Wilcox, David R., Phil C. Weigand, J. Scott Wood, and Jerry B. Howard, "Ancient Cultural Interplay of the American Southwest in the Mexican Northwest," *Journal of the Southwest* (Summer 2008).

David R. Wilcox

HISTORY OF ARCHAEOLOGICAL RESEARCH IN THE SOUTHWEST

By the Treaty of Guadalupe Hildalgo the northwestern half of Mexico became the American Southwest in 1848. Spanish scholarship before that had regarded the known archaeological sites such as the Casa Grande Ruins on the Gila River south of modern Phoenix as a way station on the migrations of the Aztecs, an interpretation of the Aztec native traditions that the German savant Alexander von Humboldt supported. Against this European view, Albert Gallatin, who had been secretary of the treasury for both Thomas Jefferson and James Madison and then minister to France, in the pages of the Transactions of the American Ethnological Society (which he had founded in 1842) forcefully articulated a new conception of Southwestern archaeology. Gallatin argued for the autonomous development of Southwestern culture, admitting influences from the "semi-civilized" tribes to the south, but proposing that the northerners were responsible for their own cultural advancement, just as the new American republic could chart its own path to civilization independent from the ways of Europe. The research agenda established by Gallatin, at least implicitly, influenced the next several generations of Southwestern archaeologists. In his fine synthesis of what had been learned up to 1924, *An Introduction to the Study of Southwestern Archaeology*, Alfred Vincent Kidder reiterated the conception of the indigenous, or as Kidder himself termed it, "autochthonous," development of Southwestern culture from the "germs" of outside influence provided by the diffusion of maize and pottery manufacture from Mexico.

In the interim period between 1848 and 1924, numerous national and local institutions were founded that shaped the study of Southwestern archaeology. They included the Smithsonian Institution (1846), the Peabody Museum at Harvard University (1869), the American Museum of Natural History in New York (1869), the Field Museum of Natural History in Chicago (1893), the Southwest Museum in Los Angeles (1907), and, closer to the field of inquiry, the Arizona State Museum in Tucson (1893) and the Museum of New Mexico in Santa Fe (1909). Other institutions that have played vital roles in the history of Southwestern archaeology came a little later: the Laboratory of Anthropology in Santa Fe (1928), the Museum of Northern Arizona in Flagstaff (1928), the Pueblo Grande Museum in Phoenix (1929), and the Amerind Foundation in Dragoon, Arizona (1937). All of these institutions have libraries, some have art galleries, and all exhibit the findings made during the field investigations they sponsored. Visiting them is an excellent way to learn about the history of Southwestern archaeology. Several of these museums also publish journals: *Masterkey*, *El Palacio*, and *Plateau*; *Kiva* is published by the Arizona Archaeological and Historical Society, an avocational group.

Exploration of the American Southwest involved reconnaissances and reports published by the U.S. government in their effort to inventory the archaeological resources on this landscape of big skies and little surface water where vegetation does not much hide the traces of earlier habitation or other human activity. As one example, in northwestern New Mexico, Chaco Canyon was visited by Lieutenant James Simpson in 1849, and the artist Richard Kern created the earliest images of what its ruined great houses may once have looked like, stimulating the imagination of the American public to want to know more. With the founding of the Archaeological Institute of America in 1879, in Boston, although these men were primarily interested in classical archaeology, some of its members—in particular the historian Francis Parkman and anthropologists Frederic Ward Putnam and John Wesley Powell—insisted on an American program. Lewis Henry Morgan, the pioneering ethnologist

whose synthesis of *Ancient Society* had been published in 1877, was asked to provide what may be called a research design, and his disciple, the formidable Adolph Bandelier, was dispatched to the Southwest to conduct a survey and report back. Visiting about 400 sites in New Mexico, southern Arizona, and northern Mexico, Bandelier's two-volume final report of 1890 and 1892 brilliantly described both the archaeology and the ethnography of the American Indian residents of the region, showing that the modern people were the descendents of the populations that produced the archaeological sites. He also wrote the first novel of Pueblo life, *The Delight Makers*, and after converting to Catholicism he presented to the pope in Rome a treatise of over 1,000 pages in French about his researches. Thus the nearly 400 watercolor drawings and maps made during his survey of the Southwest are today in the Vatican Library.

In 1879 a Bureau of Ethnology was established in the Smithsonian Institution by Congress, with John Wesley Powell as the director. He immediately sent an expedition to the Southwest to make collections for the U.S. National Museum. Secretary of the Smithsonian, Spencer Baird, detailed one of his young assistants, Frank Hamilton Cushing, to accompany this expedition, but Cushing soon went his own way, moving into the house of the governor of Zuni Pueblo, learning that unique language, and being initiated as a bow priest charged to protect the Zuni against outsiders. In 1886, while in Boston, Cushing met philanthropist Mary Hemenway, who soon became interested in sponsoring an archaeological expedition to the Southwest, where they hoped to recover the history of the Zuni people using Cushing's method of ethnological archaeology. They planned to build a Pueblo Museum in Salem, Massachusetts, and Cushing proposed that students be sent out to learn Indian languages, as he had, and to apply that knowledge to the interpretation of the archaeological record. But this plan came to naught. With Mrs. Hemenway's death in 1894, the collections went to the Peabody Museum at Harvard, where Emil Haury would write up some of them in his 1934 Ph.D. dissertation.

The Hemenway Expedition was the first to do scientific excavations in the Southwest. Tragically, due to Cushing's poor health and personal rivalry with his field secretary, Frederick Webb Hodge, he was relieved as director. In his place Jesse Walter Fewkes, an ichthyologist friend of the Hemenways, was put in charge of the expedition, thus beginning a long and productive career in Southwestern archaeology and ethnology, mainly for the Bureau of American Ethnology. Before that happened, however, Hemenway and her influential friends petitioned Congress to have the Casa Grande Ruins set aside from the public lands, and Cushing successfully lobbied to have that happen. The Casa Grande Ruins thus became the first prehistoric site in America to be so preserved (Lee 2000, 205–209).

Because much of the Southwest is public land, the frameworks for studying its archaeology were largely erected through federal or state laws and regulations. The most important of these was the federal Antiquities Act of 1906. This landmark statute was maneuvered through Congress by the knowledgeable southwestern educator and institution builder Edgar Lee Hewett and the conservative but conservation-minded Congressman John F. Lacy of Iowa (see articles by Lee, Thompson, Conard, and McManamon in Harmon et al. 2006). It extends the privilege of excavating archaeological sites and collecting artifacts on federal lands to public institutions that could curate them in perpetuity for educational purposes. It requires an antiquities permit from the federal agency having jurisdiction to legitimately excavate on federal lands, condemning unpermitted digging as vandalism. In addition, it entitles the president of the United States to set aside national monuments, a power presidents from Theodore Roosevelt to Bill Clinton have exercised vigorously, preserving many sites and even whole settlement systems for the continuing education and benefit of the peoples of the world.

Tourism to these special places is a key economic factor supporting modern southwestern settlement. Knowing this, Hewett quickly used the newly founded Museum of New Mexico to promote the establishment of a New Mexico State Park system of archaeological sites, the visitation of which would keep people spending money in the state for the additional days needed to see these wonders. The coming of the automobile and the good-roads movement greatly increased the accessibility of many sites. Even so, although the vast open spaces of the Southwest are gradually filling up with modern occupation as urban expansion and the subdivision of ranches proceeds, destroying many archaeological sites in the process, thousands of southwestern sites remain as though in a state of nature, something the as yet unpaved roads leading to Chaco Canyon are intended to preserve.

In 1906 Hewett was put in charge of the American program of the Archaeological Institute of America, and a School of American Archaeology was begun that one year later brought the young A. V. Kidder and Sylvanus Morley to the Southwest for the first time. Hewett also recruited the dean of arts and letters at the University of Utah, Byron Cummings, to an interest in archaeology. In 1915 Cummings became the director of the Arizona State Museum, and by 1928 he had initiated a master's degree program at the University of Arizona that produced a cadre of students who would profoundly influence the development of Southwestern archaeology, including Emil Haury and Florence Hawley Ellis. Meanwhile, in Santa Fe Hewett, with help from Morley and Jesse Nusbaum, established the "Santa Fe style," a southwestern conception of the good life that built on the aesthetics of Pueblo dwellings and colonial Spanish churches. Charles Lummis in Los Angeles similarly promoted the "mission style." Harold Colton embraced a similar craftsman aesthetic in his 1929 home, the Colton House, and the 1935 exhibition building at the Museum of Northern Arizona. Nusbaum's contributions to this aesthetic can be seen in the museum at Mesa Verde National Park and in the Palace of the Governors and Art Museum on the plaza in Santa Fe. The estate of Amelia Elizabeth White in Santa Fe, became the seat of the School of American Research (renamed the School for Advanced Research in 2006), is another fine example of this vision of what American civilization can be.

The death in 1908 of Chairman of the Board Morris Jessup of the American Museum of Natural History in New York led to the accession of Henry Fairfield Osborn to that role. He wanted new blood on the board, and one of those elected was Archer Huntington, the founder in 1904 of the Hispanic Society of America and one of the heirs to the fortune of Collis Huntington, the Union Pacific and Southern Pacific railroad magnate. Clark Wissler, the curator of anthropology at the museum, went to Huntington in 1909 to seek funding for an ethnological and archaeological survey of a region where Spanish culture had clearly influenced the Native peoples, the American Southwest. Huntington agreed, and soon a "new archaeology" was born in the Southwest based on the study of time relations derived from observations of stratigraphic relationships and of statistical changes in pottery types through time (called seriation). Anthropologists Alfred Kroeber, Robert Lowie, Nels Nelson, and Leslie Spier all contributed to this methodological revolution, and A. V. Kidder in his excavations at Pecos Pueblo, New Mexico, which began in 1915, embraced the new approach. Against the convictions of Cushing and Fewkes, as well as the Pueblo and other Indian people, Lowie argued persuasively that oral tradition was not history—a conclusion that both Hewett and Kidder accepted. For the next seventy years the Native peoples of the Southwest would essentially be shut out of the scientific study of their own past.

In hopes of overcoming controversies with consensus about proposed chronologies, A. V. Kidder in 1927 sent out postcards inviting about seventy people to gather at Pecos Pueblo in August that year to discuss matters. He was remarkably successful in that the representatives of some fourteen institutions working in the Southwest agreed on how to name pottery types and on the main features of a sequence of cultural growth from three stages of Basketmaker culture through five stages of Pueblo culture. Except for Basketmaker I, which was only hypothetical, the terminology they devised is still used today; however, some of the generalizations, such as the sequence of small houses in Pueblo I and II to communal pueblos in Pueblo III, have had to be modified. More important, the supposition that this sequence applied to the whole Southwest was soon shown to be incorrect. At a conference held in 1932 at the private research institute of Gila Pueblo in Globe, Arizona, its founder, Harold Gladwin, succeeded in showing that the distribution of red-on-buff pottery in southern Arizona was evidence of a separate cultural tradition. They agreed to call it the Hohokam culture. Soon Gladwin's assistant Emil Haury in 1936 proposed a Mogollon cultural sequence; and although that claim was more controversial,

Kidder saw that the original Basketmaker/Pueblo sequence was best defined on the Colorado Plateau and suggested the name Anasazi for it. A few years earlier a Fremont cultural tradition in Utah was defined, and Harold Colton in 1939 defined a Patayan tradition centered along the lower Colorado River in the western reaches of the Southwest. Thus it was found that unlike the eastern woodlands, where a Mississippian culture was nearly all pervasive, in the Southwest there were five different cultural traditions contemporaneous with one another.

Called the "Pecos Conference" by Katherine Bartlett in 1950 when it was first held in Flagstaff, until the late 1960s this annual August gathering of Southwestern archaeologists, still an important yearly conference, served as a mechanism for maintaining consensus and orchestrating informal and civil debate. World events, a new restlessness among American youth, and the growth of scientific knowledge then brought about a second, "new archaeology" that was to have profound effects on Southwestern archaeology. Led by then University of Chicago professor Lewis Binford, this movement was advanced by his student William Longacre, who introduced Binford to Paul Martin, the curator of anthropology at the Field Museum. Martin had helped to establish the legitimacy of the Mogollon culture concept, but he was always open to new ideas and was charmed by Binford. So he turned over direction of the research design of his field program to Longacre, James Hill, Fred Plog, Michael Schiffer, and a host of other bright, young graduate students, who began to excavate sites "their way" and to publish the results of their work. Summer field schools, a long tradition in the Southwest, became a vital context for this work. The credibility of this new archaeology was thus established, and as the students finished their degrees and were hired at universities they began spreading the word about how archaeology should now be done. Asking new questions, they implemented new methods of studying the archaeological record, including formal statistical sampling designs, computer manipulation of the data, and population thinking about past peoples. Many practitioners from earlier generations also joined in this intellectual movement in a number of interesting ways.

Coincidentally, the growth of support in America for conservation and historic preservation led to passage of the National Historic Preservation Act of 1966, whose regulations were published in 1972. Now all federal agencies had to consult with newly created state historic preservation officers about the actions they were taking on federal lands in each state, evaluating what effect those actions would have on cultural resources, and proposing how those effects could be mitigated to preserve the significant aspects of the resources. Now the National Park Service was no longer the only "lead agency" for archaeology on federal lands. Many federal agencies began to reorganize to manage their cultural resources, using the federal procurement process to contract for the expertise they needed. Thus modern "contract archaeology"

was born, and tens of millions of dollars began to be spent on archaeology in the Southwest. At first, the traditional institutions tried to reorganize to take on this work. Several of them had already been effective in an earlier era of "salvage archaeology" involving federal contracts dealing with dam and highway construction. But by the middle 1970s, private companies began to compete for the federal contracts, and they soon proved they had better business models than most of the museums and universities. By the 1990s, some of these companies began to create nonprofit organizations, such as the Center for Desert Archaeology in Tucson, publisher of the newsletter *Archaeology Southwest*. Active in the conduct of what is increasingly being called "preservation archaeology," these innovative organizations are inventing new ways to preserve archaeological sites and to learn about the past.

The result over the last thirty years has been an enormous increase in the amount of published data about Southwestern archaeology, but another result has been the fragmentation of the traditional consensus about what that data means and a failure to digest it in a systematic or coherent way. Yet serious attempts have been made to do this in a plethora of conferences and advanced seminars. A series of Anasazi, Mogollon, and Hohokam conferences have been held and published, and have advanced knowledge, but they also served to reify the traditional cultural historical categories without a real synthesis and rethinking of the data in population terms. Beginning in 1968, Douglas Schwartz, as president of the School of American Research, facilitated a superb series of advanced seminars whose publication has effectively supported the process of synthesis. The Amerind Foundation has begun a similarly stellar program. The biennial Southwest Symposium has also been a fruitful forum for synthetic efforts by scholars. What is lacking is a mechanism to bring together archaeologists from government service, contract companies, museums, and academia into a common intellectual arena where they can interact as equals and formulate comprehensive research designs that truly synthesize current knowledge and focus it on a shared set of research questions.

Yet in the early twenty-first century something more is needed. Passage in 1990 of the Native American Graves Protection and Repatriation Act (NAGPRA) and subsequent changes to the regulations for the Historic Preservation Act of 1966 have fundamentally redefined what American archaeology is about. The former privilege of public institutions to conduct archaeology on public lands, based on the rights of conquest, has now been restricted. Indian tribes that can establish their cultural affiliation with ancestral human remains and funerary objects once again have the right to dictate their disposition, and they have the formal opportunity to consult about all proposed research designs to study archaeological sites on federal lands. No longer shut out, Indian tribes are now empowered to ask for modifications of research designs in keeping with their cultural values and claims to sovereignty. A new era of dialogue about the current and future aims of Southwestern archaeology has begun. Whether this will mean the end of archaeology as it is currently known or the emergence of new forms of consensus about the study of the past, however, may not be left to archaeologists and Indians alone to decide. The juggernaut of demographic growth and the building of related infrastructure in the Southwest show no signs of moderating, and the tolerance of the driving political forces for the delays caused by disputes between Indians and archaeologists may make them largely moot. As has always been true, archaeology must be conducted in a set of personal, sociological, economic, and political contexts whose configurations fundamentally affect what archaeologists can know about the past.

Further Reading: Bandelier, Adolph F., *Contributions to the History of the Southwestern Portion of the United States*, Papers of the Archaeological Institute of America, American Series, No. 5 (Cambridge, MA: Peabody Museum of American Archaeology and Ethnology, 1890); Bandelier, Adolph F., *Final Report of Investigations among the Indians of the Southwestern United States, Part II*, Papers of the Archaeological Institute of America, American Series, Vol. 4 (Cambridge, MA: Peabody Museum of American Archaeology and Ethnology, 1892); Fowler, Don D., *A Laboratory for Anthropology: Science and Romanticism in the North American Southwest, 1846–1930* (Albuquerque: University of New Mexico Press, 2000); Harmon, David, Francis P. McManamon, and Dwight T. Pitcaithley, eds., *The Antiquities Act: A Century of American Archaeology, Historic Preservation, and Nature Conservation* (Tucson: University of Arizona Press, 2006); Hinsley, Curtis M., and David R. Wilcox, eds., *The Lost Itinerary of Frank Hamilton Cushing* (Tucson: University of Arizona Press, 2002); Kidder, Alfred V., *An Introduction to the Study of Southwestern Archaeology, with a Preliminary Account of the Excavations at Pecos*, Papers of the Phillips Academy Southwestern Expedition, No. 1 (New Haven, CT: Yale University Press, 1924); Lee, Ronald Freeman, "The Antiquities Act of 1906," *Journal of the Southwest* 42(2) (Summer 2000): 197–270, http://www.nps.gov/archeology/pubs/Lee/index.html (online June 2007); Snead, James E., *Ruins and Rivals: The Making of Southwest Archaeology* (Tucson: University of Arizona Press, 2001); Wilcox, David R., and Don D. Fowler, "The Beginnings of Anthropological Archaeology in the North American Southwest: From Thomas Jefferson to the Pecos Conference," *Journal of the Southwest* (Summer 2002); Woodbury, Richard B., *Sixty Years of Southwestern Archaeology: A History of the Pecos Conference* (Albuquerque: University of New Mexico Press, 1993).

David R. Wilcox

CLIMATE AND NATURAL ENVIRONMENT OF THE SOUTHWEST

INTRODUCTION

Traditionally defined as extending from Durango, Colorado, to Durango, Mexico, and from Las Vegas, Nevada, to Las Vegas, New Mexico, the American Southwest is a complex and diverse region that includes the Colorado Plateau, a mountainous transition zone (including the Mogollon Rim), and portions of the Basin and Range province. After about AD 1, the Colorado Plateau was the home of the Basketmaker and later Anasazi cultures, the mountainous transition zone was home to the prehistoric Mogollon, and the Basin and Range province was the domain of the Hohokam and earlier Cochise cultures. For thousands of years prior to AD 1, generalized Archaic populations reliant on gathering and hunting resources in each region pursued a semi-nomadic existence. Before the Archaic, the earliest indication of human occupation in the American Southwest comes from Paleoindian projectile points that are well dated to beginning around 11,800 years ago.

Given the climatic and environmental diversity of the American Southwest, a transect across the region recording variation in any parameter, be it elevation, slope, aspect, precipitation, temperature, species composition, or any other variable, will be characterized by extreme values and high spatial (and potentially temporal) variability. As but one example, there is a 3,600 meter (ca. 12,000 ft) change in elevation from near sea-level portions of the Colorado River valley near Yuma, Arizona, to the highest peaks in the San Francisco Mountains near Flagstaff, Arizona. Temperature decreases along this elevational gradient, while precipitation increases. Because species distributions are related to precipitation and temperature patterns, it is possible to walk, over the course of a few days, from desert ecosystems up through transitional woodlands, then through mountain forests, and finally into the treeless alpine meadows and mountaintops.

This discussion examines climate and environment in the American Southwest with an eye toward understanding how archaeologists use such information to understand the prehistoric past. Paleoenvironmental research has conclusively demonstrated that climates and environments characteristic of the American Southwest today *differ* from those that characterized this region in the past. As a result, descriptions of climate and environment that are offered in archaeological site reports must be examined critically, with the understanding that the descriptions offered describe the setting for fieldwork rather than the prehistoric climate and environment that is of interest to the archaeologist.

CURRENT CLIMATE AND ENVIRONMENT IN THE AMERICAN SOUTHWEST

The American Southwest has several climatic, topographic, and geographic features that combine to support a large array of diverse ecosystems. Climatically, a key and distinctive feature of rainfall in the Southwest is its distribution throughout the year in two seasonal peaks (Sheppard et al. 2002). Up to one-half of the total annual rainfall comes during summer, from early July through mid-September. Summer precipitation, with its moisture originating from both the Gulf of Mexico (Bryson and Lowery 1955) and the Gulf of California (Wright et al. 2001), is delivered typically by convectional thunderstorms that can be small spatially but otherwise intense with high rainfall rates. Because the precipitation comes during the warm season, much of it evaporates soon after hitting the ground.

The other half of the total annual rainfall comes during winter, a more extended season from November through March. Winter precipitation originates from the Pacific Ocean, usually from the northern Pacific but sometimes also from tropical latitudes. Winter storms are usually massively large frontal systems whose southern tails wash over the Southwest. Because it comes during the cold season, winter rainfall is not immediately evaporated. Indeed, much winter precipitation comes as snow and is therefore effectively stored until spring and early summer.

Winter rainfall over the Southwest is affected by distant ocean dynamics, notably by the so-called El Niño, an ocean current phenomenon of the equatorial Pacific (NOAA 2005). In typical years, deep cold water upwells off the west coast of South America, forcing warm surface water to the western Pacific; atmospheric convection originating over warm water that far away from the Americas does not usually flow over the American Southwest. In contrast, during El Niño, cold water fails to upwell off the west coast of South America, and the surface warm pool sits in place. Atmospheric convection originating in the central or even eastern Pacific can travel over the American Southwest, resulting in above-average winter precipitation for Arizona and New Mexico. This El Niño phenomenon, along with other sea-surface temperature variability in the Pacific Ocean, leads to high inter-annual and even decadal variability in winter precipitation in the Southwest.

Temperatures in the Southwest show the usual seasonal and diurnal patterns seen in temperate regions. Beyond that, spatial patterns in temperature of the Southwest are controlled by high topographic variability in the region. Low deserts of Arizona are notoriously warm, with summer highs exceeding 100°F (38°C) and winter afternoons reaching 75°F (24°C). Conversely, high mountain areas of both Arizona and New Mexico can experience overnight lows well below 0°F (−18°C) during winter, and daytime winter highs are not guaranteed to exceed freezing. This topographic variability in temperature presents an opportunity for life in the Southwest, leading to highly diverse vegetation as well as obvious migration strategies for animals and people. Additionally, in between frontal storms of winter, when humidity can be very low, the diurnal range in temperatures can be spectacular, especially in low deserts where an overnight low of 25°F (−4°C) might be followed by daytime high of 75°F (24°C). This diurnal variability in temperature presents challenges to life in the Southwest, forcing plants and animals as well as people to adapt to extremes on short time scales. In short, patterns of both precipitation and temperature in the Southwest can be highly variable at daily, seasonal, annual, and even decadal time scales. This climatic variability influences both plant and animal components of natural ecosystems, leading to a high level of diversity for people to utilize and make a living.

Natural ecosystems of the Southwest are profoundly rich in biotic diversity. Beginning at the lower elevations, the Sonoran Desert of the Southwest has been dubbed the world's "most interesting" desert because of its huge number of plant and animal species (McGinnies 1981). This diversity stems in part from the two separate rainfall peaks throughout the year. Some plants, for example many native grasses, are dormant during winter but revive themselves during summer rains. Other plants, dormant during summer, take advantage of winter rainfall. High plant species diversity also stems from the Southwest's mid-latitude location, allowing it to receive both tropical species from the south as well as temperate species from the north. So far, over 2,000 species of plants have been identified in the Sonoran Desert (Phillips and Comus 2000). Many Sonoran Desert cacti and other plant species have parts that can be eaten, worn, or used medicinally after only a little processing (Hodgson 2001).

The Sonoran Desert also has a large collection of tree species. Many of these tree species are particularly important ecologically because they foster natural fixing of nitrogen, a vitally essential nutrient whose (ionic) forms are rare. This ready source of plant-available nitrogen helps make Sonoran ecosystems highly productive relative to other deserts of the world.

Moving up in altitude, ecosystems shift systematically from deserts to forests. The different bands of vegetation up and down mountains appear to be stacked upon each other, and in total they combine to increase overall vegetation diversity of the Southwest. Down low and often intermixed with deserts are native grasslands. Moving upward, chaparral occupies low slopes of the mountains with manzanita as a dominant species. Above that is the Madrean woodland, named for the botanical influence of the Sierra Madres on its species composition. In some places, the Madrean woodland is dominated by pinyon and juniper, whereas in other places it has a strong component of live oak species.

Mid-level elevations of Southwest mountains are typified by ponderosa pine. One of the grand tree species of North America generally, ponderosa pine accounts for the most volume of wood fiber of all species in both Arizona and New Mexico (O'Brian 2002, 2003). Above that, Douglas fir, true firs, spruce, and southwestern white pine associate with ponderosa to form mixed-conifer forests of surprisingly high productivity. Sub-alpine tops of many mountains of the Southwest also have aspen. The very highest mountain tops have treeless alpine ecosystems.

All of this rich diversity in plant life has led to an equally rich variety of animal life throughout the American Southwest. For example, the Southwest is renowned for its spectacular number of bird species—up to 400 (Davies 1997)—some of which use the region for wintering while others use it for summer nesting. About 171 mammal species occupy the Southwest (Cockrum 1982), including the country's richest collection of bats, with at least 28 species counted during summer. Reptiles and amphibians are also well represented throughout the Southwest, with 90 snake species and 40 lizard species as well as 23 species of toads (11), frog (11), and salamanders (1) (Heymann 1975). And then there are insects: a staggering 1,000 species of bees, thousands more of beetles, and hordes of ant species just begin to quantify what is by far the most important animal group by species count in the Southwest.

Yet another geographic feature of importance to people in the Southwest has been the presence of farmable sediments and the availability of surface water to grow crops. Farmland requires both a source of sediments and a place in which to catch them. The Southwest contains both of these requisites in abundance. On the one hand, mountain ranges of Arizona and New Mexico are a ready source of sediments that erode constantly in the slow but inexorable rock cycle. On the other hand, low basins catch these sediments, making the Southwest quite flush with relatively flat expenses of unconsolidated sediments. It is therefore no surprise that domesticated plants such as maize, beans, and squash have a long pedigree in the American Southwest.

Mountain ranges of Arizona and New Mexico also form the upper headwaters of countless surface creeks and streams, all of which head for basins in their own natural cycle of water. As small tributaries coalesce, notable rivers form—the Pecos, Rio Grande, San Juan, Gila, and Salt rivers are notable perennial rivers of the Southwest. The grandfather of them all, the Colorado River, is a dominant geographic feature of the Southwest. Interestingly, because of the generally dry climate, rivers of the Southwest do not carry much water on a global scale. For example, the average annual discharge of 13.5 million acre-feet of the Colorado River (Stockton and Jacoby 1976) would barely register as a minor blip on the scale of the Columbia River. Still, rivers of the Southwest have served the water needs of humans ever since people first arrived in the region.

PALEOCLIMATE RECONSTRUCTION AND ARCHAEOLOGICAL RESEARCH IN THE AMERICAN SOUTHWEST

The understanding of paleoenvironments is more precisely resolved in the American Southwest than anywhere else in the world, because the conditions that foster environmental diversity and variability, particularly the distribution (and often lack) of water, are precisely those factors that allow for the preservation of materials useful for paleoenvironmental research. This discussion briefly considers three remarkable techniques used to reconstruct paleoenvironments in the American Southwest: pollen analysis (palynology), tree ring analysis (dendroclimatology), and pack rat midden analysis.

Palynology

Over the last fifty years, scholars have studied fossil pollen from a variety of contexts, including archaeological sites in an effort to discern changes in paleoenvironments (e.g., Clisby and Sears 1956). Martin (1963a, 1963b) used palynology to comment on the environmental contexts for the early human occupation of Arizona. Schoenwetter (1961) inferred four climatic periods for eastern Arizona and western New Mexico over the last 3,500 years that were subsequently adopted by many archaeologists: the most recent period, from AD 1000 to the present, is characterized by heavy summer rainfall, with occasional flash floods. The period between AD 350 and 1000 is characterized by lighter summer rainfall and a more balanced bi-seasonal rainfall regime, which lead to greater effective moisture in the soils. A gap in the pollen record from 1400 BC until AD 350 prevents conclusions on this period, although other portions of the Southwest seem to have experienced light summer rainfall during this time. At about 1400 BC, however, the pollen data again indicated heavy summer rainfalls.

Schoenwetter and Eddy (1964) applied alluvial and palynological data to the solution of archaeological problems in the Navajo Reservoir District of New Mexico. They postulated that the repeated occupation and abandonment of the Navajo Reservoir district is, in most cases, explainable with reference to effective moisture, and that population growth was related to agricultural potential (Schoenwetter and Eddy 1964, 127). Hall (1985) published a bibliography of all known fossil pollen studies in the Southwest, and an update of this important contribution would be welcome.

The analysis of fossil pollen has fallen into some disfavor in archaeological studies because of sampling and preservation issues that make it difficult to reliably use archaeological pollen samples in paleoclimate reconstructions. Nevertheless, this important technique provided much needed paleoenvironmental data to complement dendroclimatology and pack rat midden analyses.

Dendroclimatology

Dendroclimatology is the highly specialized science of reconstructing climate parameters from precisely dated growth rings in trees (Fritts 1976). As early as 1929, Andrew Ellicott Douglass, the founder of modern dendrochronology, posited the existence of a "Great Drought" in the American Southwest between AD 1276 and 1299 (Douglass 1929; see Nash 1999). In the nearly eighty years since, the Great Drought has become one of the most common extra-cultural causes invoked to explain the massive changes evident in the late thirteenth-century archaeological record across the Southwest, which marked the beginning of a centuries-long human abandonment of the Colorado Plateau. From a climatological standpoint, it is now known that the Great Drought was not the longest dry spell to affect the Southwest, nor was it the most severe, although it was geographically widespread.

In the 1980s, tree ring data was used to produce quantitative dendroclimatic reconstructions expressed in standard units of measurement such as inches of precipitation and degrees of temperature. Rose et al. (1981) reconstructed precipitation values using archaeological tree ring specimens from Arroyo Hondo Pueblo in northern New Mexico (Rose et al. 1982). Burns's (1983) reconstructed annual maize crop yields and simulated Anasazi storage. His study marks the first attempt to integrate tree ring data, agricultural production data, and archaeological data, the latter in the form of estimated prehistoric storage capacities. Burns concluded that the Great Drought represented the worst interval of maize storage shortfalls experienced by Anasazi populations in southwestern Colorado. Van West (1994) refined Burns's (1983) analysis using newly developed geographic information systems technology and more refined soils and drought data. Contrary to Burns's study, Van West (1994) concluded that there was always enough productive land to produce sufficient maize to support a large population, even during dry periods such as the Great Drought.

From west central New Mexico, Grissino-Mayer (1996) developed a 2,129-year tree ring chronology that indicated above-average rainfall in the area during the periods AD 81–257, 521–660, 1024–1398, and 1791–1992, and below-average rainfall during the periods AD 258–520, 661–1023, and 1399–1790. Interestingly, Grissino-Mayer noted that the amount and duration of above-normal conditions between 1791 and 1992 was unsurpassed in the record, and the drought conditions at AD 258–520 are unsurpassed.

Salzer (2000a) developed a bristlecone pine tree ring chronology (AD 663–1997) for the San Francisco Mountains that allowed him to produce a paleotemperature reconstruction for the American Southwest and to examine the implications of that data on the prehistoric occupation of the region (Salzer 2000b). The data indicates that AD 1195–1219 was the longest, if not most severe, cold period in the sequence; AD 1225–1245 was comparably long, but not so severe; and AD 1258–1271 was the shortest cold period and of intermediate severity.

Archaeologists have begun to successfully integrate dendroclimatic and archaeological data, particularly in southwestern Colorado, where excellent preservation, a long history of archaeological research and funding, and dry farming yield data combine to offer a remarkable laboratory for paleoenvironmental research (see Dean and Van West 2002; Van West 1994; Van West and Dean 2000).

Pack Rat Midden Analysis

Pack rats (*Neotoma* spp.) forage within about 30 meters of their dens and continuously bring samples of local plants and other materials back to create their dens. These materials are then cemented in place by rat urine. Because generations of pack rats can live in the same locations for thousands of years, these seemingly amorphous entities include well-preserved records of floral and faunal change through time, in some cases tens of thousands of years (Betancourt et al. 1990).

Although pack rat middens are rarely found on archaeological sites, the paleoenvironmental data they yield are useful for archaeological analysis when radiocarbon dated. For instance, the study of pack rat middens reveals conclusively that the climate and environment of the Southwest has changed dramatically since the arrival of the first humans at the end of the last Ice Age 12,000 years ago (Allen et al. n.d.). At that time, desert vegetation, which is now quite common in southern Arizona and New Mexico, was then restricted to the lowest elevations (<300 m) around Yuma, Arizona. At the other extreme, the spruce-fir, mixed-conifer, and subalpine forests that are now comparatively rare in the Southwest once covered much of the territory that is now covered by the common pinyon-juniper woodland.

Pack rat midden analysis reveals that mixed-conifer forests dominated the Chaco Canyon region during the Paleoindian period between 9,000 and 11,000 years ago (Betancourt and Van Devender 1981), when the climate was generally colder than it is today. Although there is a gap in the pack rat midden record for the area between around 6,000 and 9,000 years ago, data indicates that from 4,000 to 6,000 years ago, characterized by Early Archaic occupations, the Chaco region was substantially drier than before, with most rainfall occurring during the summer months. During the Late Holocene (2000 BC–AD 500), roughly coincident with Late Archaic, the Chaco region was dominated by pinyon-juniper woodlands, which have since disappeared from the region (Betancourt and Van Devender 1981).

The combined accumulation of palynological, tree ring, pack rat midden, hydrological, and other data gleaned as a result of decades worth of paleoenvironmental research (see Dean 1996) indicates the following. The period around AD 300–500 was characterized by summer-dominant rainfall and low effective moisture, AD 500–800 was characterized by winter-dominant rainfall and high effective moisture, and AD 800–1000 was characterized by low effective moisture and high temporal variability in rainfall patterns. The period from AD 1000 to 1300 enjoyed high effective moisture and low spatial and temporal variability in rainfall patterns. From AD 1300 to 1550, effective moisture was low, and there was high temporal and spatial variability in rainfall. From about AD 1550 to 1700 the effective moisture was again higher. Finally, between AD 1700 and the present, the Colorado Plateau has been characterized by very high spatial variability in rainfall and occasional wet periods interspersed with dry intervals.

CONCLUSION

Second perhaps only to the wonderful cultural diversity characteristic of the region, the climate and environment of the American Southwest are what make the area so attractive for tourists, scientists, and retirees. The remarkable preservation facilitated by generally arid conditions makes the archaeological record available for study at a level of detail effectively unmatched in other parts of the world. The environmental variability and attendant species diversity allows the American Southwest to serve as a laboratory in the development of new analytical techniques for paleoenvironmental research. Southwestern archaeologists are at once blessed with and burdened by the paleoenvironmental data available to them, because highly precise tree ring reconstructions, detailed pack rat midden analyses, and other data can be difficult to interpret when compared to an archaeological record in which artifact technologies and styles can remain essentially unchanged for hundreds, if not thousands, of years. Nevertheless, the American Southwest remains a remarkable laboratory for the study of climate and environment in the prehistoric past.

Further Reading: Allen, Craig D., Betancourt, Julio L., and Thomas W. Swetnam, *Land Use History of North America (LUHNA): The Paleobotanical Record*, http://biology/usgs.gov/luhna/chap9.html (n.d.); Betancourt, Julio L., and Thomas R. Van Devender, "Holocene Vegetation Change in Chaco Canyon, New Mexico," *Science* 214 (1981): 656–658; Betancourt, Julio L., Thomas R. Van Devender, and Paul S. Martin, eds., *Packrat Middens: The Last 40,000 Years of Biotic Change* (Tucson: University of Arizona Press, 1990); Bryson, R. A., and W. P. Lowery, "Synoptic Climatology of the Arizona Summer Precipitation Singularity," *Bulletin of the American Meteorological Society* 36 (1955): 329–339; Burns, Barney T., "Simulated Anasazi Storage Behavior Using Crop Yields Reconstructed from Tree-Rings: A.D. 652–1968," Ph.D. diss. (University of Arizona, 1983); Buchmann, S. L., G. P. Nabhan, and P. Mirocha, *The Forgotten Pollinators* (Washington, DC: Island Press, 1996); Clisby, K. H., and P. B. Sears, "San Augustine Plains—Pleistocene Climatic Changes," *Science* 124 (1956): 537–539; Cockrum, E. L., *Mammals of the Southwest* (Tucson: University of Arizona Press, 1982); Davies, B. L., *A Fieldguide to Birds of the Desert Southwest* (Houston: Gulf, 1997); Dean, Jeffrey S., "Dendrochronology and the Study of Human Behavior," in *Tree Rings, Environment and Humanity: Proceedings of the International Conference, Tucson, AZ, May 17–21, 1994*, edited by J. S. Dean, D. M. Meko, and T. W. Swetnam (Tucson: Radiocarbon Laboratory, University of Arizona, 1996), 461–469; Dean, Jeffrey S., and Carla R. Van West, "Environment-Behavior Relationships in Southwestern Colorado," in *Seeking the Center Place: Archaeology and Ancient Communities in the Mesa Verde Region*, edited by Mark D. Varien and Richard H. Wilshusen (Salt Lake City: University of Utah Press, 2002), 81–99; Fritts, Harold C., *Tree-Rings and Climate* (New York: Academic Press, 1976); Grissino-Mayer, Henri, "A 2,129-Year Reconstruction of Precipitation for Northwestern New Mexico," in *Tree-Rings, Environment, and Humanity: Proceedings of the International Conference, Tucson, 1994*, edited by J. S. Dean, D. Meko, and T. Swetnam (Tucson: Radiocarbon Laboratory, University of Arizona, 1996),

191–205; Hall, Stephen A., "Bibliography of Quaternary Palynology in Arizona, Colorado, New Mexico, and Utah," in *Pollen Records of Late Quaternary North American Sediments*, edited by V. M. Bryant Jr. and R. G. Holloway (Dallas: American Association of Stratigraphic Palynologists Foundation, 407–423); Heymann, M. M., *Reptiles and Amphibians of the American Southwest* (Scottsdale, AZ: Doubleshow, 1975); Hodgson, W. C., *Food Plants of the Sonoran Desert* (Tucson: University of Arizona Press, 2001); Martin, Paul Schultz, "Early Man in Arizona: The Pollen Evidence," *American Antiquity* 29(1) (1963a): 67–73; Martin, Paul Schultz *The Last 10,000 Years: A Fossil Pollen Record of the American Southwest* (Tucson: University of Arizona Press, 1963b); McGinnies, W. G., *Discovering the Desert* (Tucson: University of Arizona Press, 1981); Nash, Stephen E., *Time, Trees, and Prehistory: Tree-Ring Dating and the Development of North American Archaeology 1914–1950* (Salt Lake City: University of Utah Press, 1999); NOAA (National Oceanic and Atmospheric Administration), El Niño Web site, www.elnino.noaa.gov (online 2008); O'Brian, R. A., "Arizona's Forest Resources, 1999," *USDA Forest Service Resources Bulletin* RMRS-RB-2 (2002); O'Brian, R. A., "New Mexico's Forest Resources, 1999," *USDA Forest Service Resources Bulletin* RMRS-RB-3 (2003); Phillips, S. J., and P. W. Comus, *A Natural History of the Sonoran Desert* (Tucson: Arizona-Sonora Desert Museum Press, 2000); Rose, Martin, J. S. Dean, and William J. Robinson, *The Past Climate of Arroyo Hondo, New Mexico, Reconstructed from Tree Rings* Arroyo Hondo Archaeological Series, Vol. 4 (Santa Fe, NM: School of American Research Press, 1981); Rose, Martin R., William J. Robinson, and Jeffrey S. Dean, "Dendroclimatic Reconstruction for the Southeastern Colorado Plateau," Report submitted to the Dolores Archaeological Project, the Chaco Center, and Eastern New Mexico University (manuscript on file at the Laboratory of Tree-Ring Research, University of Arizona, Tucson, 1982); Salzer, Matthew, "Dendroclimatology in the San Francisco Peaks Region of Northern Arizona, U.S.A.," Ph.D. diss. (University of Arizona, 2000a); Salzer, Matthew, "Temperature Variability and the Northern Anasazi: Possible Implications for Regional Abandonment," *Kiva* 65 (2000b): 295–318; Schoenwetter, James, "The Pollen Analysis of Eighteen Archaeological Sites in Arizona and New Mexico," in *Chapters in the Prehistory of Arizona, I*, edited by Paul S. Martin, *Fieldiana: Anthropology* 53 (1961): 168–209; Schoenwetter, James, and Frank W. Eddy, "Alluvial and Palynological Reconstruction of Environments: Navajo Reservoir District," Papers in Anthropology No. 13 (Santa Fe: Museum of New Mexico, 1964); Sheppard, P. R., A. C. Comrie, K. Angersbach, G. D. Packin, and M. K. Hughes, "The Climate of the Southwest," *Climate Research* 21 (2002): 239–258; Stockton, C. W., and G. C. Jacoby, "Long-Term Surface-Water Supply and Streamflow Trends in the Upper Colorado River Basin Based on Tree-Ring Analyses," *Lake Powell Research Project Bulletin* 18 (1976): 1–70; Van West, Carla R., "Modeling Prehistoric Agricultural Productivity in Southwestern Colorado: A GIS Approach," Reports of Investigations, No. 67 (Pullman: Department of Anthropology, Washington State University, 1994); Van West, Carla R., and Jeffrey S. Dean, "Environmental Characteristics of the A.D. 900–1300 Period in the Central Mesa Verde Region," *Kiva* 66 (2000): 19–44; Wright, W. E., A. Long, A. C. Comrie, S. L. Leavitt, T. Cavazos, and C. Eastoe, "Monsoonal Moisture Sources Revealed Using Temperature, Precipitation, and Precipitation Isotope Timeseries," *Geophysical Research Letters* 28 (2001): 787–790.

Stephen E. Nash and Paul R. Sheppard

THE EARLIEST INHABITANTS AND SITES

Some of the oldest archaeological sites in North America are found in the American Southwest, which encompasses Arizona and New Mexico, the southern halves of Utah and Colorado, and northern Mexico. The earliest inhabitants of the Americas, called Paleoindians, are Late Pleistocene/Early Holocene American Indians, whose ancestors crossed the Bering Strait and entered the New World from Eurasia. In the American Southwest, the Paleoindian period dates between 8,000 and 12,500 years ago. The oldest identified Paleoindians, the Clovis people, were hunter and gatherers between about 10,800 and 12,000 years ago.

It is believed that the first humans to enter the New World arrived to the continent from Northern Asia and Siberia. Once in the New World people moved south and developed a distinct culture that archaeologists call the Clovis culture. The Old World Eurasian origins and continent-wide dispersal of the Clovis culture are controversial topics in American archaeology. Genetic (i.e., ancient DNA), cranio-facial/osteological (skeletal), linguistic, and stone tool (mainly projectile point typologies) evidence suggests that some Paleoindians have north Asian ancestry, but the timing, geographic route, frequency, and nature of migration(s) to North America are debated.

No human skeletal evidence of Clovis people has been found, and current information about their domestic and social life is minimal and overly focused on hunting behavior. However, some information about this group has been gleaned from archaeological investigations. As nomadic hunter-gatherers, their belongings were few and easily portable from one camp to the next. Bands of twenty-five to thirty people ranged over a territory that might have extended several thousand square miles. Movement was regulated by the seasons as well as by the amount, type, and availability of game animals and plant foods. Archaeologists have studied the territorial ranges of Clovis bands by looking at the material types of stone tools recovered from sites. Many sites have materials that were transported up to 500 kilometers from where the rock naturally occurs, suggesting that Clovis people were highly mobile.

THE PEOPLING OF THE AMERICAS AND THE PRE-CLOVIS DEBATE

Geological evidence shows that the Bering land bridge connecting Siberia and Alaska was open several times between 10,000 and 25,000 years ago, as well as much earlier from 30,000 to 50,000 years ago. The land bridge was an 1,800-kilometer-wide land mass linking the two continents consisting of an expansive steppe or tundra plain. Entry to the southwestern portion of interior North America was made possible by an ice-free corridor separating the North American

ice sheets (the Cordilleran and Laurentide ice sheets). The two continental ice sheets covered the northern portion of the continent, including all of Canada and portions of the American Midwest, making passage into North America unlikely before 25,000 years ago.

It is also possible that these first Americans reached the southern portions of the American continents not by the Bering land bridge, but by following the coast south. Unfortunately, the coastline has changed, and archaeological sites resulting from a coastal migration route into the Americas are now submerged due to higher sea levels. Coastal migration is difficult to prove due to a paucity of physical evidence supporting the theory. Therefore, the inland migration theory has the widest popularity among scholars, although new investigations along the Pacific coast are focusing attention on possible ancient coastal immigration.

Archaeologists do not know whether the first Americans to cross the Bering Strait were the Clovis people, but some believe that Clovis people were the first to enter the New World. If Clovis people were not first, they were likely the descendents of the first inhabitants of the New World. After their arrival or establishment in the New World it took less than 1,000 years for Clovis people to spread throughout North America and into portions of Mexico and South America. Clovis period radiocarbon dates from sites throughout the Americas cluster between 10,800 and 11,500 years ago, suggesting rapid migration and population movement. Clovis sites are identified by the presence of a lanceolate-shaped, fluted projectile point, often found in association with extinct megafauna including mammoth, horse, and camel.

Purported sites that date before 12,000 years ago and lack Clovis projectile points are called pre-Clovis sites. Pre-Clovis proponents believe the Paleoindian period should extend beyond 12,000 years ago. There are several sites that could be older than 12,000 years, but they have not been widely accepted due to problems with dating and geologic interpretations. In North America, well-known proposed pre-Clovis sites include Badger Springs, Bluefish Caves, Cactus Hill, Calico Hills, China Lake, Del Mar, Dry Creek, Dutton, Fort Rock Cave, Hermit's Cave, Laguna Beach, Lamb Springs, Meadowcroft Rockshelter, Pendejo Cave, Sandia Cave, Shelby, Texas Street, Topper, Tule Springs, Walker Road, and Wilson Butte Cave.

Presently, the only widely accepted pre-Clovis site is Monte Verde in Chile, dating to 12,500 years ago. It took over twenty years of interdisciplinary studies for Monte Verde to be accepted, although some still question the site interpretations. Early sites that may pre-date Clovis are intensely scrutinized and must meet minimum criteria for acceptance. They must have stone or bone tools, have datable remains such as charcoal or fire-pits, and be in undisturbed context with a clear stratigraphic position for accurate dating. Many proposed pre-Clovis sites do to not meet these criteria and have contamination problems or lack organic remains for dating, or are found in secondary eroded geologic deposits.

Some proposed pre-Clovis sites may be substantiated in the future. Debate over the peopling of the Americas and pre-Clovis sites will continue as new testing methods, hypotheses, and archaeological evidence emerge. It is possible that Clovis people were not the first New World inhabitants, but the jury is still out, and the search for pre-Clovis sites continues.

THE FOLSOM DISCOVERY

The beginning of Paleoindian archaeology can be traced to the discovery of man-made tools in association with the bones of extinct animals in Folsom, New Mexico, and later at Black-water Draw, near Clovis, New Mexico. The Folsom site, the type site for the Folsom culture, was discovered in 1925 by George McJunkin, a cowboy who spotted large bones protruding from an arroyo following heavy summer rains. At the time, the antiquity of humans in the Americas was uncertain, and there was intense skepticism about the finds. It took three years to convince the scientific community of the authenticity of the site, but it was finally accepted in 1928. Acceptance of the Folsom and Blackwater Draw (Clovis) sites had two important results: (1) it stimulated further research into the Paleoindian period; and (2) it provided evidence of human occupation of the New World earlier than scholars thought, allowing for the time depth needed to account for the diverse indigenous cultures of the Americas.

PALEOINDIAN STONE TOOLS

Stone tools are the most common artifacts found at Paleoindian sites and were essential survival tools for 99 percent of humankind's history. Stone tools are more commonly found than tools made of wood or bone, mostly due to preservation. Tools made of perishable material such as antler, bone, and wood do not survive in open-air sites, and Paleoindian cave sites, where dry conditions that might permit long-term preservation, are extremely rare. Projectile point styles have been described by archaeologists to distinguish different Paleoindian technological complexes and cultures. Projectile point styles and production techniques were taught, learned, and replicated by members of related kinship or social groups. The categories of projectile point styles and how they were made and used changed over time, making them useful temporal markers for dating archaeological sites.

Once enough archaeological sites with projectile points were dated using C-14 radiocarbon dating, a sequence of absolute dates for periods during which certain projectile point styles were manufactured and used was established. This allowed archaeologists to distinguish different Paleoindian complexes or cultural groups. Each Paleoindian culture has its own diagnostic projectile point style or type that can

be found over large geographic areas. Some areas of the Southwest have a variety of contemporaneous projectile point types that reflect the presence of a number of different cultural groups in the area and/or diverse local adaptations.

THE CLOVIS CULTURE
Stone Tool Technology

Clovis sites are recognized by the presence of a large lanceolate, fluted projectile point with a concave base, and biface/blade lithic technology. The Clovis projectile point or spear point averages 7 centimeters in length and often has flutes on both sides. A flute is a long indentation or flake scar that runs from the base of the point toward the tip. Fluting is a technologically specialized technique; it thins the piece by removing a long flake that originates from the base of the point. The fluting technique continued after Clovis. Later Folsom style projectile points (10,000–11,000 years ago), although in general shorter than Clovis points, also have flutes. Finished Clovis points often have basal and lateral grinding, which was done to ensure that the sharp edges of the point did not tear the sinew spear mount or haft. Clovis points were hafted onto spear shafts that could be removed and replaced with new points. The spear was thrust or propelled into an animal by hand. Later, during the Archaic period, hunter-gatherers used the *atl atl*. An *atl atl* is a spear or dart thrower that works as a lever to propel the projectile for greater distance and with greater force. In addition to projectile points, the Clovis stone tool kit includes spurred end scrapers, large unifacial end scrapers, backed blades, crescent-shaped knives, gravers, and perforators. Bone tools include points, fore-shafts for spears, awls, punches, scrapers, fleshers, and shaft wrenches.

The manufacture of Clovis projectile points followed a careful systematic reduction strategy. First, a biface preform or a roughly shaped piece was produced from a flake. A biface preform is a piece of rock shaped along at least three-fourths of its surface on both sides. The biface preform was further shaped and thinned using direct soft hammer percussion with a billet of antler, bone, ivory, or possibly hardwood. The Clovis biface thinning technique is termed "alternating opposed biface thinning," and it involved detaching thinning flakes beyond the midline of the biface across both faces, which often resulted in the removal of a portion of the biface edge. Evidence of the use of this thinning technique is widespread in sites of this period and is particular to the Clovis period. Once the biface was laterally thinned, it was basally thinned by removing a large, thin flake or flute from the base toward the tip; then the edge was ground before the point was hafted to a spear fore-shaft.

Some archaeologists believe that Clovis technology evolved from Old World Paleolithic tool technology. Stone tool complexes of Lake Baikal, north Asia, and areas of Siberia show some similarity to Clovis technology, indicating a possible relationship between Clovis and people in parts of Asia and Siberia.

In northwestern Alaska there are numerous sites that have stone tool assemblages with bifaces that have basal thinning and concave bases similar to Clovis points. Some of these sites appear to date before Clovis occupation in the middle part of the continent, while others overlap in age with Clovis sites. Therefore, although there is some evidence of Clovis antecedents in Siberia and northern Alaska, there is also evidence of different tool traditions that may have co-existed during and possibly before Clovis occupation of North America. The search for a technological precursor to Clovis blade and biface technology is ongoing and will likely continue.

Subsistence and Hunting

Besides the remains of stone tool technology, most Clovis sites also have remains of extinct Pleistocene fauna, with mammoth being common. The Clovis culture is often characterized as big-game hunters who followed mammoth and bison herds. However, smaller animals are also recovered from Clovis sites. Hunting strategies that focused on one type of game, such as mammoth or bison, are called specialized. At Clovis sites where remains of small animals are found, a more generalized hunting strategy focusing on more animals than just mammoth and bison is evident.

Plant gathering probably provided a significant portion of the Clovis diet. Remains of wild plant collection and processing sites are rarely preserved. Therefore, archaeologists do not know the exact proportion or varieties of wild plants utilized. Most current and past hunter-gatherers rely on wild plant foods and hunt only to supplement their diet and for the hides and other useful byproducts that remain after the meat is removed. Since Clovis bands exploited many environments across large territories, their hunting and gathering behavior was fluid and adjusted to the resources available in different ecosystems and seasons. This means that although hunting was a common pursuit, there were also numerous occasions when only plant foods were processed and eaten, and meat was not the main focus.

Many of the animal bones found at Clovis sites are of extinct mammals, including mammoth (*Mammuthus columbi*), mastodon (*Mammut americanum*), bison (*antiquus*), horse (*Equus* spp.), camel (*Camelops* spp.), American lion (*Panthera leoatrox*), giant ground sloth (*Northrotheriops shastensis*), and the dire wolf (*Canus dirus*). Remains of extant animals include certain species of antelope, bears, turtles, canids, jackrabbits, and other rodents.

Many of the extinct animals listed so far are called megafauna. Megafauna, like the mammoth, were indeed "big animals." Mammoths were as tall as 13 feet, had enormous curved tusks, and weighed 8–10 tons. To successfully kill a mammoth took group cooperation, knowledge of elephant behavior, and sturdy hunting weapons. Knowledge of landforms and watering holes was also crucial to successfully hunting a mammoth. Most Clovis kill sites occur in marshy, spring, or lake environments where landforms restricted mammoth movement or escape and animals congregated near drinking water.

Clovis people were hunter-gatherers who used a wide range of natural resources. The idea that they focused on big-game hunting primarily comes from the consistent association of hunting weapons (projectile points) and megafauna (i.e., mammoth, bison, horse) at Clovis sites. Kill sites represent only the hunting aspects of Clovis life. Few habitation or campsites have been found. In fact, almost all known Clovis sites are kill sites, although some kill sites have nearby short-term campsites and butchering areas. There are a few archaeological and geological reasons for this. First, kill sites are more visible than campsites or plant-gathering sites due to the presence of large animal bones. Second, kill sites are commonly near old or present water sources because hunters often waited for animals to drink water and hunted them at a water source. In these environments rapid burial of sites due to flooding and sediment buildup actually preserves sites more quickly compared with other areas. Since many Clovis kill sites are near old or present streams, ponds, and marshes, where preservation is better and where the remains are later exposed by erosion, more of these kill sites are found by archaeologists. Campsites, which may be located in different environments than kill sites, have a lesser chance of being preserved.

THE EXTINCTION OF MEGAFAUNA

The extinction of megafauna coincides with the continental dispersal of Clovis people. Paul S. Martin first proposed that Clovis hunters hastened the extinction of the Pleistocene megafauna. Martin hypothesized that the animal populations of North America were not adapted to human predation and had no defensive responses to human hunters. Martin created a computer simulation using a number of assumptions concerning variables such as Clovis reproductive rates, number of animals hunted per person, population movement rate, and group size. The simulation seems to show that Clovis hunters could have caused the extinction of megafauna.

Several of Martin's assumptions have been challenged. There appear to have been other processes, mostly environmental, during that time that may have contributed to megafauna extinction. For example, the continent was going through large-scale climate changes, and the habitat was changing, causing the extinction of many animals, some of which were not hunted by humans. Large numbers of bird species and whole insect genera went extinct along with the hunted megafauna. Large mammals that survived the mass extinction became smaller in size beginning in the early Holocene.

Climate change, the subsequent reduction of megafauna habitat, and Clovis hunters may have had a cumulative effect on megafauna populations that resulted in extinction, but Clovis hunters were not the main cause of the mass extinctions of the end of the last Ice Age. Plant and animal responses to the changing climate also had an effect on extinctions. Recent paleo-environmental studies reveal that the Pleistocene witnessed less seasonal variation than today. Summers became warmer and winters cooler. The change in climate pattern and seasonal precipitation affected plant communities. Many of the large mammals that became extinct were herbivores (plant eaters) and their predators. Reductions in mammal body size and changes in availability and types of plants influences reproduction and overall fitness. Smaller animals typically have shorter gestation periods, giving them the ability to recover and making them less vulnerable to extinction. For instance, it is estimated that mammoths had a gestation period of 2.5 years, which means that it would be difficult for the species population to reproduce fast enough to recover from the loss of breeding individuals. This scenario could hasten extinction of larger animals and enhance the competitive advantages of smaller species exploiting the same ecological niches as the larger ones.

Climate also affected water sources: streams became smaller, and lakes dried up. Animals had to travel large distance to find plant food and water. The decline in available watering holes meant that the locations of animals became more predictable. Hunters who took advantage of the predictability of game increased the likelihood of a successful hunt and may have put additional pressure on megafauna populations. However, Clovis hunters were probably not the sole cause of the massive extinctions at the end of the Ice Age.

CLOVIS AT THE END OF THE PLEISTOCENE

Archaeologists have an incomplete picture of Clovis adaptations to changing climatic conditions of the Late Pleistocene/Early Holocene. By the time that the last Clovis points were being made (around 10,800 years ago), the megafauna were extinct, and the continent was warmer and drier. Vegetative communities also changed, and the landscape became different from what Clovis people were used to. Clovis people had adapted their hunting and residential mobility patterns to these changing conditions. During this time, a new cultural complex appears that archaeologists term the Folsom culture. Although the relationship between Clovis and Folsom is unclear, aspects of the Clovis way of life and technology continued during the Folsom period.

The Folsom culture, which overlaps and post-dates Clovis, represents a continuation of the Clovis tradition of hunting large game using lanceolate, fluted points. Instead of hunting mammoth like their Clovis predecessors, Folsom people hunted bison herds that roamed the plains and river valleys of the Southwest. However, Folsom people also utilized a larger range of plants and animals and can be considered more generalist than Clovis people.

Folsom sites also differ from Clovis sites. There are more campsites found compared with the Clovis period. Folsom campsites are often found near kill sites, with butchering and meat-processing areas near the kill. Clovis sites can be found throughout North America, whereas Folsom sites are concentrated in the West, in the central and southern plains of the Dakotas, Montana, Wyoming, Colorado, Nebraska, Texas, and New Mexico; they are not found along the West Coast or east of the Mississippi. Population densities were higher than during the Clovis period but still low overall. Bands of Folsom hunter-gatherers roamed over areas as large as 300 square miles.

CLOVIS ARCHAEOLOGY IN THE AMERICAN SOUTHWEST

Clovis sites are usually found in stream banks or in eroded river deposits exposed following heavy rains. Most Clovis sites are located at low elevations near old waterways, ponds, marshes, and plains that once offered a variety of forage for large Pleistocene mammals.

Clovis sites are distributed over much of the southwestern United States, often in the form of isolated finds of projectile points. More substantial sites occur in southern Arizona, which has some of the better-known Clovis sites. Significant Clovis sites also occur in New Mexico, especially in the Llano Estacado (Staked Plains) area in the eastern and southern portions of the state. Clovis sites are found in most areas of Texas and are more common in the Trans-Pecos region and near ancient lakes. A few Clovis sites have also been found in Utah and northern Mexico.

CLOVIS SITES OF THE SAN PEDRO RIVER VALLEY IN ARIZONA

The San Pedro River valley in southeastern Arizona has yielded some of the best-known Clovis sites in North America, including the Lehner Ranch, Murray Springs, Naco, Escapule, and Leikem sites. The valley has the largest concentration of Clovis sites in the Americas. Overbank flooding buried the sites after Clovis people left, and stream erosion and downcutting that began in the 1880s exposed the sites. The most significant Paleoindian sites in the San Pedro River valley are the Lehner Ranch, Murray Springs, and Naco sites.

Lehner Ranch

The Lehner Ranch site was discovered in 1955 following heavy rains. It has provided valuable geological, paleontological, and palynological data concerning the Late Pleistocene/Early Holocene. The evidence suggests that the area underwent a rather rapid climate change at the end of the Pleistocene just before the arrival of Clovis peoples. Invertebrate fauna, pollen, and soils from the bottom layer of the site suggest cooler and wetter conditions prevailed before 11,500 years ago. This climate locally supported stands of pine, oak, and juniper before 11,500 years ago.

At Lehner, Clovis artifacts and faunal remains are found stratigraphically above an erosional unconformity caused by desiccation (drying). Pollen found in the same layer as Clovis artifacts represent typical desert plant communities, which provides evidence of climate change that altered vegetative communities resulting in similar desert conditions as exist today. The megafauna remains at the Lehner site are mostly mammoth. The mammoth bones appear to represent a typical mammoth family unit, suggesting that at Lehner Clovis people did not cull out the weakest mammoths of the herd. Instead they were able to kill a whole family unit, perhaps during multiple hunting events. Evidence of butchering activities and cooking or warming hearths was found near the animal remains. Animal remains include nine mammoths and bones of horse, bison, and tapir scattered near the hearths. Among the Clovis projectile points recovered were three extremely rare small, basally thinned quartz-crystal points.

Murray Springs

The Murray Springs Clovis site was excavated by the University of Arizona under the direction of C. Vance Haynes from 1966 to 1971 with funding from the National Geographic Society. It is located just south of the Lehner Ranch site. Murray Springs is significant due to the presence of intact Clovis occupation surfaces. The site has 40,000 years of undisturbed stratigraphy, and radiocarbon dates suggest Clovis occupation around 11,000 years ago. Bones, stone tools, and hearths were found just as Clovis people left them 11,000 years ago. Clovis activity areas were preserved by the rapid deposition of a soil layer called the "black mat." The black mat is actually the Clanton clay soil layer, which is richly organic, giving it the black mat appearance and texture. The black mat is a time index since it was laid down immediately following Clovis occupation. This means that Clovis artifacts are usually found directly below the black mat, and more recent artifacts are found above the layer.

Murray Springs is unique for three preserved Clovis activity areas: one where at least eleven bison of an extinct form were killed, a second location where a mammoth was partially butchered, and a hunter's campsite where portions of the game were prepared and where stone tools were used, repaired, and lost or discarded. Bones of several extinct animals were found, including mammoth, horse, camels, bison, lion, and dire wolf. A very special bone artifact was also recovered from the site—a bone wrench, which may have been a tool for straightening wooden spear shafts. Similar examples have been found in Russia, the Ukraine, and Europe at Upper Paleolithic sites. The artifact is 10 inches long and made from a mammoth long bone.

The paleo-environment of the Murray Springs site typifies Clovis kill/butchering sites. The area was a marshland with shallow spring-fed pools and abundant swampy forage for large animals. The clay soil surrounding the marsh was so well preserved that the footprints of mammoth and other large mammals were found during excavations.

Naco

The Naco site is a Clovis kill site consisting of the remains of a single mammoth with eight Clovis points between the skull and ribcage. The site was excavated in 1952 by Emil Haury of the University of Arizona. It appears that the thorax was the target for throwing or thrusting spears into the giant animal. No evidence of camping or butchering activities was found. No artifacts except projectile points were found at Naco, which differs from the nearby Lehner site, where there was greater artifact diversity. The Lehner site also had clear evidence of camping, whereas evidence of camping at Naco was less conclusive; however, there was some scattered charcoal nearby, suggesting that hearths may have been present but were eroded.

OTHER CLOVIS SITES IN THE SOUTHWEST AND NEARBY

At Blackwater Draw in eastern New Mexico, Clovis points were found in association with megafauna remains. Archaeological evidence at Blackwater Draw was first discovered in 1929 by a fourteen-year-old named James Ridley Whiteman. Whiteman sent a Clovis point and an associated mammoth tooth fragment to the Smithsonian Institution. It caught the attention of E. B. Howard, who made his first visit to Blackwater Draw in the summer of 1932. In 1936 and 1937, Howard and John Cotter (later in his career to be one of the founders of historic period archaeology in the United States) were the first professional archaeological investigators. E. H. Sellards's excavations from 1948 to 1956 documented the existence of Clovis people dating before Folsom people. The site has been extensively studied over the years and is currently protected by Eastern New Mexico University.

Like many Clovis sites, the paleo-environment of Blackwater Draw was marsh-like with drying playas or small lakes where animals would come to drink. Blackwater Draw has an intact stratigraphic record of the last 13,000 years, with abundant later Paleoindian and Archaic remains. Decades of scientific research at Blackwater Draw has given archaeologists a better understanding of Paleoindian groups and of the paleo-environment of the southern high plains.

Blackwater Draw also is significant due to re-use of the site from Paleoindian times into the Archaic period. The site was occupied by different Paleoindian groups. Further, the site has evidence of an overlap between Clovis and Folsom of about 500 years. Another interesting part of the site is a hand-dug well dating to the Clovis period. This is considered the earliest water control feature in the New World. The well and some bone beds are protected by metal buildings constructed around the remains. Fourteen other hand-dug wells dating to the Archaic period were also found. Identified animal remains include mammoth, bison, camel, giant turtle, large horses, short-faced bear, giant beaver, and peccary.

The Gault site, located in south central Texas, is a large site possibly representing a Clovis camp. The site is significant due to the diversity and the fact that few Clovis campsites have been excavated. Other Clovis sites in Texas appear to be within similar environments along mountain fringes bordering plain grasslands. The Gault site has produced numerous flat limestone artifacts with incisions and markings that have baffled researchers, but these appear to be early representational art or possibly counting systems. Continuing research at the Gault site could help broaden understanding of Clovis adaptation.

In southeastern Utah, the remains of a Clovis campsite were found at the Lime Ridge site. Artifacts include end scrapers, blades and blade tools, and several projectile-point fragments. The site is important because few Clovis campsites have been found. Clovis finds in Utah mostly consist of isolated projectile points.

Paleoindian occupation of Mexico is poorly understood. In the northern part of Mexico is the site of El Bajio. Located northwest of Hermosillo, in Sonora, the site yielded evidence of Clovis spear point manufacture and use of a nearby raw material source. A re-appraisal of possible Paleoindian sites in Mexico suggests that more sites will be found in the future.

CONCLUSION

Over the last two decades the media has popularized Clovis finds and the pre-Clovis debate. Indeed, the search for pre-Clovis sites and addressing hypotheses concerning the first entry of humans into the New World are two of the most important current research endeavors in American archaeology. This essay provides an overview and introduction into the Paleoindian period and Clovis archaeology in the Southwest.

The full history of the Clovis people continues to be investigated and remains to be written. In many ways Clovis is an enigma. It is difficult for most people to imagine what life was like at the end of the last Ice Age. How do we relate to predators two to three times the size of modern predators, prey animals that weight between 8 and 10 tons, and changing climatic conditions during that time period? For many of us, Clovis and the Ice Age environment live within our imaginations but are poorly understood. The search for a better understanding of Paleoindian and Clovis peoples continues. Through the work of dedicated researchers, a more complete picture of Paleoindian life is emerging. With continued efforts, appreciation for the ingenuity of Paleoindians will continue to grow.

Further Reading: Antevs, E., "Geologic Age of the Lehner Mammoth Site," *American Antiquity* 25(1) (1959): 31–34; Bonnichsen, R., and Karen L. Turnmire, eds., *Clovis: Origins and Adaptations* (Corvallis: Oregon State University Press, 1991); Cordell, Linda S., *Prehistory of the Southwest*, 2nd ed. (San Diego, CA: Academic Press, 1997); Dillehay, Thomas D., *Monte Verde: A Late Pleistocene Settlement in Chile*, Vol. 2: *The Archaeological Context* (Washington, DC: Smithsonian Press, 1989); Dillehay, Thomas D., *The Settlement of the Americas: A New Prehistory* (New York: Basic Books, 2000); Dillehay, Thomas D., and David J. Meltzer, eds., *The First Americans: Search and Research* (Boca Raton, FL: CRC Press, 1991); Greenberg, J. M., C. G. Turner II, and S. L. Segura, "The Settlement of the Americas: Comparison of the Linguistic, Dental and Genetic Evidence," *Current Anthropology* 27 (1986): 477–497; Haynes, C. V., "The Earliest Americans," *Science* 166 (1967): 709–715; Haynes, C. Vance, and E. T. Hemmings, "Mammoth Bone Shaft Wrench from Murray Springs, Arizona," *Science* 159 (1968): 186–187; Haury, Emil W., E. B. Sayles, and W. W. Wasley, "The Lehner Mammoth Site, Southeastern Arizona," *American Antiquity* 25(1) (1959): 2–30; Hester, J., *Blackwater Draw Locality No. 1*, (Fort Burgwin, NM: Fort Burgwin Research Center, Southern Methodist University, 1972); Justice, Noel D., *Stone Age Spear and Arrow Points of the Southwestern United States* (Bloomington: Indiana University Press, 2002); Kelly, Robert L., and Larry C. Todd, "Coming into the Country: Early Paleoindian Hunting and Mobility," *American Antiquity* 53 (1988): 231–244; Krech, Shepard, III, *The Ecological Indian: Myth and History* (New York: W. W. Norton, 1999); Martin, Paul S., and H. E. Wright, eds., *Pleistocene Extinctions: The Search for Cause* (New Haven, CT: Yale University Press, 1967); Meltzer, D., *Search for the First Americans* (New York: St. Remy Press, 1993); Mosimann, James E., and Paul S. Martin, "Simulating Overkill by Paleoindians," *American Scientist* 63 (1975): 304–311; Roberts, Frank H. H., Jr., "The Folsom Problem in American Archaeology," *Annual Report of the Smithsonian Institution* (1938): 531–546; Steele, G., and Joseph F. Powell, "Peopling of the Americas: Paleobiological Evidence," *Human Biology* 64 (1995): 303–336; Turner, Christy G., "Relating Eurasian and Native American Populations Through Dental Morphology," in *Method and Theory for Investigating the Peopling of the Americas*, edited by R. Bonnichsen and D. Gentry Steele (Corvallis: Oregon State University Press, 1994).

Jeremy M. Moss

EARLY AGRICULTURE AND RELATED CULTURAL DEVELOPMENTS

SOUTHWESTERN UNITED STATES AND NORTHWESTERN MEXICO

The chronology, circumstances, and consequences of the transition from a hunting and gathering way of life to one based on agriculture in southwestern North America (the Southwest) has been an important research focus in American archaeology since the 1930s, with a burst of new data and interpretations beginning in the 1980s and continuing today. Debate continues about whether maize and other tropical cultigens (plants that were cultivated, e.g., maize, squash, gourds, beans) were initially introduced to the Southwest by the migration of people from the south who already were agriculturalists or through the diffusion of information about cultivating plants and trade for domesticated plant seeds. There are additional questions about whether the transition to agriculture was rapid or gradual and whether this shift in economic focus was primarily a strategy for reducing subsistence risks or for maximizing returns to subsistence efforts.

Recent interpretations of the transition to agriculture in the Southwest variously argue for active manipulation of indigenous plants prior to the arrival of tropical cultigens; crops spreading through combinations of migration and diffusion; multiple waves of these processes introducing new crop complexes and multiple crop varieties; local domestications of native plants; local breeding of new varieties of tropical cultigens; early farmers developing portfolios of diverse cultivation techniques; and agricultural decision making that simultaneously weighed risk, effort, productivity, and efficiency. More details about all of these interpretations can be found in the articles, books, and reports listed in the "Further Reading" section of this essay.

ARRIVALS AND DISPERSALS OF MESOAMERICAN CULTIGENS

Beginning in the 1950s, radiocarbon dates on wood charcoal from the same sediment deposits provided indirect dates for early cultigen remains in the Southwest. Because the early radiocarbon dating technique required large amounts of material, only a few radiocarbon dates were directly obtained from combined samples of multiple maize cobs. At the time, individual charred seeds simply were too small to be radiocarbon dated using the technology available. Also, the ranges of probability for these first dates were quite large, encompassing several centuries. It was not until the AMS (accelerator mass spectrometry) dating technique was developed during the 1980s that direct radiocarbon dating of small samples of individual cultigen remains was possible, and statistical ranges of probability for the dates obtained were reduced to half a century or less. This important technological advance allowed reassessment and significant revision of the chronology of arrivals and dispersals of tropical cultigens in the Southwest.

Based on currently available direct dates on cultigen remains, it was during the period 2500–750 BC, an interval of increased effective moisture (the net effect of precipitation after evaporation) in the Southwest, that several tropical cultigens spread northward from Mesoamerica and then dispersed across the region. Maize and squash both arrived in the southern Basin and Range province (the desert borderlands of the southwestern United States and northwestern Mexico) between 2500 and 2100 BC. Maize spread rapidly northward, reaching the Mogollon Highlands and the southern Colorado Plateau by 2200 BC. Maize did not spread east of the middle Rio Grande valley until 1100 BC, and dispersal farther northward and eastward on the Colorado Plateau did not occur until between 750 and 50 BC. Pepo squash (the most widely

cultivated variety of pumpkin) reached the Mogollon Highlands and the southern Colorado Plateau between 1200 and 1100 BC. Bottle gourd and common bean arrived in the southern Basin and Range province between 1200 and 750 BC.

The data currently available indicates that maize and pepo squash were the first tropical cultigens to arrive (possibly together, as a crop complex), and they spread rapidly to all parts of the Southwest. Common beans and bottle gourds arrived about a millennium later and spread gradually northward. However, new archaeological investigations continue to push back the earliest known ages of cultigens in the Southwest and its subregions, so the chronology of cultigen arrivals and dispersals will continue to change.

POSSIBLE INDIGENOUS CULTIGENS AND PROTO-AGRICULTURE

Evidence is accumulating that some native plants were also cultivated by early farmers in the desert borderlands, including cotton (either wild or domesticated), tobacco, and possibly amaranth. In addition, many researchers have suggested that other native plants were semi-cultivated in the Southwest prior to the arrival of tropical cultigens. Plant remains recovered from Middle and Late Archaic sites dating between 3000 and 1000 BC (hunter-gatherer sites temporally overlapping the earliest sites with remains of tropical cultigens) often include weedy, large-seeded, and leafy annuals and perennial grasses, including goosefoot, amaranth, Indian rice grass, dropseed grasses, tansy mustard, and beeweed. Most of these plants grow in naturally disturbed, damp alluvial soils.

Their regular occurrence in archaeological sites from this early time period and their abundance suggest that these wild native plants were intensively gathered by Late Holocene Archaic groups, and in some locations may have been protected, encouraged, or even cultivated. In addition to tropical cultigens and local cultigens and semi-cultigens, subsistence remains from early farming sites in the Southwest often include these specific native wild species and a wide variety of other wild plants and animals, showing that early southwestern farmers were also intensive foragers, hunters, and fishers.

EARLY CULTIVATION TECHNIQUES

Prehistoric cultivation techniques such as fallowing, staggered planting, intercropping, and multiple cropping are not archaeologically visible. However, several different early cultivation techniques can be identified or inferred from physical traces. These include the locations of early farming settlements and fields on specific landforms and soils favorable for agriculture; built structures and surface modifications that enhanced and directed runoff; canals that diverted perennial river flows; and signs of fire to clear weeds and brush from fields and canals. These types of archaeological evidence indicate varied forms of dry farming (exploiting residual soil moisture), runoff farming (diverting slope runoff to fields), flood farming (locating fields in naturally flooding areas), water-table farming (locating fields in areas with high water tables), and irrigated farming (diverting perennial river or spring flows into canals) in use by early farmers in several parts of southwestern North America between about 2200 BC and AD 250.

The earliest cultivation techniques were water-table farming and flood farming, practiced in similar alluvial settings in the southern Basin and Range province and the southern Colorado Plateau by 2200–2100 BC. Runoff farming using hillside terraces was practiced in northwestern Chihuahua by 1500 BC, and using diversion ditches at the bases of slopes on the southern Colorado Plateau by 1200 BC. Irrigated farming was practiced in the southern Basin and Range province by 1250 BC (and possibly as early as 1500 BC), and by 1200 BC on the southern Colorado Plateau. Dry farming in dune fields and other areas with naturally mulching sandy soils developed on the southern Colorado Plateau by 1700 BC (and possibly as early as 2100 BC), and in the Mogollon Highlands by 1300 BC. Historical and ethnographic evidence suggest that rain-fed farming (relying on correctly timed and adequate rainfall) was practiced only during brief wet intervals in later southwestern prehistory, and only at higher elevations.

All of the early forms of farming in the Southwest relied on some form of supplemental water or residual soil moisture. Except for dry farming, all of the early cultivation techniques were focused specifically on alluvial landforms with naturally replenished soil nutrients. However, replenishment from natural floods was sporadic, and deposition was often spotty. The most regular and spatially uniform fertilization with sediments and organic detritus occurred in irrigated fields, and was therefore artificial. Flood farming, runoff farming, and water-table farming were all permanent, fixed-plot, sustainable systems. In contrast, dry farming and irrigated farming might have required shifting field locations in certain locales, allowing fallow cycles to restore soil fertility and, in irrigated systems, to reduce water logging and salinization.

These early cultivation techniques and their associated water management technologies were not entirely discrete but were overlapping modes. Each group of early farmers probably practiced multiple types simultaneously and shifted emphasis when necessary. However, it is likely that some groups specialized in certain techniques.

RELATED SOCIAL AND ECONOMIC CHANGES

Current evidence indicates that agriculture was practiced in the Southwest for many centuries before cultigens became a subsistence focus, before crop productivity increased through labor investments in canals and terraces, before settlements became larger and more permanent, and before the village became an important form of social organization. As in many other parts of the world, the transition to agriculture in this region occurred over a long period of time and had delayed social and economic consequences.

Archaeological patterns show that as the subsistence importance of agriculture increased residential mobility decreased. In turn, agricultural production and reduced mobility were associated with the development of food storage technologies and specialized resource procurement strategies, increased human fertility, decreases in nutrition and health, and numerous changes in social organization. Some of the most important social shifts included changes in territoriality, trade, male-female division of labor, processes of passing cultural knowledge between generations, and concepts of property, privacy, cooperation, and competition.

The pooling of labor to construct canal systems and hillside terraces as early as 1500–1200 BC in the southern Basin and Range province represents corporate organization. A shift in the primary location of pit storage from outdoor common areas to inside houses, evident in early irrigation communities in the southern Basin and Range province before 800 BC, and in some farming settlements on the Colorado Plateau after AD 500, has been interpreted as reflecting a change from sharing food with the group to sharing food only within the family, and the rise of the household as the fundamental social and economic unit. This shift to private storage of food surpluses also represents the development of the concept of private property, as differentiated from common property and open-access resources.

The typical placement of burials within habitation areas and use of anthropomorphic figurines in domestic spaces may reflect ancestor veneration related to the increasing importance of lineages to legitimize household property rights and inheritance in these early farming communities. In the southern Basin and Range province, the appearance of courtyard groups of houses, large special-function buildings, and formal cemeteries spatially separated from habitation areas between 800 and 400 BC in the largest agricultural settlements may represent a transition to extended family households and integration of multiple households. These social and economic changes in early farming communities were the basis of development of later southwestern cultures.

Further Reading: Doolittle, William E., and Jonathan B. Mabry, "Environmental Mosaics, Agricultural Diversity, and the Evolutionary Adoption of Maize in the American Southwest," in *Histories of Maize: Multidisciplinary Approaches to the Prehistory, Biogeography, Domestication, and Evolution of Maize*, edited by John Staller, Robert Tykot, and Bruce Benz (San Diego, CA: Elsevier, 2006), 109–121; Huckell, Bruce B., Lisa W. Huckell, and K. K. Benedict, "Maize Agriculture and the Rise of Mixed Farming-Foraging Economies in Southeastern Arizona during the Second Millennium BC," in *Traditions, Transitions, and Technologies: Themes in Southwestern Prehistory*, edited by Sarah Schlanger (Boulder: University Press of Colorado, 2002), 137–159; Mabry, Jonathan B., "Diversity in Early Southwestern Farming Systems and Optimization Models of Transitions to Agriculture," in *Subsistence and Resource Use Strategies of Early Agricultural Communities in Southern Arizona*, edited by Michael W. Diehl, Anthropological Papers No. 34 (Tucson: Center for

Desert Archaeology, 2005), 113–152, Web site, http://www.cdarc.org; Matson, R. G., *The Origins of Southwestern Agriculture* (Tucson: University of Arizona Press, 1991); Sliva, R. Jane, ed., *Material Cultures and Lifeways of Early Agricultural Communities in Southern Arizona*, Anthropological Papers No. 35 (Tucson: Center for Desert Archaeology, 2005), Web site, http://www.cdarc.org; Vierra, Bradley J., ed., *The Late Archaic Across the Borderlands: From Foraging to Farming* (Austin: University of Texas Press, 2005); Wills, W. H., "Plant Cultivation and the Evolution of Risk-Prone Economies in the Prehistoric American Southwest," in *Transitions to Agriculture in Prehistory*, edited by A. B. Gebauer and T. D. Price, Monographs in World Archaeology Vol. 4 (Madison, WI: Prehistory Press, 1992), 153–176.

Jonathan B. Mabry

CLASSIC PERIOD CULTURAL AND SOCIAL INTERACTIONS AND MIGRATIONS

The Southwest is conventionally divided into three major cultural regions: Anasazi, Hohokam, and Mogollon. Anasazi (also Ancestral Pueblo) denotes the "Four Corners" area of the Colorado Plateau, around the common corners of Colorado, Utah, Arizona, and New Mexico. Hohokam refers to the Sonoran Desert region of Phoenix and Tucson, in southern Arizona. Mogollon takes its name from the mountain range and highlands that separate the Anasazi and Hohokam regions. The Mogollon Highlands run in a broad band from southwestern New Mexico to north central Arizona. Anasazi was to the north and northeast, and Hohokam to the southwest and west of the Mogollon Highlands.

AD 900–1125

During the period from AD 900 to 1125, these three areas were the settings of notable cultural developments: Chaco in Anasazi, the Sedentary period in Hohokam, and Mimbres in Mogollon. Chaco was a "regional system" centered on the extraordinary regional center in Chaco Canyon: a dozen huge "Great Houses" at Chaco and 200 smaller versions scattered throughout the Anasazi area represent a degree of political integration unique in Pueblo prehistory. The Sedentary period in Hohokam represents the maximum extent of the Hohokam ball-court system. About 200 sites with large oval, earthen features (interpreted as local expressions of Mesoamerican ball courts) were found over an area comparable to that of Chaco's regional system. A cluster of large sites in the area of modern Phoenix clearly represent the Hohokam center, but it appears that the Hohokam region was less centralized than Chaco's. The third cultural climax of the AD 900–1125 period was Mimbres, in the Mogollon region of southwestern New Mexico.

Chaco and Hohokam were the two major cultural developments of the era, but they were dramatically different. Hohokam had red-on-buff pottery, large towns composed of scores of courtyard groups (three to five single-room thatch houses facing inward into a small courtyard or patio), and ball courts, with a market economy supported by canal-irrigated farming. Chaco had black-on-white pottery, largely self-sufficient villages composed of multiple unit pueblos (small stone masonry structures behind a "kiva," or masonry-lined pit structure), Great Houses, and Great Kivas, all supported by rainfall farming. Hohokam, nearer (but not near) the ocean, developed shell jewelry production on almost industrial scales; Chaco, perhaps controlling the important turquoise mines near modern Santa Fe, is renowned for its quantities of that gemstone. It is likely that some of the shell jewelry found at early Chaco sites came from Hohokam sources; the small amounts of turquoise found in Hohokam sites may have come from Chaco or from turquoise sources closer to Phoenix.

Both Chaco and Hohokam peoples were interested in their larger worlds: both obtained objects from western Mexico (e.g., copper bells and colorful birds for feathers). But the most remarkable aspect of cultural and social interactions *between* Chaco and Hohokam is their near absence. Chaco and Hohokam did not interact in archaeologically visible ways. There is almost no Hohokam pottery at Chaco Canyon and very little Anasazi pottery in Phoenix (and most of that comes from the westernmost Anasazi region, a region only loosely involved with Chaco, if at all). Anasazi unit pueblos do not appear at southern Arizona, and Hohokam courtyard groups are not seen in the Four Corners. Only two or three sites are known that have both Hohokam ball courts and Anasazi-style Great Kivas. These sites are in the Mogollon Highlands, with the exception of the remarkable site of Wupatki (discussed later). Political and religious leaders in Chaco Canyon and the Phoenix area must have been very aware of each other, but the Mogollon Highlands apparently formed a sufficient buffer zone between Chaco and Hohokam. The exceptions came around the ends of the Mogollon Highlands: at the southeast end, in Mimbres; and at the northwest end, at Wupatki.

The Mimbres area of the Mogollon region is most famous for its remarkable black-on-white pottery. Images painted on

Mimbres bowls depict people and events using an artistic style that merits inclusion in the world's major art museums. Images also show Mimbres's wide interests: Pacific Ocean fish, tropical birds from western Mexico (and, perhaps, monkeys from the same area), and armadillos, the latter centuries before those interesting animals expanded their range into the U.S. Southwest. Although the Mimbres region was the setting for a long local history, the area was something of a cultural crossroads. From AD 700 to 950, Mimbres was clearly engaged with Hohokam, to the west (cremation burials, red-on-brown pottery, a number of minor artifacts, canal irrigation, and courtyard groups, but no ball courts). After AD 950, Mimbres looked more to the north and to the rapidly developing Chaco Anasazi (black-on-white pottery, other ceramic developments, and unit pueblos, but no Great Houses). Mimbres was an independent, local development, closely tied to the larger world around it. Like Chaco and Hohokam, Mimbres engaged western Mexico, perhaps in parallel or even competition with Hohokam. The Mexican objects and birds found at Chaco might well have come through Mimbres channels. Mimbres's location, south of Chaco and east of Hohokam, probably influenced the shifting emphasis in regional interactions. To the west, Hohokam's energy dissipated during the Sedentary period, while Chaco rose to prominence in the north, and Mimbres registered those shifting fortunes.

At the opposite end of the Mogollon Highland zone, far to the northwest, a natural event profoundly affected cultural interactions: the eruption of Sunset Crater (near Flagstaff, Arizona). The volcano erupted sometime in the very late eleventh or early twelfth century AD. The southwestern region had not seen active volcanism for millennia, and Sunset Crater (although a small volcano) must have been a major phenomenon. The fire cloud and plume were visible over much of the Southwest, including much of the Chaco and Hohokam regions. Prior to the Sunset Crater eruption, the area was a backwater, populated with small farming villages beyond both Chaco and Hohokam spheres. Very shortly after the brief but spectacular eruption, the site of Wupatki combined one of the last Hohokam ball courts ever built, a late Chaco Great House, and a Great Kiva–like building. Wupatki was a remarkably rich site, producing extraordinary quantities of western Mexican and locally made high-value items denoting ritual and political power. The combination of volcano, Hohokam, and Chaco, over a base of strong local traditions, was a rich mix. It produced new ritual and social formations that contributed importantly to later Pueblo history.

AD 1125–1350

The early Sedentary period marked the apogee of Hohokam, and the ball-court system unraveled thereafter, during the middle and late Sedentary period. As noted, while Hohokam diminished, Chaco expanded, reaching its maximum geographic extent around AD 1100. Building ceased at Chaco Canyon by AD 1125, and its Great Houses fell into decay. But the idea of an Anasazi regional center did not end. After AD 1110, a second center was built 60 kilometers north of Chaco Canyon, at the misnamed Aztec Ruins complex. Construction of Great Houses at Aztec Ruins continued through AD 1280.

Aztec Ruins represented a retrenchment and decline: while the Chacoan regional system was characterized by widespread trade and exchange of both local and Mesoamerican objects, the northern Anasazi region from AD 1125 to 1300 saw little exchange of "exotics," or objects from beyond the local area. Aztec's region was also smaller than Chaco's, and less well integrated. Mesa Verde, for example, was probably within Aztec's sphere (as it had been within Chaco's) but was far more independent of Aztec than it had been from the earlier regional center. Social controls deteriorated, and the period from AD 1125 to 1300 was marked by increasing inter-village violence, eventually approaching warlike severity.

Far to the south, Mimbres ceased at the same time as Chaco, that is, about AD 1125. No one made the beautiful black-and-white pottery. Architecture shifted from stone masonry to adobe-walled pueblos, burial practices changed, and a range of cultural practices were abandoned and replaced over a notably short time. Population dropped in the core Mimbres area. Old Mimbres villages were abandoned, with the population moving up into the surrounding hills or shifting south out into the deserts. The changes were dramatic, and there is much debate about continuities and discontinuities between Mimbres and the role of Mimbres and post-Mimbres populations in subsequent developments, such as the great fourteenth century of Paquimé (discussed later). The timing of Mimbres's and Chaco's collapses was almost certainly not coincidental, but the precise historical linkages are (like Mimbres's fate) the subject of much debate.

In the Hohokam region, in the late eleventh or early twelfth century, ball courts fell into disrepair and were replaced (in larger towns) by a new architectural form: platform mounds. Platform mounds were large, flat-topped, rectangular, solid-fill structures, originally built as stages for village ceremonies but later co-opted by ruling elites, who (after about AD 1250) built their homes atop what were previously communal sacred spaces. Many other traditions that defined Hohokam disappeared or abruptly changed, including burial ritual and ceramic decoration. The courtyard group continued or transformed into adobe-walled compounds, and shell jewelry production continued at diminished scales. The early twelfth century AD shifts in Hohokam were less dramatic than those of Mimbres, which essentially ended, but were more marked than the attenuated continuation of Chaco in a new center at Aztec Ruins.

The remarkable disruptions in Chaco, Hohokam, and Mimbres around AD 1125–1150 were mirrored in decreased social and cultural interactions. As noted, the Aztec area (including Mesa Verde) was more or less cut off from the flow of objects and ideas that characterized Chaco's era. Perhaps this inward focus explains why Mesa Verde pottery and regional architecture became more and more stylized. Mesa Verde–style pottery, unit pueblos, and kivas attained a cookie-cutter sameness across this broad area compared to the wider variation in ceramics and architecture encompassed by Chaco. Conversely, Hohokam fragmented into a number of subregions, with the Tucson area (for example) spinning off in its trajectory of pottery and architecture. Platform mounds were found through much (but not all) of the area previously marked by ball courts, but their histories varied from site to site, in Phoenix to Tucson and beyond.

While Mimbres and Hohokam were, in effect, reforming during the late thirteenth century, Aztec and the Mesa Verde region reached a cultural peak with the magnificent cliff dwellings of Mesa Verde National Park and elsewhere. The cliff dwellings, wonderful in their architecture, were unfortunately symptoms of troubled times: warfare forced villagers to move into protective alcoves in the cliffs. Although less commonly known, Mesa Verde people also clustered into very large, sometimes walled towns in the plains below Mesa Verde—again, it is thought, at least in part for defense. Social disruption across the whole Four Corners area spurred out-migration, first a trickle and then a flood. At its peak, the Mesa Verde region was home to tens of thousands of people, perhaps as many as 40,000. Out-migration of families, clans, and whole villages began as early as AD 1250 (and probably decades earlier), punctuated finally by a severe drought about AD 1275–1300. By 1300, everyone was gone.

Whole villages moved hundreds of kilometers to the south, to the edge of the old Mimbres region and well into the old Hohokam area. Migrant village sites are known from near Truth or Consequences, New Mexico, on the east to near Tucson, Arizona, on the west. Not everyone went that far; indeed, most of the people leaving the Four Corners went to the Rio Grande area, the areas around modern Acoma and Zuni pueblos, Mogollon Highlands of Arizona, and the Hopi area. Scores of substantial towns already occupied those areas. The influx of new peoples from the north strained farmlands and existing social arrangements. Absent effective central authority (such as Chaco), villages and towns experimented with new ways to arrange their societies. A burst of ritual and religious ideas swept the Pueblo southwest (climaxing in the late fourteenth and early fifteenth centuries AD). Some of those new ideas came from the remarkable ritual synthesis at Wupatki; others expanded concepts first developed in Mimbres (as shown on Mimbres bowls); still others were adapted from Mesoamerican or Hohokam ideas; and of course many religious developments were wholly internal to Pueblo peoples and their earlier histories. The Pueblo region, from Hopi on the west to the Rio Grande on the east, shared these ideas, which are seen archaeologically as remarkable widespread art styles on wall murals and painted pottery. Although Pueblos of the fourteenth century AD (and later) formed tight clusters, with broad areas of empty lands

between, the art styles and the ideologies they represented spread rapidly back and forth between Hopi and the Rio Grande. There were almost certainly substantial population movements within the Pueblo region, east and west, at the same time migrations came from the north. The cultural and social interactions between Four Corners peoples and existing populations in the areas of modern Pueblos created the distinctive Pueblo ways of life, which clearly rejected central political authority on the models of Chaco and Aztec Ruins. It was a new and vibrant synthesis but also a reaction against the failed political systems of the eleventh through twelfth centuries AD.

Hohokam, in decline, experienced a brief burst of superficial glory in the misnamed Classic period—the era of platform mounds. Initially, as noted earlier, the platform mounds were built for public ritual; however, sometime after AD 1200 (coincident with out-migrations from the Four Corners), platform mounds expanded into truly monumental structures, supporting the homes of ruling elites. Populations in many Phoenix area towns boomed as people moved in from outlying valleys and settlements. Trade and exchange returned to levels seen at the height of Hohokam. But the apparent prosperity was short-lived. Rising numbers of people outstripped the capacities of canal farming. Health declined, and population was maintained only by local in-migration, which soon ceased. The Classic period of Hohokam sputtered to an end sometime after AD 1400, punctuated by dramatic floods in the late fourteenth and early fifteenth centuries AD, which destroyed the irrigation canals.

The decline of Classic period Hohokam was matched by the rise of a possible rival, far to the southeast: Casas Grandes, in northern Chihuahua, Mexico. (Casas Grandes was about as far from Phoenix as Phoenix was from Chaco.) The center and capital of the Casas Grandes region was Paquimé, the last and most impressive of the Southwest's ancient cities. Paquimé rose quickly, sometime after AD 1250. Its massive adobe walls rose up to four or even five stories in dense, pueblo-like compounds. Beyond the residential area stood a remarkable variety of monumental structures: effigy mounds, small pyramids, and several large I-shaped ball courts. (Hohokam ball courts were ovals formed by earthen berms, with no known parallels in Mesoamerica; Paquimé's I-shaped ball courts were identical in form to those of Tula and central Mexico.)

Casas Grandes had its own distinctive pottery, likely the artistic heir of earlier Mimbres traditions; Mimbres descendants probably constituted a major part of the Casas Grandes regional population. Paquimé's cosmopolitan connections were evident in pottery: a wide variety from across the Southwest was found at the site, with a great deal of Classic period Hohokam's distinctive polychrome pottery. Beyond pottery, the range and quantities of shell, copper, and other exotic objects and artifacts at Paquimé greatly exceed those from Chaco and Hohokam. Paquimé had more copper objects, of finer craftsmanship, than have been found at many Mesoamerican cities.

Most of these objects came from western Mexico. Shell was also important. Paquimé was over twice as far from the ocean as Phoenix (and Paquimé's distance included a major mountain range), yet Casas Grandes worked shell on levels rivaling Hohokam's. Paquimé has been interpreted as a mercantile trading center with powerful rulers who forged trading alliances and perhaps political alliances with Mesoamerican elites.

Paquimé was on the southern margin of the Southwest. Its relationship to the protohistoric Pueblos, far to the north, remains unclear. Paquimé raised macaws (tropical birds imported from the south) on commercial scales, presumably for their colorful feathers. Macaws figure prominently in the ritually charged Pueblo art of the fifteenth century AD, but few actual birds have been found in protohistoric Pueblo sites (with the curious exception of two late Mogollon pueblos). It seems likely that Paquimé supplied these exotic birds, shell jewelry, and other objects important to rapidly developing Pueblo ceremonial systems. It is also possible that Paquimé—with its strong connections to the south— funneled ideologies and ceremonies from Mesoamerica to the Pueblos, which then reinterpreted those models in southwestern idioms. Thus, several Mesoamerican deities may have been transformed into Pueblo supernaturals.

The Southwest's last city was also its most cosmopolitan, most clearly connected to its region and to the larger continent of which the Southwest was a part. From the earliest appearance of maize, however, the Southwest was linked to Mesoamerica; the strength and significance of Southwest-Mesoamerican interactions varied with time and circumstance. The rulers of Chaco appealed to Mesoamerican symbols, objects, and architectural styles to legitimize their regime and may have shipped turquoise south in return, but direct contacts between Chaco and Tula (for example) were probably few. More significantly, Hohokam itself may represent (at least in part) a very early migration of peoples from western Mexico, based on linguistic, architectural, and artifactual evidence. Conversely, many Pueblo traditions recall clans or groups that migrated south, never to return. It is possible that southwestern groups played roles in the cascade of Chichimec migrations remembered by Aztecs, Tarascans, and other Mesoamerican groups. Southwestern migrants may or may not have reached central Mexico, but their peregrinations were part of the larger fabric of interaction and migration that shaped the later history of North and Central America.

Historic claims that the Southwest was Aztlan, the original homeland of the Aztec Chichimeca, are primarily political statements—first put forth in the run-up to the Mexican War (1846–48) and later in the Chicano civil rights movement (beginning in the 1960s and continuing today). There are threads of truth, however, in the deep engagement of what today is the U.S. Southwest and the Mesoamerican civilizations of Mexico. Southwestern societies would not have forged the histories they followed without long, fundamental interactions (including migrations) from south to north, and north to south.

Further Reading: Abbott, David R., ed., *Centuries of Decline during the Hohokam Classic Period at Pueblo Grande* (Tucson: University of Arizona Press, 2003); Adams, E. Charles, and Andrew I. Duff, eds., *The Protohistoric Pueblo World, A.D. 1275–1600* (Tucson: University of Arizona Press, 2004); Adler, Michael A., ed., *The Prehistoric Pueblo World, A.D. 1150–1350* (Tucson: University of Arizona Press, 1996); DiPeso, Charles C., *Casas Grandes: A Fallen Trading Center of the Gran Chichimeca*, Vols. 1–3 (Dragoon, AZ: Amerind Foundation, 1974); Lekson, Stephen H., ed., *The Archaeology of Chaco Canyon: An Eleventh-Century Pueblo Regional Center* (Santa Fe, NM: School of American Research Press, 2006); Whalen, Michael E., and Paul E. Minnis, *Casas Grandes and Its Hinterland: Prehistoric Regional Organization in Northwest Mexico* (Tucson: University of Arizona Press, 2001).

Stephen H. Lekson

RITUAL AND IDEOLOGY AT SOUTHWESTERN SITES

Many people living in the modern world may have a hard time envisioning the vital importance of religious life to the ancient peoples of the U.S. Southwest. From what is understood of the rituals and beliefs of ethnographically studied peoples, however, it seems that religious beliefs and practices permeated every aspect of daily life. Religion was a bulwark for survival, a means of coping with an uncertain life and a sometimes dangerous environment. Ritual practices helped ensure that the sun kept rising, the seasons continued turning, and all plant, animal, and human life remained safe and at peace.

Again inferring from what living Native Americans have shared with archaeologists, a general belief system probably covered most of the U.S. Southwest. This is best described as a complex suite of beliefs centered on the universe, a creator, spirit beings, and the ancestors. In many native belief systems, the universe is visualized as divided into a lower, middle, and upper world, and certain beings, plants, animals, colors, and so on are associated with these worlds. Creation stories often tell of rising from the underworld or a series of underworlds into the middle world; the upper or celestial world is often viewed as the home of the creator, spirit beings, and humanized celestial objects.

Most farming peoples, such as the Hopi, further focused on the agricultural year, propitiating the spirits so that ample rain would fall, celebrating the seasons and planting and harvesting times with rituals and feasts, and praying to the ancestors to help bring rain and bountiful crops. The entire community usually participated. The more mobile groups who farmed less, such as the Yuman-speaking peoples of the lower Colorado River area, tended to have belief systems that were more individualistic and focused on shamanistic rites and dreaming.

When archaeologists look at the ancient Southwest, three major religious and ceremonial systems emerge that were expressed in the built environment and whose iconography can be interpreted to some degree. The first was the ball court–cremation complex of the Hohokam peoples, who lived primarily in southern Arizona. Archaeologists dispute the temporal range of their culture, but all would agree that it began around AD 750 and continued until at least AD 1150, if not later. Perhaps best envisioned as a religious cult to which peoples of different ethnicities may have belonged, this system was focused on a complicated ritual practice using fire and water symbolism.

Ball courts were the primary religious facility (although some archaeologists think they may have served as market areas, dance grounds, or other functions). These were oval, earthen, bowl-shaped constructions where a sacred ball game may have been played. They also may have served some role in water control and distribution, because ball courts are invariably located along major watercourses, sometimes at the confluence of streams. The most important sites had more than one court. The great court at the site of Snaketown along the Gila River south of Phoenix measured more than 60 meters long and 30 meters wide and was about 6 meters deep. Ancillary ritual features were flat-topped mounds built of trash and capped or constructed of clean earth. At least one, located at the site of Snaketown, was surrounded by a wooden palisade.

Fire was used as a cleansing and transforming mechanism. The dead were cremated, and the remains were placed in ceramic urns or pits and buried. Dwellings and possessions were burned as a termination ritual performed at abandonment or when one of the residents died. Offerings such as ceramic containers placed with cremations or caches of pottery figurines, miniature vessels, and other objects were ritually broken, burned, and buried. Stone palettes and carved stone censors were used together in the ritual burning of mineral substances, perhaps to create colored flames.

Water symbolism also figured prominently. Pottery vessels, shell ornaments, and stone objects were decorated with images of water birds, frogs, and snakes. The utilitarian pottery was tempered with pulverized micaceous schists, and the shiny bits of mica gave the pots a glittering appearance, as if the sun was shining on water.

All of these aspects of Hohokam religious life point to a link with the ancient peoples of Mesoamerica and to a cult

dedicated to bringing rain, such as that associated with the Mesoamerican deities Tlaloc and Chac. Such rain cults had strong mountain-cave symbolism, because the mountain was thought to be the source of water, and caves were the link to the underworld and the ancestors to whom one prayed for rain. Also associated with rain deities were shells, the color blue-green, snakes, and zigzag symbols representing lightning. The ball court was, of course, a prominent feature at many Mesoamerican sites.

In many parts of southern Arizona, the ball-court ceremonial system essentially disappeared around AD 1000. Ball courts were no longer built, and existing ones were abandoned. New forms of burial appeared, and there was new symbolism.

A second important religious system took place in kivas, plazas, and Great Kivas and was associated with the Puebloan peoples living in the mountain zone of central Arizona and on the Colorado Plateau. Kivas were special ceremonial chambers built of masonry much as dwelling rooms were built, but with special architectural features. Among the Mogollon people, kivas were rectangular, as at modern Hopi and Zuni. The Ancestral Puebloans built circular kivas. Both types typically were underground. The special architectural features included a ventilator shaft, a fire pit or hearth with a deflector slab, and a masonry bench lining one of the short walls of rectangular kivas. Often, the hearth was circular and lined with stone slabs, unlike the rectangular hearths used for cooking. Kivas often had small holes in the floor thought to be *sipapus*, which is a Hopi word for the entrance to the underworld, and some have stone floors. Archaeologists believe private religious rites were conducted in kivas, as among the modern Pueblo peoples, such as the Hopi and Zuni.

Ancillary ceremonial facilities were enclosed plazas. At Mogollon settlements, these open-air features were located in the center of the village and were bounded by masonry rooms where people lived. Plazas probably were used for dance rituals or other public performances. The Great Kiva was, as its name suggests, an extremely large, roofed facility that could have accommodated many people. Like small kivas, these were also rectangular or circular, depending upon who built them. The roof of the Great Kiva at Grasshopper Pueblo was supported by two rows of huge juniper posts. Unlike small kivas, Great Kivas had no special architectural features. Some Great Kivas had a feature called a foot drum on the floor. It was basically a stone-lined trench covered with a wooden roof, which would create a drumming sound when danced upon.

Macaws were associated with the kiva ceremonial complex. At Grasshopper Pueblo, many macaws (as well as formal burials of other birds) were buried in kivas, either behind the bench of small kivas or below the floor of the Great Kiva. The modern Hopi ritually dispatch eagles, and the people of the kiva ceremonial complex may have participated in similar rites involving birds. The macaws were obtained from south of the international border; archaeologists know that the site of Paquimé, or Casas Grandes, in Chihuahua was a distribution center for the macaws that were bred and raised there. Young macaws are seldom found outside Paquimé. Macaws in stylized, abstract form are a prominent iconographic image on the polychrome pottery made along the Mogollon Rim. A mortuary complex including extended inhumation and graves that often were roofed like pueblo rooms was associated with this religious system.

Many of the similarities between modern Hopi beliefs and the kiva ceremonial complex suggest that the latter may have been associated with the *katsina* religion. *Katsinas* are spiritual beings who live half of the year on the San Francisco Peaks and the remainder with the people. Masked *katsina* dancers represent these beings at public dances sponsored by religious societies, which are associated with clans at Hopi. These dances are held in the plazas, whereas the societies prepare for the dances and hold the associated ceremonies in secret within the kivas. *Katsinas*, also called Cloud People, bring rain and blessings.

A third ceremonial complex was associated with platform mounds. These large, often massive constructions were built of earth and cobble masonry, usually with retaining walls to protect against erosion. They served as elevated surfaces for private and public functions. Platform mounds are found throughout southern and central Arizona, and their distribution extends to Paquimé and possibly other areas. In some regions, platform mounds were built when ball courts were abandoned; in other areas, platform mounds were built where no ball courts had ever been constructed. Archaeologists debate the function of platform mounds and their origins, but regardless, most were built late in prehistory, around AD 1250 or so.

The ritual complex associated with platform mounds appears to have included the use of Gila Polychrome, one of the later types in a series of painted ware called Roosevelt Red Ware, but did not incorporate macaws, unlike the kiva ceremonial complex. Based on the unusual items found in mound contexts, some archaeologists believe that the rituals performed atop the mounds were shamanistic rites, that is, ceremonies associated with burial of the dead, divination, and feasting.

This discussion of ritual and ideology cannot be concluded without considering the Chaco complex of New Mexico. More ink has been spilled over Chaco than almost any other cultural construct in southwestern archaeology, yet the theories and hypotheses about Chaco continue to proliferate and flourish. In Chaco Canyon between about AD 900 and 1130, Ancestral Puebloans—perhaps heavily influenced by peoples living south of the international border—built massive, multistoried Great Houses of core-veneer masonry with planned symmetry and many huge, circular Great Kivas with foot drums and other special features. They also constructed an elaborate road system connecting Chacoan outliers; these roads appear to have had little practical utility. Archaeologists believe that many aspects of Chaco architecture were connected with various celestial and solar events; for example, the famous Sun Dagger atop Fajada Butte was associated with solar and lunar cycles. Whatever its ultimate function—a ceremonial center, homes of the political elite, the heart of a trading empire, an outpost of Mesoamerican peoples—Chaco Canyon was a cosmological map built in stone.

Further Reading: Abbott, David R., ed., *Centuries of Decline during the Hohokam Classic Period at Pueblo Grande* (Tucson: University of Arizona Press, 2003); Dean, Jeffrey S., ed., *Salado* (Albuquerque: University of New Mexico Press, 2000; and Dragoon, AZ: Amerind Foundation, 2000); Gabriel, Kathryn, *Roads to Center Place: A Cultural Atlas of Chaco Canyon and the Anasazi* (Boulder, CO: Johnson Books, 1991); Haury, Emil W., *The Hohokam: Desert Farmers and Craftsmen: Excavations at Snaketown, 1964–1965* (Tucson: University of Arizona Press, 1976); Lekson, Stephen H., *The Chaco Meridian: Centers of Political Power in the Ancient Southwest* (Walnut Creek, CA: Altamira Press, 1999); Reid, Jefferson, and Stephanie Whittlesey, *The Archaeology of Ancient Arizona* (Tucson: University of Arizona Press, 1997); Reid, Jefferson, and Stephanie Whittlesey, *Grasshopper Pueblo: A Story of Archaeology and Ancient Life* (Tucson: University of Arizona Press, 1999).

Stephanie M. Whittlesey

TRADITIONAL INDIAN HISTORIES AND PERSPECTIVE ON HISTORY

Southwestern Indian peoples have preserved their histories from time immemorial. All tribes have accounts of their origins, clan migrations, and social interactions. Traditionally, these accounts are not written down as in Western culture, but rather are transmitted orally from elders to juniors. These "oral histories" tend to be communicated in religious

contexts, such as initiations into a kiva society or a puberty ceremony. This is one reason that they are jealously guarded and only infrequently shared with non-initiates. These accounts often identify special places in the landscape where particular events took place. The events can be mythological, such as the place where a supernatural deity performed a certain task, or historical, such as the site where a man killed an enemy. Generally speaking, no one individual knows a tribe's entire oral history, since these narratives are typically distributed across traditional leadership roles and by gender. For example, women's stories are sometimes kept separate from men's stories. Oral histories thus constitute a dynamic, community-focused, place-based knowledge system that allows people to know their position in the world and to determine the right course of action.

ETHNOGRAPHY AND ORAL HISTORY

Early ethnographers, such as Elsie Clews Parsons and Ruth Benedict, were immediately attracted to oral histories and sought to classify them into discrete categories. For example, Parsons (1926) classified Tewa oral history into two kinds: emergence/migration tales and animal tales. Benedict (1931) expanded on this framework and classified Cochiti Pueblo oral history into six categories: origin stories, hero tales, novelistic tales, animal tales, European tales, and true stories. As Alfonso Ortiz (1981, vi) points out, these categories are not easy to maintain since what are categorized as "true stories" are no more "true" than those in the other categories. While her typological approach can be critiqued, Benedict (1931, 221) was successful in drawing attention to the importance of myth as a "native comment on native life." Oral history thus reveals the kinds of daily life events that are appropriate for commemoration. It demonstrates the operation of indigenous narrative art forms with specific linguistic tropes. Finally, it reveals distinctive cultural attitudes and dispositions toward being-in-the-world.

Today most scholars deemphasize the classification approach and focus on the agentive quality of oral history. That is to say, they emphasize that oral history is not simply a remembering, but also a doing. When Apache elders tell a story, they do so to establish a connection between people and aspects of the natural landscape, and this connection has the direct effect of causing people who have acted improperly to reflect critically upon their actions and seek to improve them. As Keith Basso (1996, 134–135) explains, Western Apache narratives often juxtapose a character whose mind is insightful (smooth) with characters whose minds are not. The latter characters often fail to understand their true situation and act impulsively in ways that threaten the stability of the group. The former character recognizes the true nature of situation and acts responsibly, contributing to the success of the group. These stories thus highlight the differences between the two kinds of characters and the value of right thinking, which is the mark of wisdom.

Similarly, Ekkehart Malotki states that among the Hopi people oral narratives reinforce bonds of ethnic and cultural identity and create a sense of continuity linking past and present. This linking often takes the form of prophesy. For example, when Sidney Namingha Jr. narrated to Malotki the story of the destruction of the village of Histsongoopavi (Old Shungopavi) by an earthquake, he used it to interpret recent events at Hopi (Malotki 1993, 45). He recounted a Hopi saying proclaiming that if the traditional rituals are not carried out properly, the village of Shungopavi will sink into the ground, which happened to Histsongoopavi. He then pronounced that the time for the prediction was at hand and the process of disintegration had already started. As evidence, he noted that a rock outcrop at Shungopavi had recently toppled over. The clear implication was that ceremonies must be performed correctly and in the right spirit to prevent this potential outcome.

Among the most sophisticated of recent studies are those by Peter Whiteley (2001, 2002), who has conducted extensive research into the Hopi on the complex relationships between oral histories and historical consciousness. Whiteley holds that it is incorrect to suppose that Hopi oral history relies upon a wholly mystical sense of causation. Rather, it emphasizes the thoughts and actions of conscious agents, who are actively conceiving and carrying out plans of action. It encompasses that which is cosmically ordained and that which is pragmatically determined. In a careful analysis of the oral narratives associated with the village of Awat'ovi, Whiteley (2002) shows that the re-imagining of community that occurred after the Pueblo Revolt was due to direct transfers of people and ideas from the Rio Grande region, as well as internal reorganizations within the Hopi villages. He finds that this re-imagining was likely orchestrated by a charismatic leader, known as Espeleta, and likely involved the use of peyote ceremonialism. He concludes from his study that what we know of Hopi social structure ethnographically is not the result of some timeless, changeless structure, but rather the product of historically situated, consciously created social practices.

ARCHAEOLOGY AND ORAL HISTORY

Early Southwestern archaeologists routinely documented oral history in the course of their fieldwork. Adolph Bandelier, for example, collected both Spanish and Cochiti accounts of the Spanish attack on Kotyiti Pueblo in 1694. "I was repeatedly shown the different trails, and I find the report of the Spanish commander (Diego de Vargas) to be very exact and graphic. The condition of the ruins resembles that of a pueblo destroyed by fire, and there is considerable charred corn to be seen. As in every other instance where I have compared the Spanish documents with the localities, and with current tales, I have found them to be of great accuracy, and in substantial agreement with the traditions of the people" (Bandelier 1892, 168–178). This statement demonstrates Bandelier's scientific interest in cross-checking multiple lines of evidence—in this case, Pueblo Indian oral history, Spanish documents, and archaeology—to arrive at a robust historical account.

It was Jesse Walter Fewkes, however, who paid the most attention to oral history. He documented Hopi clan migration stories and discovered far-ranging connections to diverse areas of the Southwest (Fewkes 1900). He then conducted archaeological research to identify the sites mentioned in the narratives. For example, Spruce Tree House at Mesa Verde has been identified by the Hopi Badger clan as one of their ancestral villages and a rock art panel as a record of their migration story. Most of the Hopi clan migration stories probably date to the population relocations associated with the Great Drought between AD 1263 and 1299. However, some are more recent and are clearly associated with the migrations of Rio Grande peoples to Hopi regions after the Pueblo Revolt of 1680.

Oral history, however, fell into disfavor with the rise of the culture historical paradigm. Robert Lowie, in particular, was a leading critic of the use of oral history. He wrote, "I cannot attach to oral traditions any historical value whatsoever under any conditions whatsoever" (Lowie 1915, 598). He castigated Fewkes, by name, for his naive faith in the historic value of clan migration narratives (Lowie 1956). On the strength of this critique, culture historical archaeologists turned away from oral history to the study of cultural traits and their spatial distributions to reveal past migrations and the diffusion of ideas. Archaeologists were not so much interested in what Indians had to say about their motivations and behavior as they were in their technologies, especially pottery manufacture, which were seen as useful in developing analogies for interpreting prehistoric technologies.

This critique of oral history also was embraced by advocates of the processual archaeology paradigm of the 1960s. Processualism focused on long-term "culture process"—the ways in which different cultures adapted to changing environmental conditions. The historical period is acknowledged but deemed of limited theoretical interest because of its shallow time depth. Processual archaeologists were especially critical of the use of ethnographic analogy and oral history, arguing that cultural variability of the past is greater than that in the present and that oral history is a form of biased knowledge. This approach was denigrated with the phrase "the tyranny of ethnographic analogy." This represents a case of misplaced agency since it is people who are tyrannical and not analogies. While processual archaeology has permitted valuable contributions to our knowledge of prehistory, it inadvertently created a divide between Southwestern archaeology and contemporary Indian peoples.

In the past fifteen years or so, archaeologists have returned to oral history as a means of bridging this divide. This new commitment should be understood in conjunction with several international and national developments. First, archaeology worldwide has started to implement a landscape-based approach that emphasizes the construction of place through local beliefs and practices. In many ways, this is a natural outgrowth of a long-term interest among archaeologists in settlement patterns, that is, the nature and distribution of archaeological sites, and reflects a new humanistic interest in phenomenology. Second, there is a growing international focus on multivocality and an appreciation of the importance of integrating contemporary indigenous views of the past. These insights are part of the emergence of a more equitable or democratic archaeology. In the Southwest, archaeologists have worked both for and with tribes, and this has led to the development of collaborative or indigenous archaeology. Third, at both the national and state levels, legislation is changing the power relationships between archaeologists and Native Americans. Perhaps the most important new piece of legislation is the Native American Graves Protection and Repatriation Act (NAGPRA), passed into law in 1990. It explicitly identifies oral history as once of the categories of data that must be considered in weighing the preponderance of evidence.

A recent example of the integration of oral history and archaeology is Robert Preucel's (2005) study of the Cochiti migrations. He has compiled the published oral history accounts of the migrations of the Cochiti people from Frijoles Canyon in what is now Bandelier National Monument to the village they occupy today. These accounts all identify Yapashi and Kuapa as two villages successively occupied. This is reasonable on the basis of archaeological data, particularly ceramic dating. Moreover, there is a formal connection. The two villages exhibit a distinctive sacred landscape—both are located near a Stone Lions shrine. He concludes from this pattern that the people of Yapashi moved south to Kuapa, where they replicated their sacred landscape. This is consistent with stories recorded by Benedict (1931) indicating that there was a factional split at Yapashi, and the ancestors of the Santo Domingo people moved east of the Rio Grande to establish their village while the ancestors of the Cochiti (and perhaps the San Felipe) people moved south to Kuapa.

Another example is the "archaeological ethnohistory" of the San Pedro Valley by T. J. Ferguson, Roger Anyon, and Chip Colwell-Chanthaphonh (Ferguson and Colwell-Chanthaphonh 2006). Ferguson and Anyon approached the Hopi, Zuni, T'ohono O'odam, and San Carlos Apache tribes, four groups with historic ties to the valley, and invited them to participate in the project. Joined by Colwell-Chanthaphonh, they carefully worked out protocols with each tribe to elicit information about past and present meanings of places that together constitute dynamic cultural landscapes. This involved identifying tribal advisors and visiting archaeological sites, examining artifacts from museum collections, and documenting oral histories. The research was conducted with each tribe separately in order to maintain the confidentiality of sacred information, and each tribe had the final authority to determine what information was to be released to the public. This study is an excellent example of how productive collaborations can be established between archaeologists and Indian peoples for mutual benefit.

Further Reading: Bandelier, Adolph, *Final Report of Investigation among the Indians of the Southwestern United States, Carried on Mainly in the Years from 1880 to 1885: Part II*, Papers of the Archaeological

Institute of America, American Series, Vol. IV (Cambridge: Cambridge University Press, 1892); Basso, Keith H., *Wisdom Sits in Places: Landscape and Language among the Western Apache* (Albuquerque: University of New Mexico Press, 1996); Benedict, Ruth, *Tales of the Cochiti Indians*, Bureau of American Ethnology Bulletin No. 98 (Washington, DC: Government Printing Office, 1931); Ferguson, T. J., and C. Colwell-Chanthaphonh, *History is in the Land: Multivocal Tribal Traditions in Arizona's San Pedro Valley* (Tucson: University of Arizona Press, 2006); Fewkes, Jesse Walter, *Tusayan Migration Traditions*, 19th Annual Report of the Bureau of American Ethnology for the Years 1897–1898 (Washington, DC: Government Printing Office, 1900); Lowie, Robert H., "Oral Tradition and History," *American Anthropologist* 17 (1915): 597–599; Lowie, Robert H., "Reminiscences of Anthropological Currents in America Half a Century Ago," *American Anthropologist* 58 (1956): 995–1014; Malotki, Ekkehart, ed., *Hopi Ruin Legends: Kiqotutuwtutsi* (Lincoln:

University of Nebraska Press, 1993); Ortiz, Alfonso, "Introduction," in *Tales of the Cochiti Indians*, 2nd ed., by Ruth Benedict (Albuquerque: University of New Mexico Press, 1981), v–viii; Parsons, Elsie Clews, *Tewa Tales*, Memoirs of the American Folk-Lore Society, No. 19 (New York: 1926); Preucel, Robert W., "The Journey from Shipap," in *The Peopling of Bandelier: New Insights from the Archeology of the Pajarito Plateau*, edited by Robert P. Powers (Santa Fe, NM: School of American Research Press, 2005); Whiteley, Peter, "Hopi Histories," in *Katsina: Commodified and Appropriated Images of Hopi Supernaturals*, edited by Zena Pearlstone (Los Angeles: University of California, Fowler Museum of Cultural History, 2001), 22–33; Whiteley, Peter, "Re-imagining Awat'ovi," in *Archaeologies of the Pueblo Revolt: Identity, Meaning and Renewal in the Pueblo World*, edited by Robert W. Preucel (Albuquerque: University of New Mexico Press, 2002), 147–166.

Robert W. Preucel

COLONIAL PERIOD ARCHAEOLOGY AND SITES

INTRODUCTION

Spanish mission and military establishments across the southwestern United States were each put in place to control interactions with resident Native American groups—albeit for different reasons—and efforts to locate and excavate such sites constitute the bulk of the archaeological literature from southern Arizona to western Texas.

Intimate relationships of a different nature between Spaniards and Native Americans were systematically carried out at what has been termed a micro-frontier level of interactions, where contacts between native and conqueror focused primarily on maintaining a living. Those frequent face-to-face encounters both required and were characterized by less coercive, more cooperative and cordial relationships between colonists—such as Franciscan or Jesuit priest or military personnel—and their Native American neighbors and kin. That more mundane cultural landscape contains potential contributions to Southwestern history that have barely been tapped. Northern New Spain's "everyman," like those "people without history" of the post-Renaissance world (Wolf 1982), until recent years, has been virtually neglected by archaeologists.

The "Spanish" population of the Southwest, in reality, was a heterogeneous one, comprising from the outset very few Iberian-born colonists, who created a hybrid culture neither Iberian nor Mexican, partaking and melding elements of both with Native American societies, resulting in a unique "Indo-Hispanic" culture that contrasts sharply with that of other North American European colonial experiences (e.g., Rothschild 2003; Gonzalez 1967). In particular, the survival of Native American populations and the continuing vitality of

their cultures in Arizona and New Mexico remains a unique aspect of Spanish colonization, in part because of Spanish law, which granted rights in perpetuity to land and resources traditionally required by the agricultural Pueblo peoples of the Rio Grande.

Archaeological investigations in non-mission and non-military sites in Spanish New Mexico and west Texas are the focus of this essay. No sites of this nature have been excavated on the Spanish frontier in southern Arizona. Reports from the work discussed here, for the most part, are difficult to access for the layman and are buried in the "gray literature" of cultural resource management projects or in unpublished doctoral dissertations. The limited excavation and surface survey information provided by this material, nevertheless, brings important insights into the life of "everyman" on the frontiers of New Spain's northern province for nearly 400 years, filling gaps in the surviving documents that only archaeology can provide. Nevertheless, the list of further reading provided will provide access to greater detail than is possible in this brief review of archaeological research beyond mission and presidial walls.

EXPLORATION AND SETTLEMENT, 1536–1598

Of seven known exploration parties that entered the Southwest during the sixteenth century, that of Cabeza de Vaca (1536–1538) from the gulf coast of Texas to the Pacific is the first recorded. Although no hard evidence for de Vaca's route across western Texas has yet been found, Thomas R. Hester (in Perttula 1999) has reviewed Native American archaeological materials from west Texas that closely resemble items described in de Vaca's accounts of his peregrinations. Their distribution suggested to Hester that de Vaca's route lay farther south than some researchers previously believed.

Convincing evidence of campsites of Coronado's army in 1540–41 have been identified near Albuquerque (Vierra 1989) and at the Jimmy Owens site in Floyd County on the eastern edge of the caprock in the Texas panhandle (Flint and Flint 2003). Recovery of chain mail fragments and particularly crossbow bolt heads, many from surface finds in the vicinity of Albuquerque, at Santiago Pueblo ruin, and at the Jimmy Owens site, are indisputable evidence of those mid- to late-sixteenth-century Spanish *entradas*.

The site of Juan de Oñate's temporary settlement at San Gabriel del Yunque in 1598 also was partially excavated, revealing thirteen room or apartment "suites" modified by the colonists in the Native American pueblo vacated at the insistence of the Spaniards for their use. Also revealed at that site were the foundations of the first church built in the Southwest, as well as the earliest evidence for the ubiquitous Moorish dome-shaped bread oven (*horno*) characteristic of today's Pueblo villages (Ellis 1989).

Fragments of imported European glazed earthenwares probably reflect the Spanish origins of many of the earliest European settlers, as does the engraved ivory gun-stock depicting a European scene. Chain mail fragments, a fragmentary archer's *salade* (a type of sixteenth-century iron helmet), brass buttons, horseshoe and furniture nails, and a European candlestick base of brass or copper are among the materials from the excavations housed at the University of New Mexico's Maxwell Museum of Anthropology.

THE SEVENTEENTH CENTURY

Even before the majority of Juan de Oñate's disillusioned colonists returned to Mexico in 1601, a small number of families had already left San Gabriel to establish their residences away from the crowded settlement and engage in subsistence farming and ranching. That trend away from "urbanization" characterizes much of the subsequent settlement strategy of the Spanish Southwest until the early decades of the nineteenth century. In addition to excavations in Santa Fe, founded as early as 1605 and designated a formal villa in 1609–10, seven residential sites of the rural seventeenth-century landscape have been partially or completely excavated, most of them near Santa Fe, New Mexico.

The earliest site produced tree ring dates for construction between 1629 and 1632, and the associated features cover nearly 2 acres. This large *estancia*, or ranching complex, appears to have been torched during the Pueblo Revolt of 1680. Other residential units of this period of settling in appear to have utilized abandoned rooms in pueblo ruins (Kuaua, Santiago, Tunque, Cieneguilla, and other pueblos).

Three sites possess interior room features (centrally located firepits dug into the floors) that suggest the presence of Native Americans, most likely household servants; one features a pueblo-style adobe mealing bin affixed to the floor for use with a *metate* and *mano* to produce corn meal flour. Two sites have very large rectangular corrals that likely were used for personal and working horses, rather than the extensive herds of free-ranging sheep and cattle. Artifacts recovered indicate a wide-ranging network of trade relations with the native Pueblos of the region.

Among other items are thousands of fragments of Native American pottery vessels, which the Spanish colonists depended on for their daily needs. These include occasional vessels of introduced forms made by Pueblo potters—the European soup plate (or bowl) and candlestick holders. In addition, stone griddles (*comales*), traded from their Pueblo neighbors for making the traditional wheat flour tortilla, are present at these domestic sites. Similarly, because of the scarcity of metal implements on the frontier, the colonists often used local stone to chip expedient cutting and scraping tools, gunflints, and strike-a-lights (for making sparks to light tinder for fire).

The presence of spindle whorls made on broken pottery fragments not only indicates that spinning was a substantial aspect of the household economy, but it also reflects the preparation of yarn from wool rather than the cotton thread of traditional Pueblo cloth. These items reflect a substantial activity characteristic of colonial households throughout succeeding centuries in New Mexico, but so far little documented elsewhere in the Spanish Southwest.

Santa Fe was the first state capital in the Spanish Southwest, and excavations in the historic downtown district reveal the remains of numerous seventeenth-century building foundations and artifacts, as well as abundant trash deposited in prepared pits and as landfill in the once-marshy area adjacent to the Palace of the Governors. Excavations within the old Palace of Governors exposed wall footings of colonial era construction at several locations offset from the current foundations, as well as many artifacts relating to the continued occupation of the site to the present day.

Those foundations attest to seventeenth-century modifications to the present building for which documentation is lacking (C. T. Snow 1974; Post 2005). In one of the rooms excavated a unique floor of adobe bricks laid in diagonal fashion attests to efforts to re-create the visual impression of the tiled flooring of the more grandiose buildings in viceregal Mexico. Elsewhere on the more mundane residential landscape, floors were simply of bare earth, packed hard with use.

Test excavations in Santa Fe's present plaza fronting the palace failed to find evidence for its use earlier than the nineteenth century, suggesting that the present layout of the downtown is not necessarily indicative of the past. Additional excavations, some of them only recently completed in the downtown area and not yet reported, have produced considerable information about the colonial uses and changes in the core historic district. For example, excavations behind the present Palace of Governors revealed extensive trash and stratified deposits from the earliest years of Santa Fe through the eighteenth century and later.

Footings throughout the area match closely the structural details of the former extent of the palace compound illustrated in a 1767 map of the villa (Post 2005), as well as confirming additional details of changes to the compound up to the U.S. territorial period and beyond.

Large numbers of artifacts from excavations in the palace point to the higher status of its various governors and their retinues, including three carved ivory chess pieces, fragments of silver galloon and gold leaf, Chinese porcelains, the carved bone handle of a fork or table knife, a silver fork probably of eighteenth-century style, and a necklace of Blue Sucker vertebrae (probably of Native American make). The majority of the material was recovered from trash pits that included debris from twelve years of occupation by Pueblo rebels (C. T. Snow 1974) and reflects, like the above-mentioned trash deposits, efforts by the returning Spaniards to clean up the accumulated debris.

Animal food bones and plant remains from these sites provide significant information on the colonial diet (Bowen 1995; Snow and Bowen 1995). Surviving documents suggest that cattle were the mainstay of the Spanish colonial diet. Nevertheless, sheep bones dominate the deposits in all cases. Native wild game is represented by twelve different species, versus only six domestic European imports. Nevertheless, wild game such as elk, deer, antelope, and rabbits, as well as fish—as evidenced by the many fish bones from excavations in the Palace of the Governors (along with, surprisingly, a toe bone from a Thomson's gazelle, native to Africa!)— contributed only occasionally to the colonial diet in New Mexico. This is in strong contrast to the colonial diet, for example, in Spanish Florida and other contemporary colonial settlements on the Atlantic coast.

Plant remains indicate a limited variety of introduced European species, with native plants constituting significant additions to the diet. Ten or more introduced species (wheat, peaches and apricots, peas, grapes, plums, watermelons, lentils, chiles, and coriander) have been recovered from these sites, and they were supplemented by pinyons, pigweed, goosefoot, purslane, cactus fruits, and sunflower seeds. Other plants utilized by the Native Americans found in colonial sites include cotton, tobacco, squash, beans, and, of course, corn—the latter exclusively varieties grown by native Pueblo people.

Evidence of extensive mining for copper, lead, and silver, and the remains of primitive smelting operations during the seventeenth and eighteenth centuries in the Rio Grande region of New Mexico, are being investigated by archaeologists at present (but see Bice et al. 2003). Two such smelting operations occurred in historic pueblos nearby the deposits, and native labor from those villages might have been used in the process. In contrast to silver (never recovered in significant quantities), lead and copper were extracted for local use

as musket balls and copper household implements, since their importation from Mexico over the Camino Real was prohibitively expensive. Portions of that route have been identified on the ground (Marshall 1999), and its history and archaeology are portrayed in the Camino Real International Heritage Center between Socorro and Truth or Consequences, New Mexico.

REBUILDING AND GROWTH, 1700–1846

In New Mexico, the nearly 150 years following the reconquest in 1693 until U.S. intervention in 1846 is scarcely represented in the archaeological record. One of the more interesting sites, however, provides evidence for the colonists' use of standing walls in abandoned prehistoric (and early historic) pueblo ruins, perhaps for temporary habitation (Snow 1992). These were modified in much the same manner as at San Gabriel in 1598. A number of eighteenth-century residential sites have been located by survey within the western limits of Santa Fe, continuing for some miles down the Santa Fe River; and survey of Albuquerque's north valley floodplain along the Rio Grande have identified the locations of well-known former "plazas," or individual small clusters of Hispanic farming communities dating from the mid- to late eighteenth century. None of these potentially informative sites have been excavated. David Weber (1996) provides a fascinating and detailed account of life at a typical estate of the period in Taos, New Mexico, that incorporates information obtained through minor excavations there.

Alan Ferg (1984) excavated at Las Huertas in the Placitas area near Albuquerque. His report, together with a more recent report of excavations on the Chama River, provide much of our archaeological information about the period in New Mexico. The small two-room structure demonstrating Spanish construction techniques and interior features at Las Huertas contained very little in the way of materials imported from Mexico, and was occupied no later than about 1810 or 1820. Two rural houses in the Chama River valley, upriver from San Gabriel, provide important data on the gradual accumulation of goods imported from the eastern United States by Hispanic families during the Mexican period (Moore et al. 2004). Items such as cheap but durable ceramics (for example, ironstone and "china" wares), nevertheless, did not replace traditional local earthenwares until late in the nineteenth century.

The city of Santa Fe sponsored a project to identify remnants of colonial irrigation ditches (acequias) within the city, with an eye toward preserving the extant segments (Snow 1988). Dating from the earliest settlement, some of them remain in use today, but most reflect the expanding agricultural base that accompanied population growth during the eighteenth and nineteenth centuries. Similar inventories of irrigation systems and technology, dating from colonial times in Rio Grande valley farming communities, also have been conducted and provide important data on land use patterns, settlement strategy, and village formation and continuity (Rodriguez 2006).

An especially interesting and informative location that portrays New Mexican village life at the turn of the nineteenth century (ca. 1790–1820) is the living history museum at Rancho Las Golondrinas, near Santa Fe. Although not an archaeological site, this reconstructed village—much like Sturbridge or Deerfield, or even old Williamsburg—is an accurate replica based on documentary accounts, oral history, and archaeology that illustrates and actively demonstrates many aspects of the *imponderabilia* of daily colonial life on this far northern frontier.

The remains of eighteenth- and early-nineteenth-century hamlets and *ranchos*, some of which have been partially investigated by archaeologists, now lie beneath the waters of Falcon Reservoir in the Big Bend region of extreme west Texas (Pertulla 1999). Much of the research there remains unpublished, but significant differences in architecture (stone vs. adobe bricks) from contemporary structures in New Mexico are evident; the two areas have in common, however, the use of round stone towers, either attached or isolated, for purposes of defense and observation in response to continuing hostilities by Apache and other Native American groups well into the mid-nineteenth century. Many of those small ranches and hamlets, occupied since the 1750s and 1760s, were still in use until the reservoir began filling in the 1950s.

Investigations in advance of surface-disturbing projects in the valley south of El Paso, Texas, revealed colonial and Mexican period remains possibly representative of small ranches occupied by presidial troops and their families in the vicinity of San Elizario. Additional projects of the same nature in the greater El Paso area monitored or tested by archaeologists have identified a number of post-1700 through mid-nineteenth-century sites that reflect the growth of this major urban center from its beginnings in 1659. Most of these locations have been identified from pottery fragments that reflect indigenous and, perhaps, Spanish earthenware traditions, as well as imported majolica (glazed earthenware) types from Mexican factories.

Majolica wares from Mexico, and small quantities of Chinese porcelain shipped from the Philippines, are found at all colonial and Mexican period sites in the Southwest, but together they consistently make up less than 1 percent of all pottery found. Their presence clearly reflects their owners' participation in a "European" rather than a Native American culture, regardless of the great extent to which the two were intimately involved as well as related through intermarriage. Beyond these imported wares, the ethnicity of the inhabitants cannot be determined from the archaeological remains alone.

With the establishment of trade restrictions on foreign imports from Europe and the United States by the newly formed Mexican Republic in 1821—over the Santa Fe Trail, for example—imported goods began to flood the local communities and rural households. Segments of that famous trail have been identified in residential neighborhoods of modern Santa Fe. The economies and subsistence basis of traditional Hispanic lifeways in the Southwest were irrevocably altered by the increasing availability of cheaply manufactured goods, particularly those from the eastern United States, which gradually replaced traditional artifacts such as Pueblo pottery, stone griddles and other expedient stone tools, mica for window panes, and so on. This was especially the case in the more "urbanized" centers at Santa Fe, Albuquerque, and El Paso, where limited excavations have revealed the increasing popularity of (and accessibility to) luxury items, household accessories (including window glass), and farm and related equipment and tools.

Further Reading: Ayres, James E., comp., *The Archaeology of Spanish and Mexican Colonialism in the American Southwest*, Guides to the Archaeological Literature of the Immigrant Experience in America, No. 3 (Rockville, MD: Society for Historical Archaeology, 1995); Bice, Richard A., P. S. Davis, and William M. Sundt, *Indian Mining of Lead for use in Rio Grande Glaze Paint: Report of the AS-5 Bethseba Project Near Cerrillos, New Mexico* (Albuquerque, NM: Albuquerque Archaeological Society, 2003); Bowen, Joanne, "Seventeenth Century Faunal Remains from Santa Fe's Downtown Historic District," manuscript submitted to the Santa Fe Archaeological Review Committee (1995); Ellis, Florence Hawley, *San Gabriel del Yungue as Seen by an Archaeologist* (Santa Fe, NM: Sunstone Press, 1989); Ferg, Alan, *Historic Archaeology on the San Antonio de las Huertas Grant, Sandoval County, New Mexico*, CASA Papers, No. 3 (Cortez, CO: Complete Archaeological Service Associates, 1984); Flint, Richard, and Shirley Cushing Flint, eds., *The Coronado Expedition from the Distance of 460 Years* (Albuquerque: University of New Mexico Press, 2003); Gonzalez, Nancie L., *The Spanish Americans of New Mexico* (Albuquerque: University of New Mexico Press, 1967); Marshall, Michael P., "Journal of a Reconnaissance," in *El Camino Real de Tierra Adentro*, edited by Gabrielle G. Palmer and Stephen L. Fosberg, Cultural Resources Series, No. 13 (Santa Fe: New Mexico Bureau of Land Management, 1999), 15–40; Moore, James L., J. L. Boyer, and D. F. Levine, *Adaptations on the Anasazi and Spanish Frontiers: Excavations at Five Sites Near Abiquiu, Rio Arriba County, New Mexico*, Office of Archaeological Studies, Publication AN 187 (Santa Fe: Museum of New Mexico, 2004); Perttula, Timothy K., and Linda W. Ellis, eds., *Bulletin of the Texas Archeological Society* 70, 1999; Post, Stephen S., "Archaeology, History and Cartography of Pre-Statehood New Mexico: A View from the Backyard of the Palace of the Governors," in *Inscriptions: Papers in Honor of Richard and Nathalie Woodbury*, edited by R. N. Wiseman, T. C. O'Laughlin, and C. T. Snow, Publication No. 31 (Albuquerque: Archaeological Society of New Mexico, 2005), 171–186; Rodriguez, Sylvia, *Acequia Water-Sharing, Sanctity, and Place* (Santa Fe, NM: SAR Press, 2006); Rothschild, Nan A., *Colonial Encounters in a Native American Landscape: The Spanish and Dutch in North America* (Washington, DC: Smithsonian Books, 2003); Snow, Cordelia T., "A Brief History of the Palace of the Governors and a Preliminary Report on the Excavations," *El Palacio* 80(3) (1974): 1–22; Snow, David H., *The Santa Fe Acequia Systems* (Santa Fe, NM: City Planning Division, 1988); Snow, David H., ed., *The Native American and Spanish Colonial Experience in the Greater Southwest*, Vol. 10: *Spanish Borderlands Sourcebooks* (New York: Garland Press,

1992); Snow, David H., and Joanne V. Bowen, "No Scum, No Vermin: Seventeenth Century Faunal Remains from Santa Fe's Downtown Historic District," report prepared for the Santa Fe Archaeological Review Committee (1995); Thomas, David Hurst, ed., *Columbian Consequences*, Vol. 1: *Archaeological and Historical Perspectives on the Spanish Borderlands West* (Washington, DC: Smithsonian Institution Press, 1989); Trigg, Heather B., *From Household to Empire: Society and Economy in Early Colonial New Mexico* (Tucson:

University of Arizona Press, 2005); Vierra, Bradley J., *A Sixteenth-Century Spanish Campsite in the Tiguex Province*, Laboratory of Anthropology Notes No. 475 (Santa Fe: Museum of New Mexico, Research Section, 1989); Weber, David J., *On the Edge of Empire: The Taos Hacienda of Los Martinez* (Santa Fe: Museum of New Mexico Press, 1996); Wolf, Eric R., *Europe and the People without History* (Berkeley: University of California Press, 1982).

David H. Snow

MISSION PERIOD ARCHAEOLOGY AND SITES

After the discovery of the New World by Spain in 1492, a wave of exploration and settlement swept across the continent of North America. Spain established the colony of New Spain in the area now called Mexico beginning in 1520, and this colony rapidly expanded across present Mexico into territory now part of the United States. The Mexican Revolution of 1821 broke Spain's hold on North America and established the state of Mexico, only to witness the loss of the northern Mexican territories to the United States in the period from 1836 to 1848. Spain left a legacy of cultural traits and lifeways that strongly characterizes Mexico and the American southwest. The multicultural American Southwest cannot be understood without a clear understanding of its Spanish colonial and Mexican heritage. One critical component of that heritage is the mission system.

The Spanish method of conquest included a way of subduing indigenous peoples and incorporating them into the European cultural system Spain imposed on the conquered areas. This was the mission system. Missions were both Indian reeducation centers and Spanish economic centers in frontier areas. Although Spanish colonial records document the mission system itself, most of the essential information about indigenous cultural change and the effects of the mission on the frontier economy was not recorded. Our only hope for understanding the powerful effect this system had on both indigenous and Spanish frontier society, beyond the rather simple level allowed by historical records, is through the use of archaeology.

Missions varied in their physical pattern through time and from place to place on the northern frontier of New Spain. However, the core structures remained fairly similar for both the Jesuits and the Franciscans, the two major missionary orders working the northern frontier of New Spain in the American Southwest. All missions had a church, a priest's residence, a complex of workshops and storerooms, and areas devoted to livestock, from chickens and pigs to goats and sheep, milk cows, mules, horses and cattle, although Jesuit plans for this core group of structures differed from the

Franciscan plans. The structure and daily life of a mission bore the stamp of both the Spanish and the local indigenous way of life, and had clear variations according to the specific "missionary culture," whether Jesuit or Franciscan, that built it, the period in which it was built, and the indigenous culture for which it was established.

MISSION ARCHAEOLOGY

As the United States expanded west of the Mississippi into the old Spanish colonies of northern New Spain during the middle and late nineteenth century, its explorers and scholars encountered missions, missionized Indians, and the remains of Spanish colonial and Mexican frontier society all across the American Southwest. However, their knowledge of the history and culture of this vast new territory was limited. How these Spanish settlements, forts, and missions had arrived in the newly acquired American lands was only vaguely known, and the history and purpose of these sites was poorly understood at best. In general, new Anglo-American settlers had the erroneous impression that all Spanish settlement was for the purpose of finding and mining gold and silver, and enslaving Indians to work in those mines.

The earliest investigation of Spanish missions in the American Southwest that could be called "historical archaeology" was that by the ethnologist Adolph Bandelier. From 1880 to 1892 Bandelier conducted what today we would call a surface survey of many of the mission sites of New Mexico and collected ethnographic and historical information about the people and places of the missions. He studied the Indians, missions, and colonial history of New Mexico as part of the history of Mexico to the south. His collected information included measured plans of the ruins of abandoned missions and pueblos, as well as of missions and pueblos still in use. Bandelier had a deep natural talent for evaluating sites. His suggestions about the probable developmental and occupational history of various mission sites have frequently been found to be correct upon subsequent excavation.

Extensive excavation of mission sites began in the twentieth century. The two most complete and best-documented excavations of missions in the southwest remain La Purísima Concepción de Hawikuh and San Bernardo de Awatovi, seventeenth-century missions located in northwestern New Mexico and northeastern Arizona, in the old province of New Mexico. Both are on Indian lands and are not open for visitation. Hawikuh was excavated very early in this developmental period of Southwestern mission archaeology, in 1917. The archaeologist and ethnologist Frederick Webb Hodge directed the excavation of the Zuñi pueblo of Hawikuh as a whole, but Jesse Nusbaum, a jack-of-all-trades who worked for the Museum of New Mexico, directed most of the work of excavating the mission buildings. Nusbaum, who would be hired a few years later as the first professional archaeologist of the newly formed National Park Service and superintendent of Mesa Verde National Park, was fresh from his excavation and stabilization of the eighteenth-century adobe colonial mission church of Nuestra Señora de Los Ángeles de Porciúncula at Pecos Pueblo in 1915. At Pecos, his investigations were done in association with archaeologist Alfred V. Kidder's excavations of the prehistoric pueblo site, probably the single most important series of excavations in the history of Southwestern archaeology because it established the relative chronology and broad pattern of development of Southwestern Indian cultures. Kidder's interests were primarily directed toward the pueblo, and Nusbaum's work, carried out for the Museum of New Mexico, was to stabilize the church ruins; the ruined convento was not part of the project. As a result, very little information about the mission at Pecos resulted from the Kidder work, although during his work there Nusbaum was able to make an accurate plan of the eighteenth-century convento based on the visible surface traces of the adobe walls of the building.

Nusbaum uncovered virtually the entire plan of the principal church and convento at Hawikuh. The detailed discussion and plans included in the published report demonstrate that Nusbaum kept detailed notes and drawings of his work. The excavations found that the convento had been reoccupied by the people of Hawikuh after the Pueblo Revolt; they had subdivided the large rooms into smaller spaces that met their own cultural preferences.

The Hawikuh excavations were not published until 1966, and during the years from 1923, when the project's fieldwork was completed, to 1955, when Hodge gave the task of overseeing the writing of the report to Watson Smith (who subsequently convinced Richard Woodbury to carry out the work), the field notes, plans, drawings, and photographs remained in Hodge's personal papers. Because of this long delay and the seclusion of the records of the fieldwork, the Hawikuh excavations contributed little to the knowledge of Southwestern mission archaeology before 1966.

A detailed artifact analysis of the material culture found in the convento has not yet been carried out. This is unfortunate, because the mission was burned suddenly, with little chance for the Franciscans to remove anything. The result was that virtually everything that was not consumed by the fire on the day of the Pueblo Revolt was preserved in charred form in the ruins of the rooms.

John Otis Brew directed the Peabody Museum excavations at the Hopi pueblo of Awatovi from 1935 to 1939. As at Hawikuh, the excavation uncovered virtually the entire convento and church, as well as a second, incomplete church and several other Spanish colonial structures associated with the pueblo. And as at Hawikuh, the excavations found that the convento had been reoccupied by the people of Awatovi, who divided the large rooms into smaller spaces for their own use. Brew planned a volume to present an analysis of the Spanish colonial cultural material found in the mission, but this was never published. In general, the preservation of the material culture of the Franciscan occupants of the mission was poorer at Awatovi than at Hawikuh.

The Awatovi report became the single most important archaeological report on a southwestern mission because of its interpretive section, written by the architect and architectural historian Ross Montgomery. Montgomery had considerable experience in California in the design and construction of buildings in the California Mission style. In the mid-1930s he had designed and built a church in Montecito, California, between Los Angeles and Santa Barbara, in the Pueblo Revival style then popular in New Mexico. Montgomery had been introduced to the architectural analysis of Spanish colonial churches during his direction of the repair of Mission Santa Barbara after the earthquake of 1925. Montgomery applied this expertise to the ruined buildings of San Bernardo de Awatovi, and he wrote what remains the best overall description of mission life and architecture for the Awatovi report. This was intended to explain why the building had the plan it did, what the uses of the various rooms were, and the significance of the changes to the structure.

Other missions were excavated during this period before the Second World War, although none of them were as thoroughly documented and well published as the Hawikuh and Awatovi excavations. In the 1920s, the first organization of mission sites as parks designed for tourist visitation began, with excavation and restoration work at Tumacácori in Sonoran Arizona, and San José de Giusewa and Gran Quivira (San Buenaventura de Las Humanas) in New Mexico, two of the five "archaic" missions of New Mexico. The other three were Purísima Concepción de Quarai, San Gregorio de Abo, and Pecos; all five were abandoned mission ruins thought— correctly in every case except that of Pecos—to be seventeenth-century structures. Similar site preparation projects continued during the 1930s, as part of the "New Deal" work relief programs of the Depression. These projects usually focused on the quick emptying of a church and convento and some stabilization for the purpose of making the site ready for tourist visitation and interpretation. The other four of the five "archaic" ruined missions in New Mexico were the principal examples of Depression-era projects. In Texas, the major mission project during this period was San José y San Miguel de Aguayo in San Antonio, one of the five missions in the "Alamo Chain" along the San Antonio River. In Arizona, a work relief archaeological project was the excavation of the convento of Tumacácori.

After World War II, the archaeological investigation of missions in the Southwest became increasingly a testing regime rather than complete excavations. For publicly owned sites, which included most of the known mission sites in the Southwest, most excavations were undertaken to document the archaeological remains impacted by construction projects for improving drainage and stabilization of the sites; however, a few sites received more extensive study. The National Park Service acquired the Pecos mission ruins in 1965 and carried out an extensive excavation and stabilization of the church and convento in the 1960s and 1970s. Guevavi and Calabasas in Sonoran Arizona were partly excavated in the 1950s through the 1970s, as were Concepción, San Juan, and Espada, three of the four "Alamo Chain" missions of San Antonio, Texas. The four missions other than San Antonio de Valero (the Alamo) were included in the new San Antonio Missions National Historical Park in the late 1970s, and the three "Salinas" missions of Quarai, Abó, and Gran Quivira became a National Historical Park in 1980. Guevavi and Calabasas were acquired by the National Park Service and incorporated with San José de Tumacácori into Tumacácori National Historical Park.

During the last few years of the twentieth century and the first few of the twenty-first century, interest increased in the last several ruined missions of New Mexico that were not protected by public or semipublic agencies. These were San Marcos, Galisteo, and San Cristóbal, three of the four missions of the Galisteo Basin, held on private land. The fourth mission, San Lazaro, was on public land and protected by the Bureau of Land Management. In 2005 the Galisteo Basin Initiative, a public effort to preserve the ancient and historic sites in the region, included these three missions in a broad protection and research program. Investigations and stabilization treatments were planned and carried out through cooperative agreements among federal agencies, the state of New Mexico, and the Archaeological Conservancy. San Marcos was extensively tested by David Hurst Thomas and the American Museum of Natural History over several years beginning in 1999, before the Galisteo Basin Initiative, and Galisteo and San Cristóbal were mapped in 2005–06 as part of the initiative.

ARCHAEOLOGY AND MISSION CULTURAL STUDIES

Archaeological studies of missions fall into two general categories. Missions were both Indian reeducation centers and Jesuit and Franciscan economic centers. Archaeological investigations usually have looked at both of these aspects as part of most excavations.

The plan of the core structure of a mission in the north varied according to time, the missionary group that established it, and the Indian group to which it was assigned. Missions were fairly similar in the sixteenth century in central and northern Mexico, and in the seventeenth century in New Mexico, laid out around a well-defined central courtyard called the "patio," with the priest's residence adjacent to the church. They began to vary in plan in Texas and southern Arizona in the eighteenth century, where the residential layout around the patio followed the general pattern early in the period, but a less standardized plan became common in the later years. Late-eighteenth- and early-nineteenth-century California missions used a plan distinctly different from that seen elsewhere on the frontier, with the church and the priest's residence forming two sides of an enclosure and the workshops and women's dormitories forming the other two sides.

Jesuits tended to let indigenous people live in their own settlements, regardless of how insubstantial and impermanent the structures of the settlement might be, and built missions near a given village or in an area close to several villages. Franciscans, on the other hand, believed that the mission indoctrination program should include how to build and live in European-style houses. With indigenous people who preferred the more temporary structures, Franciscans would insist on establishing a European-style village for those who chose to enter the mission program.

Texas and California mission design and systems were similar because Indians in both areas were semi-sedentary, and the mission included a residential area for the Indians. Where Franciscans took over Jesuit missions, they added this little European-style town to the existing mission. In New Mexico the Indians were Puebloan, with their own permanent towns and farming enterprises, and the missions were self-contained Franciscan operations, each with a direct connection to a specific pueblo. In Arizona the Jesuits began with a design similar to that used by the Franciscans in New Mexico, but the Franciscans decided to develop a more European style of construction for houses and villages, leading to a more Texas/California approach after 1768, with Indians induced to move to the mission sites and to live in mission-built housing.

Archaeological studies have shown that the depth of culture change varied from mission to mission, and from province to province. Debate continues over the extent of this cultural change at any given mission or mission system; for example, California archaeologists and historians consider that culture change in the California mission system was extensive, even though the physical and documentary evidence seems to indicate that the mission program in California was no more successful than that in New Mexico, and was considerably less effective than that in Texas. A parallel debate addresses whether and to what extent superficial material culture changes indicate deeper cultural changes. In general, the process of culture change is fairly well recorded, but the results are unclear.

ARCHITECTURAL STUDIES

The architectural study of missions is still a relatively young discipline. Although a number of studies of the broad development of missions have been written, as well as several similar syntheses of mission development in single provinces such as California or Texas, the examination of the history of the design and construction of individual missions, and the assembly of histories of province-wide and frontier-wide developmental histories that compare and contrast local and regional design and construction patterns has only just begun. Objectives include the recognition of patterns of mission design peculiar to a specific province, and an effort to determine why these designs vary from province to province. Other topics now being pursued are the recognition of building methodologies and the identification of master masons and master architects. The tracing of the building careers of these master craftsmen across the frontier and the comparison of their major works is a new area of research.

A second area of mission studies still in its relative infancy is the analysis of the decorative programs of individual missions, both as described in historical documentation and as surviving painted decoration and artifacts. One focus within this broader art-historical endeavor is the discovery, cleaning, and stabilization of painted decoration in missions. Examples of this may be found all across the mission frontier. An excellent example is the work recently carried out at San Xavier del Bac, a Franciscan mission still in operation and open for public visits, near Tucson, Arizona. The project to clean and preserve its painted decorations in the interior of the church has been ongoing since the 1980s.

HISTORICAL RESEARCH

Because of the nature of historical archaeology, the development of American scholarship on the Spanish colonial Southwest has directly influenced the interpretation of the results of archaeological investigations of mission sites. It was in California in the 1870s that the first concerted effort to define the history of the province and the function of the missions, forts, and settlements was carried out, under the direction of bookseller-turned-historian Hubert Howe Bancroft. Bancroft compiled documents, document summaries, and interviews with old residents to determine how and why California had been established. His interpretation of the purpose and function of the missions was the first detailed examination of these institutions in the United States.

However, because the California missions were established late in the development of New Spain and of the mission system, and because of their location in a province that itself had a unique relationship to central authority, a number of peculiarities of legal and social practice set them apart from other mission systems in northern New Spain. Because the mission system of California was set up at a time when Bourbon reformation policies for the northern frontier had become particularly influential, they were developed in the context of an ongoing humanist debate about the nature of Indians and their relationship to Spanish colonial society that did not significantly affect the other mission territories of the north. As a result, the history of the California missions is embedded in contemporaneous controversies over the rights of Indians as human beings that colored Bancroft's interpretation of their evolution and nature.

Bancroft's interpretation of California mission history prompted a rebuttal by Franciscan apologists, especially Father Zephyrin Engelhardt. These Franciscan historians perceived his evaluation as negative, and they countered it with a view of the Franciscan missionaries as heroic saviors of the primitive people of California. However, Bancroft's picture of the development of California, set in the context of the broader history of the northern frontier of New Spain, was well balanced and presented the history of the missions of California in a fairly matter-of-fact way.

The conflict between the pro- and anti-mission schools of thought within California historiography led to strong polarization in how the missions were perceived by scholars in both history and archaeology. The general picture presented by California mission scholarship has been characterized by several basic assumptions: Franciscans controlled the lives of the Indians in the mission twenty-four hours a day; Franciscans operated the missions as though they were prisons or labor camps, with little regard for the well-being of the Indian converts; secular authority accepted Franciscan control over most of the land of coastal California, which prevented the non-Indian citizens of California from acquiring land; and Franciscans exercised dominating influence over the secular government of the province. In this period of historiography, at least, the Indians were viewed as thoroughly indoctrinated, with little of the aboriginal culture surviving.

Bancroft's and Engelhardt's published views on the nature of missions and their relationship to the rest of Spanish colonial society in California influenced subsequent historical interpretation of the missions everywhere else across the Southwest. Bancroft himself expanded his study into Arizona and New Mexico, although only as areas of peripheral interest to the history of California. Other researchers took up the search for the story of these provinces. In the early years of the twentieth century, Herbert E. Bolton, the director of the Bancroft Library at Berkeley for twenty-five years, began constructing hypotheses about the nature of colonial society in northern New Spain that had frontier-wide influence. Bolton had been a professor at the University of Texas, where he became involved with the *Handbook of North American Indians* and the *Guide to Mexican Archival Materials Relevant to United States History*. He became a professor at Berkeley in 1911. Bolton defined the "Spanish Borderlands" as a recognized area of study, with Bancroft's well-defined ideas about California missions and their relationship to Spanish colonial society forming a core of influence within Bolton's broad, frontier-wide focus.

In New Mexico and northern Arizona, it was the work of Adolph Bandelier that began to shed light on the formation of the province of New Mexico. Beginning his work in 1880, Bandelier was not significantly influenced by the conclusions of Bancroft in California. However, as the work of Bancroft and Bolton became generally available, New Mexico fell under the influence of the California imprint as well.

France V. Scholes, who received his master's degree from Harvard and who was pursuing a doctorate there, was diagnosed with tuberculosis and moved to New Mexico in 1924. He recovered and became an assistant professor in history at the University of New Mexico. He began correspondence with Bolton at the Bancroft Library and developed his program of research on the seventeenth-century history of New Mexico with Bolton's advice. Bolton's input and Bancroft's scholarship had a strong influence on Scholes's interpretation of the history of New Mexico.

Scholes conducted extensive research in Mexico on the history of New Mexico in the late 1920s, and he began writing his seminal two-volume history of the province in the 1930s. Scholes's achievement was remarkable because most of the documents of local origin, usually so critical to the history of a region, had been destroyed in the Pueblo Revolt of 1680, and Scholes had to reconstruct a past for the province from those documents sent out of the province to other repositories in New Spain and Spain.

While Scholes was reconstructing the history of New Mexico, other scholars were doing the same for Texas. Carlos Castañeda, a follower of Bolton, wrote the first definitive history of the province of Texas beginning in the 1930s. Fray Marion Habig, who had studied at Berkeley, wrote the most detailed study available to date of the development of the missions of San Antonio, Texas, using original research into the archives of Mexico but with Castañeda's broader history as its foundation.

Mission archaeology as an area of study has several unresolved critical methodological and theoretical problems. Perhaps the single most disturbing of these is that room use in a mission cannot be determined by artifact content. Instead, some room uses must be determined based on the specific structure in a given room; and although historical documents, especially inventories, sometimes give full-mission descriptions of room use, so far archaeology has not demonstrated the ability to recognize a friar's cell or a storeroom, or to tell a school room from a dispensary by artifact content. A second major area of concern is that there has been no compilation of Franciscan or Jesuit mission culture and its variations on the frontier.

Further Reading: Elliot, Melinda, *Great Excavations* (Santa Fe, NM: School of American Research Press, 1995); Ivey, James E., *In the Midst of a Loneliness: The Architectural History of the Salinas Missions*, Southwest Cultural Resources Center, Professional Papers, Vol. 15 (Santa Fe, NM: National Park Service, 1988); Ivey, James E., *The Spanish Colonial Architecture of Pecos Pueblo, New Mexico*, Professional Papers, No. 59 (Santa Fe, NM: National Park Service, 2005); Fontana, Bernard L., *Entrada: The Legacy of Spain and Mexico in the United States* (Tucson, AZ: Southwest Parks and Monuments Association, 1994); Lightfoot, Kent G., *Indians, Missionaries, and Merchants: The Legacy of Colonial Encounters on the California Frontiers* (Berkeley: University of California Press, 2004); Montgomery, Ross G., Watson Smith, and John Otis Brew, *Franciscan Awatovi: The Excavation and Conjectural Reconstruction of a 17th-Century Spanish Mission Established at a Hopi Indian Town in Northeastern Arizona*, Vol. 36: *Papers of the Peabody Museum of American Archaeology and Ethnology, Harvard University* (Cambridge, MA: Peabody Museum, 1949); Smith, Watson, Richard B. Woodbury, and Nathalie F. S. Woodbury, *The Excavation of Hawikuh by Frederick Webb Hodge: Report of the Hendricks-Hodge Expedition, 1917–1923*, Vol. 20: *Contribution from the Museum of the American Indian* (New York: Heye Foundation, 1966).

James E. Ivey

HISTORIC PERIOD ARCHAEOLOGY IN THE SOUTHWEST

The historic period in the Southwest covers nearly 400 years and is unique in the United States, with the continuation of many prehistoric tribal cultures into the historic period and the present. Historic archaeology can be broken into three basic periods: (1) the Spanish incursion and settlement, (2) Mexico's influence, and (3) the United States taking control over what is considered the contemporary southwestern United States. The Southwest includes Arizona and New Mexico along with parts of west Texas, southeast Utah, southeast Nevada, and southwest Colorado.

HISTORY OF THE SOUTHWEST
In 1540 Francisco Vasquez de Coronado traveled from Mexico City on his failed search for the fabled "Seven Cities of Cibola." In 1598 a large group of Spanish and Mexican settlers led by Juan de Oñate arrived in the Southwest, claiming the land for Spain and naming it New Mexico. The route they took from Mexico City become known as El Camino Real, the royal road. The Spanish responded to any resistance on the part of the Indians with ruthlessness. By 1608 Spain replaced Oñate with a new governor.

The new governor, Pedro de Peralta, founded the city of Santa Fe as his capital. Santa Fe remains the capital of New Mexico today, and it holds the title of oldest capital in the United States. In comparison, the British established their first colony in North America at Jamestown, Virginia in 1607, and the Pilgrims arrived at Plymouth, Massachusetts, in 1620.

In 1675 the Spanish attempted the complete subjugation of the Indians by destroying their religious and ceremonial objects. In response, the tribes united and in 1680 revolted against the Spanish and forced them out of New Mexico in what became known as the Pueblo Revolt. The Spanish regained control in 1692 by means of a severe military campaign.

On September 16, 1810, Mexican independence from Spain was declared by Miguel Hidalgo, causing a long war that eventually led to independence in 1821 and the creation of the First Mexican Empire, with Agustín de Iturbide as first and only emperor. In 1824 the new republic proclaimed Guadalupe Victoria its first president.

When Mexico became independent from Spain, trade was encouraged with the United States. The Santa Fe Trail was established and American pioneers began migrating westward.

Following the Mexican-American War in 1846, Mexico ceded all lands between Texas and the Pacific Ocean to the United States of America. In 1853 the Gadsden Purchase added 30,000 square miles in southern Arizona and New Mexico.

The Southern Pacific Railroad completed the first rail line through the Southwest in the early 1880s. Along with the railroad came a host of workers, including the Chinese. Although the earliest Chinese settlers arrived in Arizona and New Mexico in the 1860s, work on the railroad brought them in large numbers. After the rail lines were completed, many of the Chinese stayed in the region, finding work in mining, ranching, and truck farming. They also opened retail stores, restaurants, and groceries. In Arizona Chinese communities formed in Guthrie, Fairbanks, Tombstone, Benson, and Holbrook. The largest communities were in Prescott and Tucson. The 1880 census listed 1,630 Chinese residents in Pima County, 159 of them in Tucson, Arizona. In Arizona the Chinese were not welcomed, but a movement to remove them never formed. In New Mexico Chinese communities developed in Silver City, Albuquerque, Raton, and Las Vegas. Many of the Chinese left New Mexico amidst anti-Chinese hysteria in the 1880s. In Arizona many of the Chinese stayed, with some communities remaining today.

Life for the Indians did not improve as Americans came to the Southwest; in many ways it became even more difficult. Whole tribes were forcibly moved from their traditional homelands. Those who resisted were often killed. The United States constructed a series of forts across the Southwest to enforce the subjugation of Native Americans, particularly when they resisted.

Despite the failure of relocation, the United States continued its practice of cultural integration. Some Indian children were removed from the tribes and raised by white families. Education was provided by means of boarding schools, requiring children to leave the reservations to receive any form of advanced education. This practice continued through the 1950s. Native Americans were granted U.S. citizenship in 1924, and they received voting rights in 1948 in Arizona and New Mexico, and in 1957 in Utah.

HISTORIC ARCHAEOLOGY IN THE SOUTHWEST

The southwestern United States has a history of more than fifty years of professional historic site excavation and interpretation. One important early historic site excavation report was the classic *Johnny Ward's Ranch: A Study in Historic Archaeology* by Bernard L. Fontana and J. Cameron Greenleaf. This 1962 publication reported the results of the excavation of a ranch site occupied from the 1850s through 1900s. This report marked the beginning of archaeological investigations of sites dating after the colonial period. Since its publication, most excavations of sites from the historic period in the Southwest have been conducted as part of the reconstruction and interpretation of public historic sites (some of which are listed later) or as investigations to document sites and preserve archaeological information that would be destroyed from new construction or developments that involve removal or alteration of the ground and lead to the destruction or disturbance of archaeological remains.

The southwestern Pueblos, with their unique culture and long history, have always fascinated Americans. The Pueblo people have attempted to protect their cultural resources, and thus there have been few large-scale excavations of the "living pueblos" although there have been major excavations at historic pueblos not currently occupied, such as Hawikuh and Salinas pueblos.

In addition to the Puebloan tribes, there are a host of other Indian tribes who lived during prehistoric times and historically in the Southwest, including the Chemehuevi, Chiricahua, Cocopa, Diné, Dilzhe'e Apache, Havasupai, Hopi, Hualapai, Jicarilla Apache, Kohuana, Maricopa, Mescalero, Mohave, Paiute, Akimel O'odham, Quechan, San Carlos Apache, Tewa, Tohono O'odham, Southern Ute, White Mountain Apache, and Yavapai. Many historic period sites include archaeological deposits related to these tribes. Archaeologists have excavated many tribal historical sites, frequently for or in cooperation with individual tribes.

Early Spanish sites have always been of interest to people in the Southwest, and today many are national or state parks. Archaeological excavations frequently were conducted to prepare these sites for tourism and as part of their maintenance and interpretation.

Archaeological sites from the Mexican period also have been investigated, but most often sites with Mexican period artifacts also have earlier and later deposits associated with them, indicating a continuity of settlement at these locations. There are many multiple-period occupation sites that contain substantial archaeological data from the Mexican and the later American period, including parts of the Rio Nuevo District and the Presidio area in Tucson, Arizona. This continuity in settlement pattern also was found in association with archaeological excavations in downtown Yuma, Arizona, and Santa Fe, New Mexico.

Archaeological investigation of the earliest American settlements has been conducted in Yuma, Tucson, Phoenix, Albuquerque, and Santa Fe. Reports on these excavations can be found at the Web sites of Old Pueblo Archaeology (www.oldpueblo.org), the Center for Desert Archaeology (www.cdarc.org), Statistical Research Incorporated (www.sri crm.com), and the Office of Archaeological Studies of the Museum of New Mexico (http://www.nmculturaltreasures. org/cgi-bin/instview.cgi?_affil=Museum%20of%20New% 20Mexico). Those areas that are available for public visitation are identified below.

Many forts were constructed to protect the growing American settlements. Most were abandoned in the early 1890s with the end of the "Indian wars." They represent a unique period in American history and can be found all over the Southwest, many maintained by public agencies as historic parks.

Substantial archaeological excavation was conducted in the Tucson Chinatown area in the late 1960s and early 1970s and in the Phoenix Chinatown in 1990. Exhibits can be found at the Arizona State Historical Society Museum in Tucson and at the Pueblo Grande Museum in Phoenix.

Archaeological investigations were conducted at the historic African American settlement of Mobile, Arizona, by Mark Swanson and represent a unique work of research on African Americans in the Southwest.

Mining played a significant role in the Southwest's historic period development. Significant archaeological investigation has been conducted at a number of popular tourist towns, including Tombstone, Bisbee, and Jerome, Arizona; and Silver City and Madrid, New Mexico. The Bureau of Land Management conducted large-scale archaeological investigations of the Silver Bell Mining District northwest of Tucson, Arizona. An informative presentation on this historical district can be found at http://www.statemuseum.arizona.edu/exhibits/blm_vignettes/index.shtml.

There are few archaeological and historical sites representing the ranching industry in the Southwest. The Bureau of Land Management maintains the Empire Ranch as a historic treasure as well as a modern-day, working cattle ranch southwest of Tucson, Arizona. You can see the preserve at http://www.blm.gov/heritage/adventures/menu/featured_site_az.html

MAJOR HISTORIC SOUTHWEST SITES

Southwest historic sites can be ordered into a variety of categories. Several categories are used to organize the information that follows about places and sites that can be visited.

Readers should check with the locations or sites that they plan to visit to learn of hours of operation or of limitations or restrictions on visitors. The latter is particularly important for planning visits to Native American pueblos or towns that are still occupied. Categories of places and sites available for visitation include historic Native American pueblos (either currently occupied or maintained as historic sites but not occupied); Spanish period forts (presidios), settlements, missions, and other sites; and American period forts and settlements. Sites and historic districts that represent multiple periods are listed last as multiple-period sites.

Historic Native American Pueblos

According to the 2000 U.S. Census, more than 10,000 Native Americans live on pueblo lands that have been occupied since ancient times.

Currently Occupied ("Living") Pueblos

Acoma. The People of the White Rock have occupied this pueblo since the twelfth century. It is considered by many to be the longest-occupied settlement in the United States. The pueblo is located atop a high mesa with spectacular views from the top. This is perhaps the site that best provides the visitor with a sense of what life was like in a prehistoric pueblo. It is a National Historic Landmark. (http://www.indianpueblo.org/ipcc/acomapage. htm, http://tps.cr.nps.gov/nhl/detail.cfm?ResourceId= 357&ResourceType=District)

Isleta Pueblo. Established in the 1300s, this pueblo was burned when the Spanish reconquered the area following the 1680 Pueblo Revolt. During the eighteenth century the pueblo was rebuilt, and it has continued as a prosperous community to the present. An outstanding historic structure at the pueblo is the adobe Church of San Augustine, built 1709–10.

San Ildefonso. This smaller pueblo has been occupied since the fourteenth century and is famous for the black-on-black pottery by Maria and Julian Martinez. (http://www.indianpueblo.org/ipcc/sanildefonsopage. htm)

San Juan Pueblo. Known by its people as O'Kang, this pueblo was first visited by the Spanish in 1541, and in 1598 the headquarters for Spanish colonization was established here. It was lost by the Spanish in the 1680 Great Pueblo Revolt. In 1692 a mission complex was built. (http://www.indianpueblo.org/ipcc/sanjuanpage.htm)

Santa Clara. Santa Clara was first visited by the Spanish in 1541, and a mission was established in 1628. The historic section consists of one- and two-story adobe houses around two main plazas. (http://www.indianpueblo.org/ipcc/santaclarapage.htm)

Taos Pueblo. This site's multi-story adobe buildings have been continuously inhabited for centuries. Estimates of the original date of construction for the oldest parts of the pueblo range from AD 1000 to 1450. It was first visited by Europeans in 1540 and was the center of the 1680 Pueblo Revolt. It has been designated a World Heritage Site and a National Historic Landmark. (http://www.taospueblo.com/, http://www.nps.gov/world heritage/taos.htm)

Zia. This large "living" pueblo with two plazas surrounded by one- and two-story rock structures has been occupied since the thirteenth century. Many have proclaimed it the finest living pueblo. (http://www.indianpueblo.org/ipcc/ziapage.htm)

Zuni. This pueblo stands on the site of Halona, occupied at the time the Spanish entered New Mexico. The site, still occupied by the Zuni, gives visitors a feel for life in ancient times. It is listed on the National Register of Historic Places. (http://www.indianpueblo.org/ipcc/zunipage.htm)

Pueblo Historic Sites

Hawikuh. This Zuni pueblo was founded in the 1200s but abandoned after the Pueblo Revolt of 1680. (http://www.nps.gov/nr/travel/amsw/sw30.htm)

Salinas Pueblo Missions National Monument. This park contains the ruins of three prehistoric/historic pueblos and late Spanish missions in the Salinas valley near Mountainair, New Mexico. It was abandoned in the 1670s. (http://salinaspueblomissions.areaparks.com/)

Spanish Presidios (Forts) and Missions

San Felipe de Neri Church. This adobe church, built in traditional Colonial style with Spanish architectural traits, was constructed to replace the original 1706 mission church. It is located in Old Town Plaza in downtown Albuquerque. (http://www.nps.gov/nr/travel/amsw/sw35.htm)

San Jose de la Laguna Mission and Convento. This exceptionally well-preserved Spanish Colonial church and mission complex, built between 1699 and 1701, is located on the Laguna reservation. (http://www.nps.gov/nr/travel/amsw/sw33.htm)

San Xavier del Bac Mission. Founded in 1692, this mission contains the most beautiful and intact churches in the Southwest. The present church was built between 1783 and 1797 and is considered by many to be one of the most spectacular historic buildings in the United States, with many original paintings, sculptures, and architectural features. It well deserves its title, "White Dove of the Desert." (http://www.sanxaviermission.org/)

Tubac Presidio. This site contains the ruins of the original 1752 fort established to protect the missions and to quell Native American uprisings. (http://www.azparks.gov/Parks/parkhtml/tubac.html)

Tumacacori Mission. Founded in 1691, this site contains a fairly intact church built in 1799, with associated structures. President Theodore Roosevelt declared it a National Monument in 1908. Today it is part of Tumacacori National Historical Park and managed by the National Park Service. (http://www.nps.gov/tuma/)

Spanish Settlements

Barrio de Analco Historic District. Established during the Spanish recolonization following the 1680 Pueblo Revolt, this Spanish Colonial neighborhood housed workers and others who built Santa Fe. (http://www.cr.nps.gov/nr/travel/amsw/sw54.htm)

Blumenschein, Ernest L., House. This early Spanish structure built in 1797 was home to the famous artist and is now a house museum. (http://www.taoshistoricmuseums.com/blumenschein.html)

El Santuario de Chimayo. This private chapel, constructed from 1813 to 1816, is noted for its Spanish Colonial architecture and quality of preservation. (www.nps.gov/nr/travel/amsw/sw42.htm)

Las Trampas Historic District. This agricultural settlement, established in 1751, is a well-preserved eighteenth-century community. (http://tps.cr.nps.gov/nhl/detail.cfm?ResourceId=737&ResourceType=District)

San Francisco de Asis Mission Church. This 1772 mission church lies just outside of Taos, New Mexico, in the Ranchos de Taos plaza. The building has been recognized for its twin bell towers and arched portal entrance. (http://tps.cr.nps.gov/nhl/detail.cfm?ResourceId=949&ResourceType=Building)

San Jose de Gracia de Las Trampas. This Spanish mission church in the colonial village of Las Trampas, New Mexico, was completed in 1780 and is a well-preserved example of a Spanish Colonial mission. (http://tps.cr.nps.gov/nhl/detail.cfm?ResourceId=948&ResourceType=Building)

Santa Fe Plaza. Since about 1610 this plaza has served as the commercial, social, and political center of Santa Fe. The plaza is ringed with structures in the Pueblo, Spanish, and Territorial styles. Notable structures include the Palace of the Governors, the oldest existing European public building in the United States (which served the Spanish royal governor), the territorial capitol, the state capitol, and the San Miguel Mission. (http://www.nps.gov/nr/travel/amsw/sw53.htm, http://www.palaceofthegovernors.org/)

Taos Downtown Historic District. This historic district was established in 1780–1800 and consists of a central plaza and surrounding residences. Building styles include Spanish Colonial, Territorial, Mission Revival, and Pueblo Revival. (http://www.nps.gov/nr/travel/amsw/sw45.htm)

Other Spanish Period Sites

Coronado National Monument. This site commemorates the first major European exploration of the American Southwest by the 1540–42 expedition led by Francisco Vasquez de Coronado. (http://www.nps.gov/coro/)

Mexican Settlements

La Casa Cordova. Though built at the end of the period, this Mexican town house is the oldest surviving building in Tucson and provides a feel for life during this period.

United States Forts

Fort Apache Historic District. Constructed between 1874 and 1932, this complex contains thirty structures, including structures in the Fort Apache military post and the Theodore Roosevelt Indian School.

Fort Bowie National Historic Site. Built in 1862 and abandoned in 1894, this fort now exists in the form of ruins of its post buildings. (http://www.nps.gov/fobo/)

Fort Huachuca. Constructed in 1877, this fort was a major base for U.S. military forces in their wars with regional Native Americans, such as the Chiricahua Apaches and one of their leaders, Geronimo. Many historic post buildings and houses are present in this complex. (http://www.nps.gov/nr/travel/amsw/sw3.htm)

Fort Selden State Monument. Constructed near Las Cruces, New Mexico, in 1865, this facility housed soldiers who protected local residents until it was abandoned in 1891. (http://www.nmculturaltreasures.org/cgi-bin/instview.cgi?_recordnum=SELD)

Fort Stanton. Established in 1855 to defend against the Mescalero Apache, the fort was abandoned in 1896. Located southeast of Capitan, New Mexico, the site was later used for various purposes, serving, for example, as the first German internment camp during World War II. (http://www.nps.gov/nr/travel/amsw/sw57.htm)

Fort Sumner State Monument. As American settlers forced their way into Native lands, the Mescalero Apache and Navajo fought to retain control over their lands and way of life. This fort was established to subjugate the Native people, who were then marched to Fort Sumner and the surrounding Bosque Redondo reservation, where many died. (http://www.nmculturaltreasures.org/cgi-bin/instview.cgi?_recordnum=SUMN)

Fort Union National Monument. A U.S. Army post and supply depot from 1851 to 1891, it was the base for campaigns against Native peoples in the late 1800s. It is located near Watrous, New Mexico. (http://www.nps.gov/nr/travel/amsw/sw48.htm)

Euro-American United States Period Settlements

Barrio Libre. This historical neighborhood is located in Tucson, Arizona, with many Territorial and Victorian homes from the late 1800s.

Historic Heritage Square. This site consists of historic museums and homes in downtown Phoenix, Arizona, depicting the American settlement of the city. (http://www.phoenix.gov/PARKS/heritage.html)

Las Vegas Plaza. This historic Las Vegas, New Mexico, town plaza contains many structures dating to the second half of the 1800s. (http://www.nps.gov/nr/travel/amsw/sw49.htm)

Lincoln Historic District. This well-preserved cattle town is a fine example of the towns that sprang up after the Civil War. It is renowned as the home of the Lincoln County War of 1878. (http://tps.cr.nps.gov/nhl/detail.cfm?ResourceId=338&ResourceType=District)

Old Governor's Mansion/Sharlot Hall Museum. This historic log building, erected in 1864, served as the residence for the territorial governor and the hall for the territorial government. (http://www.nps.gov/nr/travel/amsw/sw15.htm)

Other United States Period Sites

Empire Ranch. This is a working and historic cattle ranch maintained by the Bureau of Land Management outside of Tucson, Arizona. (http://www.blm.gov/heritage/adventures/menu/featured_site_az.html)

Hubbell Trading Post. Founded in 1878, this trading post served as the interface between the Navajo and the dominant American culture.

Kitt Carson House. From 1843 until his death, this was the home of Christopher "Kit" Carson (1809–68), American frontiersman and legendary hero of the "Old West." The site is a National Historic Landmark. (http://www.taosmuseums.org/kitcarson.php)

Locations that Span Multiple Periods

Barrio de Analco Historic District. First settled in 1620, this barrio is unique because it represents an active working-class neighborhood of Spanish Colonial heritage. The area continues to be occupied, though it has become highly commercial. It is listed as a National Historic Landmark. (http://tps.cr.nps.gov/nhl/detail.cfm?ResourceId=789&ResourceType=District)

El Presidio Historic District. This historical neighborhood near downtown Tucson contains adobe and brick homes from the Spanish-Mexican and Anglo-American period, as well as much of the original presidio (fort). (http://www.nps.gov/nr/travel/amsw/sw7.htm)

Pecos National Historical Park. Located near Pecos, New Mexico, this multi-period park includes the prehistoric/historic Pecos Pueblo, Colonial Missions, and Santa Fe Trail sites; the twentieth-century Forked Lightning Ranch; and the site of the Civil War battle of Glorieta Pass. (http://pecos.areaparks.com/)

Santa Fe Historic District. Founded in 1610, Santa Fe is the oldest capital city in the United States. The original Spanish Colonial buildings are intact here along with later Territorial and nineteenth-century buildings. (http://www.nps.gov/nr/travel/amsw/sw51.htm)

Further Reading: Ayres, James E., "The Archaeology of Chinese Sites in Arizona," in *Origins and Destinations: 41 Essays on Chinese America* (Los Angeles: Chinese Historical Society of Southern

California, UCLA Asian American Studies Center, 1994); Ferg, Alan, and Karen Wilhelm, eds., "Mormon History and Archaeology in Northern Arizona," *Southwestern Archaeology* 19(2) (2005); Sheridan, Thomas, Los Tucsonenses: *The Mexican Community in Tucson, 1854–1941* (Tucson: University of Arizona Press, 1986); Thiel, Homer, *Phoenix's Hidden History: Archaeological Investigations at* *Blocks 72 and 73 (Phoenix Courthouse)*, Anthropological Papers, No. 26 (Tucson, AZ: Center for Desert Archaeology, 1998); Thomas, David Hurst, ed., *Columbian Consequences*, Vol. 1: *Archaeological and Historical Perspectives on the Spanish Borderlands West* (Washington, DC: Smithsonian Institution Press, 1989).

Timothy W. Jones

SAN PEDRO VALLEY SITES

Southern Arizona

Paleoindian Hunters to Spanish Colonists

The San Pedro River is a riparian desert stream remarkably rich in its biological diversity and cultural history. Today a world-famous destination for bird watchers, the river preserves abundant evidence of human explorers who hunted mammoth and bison nearly 13,000 years ago; various Native American village farmers whose crops flourished along its banks for nearly 2,500 years; and Anglo-American homesteaders, soldiers, and miners, including those associated with the Camp Grant massacre in 1871, as well as the founders of the notorious town of Tombstone, Arizona.

The largest undammed river in the American Southwest, the San Pedro begins high in the Sierra de los Ajós, foothills to the Sierra Madre Occidentals, near the mining town of Cananea, Mexico. The river flows northward through northern Mexico and southern Arizona until it reaches the Gila River, draining approximately 11,600 square kilometers of the lower Colorado River basin. The physiography of the basin includes the upper valley in the Chihuahuan grasslands, the transitional middle valley, and the lower valley in the Sonoran desert scrub. The upper San Pedro is located in Mexico, whereas the middle and lower valleys are found in Arizona.

CLOVIS COMPLEX SITES

The archaeology of the middle San Pedro valley is best known for its density of human-mammoth sites, such as Murray Springs, Naco, and Lehner. The Murray Springs site is the most extensive, diverse, and best-preserved Clovis kill site and camp recorded to date. Discovered by C. Vance Haynes Jr. and Peter J. Mehringer Jr. in 1966, six field seasons of archaeological excavation between 1966 and 1971 uncovered the bones of one Columbian mammoth, eleven extinct bison, and a nearby campsite. Other Ice Age fauna discovered at the site, but probably not killed by Clovis hunters, include two additional mammoths, as well as an extinct horse, camel, and dire wolf. Stone tool manufacture, use, and discard is represented by nearly 15,000 individual flakes of chipped stone recovered from discrete knapping (chipped-stone tool manufacture or maintenance activity) loci, as well as by end scrapers, gravers, bifaces, blades, and eighteen Clovis points. Bone technology at the site includes an apparent spear shaft wrench made from mammoth bone. Eight radiocarbon dates indicate an age of approximately 10,900 years ago, making Murray Springs one of the more recent Clovis sites.

The archaeological preservation at Murray Springs benefits from a famous but poorly understood stratigraphic soil layer referred to as the "black mat." Radiocarbon-dated to between 10,800 and 9,800 years ago and contemporaneous with the Younger Dryas cold event, this thin layer of black organic clay draped the Clovis surface immediately after hunters abandoned the site and Pleistocene megafauna extinctions took place; mammoth and other extinct fauna occur below the black mat in the valley, but never within or above it. Maintained by the Bureau of Land Management, an interpretive trail demonstrates the exceptional stratigraphic situation in the arroyo and re-creates the archaeology of the site. Deposition of the black mat was so rapid that approximately 98 percent of the Murray Springs artifacts occur in their precise original locations, and numerous small depressions resembling mammoth tracks were found, similar to those left by modern elephants near waterholes.

The large adult Columbian mammoth and eight spear points discovered in 1951 at the Naco site, located in Greenbush Draw, approximately 2 kilometers from the U.S.-Mexico border, represent the first buried Clovis site reported west of the continental divide. Excavations led by Emil W. Haury and his interdisciplinary team of scientists provides compelling evidence that Clovis groups practiced big game hunting rather than opportunistic scavenging. Subsequent exploration at the nearby Liekem and Navarette sites indicates that Greenbush Draw preserves

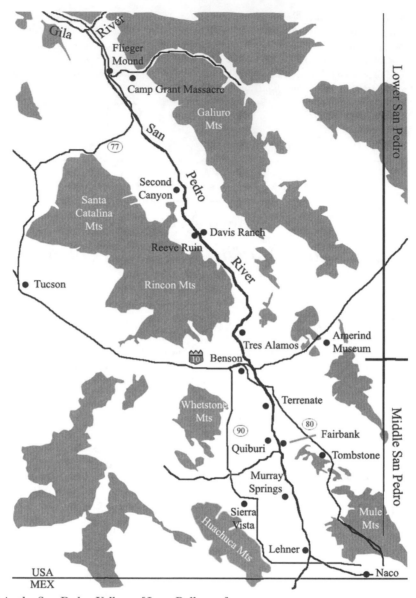

A map of significant sites in the San Pedro Valley.   [Jesse Ballenger]

multiple mammoth skeletons with a complex story of human-mammoth interaction.

In the midst of the excavations at Naco, only 18 kilometers away, Ed Lehner discovered abundant large bones eroding from the side of an arroyo. Also excavated by Emil Haury in 1954 and 1955, the Lehner Mammoth Kill site ultimately revealed thirteen mammoths, thirteen Clovis points, and a small assortment of flake tools directly beneath the black mat. Charcoal recovered from two hearths provided the first radio-carbon dates associated with Clovis projectile points. Twenty years later, Vance Haynes returned to Lehner in search of its camp site. This effort located an archaeological feature inferred to be a Clovis roasting pit containing the remains of immature mammoth, bison, jackrabbit, tortoise, and bear.

ARCHAIC LEHNER AND FAIRBANK SITES
The seminal 1941 work of Edward B. Sayles and Ernst V. Antevs defined what archaeologists refer to as the Sulphur Spring, Chiricahua, and San Pedro stages of the Cochise culture based partly on sites in the San Pedro valley. First recognized at the Double Adobe site in the neighboring Whitewater Draw, the Sulphur Spring stage began as early as 10,000 years ago and continued until 8,000 years ago. In the San Pedro valley, a small amount of fire-cracked rock and charcoal discovered above the black mat at the Lehner site provided radiocarbon dates of approximately 9,350 years ago, the earliest post-Clovis archaeological feature from the valley. A critical shortage exists for buried, in situ Early and Middle Archaic time period sites in the valley, resulting in immense

surface collections but limited archaeological information. Hearths exposed in arroyo cutbanks generally do not pre-date 4,000 years ago; earlier Archaic time period sites are rarely preserved in the arroyos.

Situated near the historic ghost town of Fairbank, the type site of the San Pedro stage was first excavated by Sayles in 1938. Distinctive artifacts include marine shell ornaments, clay human figurines, and the widespread San Pedro projectile point type. Revisited by Bruce Huckell in 1989, the Fairbank site also preserves subsurface pit structures, maize, storage pits, and other evidence of permanent village farming around 900 BC. This led Huckell to revamp the definition of the Early Agricultural period, which includes the San Pedro (1200–800 BC) and Cienega (800 BC–AD 50) phases. The discovery of similar residential features and maize as early as 2100 BC in the Santa Cruz valley indicates that continued exploration is needed for better understanding of just how far into the past early village farming in the San Pedro valley extends.

TRES ALAMOS BALL COURT SITE

Tres Alamos, visited by Adolph F. Bandelier in the 1880s, is the only San Pedro ball-court site managed by the Bureau of Land Management. The fruitful efforts of Carr Tuthill of the Amerind Foundation, Dragoon, Arizona, resulted in the recovery and curation of approximately 1,000 items from the site for display and study. With the accompanying pit house dwellings, cremation burials, and decorated buff ware pottery, the construction of Tres Alamos and five other ball courts beginning around AD 800 demonstrates expansion of the Hohokam culture's sphere of influence, which often is associated with ancient ball courts, pit house dwellings, cremations, and this type of pottery, into the lower valley. A visible lack of similar public architecture farther south in the middle reaches of the San Pedro marks the traditional limit of Hohokam influence in the valley.

SECOND CANYON, REEVE RUIN, AND DAVIS RANCH SITES

The events that unfolded during the late 1200s left a visible mark on the San Pedro landscape. Most impressive are the eleven platform mounds constructed during this time that have been documented in the lower valley, located between 6 and 8 kilometers apart. Research conducted by the Center for Desert Archaeology indicates that these public monuments marked the territories of irrigation communities. Second Canyon and other upstream platform mounds were gradually abandoned during the 1300s; local populations coalesced downstream between the Aravaipa Creek and Gila River confluences. This concentration of people was short-lived, as aggregated communities witnessed population decline. Flieger Ruin, one of the last platform mound sites to be abandoned, was probably depopulated by AD 1450.

The arrival of immigrants from northern Arizona accompanied platform mound construction and aggregation in the lower San Pedro. At Reeve Ruin, Charles C. Di Peso found a walled masonry room block with abundant, locally produced Roosevelt Red Ware style pottery and perforated plates, as well as other distinctively Puebloan traits new to the valley. Directly across the river at the Davis Ranch site, Rex Gerald excavated a rectangular kiva typical of ceremonial structures in distant northeastern Arizona. These sites indicate the practice of migrants forming segregated enclaves but then interacting and trading with local groups within decades. There is evidence that intermarriage and population mixing had taken place by the time both sites were abandoned in the late 1300s, suggesting the emergence of a new ethnic group that combined elements of both local and migrant cultures.

QUIBURI, THE PRESIDIO, AND HISTORIC FAIRBANK

Although the San Pedro valley was probably visited by friar Marcos de Niza in 1539, and possibly again by Don Francisco de Coronado in 1540, the first sustained European influence in the valley developed from the explorations and investments of Father Eusebio Francisco Kino, the charismatic Jesuit missionary responsible for the Pimería Alta region. Described by Kino in 1696, the fortified rancheria of San Pablo de Quiburi was a central agricultural community that supported approximately 100 houses and 500 Sobaipuri Indians amid the tension of Jano, Jocome, and raiding Chiricahua Apache. Sobaipuri livelihood in the San Pedro Valley was brief but productive. Beginning in the fifteenth century, small Sobaipuri communities constructed reed mat–covered houses arranged in open rancheria-style clusters, typically located on high terraces, and maintained irrigated crops on the floodplain below. The geographic location of the Sobaipuri invited hostilities with the Apache but also protected Spanish interests by separating the heart of the Pimería Alta from the Apache threat. Eventually pressured by Apache aggression, the majority of the Sobaipurian population relocated west to the Santa Cruz River basin (including San Xavier del Bac) in 1762.

Spanish efforts to secure the San Pedro valley with a military surge in 1775 were thwarted by the resistance of local Native American inhabitants. Spanish soldiers constructed Presidio Santa Cruz de Terrenate in the valley. However, they were terrorized by the Apache. Unable to sustain itself, the fort lost more than eighty soldiers and lasted less than five years. Investigated by Di Peso and listed on the National Register of Historic Places as one of the best-preserved presidios in America, the adobe and stone walls of the chapel, commandant's quarters, and other structures are still visible at the site. An interpretive trail within the presidio describes the fortifications and re-creates the isolation experienced by the fort's unlucky occupants.

One hundred years after the presidio's abandonment, a stage-coach stop was established at the nearby site of Fairbank. The Gadsden Purchase of 1853, as well as a treaty with Chief Cochise and his raiding Apaches, made this and other Anglo-American communities possible. Inspired by the 1878 discovery of silver in Tombstone, the town of Fairbank became a railroad depot for the movement of cattle and ore. Not immune to the lawlessness of Tombstone, the site witnessed a train robbery attempt, as well as whatever social dynamics spilled through the doors of its saloon. The community that endured in Fairbank maintained a small schoolhouse until 1944; the post office closed in 1970. Restored by the Bureau of Land Management in 2007, a self-guided trail and museum is open to the public.

Further Reading: Carpenter, John P., and Guadalupe Sanchez, eds., *Prehistory of the Borderlands: Recent Research in the Archaeology of Northern Mexico and the Southern Southwest* (Tucson: University of Arizona Press, 1997); Clark, Jeffery J., and Patrick D. Lyons, eds., *Migrants and Mounds: Classic Period Archaeology of the Lower San Pedro Valley*, Anthropological Papers, No. 45 (Tucson, AZ: Center for Desert Archaeology, 2007); Colwell-Chanthaphonth, Chip, *Massacre at Camp Grant* (Tucson: University of Arizona Press, 2007); Di Peso, Charles C., *The Reeve Ruin of Southeastern Arizona: A Study of a Prehistoric Western Pueblo Migration into the Middle San Pedro Valley*, Publication No. 8 (Dragoon, AZ: Amerind Foundation, 1958); Haury, Emil W., Ernst V. Antevs, and John F. Lance, "Artifacts with Mammoth Remains, Naco, Arizona: Discovery of the Naco Mammoth and the Associated Projectile Points," *American Antiquity* 19 (1953): 1–14; Haury, Emil W., E. B. Sayles, and William W. Wasley, "The Lehner Mammoth Site, Southeastern Arizona," *American Antiquity* 25 (1959): 2–32; Haynes, C. Vance, Jr., and Bruce B. Huckell, eds., *Murray Springs: A Clovis Site with Multiple Activity Areas in the San Pedro Valley, Arizona* (Tucson: University of Arizona Press, 2007); Hill, J. Brett, Jeffery J. Clark, and Patrick D. Lyons, "Prehistoric Demography in the Southwest: Migration, Coalescence, and Hohokam Population Decline," *American Antiquity* 69 (2004): 689–716; Seymour, Deni J., "Sobaipuri-Pima Occupation in the Upper San Pedro Valley," *New Mexico Historical Review* 78 (2003): 147–166.

Jesse Ballenger

ARROYO CUERVO AREA ANCIENT SITES

Northwestern New Mexico
Searching for the Ancestors of the Anasazi

The Anasazi Origins Project was initiated by Dr. Cynthia Irwin-Williams as part of a long-term research program to identify the Archaic hunting and gathering predecessors of Pueblo culture. This work was conducted in the Arroyo Cuervo area located northwest of Albuquerque, New Mexico. The fieldwork for the original Anasazi Origins Project (AOP I) began during the summer of 1967 and was completed by the summer of 1971. The work conducted during the summers of 1970 and 1971 also included long-range surveys into the adjacent Puerco River valley. Excavations were carried out at about eighteen major archaeological sites, consisting of both open-air sites and rockshelters: Armijo Shelter, Casa Redondo, Collier Dune, Cuervo Shelter, Dunas Altas, En Medio Shelter, Mosca Dunes, Mud Lump, Ojito Dune, Ojito Shelter, Sandoval Springs, Shelten's Shelter, Sky Village, Tompsett Shelter, and Westover Shelter. All of these sites were located in the Arroyo Cuervo area; however, work was also conducted at the Moquino and Jackpile sites located near Laguna, New Mexico, and there was limited testing with the analysis of previously collected materials from the La Bajada site near Cochiti, New Mexico. Besides the excavations, a number of sites were tested and surveyed, with archaeological materials also being collected from various locales in the Arroyo Cuervo area. A second field campaign was conducted during the summers of 1982 to 1986. This is referred to as the AOP II project. Most of the work consisted of archaeological survey and in-field collections, with a limited amount of excavation and some new documentation of the earlier AOP I sites. All the collections are currently curated at Eastern New Mexico University.

The concept of the Archaic in the Southwest was poorly defined prior to the Anasazi Origins Project, but had its beginnings with the Basketmaker remains identified by the Wetherills at the turn of the last century. During the 1920s, Alfred Kidder first postulated the existence of the hypothetical Basketmaker I stage in his development of the Pecos chronology, consisting of nomadic hunter-gatherers who used the *atl atl* and made coiled baskets (pre–AD 1). This stage was followed by Basketmaker II, which Kidder represented by the addition of maize, but no pottery (AD 1–500). Much of this evidence was based on the fieldwork of Kidder and Guernsey in the Four Corners region. Excavations subsequently conducted at Jemez Cave in north central New Mexico yielded Archaic dart points, sandals, and maize. The relationship between these artifacts was unclear, and not until the 1950s and the advent of radiocarbon dating would the

Absolute Chronology	Cultural Identity	Dunas Altas	Collier Dunes	Ojito Dunes	La Bajada	Armijo Shelter	En Medio Shelter	Sandoval Springs	Shelten Shelter	Querencia Cliff	T Bar I	Piedras Del Cielo	Pueblo Groups Collected and/or Tested	Puname (ELLIS 1966)
PRESENT	(ZIA) V / Pueblo IV–I / BM III	1/A1	Surf / Surf	Surf	A1	A1	A1 / A2	1/A	A / B		A / B	A / B	Loma Alta, Cañon Salado, Sky Village, Loma Fria, Prieta Vista, Esquinita	I
1500 / 1000 / 500		Surf	Surf	Surf		A2 / B / C			C	A				
A.D. / B.C. 500	(LATE BM II) EN MEDIO	Surf	Surf / 3-4aA1	Surf	Surf	D / E	B1 / B2	3/B1 / 3/B2	D					
1000	(EARLY)		3-4aA1			F / G		3/B3						
1500	ARMIJO	3-4aA2	3-4aA2	3-4aA		H / I1	C / E D / F	3-4/B4						
2000	SAN JOSE	4a/B / 4a-b/C	4a/B / 4a-b/C	4b/B	Surf			4b/C						
2500 / 3000 / 3500														
4000	(LATE) BAJADA	Surf	4c/D / Surf	Surf	A2 / B									
4500 / 5000	(EARLY)	4b/D												
5500	JAY	4b/E	Surf	Surf										
6000		~~~~~~												
6500	CODY COMPLEX	5/F		Surf	Surf									
7500														
8500	(FOLSOM)	Surf	Surf	Surf	Surf									
9500	(CLOVIS)													

Archaeological site stratigraphic sequences for the Oshara tradition.   [Chart by Cynthia Irwin-Williams, original on file at Department of Anthropology, Eastern New Mexico University]

Archaic context of this early maize be confirmed at the first few centuries BC. Otherwise, systematic studies of the Archaic shifted from rockshelters to open-air sites during the 1940s and 1950s. Various regional traditions were defined, with the antiquity of these Archaic deposits being substantiated by the geomorphologic evidence and the radiocarbon dating of amaranth seeds to about 4000 BC.

This was the state of Archaic hunter-gatherer research when Cynthia Irwin-Williams initiated the Anasazi Origins Project. Her systematic excavations at numerous stratified rockshelters and open-air sites provided the basis for defining the Oshara tradition. This was a cultural-historical framework that divided the Archaic into five phases: Jay (5500–4800 BC), Bajada (4800–3200 BC), San Jose (3200–1800 BC), Armijo (1800–800 BC), and En Medio (800 BC–AD 400). She proclaimed that "the earliest archaeological materials which can be directly connected with the development of Anasazi (Ancestral Pueblo) culture belong to the general group termed Archaic, defined in terms of a broadly based mixed hunting and gathering economy" (Irwin-Williams 1973, 4).

As previously noted, this data was collected from a series of excavations conducted in the Arroyo Cuervo area and adjacent regions. Nonetheless, the results of this project have been presented in a single synthetic monograph that defines the Oshara tradition. Otherwise, a single excavation report has been provided for En Medio Shelter. The Jay phase was defined at Dunas Altas, the Bajada phase at the La Bajada site, the San Jose phase at Dunas Altas and Collier Dune, and the Armijo and En Medio phases at Armijo Shelter, En Medio Shelter, and Sandoval Springs. The evidence for early maize was primarily based on the presence of maize pollen in deposits at En Medio Shelter (Strata A–D) dating from the first centuries AD to circa 1500 BC. Irwin-Williams suggested that maize represented only a minor supplement to the Armijo and En Medio phase diet, being grown in nearby floodplains and canyon head environments. Although the antiquity of this maize pollen has been questioned, maize cobs from nearby Jemez Cave have recently been dated to around 1200 BC.

Even after thirty years, the Oshara tradition remains the basic chronological framework for the Archaic in northwestern New Mexico. Although numerous excavation projects have been conducted during the intervening period, little has changed. Irwin-Williams's original argument that the beginnings of the Oshara tradition represent the eastern movement of western-based hunter-gatherer groups into areas abandoned by Paleoindians has yet to be fully evaluated. Rather than the San Jose phase, ground-stone artifacts have now been identified at earlier Jay and Bajada phase sites. The antiquity of maize has been substantiated, and most researchers would agree that maize was integrated into local foraging economies and is not associated with the movement of farmers into the region. However, too few projectile points have been recovered from well-dated contexts to independently evaluate the proposed sequence. Finally, the Oshara tradition was developed as a region-specific chronological framework and was never meant to be used as a generalized hunter-gatherer model. Those researchers who do employ the chronology as a more general model do so at their own risk.

Further Reading: Irwin-Williams, Cynthia, *The Oshara Tradition: Origins of Anasazi Culture*, Contributions in Anthropology 5(1)

(Portales: Eastern New Mexico University, 1973); Irwin-Williams, C., and S. Tompkins, *Excavations at En Medio Shelter, New Mexico*, Contributions in Anthropology 1(2) (Portales: Eastern New Mexico University, 1968); Vierra, Bradley, and Richard Ford, "Early Maize Agriculture in the Northern Rio Grande Valley, New Mexico," in *Histories of Maize: Multidisciplinary Approaches to the Prehistory, Linguistics, Biogeography, Domestication and Evolution of Maize*, edited by John Staller, Robert Tykot, and Bruce Benz (Boston: Academic Press, 2006), 497–510.

Bradley Vierra

VENTANA CAVE, CIENEGA VALLEY, AND SAN PEDRO VALLEY SITES

Southern Arizona

The Cochise Tradition: Defining the Archaic Period

The Cochise culture represents the first recognized preceramic cultural entity defined for the North American Southwest. It was originally proposed by E. B. "Ted" Sayles and Ernst Antevs from their 1935–41 comprehensive survey and limited excavation of surface and deeply buried sites exposed along the arroyos (deeply entrenched stream channels) in the Sulphur Spring, San Pedro, Santa Cruz, and San Simon valleys in southeastern Arizona. Representing the first sustained effort to deal with the earliest human occupation of southern Arizona, southwestern New Mexico, and northern Sonora, Mexico, this pioneering research was noteworthy because it defined a cultural entity spanning several thousand years. Further, it was one of the earliest interdisciplinary projects conducted in the region, involving archaeologists, Quaternary geologists, paleontologists, botanists, and other scientists.

As originally presented by Sayles and Anevs (1941), the Cochise culture consisted of three stages or phases, each keyed to a type site: Sulphur Spring (ca. 10,000–6,000 years ago), Chiricahua (ca. 6,000–3,000 years ago), and San Pedro (ca. 3,000–1,500 years ago). Sulphur Spring stage sites were identified by their occurrence in deposits of Late Pleistocene or Early Holocene age, often in association with (or in strata beneath others containing) the bones of extinct species such as horse, mammoth, dire wolf, and bison. Lacking projectile points, Sulphur Spring sites instead produced large quantities of simple ground-stone seed milling equipment such as slab metates and one-hand manos, fire-cracked rock, and simple percussion-flaked stone tools. This was in great contrast to what was then known about other Late Pleistocene cultures, such as Folsom and Clovis, which seemed to have economies largely founded on the hunting of large mammals, in particular bison and mammoths, respectively. Most Sulphur Spring stage sites were found along Whitewater Draw and were thought to represent economic adaptations focused on plant gathering.

The Chiricahua stage was defined principally from excavations at a site on the northeastern margin of the Chiricahua Mountains in southeastern Arizona. It too yielded substantial quantities of ground-stone milling equipment, including new types such as basin metates and pebble mortars. Percussion-flaked stone tools were also recovered, along with pressure-flaked projectile points believed to be intrusive.

Definition of the San Pedro stage was predicated on the results of excavations at a site deeply buried in alluvium near Fairbank on the San Pedro River. A thick midden deposit there yielded basin metates and typical one-hand manos, mortars and pestles, as well as numerous flaked-stone tools including pressure-flaked side- to corner-notched projectile points (thought to be of indigenous origin). In addition, excavations at the Fairbank site revealed a few large pits, bell-shaped in cross section, and shallow basin-shaped hearths. Sayles noted that this site and others representing the same stage had the appearance of later pit house communities from the pottery-producing Mogollon and Hohokam cultures. In fact, Sayles (1945) later reported on two other San Pedro sites at which he discovered small, 2-meter-diameter pit structures as well as other bell-shaped pits.

In 1941–42, Emil Haury and Julian Hayden excavated Ventana Cave, some 115 kilometers west of Tucson in southeastern Arizona. Haury had participated in the fieldwork with

Sayles and Antevs, and he was familiar with the artifacts diagnostic of the Cochise culture. Ventana Cave contained a record of occupation that extended back to the Late Pleistocene, but particularly impressive were the deposits from the Middle Holocene. Those produced numerous projectile points of a form similar to those of the San Pedro stage, as well as abundant evidence of points from deeper deposits. Their abundance convinced Sayles that pressure-flaked points were part of the Chiricahua stage. Haury viewed Ventana Cave as near the western boundary of Cochise, with the San Dieguito–Amargosa industry defined by Malcolm Rogers (1939), and he described the older cultural remains present in Ventana Cave as Ventana-Amargosa I and Chiricahua-Amargosa II; he used San Pedro for the later pre-ceramic occupation.

Sayles continued his collaborative research with Antevs in southeastern Arizona in 1953–55, and a report on that work was ultimately published posthumously (Sayles 1983). He redefined the Sulphur Spring stage as dating between 11,000 and 14,500 years ago, and he added a new stage, Cazador, between Sulphur Spring and Chiricahua; it contained projectile points and was dated to between 8,000 and 11,000 years ago. A variety of projectile points were added to the Chiricahua stage, and its age range was changed to 6,000–3,500 years ago. The material culture–based definitions of the San Pedro stage remained unchanged, and its age was adjusted to 3,500–2,000 years ago. Work had shown that maize and perhaps other cultigens were part of the San Pedro and perhaps Chiricahua stages in New Mexico.

Expanded definitions of the Chiricahua and San Pedro stages were also made possible by research in southeastern Arizona conducted by Frank Eddy (Eddy and Cooley 1983), Larry Agenbroad (1970), Norman Whalen (1971), and Rick Windmiller (1973). The Cochise culture concept was also adopted and employed in research in west central New Mexico (Dick 1965; Martin et al. 1949, 1952) and northern Sonora. It was also during the 1960s that pre-ceramic manifestations in the Southwest began to be integrated into larger frames of reference such as the Desert Culture (Jennings 1957;), Picosa (Irwin-Williams 1967), or simply Archaic (Kelley 1959).

Beginning in the 1970s, new research questioning the Cochise culture concept itself and the age and definition of its component stages began to appear. Whalen's (1971) critique of the concept as a whole, based on his work in the San Pedro valley, was the first attempt to address it systematically. Investigations by Michael Waters (1986) along Whitewater Draw demonstrated that the Sulphur Spring stage was younger than previously thought, with radiocarbon ages from three of Sayles's sites along Whitewater Draw falling in the range of 8,100–8,800 years ago. He also showed that the Cazador stage was probably a mixture of Sulphur Spring stage and younger artifacts from secondary geologic contexts, and that in neither stage was there any certain evidence for association with extinct fauna.

By the mid-1980s it became clear that the suite of material traits on which the definition of the Cochise culture was founded was, with the benefit of new knowledge about the North American Southwest as a whole, no longer the unique or distinctive cultural complex it was thought to be. Instead, most artifacts from the Cochise culture area showed close similarities to those from other parts of this region, and proposals were made that use of the concept be terminated and replaced by some system that simply recognized these manifestations as Archaic (Berry and Berry 1986; Huckell 1984, 1996). Most researchers today treat the post-Paleoindian, pre-pottery record as the Southwestern Archaic, and typically employ a tripartite Early-Middle-Late subdivision into periods. Further complexity has been recognized in that the arrival of maize agriculture and the rise of mixed farming-foraging economies and at least semi-sedentary village formation is now know to have occurred between about 4,000 and 3,000 years ago. The San Pedro stage (or phase, as is now commonly used) clearly belongs to this time period, for which the designation Early Agricultural period has been proposed (Huckell 1995). New research at Sayles's San Pedro type site at Fairbank, as well as at others in southeastern Arizona (Mabry 1998), have been instrumental in developing understanding of this significant socioeconomic change.

Thus, while no longer seen as a viable cultural-historical formulation, the Cochise culture holds an important place in the history of Southwestern archaeology as the first sustained attempt to bring order to the sequence of pre-ceramic occupations in the region.

Further Reading: Agenbroad, Larry D., "Cultural Implications from the Statistical Analysis of a Prehistoric Lithic Site in Arizona," master's thesis (University of Arizona, 1970); Berry, Claudia F., and Michael S. Berry, "Chronological and Conceptual Models of the Southwestern Archaic," in *Anthropology of the Desert West: Essays in Honor of Jesse D. Jennings*, edited by Carol J. Condie and Don D. Fowler, University of Utah Anthropological Papers, No. 110 (Salt Lake City: University of Utah Press, 1986), 253–327; Dick, Herbert W., *Bat Cave*, Monograph No. 27 (Santa Fe, NM: School of American Research, 1965); Eddy, Frank W., and Maurice E. Cooley, *Cultural and Environmental History of Cienega Valley, Southeastern Arizona*, Anthropological Papers of the University of Arizona, No. 43 (Tucson: University of Arizona Press, 1983); Huckell, Bruce B., *The Archaic Occupation of the Rosemont Area, Northern Santa Rita Mountains, Southeastern Arizona*, Arizona State Museum Archaeological Series, 147(1) (Tucson: Arizona State Museum, University of Arizona, 1984); Huckell, Bruce B., *Of Marshes and Maize: Preceramic Agricultural Settlements in the Cienega Valley, Southeastern Arizona*, Anthropological Papers of the University of Arizona, No. 59 (Tucson: University of Arizona Press, 1995); Huckell, Bruce B., "The Archaic Prehistory of the North American Southwest," *Journal of World Prehistory* 10 (1996): 305–373; Irwin-Williams, Cynthia, "Picosa: The Elementary Southwestern Culture," *American Antiquity* 32 (1967): 441–457; Jennings, Jesse D., *Danger Cave*, University of Utah Anthropological Papers, No. 27 (Salt Lake City: University of Utah, 1957); Kelley, J. Charles, "The Desert Culture and the

Balcones Phase: Archaic Manifestations in the Southwest and Texas," *American Antiquity* 24 (1959): 276–288; Mabry, Jonathan, ed., *Archaeological Investigations of Early Village Sites in the Middle Santa Cruz River Valley*, Anthropological Papers, No. 19 (Tucson, AZ: Center for Desert Archaeology, 1998); Martin, Paul Sydney, John B. Rinaldo, and Ernst Antevs, "Cochise and Mogollon Sites, Pine Lawn Valley, Western New Mexico," *Fieldiana Anthropology* 38(1) (1949); Martin, Paul Sydney, John B. Rinaldo, Elaine Bluhm, Hugh C. Cutler, and Roger Grange Jr., "Mogollon Cultural Continuity and Change: The Stratigraphic Analysis of Tularosa and Cordova Caves," *Fieldiana Anthropology* 40 (1952); Rogers, Malcolm J., *Early Lithic Industries of the Lower Basin of the Colorado River and Adjacent Desert Areas*, San Diego Museum Papers, No. 3 (San Diego, CA: San Diego Museum of Man, 1939); Sayles, E. B., *The San Simon Branch: Excavations at Cave Creek and in the San Simon Valley*, Medallion Papers, No. 34 (Globe, AZ: Gila Pueblo, 1945); Sayles, E. B., *The Cochise Cultural Sequence in Southeastern Arizona*, Anthropological Papers of the University of Arizona, No. 42 (Tucson: University of Arizona Press, 1983); Sayles, E. B., and Ernst Antevs, *The Cochise Culture*, Medallion Papers, No. 29 (Globe, AZ: Gila Pueblo, 1941); Waters, Michael R., *The Geoarchaeology of Whitewater Draw, Arizona*, Anthropological Papers of the University of Arizona, No. 45 (Tucson: University of Arizona Press, 1986); Whalen, Norman M., "Cochise Culture Sites in the Central San Pedro Drainage, Arizona," Ph.D. diss. (University of Arizona, 1971); Windmiller, Ric, "The Late Cochise Culture in the Sulphur Spring Valley, Southeastern Arizona: Archaeology of the Fairchile Site," *The Kiva* 39 (1973): 131–169.

Bruce B. Huckell

BAT CAVE

West Central New Mexico

The Long and Complex History of Rockshelter Use

Bat Cave is a large rockshelter located in a volcanic escarpment overlooking the plains of San Augustin in west central New Mexico. Archaeological excavations in the 1940s in a joint project of Harvard University and the University of New Mexico produced small maize (*Zea mays*) cobs in association with wood charcoal dated by radiocarbon methods at approximately 6,000 years old. Subsequent excavations in the 1980s by the University of Michigan, coupled with reanalysis of the original archaeological collections, resulted in a revised date for maize between 4,000 and 3,500 years ago.

When the first radiocarbon dates associated with the Bat Cave maize were published in the early 1950s, the site became an immediate sensation in the scientific community and among the general public for two reasons. First, the dates were among the first obtained on archaeological material by the world's original radiocarbon dating laboratory at the University of Chicago, and were thus part of a revolutionary breakthrough in scientific understanding of the past. Second, the Bat Cave maize was apparently many thousands of years older than researchers had expected. Scientists knew at the time that maize was a domesticated version of a wild plant native to Central America and that it was a major crop through the New World when Europeans began exploring the continent, but archaeologists had no clear sense of when maize first arrived in North America. Archaeologists working in the arid American Southwest prior to the work at Bat Cave had assumed that agriculture in the region was probably about 2,000 years old because they had not recovered specimens of maize or other domesticated plants in archaeological contexts that seemed any older than that based on associated tree ring dates. Hence the apparent antiquity of the Bat Cave maize was a surprising revelation.

This initial surprise gave way to a minor archaeological "gold rush" as other researchers initiated excavations in rockshelters near Bat Cave in an attempt to find more sites with evidence for the earliest phases of agricultural development; famous sites such as Tularosa Cave, O Block Cave, and Cordova Cave were explored during the 1950s as part of this process. However, none of these rockshelters produced radiocarbon-dated maize as old as that from Bat Cave. In fact, the oldest maize recovered from sites other than Bat Cave was only about 2,500 years old.

And that remained the standard chronological benchmark for early agriculture in the Southwest until the 1980s. During the 1950s and 1960s, researchers continued to look for ancient maize and other domesticated plants such as beans and squash in rockshelters throughout the Southwest, but Bat Cave remained the oldest agricultural site. Therefore, efforts to explain the diffusion of food production into the region were based on the assumption that that the earliest efforts at maize cultivation began in west central New Mexico, a vast area of high, rugged mountains that separates the hot, dry deserts of the Basin and Range geographic province to the south from the cooler, more temperate Colorado Plateau to the north. Still, archaeologists were puzzled that maize did not

Archaeologists working at the 1947 Bat Cave excavation.   [W. H. Wills]

occur in sites very close to Bat Cave until more than 3,000 years later. Why, they wondered, was the area around Bat Cave attractive to the first farmers, and especially, why would the first maize in the Southwest be grown only at Bat Cave for so long? A possible answer was that the dating of the site was incorrect, and between 1981 and 1983 the Museum of Anthropology at the University of Michigan conducted excavations in Bat Cave to determine if the dating of the Bat Cave maize was accurate.

These new field studies at Bat Cave produced a detailed history of site use. Bat Cave was formed when waves from an extinct lake cut into surrounding volcanic cliffs during the Pleistocene geological period. The lake had dried up by at least 12,000 years ago, and evidence for human activity in the rockshelter is dated from 8,550 BC to the historic period. Archaeological remains in the site dating before about 2000 BC were scarce, consisting primarily of scattered hearths and stone debris produced by the making of stone tools such as projectile points. This is the kind of material that indicates occasional use by small hunter-gatherer bands.

The appearance of maize in the deposits at Bat Cave between 4,000 and 3,500 years ago was associated with a change in site use patterns as a more intensive occupation produced densely compacted "living floors" or occupation surfaces, storage pits, thick layers of domestic debris such as bones and fragments of rabbit fur blankets, and a wide range of stone tools. This contrast with earlier site use suggests a shift to longer periods of occupation during which farmers tending local fields lived in the natural shelter of Bat Cave. However, there is not enough material or substantial living structure remains to indicate year-round occupation, and therefore the site seems to have been used seasonally during the summer agricultural cycle.

After AD 150, following the introduction of ceramic technology to the region, the use of Bat Cave shifted to a specialized hunting camp, as inferred from the presence of several thousand bison bones, less artifact diversity, and only sparse indications of maize. It appears that farming during the ceramic period was conducted mainly at more permanent settlements along stream drainages in the surrounding mountains. In the historic period, particularly toward the end of the nineteenth century, sheepherders used Bat Cave to shelter their flocks, which destroyed much of the upper prehistoric deposits in the site.

Since the 1980s it has become clear that maize entered the Southwest through a number of routes around 4,000 years ago, and that the earliest development of fully agricultural economies occurred about 2,000 years later, especially along major river systems. Bat Cave is still considered one of the earliest locations for maize cultivation in the region, but it is no longer thought to represent the first evidence for the arrival of this important new food resource.

Bat Cave is currently managed by the Bureau of Land Management, but visits are largely restricted to scientists because the surface of the site is extremely fragile and access requires passing through private land. However, an excellent example of the prehistoric use of rockshelters in the region can be found at Gila Cliff Dwellings National Monument, just north of Silver City, New Mexico.

Further Reading: Dick, Herbert W., *Bat Cave*, School of American Research Monograph No. 27 (Santa Fe, NM: School of American Research Press, 1965); Mangelsdorf, Paul C., "The Mystery of Corn," *Scientific American* 183 (1950): 20–29; Wills, W. H., *Early Prehistoric Agriculture in the American Southwest* (Santa Fe, NM: School of American Research Press, 1988).

W. H. Wills

CERRO JUANAQUEÑA

Chihuahua State, Northwestern Mexico
Early Agriculture and Terraced Household Sites

About 1200 BC indigenous people constructed numerous terraces and walls on the top and sides of a 140-meter-high hill known as Cerro Juanaqueña, located in northwestern Chihuahua, Mexico, about 190 kilometers southwest of El Paso, Texas. It is one of the earliest large settlements in the American Southwest or northwestern Mexico where maize played a significant role in the economy. About 200 people lived here at a time known as the Early Agricultural period (ca. 2000 BC to AD 100), when maize was being introduced into the general region. The occupation of Cerro Juanaqueña preceded a widespread regional agricultural economy by 1,500 to 2,000 years. In addition, the site served as a defensive settlement.

The site occupies a 10-hectare (approximately 25 acres) area with a total of about 550 constructed terraces divided into two groups. The largest one covers about a 6-hectare area on the top and upper slopes of the hill. This area was totally modified through the clearing of stones and construction of the terraces, and here artifact density is typically high. The occupation of this main area was under way between 1350 and 1300 BC, yet the area was abandoned by 1100 BC. The second, smaller group of terraces is on the toe of the hill, about 20 to 40 meters above the floodplain. Most of these terraces were utilized at the same time as the upper ones, but at least two of these terraces indicate that a second occupation occurred between 400 BC and AD 1.

The site's inhabitants constructed the terraces by piling the stones that dominate the surface to form berms, which were then filled on the upslope side with stone and sediment to create level surfaces. The terraces are parabola-shaped and individually are not large, averaging 15 meters long and 6 meters wide. However, the terraces form linked groups that make a continuous surface. In one case twenty-two terraces form a continuous berm wall that in turn forms a 400-meter perimeter around the north, east, and south sides of the hill. This large feature is but a fraction of the total 8 kilometers of berm walls constructed on the site.

Excavations from 1997 to 2000, funded by the National Science Foundation (BCS-0219185, SBR-9809839, SBR-9708610) and the National Geographic Society, revealed terrace details. Thirty-one thousand cubic meters of stone and sediment were incorporated into the terrace constructions at Cerro Juanaqueña, representing about 30 person-years of labor, an effort similar to that required to build a 550-room stone pueblo, and far more than what is expected for this time period in the southwestern United States or northwestern Mexico. Despite the effort required to construct the terraces, their total surface area is only 3.6 hectares. If planted in maize, this would feed only six adults for a year even assuming greater rainfall than present. With their costly construction and low potential yield, the terraces were apparently not agricultural features; farming was likely conducted on the fertile floodplain immediately below the site.

Cerro Juanaqueña is situated on the edge a large flood basin formed by volcanic bedrock that pinches the wide floodplain some distance downstream, which promotes overbank flooding and the formation of deep soils upstream. Good maize yields may have required minimal planting effort in such a setting, particularly since it would have occurred during a period of increased moisture when water tables were likely high.

Maize dependence was high, but there were many other items in the diet. People may have also cultivated domesticated amaranth; if so, it would be the earliest example of this domesticated plant north of Mesoamerica. Wild plant use at Cerro Juanaqueña includes an array of forbs and grasses that were harvested for their small seeds. Leporids, particularly black-tailed jack rabbits (*Lepus californicus*) and desert cottontail rabbits (*Sylvilagus audubonii*), represent by far the majority of bones recovered, but small fish were also important in the diet. Deer and pronghorn were hunted, but their bones were far less common. Most terraces were constructed to form flat living spaces on this steep-sloped hill, rather than for agriculture. The material culture associated with the terraces include midden deposits with ample burned and unburned animal bone, wood charcoal and other plant remains, lithic debris, and food-grinding implements and rock ring features. About 100 rock rings are present, averaging 2.5 meters in diameter. Excavations indicate that some of these rock rings served as foundations for small, hut-like structures. The ground stone assemblage indicates that maize and seed processing activities were major elements of domestic life. The deeply worn, trough-like metates (lower grinding stones) and intermediate-size manos (upper stones) suggest a level of maize processing not seen in typical hunter-gatherer sites in this area. Most of the nearly 700 whole and fragmentary basin-shaped metates recovered from Cerro Juanaqueña exhibit heavy wear; in fact, many are worn out. Small mortars and pestles, some carefully manufactured, are also elements of the grinding stone assemblage. Projectile points, hammer stones, and cores are abundant on the site, and all stages of chipped-stone manufacture utilizing local material are in evidence. Rare artifacts include cylindrical stone pipes made from volcanic tuff, bone awls, and small, cross-shaped ("cruciform") objects of unknown function.

Archaeological fieldwork also involved testing three other, similar, though smaller, cerros de trincheras sites plus mapping nine other hilltop sites along a 70-kilometer stretch of the Rio Casas Grandes floodplain and that of an adjacent major stream. These hilltop settlements display many of the attributes of defensive sites, including use of defensible land forms, evidence of planning and coordinated rapid construction, and a defensive layout, exemplified by the perimeter berms and 360-degree views. From atop most of the twelve cerros de trincheras sites, one or more other, nearby cerros de trincheras sites can be seen; such intersite visibility is another characteristic of defensive sites, as it facilitates line-of-sight signaling.

Cerro Juanaqueña and the other Early Agricultural period cerro de trincheras sites in northwest Chihuahua were likely constructed in response to raiding and warfare at a time when populations were relatively high. In this competitive environment, the residents of Cerro Juanaqueña maintained a defensive posture while participating in a mixed farming, hunting, gathering, and fishing economy. Today the site is protected by the regulations of Mexico's Instituto Nacional de Antropología y Historia. It lies on a combination of private and community-owned land and is not currently accessible to the public. Information about the sites can be found at the Museo de las Culturas del Norte in Casas Grandes, Chihuahua.

Further Reading: Hard, Robert J., MacWilliams, A. C., Roney, J. R., Adams, K. R., and Merrill, W. L., "Early Agriculture in Chihuahua, Mexico," in *Histories of Maize: Multidisciplinary Approaches to the Prehistory, Linguistics, Biogeography, Domestication, and Evolution of Maize*, edited by J. Staller, R. Tykot, and B. Benz (Burlington, MA: Academic Press, 2006), 471–485; Hard, R. J., and Roney, J. R., "A Massive Terraced Village Complex in Chihuahua, Mexico, 3000 Years before Present," *Science* 279(5357) (1998): 1661–1664; Hard, R. J., J. E. Zapata, B. K. Moses, and J. R. Roney, "Terrace Construction in Northern Chihuahua, Mexico: 1150 B.C. and Modern Experiments," *Journal of Field Archaeology* 26(2) (1999): 129–146; Roney, J. R., and R. J. Hard, "Early Agriculture in Northwestern Chihuahua," in *Traditions, Transitions, and Technologies: Themes in Southwestern Archaeology, Proceedings of the 2000 Southwest Symposium*, edited by S. Schlanger (Boulder: University of Colorado Press, 2002), 163–180; Roney, J. R., and R. J. Hard, "A Review of Cerros de Trincheras in Northwestern Chihuahua," in *Surveying the Archaeology of Northwest Mexico*, edited by G. E. Newell and E. Gallaga (Salt Lake City: University of Utah Press, 2004), 127–148.

Robert J. Hard and John Roney

CIENEGA PHASE SITES

Near Tucson, Arizona

Early Agriculture in the Tucson Basin

Since the 1980s an explosion of discoveries at early farming settlement archaeological sites in the Tucson Basin in southeastern Arizona has pushed the earliest dates farther and farther back in time in southwestern North America for agriculture, canals, pottery, cemeteries, communal buildings, and possibly for courtyard house groups, plazas, and the bow-and-arrow. The majority of the new data has emerged since 1993 from government agency–funded archaeological projects, required to comply with environmental and historic preservation laws, conducted at sites in the path of new construction along Interstate 10 and in the west side of downtown Tucson, both of which are located in the former floodplain of the Santa Cruz River in the western basin. Important early agricultural sites where excavations have been conducted include the Clearwater, Cortaro Fan, Cortaro Road, Costello-King, Dairy, Las Capas, Los Pozos, Milagro, Santa Cruz Bend, Stewart Brickyard, Stone Pipe, Tumamoc Hill, Valley Farms, and Wetlands sites.

The resulting rapid expansion of archaeological knowledge led to revisions of chronology and the terms used to describe different time periods, with those sites having early evidence of agriculture now assigned to the "Early Agricultural period," and the previously used term "Late Archaic" reserved for nonagricultural sites dating to the same interval. The term "Early Formative period" has also been proposed for this interval, but "Early Agricultural period" has gained wider acceptance and is used here.

In the Tucson Basin and the rest of southeastern Arizona and northwestern Mexico (often referred to as the desert borderlands), the Early Agricultural period is divided into two phases based on differences in age, projectile point styles, architectural forms, and types of ground-stone tools, marine shell jewelry, and some other categories of material culture. Sites of the earlier San Pedro phase (1200–800 BC) typically have large-bladed points with shallow side-to-corner notches, oval or round pit structures, and limited varieties of ground-stone tools and shell ornaments, while sites of the Cienega phase (800 BC to AD 50) have triangular points with deep corner notches, round pit structures, and diverse ground-stone and marine shell assemblages.

Common to the two phases in sites are abundant maize remains, bell-shaped storage pits, specialized storage structures, rock-filled roasting pits, canals, wells, human burials with individuals placed in flexed positions, canid (dog) burials, untempered pottery, fired-clay anthropomorphic (human-shaped) figurines, Western Basketmaker–style dart points, stone pipes, a variety of bone and antler tools, personal adornments made of various materials, and the processing and use of red ocher pigment. Perishable types of material culture that can be inferred for the San Pedro phase include coiled basketry (detected based on impressions left in fired clay) and cotton textiles (inferred from the presence of both cotton pollen and ceramic and stone spindle whorls). Simultaneous use of the *atl atl* and the bow-and-arrow during the Cienega phase is suggested by arrow-size points found along with dart-size points and stone *atl atl* weights and finger loops.

While primary inhumations (human burials) were the most common burial type during both phases (and included infants and children), secondary inhumations and secondary cremations are also known from Cienega phase sites. During the San Pedro phase, primary inhumations were found within habitation areas, sometimes in small groups. Graves were dug in abandoned houses or open areas within the habitation site, sometimes bodies were placed in former storage pits. The first discrete, spatially separated cemetery areas developed during the Cienega phase, although some inhumations continued to be placed in habitation zones. Bodies were usually tightly flexed, and individuals were placed on their side or back, or in a seated position. They were sometimes sprinkled or painted with red ocher, particularly in the mouth and pelvic areas. Red ocher lumps were the most common type of nonperishable grave offering, often placed near the mouths of both adults and infants. Other typical grave offerings during both phases included broken metates (smoothed stone slabs used for grinding maize) and whole ground-stone tools, lumps of black pigment, stone dart points and bifaces, ceramic figurine fragments, marine shell beads, stone pipes, and bone awls.

The locations, sizes, and artifact and feature diversity of Early Agricultural period sites in the Tucson Basin indicate a settlement pattern of long-term, multiple-function residential sites where the majority of people lived most of the year, concentrated in the Santa Cruz River floodplain; and short-term, special-function base camps of task groups who ventured out of the residential site to exploit seasonal resources concentrated in upper bajada zones.

Because residential sites in the floodplain were frequently inundated by overbank floods, these settlements were characterized by a relatively ephemeral architectural style, and particular locations were periodically abandoned and reoccupied over time, creating extensive and overlapping archaeological sites, often with large numbers of superimposed cultural features. The San Pedro phase site of Las Capas has thick midden deposits with unusually high artifact and feature densities, indicating longer and more intensive occupations relative to most other known Early Agricultural period sites in the desert borderlands.

At the Cienega phase site of Santa Cruz Bend investigators found the earliest known examples in the Southwest of a large communal structure ("Big House"), courtyard house groups, cremation burials, and possibly a plaza. Since the fieldwork at that site, Cienega phase "Big Houses" have also been found at the Clearwater site and possibly other sites in southeastern Arizona. These structures, which are up to three times larger than the average houses and lack internal storage pits, likely functioned as communal-ceremonial buildings and represent a level of social organization above the household. At the Tumamoc Hill site, terraces were constructed for house platforms and possibly gardens during the Cienega phase. The Wetlands site is a Cienega phase cemetery possibly related to the nearby Los Pozos habitation site. Jewelry made from marine shell species native only to the Pacific coast, and projectile points made from obsidian from distant sources, indicate the development of long-distance trade during the Cienega phase.

Discoveries since the mid-1990s have demonstrated that Mesoamerican cultigens (plants that are cultivated, e.g., maize, squash, gourds, beans) and many material culture elements of the Early Agricultural period were present in the Tucson Basin long before the San Pedro phase. Pit structures, storage pits, and maize radiocarbon-dated at between 2100 and 1200 BC have now been reported from the Clearwater, Las Capas, and Los Pozos sites along the Santa Cruz River. Untempered, fired-clay pottery shards decorated with incised designs and probable ceramic figurine fragments, along with charred maize and a Southwest style of dart point (Armijo or San Jose), were recovered from pit structures and storage pits dating to 2100 BC at the Clearwater site. Currently, these are the oldest known fired ceramics in the Southwest, rivaling in age the oldest ceramics in Mexico.

It is not yet possible to define more precise time periods, referred to as phases, within the long interval of agriculture preceding the San Pedro phase, and for now the period 2100–1200 BC in southeastern Arizona is referred to simply as the "unnamed interval" of the Early Agricultural period. No major interruptions or shifts in regional occupation or material culture have been identified for the full span of the Early Agricultural period (2100 BC to AD 50), and it appears to have been a long interval of cultural continuity in the desert borderlands.

Considerable evidence of water control by early farmers along the Santa Cruz River has been found since 1993. Currently, the earliest identified canal is at the Clearwater site and dates to approximately 1500 BC. Canals and a well at the Las Capas-Costello-King site complex indicate exploitation of both surface flows and water tables by 1200 BC. At Las Capas were found a secondary canal branching off a primary canal, and evidence of operation of canal headgates to control diversions from a perennial river flow. Based on its calculated capacity, a late San Pedro phase canal at Las Capas is estimated to have had a total length of 1.5–2.0 kilometers and to have irrigated an area of 24–38 hectares. Uncovered at the Stewart Brickyard site was a portion of an irrigated field with canals and hundreds of planting holes arranged in a regular, staggered pattern; associated maize remains were radiocarbon-dated to 1100 BC. With these recent discoveries, the famous canal systems of the later Hohokam culture (ca. AD 550–1450) now have a local precedent, implying a long history of irrigation development (possibly indigenous) in the northern Sonoran Desert.

Archaeologists now recognize that early agriculture in this region included diverse technologies, techniques, and crops. In addition to canals indicating irrigated farming (diversion of perennial flows from rivers, streams, or springs to fields), Early Agricultural period site locations in the Tucson Basin also imply the practice of water-table farming (locating fields in areas with naturally high water tables), flood farming (locating fields in naturally flooding areas), and runoff farming (diversion of slope runoff or seasonal stream flows to fields). Direct radiocarbon dates demonstrate that maize was cultivated in the basin by at least 2100 BC. Pepo (pumpkin-type) squash remains dating to approximately this time have been found in McEuen Cave in southeastern Arizona, and this plant was probably also cultivated in the Tucson Basin by then. Pollen of cotton (either wild or domesticated) found at the Valley Farms site, and charred seeds of a wild tobacco variety found at Las Capas, indicate that these plants were also cultivated by 1200 BC. A possible common bean from Las Capas has also been radiocarbon-dated to about that time.

In addition to cultivating Mesoamerican crops, Early Agricultural period farmer-foragers in the Tucson Basin hunted rabbits, deer, and bighorn sheep; caught fish, turtles, waterfowl, and freshwater mussels in the Santa Cruz River; and intensively collected, probably protected and encouraged, and possibly cultivated several weedy, large-seeded, and leafy annuals (including amaranth, goosefoot, tansy mustard, dropseed grasses, and others) that pioneered the damp, disturbed soils of the active floodplain and cultivated fields and canals. The diversity of wild food resources was much higher than during later periods of prehistory and reflects a gradual transition to dependence on cultigens in this region.

Further Reading: Diehl, Michael W., ed., *Subsistence and Resource Use Strategies of Early Agricultural Communities in Southern Arizona*, Anthropological Papers, No. 34 (Tucson, AZ: Center for Desert Archaeology, 2005), www.cdarc.org; Fish, Paul R., Suzanne K. Fish, Austin Long, and Charles Miksicek, "Early Corn Remains from Tumamoc Hill, Southern Arizona," *American Antiquity* 51(3) (1986): 563-572; Gregory, David A., ed., *Excavations in the Santa Cruz River Floodplain: The Early Agricultural Period Component at Los Pozos*, Anthropological Papers, No. 21 (Tucson, AZ: Center for Desert Archaeology, 2001), www.cdarc.org; Huckell, Bruce B. "Late Preceramic Farmer-Foragers in Southeastern Arizona: A Cultural and Ecological Consideration of the Spread of Agriculture into the Arid Southwestern United States," Ph.D. diss. (University of Arizona, 1990); Mabry, Jonathan B., "Changing Knowledge and Ideas about the First Farmers in Southeastern Arizona," in *The Late Archaic across the Borderlands: From Foraging to Farming*, edited by Bradley J. Vierra (Austin: University of Texas Press, 2005), 41–83; Mabry, Jonathan B., ed., *Las Capas: Early Irrigation and Sedentism in a Southwestern Floodplain*, Anthropological Papers, No. 28 (Tucson, AZ: Center for Desert Archaeology, 2007), www.cdarc.org; Roth, Barbara J. "Late Archaic Settlement and Subsistence in the Tucson Basin," Ph.D. diss. (University of Arizona, 1989); Sliva, R. Jane, ed., *Material Cultures and Lifeways of Early Agricultural Communities in Southern Arizona*, Anthropological Papers, No. 35 (Tucson, AZ: Center for Desert Archaeology, 2005), www.cdarc.org; Thiel, J. Homer, and Jonathan B. Mabry, eds., *Rio Nuevo Archaeology, 2000–2003: Investigations at the San Agustín Mission and Mission Gardens, Tucson Presidio, Tucson Pressed Brick Company, and Clearwater Site*, Technical Report No. 2004–11 (Tucson, AZ: Desert Archaeology, 2006), http://www.cdarc.org/pages/library/rio_nuevo/.

Jonathan B. Mabry

SHABIK'ESCHEE VILLAGE SITE

Chaco Canyon, New Mexico
Early Agriculture on the Colorado Plateau

Shabik'eschee Village is an early farming settlement in the Colorado Plateau region of the American Southwest. Excavated by the Smithsonian Institution from 1926 to 1927, and again in 1975 by the National Park Service, Shabik'eschee Village is one of the best-known examples of the Basketmaker III period (ca. AD 400 to 750). Although maize agriculture began in the Colorado Plateau around 2000 BC during the Late Archaic period (ca. 2000 BC to AD 400), evidence for relatively permanent agricultural settlements does not appear until much later, in conjunction with the development of pottery—a technological innovation that defines the beginning of the Basketmaker III period. Shabik'eschee Village illustrates several important socioeconomic aspects of the transition from highly mobile lifestyles to more sedentary adaptations characterized by changes in architecture, settlement size, and technology.

Shabik'eschee Village is located on the southern edge of a mesa that overlooks Chaco Canyon, a shallow but wide canyon that runs for approximately 30 kilometers east-west through the San Juan basin in northwest New Mexico. The original excavation of the site, directed by Frank H. H. Roberts, uncovered nineteen circular and rectangular dwellings—called pit houses—and forty-five smaller storage features. A pit house is a single-room structure constructed partially or wholly below ground level. During the Basketmaker III period, these dwellings became fairly elaborate, with substantial timber roofs, stone slab walls, and thick plaster floors. The amount of effort needed to build these structures indicates that the occupants planned to use them for extended periods of time, in contrast to less substantial dwellings of earlier time periods. The large number of probable storage features also points to prolonged episodes of site use.

In addition to pit houses and storage features, Shabik'eschee Village had a very large (95 m² in floor area), circular, semi-subterranean building that Frank Roberts called a kiva. Among modern Pueblo communities in the Southwest, a kiva is a non-residential structure or room that is owned and used by specific social groups, such as clans or religious societies. The activities that take place in kivas are different from the daily, domestic activities—such as food preparation and pottery manufacture—that occur in dwellings. Because of this historic affiliation of sociopolitical functions with kivas, archaeologists tend to interpret unusually large pit structures lacking evidence for domestic functions as public buildings, rather than household dwellings. The Shabik'eschee Village kiva was one of the first public buildings identified at an early agricultural settlement in the Southwest.

In the early 1970s, the National Park Service excavated two more pit houses at Shabik'eschee Village and conducted a thorough survey of the mesa around the site. These additional investigations indicate that Shabik'eschee Village is much larger than originally described, with a total of at least sixty-eight pit houses. However, it is clear from both excavations that all of the pit houses were not contemporaneous. Many had been partially dismantled and then filled with debris during the occupation. Similarly, the kiva had burned and then been used as a trash dump for nearby households. An analysis by W. H. Wills and Thomas C. Windes of these "abandonment" patterns suggested that no more than forty-three pit houses were likely to have been used at any one time (and probably fewer).

This is still a very large site by Basketmaker III standards. Of the more than 160 known Basketmaker III sites in Chaco Canyon, only one approaches Shabik'eschee Village in size. Most consist of only two or three pit houses, a pattern that is typical throughout the Colorado Plateau. Shabik'eschee Village was therefore an unusual settlement for its time, even though it is often referred to in textbooks as characteristic of the Basketmaker III period. The largest population estimate for the site at any time during its occupation is around seventy-seven individuals, or perhaps fifteen households, compared to estimates of five to fifteen people for the more common small Basketmaker III sites.

Researchers see the larger population figures associated with Shabik'eschee Village as evidence that the site was produced by the aggregation of a number of households exceeding the size of an extended family or similar closely related social group. No agricultural sites in the Colorado Plateau preceding the Basketmaker III period suggest population aggregation at the scale of Shabik'eschee Village, which makes the site a critical source of information for the conditions that gave rise to the first permanent communities in this part of North America.

Given that farming was the economic foundation for Basketmaker III society, it would seem likely that the conditions supporting early sedentary communities of multiple households like Shabik'eschee Village were ones that favored successful crop cultivation.

But this is not as obvious as we might expect. Chaco Canyon today is not a very good place for farming, nor an attractive place for living. Elevations range from 6,200 to 6,600 feet, annual precipitation is less than 10 inches, summers are hot,

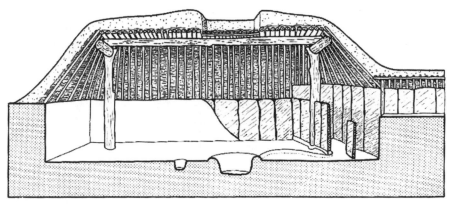

Cutaway drawing of a typical Shabik'eschee pit house.   [W. H. Wills]

and winters are extremely cold. In January, the temperature at Chaco has dropped to 37 degrees Fahrenheit six times in the past sixty years. Experiments to assess agricultural potential in Chaco Canyon have concluded that under modern climate conditions, maize farming is a highly risky endeavor prone to frequent failure due to lack of water, short growing seasons, and poor soils. However, studies of past environments point to somewhat wetter regimes and higher ground water levels during the Basketmaker III period, which might have been sufficient to support small-scale cultivation. In either case, the archaeological evidence for maize farming, storage, and processing at Shabik'eschee Village is very strong. Therefore, it is clear that agriculture was successful.

The persistent archaeological question is whether successful farming was in itself enough to promote the coming together of up to fifteen households as co-residents of a single settlement. W. H. Wills and Thomas C. Windes have argued that such an aggregation must have also required a significant economic contribution from wild plants and animals in the area. The data from the original excavations is not adequate to address this question directly at Shabik'eschee Village, but recent research at Basketmaker III sites near Chaco Canyon indicates that non-agricultural resources were critical to overall diets. Hence, aggregated settlements would have certainly been heavily dependent on a wide range of domesticated and non-domesticated foods.

Shabik'eschee Village is located in Chaco Culture National Historic Park but is only accessible by special permission of the National Park Service, usually for specific research requests. However, excavated Basketmaker III pit houses can be seen at various interpretive stops open to the public in Mesa Verde National Park in southwest Colorado; and exhibits of Basketmaker III artifacts can be seen at Mesa Verde and at the nearby Anasazi Heritage Center in Dolores, Colorado, managed by the Bureau of Land Management.

Further Reading: Reed, Paul F., ed., *Foundations of Anasazi Culture: The Basketmaker-Pueblo Transition* (Salt Lake City: University of Utah Press, 2000); Roberts, Frank H. H., *Shabik'eschee Village: A Late Basket Maker Site in the Chaco Canyon*, Bulletin No. 92 (Washington, DC: Bureau of American Ethnology, 1929); Steward, Julian H., "Ecological Aspects of Southwestern Society," *Anthropos* 32: 87–104; Wills, W. H., and Thomas C. Windes, "Evidence for Population Aggregation and Dispersal during the Basketmaker III Period in Chaco Canyon, New Mexico," *American Antiquity* 54 (1989): 347–369.

W. H. Wills

THE SU SITE

Southwest New Mexico

Early Agriculture and Pit House Villages in the Mogollon Highlands

The SU site is an early farming settlement in the rugged, high-elevation Mogollon Mountains of southwestern New Mexico excavated by the Field Museum of Natural History (Chicago) between 1939 and 1946, and by the University of New Mexico from 1987 to 1988. SU is one of the largest and best-known sites of the Early Pit House period (ca. AD 200 to 700) in the Mogollon cultural tradition. Archaeological sites assigned to the Mogollon tradition date to between about AD 200 and

Aerial photographs of the excavations of two of the twenty-eight pit houses found at the SU site, New Mexico, during investigations between 1939 and 1946.   [© The Field Museum, Chicago, Field-A88111_A88142]

1450, and occur over a vast, ecologically diverse geographic area in southwestern New Mexico, southeastern Arizona, and northwestern Mexico. The SU site is illustrative of economic and social changes associated with the shift from highly mobile settlement systems of the preceding Archaic period (ca. 8000 BC to AD 200) to more sedentary lifeways characterized by substantial residential architecture, pottery manufacture, and household production strategies.

The SU site is located at an elevation of more than 2,000 meters along a broad ridgeline at the center of the Pine Lawn Valley in west central New Mexico, deep within the heavily forested volcanic mountains that form the Mogollon Highlands, a natural boundary between the cool-temperate Colorado Plateau and the hot deserts of the southern Basin and Range province. The site was first investigated by Paul S. Martin and John B. Rinaldo, who identified twenty-eight large semi-subterranean structures called "pit houses" and numerous smaller features such as refuse pits and human burials. Later fieldwork by the University of New Mexico investigated areas between previously excavated pit houses, with the objective of obtaining new economic and chronometric data. The SU site was occupied sometime around AD 500, based on tree rings and radiocarbon dates, and inhabited over a span of perhaps several human generations.

Pit houses are single-room dwellings constructed by excavating a large hole or pit, building a timber framework inside the pit, then covering the framework with the excavated dirt, resulting in a house that is very thermally efficient but prone to rapid deterioration from the effects of moisture on the covered timbers, as well as vermin infestation. SU pit houses average about 40 square meters in floor area, and some are nearly 100 square meters, with depths exceeding 1 meter. These dimensions are quite large for a single-household dwelling during this time period, and it seems likely that these structures required more labor than any single family could muster to procure and erect the substantial numbers of large timbers required for roof supports and walls. For that reason it is possible that SU pit houses were built by work parties drawn from the entire community, and perhaps that they were used by extended households composed of more than one family.

Archaeological patterns at the SU site indicate that only about a third of the pit houses were occupied at the same time and many were dismantled or burned during the occupation of the settlement, probably reflecting the short-term viability of these structures in relatively wet, high-elevation forests. Abandoned pit houses were used as dumps for household refuse and for interring human remains. A total of fifty-five burials have been recovered from the SU site, of which fifty-three definitely date to the Early Pit House period. In addition to those in abandoned structures, some burials were placed beneath house floors, and many appear to have been interred in a specialized mortuary building constructed of upright posts surrounding several large pits containing

burials. Very few artifacts were found in association with the SU burials, a pattern that probably indicates a low level of status differentiation. However, the large number of burials at SU is a distinct change from the preceding Archaic, when burials in general were rare in the region, and may therefore point to an increasing concern with establishing property rights, or land tenure, through formal burials and mortuary locations.

Evidence for agriculture is abundant during the Early Pit House Period in the form of maize, squash and beans, but foraging for wild plants and hunting also were a critical part of local economies. Although charred fragments of maize and maize pollen are common at SU, preservation of plant remains is not good. Our best information for food production and wild resource procurement at this time comes from nearby rockshelters, especially Tularosa Cave (excavated by the Field Museum in the early 1950s) and a remarkable pit house site in the Gallo Mountain area (LA 5407) that burned while occupied, leaving complete household assemblages of pots containing stored seeds from many species of wild and domesticated plants.

The earliest maize in the Mogollon region dates to around 2000 BC, with low levels of food production forming a consistent portion of local economies for the next two millennia of the Archaic period. The increase in sedentism and settlement size found in Early Pit House period sites such as SU was probably a result in part of greater investment in agricultural production, and much archaeological research over the past two decades has attempted to understand the basis for this development. A key aspect of changing food production strategies was the adoption of ceramic technology. The SU inhabitants made a plain or undecorated pottery that fired a red or reddish-brown color. This is the first well-dated example of ceramic manufacture in the Mogollon Highlands, and it represented a major technological innovation that had a significant impact on subsistence economies, particularly the agricultural components, by enhancing nutritional qualities of foods through slow cooking and allowing long-term storage of both dry grain and water.

The SU site was probably occupied seasonally, during the winter months, with individual households dispersing in the summer throughout the stream systems of the Mogollon Highlands to cultivate small agricultural plots in the narrow valleys while foraging and hunting in adjacent forests. Early Pit House period sites in other parts of the Mogollon tradition appear to have followed similar seasonal patterns of dispersal and aggregation, adjusting settlement patterns flexibly to annual variation in wild resources and investing minimally in agricultural features or localities.

A significant difference between highland sites like SU or LA 5407 and Early Pit House period sites at lower elevations, especially those in non-forested settings, is the size and complexity of pit house architecture. High-elevation dwellings are much larger, are much more substantial. and include much greater potential food storage capacity in floor pits than lower-elevation pit houses. Some of this variation may be a response to colder upland climates (favoring more thermally efficient buildings), but it is also possible that the larger pit houses indicate a shift from small households of perhaps a single nuclear family to bigger households characterized by multiple or extended family units. Greater household size may be a function of more intensive agricultural practices requiring larger labor pools associated with more emphasis on the production and control of surpluses. The existence of such socioeconomic differences during the Early Pit House period seems to correspond to environmental and demographic variability within the Mogollon tradition found during the initial transition from the pre-ceramic to ceramic periods.

Further Reading: Akins, Nancy J., *Excavations at the Gallo Mountain Sites, NM 32, Catron County, New Mexico*, Archaeology Notes, No. 65 (Santa Fe: Museum of New Mexico, Office of Archaeological Studies, 1998); Diehl, Michael W., and Steven A. LeBlanc, *Early Pithouse Villages of the Mimbres Valley and Beyond: The McAnally and Thompson Sites in Their Cultural and Ecological Contexts*, Papers of the Peabody Museum of Archaeology and Ethnology, Vol. 83 (Cambridge, MA: Harvard University, 2001); Gilman, Patricia A., "Multiple Dimensions of the Archaic-to-Pit Structure Period Transition in Southeastern Arizona," *The Kiva* 60 (1998): 619–632; Haury, Emil W., *The Mogollon Culture of Southwestern New Mexico*, Medallion Papers, No. 20 (Globe, AZ: Gila Pueblo, 1936); Martin, Paul S., and John B. Rinaldo, *The SU Site: Excavations at a Mogollon Village, Western New Mexico, Third Season, 1946*, Anthropological Series, Vol. 32, No. 3 (Chicago: Field Museum of Natural History, 1947); Whalen, Michael E., *Turquoise Ridge and Late Prehistoric Residential Mobility in the Desert Mogollon Region*, Anthropological Papers, No. 118 (Salt Lake City: University of Utah Press, 1994); Wills, W. H., "Patterns of Prehistoric Food Production in West-Central New Mexico," *Journal of Anthropological Research* 45 (1988): 139–157; Wills, W. H., "The Transition from the Preceramic to Ceramic Period in the Mogollon Highlands of Western New Mexico," *Journal of Field Archaeology* 23 (1996): 335–359.

W. H. Wills

THE HOUGHTON ROAD SITE

Pima County, Tucson Basin, Southern Arizona
A View of the Transition to Settled Village Lifeways

The Houghton Road site (AZ BB:13:398 in the Arizona State Museum site-numbering system) is an Early Formative, or early ceramic period, site located in the eastern Tucson Basin, Pima County, southern Arizona. Houghton Road is important for several reasons. It was one of the first Early Formative sites in the area to be investigated, and the Agua Caliente phase was defined there. Perhaps most significant, investigations at the site highlighted an important period of transition and cultural development in the prehistory of the U.S. Southwest.

The site was located near the confluence of Agua Caliente and Tanque Verde washes. It was excavated because Pima County was re-aligning a portion of Houghton Road—hence the name. Pima County sponsored the project as part of its innovative cultural resource management program.

Although set in the arid and hot Sonoran Desert, this part of the Tucson Basin was well watered in prehistoric times. Floodwater farming was productive. Ancient pollen and charred plant remains demonstrate that the residents were successful farmers, growing maize (corn) and beans. They also exploited a wide range of edible desert plants, such as cactus, mesquite, grasses, agave (century plant), and herbaceous annuals. Small mammals, such as rabbits, were the major game.

The Early Formative period spanned the time between about AD 1 and AD 650. It is distinguished from the preceding Late Archaic period by the appearance of true ceramic containers. Some archaeologists divide the Early Formative period into two horizons based on characteristic pottery: the Plain Ware horizon, from the appearance of plain ware ceramics to AD 400, and the Red Ware horizon, from AD 400 to 650/700. The Agua Caliente phase represents the Plain Ware horizon in the Tucson Basin and is broadly dated to between about AD 1 and 475. The equivalent phase in the Phoenix Basin is the Red Mountain phase. In the Tucson Basin, the Red Ware horizon is called the Tortolita phase; in the Phoenix Basin, it is labeled the Vahki phase. In the Mogollon areas of Arizona and New Mexico, the Early Formative equivalent is the Early Pit House period. Radiocarbon dates indicate that Houghton Road was occupied during the transition between the Plain Ware and Red Ware horizons.

As the name suggests, the Plain Ware horizon was characterized by plain (undecorated) pottery made from brown-firing volcanic clays containing sand-sized particles. The ancient potters used the coil-and-scrape method, building up coils of clay, pinching them together, and scraping the surface smooth. These were true ceramic containers that were thin walled and well fired, not the crude, thick, low-fired, baseball-size bowls that were made in the Late Archaic period. The containers were used for multiple purposes, although most appear to have been designed to store foods such as corn kernels. These so-called seed jars are globular containers that lack necks.

The Red Ware horizon was characterized by the addition of red-slipped pottery; plain ware continued to be made. Most red ware was highly polished, so much so that it had a dimpled or hammered surface from the pressing down on and compacting of the coils during polishing. At Houghton Road, container shapes were similar to the plain ware; later in the Early Formative period, red ware containers would diversify in shape and size.

Fourteen pit structures or possible structures were excavated at the site. Two were the round, shallow, ephemeral kinds of houses associated with the Late Archaic period. Four were constructed more formally and appeared to have been used as habitation (living) structures. They were circular or rectangular with rounded corners, constructed by digging a pit and plastering the walls. Roof support posts were placed in the interior, and the upper walls presumably were of pole-and-mud construction (in the Southwest, called *jacal*; elsewhere this type of construction is often labeled wattle and daub). The covered entries had plaster lobes supporting posts on either side of the entry's opening. The circular hearths were located in alignment with the entry, and the floors, hearths, and an apron extending from the hearth to the entry were plastered.

Feature 18, another pit structure, probably served communal religious or social functions. Although constructed much like the domestic structures, it was larger and deeper and was bean shaped in plan view. Plastered adobe pillars or pilasters at the juncture of the entry with the main structure created the "bean's" indentation. This type of communal structure was common at Mogollon Pit House period sites, but the later Hohokam had a completely different religious and ceremonial system based on structures called ball courts and a cremation mortuary complex.

The dead were buried in various ways. Children were placed in a tightly flexed, fetal position. Adults were either cremated or inhumed. One burial, that of an adult woman, had been placed in a seated position. A dog had been buried with her and was placed directly below her knees. Another burial was a primary, or in-place, cremation. The individual of indeterminate sex had been laid on a wooden platform supported by four posts, cremated, and buried in place. This type of cremation also is found in central and northern Arizona. Several formal dog burials were found on pit house floors. Clearly, dogs were important to the Houghton Road residents and were treated with care.

Not surprisingly, many aspects of the material culture found at the Houghton Road site and the way of life they indicate depict transitional qualities. The dead were buried primarily in flexed positions during the earlier Late Archaic period, and the Hohokam who settled later in the Tucson Basin typically cremated their dead and then buried the remains in a separate pit or container (called a secondary cremation). Formal dog burials are not common at Hohokam sites but are found at Archaic period sites. The flaked-stone artifacts combined elements from the preceding Late Archaic period and the following early Hohokam period. The ground-stone tools were identical to those of the Late Archaic period and were designed to grind seeds. The troughed metates, or bottom grinding stones, which signify maize processing, would not appear until the end of the Red Ware horizon. Deep, bell-shaped storage pits located below the floors of houses were typical of the Late Archaic period and also were found at Houghton Road. Roasting pits—rock-filled pits for pit-baking foods—were a common outdoor feature that spanned the Late Archaic and Hohokam periods. The houses at Houghton Road indicate increased permanence of occupation and the dedication of architecture to habitation purposes. In the Late Archaic period, structures appear to have served primarily as specialized storage facilities, and the people were mobile. But at Houghton Road, the settlement was of hamlet size; there were no large villages at this time.

This time was critical in the development of Southwestern cultures, because it represents the addition of important new technologies to the basic cultural pattern already in place. Late Archaic farmers cultivated maize and probably other cultigens, but their food-processing equipment and techniques were not suited to maximizing the nutritional value of this food, which is naturally deficient in minerals, particularly iron, amino acids, and protein. The development of ceramic containers allowed cooks to boil maize and perhaps process it with an alkali solution, which increases its nutritional value. Pots also were invaluable for soaking and boiling dried beans. Ceramic containers also were vastly superior to basketry containers for storage. They could be heated to kill insect pests and molds and were impervious to rodent teeth. Seed jars have been found in pits, indicating their use as storage facilities. Pottery vessels thus allowed Early Formative period farmers to depend on cultivated plants foods more intensively than in earlier times.

It is intriguing that these patterns were replicated over much of the southern Southwest, in diverse geographic and environmental areas whose later residents would be labeled Mogollon, Ancestral Pueblo (or Anasazi), and Hohokam. In fact, the resemblances between sites such as the Houghton Road site and Mogollon sites found in the mountain Transition Zone of Arizona and in west central New Mexico were so great that they were originally labeled Mogollon, although they were in the middle of Hohokam territory. This uniformity suggests that whoever the Early Formative period people were, they were culturally similar regardless of where they lived. The pattern recalls the O'otam culture concept formulated by archaeologist Charles D. Di Peso of the Amerind Foundation to explain the archaeological culture of southern Arizona—a basic culture that gave rise to many diversified groups.

Since the site was excavated, several other, similar sites have been investigated by cultural resource management firms. These are located along the Santa Cruz River, the only major watercourse in the Tucson Basin, and although they demonstrated many aspects of economy and material culture in common with Houghton Road, there were differences suggesting that local peoples were beginning to diversify their lifeways.

Houghton Road has not been developed for public access. The site is now backfilled and landscaped. Few but the archaeologists who excavated there know that an important site is buried on a strip of land adjacent to the bridge that carries the new alignment of Houghton Road.

Further Reading: Reid, Jefferson, and Stephanie Whittlesey, *The Archaeology of Ancient Arizona* (Tucson: University of Arizona Press, 1997); Ciolek-Torrello, Richard, ed., *Early Farmers of the Sonoran Desert: Archaeological Investigations at the Houghton Road Site, Tucson, Arizona*, Technical Series, No. 72 (Tucson, AZ: Statistical Research, 1998).

Stephanie M. Whittlesey

AN OVERVIEW OF THE ARCHAEOLOGY OF CHACO CANYON

Chaco Canyon, Northwestern New Mexico
Chaco Culture National Historical Park

The magnificent, multi-story, masonry pueblos of Chaco Canyon have fascinated people for centuries. Initial speculation held that the Aztecs of Central Mexico had built these amazing edifices prior to migrating south to the Valley of Mexico. Subsequently, reasoned and careful scientific study replaced the rampant conjecture of the late nineteenth century, and the direct-historical method of twentieth-century archaeology revealed that the ancestors of the modern Pueblo people of New Mexico and Arizona had built the abandoned dwellings in Chaco and across the northern American Southwest.

Chaco Cultural National Historical Park protects and preserves about a dozen sites that have been described as the greatest monuments of pre-Columbian construction in the United States. Beyond the Great Houses, the park also contains thousands of additional archaeological and historic sites that date from 9000 BC to AD 1900. The most significant structures in the park include Great Houses, such as Pueblo Bonito, Chetro Ketl, Hungo Pavi, Penasco Blanco, and Pueblo del Arroyo (see Table 1 for a complete list).

President Theodore Roosevelt designated Chaco Canyon a national monument in 1907, with nearly 27,000 acres protected. Throughout its status as a monument, Chaco was far larger than other archaeological monuments in the park system. It was renamed as a national historical park in 1980, with the acreage expanded to almost 33,000 and the name changed to Chaco Cultural National Historical Park.

CHACO'S REDISCOVERY AND BRIEF HISTORY
The history of rediscovery and exploration in Chaco Canyon is sufficiently rich and detailed to fill many pages. Rendered briefly, it seems likely that early Spanish explorers in the sixteenth and seventeenth centuries were aware of the Chacoan sites. However, the first documented visit was in 1823, by a Spanish military expedition led by Governor Jose Antonio Vizcarra. In 1849 Lt. James Simpson visited Chaco on an American army exploratory expedition

Table 1   Chaco Canyon Great Houses

Name	Size
Pueblo Bonito	650 rooms
Chetro Ketl	580 rooms
Pueblo del Arroyo	290 rooms
Penasco Blanco	220 rooms
Wijiji	190 rooms
Una Vida	160 rooms
Tsin Kletzin	155 rooms
Hungo Pavi	150 rooms
Kin Kletso	140 rooms
Pueblo Alto	130 rooms
Casa Chiquito	80 rooms
New Alto	50 rooms

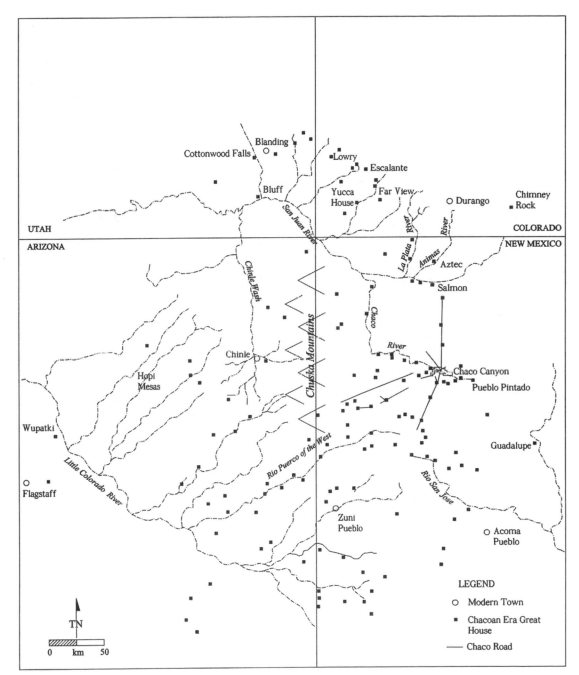

Map showing Chaco Culture National Historical Park and the distribution of Chacoan-affiliated sites across the modern Four Corners states.   [Paul F. Reed]

dispatched to the Navajo country. Together with artist Richard Kern, Simpson provided the first detailed written and cartographic documentation of the huge, abandoned pueblos of Chaco. Subsequent visitors and explorers added to knowledge of the sites.

Large-scale excavation of the Great Houses commenced at the end of the nineteenth century and continued into the 1930s, with projects sponsored by the American Museum of Natural History, the National Geographic Society, the

School of American Research, and the University of New Mexico. Finally, Park Service personnel completed much of the later research at Chacoan sites during the multi-year Chaco Project, led first by Robert Lister and later by James Judge.

Many archaeologists have studied the sites in Chaco Canyon; a few of the many books and articles about Chaco are listed at the end of this summary. I have drawn on all of that research in this article.

Aerial photograph of Pueblo Bonito.   [Aerial photograph © Adriel Heisey]

CHACO'S GREAT HOUSES

Although thousands of sites have been recorded within the park's boundary, I'll focus primarily on the dozen large structures—Chaco's Great Houses—that comprised the centers of Chacoan society. This society peaked around the year AD 1100, when more than 150 Chacoan towns (or outliers) were affiliated with Chaco, as were the twelve Great Houses in Chaco Canyon and perhaps 30,000 people across the greater San Juan basin of the southwestern United States. This Chacoan territory, which extended across portions of the four modern states of New Mexico, Arizona, Utah, and Colorado, was roughly equal in size to the country of Ireland.

Chacoan Great Houses were distinct from the majority of Puebloan structures of earlier and later periods for several reasons. First, Great Houses were constructed symmetrically and massively, with a specific type of architecture (described as core-veneer). The massive walls (up to a meter thick) consisted of a rubble, dirt, or masonry core with inner and outer veneers of carefully selected and shaped sandstone slabs.

The primary purpose of these thick walls was to support construction that rose as high as four and five stories at sites such as Pueblo Bonito and Chetro Ketl. However, even single-story sites, like Pueblo Alto, were constructed using the massive core-veneer technique. Core-veneer was more than just a construction technique and may have had intrinsic importance to the Chacoans.

Beyond massive core-veneer construction and distinctive masonry types, Chacoan Great Houses were also characterized by kivas (round ceremonial rooms) built directly into the pueblo structures (described as "blocked-in" kivas); some kivas were built at the second- and third-story levels. The rooms built within Chacoan structures were also huge by pueblo standards—up to 12 feet square, with ceilings sometimes over 10 feet high. Table 1 summarizes the room counts for Great Houses in Chaco.

Beyond these extraordinary construction approaches, the actual construction of the Great Houses required a major effort. More than 200,000 trees (varieties of pine, fur, and spruce, with some juniper and other species) were used to build roofs and support walls in the twelve primary Chaco Canyon Great Houses. Fine sandstone slabs and blocks were quarried at sites in the canyon and from areas beyond.

The overwhelming size and height of these structures, along with other factors, supports the idea that the Great Houses were intended to be landscape monuments (in addition to having other functions). As monuments, the Great Houses were intended to impress and awe local residents, as well as outsiders. They were visible across the landscape for miles.

Beyond Chaco Canyon, Great Houses were often built on hills, ridges, and other high points to increase their visibility. Pueblo Pintado (located several miles east of Pueblo Bonito), for example, is visible today for several miles when one is approaching from the north. These Chacoan Great Houses were the economic and social centers of the eleventh- and twelfth-century Puebloan landscape.

SUBSISTENCE: MAKING A LIVING IN ANCIENT CHACO

Chacoan subsistence, like that of all ancient Pueblo groups, depended on the production of three primary agricultural crops: corn, beans, and squash (including various types, such as pumpkins and gourds). One can easily envision the fertile plain of the canyon floor at AD 1075 covered with these crops, with corn particularly dominant and visible, as far as the eye can see.

We can infer that the Chacoans (in good years) produced significant agricultural surpluses that went well beyond their yearly needs; these surpluses provided the basis for the monumental construction of Great Houses. We can suggest further that crop surpluses funded monumental construction of Chacoan Great Houses, Great Kivas, roads, and agricultural support facilities in several ways. First, surplus food was used to feed and thus compensate workers who undertook construction activities. Second, food surpluses were traded for more durable goods, such as finished pottery, stone tools, basketry, woven items (such as clothing and pouches), digging sticks, and bows and arrows. These items could then be offered as payment for work completed.

Aside from situations that may have led to direct compensation for labor, more indirect means were probably also operating. For example, as some Chacoan leaders had success with agricultural pursuits, they were able to attract additional people to live in or near Great Houses. Thus the overall pool of people available for a variety of tasks involving construction, farming, or craft production would have increased and contributed to the rise of these leaders.

An important aspect of Chacoan agriculture involved the raising of domesticated turkeys. Archaeologists have recovered large amounts of turkey bone and eggshell from Great Houses and small pueblos, indicating that these birds provided not only an important source of feathers for ritual, but also a predictable food supply. Later in time, in the AD 1200s, turkeys took on an even more important role as the primary protein source in the ancient Pueblo diet.

Beyond agricultural pursuits, the Chacoans undertook a number of other subsistence activities in the course of their lives. Hunting a variety of game animals, including deer, antelope, elk, and rabbit, was very important, providing much-needed protein. Bears, mountain lions, and smaller predators and birds were hunted to provide hides, claws, and other animal parts for rituals. A great variety of natural plants were gathered—some for food (such as pigweed and wild mustard) and others for ritual or medicinal purposes (including sage, Mormon tea, and wild tobacco).

THE POPULATION OF CHACO: HOW MANY PEOPLE?

Nearly all of the land area in Chaco Culture National Historical Park has been archaeologically surveyed. As a result, we have a good idea of how many sites were in use and how many of these were Great Houses. At least eighteen Great Houses exist in the greater Chaco Canyon area (what has been called the Chaco core).

With eighteen Great Houses, numerous Great Kivas, and dozens of smaller pueblos going full throttle by AD 1050, Chaco was home to thousands of people. Exact estimates of Chaco's population provoke some of the most spirited debate among Southwestern archaeologists. Estimates over the 150 years of research have varied from below 1,000 to over 10,000. Early archaeologists counted rooms in all the Great Houses and small pueblos and applied a standard number of three persons per room to get these very high estimates. Most Chacoan archaeologists would probably agree that the number of people living in Chaco Canyon at AD 1075 (what archaeologists term a momentary population) was between 1,500 and 4,000.

Some recent studies have minimized the amount of labor that would have been necessary to build and maintain the Great Houses, to undertake agricultural activities, to maintain water and soil control facilities, and to build the Chaco roads. Nevertheless, the scale of these undertakings, along with their often simultaneous scheduling, required a substantial, properly scheduled, and well-organized labor force.

Research by archaeologist Nancy Akins on the Park Service's Chaco Project revealed a very diverse genetic population. Analysis of human burials from Pueblo Bonito in particular revealed at least two distinct populations, based on skeletal studies. This research has also shown that the residents of Pueblo Bonito were taller, healthier, and better nourished than contemporary residents of small-house sites. This suggests a hierarchy, with individuals of higher status living in the Great Houses.

More recent studies have confirmed the diversity of Chaco Canyon—and Pueblo Bonito specifically. A population from the western part of Pueblo Bonito showed a close relationship with Rio Grande populations, while burials from the north portion of Pueblo Bonito matched a Basketmaker group from Grand Gulch, Utah. Remains from several small-house sites in Chaco revealed a relationship with some from the village of the Great Kivas, to the south near Zuni Pueblo.

Although these results represent only the beginning of what will be a much larger study, they are nevertheless significant. Chaco Canyon appears to have been the home of a very diverse group of people who probably represented a number of ethnic and linguistic populations.

The presence of numerous macaws (parrots) in Pueblo Bonito suggests an ancestral connection to what became the macaw-parrot clans at Zuni and Hopi pueblos. The macaws found include primarily two species: scarlet macaws, with beautiful red, yellow, blue feathers; and military macaws, which are predominantly green. Together, these findings indicate that Chaco Canyon was probably the ancestral home to people who live today at Hopi, Zuni, many of the Rio Grande pueblos, and probably other pueblos.

SOCIAL AND POLITICAL ORGANIZATION OF CHACOAN SOCIETY

What type of social organization did the Chacoans have? Were they organized like the Hopi and other Western Pueblos, with matrilineal and matrilocal (living near the woman's family) clans? Or were they more like the Eastern Pueblos, with weak or nonexistent clans, a village-wide bilateral moiety organization, and various ceremonial societies or sodalities? Or were they governed with a type of organization that is not present among the contemporary Pueblos?

Various views of Chacoan social organization have been offered over the years. Here we can explore a few possibilities. One early suggestion linked the inhabitants of the Great Houses with one type of social order and the small pueblo dwellers with a simpler form of organization. Expanding on this view, archaeologist Gwinn Vivian further proposed that two distinct ethnic groups built and lived in the Great Houses and small pueblos, respectively.

In the late 1970s and 1980s, archaeologists (Steve Lekson, for example) put forth several models that viewed Chacoan society as hierarchical and ranked, with distinct differences among social classes. In this view, Chacoan developments were led by a group of permanent leaders who made important decisions and directed the course of Chaco's evolution. Putting Chaco into an anthropology typology developed to classify societies, proponents of this position described Chacoan society as a chiefdom.

By the late 1980s, it was clear to many archaeologists that simply classifying Chacoan sites and trying to fit them into a rigid typology were not going to lead to enlightenment or fuller understanding. Getting away from conventional anthropological categories, Chacoan archaeologists interested in social organization began exploring a variety of issues, including power, competition, status, ritual, and complexity. From this reconsideration of issues, a number of new and innovative perspectives on Chacoan social relations emerged.

Limitations of space preclude me from discussing all of these approaches. I will, however, highlight several contrasting views of Chacoan societal organization.

One recent school of thought among Chacoan archaeologists (for example, Lynne Sebastian) emphasizes the role of competition in driving the construction of Great Houses and other Chacoan developments. To explain the presence of so many Great Houses in Chaco Canyon, the notion of competition among rival leaders is invoked. In this view, Chacoan leaders built Great Houses to improve their status—a type of self-aggrandizement—and to outcompete other aspiring leaders. To succeed, leaders needed to control prime agricultural lands and produce an agricultural surplus to feed supporters and for trading purposes, and they needed to attract a loyal group of followers. These leaders are not seen as situational; they were permanent, and they had higher social status than other individuals in the pueblo.

In contrast to models that view Chacoan society as driven by competition and hierarchy, other approaches to social organization envision a unified, cooperative endeavor. Chacoan society is seen as the result of an integrated, cooperative, and largely egalitarian effort without significant competition or social hierarchy. According to this view, ritual and ceremony were paramount concerns, and ritual specialists, or priests, were the Chacoan leaders.

Between these two viewpoints lies significant middle ground. Not surprisingly, some archaeologists have drawn from both models, suggesting that neither extreme is correct. Marxist views of Chacoan archaeology reject the false dichotomy between hierarchical and egalitarian social relations. Instead, Marxist archaeologists view Pueblo society as a complex, communal organization with elements of hierarchy present, but subsumed within the communal structure.

Our understanding of Chacoan society is currently in a state of considerable flux. Even after more than 150 years of exploration and archaeological research, many questions remain. Recent publications, such as archaeologist Steve Lekson's edited volume *The Archaeology of Chaco Canyon*, have summarized and synthesized much of what is known. Nevertheless, significant issues remain unresolved, and Chaco Culture National Historical Park will remain a primary focus of research for years to come.

CONTEMPORARY NATIVE AMERICAN CONNECTIONS TO CHACO CULTURE NATIONAL HISTORICAL PARK

Numerous contemporary Native American tribes have connections to the sites or the landscape of Chaco Canyon. Most modern Pueblo villages have ancestral stories that connect them to Chaco. In particular, Zuni, Acoma, and Hopi oral history describe migrations that include stops at sites in Chaco

Canyon. Acoma oral tradition describes a place known as White House that is believed to be Pueblo Bonito. The Zuni Sword Swallower society traces it roots to a migration from Chaco.

The Navajo tribe has a strong ritual and landscape connection to Chaco Canyon. Arriving between AD 1700 and 1750, the Navajo quickly adapted to the dramatic landscape and abandoned pueblos of Chaco. Navajo lands of today, west of the main Navajo Indian reservation but part of the tribe's preserve, surround Chaco Canyon.

ACCESSING CHACO CULTURE NATIONAL HISTORICAL PARK

Chaco Culture National Historical Park is among the more remote of the nation's treasures, and a large part of the appeal for many visitors is the isolated setting that allows one to travel back in time and imagine Chaco as a thriving ancient city.

Chaco's visitor center lies at the end of a drive of more than 20 miles from U.S. Highway 550. The first 7 miles of this road are paved; thereafter the road is gravel, with frequent sandy spots and a lot of bouncy washboard. Once visitors make it inside the park, a paved road leads to the visitors' center and to many of the biggest attractions: Pueblo Bonito, Chetro Ketl, Hungo Pavi, and Una Vida. Short hikes are required to access some of the Great Houses (for example, Tsin Kletzin), while others can be seen only with longer or steeper hikes (for example, Penasco Blanco and Pueblo Alto).

Further Reading: Chaco Culture National Historic Park Web site, National Park Service, http://www.nps.gov/chcu; Cordell, Linda S., and W. James Judge, eds., *Chaco Society and Polity: Papers from the 1999 Conference*, Special Publication 4 (Albuquerque: New Mexico Archaeological Council, 2001); Fagan, Brian, *Chaco Canyon: Archaeologists Explore the Lives of an Ancient Society* (Oxford: Oxford University Press, 2005); Lekson, Stephen H., ed., *The Archaeology of Chaco Canyon* (Santa Fe, NM: School of American Research Press, 2006); Lister, Robert H., and Florence C. Lister, *Chaco Canyon: Archaeology and Archaeologists* (Albuquerque: University of New Mexico Press, 1981); Chaco Digital Initiative, online archive for Chacoan archaeology, http://www.chacoarchive.org; Judd, Neil M., "The Excavation and Repair of Betatakin," *Proceedings of the National Museum* 77 (article 5) (1930): 1–77; Noble, David Grant, ed., *In Search of Chaco: New Approaches to an Archaeological Enigma* (Santa Fe, NM: School of American Research Press, 2004); Pepper, George, *Pueblo Bonito*, Anthropological Papers of the American Museum of Natural History, Vol. XXVII (New York: 1920) (reprint Albuquerque: University of New Mexico Press, 1996); Reed, Paul F., *The Puebloan Society of Chaco Canyon* (Westport, CT: Greenwood Press, 2004); Sebastian, Lynne, *The Chaco Anasazi: Sociopolitical Evolution in the Prehistoric Southwest* (Cambridge: Cambridge University Press, 1992).

Paul F. Reed

PUEBLO BONITO

Chaco Canyon, Northwestern New Mexico

Investigations of the Greatest of the Great Houses at Chaco

Pueblo Bonito is the largest of thirteen multi-story buildings, often referred to as Great Houses, located in Chaco Canyon, a remote canyon in northwest New Mexico. The structure was constructed of fine stone masonry, beginning in the early AD 800s and continuing into the early 1100s. At its peak, it was four stories tall, covered almost 3 acres, and contained perhaps as many as 800 rooms. Pueblo Bonito was the political, economic, and religious center of a hierarchically organized society whose influence extended far beyond Chaco Canyon.

Today members of the Hopi and Zuni tribes, modern-day Pueblo groups descended from the people who once occupied Chaco Canyon, view Pueblo Bonito as a sacred place. The United States government officially recognized the significance of Pueblo Bonito and its neighboring sites in 1907, when Chaco Canyon was designated a national monument. In 1980 the monument boundaries were expanded and the canyon became part of Chaco Culture National Historical Park. Further recognition came in 1987, when Chaco Canyon was added to UNESCO's list of World Heritage Sites.

The Chacoans were part of the Anasazi (or Ancestral Pueblo) culture, which encompassed the semi-arid plateau of the northern Southwest from approximately AD 0 until the arrival of the Spanish in the early sixteenth century. Ancestral Pueblo culture had three defining traits: corn agriculture, black-on-white pottery, and (in later periods) settlements composed of contiguous, rectangular surface rooms that were organized in room blocks called pueblos. The latter were often associated with round, ceremonial structures known as kivas. After modest beginnings in the AD 800s, the Chacoans elaborated these characteristics over the next four centuries.

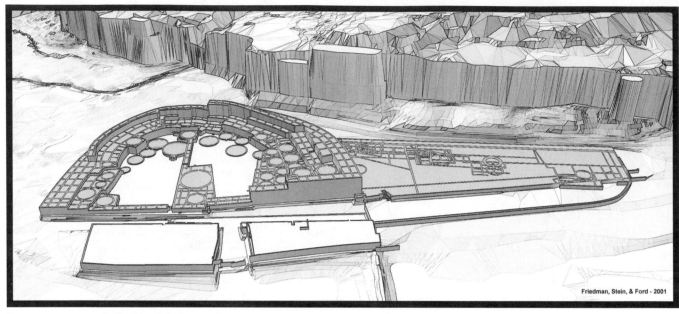

Friedman, Stein, & Ford - 2001

Perspective view of all of Pueblo Bonito between AD 1070 and 1115.   [Adapted from Stein, Ford, and Friedman (2003)]

Between AD 900 and 1000, the Chacoans intensified their varied farming methods by developing complex water and soil control systems. Many of their black-on-white ceramics were decorated with distinctive hatched designs on a variety of forms—including unique, cylinder-shaped vessels found almost exclusively in a ritual cache at Pueblo Bonito.

The Chacoans built two types of pueblos. Whereas small houses resembled typical Ancestral Pueblo villages, Great Houses were the Chacoans' singular architectural achievement. Constructed in formal layout with sophisticated masonry, Great Houses were large, often had multiple stories, and usually contained Great Kivas, which were very large kivas with distinctive features. The highest concentration of Great Houses was in Chaco Canyon, but approximately 200 others were built throughout the surrounding San Juan basin. The Chacoans also constructed two long road systems extending north and south from the canyon, and many Great Houses were associated with short road segments.

Pueblo Bonito is a D-shaped structure whose curved back wall is located just below Chaco Canyon's north cliff face. The building's interior consists of two plazas, hundreds of rectangular rooms, perhaps as many as sixty kivas, and at least three Great Kivas. The site also has two large mounds at its front, an unfinished expansion extending to the east, and two sets of burial rooms in its oldest section. The grave goods in the richest burial room included approximately 50,000 pieces of turquoise and 6,000 pieces of marine shell, mostly in the form of jewelry. The turquoise and shell had been imported to the site, as had many other materials, including copper bells and macaws from Mexico and enormous volumes of ceramics and tree beams from various parts of the San Juan basin.

Based on analyses of masonry styles, wall abutments, and tree ring dates, archaeologists have traced Pueblo Bonito's construction over seven major stages. The initial building, which may date to as early as AD 828, consisted of a crescent-shaped cluster of rooms. In the AD 1070s and early 1080s, large room blocks were added to each end of the crescent. Further building around AD 1085 enclosed the plaza and completed the structure's D-shaped plan. After a peak period of roughly thirty-five years, site use declined sharply over the following two decades. The structure was essentially abandoned by AD 1150, although very limited use by small numbers of people continued into the AD 1200s.

The first descriptions and maps of Pueblo Bonito were published in the mid-nineteenth century. Excavations began in 1896, when the American Museum of Natural History sponsored the three-year Hyde Exploring Expedition. The National Geographic Society, together with the Smithsonian Institution, conducted further excavations from 1921 to 1927. These two projects uncovered almost the entire site and produced detailed maps, enormous artifact collections, and extensive reports by project directors George Pepper and Neil Judd. Another major development occurred in 1971, when the National Park Service initiated a decade-long, multidisciplinary study of Chaco culture. The Chaco Project prompted a number of archaeologists to initiate further analyses of all aspects of Pueblo Bonito.

As the largest and most important building in a broader community, Pueblo Bonito served as both an elite residence and a

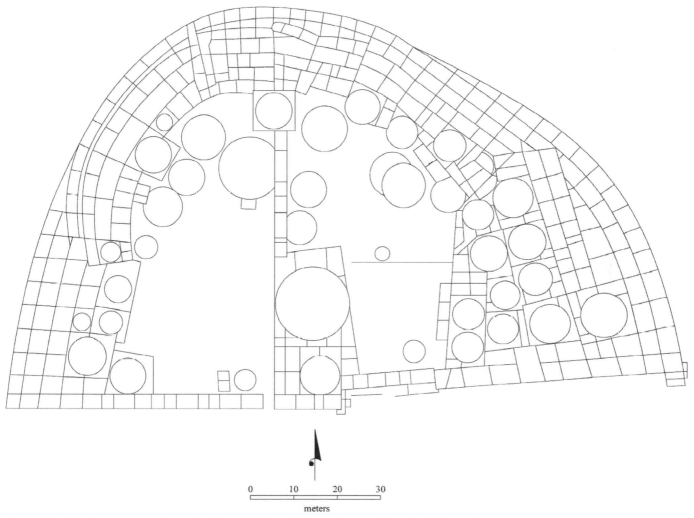

Plan of Pueblo Bonito proper drawn by Oscar Walsh in 1925. [Adapted from Judd (1964)]

ceremonial center throughout most of its history. The preeminence of the residential function was eclipsed around AD 1050, when the ceremonial role became dominant. Mortuary and settlement pattern analyses indicate that Chacoan society was hierarchically organized, and that the residents of Pueblo Bonito were at the top of the hierarchy. Although most archaeologists think that no more than several hundred people ever lived within the structure, they continue to debate whether its associated community should be considered proto-urban.

Pueblo Bonito's role as a ceremonial center may have been related to its location next to a lone pine tree and a huge sandstone monolith, as well as to its central position within the canyon, which in turn is situated roughly in the middle of the San Juan basin. Studies of Pueblo Bonito's layout, astronomical alignments, kivas, ritual caches, and burials suggest that multiple kinds of religious ceremonies were conducted at the structure. These ceremonies were probably connected with those at other canyon sites—most notably the sun dagger pet-

roglyph that marks solar and lunar events on nearby Fajada Butte. Several researchers have suggested that numerous religious pilgrims attended at least some of the ceremonies.

Key factors in the rise and fall of Pueblo Bonito and the other Great Houses were climate change, the spread of a new religion, and trade. A period of fluctuating rainfall from AD 900 to 1050 may have offered advantages for an emerging leadership hierarchy and for the initiation of trading relationships outside the canyon. Above-average rainfall between AD 1050 and 1130 made farming more productive, which enabled population growth and increased societal complexity. The spread of a new religious ideology, as evidenced by the distribution of Great Kivas, the astronomical alignments of many Great Houses, and the roads connecting Great Houses to prominent geological features, also contributed to the expansion of the Chacoan system.

Another factor was turquoise, which may have been traded to buffer food shortages and which served as both a marker of high status and an important ritual item. The widespread distribution of Great Houses probably represents a number of polities that were influenced to varying degrees by the political, economic, and religious power of Pueblo Bonito.

The decline of the Chacoan system coincided with four decades of below-average rainfall between AD 1130 and 1170. This climate change caused successive years of crop failure, which resulted in the disintegration of trading networks, the dissolution of the leadership hierarchy, the weakening of the Chacoan religion, and the abandonment of both Great Houses and villages as their occupants moved to other areas.

Pueblo Bonito and the other archaeological sites located in Chaco Culture National Historical Park are open to the public year-round. A trip to the park requires planning; visitors must travel over rough dirt roads and will find no food services or accommodations except for a campground. Within the park, Pueblo Bonito and four other major sites can be reached by a paved road and toured by walking self-guided trails. Other ruins can be reached by backcountry hiking. The park's visitors' center contains a small museum and theater. The center sponsors guided tours and hikes, as well as evening programs from May through October. Further information can be found on the park's Web site, which is listed below.

Further Reading: Chaco Canyon tour map, http://www.colorado.edu/Conferences/chaco/tour/chacomap.htm; Fagan, Brian, *Chaco Canyon: Archaeologists Explore the Lives of an Ancient Society* (Oxford: Oxford University Press, 2005); Frazier, Kendrick, *People of Chaco: A Canyon and Its Culture*, rev. ed. (New York: W. W. Norton, 1999); Judd, Neil M., *The Architecture of Pueblo Bonito*. Smithsonian Miscellaneous Collections, Vol. 147, No. 1, Publication 4524; 1964, Washington, DC; National Park Service, *Chaco Culture*, http://www.nps.gov/chcu; Neitzel, Jill E., ed., *Pueblo Bonito: Center of the Chacoan World* (Washington, DC: Smithsonian Institution Press, 2003); Noble, David G., *In Search of Chaco: New Approaches to an Archaeological Enigma* (Santa Fe, NM: School of American Research Press, 2004); Reed, Paul F., *The Puebloan Society of Chaco Canyon* (Westport, CT: Greenwood Press, 2004); Stein, J. R., D. Ford, and R. Friedman, "Reconstructing Pueblo Bonito." (2003) in *Pueblo Bonito: Center of the Chacoan World*, ed. Neitzel, J. E. (Smithsonian, Washington, DC), pp. 33–60; Vivian, R. Gwinn, *Chaco Handbook: An Encyclopedia Guide* (Salt Lake City: University of Utah Press, 2002).

Jill E. Neitzel

PUEBLO ALTO SITE

Chaco Canyon, Northwestern New Mexico
Link to the Chacoan Roadway Network North

Chaco Canyon, in the San Juan basin of northwestern New Mexico, is one of the premier archaeological areas in the nation. Many multi-storied, stone masonry pueblos, called Great Houses by archaeologists, were built in Chaco Canyon between the late AD 800s and early 1100s. These have long fascinated archaeologists as they try to understand the events and social organization of the people who built and lived in this desolate, arid environment, which lacks subsistence resources for such a large population—once postulated as high as 25,000 inhabitants. The best-known Great House is Pueblo Bonito, excavated in the 1890s and 1920s, which yielded many rare minerals and unique artifacts. These are now housed at the American Museum of Natural History, New York, and the National Museum of Natural History, Washington, D.C.

Pueblo Alto was first discovered and documented in 1877 by famed western photographer William Jackson. In the late 1800s, Alto was the focus, along with Pueblo Bonito, of Native American legends of a powerful gambler who controlled the lives of the ancients who lived there, which shares interesting parallels with theories developed in the 1970s about the Chacoan system. In the late 1960s, a new research program, the Chaco Project, developed by the National Park Service, investigated the occupations in Chaco Canyon with a focus on the Puebloan occupations between AD 500 and 1300. Aside from investigations in the small early sites, a Great House was selected to gain new insights into the rise, use, and abandonment of these large, magnificent structures.

Increased archaeological work in the American Southwest during the 1970s revealed the presence of many Great Houses throughout an area of 100,000 square miles or more. This area centered around the Four Corners, where the states of Arizona, Colorado, New Mexico, and Utah come together. The greatest concentration of Great Houses, however, is in Chaco Canyon, a wide canyon bordered by high cliffs and a deeply incised but intermittent drainage, Chaco Wash, that bisects the canyon. Nine Great Houses are found in the canyon bottom, including Pueblo Bonito, while another five are placed on the high mesas overlooking the canyon, including one at each end of the 21-mile-long canyon. At Chaco Canyon, one site built on top of the North Mesa is the nexus for many of these road alignments and control points: Pueblo Alto.

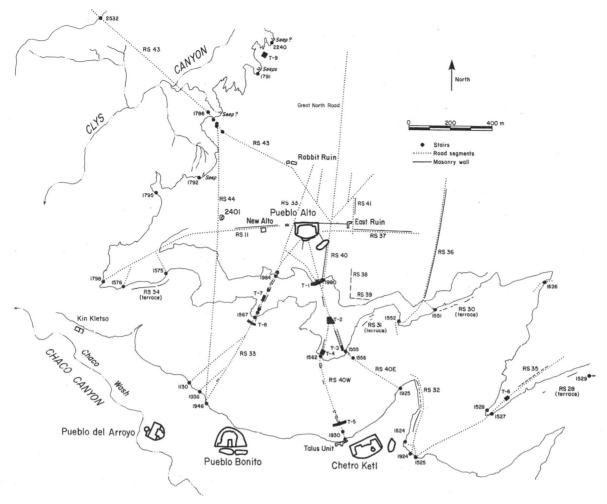

The prehistoric road network in the Pueblo Alto vicinity. Road segments are designated RS. Site numbers identify many of the associated road features, such as stairways and ramps. [Original by Tom Windes]

Pueblo Alto provides a number of characteristics that drew the attention of the Chaco Project staff. Most important was its association with numerous prehistoric roads that connected Chaco Canyon with sites to the north in the San Juan River area, where a new center of Great Houses arose in the late AD 1000s and early 1100s at Salmon—and later at the Aztec Ruins. Although archaeologist Neil Judd, who excavated at Pueblo Bonito and Pueblo del Arroyo in the 1920s, was aware of the numerous prehistoric roads that connected Chaco Canyon to areas outside, remote sensing work during the Chaco Project expanded on Judd's observations and provided a comprehensive view of a broad network of connections throughout the San Juan basin. This association provided direct evidence of links between the canyon and the greater world of the San Juan basin (bordered by several mountain ranges) and beyond. In addition, Pueblo Alto is situated so that it has visibility to all the mountain ranges surrounding the San Juan basin and many of its prominent volcanic peaks, which are important landmarks and sacred places to present-day Native Americans. Even Sandia

Mountain—next to Albuquerque, New Mexico, 110 miles (176 km) to the southeast—is visible from Pueblo Alto.

Some Native American groups trace their ancestry to Chaco Canyon. Experiments revealed that Pueblo Alto was part of a large line-of-sight communications network that probably linked all Great Houses and numerous, special network shrines located at high points around the canyon and throughout the San Juan basin. Pueblo Alto was an ideal site to investigate because of its placement overlooking Chaco Canyon and its ties, both physical and visible, to the greater San Juan Basin world.

Another point in Pueblo Alto's selection was the concurrent excavations at the Salmon Ruin, located along the San Juan River about 40 miles (64 km) north, and its possible connection via the Great North Road to Pueblo Alto. The task of investigating the Alto complex was limited to ten archaeologists and their laborers over a 3-year period. Approximately 10 percent of Pueblo Alto was excavated between 1976 and 1978, saving much for the future. The major points of inquiry at the site focused on room suites, the interior plaza, the trash

PUEBLO ALTO

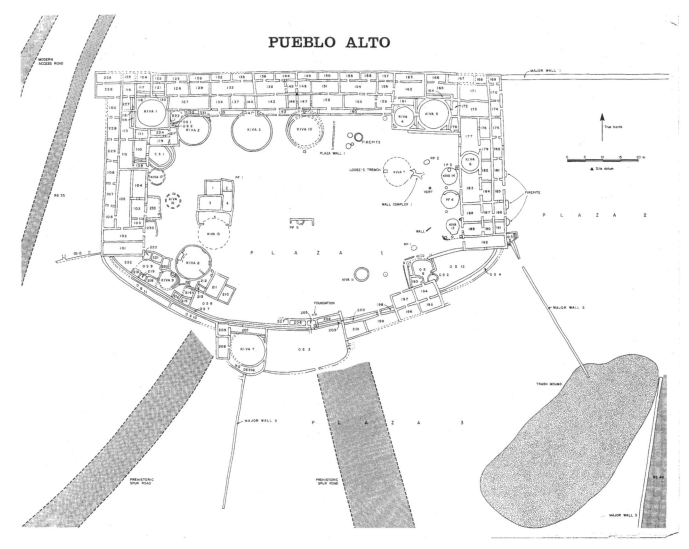

Plan view of Pueblo Alto. Dark linear strips are prehistoric roads entering Pueblo Alto or adjacent to it.   [Courtesy of the National Park Service]

midden, the adjoining isolated structures and walls, and the east exterior plaza—the nexus for several roads and direct entries into the pueblo.

Pueblo Alto contains 77 single-story rooms built about AD 1040, but modifications and additions increased the number to 133 rooms during the final use of the site in the early AD 1100s. Pueblo Alto was not only large, but also connected other room blocks just east and west of it by low masonry walls. The room blocks and central plaza cover 20 acres (8 hectares), but the two adjacent external plazas increase the built and modified landscape to about 42 acres (17 hectares). There are few spectacular artifacts among the 203,000 recovered from the site, but the abundant suite, plaza, and refuse information greatly expand our understanding of Chacoan Great Houses.

The first season, in 1976, focused on exposing the tops of all the masonry walls at the site and its adjoining units, while

in 1977, work continued to expose and map the door connections and to define the many room suites. After the tops of the walls were exposed, aerial photographs provided the basis for the site architectural layout map. Excavations focused on clearing a few representative redundant room suites in the site; understanding one suite in a group helps to interpret the others and to understand similar ones in other Great Houses.

Based on excavation of a few room suites that are duplicated at the site, the function of 74 percent of the different layouts of suites could be interpreted. No excavations occurred in the east wing of the Pueblo Alto, but work in the central and west room blocks provides new insights into room function—and good estimates of the number of residents. The size of the resident population in the Chaco Canyon Great Houses is key to understanding how sparse local resources could have supported a large number of people. A drastically reduced population, much of it possibly seasonal, may also explain the lack of burials.

View of Pueblo Alto, looking north across the west wing and the five primary habitation rooms now buried. The indistinct bumps on the far horizon to the right make up Huerfano Butte, a sacred place and link in the visible communications system. [John M. Campbell]

From the excavations, three prominent types of room suites are evident: big-room, habitation, and storage-room suites. The big-room suites are similar in layout to site habitation suites from earlier periods (between AD 700 and 900) but lack the large habitation room. Identical big-room suites are found in several Great Houses, including Una Vida and Pueblo Bonito, and were the first large units constructed in the early Great Houses.

There are five Pueblo Alto habitation suites, all located along the west wing. Internal features, which include fire pits, mealing bins, and many storage pits, suggest that one or two domestic groups occupied each habitation room. About five families, or about 25 to 50 people, lived intermittently at Pueblo Alto when it was first built. Former estimates of about 800 inhabitants for the site were based on the similarity of Pueblo Alto (and other Great Houses) to historic apartment houses such as the Acoma and Taos pueblos.

Finally, contiguous units of storage rooms accessed by doorways along the pueblo exterior and laterally through the suite are designated as road-associated suites, generally built between about AD 1040 and 1050 at several Great Houses. In every case, prehistoric roads are known to have occurred in very close proximity to these types of suites, although we know very little about the former activities within these units.

A 4-meter trench across the trash mound revealed layers of materials separated by bands of eolian sand. This arrangement suggests intermittent deposition rather than the steady, mixed accumulations typical of full-time household disposal. Charcoal, ash, and decayed vegetal material—common indicators of household refuse—are noticeably absent compared to the small-house refuse heaps excavated in the canyon. Debris from stone tool production along with fragments of pottery revealed materials that were procured in the Chuska Mountains 50 miles (80 km) to the west. Roofing elements of nonlocal tree species also attest to long-distance procurement.

The findings from the work at the Pueblo Alto complex provide our most detailed information about Great Houses since the work of Neil Judd in the 1920s. While not every Great House served the same functions, Pueblo Alto provides a much-reduced estimate of resident numbers, with clear ties to other Great Houses—and to resources far to the west and north, via prehistoric roads and a visual signaling system. While large amounts of materials were discarded at the site, it is unlikely that so few residents produced it. Instead, evidence from the trash mound reveals periodic deposition from events that may have been staged at Alto and other Great Houses.

While consensus among archaeologists is still lacking for why the Chacoan Great Houses appeared, the power and kind of leadership that produced the complex Chacoan society, and what happened to this society, the excavations at Pueblo Alto provide considerable new information to be interpreted for understanding Pueblo Alto and Chacoan society.

Pueblo Alto was backfilled after the excavations to help preserve its architecture, plastered walls, and room features. Its outline is still visible, along with some walls that project above the fill. Trails to the site and adjacent New Alto, a small, late two-story structure, lead from behind Kin Kletso on the canyon floor to the 100-foot-high cliff tops, where a half-mile walk leads to an overlook above Pueblo Bonito. A trail leaves this route for Pueblo Alto and Jackson's Staircase along a 3-mile loop. Visitors must obtain a free back-country permit to use the trail. A museum at the visitors' center provides information about Chaco, and films are shown daily.

Further Reading: Chaco Culture National Historical Park, National Park Service Web site, www.nps.gov/chcu (online January 2007); Frazier, Kendrick, *People of Chaco: A Canyon and Its Culture*, rev. ed. (New York: W. W. Norton, 2005); Lekson, Stephen H., Thomas C. Windes, John R. Stein, and W. James Judge, "The Chaco Canyon Community," *Scientific American* 259(1) (1988): 100–109; Windes, Thomas C., *Investigations at the Pueblo Alto Complex, Chaco Canyon, New Mexico, 1975–1979*, Vol. I: *Summary of Tests and Excavations at the Pueblo Alto Community*, Publications in Archeology No. 18F, Chaco Canyon Studies (Santa Fe, NM: U.S. National Park Service, 1987).

Thomas C. Windes

GREAT HOUSE ARCHITECTURE AT CHACO CANYON AND BEYOND

Chaco Canyon, Northwestern New Mexico
The History and Anthropology of Ancient Great Houses

"Great House" is an archaeological term for exceptionally large, remarkably geometric ancient structures of Chaco Canyon, New Mexico. Chaco Canyon was the largest settlement and a major regional center of the Anasazi (or Ancestral Pueblo) region from AD 850 to 1150. Chaco Culture National Historical Park protects a dozen Great Houses, including the two largest, Pueblo Bonito and Chetro Ketl. (Such Great House names were given by

Chetro Ketl.   [Stephen H. Lekson]

archaeologists and explorers and probably do not reflect the original names of these buildings.)

The word "great" in Great House refers to the extraordinary size and formality of these structures compared to the typical residence of the time: a small, roughly built, single-story pueblo of six to ten rooms arranged in a shallow arc, with a single nearby kiva (a subterranean pit structure). In the eleventh century AD, roughly 95 percent of Anasazi people lived in small houses of that type; approximately 5 percent lived in Great Houses. In contrast to small houses, Great Houses had up to 800 rooms, rising five stories tall, in formal geometric ground plans, over areas equivalent to several football fields.

Great Houses were massively (even monumentally) built, with great craftsmanship. Their masonry is among the finest of ancient North America. Compared to small houses, Great Houses represented a major investment of labor and time, with sandstone walls 2 to 3 feet thick and strongly built ceilings comprising thousands of large pine beams procured from forests 40 miles or more away. Consequently, many Great Houses are still standing today (with intact roofs) while the far more numerous ruins of small houses have been reduced to low rubble mounds.

The earliest Great Houses (AD 700 to 900) shared ground plans with small houses; that is, early Great Houses consisted of repeated units of six to ten rooms, each with an associated kiva. But the scale of Great House building vastly exceeded that of small houses. An entire small house could fit into a single room of an early Great House. Similarities in ground plans strongly suggest similar functions: Great or small, both were houses.

The Great House tradition began far north of Chaco, in the Mesa Verde region of southwestern Colorado. There, in the AD 700s, most villages consisted of clusters of small houses and one or two much larger houses that were conspicuously more massive in plan and construction. These were the first Great Houses, probably the homes of village leaders or elite families. Early Great Houses were short-lived, as were the villages they served. Anasazi villages in the eighth and ninth centuries typically lasted only a generation, after which their residents moved and re-established their towns in new places.

The tradition took root in Chaco Canyon at three key Great Houses: Peñasco Blanco, Pueblo Bonito, and Una Vida. Through the tenth century AD, these three early Great Houses were maintained and expanded, continuing the original house form: arcs of six- to ten-room units with associated kivas. Then, about AD 1020, a building boom began at each of the original Great Houses and at several new buildings, including Chetro Ketl, Hungo Pavi, and Pueblo Alto. The explosion of Great House construction also saw changes in form and design. The irregular arcs of the old house form gave way to rigidly geometric plans, most easily described as various letter forms: D, E, O, and others. Remarkably large blocks of non-residential rooms and structures were added to the older, residentially styled Great Houses. Great care was taken in laying out new building projects, and their construction required mobilization of labor from the surrounding region and significant centralized planning and coordination.

Many of the Chaco Canyon Great Houses were positioned below the towering cliff walls of the canyon, and the ground plans could be easily viewed from above. But several Great Houses were built atop surrounding mesas, where their geometry would not be readily apparent. The shapes of the buildings, whether viewed from above or from ground level, were carefully thought out.

Great Houses were not casual constructions or happy accidents. It is reasonable to speak of architectural canons and principles: Chaco Great Houses were designed buildings, answering to various geometric, astronomical, and geomantic

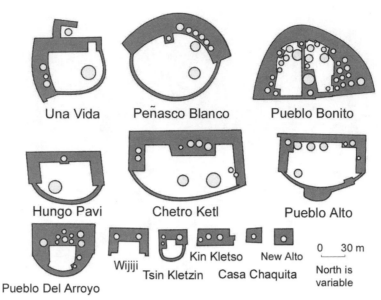

Una Vida Peñasco Blanco Pueblo Bonito

Hungo Pavi Chetro Ketl Pueblo Alto

Pueblo Del Arroyo Wijiji Tsin Kletzin Kin Kletso Casa Chaquita New Alto

0 30 m

North is variable

Ground plans of Chaco Great Houses. [Stephen H. Lekson]

rules. Many of these rules have been reconstructed by John Fritz, Anna Sofaer, John Stein, and other researchers through analysis of the buildings and their arrangement in the canyon. While no one architect or group of architects was responsible for all Great Houses, the buildings share ideas and principles that were clearly understood by the many individual architects, builders, and users. Chaco Great House architecture was one of the great Native building traditions of ancient North America, in a class with Hopewell earthworks and Mississippian town planning.

Building continued at Chaco Canyon through the eleventh and early twelfth centuries. After about AD 1090, construction focused on compact, rectangular buildings with scores or even hundreds of smaller rooms and only one or two kivas (such as Kin Kletso or New Alto); similar construction took place as additions to existing Great Houses. By about AD 1130 (based on tree ring evidence), building ceased at Chaco Canyon Great Houses.

The canons of Great House building were also evident in over 200 smaller Great Houses located at communities outside Chaco Canyon. And the tradition continued after the end of active construction in Chaco Canyon (ca. AD 1130), but in a variety of ways, depending on local situations. To the north, the formal canons of Chacoan architecture were followed at one later, major regional center at Aztec Ruins (AD 1110 to 1280); and, perhaps, Great House architecture influenced the form of enigmatic D-shaped structures found at many Mesa Verde sites dating to the thirteenth century AD. These sites may reflect the shapes of Pueblo Bonito or Chetro Ketl. To the south, the remarkable geometric formality of many AD thirteenth- and fourteenth-century Zuni area sites probably echoes Chaco principles, transferred from Great Houses to

compact towns. Many Zuni-area sites began with a master plan of rigid geometric proportions (circles, squares, etc.) defined by massive enclosing walls, which were then filled in with normal domestic architecture. And, taking a longer view, Chaco Great Houses can be seen as the origins of the Pueblo style: massed multi-story structures, terraced down to an enclosed plaza. That form, archetypical of Pueblo building in the fifteenth and sixteenth centuries AD, began at Chaco Canyon in the eleventh century AD.

What were Great Houses? They were originally interpreted as crowded farming villages, with (for example) Pueblo Bonito being equivalent to a modern Pueblo town like Taos or Zuni. Recent research discovered that the largest Great Houses had relatively few permanent residents, and those residents were of notably higher status than their contemporaries living in surrounding small houses. Great Houses are now interpreted to be ritual structures, monuments, warehouses, or palaces—or, most likely, a combination of all those functions. Indeed, functions changed (or were added) over the three centuries of Chaco Great House construction from AD 850 to 1150, and Chaco architectural principles used after AD 1150 undoubtedly addressed different goals or solved new architectural problems.

While Great Houses were without question in the history and traditions of modern Pueblo people, these magnificent structures were probably not Pueblo in the sense of a small, egalitarian, farming village. It is, of course, important to look to modern Pueblos for insights about Chaco and its Great Houses, but it is also useful to look at Chaco's contemporary world—North America and Mexico around the eleventh and twelfth centuries AD. Chaco Great Houses developed on a continent marked by politically complex

Chaco masonry. [Stephen H. Lekson]

societies: the kings and states of Mesoamerica, the impressive chiefdoms of the Mississippi valley, and even the hierarchical hunter-gatherers of California. Chaco was almost literally surrounded by kings and chiefs, and Great Houses probably represent a local, southwestern reflection of that era in Native North America—more palaces than pueblos, but still profoundly Puebloan.

Further Reading: Lekson, Stephen H., *Great Pueblo Architecture of Chaco Canyon* (Clinton Corners, NY: Percheron Press, 2007); Lekson, Stephen H., ed., *Archaeology of Chaco Canyon, An Eleventh-Century Pueblo Regional Center* (Santa Fe, NM: School for Advanced Research Press, 2006); Lekson, Stephen H., ed., *Architecture of Chaco Canyon* (Salt Lake City: University of Utah Press, 2007).

Stephen H. Lekson

CHACO OUTLIER SITES: CASAMERO, KIN YA'A, AZTEC, AND OTHER SITES

The Four Corners Region, Northern Southwest
The Wider Chacoan World

Many people know about the phenomenal archaeology of Chaco Canyon, located in northwestern New Mexico. Massive masonry buildings constructed with enormous beams carried by hand over dozens of kilometers, sophisticated solar and perhaps even lunar observatories, and great quantities of valuables imported from as far away as Mesoamerica—all set in a seemingly inhospitable and isolated environment—make Chaco Canyon a fascinating place for archaeologists and the public alike. What is perhaps even more impressive, however, are the innumerable communities outside of Chaco Canyon that were directly or indirectly influenced by the central canyon as it developed from the late AD 800s into the early AD 1100s. Almost 250 of these sites have been identified so far, some seemingly connected to Chaco Canyon with lengthy, prehistoric roadways that cross the high-desert floor.

Variously referred to as "Chacoan outliers" or "Great House communities," each outlying Chacoan site is characterized by dozens of family households closely scattered around one or more Great Houses, each reminiscent of the monumental architecture of Chaco Canyon. Great Kivas,

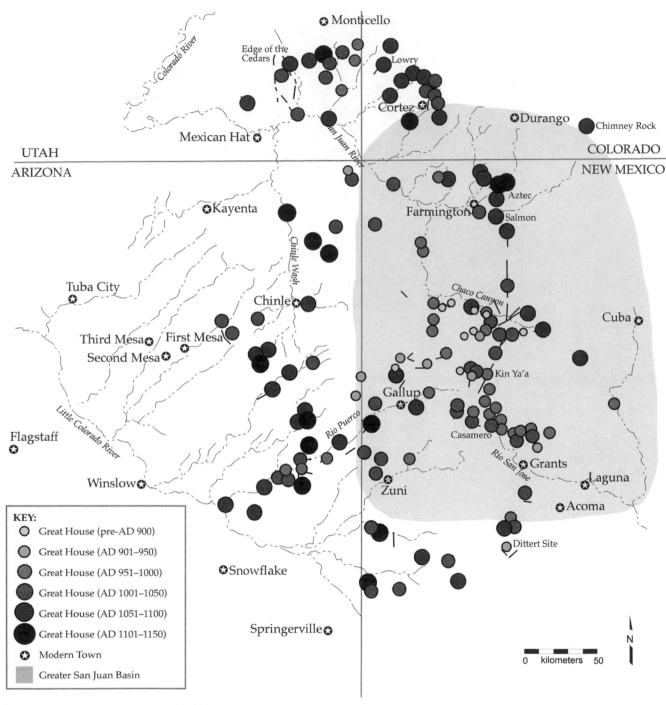

Outlying ancient communities in the Chaco World, showing dates of great house construction.   [John Kantner]

another ceremonial feature common in the central canyon, are often found in these distant communities, as are the remains of roadways.

Beyond this basic characterization, however, considerable variability is present, with some communities exhibiting small Great Houses that barely qualify for such a status, while others rival the size and complexity of the largest Great

Houses in Chaco Canyon. Some outlying communities have Great Kivas and roadways; others do not. Most Chacoan outliers started long before the Chaco era as ancient villages that later saw the addition of Great House architecture and related Chacoan features, but a handful known as "scion communities" were established during the Chaco era in previously unoccupied areas. And, in a few mysterious cases, isolated

The stabilized tower kiva at the Kin Ya'a Great House stands two stories above the rest of the structure.   [John Kantner]

Great Houses without accompanying residential architecture are found.

THE CHACO WORLD

Archaeologists know that we cannot understand the development of Chaco Canyon without knowing what was happening in the multitude of Great House communities found across the northern Southwest, an area often referred to as the Chaco World. Over the past several decades, but particularly in recent years, a small number of scholars have studied these outliers in detail. Complicating their efforts, however, are the sheer number and size of these communities and the diversity of lands on which they are found; many are spread across multiple public, tribal, and private jurisdictions, making access a significant challenge. Unfortunately, many also are disturbed by illegal pot hunting activity, compromising archaeologists' ability to reconstruct their history.

Despite these challenges, archaeologists are slowly identifying how the Chaco World developed and how this relates to events inside Chaco Canyon. Although some evidence suggests that Great House communities emerged simultaneously all around the central canyon, the growth of the Chaco World was in fact quite uneven.

Those communities located to the south were the first to have Great Houses built in them, probably as early as the tenth century. As far as can be determined in the absence of sufficient excavation, archaeologists believe that people were living in these southern communities well before the construction of the Great Houses. From that point in time, the impact of Chaco spread into other existing communities— down the Rio Puerco of the west drainage in the late AD 900s, into the foothills of the Chuska Mountains by about AD 1000, and north into the San Juan River area beginning in the mid-1000s.

Another intriguing pattern in the Chaco World is that Great Houses in communities situated closest to Chaco Canyon were built earlier than those found farther away. The former also exhibit the strongest fidelity: Communities near the central canyon are more likely to exhibit an impressive Great House with a compelling suite of Chacoan features, such as massive masonry and roadways. Those farther away are more likely to have Great Houses with the weakest Chacoan signature. Interestingly, when Chaco Canyon began to fade in importance during the early eleventh century, those most distant communities were least impacted. Some, in fact, continued to build Chacoan-influenced architecture for a few generations after Chaco's Great Houses had fallen into ruin.

EXAMPLES OF GREAT HOUSE COMMUNITIES

Despite the large number of outlying Chacoan sites, few are accessible to the public, and even fewer are professionally excavated. Visitors, however, can explore several outlying

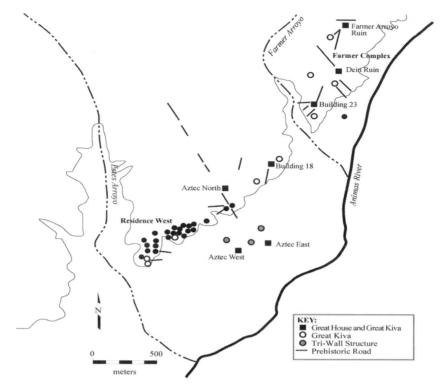

Ancient building at Aztec: the well-known Aztec West Great House is only one of possibly seven Great Houses, as well as many small residences, found in the extensive Aztec community.   [John Kantner]

Great Houses, each of which provides excellent insight into the great variety that characterizes the Chaco World. Some sites also provide access to the households whose residents likely constructed the Great Houses, Great Kivas, and roadways. In southwestern Colorado, Chimney Rock and Lowry provide three very different Great Houses to explore, while in Utah, Edge of the Cedars is open to the public. Accessible New Mexico communities include Salmon Ruin, Aztec, Casamero, Kin Ya'a, and the Dittert site. Three of these are described below: a small village with an early Great House distant from Chaco Canyon, a larger community with a more formal Great House closer to the canyon, and an even larger community with several large Great Houses that flourished late in the Chacoan sequence and may represent the last gasp of the Chacoan way of life.

CASAMERO

More than 70 kilometers to the south of Chaco Canyon, nestled against the red sandstone walls of the Red Mesa valley, is the small village of Casamero. Its first permanent inhabitants arrived by the AD 700s, building pit houses on top of the mesa before establishing small masonry homes at the base of the cliffs.

These modest structures were small—none more than a dozen rooms—and the architecture was simple, consisting

of roughly shaped cobbles of readily available sandstone. By the AD 900s, the village consisted of no more than twenty of these homes. At some point in the late AD 900s or early AD 1000s, the residents of Casamero built something new: a two-story Great House of over twenty rooms. Made of carefully shaped limestone blocks fitted in such a way as to make comparatively massive walls, the new building was designed with unusually large rooms and constructed around an open plaza.

At roughly the same time, in virtually every village throughout the Red Mesa valley, Great Houses such as the one at Casamero appeared, just as would eventually happen across the northern Southwest in the tenth and eleventh centuries. Not far from Casamero, for example, in the village of Andrews, a comparable Great House was constructed, and residents in the nearby Blue J community augmented an older home by adding thick limestone walls similar to those at Casamero. Short roadways emanated from the Casamero and Andrews Great Houses, but rather than creating highways between communities, they almost certainly formed ceremonial alignments that symbolically connected the Great Houses with prominent landscape features.

Casamero is owned by the Bureau of Land Management, and visitors can follow a short path from a small parking area to explore the stabilized Great House. Although no information about the surrounding community is provided, interpretive signs describe what archaeologists discovered during their excavations of the Great House.

KIN YA'A

The most impressive Great Houses in the Chaco World tend to be located closer to Chaco Canyon than are the ones whose identities as Great Houses are questionable. Those situated on the edges of the San Juan basin are particularly striking. A bit over 40 kilometers southwest of Chaco Canyon, for example, is Kin Ya'a. This large structure once included over forty rooms built of massive masonry walls rising three stories; one of the four original kivas built into the structure is a tower kiva that still stands nearly four stories tall. Although the Great House itself may have been built as early as the AD 1020s, tree ring dates from the tower kiva suggest at least some construction in the AD 1080s.

Surrounding the Kin Ya'a Great House is a dense community of eighty residences, as well as at least one and perhaps two Great Kivas. One of the most impressive roadways connected with Chaco Canyon—known as the South Road—passes through the community, ascends the nearby Dutton Plateau, and disappears into the shrubby forest near a simple stone shrine, a feature often found along these roadways. Archaeologists once assumed that the South Road connected Chaco Canyon with communities on either side of the Dutton Plateau, but its arrow-straight alignment points most obviously at Hosta Butte, a prominent geographical feature that sits on top of the plateau and is visible even as far away as Chaco Canyon itself. Along with the roadways in the Red Mesa valley, such discoveries are leading archaeologists to interpret the Chacoan roads as a symbolic, rather than economic, network that tied the Chaco World to a broad cultural landscape.

Although the short dirt road into Kin Ya'a is challenging to find and negotiate, the National Park Service provides interpretive signage and an informative pamphlet to visitors of the stabilized Great House. Low rubble mounds—the remains of a once-thriving community—can be seen along the road into Kin Ya'a.

AZTEC

Approximately 100 kilometers to the north of Chaco Canyon, a cluster of Great Houses built in the early AD 1100s rival the scale of architecture seen in Chaco Canyon. Today, the site is known as "Aztec," since ethnocentric nineteenth-century Anglo-European visitors thought the buildings were too monumental to have been built by southwestern Native Americans.

As many as six Great Houses were ultimately built here. One of the buildings, known as Aztec East, is mostly unexcavated and not well known, but its neighbor, Aztec West, was fully excavated and can be visited today. Containing an astounding 437 rooms arrayed around a plaza and an impressive Great Kiva, Aztec West was built rapidly in two labor-intensive construction episodes in AD 1113 and 1119. Containing substantial quantities of imports and rich burials, Aztec West has no peers among the nearly 250 outlying Great Houses recorded so far.

Aztec was the last bastion of the Chaco tradition, gaining prominence as Chaco Canyon faded in importance. Most of Aztec's Chacoan features continued to be used well into the AD 1200s, including its Great Kivas and roadways. The surrounding community was quite large, and elaborate burials from the excavated Great House indicate inequities in wealth and status comparable to that seen in Chaco Canyon. Aztec, however, did not have the same impact that Chaco did during its height. Areas surrounding Aztec appear to have given up on the Chaco tradition as the central canyon itself faded in prominence. Most outlying Great Houses built in the late eleventh century fell into disuse or were remodeled to serve other purposes.

The last tree ring dates from Aztec are in the AD 1230s to 1250s. What happened to Aztec remains a mystery. It is likely that, similar to the fate of Chaco Canyon, people likely lost interest in Aztec as the extravagance of its leaders exceeded the benefits that local populations received. After several decades of disuse, Aztec too was eventually reoccupied by people who remodeled the buildings for their own domestic uses. By then, all surviving Great Houses were purely residential, and the power of Chacoan architecture just a memory.

The National Park Service unit of Aztec Ruins National Monument maintains the stabilized architecture of Aztec West, and a small museum offers exhibits, trail guides, tours, and an excellent summer lecture series. In contrast to Casamero and Kin Ya'a, Aztec is readily accessible, located on the edge of the modern town of Bloomfield, New Mexico.

Further Reading: Fagan, Brian, *Chaco Canyon: Archaeologists Explore the Lives of an Ancient Society* (Oxford: Oxford University Press, 2005); Frazier, Kendrick, *People of Chaco: A Canyon and Its Culture*, 3rd ed. (New York: W. W. Norton and Company, 2005); Kantner, John, *The Ancient Puebloan Southwest* (Cambridge: Cambridge University Press, 2004); Kantner, John, *Sipapu: The Anasazi Emergence into the Cyber World*, http://sipapu.gsu.edu (online March 2007); Kantner, John, and Nancy M. Mahoney, eds., *Great House Communities Across the Chacoan Landscape* (Tucson: University of Arizona Press, 2000); Lekson, Stephen H., ed., *The Archaeology of Chaco* (Santa Fe, NM: School for Advanced Research Press, 2006); Noble, David Grant, ed., *In Search of Chaco: New Approaches to an Archaeological Enigma* (Santa Fe, NM: School for Advanced Research Press, 2004).

John Kantner

POST-CHACOAN SITES: AZTEC, LOWERY, AND BLUFF

Northern San Juan River Drainage, Colorado, New Mexico, and Utah
The Archaeology of the Declining Chaco World

The northern San Juan region includes southwestern Colorado, southeastern Utah, and that part of northwestern New Mexico north of the San Juan River. It was a key part of the Chacoan regional system during the AD 1000–1150 period. Many Chacoan Great Houses, such as Aztec Ruins in New Mexico, Lowry Ruins in Colorado, and the Bluff Great House in Utah, were built here and functioned as focal points for their surrounding community.

After the fall of the great center at Chaco Canyon in the mid-twelfth century, scholars believe that Chacoan leaders retreated north and re-established their regional center at Aztec Ruins. Some Great Houses were abandoned at this time, but others, such as Bluff and Lowry, continued to be occupied, and large communities without Great Houses were established. During this post-Chaco era, Great Houses seem to have changed function. Rather than serving as community centers inhabited by a few leaders or priests, as may have occurred in Chaco Canyon, these later sites show evidence of many inhabitants carrying out their daily lives. Post-Chacoan Great Houses were used until the entire region was abandoned before AD 1300.

Chacoan Great Houses were built by the Ancestral Pueblo, an agricultural people who had lived in the northern part of the Southwest for centuries. Although the typical settlement in the northern San Juan region was a small hamlet, by AD 700 these hamlets were forming into large villages. Recent work by Richard Wilshusen has shown that by about AD 900, some people from these short-lived villages were moving into the Chaco region. After Chaco Canyon fell, descendants of these migrants moved back to the northern San Juan region, significantly increasing population there.

Chacoan Great Houses in the northern San Juan region are multi-storied buildings generally located in prominent locations, where they overlook the surrounding landscape. They seem to have been built very late in the Chaco era, around AD 1100. These buildings have the same architectural characteristics as the Great Houses built in Chaco Canyon itself. They consist of many of large square or rectangular rooms, as well as round rooms (called kivas). Walls are thick stone constructions made with a technique called core-and-veneer masonry. These buildings were built to last, and many walls still stand after almost 1,000 years.

During the post-Chaco era, residents modified Chacoan Great Houses. They subdivided the large rooms to make cozy living spaces. The post-Chaco dividing walls are often thin and poorly made. Post-Chaco residents also added many kivas, usually modifying an existing room with the addition of a round room. Whereas Chaco-era Great Houses might have only one or two kivas, post-Chaco Great Houses featured an abundance of them. Kivas are thought to be religious rooms, based on analogy with structures at modern pueblos. However, the kivas used at post-Chacoan Great Houses were likely domestic as well as ritual structures.

Chacoan Great Houses are not simply isolated buildings. They are usually at the center of a carefully constructed landscape of other structures and features. Great Houses generally have a nearby large, circular, subterranean ceremonial Great Kiva, mounds of earth (called berms), and prehistoric roads. There is evidence that Great Kivas continued to be used and modified during the post-Chaco era, that additional material was added to berms, and that prehistoric roads continued to be used.

Chacoan Great Houses are usually surrounded by a dispersed community of small houses (called unit pueblos), which served as residences for the people whose lives centered on the Great Houses. In some parts of the northern San Juan region, this pattern changed during the post-Chaco era, and people aggregated into large settlements, of which the Great House was only one element. In other parts of the region, however, dispersed communities of unit pueblos still surrounded large, prominently placed buildings, but these buildings lack many Great House characteristics. Aztec Ruins, Lowry Ruins, and the Bluff Great House exemplify the patterns of post-Chaco use and modification of Chacoan Great Houses.

AZTEC RUINS

Aztec Ruins is the largest Great House in the northern San Juan region and is second only to Chaco Canyon in size and architectural development. Now a national monument, it consists of a number of Great Houses, Great Kivas, tri-wall structures, prehistoric roads, and many other structures and features that date to both the Chaco and post-Chaco eras. It was excavated by pioneering Southwestern archaeologist Earl Morris for the American Museum of Natural History in the early twentieth century, although the full extent of the Aztec complex was only recognized during work by John Stein and Peter McKenna in the 1980s. Stein and McKenna demonstrated that Aztec consisted of highly structured and symmetrically ordered set of ritual structures that were the focus for

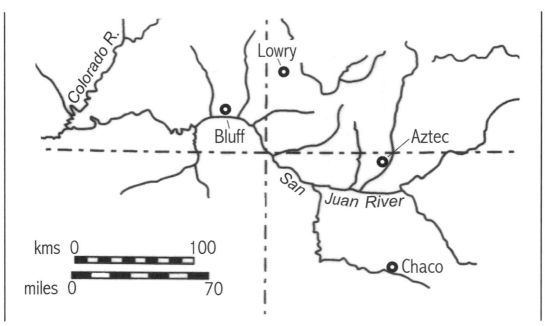

A map of important post-Chacoan sites in the northern San Juan region.   [Catherine M. Cameron]

an extensive community of smaller sites stretching along the Animas River for more than 2 miles.

The core of the Aztec complex is composed of four Great Houses: Aztec West, Aztec East, Aztec North, and the Earl Morris Ruin. These Great Houses were built consecutively, with construction beginning in the Chaco era and continuing until the end of the post-Chaco era. Only Aztec West has been extensively excavated. It consists of a bracket-shaped building with more than 400 rooms and 28 kivas, mostly added during the post-Chaco era. Adjacent to Aztec West is an enormous Great Kiva, more than 12 meters across and 3 meters deep. Tall stone and wood pillars hold a massive wooden roof, and the kiva was surrounded at ground level by more than 15 peripheral rooms.

Aztec West is open to the public, and visitors can wander through several extraordinarily well-preserved rooms and marvel at the sturdy walls and the beautifully constructed wooden ceilings. Earl Morris reconstructed the Great Kiva, and it too is open to the public. Morris's reconstruction is generally accurate, and the visitor can experience this vast subterranean chamber as it was almost 1,000 years ago. Aztec Ruins National Monument is located in the town of Aztec, New Mexico, and includes a museum, interpretive signs and brochures, and a knowledgeable NPS staff.

LOWRY RUIN

The Lowry Ruin Great House and its Great Kiva were excavated by Paul Martin as part of a Field Museum of Natural History expedition during the 1930s. Martin uncovered a rectangular building with perhaps fifty multi-story rooms, some of which were two or three stories high. Eight kivas are located in or near the building, and a Great Kiva and prehistoric roads are nearby. The Lowry Ruin was built during the Chaco era but underwent extensive remodeling and continued to be used well into the post-Chaco era. Martin was able to identify at least five different construction episodes, including the addition or reconstruction of kivas.

Recent work by James Kendrick and James Judge have found that Lowry Ruin is part of an extensive community that included several Great Houses, many small unit pueblos, specialized ceremonial sites, shrines, reservoirs, and roads.

The Lowry Ruin is part of the Canyon of the Ancients National Monument. It is located about 30 miles northwest of Cortez Colorado and is open to the public. One of the kivas excavated by Martin had a decorative mural. Visitors can enter the kiva, although the mural is no longer visible. Or they can visit the Anasazi Heritage Center near Dolores, Colorado, to see a surviving fragment of the mural. The Great Kiva is also open for viewing by visitors.

BLUFF GREAT HOUSE

The Bluff Great House is located in the small town of Bluff, Utah, on a prominent terrace above the San Juan River. It was excavated between 1995 and 2004 as part of the University of Colorado archaeological field school, under the direction of Catherine Cameron and Stephen Lekson. It consists of a Great House, Great Kiva, berm, and prehistoric roads. The Great House was initially built between AD 1075 and 1150, but continued to be used and extensively remodeled until about AD 1250. It was three or perhaps even four stories high and had tall rectangular or square rooms. At least one kiva was part of the Chaco-era construction, and several others were inserted along the front of the Great House—likely during the post-Chaco era.

The Great House is surrounded by an earthen berm that forms a flat terrace north of the Great House. This terrace is almost unique in Chacoan architecture and may have been a platform used for ceremonial activities. Other portions of the berm encircle the Great House and are broken by the entry of prehistoric roads. The adjacent Great Kiva is almost 13 meters in diameter and more than 3 meters deep.

The Bluff Great House was once the center for a community of surrounding unit pueblos, but modern development and the San Juan River have destroyed or buried most of these sites. The Bluff Great House is owned by the Southwest Heritage Foundation, a preservation group based in Bluff. Although excavation units have been mostly filled, visitors are welcome to visit the site, and informational signs are located in an adjacent kiosk.

Further Reading: Cameron, Catherine M., *Chaco and after in the Northern San Juan: Excavations at the Bluff Great House* (Tucson: University of Arizona Press, 2008); Lipe, William D., "Notes from the North," in *The Archaeology of Chaco Canyon: An Eleventh Century Pueblo Regional Center*, edited by Stephen H. Lekson (Santa Fe, NM: School of American Research Press, 2006), 261–314; Lister, Robert H., and Florence C. Lister, *Aztec Ruins on the Animas: Excavated, Preserved, and Interpreted* (Albuquerque, NM: University of New Mexico Press, 1987); Noble, David, ed., *The Mesa Verde World* (Santa Fe, NM: School of American Research Press, 2006); Varien, Mark D., and Richard H. Wilshusen, eds., *Seeking the Center Place: Archaeology and Ancient Communities in the Mesa Verde Region* (Salt Lake City: University of Utah Press, 2002).

Catherine M. Cameron

BANDELIER NATIONAL MONUMENT

North Central New Mexico

The Development of Puebloan Agriculture and Towns

Bandelier National Monument, in north central New Mexico, is both a place of striking natural beauty and an ancestral home for peoples of at least two Pueblo ethnolinguistic groups, the Tewa and the Keres. Although use of the monument began in Paleoindian times, the vast majority of the many known sites document a fairly recent Pueblo occupation, between about AD 1150 and 1550. The monument is named after Adolph (or Adolf) Bandelier (1840–1914), a pioneer explorer, ethnographer, and archaeologist who was the first Euro-American to describe this area and to attempt to understand its archaeology. The most accessible portions of the monument are in Frijoles Canyon and can be easily visited in a day trip from Santa Fe, New Mexico's capital, which is about an hour's drive to the southeast of the monument. But there is enough to see in Bandelier's awesome backcountry to reward several days of backpacking.

The land on which the monument sits, in the southern portion of the Pajarito Plateau, was, like the rest of the plateau, formed by massive pyroclastic flows of hot gas, ash, and rock from the volcanic Jemez Mountains to the west around 1.6 and 1.2 million years ago. Erosion subsequently cut deep canyons running from northwest to southeast into the plateau. These canyons separate mesas—locally known as *potreros*—and eventually drain into the Rio Grande, which forms the southeastern boundary of the monument.

With elevations that vary from about 10,000 feet in the Jemez to 5,000 feet along the Rio Grande, Bandelier's 33,000 acres are remarkably diverse in vegetation and wildlife. Archaeological sites or isolated artifacts can be found at all elevations, but habitation sites of the Ancestral Pueblo (or Anasazi) populations are particularly dense on mesa tops between about 6,300 and 7,200 feet. This approximate range presumably marks the elevations that were high enough to receive adequate precipitation for farming without irrigation in normal years, but not so high that the growing season was too short for maize to mature. Current research is attempting to discover the advantages and limitations for agriculture of the distinctive pumice-derived soils on the Pajarito.

Use of the Bandelier area by Pueblo farmers began in the mid-1100s AD, about the same time as a long drought in the lower elevation San Juan basin to the west. This drought was disrupting the political system centered in Chaco Canyon, which had dominated eastern Pueblo societies for 200 years. Following Bandelier's initial colonization, populations in the monument grew rapidly.

Until the mid- or late 1200s, habitation sites generally consisted of ten to fifteen surface rooms, sometimes with a round or D-shaped surface or semi-subterranean kiva to the east or southeast. Kivas seem to have been used as places both for

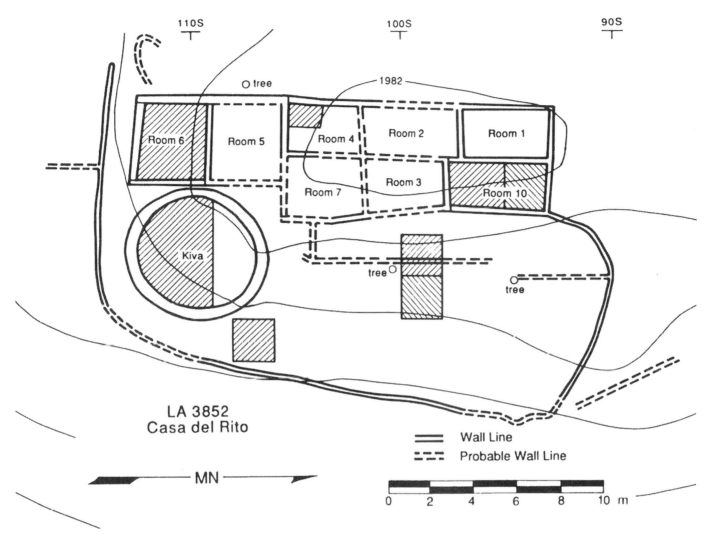

110S   100S   90S

O tree

1982

Room 6   Room 5   Room 4   Room 2   Room 1

Room 3   Room 10

Room 7

Kiva

tree O   tree O

LA 3852
Casa del Rito

Wall Line
Probable Wall Line

◄— MN —►

0   2   4   6   8   10 m

Plan map of LA 3852, Casa del Rito, an AD 1200s hamlet south of Frijoles Canyon, showing portions sampled in 1988 and 1990 by the Bandelier Archaeological Excavation Project of Washington State University.   [Timothy A. Kohler]

ceremonies and for daily living. Surface residential rooms are rectangular or square and usually occur in two rows, with rooms in the front row (to the east or southeast) often containing a hearth, and those in the back row probably used for storage. One such hamlet was partially excavated by the Bandelier Archaeological Excavation Project in the early 1990s. Only one excavated site of this type and period in the monument is prepared for public visitation: Sterile House, excavated by James Maxon and located along the Frijoles Overlook trail. Several unexcavated hamlets can be seen along the trail that begins from the Burnt Mesa trailhead on Highway 4, which forms the northern boundary for much of the monument's main unit. Small shards of black-on-white painted pottery on and around these sites, usually of the type known as Santa Fe Black-on-White, help archaeologists date most of them to the thirteenth century AD.

By the late 1200s, as populations grew, some habitation sites grew considerably larger than any of these hamlets.

Higher population levels resulted in depletion of large game and wild plant foods such as pinyon seeds, which in turn required these populations to rely more on growing maize and on raising turkeys for protein. Perhaps living in somewhat larger settlements that included non-kin among its residents was useful in exchanging maize, especially since crop failure for dry land farmers must have been common. This site form probably also had defensive advantages. The late 1200s were a generally violent time in the Pueblo Southwest, and populations on the Pajarito were dense enough to be in competition with their neighbors, particularly for access to superior areas for hunting and agriculture.

Around 1325, a series of changes began that are most detectible archaeologically in things like site plans and rock art styles, but that eventually permeated almost every aspect of life at the time. Together, these changes mark the onset of the Classic (or Pueblo IV) period throughout the northern Rio Grande region and in the monument. New and highly

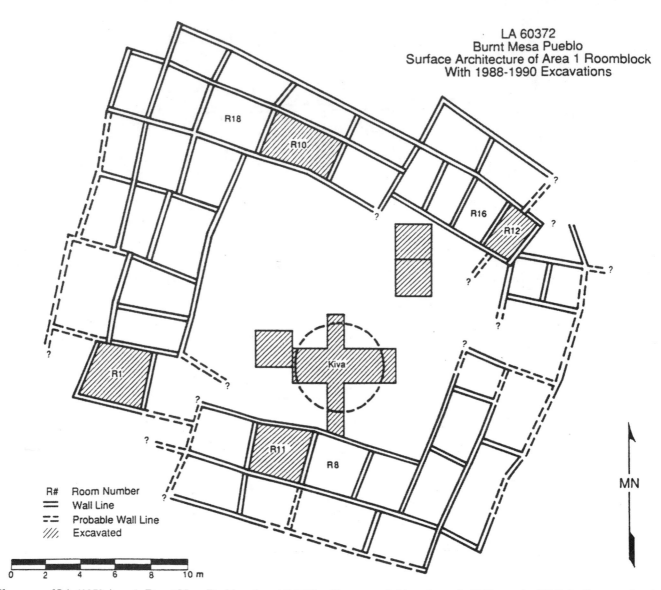

LA 60372
Burnt Mesa Pueblo
Surface Architecture of Area 1 Roomblock
With 1988-1990 Excavations

R18

R10

R16

R12

R1

Kiva

R11

R8

R#   Room Number
==   Wall Line
- -   Probable Wall Line
////   Excavated

0   2   4   6   8   10 m

MN

Plan map of LA 60372 Area 1, Burnt Mesa Pueblo, a late AD 1200s village occupied into the early 1300s north of Frijoles Canyon, showing portions sampled in 1988–90 by the Bandelier Archaeological Excavation Project of Washington State University.   [Timothy A. Kohler]

distinctive ceramic wares were made and widely exchanged. Biscuit wares dominated the area north of Bandelier, and glaze wares the areas to the south and east. The monument itself straddles the line dividing these two production areas, which were associated with Tewa populations to the north, and Keres and southern Tanoan populations to the south and east. Villages such as Burnt Mesa Pueblo gave way to much larger towns, some with hundreds of rooms and multiple plazas, as the largest habitation sites. Three of these are described below.

TYUONYI PUEBLO
Projects directed by Edgar Lee Hewett excavated much of this Classic period town in Frijoles Canyon in the early twentieth century. These excavations served to generate great

interest in the archaeology of the Southwest and its Native peoples. But techniques and record-keeping standards of the day were not sufficient to allow us to answer with clarity many basic questions about this important site, such as how many stories it had, how many households lived here, and how those households were distributed across the site.

Tyuonyi is an ancestral Keresan site whose name may mean "place of council"—possibly reflecting its location adjacent to Tewa groups to the north. Some Pueblo oral histories also identify this as an ancestral site for other Pueblo peoples in addition to the Keres. In any case, Tyuonyi was the center of a large community that included the cavates lining the north side of the canyon and several smaller sites in the canyon bottom. The latter include a down-canyon site

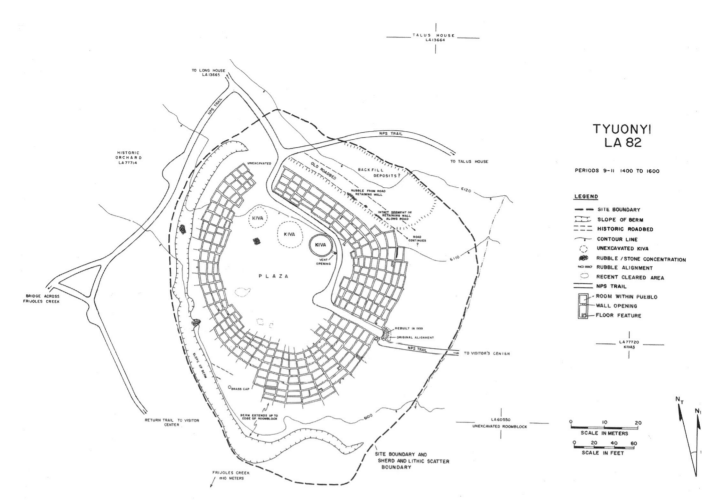

Plan map of Tyuonyi, LA 82, as mapped by the Bandelier Archaeological Survey Project in the 1990s. [Powers and Orcutt, editors, 1999]

known as Rainbow House that until recently was open to public visitation.

Although Frijoles Canyon is the only part of the monument that most people visit, it is, somewhat ironically, not representative of the local prehistoric sequence. Frijoles Canyon reached its maximum population around AD 1500, just as population levels elsewhere in Bandelier were in precipitous decline. Tree ring records document a general trend toward increasing dryness from the mid-1300s through the mid-1500s, and concentration of population in Frijoles Canyon may well be connected with the presence there of El Rito de los Frijoles, one of the most reliable streams on the Pajarito.

Tyuonyi contains about 240 ground-floor rooms, and if the site had a second and third story in places, as seems likely, the total room count may have been as high as 400. The rooms are arranged in an unusual, almost circular pattern surrounding a plaza that contains three kivas (one of which was excavated by Hewett) in an east-west line on its north side. Entrance to the plaza was through a restricted opening on the east side. Although small amounts of Santa Fe Black-on-White

in some excavation units suggest an earlier occupation, the available tree ring dates are broadly dispersed from the mid-1300s to the mid-1500s. Tyuonyi, like most Classic period pueblos, was a long-lived site, which sets it apart from Early Coalition period hamlets, which seem to have been occupied for only ten to twenty years, and Late Coalition period villages, with spans of occupation apparently on the order of fifty years.

Archaeologists have long noted that even as Classic period sites such as Tyuonyi began to be built with many more rooms, the number of kivas did not increase correspondingly. This led to an arrangement similar to that in nearby contemporary pueblos like San Ildefonso (Tewa) and Cochiti (Keres), which have many rooms but only two or three large kivas in broad plazas that are completely or partly surrounded by room blocks. This similarity (as well as some specific continuity in these cultures) encourages us to believe that ceremonial practices at Classic period towns like Tyuonyi may have been similar to traditional practices at these still-occupied pueblos. For example, enclosed spaces like the kivas—and perhaps

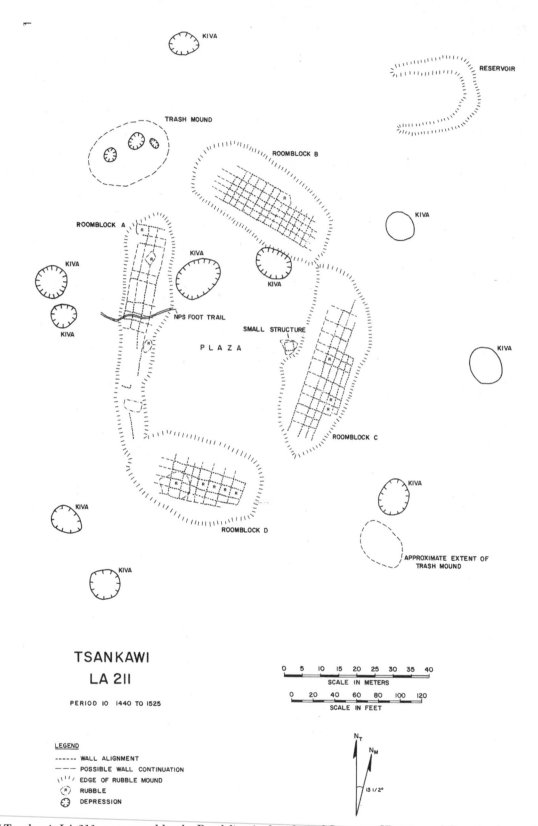

KIVA

RESERVOIR

TRASH MOUND

ROOMBLOCK B

KIVA

ROOMBLOCK A

KIVA

KIVA

KIVA

KIVA

NPS FOOT TRAIL

SMALL STRUCTURE

KIVA

PLAZA

KIVA

ROOMBLOCK C

KIVA

KIVA

ROOMBLOCK D

APPROXIMATE EXTENT OF
TRASH MOUND

KIVA

TSANKAWI
LA 211

PERIOD 10 1440 TO 1525

| 0 | 5 | 10 | 15 | 20 | 25 | 30 | 35 | 40 |
SCALE IN METERS

| 0 | 20 | 40 | 60 | 80 | 100 | 120 |
SCALE IN FEET

LEGEND

------ WALL ALIGNMENT
— — — POSSIBLE WALL CONTINUATION
\|''/ EDGE OF RUBBLE MOUND
(R) RUBBLE
DEPRESSION

N_T
N_M
13 1/2°

Plan map of Tsankawi, LA 211, as mapped by the Bandelier Archaeological Survey. [Powers and Orcutt, editors, 1999]

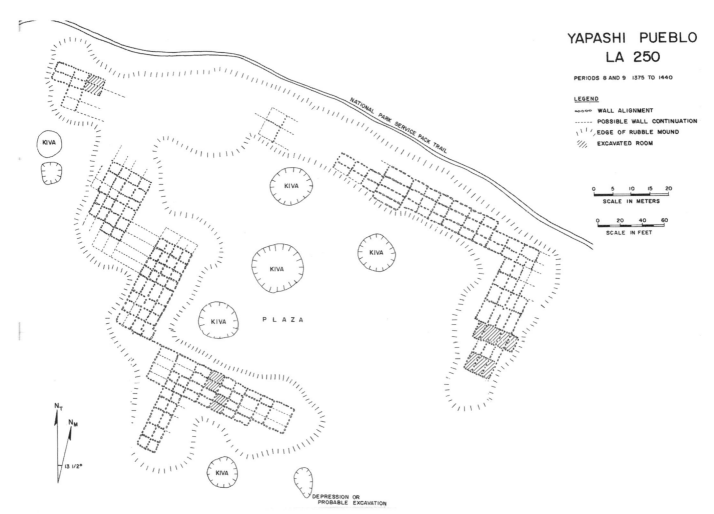

Plan map of Yapashi, LA 250, as mapped by the Bandelier Archaeological Survey Project in the 1990s.   [Powers and Orcutt, editors, 1999]

other rooms that served as headquarters for various societies (social groups within the community)—may have housed secret ceremonies restricted to initiates in that society, whereas large public ceremonies, such as dances that united the entire pueblo and even involved members of neighboring communities, may have been performed in the plazas.

Some archaeologists have suggested another similarity. Today if you go to a public dance at a pueblo, you will pass by stands with vendors hawking food, pottery, ornaments, traditional cotton and wool garments, and so forth. We know that in the Classic period, the kinds and amounts of materials traded among communities along the Rio Grande, and between them and groups on the Plains, increased dramatically. Perhaps the plazas in these large towns also served as periodic marketplaces facilitating exchanges with people from smaller sites in the same community, and between communities—even those of different ethnic groups.

The cavates—small rooms hollowed out of the soft volcanic tuff bedrock exposed along portions of the north wall of Frijoles Canyon—are set farthest back in room blocks that for the most part have disintegrated. Some of these room blocks were as much as four stories tall. In many places, the height of the original room block can be reconstructed from the beam holes still visible in the cliff face. Many of the cavates (there are over a thousand in Frijoles Canyon alone) are sooted by fire in their top halves and plastered in their lower halves. These treatments may have helped minimize dust from the soft tuff walls, though presumably they also were stylistic in nature.

Cavates had several functions. Most were used for habitation, others for a secure and relatively weatherproof storage; a few (about a dozen) apparently served ceremonial purposes. These typically have paintings or incised designs, including birds, snakes, and various geometric shapes, as well as outlined humanlike figures. These rooms are smaller, though, than the kivas in the valley bottom. In his novel *The Delight*

Makers, about Pueblo life in Frijoles Canyon, Bandelier makes one of these a society house, which remains a very plausible interpretation.

Quite a few cavates contain features such as loom anchors that are poorly preserved elsewhere—or perhaps weaving was an especially common activity in cavates for some reason. A few ceramics suggest that some cavates were re-used as refuges following the Pueblo Revolt of 1680, long after Frijoles Canyon had been abandoned for residential purposes.

TSANKAWI PUEBLO

The other easily accessible Classic period pueblo in Bandelier is in a detached section north of the main monument, near the towns of White Rock and Los Alamos. Tsankawi, a large pueblo whose name means "gap of the sharp, round cactus," sits on top of a small, abrupt mesa and comprises four room blocks enclosing a large plaza containing two kivas. Eight more kivas are located outside the room blocks on the mesita, as are three reservoirs for catching and holding water for domestic uses. Reservoirs are common near Classic period pueblos on the Pajarito—except for those, like Tyuonyi, that are adjacent to running water.

Tsankawi seems to be the only large mesa-top site that was still in use in the monument in the mid-1500s, when most of its declining population had relocated to Frijoles Canyon. As expected within the ancestral Tewa area, biscuit-type pottery wares are more common among the surface artifacts, and glaze wares are less common than in Frijoles Canyon. Ceramic types such as Sankawi Black-on-Cream and Potsuwi'i Incised represent continued use of this area by Tewa populations as late as 1700; these are much more common here than elsewhere in the monument. Some small-scale excavations were undertaken at the site in the 1930s, but overall, the site is poorly known.

Numerous cavates were excavated into the tuff below the pueblo, and these same tuff faces include the remains of many petroglyphs incised or pecked into their surfaces. Outlined human figures and ungulates (hoofed mammals like deer) are particularly common in the ancestral Tewa areas on the Pajarito and are notable here as well; look for figures depicting flute players, shield bearers, weapons, sword swallowers, and thunderbirds.

The National Park Service trail up to Tsankawi partly intersects Classic period trail systems that extend up and down the Pajarito Plateau. In several places, particularly around Tsankawi, these trails wore deep into the tuff bedrock. It is no coincidence that trails pre-dating the Classic period are uncommon, since site locations prior to the 1300s tended to be less stable. Classic trails seem to join the large towns together, but also link these towns to important nearby features. Trails approaching Tsankawi from the north and the east feature formal staircases carved into the tuff with considerable effort. The northern staircase links Tsankawi to a nearby pueblo—reworked in the early twentieth century as an artist's house—called Duchess Castle. This pueblo may have served to guard the northern approach to Tsankawi, much as Rainbow House in Frijoles Canyon may have surveyed the southeastern approach to Tyuonyi.

YAPASHI PUEBLO

Yapashi is only about 3 miles south of Frijoles Canyon, but is much less visited than either Tyuonyi or Tsankawi. Though short, this distance from Frijoles Canyon is a hard one-day round-trip hike that cuts across the grain of a rugged landscape.

Yapashi has a somewhat more irregular layout than the two towns already discussed, with five main rectangular room blocks loosely enclosing a plaza with four kivas. The plaza is open on the southeast side. Also to the southeast is a reservoir. Two to four kivas are outside the room blocks to the south and west.

Hewett's crews conducted some small-scale excavations at this site in 1908, but our current inferences about its chronology—like that of Tsankawi—are based mostly on surface ceramics. Although settlement probably began in early 1300s or even the late 1200s, Yapashi grew to be one of the Pajarito's major towns in the late 1300s—a time when many smaller pueblos were abandoned and populations concentrated in just a few large centers. Yapashi seems to have been abandoned by 1525, leaving Tsankawi and Tyuonyi as the only remaining population centers in Bandelier.

Yapashi is also called Pueblo of the Stone Lions; a nearby shrine contains two carvings of crouching mountain lions presently enclosed by a ring of vertical slabs about 70 feet in circumference, with an opening toward the east. (The name Yaspashi itself means "sacred enclosure.") Hewett called this the most important hunting shrine in the entire Pueblo region, and it is still used by many Pueblo people, including the distant Zuni. The Park Service has removed the location from current backcountry maps at the request of a local tribe. If someone asks about it, though, the visitors' center has a handout that interprets the site, then asks visitors to be aware of its significance and act in an appropriately sensitive manner.

In fact, both Tyuonyi and Yapashi figure prominently in oral histories collected early in the twentieth century at Cochiti Pueblo (though they are still current today). These stories relate a southward drift from Tyuonyi eventually arriving at Cochiti, with several stopping points in between. Yapashi is always mentioned among the places where the southward migration paused. Elements of these stories are shared by most other Keres groups, and Tyuonyi is often mentioned as a point of common origin for them all. In visiting Bandelier's pueblos, it is important to remember that they are more than just archaeological ruins. Living Pueblo peoples retain strong spiritual ties with these places and landscapes.

Archaeological data suggest that when Vázquez de Coronado's expedition arrived in New Mexico in 1540, small populations still lingered at Tsankawi and Tyuonyi. If so, they were not noticed, or at least not mentioned, by the Spaniards. Perhaps by that time, these sites were only revisited by people already living in pueblos along the Rio Grande, where they remain today.

Acknowledgments: This article benefited from comments by Rory Gauthier of Bandelier National Monument; Robert Powers of the National Park Service, Intermountain Region, Santa Fe; and Robert Preucel, University of Pennsylvania.

Further Reading: Bandelier, Adolf F., *The Delight Makers: A Novel of Prehistoric Pueblo Indians* (New York: Harcourt Brace Jovanovich, 1971); Bandelier National Monument, National Park Service Web site, www.nps.gov/band (online February 2007); Harrington, John P., "Ethnogeography of the Tewa Indians," in *Bureau of American Ethnology 29th Annual Report* (Washington, DC: Smithsonian Institution, 1916), 29–618; Hewett, Edgar L., *Pajarito Plateau and Its Ancient People*, 2nd rev. ed. (Albuquerque: University of New Mexico Press and Santa Fe, NM: School of American Research Press, 1953); Kohler, Timothy A., ed., *Archaeology of Bandelier National Monument: Village Formation on the Pajarito Plateau* (Albuquerque: University of New Mexico Press, 2004); Lange, Charles H., and Carroll L. Riley, *Bandelier: The Life and Adventures of Adolf Bandelier, American Archaeologist and Scientist* (Salt Lake City: University of Utah Press, 1996); Powers, Robert P., ed., *The Peopling of Bandelier: New Insights from the Archaeology of the Pajarito Plateau* (Santa Fe, NM: School of American Research Press, 2005); Powers, Robert P., and Janet D. Orcutt, eds., *The Bandelier Archaeological Survey*, 2 vols. (Santa Fe, NM: Intermountain Region, National Park Service, 1999); Preucel, Robert W., ed., *Archaeologies of the Pueblo Revolt: Identity, Meaning, and Renewal in the Pueblo World* (Albuquerque: University of New Mexico Press, 2002); Rohn, Arthur, William M. Ferguson, and Lisa Ferguson, *Bandelier National Monument Rock Art* (Albuquerque: University of New Mexico Press, 1989); Smith, Monica, *The Historic Period at Bandelier National Monument* (Santa Fe, NM: Intermountain Region, National Park Service, 2002).

Timothy A. Kohler

KUAUA PUEBLO SITE

Coronado State Monument, Bernalillo, New Mexico

A Late Prehistoric–Early Historic Village along the Northern Rio Grande

Kuaua Ruin is an ancient and historic period Pueblo Indian village located 17 miles north of Albuquerque, New Mexico, on a west-bank terrace of the Rio Grande. The village dates from as early as the mid-1200s to the late 1600s AD and consists of over 1,200 adobe rooms. Although not confirmed by either historic documents or archaeological data, legend has it that the Spanish explorer Francisco Vasquez de Coronado stayed in Kuaua during the winter of 1540–41. To commemorate Cuarto Centenario, the four hundredth anniversary of the first contact between Pueblo Indians and Coronado, Kuaua was proclaimed the Coronado State Monument in 1935. An interpretive center built near the ruin provides visitors an opportunity to learn about an important period in New Mexico's past.

Kuaua Ruin was one of many large Native American villages located along the Rio Grande when the Spanish first explored the region. The ruin has a typical village layout and architecture for this time period, in which blocks of apartment-like rooms enclose numerous plaza areas. It is these apartment-like structures that led early Spanish explorers to use the term "pueblo" (Spanish for "town") to describe these sedentary agriculturalists descended from the Anasazi (or Ancestral

Pueblo) culture; "pueblo" continues to be the term used to describe many modern Native American groups living in northern New Mexico and Arizona.

Regional archaeological data informs us about the lives of Kuaua's inhabitants and their neighbors. Pueblo villages encountered by Spanish explorers were the result of local populations aggregating into plaza-oriented towns that began forming in the 1200s. Over time, villages increased in size but decreased in number. This has been interpreted as evidence that there was limited population growth within the region; however, individual villages were supporting larger populations. Residents cultivated crops in the Rio Grande floodplain using a variety of agricultural techniques. For example, aerial photographs of land west of Kuaua show the possible presence of numerous rectangular garden plots that may have been dry-farmed. It has also been suggested that the Native Americans of this region used irrigation to farm some portions of the floodplain.

Although the primary food crop was maize, archaeological evidence indicates the presence of domesticated beans and squash, as well as cotton at some villages. Further, Pueblo Indians ate domesticated turkey. Climatic reconstruction for

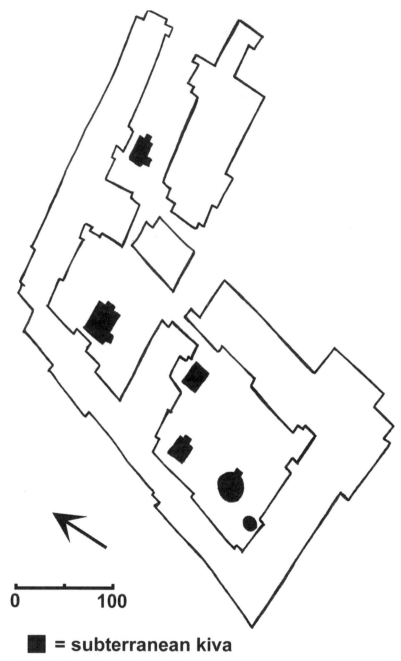

= subterranean kiva

Village layout of Kuaua Ruin. Drawing by Eckert after sketch maps on file at ARMS, the Laboratory of Anthropology, Santa Fe, New Mexico.   [Suzanne Eckert]

the region suggests dry periods that were probably devastating for agriculture; not surprisingly, then, excavation data indicate that hunting antelope and deer, and gathering wild plants, were also important activities that contributed to the inhabitants' diet.

Skeletal data from village sites such as Kuaua, Arroyo Hondo, Pindi Pueblo, and Tijeras provide insight into the health and life expectancy of the Rio Grande region's occupants during the late pre-Hispanic era. Analyses show high infant and child mortality; if an individual lived past five years, however, then he or she had a good chance of living into the late 30s or early 40s. Malnutrition and related diseases were common, possibly as a result of periodic food shortages or a high dietary reliance on maize.

Kuaua Ruin was excavated from 1934 to 1939 under the direction of Edgar Lee Hewett, an influential figure in early American archaeology who at the beginning of the twentieth century played a leading role in the passage of legislation

Kuaua Kiva mural on display at Coronado State Monument.   [Blair Clark, 1989, Museum of Indians Arts & Culture/Laboratory of Anthropology, Santa Fe, New Mexico. Courtesy of The Museum of Indian Arts and Culture, www.miaclab.org]

that became the Antiquities Act of 1906, a key federal statute for the protection of American archaeological sites. Hewett's excavations at Kuaua Ruin included the reconstruction of the ruin as part of the Cuarto Centenario celebrations; as with many preservation treatments, these efforts were met with some controversy. Hewett's efforts, and the debate that followed, are now being re-examined as the Coronado State Monument plans new restoration efforts of the site.

Approximately 95 percent of the ruin was excavated by Hewett, revealing residential rooms, storage rooms, ceremonial rooms, plazas, trash dumps, and burials. Although a precise chronology for Kuaua cannot be constructed, pottery assemblages, architectural construction and remodeling, and trash accumulation suggest that the village was constructed over several building stages. Further, sections of the village appear to have been abandoned, while other sections continued to be constructed, remodeled, and occupied.

Residential rooms at Kuaua Ruin were identified based on the presence of hearths, sleeping platforms, and grinding bins, while rooms that lacked such domestic features were considered to be for storage. Two types of ceremonial rooms were identified: subterranean kivas normally located in plazas, and kiva-like rooms situated within room blocks. These ceremonial room types shared certain ritual features, including altars, ventilators, and evidence of vertical looms. One of the most distinguishing features of Kuaua Ruin is the discovery of painted wall murals in two of its six kivas. These murals depict water (especially rain), katsina (beneficial and ancestral spirits), plants (especially corn), animals, and birds; they provide a unique glimpse into the religious practice of the Pueblo people prior to European contact.

A large amount of unpainted and glaze-painted ceramic vessels, both whole and broken, were recovered. Unpainted vessels are normally rough-surfaced jars assumed to have been used for cooking. Glaze-painted vessels are normally jars (assumed to have been used for storage) or bowls

Some of the glaze-painted pottery recovered from Kuaua Ruin. [David McNeece, 2005, Museum of Indians Arts & Culture/Laboratory of Anthropology, Santa Fe, New Mexico. Courtesy of The Museum of Indian Arts and Culture, www.miaclab.org]

(assumed to have been used for food service), but canteens, ladles, pipes, and effigies were also recovered. All of the vessels from Kuaua were built by hand (there was no potter's wheel in pre-contact North America) and presumed to have been fired in pit kilns. The great variety of glaze-painted vessels recovered from Kuaua suggest that the residents of this village not only made pottery, but were active in the extensive exchange networks that characterized inter-regional interaction along the Rio Grande during this period.

Kuaua was abandoned in the 1600s. This abandonment may have been due to the devastating effects of European-introduced diseases, or as a result of the Pueblo Revolt of 1690, or part of the Pueblo settlement cycle that characterized their culture prior to restriction on reservations. The name Kuaua was given to the site by the modern-day Pueblo Indians of Sandia Pueblo, located a few miles south of the ruin. The ruin is claimed as an ancestral village by both the Tiwa-speaking Indians of Sandia Pueblo as well as the Keresan-speaking people of Santa Ana Pueblo. This has made determining the linguistic affiliation of Kuaua's residents a bit difficult, but most historians and anthropologists agree that it was probably a Tiwa-speaking village.

Coronado State Monument is open to the public year-round through a site museum run by the Museum of New Mexico. A short interpretive trail leads to a reconstructed kiva that displays reproductions of some of the site's mural paintings. An on-site visitor center provides information recovered from excavations, as well as displays Native American and Spanish colonial artifacts.

Further Reading: Bliss, Wesley L., "Preservation of the Kuaua Mural Paintings," *American Antiquity* 13 (January 1948): 218–222; Cisneros, Jose, "Restoring the Kuaua Pueblo Ruins," *El Palacio* 108 (May 2003): 33–35; Cordell, Linda S., *Archaeology of the Southwest*, 2nd ed. (New York: Academic Press, 1997); Coronado State Monument, Museum of New Mexico Web site, http://www.nmculture.org/cgi-bin/instview.cgi?_recordnum=CORO; Eckert, Suzanne L., and Linda S. Cordell, "Pueblo IV Community Formation in the Central Rio Grande Valley," in *The Protohistoric Pueblo World A.D. 1275–1600*, edited by E. Charles Adams and Andrew I. Duff (Tucson: University of Arizona Press, 2004), 35–42; Trichy, Marjorie Ferguson, "The Kivas of Paako and Kuaua," *New Mexico Anthropologist* 2 (1938): 71–80; Sinclair, John L., "The Story of the Pueblo of Kuaua," *El Palacio* 58 (1951): 206–214.

Suzanne L. Eckert

PETROGLYPH NATIONAL MONUMENT

Albuquerque, New Mexico
Investigating and Understanding Ancient Images

Petroglyph National Monument, also known as Las Imágenes ("The Images"), is located on the outskirts of Albuquerque, New Mexico, on the west side of the Rio Grande.

This national monument is the only unit of the National Park Service system created specifically for the preservation of rock art. In this instance, protective measures were sought, beginning in the 1980s, in light of the encroachment of the city and attendant vandalism. The West Mesa escarpment is the locus of thousands of petroglyphs—carved images pecked or incised on black basalt boulders.

The escarpment itself was formed by Late Pleistocene (about 190,000 years ago) lava flows from the five small volcanoes that punctuate the western horizon. This steep, boulder-strewn slope runs for 17 miles, outlining a meandering mesa edge marked with deep rincons and jutting protrusions. The escarpment also constitutes a distinct environmental zone where rainwater accumulates and where wildlife and vegetation are diversified and abundant, in contrast to neighboring areas. This section of the Rio Grande valley is near the northern limit of the upper Chihuahuan Desert.

Historic Spanish crosses pecked in conjunction with older and more weathered Pueblo figures.   [Polly Schaafsma]

Ceremonial figure wearing a kilt and holding a feathered staff and yucca whip. Below are kachina masks.   [Polly Schaafsma]

A Rio Grande–style flute player wearing a decorative kilt and necklace.   [Polly Schaafsma]

For hundreds of years, the Rio Grande valley has been home to Pueblo villagers who built their adobe homes and farmed along the river valley. They cultivated fields of corn, beans, squash, and cotton. From the cotton they wove clothing consisting of mantas (women's dresses), kilts, and sashes. They also made pottery that they decorated with lead glazes.

Until sometime after AD 1200, there were few Pueblo villages along the Rio Grande in the vicinity of what is now Albuquerque. Shortly after AD 1300, migrations into the region from the west resulted in a number of pueblos being founded that persisted until the arrival of Coronado in 1540. Notable among these within the boundaries of Petroglyph National Monument is Piedras Marcadas, a site with over 1,000 rooms. Piedras Marcadas was inhabited for nearly 300 years between AD 1300 and 1650, and these villagers would have been responsible for many of the Pueblo petroglyphs in the vicinity.

A relatively small number of petroglyphs in Petroglyph National Monument appear to be the handiwork of hunter-gatherers who preceded the earliest Ancestral Pueblos.

Estimated dates for these now heavily weathered abstract patterns—consisting of circles, rakes, and meandering lines—range between 1000 BC and approximately AD 500. Most of the rock art, however, is more recent. The vast majority of the 17,000 or more petroglyphs were made by the ancestors of today's Pueblo Indians, who still live in villages along the northern Rio Grande. The petroglyphs document the cosmology, values, and beliefs of the Ancestral Pueblos. In addition, Christian crosses made in historic times by sheepherders occur among the Pueblo images—a legacy of the Hispanic heritage in the Rio Grande valley.

Petroglyph National Monument also includes around 100 other archaeological remains, such as prehistoric Pueblo field houses, water control features, shrines, and agricultural fields and terraces.

The earliest Pueblo rock art was made by Pueblo peoples prior to AD 1300, but most of the petroglyphs date to after approximately AD 1325. Figures typical of the earlier Pueblo period are stick figure anthropomorphs, pecked handprints, sandal prints, small solid animals, birds, lizards, and probably many of the small flute players. These are distinct in style and content from the later work known as the Rio Grande style. The Rio Grande style rock art is characterized by large-scale figures rendered in outline with interior designs.

Petroglyphs are scattered throughout the escarpment boulders from the bottom to the top of the steep slope that ascends to the rim of the West Mesa. Over 500 grinding slicks have been found in association with the imagery. Often the petroglyphs tend to occur in clusters, and groups of figures may have reference to specific aspects of Pueblo cosmology and beliefs. Kachinas, kachina masks, a variety of other ceremonial figures, and star supernaturals are among the most complex Rio Grande style images.

There are horned and/or masked serpents, shields, weapons, clouds, and large, detailed flute players. Birds, animals, and insects—all symbolically complex and, within Pueblo cosmology, invested with various powers—are also well represented. These life forms include snakes, coyotes, mountain lions, macaws, eagles, toads, frogs, and dragonflies. Animal tracks pecked in stone are perhaps a shortcut to representing the animal itself. These images play roles in bringing rain, promoting fertility, and—in some cases—success in war and the hunt. Together, they represent a belief system and worldview that is still viable among the Pueblos. The petroglyphs are visual testimony to the ancient Pueblo presence in a landscape in which the traditions are still maintained and rituals continue to be performed.

Regardless of when the rock art was made or the functional context in which it was produced, the petroglyphs preserve the ideologies of their makers. Art and symbol are important means by which basic cultural values are expressed and thereby communicated and affirmed. The rock art is a graphic document of the ideational realm of prehistory. It reaches back in time beyond the ethnographic present with information that is not commonly present in other archaeological remains.

Beginning in the 1960s, several surveys of the rock art and other archaeological sites have been conducted in the monument region. A rock art survey in 1960 led by Colonel James Bain resulted in the establishment of Petroglyph State Park of the city of Albuquerque (now the Boca Negra unit of Petroglyph National Monument). In 1985 another survey, by the Albuquerque Department of Open Space, led to the nomination of Las Imágenes (the West Mesa petroglyphs) to the National Register of Historic Places.

Petroglyph National Monument, established soon after in 1990, is managed jointly by the National Park Service, the state of New Mexico, and the city of Albuquerque, Open Space Division. There are scheduled ranger-guided tours of the petroglyphs in addition to self-guiding trails and hiking in designated areas. A National Park Service Visitor Center and bookstore is open daily (except for Thanksgiving Day, Christmas Day, and New Year's Day), where interpretive exhibits, maps, guidebooks, and more information are available.

Further Reading: Petroglyph National Monument, National Park Service Web site, http://www.nps.gov/petr; Saville, Dara, "Kachina Iconography from Piedras Marcadas Canyon, Petroglyph National Monument," *American Indian Rock Art* 28 (2002): 151–159; Schaafsma, Polly, *Rock Art in New Mexico*, 2nd ed. (Santa Fe: Museum of New Mexico Press, 1992).

Polly Schaafsma

TUSAYAN VILLAGE AND OTHER SITES IN THE GRAND CANYON

Grand Canyon, Arizona

The Archaeology of Grand Canyon National Park

The story of the people of Tusayan Village site (aka Tusayan Ruin) is the story of adaptation and life in a challenging environment. Listed on the National Register of Historic Places in 1974, Tusayan Ruin is one of thousands of archaeological sites that dot the landscape of the Grand Canyon. Tusayan Ruin is a small, U-shaped pueblo occupied sometime between AD 1190 and 1250. No more than twenty or so people ever lived at the site at any one time, and the ruin itself represents adaptation during its short occupation.

At some time in the early years of use, a fire consumed one of the rooms—a small ceremonial room, or kiva—within the room block. A separate, detached kiva was built to replace the one that had burned. At least three large living rooms formed the center of the masonry pueblo, with smaller rooms

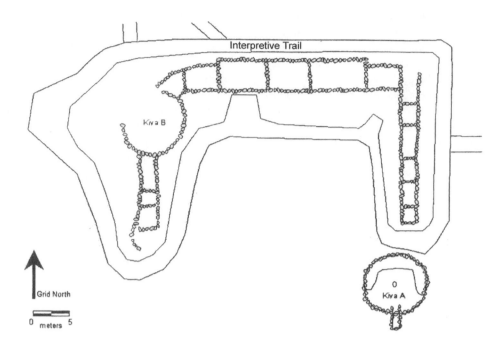

Plan map of Tusayan Village site (also known as Tusayan Ruin).   [Courtesy of the National Park Service]

on either side. A number of small storage rooms round out either side of the pueblo, with the second kiva a short distance from the storage rooms. A total of sixteen rooms have been identified; these are organized around a central plaza. The building itself is made of unshaped Kaibab limestone blocks—readily available building material for people living on the South Rim of the Grand Canyon.

The desert west is often thought of as a warm, dry place. However, the people of Tusayan Ruin, living at 7,000 feet in elevation, enjoyed a full four seasons, with summer heat and monsoon rain, moderate spring and fall, and winter cold and snow.

Tusayan Ruin was the first archaeological site recorded at Grand Canyon, given the site designation Echo Cliffs:13:1 (and later GC1) by the archaeological group known as Gila Pueblo. The site was recorded in 1927 and excavated in 1930 by Harold Gladwin and Emil Haury; it was completed in consort with the establishment of the Wayside Museum. The purpose of the excavation of Tusayan Ruin, from a scientific perspective, was to aid in the definition of the westward boundary for ancient Puebloan cultures.

At the time, this site would have represented the western extent of the Kayenta branch of the Anasazi. The excavation—sponsored, in part, by the relatively young National Park Service—was intended to provide a focal point for archaeological interpretation for the visiting public at Grand Canyon National Park. One facet of this interpretation was the desire to interpret the ruin as it was found, not necessarily as a reconstructed archaeological site. This approach was uncommon in the 1930s,

with whole-site excavations and creative reconstructions common throughout the Southwest.

As a ruin, Tusayan Ruin provided an interpretive opportunity not found elsewhere. Only two-thirds of the rooms were excavated, and both the excavated and unexcavated portions of the site were interpreted. The ruin, and the Wayside Museum (now known as Tusayan Museum), still perform their original function: to interpret a ruin and serve as a focal point for interpretation of human history at Grand Canyon National Park.

The archaeological record at Grand Canyon is dominated by the presence of remains from ancestral Puebloan peoples, dated between AD 800 and 1200. These people, often referred to as the Anasazi, hunted, gathered, and farmed throughout the Colorado plateau and Grand Canyon regions for over 500 years. The majority of known archaeological sites at Grand Canyon were occupied during the AD 950–1150 time period. Tusayan Ruin, however, was occupied slightly later, sometime between AD 1190 and the mid-1200s.

At the time of its excavation, Tusayan Ruin was thought to represent a rare example of a larger pueblo site at the end of the twelfth century. Continuing research on the South Rim of the canyon and surrounding areas suggests that Tusayan Ruin may represent one of a series of larger pueblos occupied at the end of the twelfth and into the thirteenth century. These larger pueblo sites have been located in the Desert View area of Grand Canyon and south, along major ridgelines in the upper Coconino basin portion of the Kaibab National Forest, adjacent to Grand Canyon National Park. These sites, taken

Tusayan Ruin during excavation, around 1930.   [Courtesy of the National Park Service]

Typical granary below the canyon rim.   [Courtesy of the National Park Service]

together, represent continual adaptation to the ever-changing environmental conditions of the desert west.

In this case, the drought cycles of the Southwest would have made life harsh for the inhabitants at Tusayan Ruin and the other pueblo sites in the area. The people of Tusayan Ruin did farm, on plots located near the village site. Small agricultural areas generally surrounded the Puebloan sites of the area, often with terrace systems still identifiable a thousand years after use. Numerous pieces of ground stone, manos and metates, were recovered during the excavation, attesting to considerable food production at the site. Farming, the mainstay of settled occupations, would have given way to increased hunting and gathering in order to supplement crop supplies. Dozens of small storage rooms, known as granaries, can be spotted below the canyon rim near Tusayan Ruin. The inhabitants of these areas would have stored their food near their living sites for future use, but not so close that a catastrophic event (such as a fire or animal infestation) would cause them to starve.

The early inhabitants of the canyon were not restricted to the South Rim areas near Tusayan Ruin, nor were they only Puebloan farmers. For over 10,000 years, people have used the canyon for hunting, gathering, and farming. While only 3 percent of the park's land surface has been explored scientifically for archaeological sites, remains of human use have been found in virtually every area of the park where archaeological inventories have been conducted. To date, over 4,000 sites have been documented. Sites have been found and recorded on the North Rim, in the inner canyon, along the river corridor, and on isolated rock formations (mesas) in the middle of the canyon. While these locations look improbable for comfortable living, they were ideal locations for hunters, gatherers, and farmers to make their homes and raise their families.

Sometime in the mid-1200s, the Puebloan inhabitants of Grand Canyon appear to have moved out of the area—replaced, in some areas, by non-farming groups such as the ancestral Pai, Paiute, and Navajo. With the limited archaeological information available at Grand Canyon, only a partial story can be told. The human story of Tusayan Ruin and other sites at Grand Canyon is one of adaptation to a harsh environment and adaptability to the canyon environment. People have lived in and around the Grand Canyon for over 10,000 years, adapting and moving in and out of the canyon as modern populations move in and out of cities. For these people, the trails, the Colorado River, the springs, the seeps, and the side canyons have provided a diverse homeland that has supplied everything for its people. Tusayan Ruin and surrounding sites remind us of the importance of learning from those who came before.

Further Reading: Coder, Christopher M., *An Introduction to Grand Canyon Prehistory* (Grand Canyon, AZ: Grand Canyon Association, 2000); Haury, Emil, *Kivas of the Tusayan Ruin, Grand Canyon Arizona*, Medallion No. 9 (Globe, AZ: Gila Pueblo, 1931); Jones, Anne Trinkle, and Robert C. Euler, *A Sketch of Grand Canyon Prehistory* (Grand Canyon, AZ: Grand Canyon Natural History Association, 1979); Schwartz, Douglas, *On the Edge of Splendor: Exploring Grand Canyon's Human Past* (Santa Fe, NM: School of American Research Press, 1988).

Janet R. Balsom

BETATAKIN, KEET SEEL, AND INSCRIPTION HOUSE SITES

Northeast Arizona

The Archaeology of Navajo National Monument

Three spectacular ancient Pueblo dwellings tucked into high alcoves in the canyons of northeastern Arizona might be among the most remote and best-kept secrets in the national-parks system. A broken, dissected, and rocky landscape conceals several of the best-preserved archaeological sites in the country—perhaps even in the world. Three primary dwellings (and several smaller manifestations) make up Navajo National Monument: Betatakin, Inscription House, and Keet Seel. Together these sites are among the most spectacular cliff dwellings of the ancient Pueblo people.

Archaeologists identify the surrounding region and the branch of ancient Pueblo culture as Kayenta (after the later Navajo community of the same name). Inscription House and Betatakin were built rapidly in the mid-thirteenth century; Keet Seel had a longer occupational history but also peaked during the last fifty years (AD 1250–1300) of the period archaeologists describe as Pueblo III. In the Kayenta region, archaeologists identify the last fifty years of the Pueblo III period as the Tsegi phase, after the canyon in which Betatakin and Keet Seel were built.

View of Betatakin (Talastima) showing its spectacular location in a large cave.   [Paul F. Reed]

Navajo National Monument was established by President Theodore Roosevelt in 1909 and originally covered a very large area (160 mi², or about 103,000 acres). It was significantly reduced to 360 acres in 1912 due to Navajo Nation grazing needs and Euro-American mining interests in the area.

Beyond its well-preserved vestiges of ancient Pueblo culture, Navajo National Monument is unique in the national parks system for another reason: the interdependency of the monument and the local Navajo community. From its inception in the early 1900s, the isolation of the monument has required a creative approach to management and research. In contrast to well-funded parks such as Yellowstone, Grand Canyon, and Carlsbad Caverns, Navajo saw little in the way of development or logistic support until several decades after its establishment. As a result, early superintendents and staff were challenged to secure resources, provide for visitors, and fulfill the primary mission of protecting the irreplaceable cultural resources of the monument.

A prime means of meeting these goals involved close association and partnership with local Navajos and Euro-American traders, such as John Wetherill (who founded several trading posts in the area—most notably, one at Kayenta, Arizona). Although some conflicts and misunderstandings arose from this unique partnership of NPS and local Navajo people, the net result was close cooperation and mutual benefit for both parties, which continue to this day.

Much of what we know about sites at Navajo National Monument comes from the research of archaeologist Jeff Dean, who completed a dissertation on the chronology and archaeology of Tsegi Canyon in 1967 (and a shorter publication drawing on this work in 1969). Dean's work serves as the source for some of this narrative, along with the other references listed at the end of this article. Earlier explorations began the process of understanding these sites in the 1900s, with research visits by legendary archaeologists such as Byron Cummings, Neil Judd, and Jesse Walter Fewkes.

Finally, cutting-edge research by archaeologists and close collaboration with Native tribes has greatly enhanced our knowledge of the culture and landscape of Navajo National Monument over the last twenty years.

This essay will delve deeper into the monument by examining the three best-known and researched villages: Betatakin, Keet Seel, and Inscription House.

Photograph of Keet Seel (Kawestima), with masonry rooms set against the sweeping sandstone walls of the alcove.   [Paul F. Reed]

BETATAKIN

The site name Betatakin translates as "ledge house or houses" in the Navajo language. In Hopi the site is known as *Talastima*— the place of blue corn tassels. The village was built in a tremendous, semicircular deep alcove that measures 370 feet by 135 feet, with a ceiling height of 450 feet. The site was built with at least 125 rooms and two kivas spread over two stories of habitation. A third story may have been present in a few areas.

Betatakin was rediscovered by Euro-Americans in 1909 on an exploratory expedition led by Dr. Byron Cummings; this expedition was guided by John Wetherill and a local Navajo resident. Cummings returned several times to excavate rooms and collect specimens. Jesse Fewkes visited the site and others in the Kayenta area and wrote a short description of these visits. In 1917 Neil Judd came to Betatakin to conduct preservation of its highly fragile walls and roofs. Judd's report from 1930 was the most complete publication on the site prior to the late 1960s, when Jeff Dean completed his architectural and chronological study.

Betatakin was built of coarse, sandstone masonry, with some use of adobe or jacal walls. The 125 rooms and two kivas at the site were built in a very organized manner, with rectangular rooms precisely laid out in residence groups and of very similar size and shape. Prior to the beginning of construction of the large village in the 1260s, the site had a smaller, earlier settlement of several families. This earlier dwelling (dating from the 1240s–1260s) was razed to make room for the new village. All indications suggest that the inhabitants of Betatakin constituted a social unit—a village—prior to moving into the alcove. Evidence points to a planned move from elsewhere.

In contrast to what we know about Keet Seel and Inscription House, Betatakin does not appear to have grown through the undirected accretion of rooms. Rather, the construction and occupation of room suites in the village seem to have proceeded according to a specific plan. Thus we could also conclude that the site's leadership exercised more control relative to the other sites, where individual families had greater ability to move and live where they pleased.

At its peak of population, Betatakin was home to twenty to twenty-five ancient Puebloan households, with between 130 and 150 people in residence.

KEET SEEL

"Keet Seel" translates as "broken pottery" in Navajo. In Hopi the site is known as *Kawestima*, perhaps meaning "katsina home."

Keet Seel is somewhat larger than Betatakin, with a room count of at least 165. along with six kivas. Two kivas in nearby Turkey Cave are isolated structures that are an extended part of Keet Seel. The Keet Seel alcove is smaller (350 ft by 50 ft; height of 75 ft) than Betatakin, and virtually every available square foot was used in construction of the dwelling.

Keet Seel was the first of the large cliff dwellings rediscovered in Tsegi Canyon; Richard and Al Wetherill and Charlie Mason stumbled across the site in January 1895. Richard Wetherill came back in 1897, excavated many rooms, and made extensive collections for private benefactors that are now housed at the American Museum of Natural History. Additional work by Cummings and a visit by Fewkes added information. Stabilization work between the 1930s and 1960s helped preserve the site. As with Betatakin, Jeff Dean studied the architecture of Keet Seel in the 1960s and collected numerous tree ring samples, constructing a detailed chronological history of the site.

Keet Seel has a much more complicated history than either Betatakin or Inscription House. Archaeological evidence indicates that the alcove may have been used as early as the late 700s, with sporadic occupation from the mid-900s through the early 1200s. Tree ring dates from the site range from AD 950 to 1286. Determining the configuration of habitation structures in these earlier periods is difficult, because the last occupants of the alcove leveled all existing walls prior to building the Tsegi phase village. This last occupation is dated between 1245 and 1286, with most construction and living activities occurring in the 1270s and 1280s. A retaining wall, perhaps for defensive purposes, was built in front of the village, along the edge of the alcove. Keet Seel reached its peak population of about 150 residents, with twenty to twenty-five households, by the mid-1280s.

Kivas at the site show considerable variation in construction technique and internal features and facilities—hearths, bins, pits, ventilator systems, and so on. These structures seem to reflect the idiosyncratic desires of individual families and lineages. Such individuality contrasts with the uniformity of the constructed room suites and kivas at Betatakin. Several Hopi clans are known to have ancestral ties to this pueblo village: the Bighorn Sheep, Fire, and Flute clans.

INSCRIPTION HOUSE

Inscription House (recently given the Hopi name *Tsu'ovi*, or "place of the rattlesnake") lies in Nitsin Canyon, 40 miles west of Tsegi Canyon. The site contains at least eighty rooms and three kivas spread over three stories, comprising a late Pueblo III (Tsegi phase) village. The site derives its name from an inscription scratched into a room wall, purportedly from Spanish visitors in 1661. Research has shown that the inscription was misread as "1661" when it was actually "1861"—the same year that Mormons traveling through the area visited the site. After rediscovery in 1909, the inscription was chalked for photography by archaeologist Byron

Cummings's expedition, with the 8 mistaken for a 6. Thus, it is unlikely the site was ever visited by Spanish travelers.

John Wetherill and others rediscovered the site along with Cummings in 1909. Cummings originally named the site Adobe House, as its inhabitants used numerous rectangular adobe bricks (tempered with abundant grass stems) in constructing several walls. In retrospect this name seems more appropriate, since the inscription in question had not represented an early Spanish trip to the village.

Inscription House was built in a long, narrow rockshelter, with rooms and kivas fitted into the available space. Prior to the Tsegi phase village (built after AD 1250), the site was used by early Pueblo groups from the AD 600s into the late 1100s. None of the earlier uses of the site resulted in large structures. After 1250, earlier remains in the shelter were removed or leveled, and work began on the last occupation—the eighty-room village.

Inscription House grew through a process of accretion during the last 50 years of the Puebloan occupation. Groups of rooms were added to the village as new families arrived. At peak population, the site was home to a group numbering between 70 and 100. A retaining wall was built across the entire front of the village to serve as a boundary for the site, to retain soil and possessions, and perhaps to provide protection. The site shows great variation in room size, layout, and construction, indicating that individual families built rooms according to their own specific needs. This contrasts with the uniformity of room and village construction at Betatakin during the same interval.

In contrast to that of Betatakin and Keet Seel, tree ring dating was not very successful at Inscription House. The many sampled roof and wall beams from the village produced only two tree ring cutting dates, indicative of construction activities in the years 1222 and 1273. The latter date comes from the construction of the village during the Tsegi phase; the earlier date may have come from a roof beam that had been stockpiled or recycled from earlier activity at the pueblo. Nevertheless, the architectural and ceramic data from the site, along with location in a high cliff shelter, clearly delineate the site as a Tsegi phase dwelling. The Hopi identify several clans with connections to this village, including the Lizard, Rattlesnake, and Sand clans.

Moving beyond the description of these awe-inspiring dwellings, we can address a persistent question: why were they built high in the canyon walls?

WHY BUILD LARGE VILLAGES IN REMOTE, INACCESSIBLE ALCOVES?

Two primary interpretations have been offered by archaeologists to explain the reasons behind the construction of these spectacular sites in such inaccessible locations.

The older and more conventional view offers an explanation largely based on environmental conditions. Proponents of this view (most notably archaeologist Jeff Dean) have

View inside Inscription House (Tsu'ovi) showing well-preserved adobe brick structure and masonry walls (in background).   [Paul F. Reed]

suggested that a lowered water table and resulting arroyo cutting led to reduced arable land, causing Pueblo populations in Tsegi Canyon to move into large alcoves—such as Betatakin, Keet Seel, and Inscription House, among others—in areas presumably closer to stretches of land not affected by environmental degradation. A second environmental factor invoked is the close association of large alcoves and springs for drinking water. Finally, the natural advantages of building in sheltered alcoves, with reduced wear and tear on dwellings and the reduced need for maintenance and shelter from the elements for the inhabitants, also figure prominently in this environmentally focused interpretation.

In contrast to this interpretation, other archaeologists have suggested that warfare and conflict in the Kayenta area played a significant role in the late thirteenth-century relocation into inaccessible alcoves. While acknowledging the important role that the environment played in Tsegi Canyon and the advantages of sheltered locations, archaeologists Jonathan Haas and Winifred Creamer nevertheless concluded that conflict among Pueblo III populations in the area had a great influence on settlement patterns (i.e., the places chosen for habitation). Haas and Creamer conducted several years of archaeological research in the Kayenta area, completing an intensive survey in the Kayenta, Long House, and Kletha valleys (located just east of Navajo National Monument). They found that Tsegi phase (AD 1250–1300) habitation sites in all three valleys shared several characteristics: (1) construction of large, "focal" pueblos on defensible mesas or ridges; (2) sites organized into clusters around these focal pueblos; and (3) site locations chosen such that most or all sites in a cluster were visible to nearby sites, allowing for rapid communication via smoke, fire, or pyrite mirrors. These findings suggest that the inhabitants of the Kayenta region were very concerned about, at the least, the potential for conflict with their neighbors (far or near).

Beyond identifying these specific patterns, Haas and Creamer observed that many of the alcoves occupied with large villages during the Tsegi phase had seen little or no use in prior periods. Thus one has to ask why the environmental factors invoked in the traditional explanation had little or no effect on Puebloan choice in dwelling location in earlier periods. Haas and Creamer would tell us that the potential for conflict and actual conflict were significant factors causing Kayenta families and villages to retreat into the largely unused rockshelter and alcove settings.

A significant objection that Jeff Dean and others have raised in response to the warfare-conflict hypothesis is the apparent lack of evidence. Where, they ask, are the burned dwellings, unburied bodies, and signs of skeletal trauma that would directly support the notion of warfare? In fact, many of these indications are hard to detect in the Kayenta area, although many of the sites do show evidence of fire damage.

An additional consideration in the quest for clear evidence of warfare relates to the nuances in the argument for conflict. As noted above, Haas and Creamer have suggested that the potential for conflict, not just open warfare, was enough to cause the change in settlement pattern from open, undefended sites to villages on high mesas and in high alcoves, with large, aggregated populations. Thus, the search for villages and families destroyed by large-scale, European-style warfare is barking up the wrong tree. Haas and Creamer believe that a more subtle (yet just as dangerous) type of warfare, characterized by raiding, was the key factor in producing the aggregated, defensible posture of families and villages during the Tsegi phase.

CONTEMPORARY NATIVE AMERICAN CONNECTIONS TO NAVAJO NATIONAL MONUMENT

Several contemporary Native American tribes have connections to the sites or the landscape of the Navajo National Monument: Zuni, Hopi, San Juan Paiute, and Navajo. Zuni Pueblo is located in western New Mexico, southeast of the monument. Zuni oral history describes a series of migrations prior to the group arriving at their current village site several hundred years ago. Tsegi Canyon is identified by the Zuni as an ancestral home for several of their clans.

The Hopi Tribe of northeastern Arizona has a close ancestral connection to Navajo National Monument and is geographically closest to the area. Hopi oral history tells us that several clans, including Deer, Fire, Flute, and Water, have ancestral ties to sites in Tsegi Canyon. The canyon wall east of the main dwelling at Betatakin has a large painted symbol identified as a Fire Clan marker.

The San Juan Southern Paiute may have arrived in the Navajo Monument area as early as AD 1100, migrating from the northwest. The Paiute, who historically hunted, gathered, and farmed, established sizable communities near Navajo Mountain and Tuba City, Arizona. Small Paiute groups have lived in and around Navajo National Monument for centuries. Recently the tribe was awarded several thousand acres of land as a separate, federally recognized preserve within the Navajo reservation.

Navajo use of northeastern Arizona extends back to 1800 and perhaps earlier. Navajo families have raised cattle, sheep, goats, and other livestock and planted farms in the area surrounding the monument for many generations. In addition to likely visitation by Pueblo descendants, Betatakin and Keet Seel were probably explored first by Navajo residents of the Kayenta area. As noted above, the Navajo Nation has been an active partner with the NPS in the management of the monument from its inception, and both parties have benefited from this relationship.

ACCESSING NAVAJO NATIONAL MONUMENT

Navajo National Monument is one of the more challenging areas to visit. The visitors' center is about 20 miles west of the town of Kayenta, Arizona, at the end of Arizona Highway 564. Inscription House is closed to the public because of its fragile condition. The Sandal Trail leads from the visitors' center to the Betatakin overlook—a steep distance of 1 mile. Betatakin can be reached via a different trail, with a hike of several miles. Keet Seel requires the greatest effort: a day hike of 17 miles round-trip, or a two-day backpacking trip.

ACKNOWLEDGMENTS

I want to thank several NPS staff members at Navajo National Monument for their assistance. Although Inscription House is closed to the public, I was allowed to visit, which enhanced my ability to imagine the site and its inhabitants at AD 1275. Park archaeologist Brian Culpepper organized two days of visits to Inscription House, Betatakin, and Keet Seel, generously sharing his knowledge of the area's archaeology and history. Brian asked me to make clear that his views of the founding of the cliff dwellings follows Jeff Dean's explanation, and that he is not a supporter of the conflict hypothesis.

Monument manager Curlinda Holiday expedited my visit and graciously allowed Brian to serve as my guide. Nancy Skinner, newly appointed superintendent of the monument, accompanied us on the hike to Inscription House. Archaeologist Jim Dryer provided useful data and commentary on our trip to Betatakin and Keet Seel. My sons, Kevin and Sean, accompanied me on two days of rough hiking, braving a spring snowstorm and high winds with characteristic cheerfulness.

Further Reading: Dean, Jeffrey S., *Chronological Analysis of Tsegi Phase Sites in Northeastern Arizona*, Papers of the Laboratory of Tree-Ring Research, No. 3 (Tucson: University of Arizona Press, 1969); Fewkes, Jesse Walter, *Preliminary Report on a Visit to Navaho National Monument, Arizona*, Bureau of American Ethnology Bulletin No. 50 (Washington, DC: Smithsonian Institution, 1921); Haas, Jonathan, and Winifred Creamer, "Stress and Warfare among the Kayenta Anasazi of the Thirteenth Century A.D.," *Fieldiana Anthropology* 21(n.s.) (1993); Judd, Neil M., "The Excavation and Repair of Betatakin," *Proceedings of the National Museum* 77 (1930): 1–77; Navajo National Monument, National Park Service Web site, http://www.nps.gov/nava/index.htm, http://www.nps.gov/archive/nava/adhi/adhit.htm; Noble, David Grant, ed., *Houses beneath the Rock: The Anasazi of Canyon de Chelly and Navajo National Monument* (Santa Fe, NM: Ancient City Press, 1986); Ward, Albert E., *Inscription House: Two Research Reports*, Technical Series, No. 16 (Flagstaff: Museum of Northern Arizona, 1975).

Paul F. Reed

ELDEN PUEBLO

Flagstaff, Northern Arizona
Historic Excavations to Contemporary Public Archaeology

INTRODUCTION

Elden Pueblo is one of the most significant sites in the region of Flagstaff, Arizona. The large pueblo was partially excavated in 1926 by the legendary Dr. Jesse Walter Fewkes and John P. Harrington, of the Smithsonian Institution. Elden Pueblo is the type site for the Elden phase of AD 1150–1250, although the site was occupied until about AD 1275. It was the first site of any consequence to have been professionally excavated in the Flagstaff area, which sparked an interest and awareness for archaeology that continues in the community today. These factors contributed to the founding of the Museum of Northern Arizona in 1927 and stimulated future research in the prehistoric Sinagua culture. Elden Pueblo is also recognized by the Hopi as an ancestral site, *Pasiovi*. It was listed on the National Register of Historic Places in 1986 due to its archaeological, historical, and cultural significance and for its continuing contributions as one of the first and continuously sustained public archaeology programs in the United States.

THE SITE AND ITS ENVIRONMENT

The site of Elden Pueblo occupies about 1.8 hectares (4.5 acres) in an open ponderosa pine forest adjacent to U.S. Highway 89 on the outskirts of Flagstaff, Arizona. The nearest water sources—Elden Springs, Little Elden Springs, and a seep near Robinson Hills—are 1 mile to 2.5 miles (0.6 to 2.4 km) distant.

The site had three occupation periods. The earliest is represented by twenty pit houses, and the late occupation culminates with the most impressive structure at the site: a two-story pueblo of about sixty ground-floor rooms.

Two communal structures are associated with the main pueblo: a subterranean, rectangular kiva with a raised bench across its north end, and a large community room with a seating bench around all four sides. Pueblo 2, a separate four-room pueblo with its own kiva, is east of the main pueblo and dates to the late occupation. It was also two stories high when first constructed. Four other small pueblo outliers existed around the site, but two have been destroyed by modern developments. Of particular importance is the presence of three cemetery areas, from which more than 150 burials were excavated in 1926. Besides the prehistoric component, a stone building next to the highway is the remains of a trading post and curio shop operated by a Hopi between 1927 and 1933.

THE SINAGUA

Sinagua is the name Dr. Harold S. Colton, of the Museum of Northern Arizona, gave to the prehistoric people who lived in the region of the San Francisco Peaks and the Verde valley between AD 600 and 1400. The term comes from the name the first Spanish explorers of the region gave to the San Francisco Peaks in 1583: the Sierra Sinagua, the "mountains without water."

HISTORY OF ARCHAEOLOGICAL WORK AT ELDEN PUEBLO

The history of archaeological work at Elden Pueblo begins in 1916, when Dr. Colton and his wife, Mary-Russell Ferrell Colton, began an archaeological survey that would eventually become the Archaeological Survey of the Museum of Northern Arizona, which now has records for over 28,000 sites. On October 23, 1916, Mrs. Colton went on a horseback ride and discovered the largest pueblo of their survey, which Dr. Colton named Sheep Hill Ruin, after a cinder cone a quarter mile southeast of the site.

Ten years later, during the summer of 1926, Dr. Jesse Walter Fewkes and John P. Harrington of the Smithsonian Institution came to excavate the pueblo. During Fewkes's forty-one years of anthropological work, he became a major figure in Southwestern studies, rising to the position of chief of the Bureau of American Ethnology. Fewkes renamed the site after the most prominent landmark in the area, Mount Elden—which honors John Elden, a sheep herder who was one of the earliest Euro-American settlers of the area.

Harrington was better known as an ethnologist and linguist for the bureau who had worked among southwestern tribes since 1908. But from 1911 to 1915, he supervised archaeological field schools for the School of American Archaeology. In 1923 he was part of a joint archaeological project between the Heye Foundation and the bureau at the Burton Mound in Santa Barbara.

Fewkes was keenly interested in the history and culture of the Hopi people and interpreted most of his archaeological work from the perspective of Hopi culture and clan migration traditions. He hired a crew of twelve men and started work on the site on May 27, 1926. Three months later, they had cleared thirty-four rooms, excavated about 165 burials, and collected almost 2,500 artifacts.

This was a prodigious amount of work to accomplish in such a short time, and was possible only because the techniques used to excavate the site were oriented toward the recovery of artifacts, rather than recording information about the context in which those artifacts were located. Fewkes's techniques were a far cry from those used today; they were outdated even by 1920 standards. While such practices were commonplace in the 1890s, when Fewkes began his archaeological career, by 1926 they were unacceptable, and archaeologists who visited the site criticized the excavations.

Fewkes was 75 years old and was recovering from a serious operation when he worked at Elden Pueblo. He wrote a preliminary article about the site in 1927, but his health continued to decline, and he died in 1930 before a final report could be prepared.

BURIALS

Formal cemeteries were found on the north, east, and south sides of the pueblo. More than 150 burials were excavated; all were extended and generally buried with their heads to the east. Most burials were interred in simple pits, with pottery vessels placed by the head, feet, and/or sides. Necklaces, bracelets, and earrings of shell and stone, as well as utilitarian artifacts such as manos, hammerstones, bone awls, and flaked-stone tools, were also common.

Elden Pueblo has produced the largest burial population of any site from the Flagstaff area, and its study has generated major ideas and competing interpretations about the organization and complexity of Sinagua society. The traditional picture of the Sinagua casts them as egalitarian, with limited status differentiation and little political or social organization beyond the extended family. But alternative ideas suggest the operation of a more complex society, with craft specialization, hereditary status, political leadership, and hierarchical clans and societies.

A few burials were particularly notable by their special grave treatment or the number and kind of artifacts buried with them. Burials with the greatest number and diversity of artifacts tended to be older males, who often had unique items, such as nose plugs and carved bone hairpins, with them as well. One of the most elaborate burials at the site was covered by a thick layer of clay, with fifteen pottery vessels laid out around the edge of the clay cap. Over the pelvis of another burial was a unique black-on-white pottery effigy vessel of a pregnant antelope. Fewkes speculated that this important man may have been a member of an early version of the Antelope Society. Artifact assemblages with other burials suggest some level of craft specialization, such as pottery manufacturing and flint knapping.

Elden Pueblo was an important trade center with an abundance of artifacts from places well outside the Flagstaff area. Two macaw burials and a copper bell, found in recent excavations, indicate trade with Mexico. Shells were particularly numerous, with sources from the California coast. Pendants, beads, and ornaments were made of several different types of turquoise, as well as argillite from the Chino valley, 55 miles southeast of Elden Pueblo. Bone awls, made from split deer metapodials, were unusually abundant and suggest weaving may have been an important activity. Bone "awls," decorated with finely incised grid and interlocking triangular designs, were found near the skull and shoulders of several adult male burials, identifying the bone as a hairpin rather than an awl. Fewkes believed these special items identified members of a warrior society.

Projectile points were made of local chert and basalt, but many were made of obsidian from Government Mountain, 23 miles to the northwest. Chert and petrified-wood chert from the Tolchaco deposits along the Little Colorado River 28 miles to the north were also used.

ELDEN PUEBLO AND THE MUSEUM OF NORTHERN ARIZONA

Elden Pueblo was the first site of any size to be excavated near Flagstaff, and the number of burials and the rich artifact content of the site excited the population of Flagstaff and the archaeological community of Arizona. However, those same people became upset as crate after crate of artifacts were shipped back east, with none of the material remaining in the community or in the state. There had been talk of establishing a museum in Flagstaff for several years, but Fewkes's work at Elden Pueblo was the event that brought the community together to form the Museum of Northern Arizona in 1928. Fewkes's work also stimulated the excavation of other sites in the Flagstaff area, such as Byron Cummings's excavation of Turkey Hill Pueblo in 1928–29.

ELDEN PUEBLO AND PUBLIC ARCHAEOLOGY

Although Fewkes's techniques and approach to archaeology left much to be desired, he was clearly ahead of his time in his belief that archaeologists had a responsibility to share the knowledge they acquired from their work with the public. He was one of the first practitioners of what is known today as public archaeology. In fact, Fewkes is credited with beginning the tradition of campfire talks in the national-parks system during his years of work at Mesa Verde. In his position at the Bureau of American Ethnology, he was able to use his office to support efforts to designate and protect archaeological sites as national monuments.

Fewkes brought this philosophy of public archaeology with him to Elden Pueblo and spent considerable time talking to tourists, speaking to civic groups, and giving tours of the site. He also allowed visitors to help in the excavations, providing one of the earliest examples of public archaeology in the United States.

As with many sites he worked on, there were plans to have Elden Pueblo made into a national monument, and to this end, the pueblo was stabilized. However, these plans never materialized. Over the years, the walls slowly collapsed, and the pueblo returned to a ruined state.

NORTHERN ARIZONA UNIVERSITY EXCAVATIONS, 1966–68

In 1966–68, Elden Pueblo was once more the subject of archaeological investigation. Archaeological analysis, ceramic and artifact typologies, and dating techniques had progressed considerably since Fewkes's time, and information available from Fewkes's 1926 work was inadequate to address the archaeological questions of the time.

Roger Kelly of Northern Arizona University decided to test the site to collect information needed to place Elden Pueblo in proper perspective with other sites in the Flagstaff area—and to confirm the results of Fewkes's work in the community room, which had been questioned. Kelly excavated three rooms and portions of two others; he also re-excavated the northwest quarter of the community room. One structure, first thought to be an outlier pueblo, was discovered to be a 1927–33 trading post and curio shop for tourists who stopped to visit the site.

A major result of Kelly's work was the recognition of an earlier, pre-pueblo pit house occupation of the site. He also determined that not all rooms in the pueblo were occupied at the same time, as some had been abandoned, filled with trash, and used for later activities. He confirmed that the community room was, in fact, an unusually large room with an encircling bench; he also identified several floor features.

Kelly's work resulted in the collection of 550 artifacts and 50,000 shards. The vast majority of the pottery (90 percent) was locally produced Alameda Brown Ware, with trade wares being mostly from Kayenta and Winslow Anasazi groups to the north and east. A few shards from the Prescott area indicated additional trade with that region.

Soil samples for pollen analysis were collected; these formed the basis for a major paleoclimatic reconstruction of the Flagstaff area that provides an additional perspective for understanding Elden Pueblo. Overall, the AD 1067–1250 period, during the early occupation of the site, was very warm and moist, with spring- and summer-dominant rainfall. After 1150 precipitation changed to a bi-seasonal winter- and summer-dominant rain pattern that provided optimal farming conditions. But by AD 1250, precipitation decreased and changed to a fall and winter pattern, reducing the critical summer rains. Agricultural conditions continued to worsen from 1275 to 1300 as the climate became colder and drier, with a shift to a winter-dominant precipitation pattern.

COCONINO NATIONAL FOREST AND THE ELDEN PUEBLO PROJECT, 1978–PRESENT

In 1978 the Coconino National Forest was developing a long-term land exchange program. The proximity of Elden Pueblo to U.S. 89 and the ever-growing development of adjacent private land made it a potentially choice property for exchange. Kelly's work had demonstrated that parts of the pueblo remained unexcavated, but there was still a question about the full extent of Fewkes's work, the degree to which pothunting since 1926 had impacted the site, and the condition of

extramural areas around the pueblo that Fewkes had plowed. Consequently, test excavations were made in areas where Fewkes had excavated to evaluate the extent of Fewkes's work and the remaining research potential of the site. The workforce was provided by high school students enrolled in the Youth Conservation Corps summer jobs program. It was discovered that intact deposits did exist where Fewkes had dug, but the extent of his work was quite variable.

The interest and involvement displayed by the YCC youth during the project led to the use of Elden Pueblo in 1980 as an educational site where the public, particularly schoolchildren, can participate in excavations and analysis. This hands-on experience provides an opportunity for better public understanding and support for archaeology, and develops a sense of stewardship for natural and cultural resources on public lands.

Elden Pueblo also hosts the field school for the Arizona Archaeological Society. Work is limited primarily to areas previously excavated by Fewkes or Kelly and is supervised by professional archaeologists. The concept has been tremendously successful—and now, as the Elden Pueblo Project, has received numerous local, state, and national awards. Each year, 1,500–2,000 people participate in various program activities at the site.

Current research is focused on defining the growth of Elden Pueblo through time and how it reflects environmental, social, ceremonial, and technological change. Rooms previously dug by Fewkes are re-excavated to expose construction details that permit the building sequence of the site to be determined. Systematic trenching around the pueblo is being completed to locate other structures and exterior features, so they can be related to the development of the pueblo. The project re-evaluates the work done by Fewkes and brings it up to current standards, to the extent that is possible. Fieldwork and laboratory analysis are ongoing, but much has already been learned about Elden Pueblo.

DATING ELDEN PUEBLO

When Fewkes excavated Elden Pueblo in 1926, ceramic typologies and chronometric dating techniques were not yet available, and he could only speculate that the site was inhabited about AD 1300. It now appears that the site was occupied between about AD 1067 and 1275. The earliest occupation consisted of a few pit house clusters dating to about AD 1067, part of a widespread settlement along the east side of Mount Elden and the San Francisco Peaks. Pueblo construction began around AD 1150, near the start of the Elden phase. The pueblo underwent a major expansion and rebuilding episode about AD 1250, during the Turkey Hill phase, when groups of people moved to the pueblo, more than doubling the earlier population. By AD 1275, the site was abandoned.

PIT HOUSES

Twenty pit houses have been found at the site so far. All appear to have been domestic structures, occupied on a year-round basis. The earliest pit houses date to the Angell-Winona phase

(AD 1067–1100), but surprisingly, most date to the Elden phase (AD 1150–1250). Although a few Elden phase pit houses are beneath the pueblo rooms, clearly pre-dating pueblo construction, ceramic assemblages in the Elden phase pit houses are no different from those found within the Elden phase rooms of the pueblo, suggesting contemporaneous use of both architectural forms. Upon abandonment, most pit houses had been burned, their lower levels purposefully filled with trash.

THE PUEBLOS

Pueblo construction started about AD 1150, when several two- to four-room structures were built. Through time new walls were constructed to connect what had been separate structures into larger pueblo units. A 3.5-by-6-meter kiva with a 70-centimeter-high bench across its north end was also built outside the south wall of the pueblo. About AD 1250, the pueblo expanded as blocks of two to four rooms were built around the edges of the pueblo. These multi-room units were built as single construction events, indicating that entire family groups were moving into the community. The kiva was probably closed at this time and replaced by the larger community room in response to the community's increasing size. From the height of the pueblo mound, and judging from several entries in the 1926 excavation notes, it is evident that parts of the pueblo were two stories tall. Fewkes and Harrington noted that several rooms in the pueblo had burned.

THE COMMUNITY ROOM

The community room is almost six times larger than other rooms, measuring 8.5 meters by 10.8 meters; it was originally over 2.3 meters high. A bench for seating runs along all four sides. It was partially subterranean, dug into the sterile substrate of a low, natural hill to a depth of 1 meter. The roof support pattern is not totally clear, but probably included four posts that were recessed into the four corners of the bench. Four possible sets of loom holes were also found. The ventilator reported by Fewkes is suspect, but an actual ventilator is present in the center of the east wall at the level of the bench. Another possible ventilator—or, more likely, a niche—is in the center of the west wall at floor level.

The entire central portion of the room was riddled by twenty-four firepits, pits, and basins, many of which had been intentionally filled with stones and sealed over with floor plaster. Most of the floor had been removed by Fewkes's excavation, but remnants of at least four floor re-plastering episodes, 6 centimeters thick, remained in places, perhaps indicating a cyclical cleaning or remodeling of the room.

Several macaw bones, possibly an intentional burial, were in the fill of the south bench. Another macaw burial was discovered in a room in the north end of the pueblo that may have been used for multiple animal burials.

Harrington and Colton noted that this room had burned, but they overlooked a layer of black volcanic cinders on the floor varying in thickness from a few millimeters to as much as 1 centimeter.

NORTH PLAZA AND EXTERIOR WORK AREA

During the Elden phase, the north end of the site was occupied by at least two pit house families. Associated with them was a prepared clay surface that covered an earlier deposit of trash and soil. The surface is distinctive, because it rests on top of a thin layer of black volcanic cinders and has been found beneath the pueblo in a few places. It delineates a communal work area—likely for food preparation, as it contains numerous basins, pits, and firepits, along with two roasting pits. Later, during the Elden phase, both pit houses were burned and purposefully filled with trash and rocks, with masonry rooms built over them and the activity surface.

PUEBLO 2

During the Turkey Hill phase expansion of the pueblo, Pueblo 2, a separate two-room, two-story pueblo was constructed just off the northeast side of the pueblo. Why it was built as a separate unit, rather than simply incorporated into the main pueblo, is unknown. The fact that it had its own rectangular, benched kiva (smaller than the main kiva for the pueblo) suggests its occupants were members of a different Sinagua social group. Two single-story rooms were later added to make a total of six rooms. Upon abandonment, large rocks were thrown into the kiva, and the pueblo was burned.

SUNSET CRATER AND ELDEN PUEBLO

The relationship between the aftermath of the Sunset Crater eruption(s) and the Sinagua is a long-standing topic of Flagstaff area research. A study of tree rings concluded there were two eruptions between AD 1064 and 1067. But the paleomagnetic dating of Sunset Crater lava flows suggests a much longer eruptive history extending to AD 1250. Vulcanologists, however, reject this revised dating, stating that cinder cones like Sunset Crater only erupt once or twice, but never as multiple eruptions extending over hundreds of years.

Excavations at several sites in the Flagstaff area, in addition to Elden Pueblo, have found black volcanic cinders typical of Sunset Crater in post–AD 1100 contexts. This has raised new questions about dating the eruption, as well as explaining the source of cinders in the sites. Cinders are consistently found on top of the substrate at Elden Pueblo, thought to be close to the prehistoric ground surface, and as thin lenses in the fill of other rooms and features. Cinders also occur on the floors of the kiva and community room (immediately below the outside activity surface), and within a large sealed basin in Pueblo 2.

Three explanations have been offered to explain the occurrence of cinders in these post–AD 1067 locations: (1) they corroborate the paleomagnetic dates for late eruptions, (2) they have been redeposited into the features by wind and water runoff from nearby cinder deposits, and (3) they were purposefully deposited by the Sinagua as part of the ceremonies performed when structures were abandoned. However, more work is needed to evaluate each of these propositions.

THE END OF ELDEN PUEBLO

Analysis of skeletal remains indicates deteriorating health conditions in the Sinagua population through time. Burials from Elden Pueblo show evidence of anemia, possibly tuberculosis, and dietary stress, especially in young children. Soil samples collected by Kelly were found to contain eggs from parasites that live in the human intestinal tract. Parasite eggs are absent in samples representing the early occupation period of Elden Pueblo, but they increase dramatically in later samples from trash-filled rooms that were used as latrines. This suggests a declining health of the population—probably indicating malnutrition, low population vigor, and diseases—and it is likely that the population near the end of the occupation of Elden Pueblo had decreased significantly.

Re-excavations in the main pueblo confirm 1926 observations that several rooms in the pueblo had burned, but it is not known whether this was the result of the burning of individual rooms through time as they were abandoned or of a single fire. Both pueblos may have been burned at the same time. It is clear, however, that with the burning of Pueblo 2, the occupation of Elden Pueblo came to an end. No shards, trash, or other indications of occupation are in the trench profiles above a collapsed wall of Pueblo 2.

The last occupants of Elden Pueblo likely joined the community at Old Caves Pueblo, 1.75 miles northwest of Elden Pueblo, as it is the only settlement in the Flagstaff area that lasted beyond AD 1300.

HOPI TRADITIONS

Elden Pueblo continued to be an important place to the Hopi in later centuries. Physical evidence of visitation after the site was abandoned is indicated by several shards of Jeddito Black-on-Yellow found in an undisturbed archaeological context. A number of Hopi clans trace their history through Elden Pueblo, and Hopi visitors to the 1926 excavations readily related it to the Snake Clan. Several oral traditions also have associations with the site. One identifies it as *Hovi'itstuyqa*, also a place name for Mt. Elden, and concludes with the pueblo being destroyed and burned. Others relate the site to *Pasiovi* (also *Pasiwvi* or *Pavasioki*), the "Meeting Place" where a number of clans came together and stayed for a time before continuing their migrations to the Hopi mesas. During that period, various ceremonies and religious societies developed, and ceremonial responsibilities were determined.

More recently, prior to World War II, Hopi would routinely stop at *Pasiwvi* as part of their pilgrimage to the San Francisco Peaks, and even today the site is still used to collect certain plants for ceremonial and medicinal purposes.

CONCLUSIONS

Archaeologists have studied Elden Pueblo for eighty years, and the site continues to provide significant information and ideas about the prehistory of Flagstaff and northern Arizona. Proximity to expansive areas of good agricultural soils, a unique favorable environmental location behind the mountains, and a change to a bi-seasonal precipitation pattern were important natural conditions that help explain why Elden Pueblo developed into a major center in the ponderosa pine zone when most of the population occupied the pinyon-juniper country.

However, cultural reasons that are impossible to discern from material remains may also have been significant factors that made Elden Pueblo a special place. Unlike other sites in the area, Elden Pueblo was occupied by the same families for over a century. Maintaining a presence in their ancestral area may have been important; it provided a home village for related families to return to after AD 1250, when worsening climate conditions made life in the pinyon-juniper zone no longer tenable.

The importance of place to Native American cultures aids in understanding why certain sites were maintained even through times of adversity. The oral traditions about *Pasiwvi* relate its importance to major events in the development of Hopi culture. These traditions, and the proximity of the site to the San Francisco Peaks, suggest the people of Elden Pueblo may have had special responsibilities for the sacred landscape of the peaks. Hopefully, through our efforts to understand Elden Pueblo through archaeology, those who come to the site today will be inspired to continue the stewardship of this special place.

Further Reading: Coconino National Forest, Elden Pueblo Web site, http://www.fs.fed.us/r3/coconino/forest-resources/archaeology/elden-pueblo/index.shtml (online August 2007); Colton, Harold S., *The Sinagua: A Summary of the Archaeology of the Region of Flagstaff, Arizona*, Bulletin No. 22 (Flagstaff: Museum of Northern Arizona, 1946); Downum, Christian E., "The Sinagua: Prehistoric People of the San Francisco Mountains," *Plateau* 63(1) (1992): 1–33; Fewkes, Jesse Walter, "Archaeological Field Work in Arizona: Field Session of 1926," *Smithsonian Miscellaneous Collections* 78 (7) (1927): 207–232; Hohmann, John W., "Sinagua Social Differentiation: Inferences Based on Prehistoric Mortuary Practices," *Arizona Archaeologist* 17 (1982); Hovis, Jacqueline S., "Public Archaeology at Elden Pueblo, Flagstaff, Arizona," master's thesis (Northern Arizona University, 1992); Kelly, Roger E., "Elden Pueblo: An Archaeological Account," *Plateau* 42(3) (1970): 79–91; Kelly, Roger E., and Albert E. Ward, "Lessons from the Zeyouma Trading Post Near Flagstaff, Arizona," *Historical Archaeology* VI (1971): 65–76; Partners in Resource Education, *Hands on the Land: A National Network of Field Classrooms Connecting Students, Teachers, and Parents to Our Public Lands and Waterways*, http://handsontheland.org/profiles/profile_details.cfm?sitecode=elpu (online 2006); Pilles, Peter J., Jr., "The Field House and Sinagua Demography," in *Limited Activity and Occupation Sites: A Collection of Conference Papers*, edited by Albert E. Ward, Contributions to Anthropological Studies, No. 1 (Albuquerque, NM: Center for Anthropological Studies, 1978), 119–133; Pilles, Peter J., Jr., "Sunset Crater and the Sinagua: A New Interpretation," in *Volcanic Activity and Human Ecology*, edited by Payson D. Sheets and Donald K. Grayson (New York: Academic Press, 1979), 359–385; Pilles, Peter J., Jr., "The Sinagua: Ancient People of the Flagstaff Region," in *Wupatki and Walnut Canyon; New Perspectives on History, Prehistory, Rock Art* (Santa Fe, NM: School of American Research, 1987), 1–12; Pilles, Peter J., Jr., "Hisatsinom:

The Ancient people of Sunset Crater," in *Earth Fire: A Hopi Legend of the Sunset Crater Eruption*, by Ekkehart Malotki with Michael Lomatuway'ma (Flagstaff, AZ: Northland Press, 1987), 105–119; Pilles, Peter J., Jr., "The Pueblo III Period Along the Mogollon Rim: The Honanki, Elden, and Turkey Hill Phases of the Sinagua," in *The Prehistoric Pueblo World, A.D. 1150–1350*, edited by Michael A. Adler (Tucson: University of Arizona Press, 1996), 59–72.

Peter J. Pilles, Jr.

WUPATKI, SUNSET CRATER, WALNUT CANYON, AND OTHER SITES

Northern Arizona

An Eleventh-Century Volcanic Eruption, Cultural Expansion, and Change

Sunset Crater is a late-eleventh-century AD volcano in northeastern Arizona surrounded by the archaeological remains of a late prehistoric period farming population that archaeologists call the Sinagua.

The eruption of Sunset Crater dramatically altered the course of Sinagua life. In the post-eruptive period, the Sinagua expanded their territorial range, increased their numbers, extended trade relations with surrounding populations, and experienced rapid cultural change. In the AD 1130s, the Sinagua and people of other cultural groups established Wupatki Pueblo, a 100-room, four-story building located 20 kilometers northeast of the volcano. The Sinagua also lived in cliff dwellings at Walnut Canyon (21 km south of Sunset Crater) and in hundreds of pit house and pueblo communities scattered across the adjacent pine forests and pinyon-juniper scrublands.

The local cultural florescence following the Sunset Crater eruption was relatively short-lived. The thin soils tilled by Sinagua farmers are easily exhausted of nutrients and prone to erosion, so agricultural production probably began to diminish within a few decades after the eruption. A downturn in precipitation in the early AD 1200s coincided with a great reduction in construction of new pueblo rooms. By the mid-1200s, the Sinagua had departed most of the region surrounding Sunset Crater, leaving behind a remarkably abundant and well-preserved set of archaeological sites and features.

Descendants of the Sinagua are represented today primarily by the Hopi people, a Native American tribe of approximately 7,000 members. The Hopi inhabit a reservation of about 6,500 square kilometers at the southern end of Black Mesa in northeastern Arizona. Many Hopi cultivate maize,

beans, and squash by using some of the same agricultural techniques used by the Sinagua. Hopi life features adherence to the teachings of the Katsinam—spiritual helpers and guides who mainly inhabit the San Francisco Peaks (an extinct, 3,851-meter stratovolcano located just west of Sunset Crater). The Hopi allow visitation of many of their villages, but strict rules apply to visitors, and many areas are closed to the public, especially during religious observances.

SUNSET CRATER

Sunset Crater—named *Polotsmo* ("Red Hill") by the Hopi—is a 310-meter-high cinder cone volcano of the San Francisco Volcanic Field, a geologically active region at the far southern end of the Colorado Plateau. In the late eleventh century AD, this volcano put on a spectacular display for the region's prehistoric peoples. At the peak of its eruptive power, Sunset Crater sent a column of fiery lava about 660 meters into the air. Billowing clouds of cinder, gases, and steam rose to a height of about 8,000 meters and could be seen for up to 400 kilometers. The volcano spread a blanket of black cinders over an area of about 2,300 square kilometers and extruded about 8 square kilometers of lava.

For many years archaeologists and geologists used tree ring dates to pinpoint the Sunset Crater eruption to the year AD 1065. Recent studies, however, have cast some doubt on this. The dating effort is complicated by current understanding that Sunset Crater was only the largest and among the latest of several volcanic features that erupted along a great crack in the earth stretching about 10 kilometers southeast from Sunset Crater. It is unclear exactly when each of the eruption events took place, nor is it known how long each of these events persisted. Archaeological evidence and paleo-magnetic dating, now considered more reliable than the poorly sourced tree ring specimens used in the original dating, strongly suggest that the eruption events finished no later than the last decade of the AD 1000s. Based on current dating evidence and comparison with similar volcanoes around the world, the overall eruption probably lasted for no more than a few years.

The effects of the volcano and its associated features were initially destructive but ultimately beneficial. Wind-borne basaltic cinders fell to earth in an arid, low-elevation region lying mostly north and east, toward the valley of the Little Colorado River. These cinder deposits became a moisture-conserving mulch, allowing agriculture to flourish in places previously unused for settlement. Farmers dwelling in pit houses and pueblos gradually moved into the area blanketed by the cinders and exploited the mulching properties for several decades.

Archaeological remains around Sunset Crater are sparse, owing to burial of pre-eruptive remains by volcanic deposits and the inhospitable post-eruptive landscape, which features deep cinder dunes and masses of sharp, twisted lava. Archaeologists and monument visitors have occasionally discovered prehistoric pottery vessels in crevices of the lava flows. Some of these vessels held caches of food and water intended to sustain ancient travelers, but others were probably intended as religious offerings.

Sunset Crater and its surrounding volcanic features have deep spiritual meaning to several Native American groups, especially the Hopi. A few of the Hopi's spiritual helpers, the Katsinam, inhabit Sunset Crater. The Hopi identify a small volcanic eminence west of the crater's base as the home of Yaponsa, a being responsible for the wind. In 1992 a tornado—extremely rare in this region—passed directly over Yaponsa's home, uprooting hundreds of pine trees.

The volcano and its adjacent lava flows are now preserved as a national monument. Dr. Harold S. Colton, founder of the Museum of Northern Arizona, is largely responsible for the monument's creation. In 1930 Dr. Colton and others convinced President Herbert Hoover to protect the volcano from a Hollywood film company wishing to explode dynamite along the crater's slopes to simulate a landslide. Today the Sunset Crater National Monument protects all of the natural and cultural features within its boundaries. The monument is open during daylight hours and offers an interpretive center, adjacent campgrounds, and outdoor trails and exhibits.

WUPATKI

Wupatki Pueblo lies near Deadman Wash, a seasonal stream that joins the Little Colorado River about 70 kilometers upstream from the Grand Canyon. Wupatki (a Hopi name with multiple possible meanings) occupies an intriguing location, with respect to both geography and surrounding prehistoric populations. The pueblo rests in an arid badlands tangential to lofty spruce and pine forests to the south and windswept mesas to the north. Wupatki also sits astride a cultural crossroads, a gateway to the Sinagua and Hohokam cultural traditions to the south and the various Pueblo cultural traditions to the north.

Because of its intermediate geographic and cultural position, Wupatki was well suited to serve as a regional trading center. The pueblo's residents imported (and likely exported) more than 100 types of pottery, along with macaws, copper bells, and shell jewelry from Mexico, and turquoise and mineral pigments from a broad surrounding area. Finely woven cotton cloth, made from cotton plants grown nearby, was another important craft item that likely was traded by Wupatki's inhabitants.

Wupatki Pueblo embraces a large, red sandstone outcrop about 400 meters east of a spring that supplied drinking water. The rooms of the pueblo lie atop earlier pit structures and trash deposits dating back to the AD 500s. Tree ring dates show that the first major episode of pueblo construction began around AD 1137, when builders added rooms to the east side of the outcrop, within some of its natural alcoves, and across its top. Residents expanded the pueblo by adding sets of rooms about every fifteen years from the mid-1140s through the early 1190s. The result was a massed, compact pueblo reaching up to four stories high and towering above the surrounding landscape.

A persistent puzzle in the interpretation of Wupatki concerns the multiple cultural traditions represented at the site. Early rooms were built in a style reminiscent of some of the pueblos at Chaco Canyon. Later rooms exhibit masonry similar to pueblos across the Little Colorado River. Artifacts are similarly diverse. The majority of Wupatki's pottery consists of Alameda Brown Ware, characteristic of the Sinagua culture. However, many contemporaneous pueblos yield mostly the Tusayan Gray Ware of the Kayenta branch of the Ancestral Pueblo culture, or Prescott Gray Ware originating some 140 kilometers to the southwest.

Wupatki Pueblo also features an eclectic mix of ceremonial or public architectural spaces. A Hohokam-style ball court lies a few meters north of the pueblo. It is typical of contemporaneous ball courts found in southern Arizona, except for its masonry walls. A circular subterranean structure with an encircling bench perches on a sloping surface east of Wupatki. This construction—the Amphitheater—in some respects resembles the Great Kivas associated with the Chaco culture but it also shows significant differences, including the fact that it was never roofed. A few sites surrounding Wupatki have detached, circular pit rooms akin to the kivas of the Kayenta branch.

An extensive set of archaeological remains surrounds Wupatki Pueblo. In the 1980s the U.S. National Park Service conducted a detailed survey of the 143-square-kilometer national monument surrounding Wupatki. The survey documented about 2,400 prehistoric sites, nearly all of which date to the century and a half following the eruption of Sunset

Crater. About 90 percent of the sites are agricultural fields or small masonry field houses located to take advantage of the cinder mulch originating from Sunset Crater. Many of the larger pueblos fall into geographically distinct clusters representing communities (and perhaps political entities) of several dozen to a few hundred inhabitants. This level of community size and organization had no precedent in the pre-eruptive period, and it appears that cultural developments at Wupatki were an important precursor to the very large and well-organized pueblo communities established elsewhere in northern Arizona during the late thirteenth and early fourteenth centuries.

Occupation of Wupatki and surrounding pueblos largely ceased by about AD 1250. The latest tree ring date from the pueblo is AD 1260, but no significant construction took place after AD 1215. Wupatki's residents probably moved to some of the large ancestral Hopi pueblos on Anderson Mesa to the southeast and along the Little Colorado River near modern Winslow, Arizona. There is no consensus among archaeologists regarding why Wupatki's inhabitants left the area, but most scholars today accept some combination of drought, environmental change, and social conflict as the best explanation.

Archaeologists from the Museum of Northern Arizona and the U.S. National Park Service excavated Wupatki Pueblo from the 1930s through the 1960s. Their work exposed a majority of the pueblo's rooms, the Amphitheater, and the ball court. Today Wupatki Pueblo is open for visitation during daylight hours and features a visitors' center with a gift shop and museum. Several surrounding pueblos in Wupatki National Monument are also accessible to the public, such as the Citadel (an unexcavated, fifty-room mesa-top pueblo), Nalakihu (an excavated small pueblo lying at the base of the Citadel), and Wukoki (an unexcavated, tower-like structure lying just east of Wupatki).

WALNUT CANYON

Walnut Canyon is a 134-meter-deep erosional chasm along a stretch of the Walnut Creek drainage just east of the modern city of Flagstaff, Arizona. The canyon is today dry in all but the wettest years, but it probably flowed seasonally before dams were built upstream in the early twentieth century. The canyon's water and diversity of plant and animal life made it attractive to ancient hunting-and-gathering nomads, as well as later pueblo agriculturalists.

Over the past 10,000 years, the area in and around the canyon accumulated a wide variety of archaeological sites and features. The most impressive of these are more than 300 Sinagua rooms built in the canyon's natural alcoves during the AD 1100s and 1200s. These cliff dwellings are the reason for Walnut Canyon's preservation as a national monument.

During the late AD 1000s, the Sinagua shifted their residences from pit houses to stone dwellings that lay above the ground surface. The advent of masonry architecture coincided with the expansion of settlement below the canyon rim and into the canyon itself—the result of a dramatic increase in the local population. During the early 1100s, the Sinagua began to build large masonry rooms inside natural cavities eroded into the canyon's limestone walls. They also built small pueblos above the canyon's rim. Settlements were clustered around a series of extraordinarily large stone rooms or enclosures that lie atop peninsulas of rock formed by bends in the canyon. Archaeologists of the 1930s referred to these sites as forts, but the more common view today is that they were used for ceremonial gatherings. As with Wupatki and many other surrounding settlements, the Sinagua left the cliff dwellings and forts of Walnut Canyon by the mid-1200s.

Today many of Walnut Canyon's cliff dwellings and rim-top settlements are preserved within the boundaries of Walnut Canyon National Monument. The monument has two main interpretive trails, one that leads to an excavated pueblo on the canyon's rim and another that passes alongside numerous cliff dwellings inside the canyon's walls. A visitors' center with a gift shop and museum rests on the north edge of the canyon.

RELATED SITES

Many archaeological sites are located on public lands in the region surrounding Sunset Crater volcano. Several sites on the Coconino National Forest are accessible to visitors and interpreted to the public. Elden Pueblo can be found along Highway 89 at the north end of Flagstaff, Arizona. This multi-story pueblo, occupied mostly during the AD 1100s and 1200s, features an active program of summertime excavation and a trail system with signs and interpretive brochures. Nuvaqwewtaqa, also known as Chavez Pass Pueblo, lies on Anderson Mesa, about 60 kilometers southeast of Flagstaff. This ancestral Hopi site has the ruins of two multi-story room blocks, each consisting of a few hundred rooms occupied mostly during the AD 1200s through mid-1400s. An interpretive sign can be found along the road leading to the site, and visitors can walk among the ruins via a primitive trail.

Further Reading: Anderson, Bruce A., *The Wupatki Archeological Inventory Survey Project: Final Report*, Professional Paper No. 35 (Santa Fe, NM: U.S. National Park Service Southwest Cultural Resources Center, 1990); Baldwin, Anne R., and J. Michael Bremer, *Walnut Canyon National Monument: An Archeological Survey*, Publications in Anthropology No. 39 (Tucson, AZ: U.S. National Park Service Western Archeological and Conservation Center, 1986); Downum, Christian E., "The Sinagua: Prehistoric People of the San Francisco Mountains," *Plateau* 63 (1992): 1–32; Downum, Christian E., Ellen Brennan, and James P. Holmlund, with contributions by Laurie Coveney-Thom, Kelley Hays-Gilpin, and Erik Whiteman, *An Architectural Study of Wupatki Pueblo (NA 405)*, Archaeological Report No. 1175 (Flagstaff: Northern Arizona University, 1999); Elson, Mark D., ed., *Sunset Crater Archaeology: The History of a Volcanic Landscape*, Anthropological Papers No. 30 (Tucson, AZ:

Center for Desert Archaeology, 2006); Holm, Richard F., "Field Guide to the Geology of the Central San Francisco Volcanic Field," in *Geology of Central and Northern Arizona, Geological Society of America, Rocky Mountain Section, Field Trip Guidebook*, edited by J. D. Nations (Boulder, CO: Geological Society of America, 1986), 27–43; Kamp, Kathryn, and John C. Whittaker, *Surviving Adversity: The Sinagua of Lizard Man Village* (Salt Lake City: University of Utah Press, 1999); Ort, Michael H., Mark D. Elson, and Duane E. Champion, *A Paleomagnetic Dating Study of Sunset Crater Volcano*, Technical Report No. 2002-16 (Tucson: Desert Archaeology, 2002); Pilles, Peter J., Jr., "The Pueblo III Period along the Mogollon Rim: The Honanki, Elden, and Turkey Hill Phases of the Sinagua," in *The*

Prehistoric Pueblo World A.D. 1150–1350, edited by Michael A. Adler (Tucson: University of Arizona Press, 1996), 59–72; Sullivan, Alan P., III, and Christian E. Downum, "Aridity, Activity, and Volcanic Ash Agriculture: A Study of Short-Term Prehistoric Cultural-Ecological Dynamics," *World Archaeology* 22 (1991): 271–287; Sunset Crater National Monument, U.S. National Park Service Web site, http://www.nps.gov/sucr (online April 2007); Walnut Canyon National Monument, U.S. National Park Service Web site, http://www.nps.gov/waca (online April 2007); Wupatki National Monument, U.S. National Park Service Web site, http://www.nps.gov/wupa (online April 2007).

Christian E. Downum

AGUA FRIA NATIONAL MONUMENT AND PERRY MESA

Central Arizona

Ancient History and Ways of Life in Central Arizona

Every day, Interstate 17 brings thousands of people to the edge of the Agua Fria National Monument, 40 miles north of Phoenix. As they cross the Agua Fria River and complete the long ascent to the plateau at Sunset Point, few of these travelers are aware that they are viewing an expansive vista of grasslands and canyons that was once home to a thriving network of prehistoric communities.

In January 2000 President Bill Clinton established the Agua Fria National Monument to protect a unique collection of archaeological sites within a rugged, undeveloped landscape in central Arizona. Although archaeologists have surveyed less than 10 percent of the monument's area of 71,100 acres, they have already found several hundred archaeological sites that may span some 2,000 years of human history. The monument incorporates a portion of the Perry Mesa District, listed on the National Register of Historic Places, which includes at least 500 recorded sites and extends into the Tonto National Forest to the east.

The first inhabitants were Archaic hunters and gatherers, who moved seasonally to hunt game and gather wild plant foods. Small groups of farmers related to the Hohokam tradition of southern Arizona began to live in pit houses and temporary camps near the river and on the mesa tops after AD 700. After AD 1250, the population increased dramatically as the area attracted new settlers. These migrations followed a trend that began after AD 1100 as many groups left settlements in the lower deserts and valleys and established new, larger villages in upland areas.

The settlers constructed dwellings of stone masonry. Eight major communities—called pueblos in reference to the Spanish word for towns—each contained more than a hundred rooms within one or more structures described as room blocks. Each community included at least one large structure containing thirty to ninety rooms. The pueblos and smaller hamlets may have housed a total population of 2,000 to 3,000 people. Less than two centuries later, by AD 1450, the last occupants of the Agua Fria villages left the mesa-canyon country of central Arizona and migrated onward, perhaps to join the ancestors of the modern Pueblo tribes in northeastern Arizona.

Early Spanish explorers encountered the Yavapai Indians, who lived in the Agua Fria region until they were confined to reservations in the mid-nineteenth century. The Yavapai were followed by gold miners, ranchers, and Basque sheep herders, all of whom left traces of their activities.

What is most significant about the Agua Fria National Monument is the striking dominance of the late prehistoric occupation in the distinctive natural landscape called Perry Mesa. The mesa—a plateau of desert grasslands between the New River and Bradshaw mountain ranges—is bounded and cut by canyons up to a thousand feet deep. From the vantage of the steep-walled canyons, the plateau areas appear as high mesas. Perry Mesa is the area east of the dramatic Agua Fria River Canyon; Black Mesa is the smaller plateau to the west.

The canyons of Silver Creek and Squaw Creek define the northern and southern edges of the mesas, and four other chasms slice eastward into Perry Mesa from the river. The canyons contain streams, springs, and natural waterholes. Canyon rims were favored locations for prehistoric villages. The grassy expanses on the mesa tops conceal the rocky surfaces covered with basalt from ancient lava flows out of an oozing volcano now known as Joe's Hill.

An aerial photo of Baby Canyon Pueblo. The pueblo is on a knoll jutting into Baby Canyon on Perry Mesa; the knoll casts quite a shadow at certain times of day. In the Agua Fria it is easier to see the wall alignments from the air than from the ground. [Courtesy of the Bureau of Land Management/photo by Joe Vogel]

The pueblo dwellers interacted with surrounding populations and shared many characteristics of architecture, technology, and material culture. However, archaeologists believe that the Perry Mesa occupation is distinctive enough that it cannot be easily assigned to the contemporary Salado or Sinagua cultures of central Arizona. Many researchers refer to the people of the late prehistoric (Pueblo IV) period as the Perry Mesa tradition.

The tradition's most conspicuous features are stone masonry structures ranging in size from one to more than a hundred rooms. Many of the small sites, with fewer than ten rooms, may have served as seasonal dwellings near fields. Cleared pathways, called "racetracks," that measure up to 10 meters wide and 300 meters long, extend from most of the larger pueblos. Their function is less clear than their appearance on aerial photos.

Agricultural features, such as rock-lined terraces, are widespread, as are roasting pits and other sites related to the exploitation and processing of natural resources. Rock art sites range from single designs on isolated boulders to elaborate galleries with hundreds of symbols pecked into the cliffs below large ruins. Locally produced ceramics consist of unpainted brown pottery, as well as red wares that are often highly polished. The people obtained painted pottery and other items from distant regions through trade.

Information about the Perry Mesa tradition is based largely on the results of recent archaeological surveys, surface collections, and detailed site mapping. As of 2005, scientists have conducted only limited excavations at a small number of sites. Much of our knowledge about site locations and architecture is based on the exposed walls and potholes left by vandals. Despite this past damage, the Perry Mesa region offers scientists the rare opportunity to study an entire settlement system with clear geographic and temporal boundaries in an undeveloped setting. But substantial archaeological work remains to be done to develop a more complete understanding of the late prehistoric period cultural and intercultural relationships of the monument and the wider area. Within this cultural landscape, it is possible to examine village life and subsistence, community interrelationships within the settlement system, and social and economic relations with regions beyond Perry Mesa.

VILLAGE LIFE AND SUBSISTENCE

The Perry Mesa tradition villages may have housed some descendants of the Hohokam groups that lived on the mesas prior to AD 1250. However, immigrants from surrounding areas likely contributed to the dramatic increases in the size and number of settlements. The growth of the population on Perry Mesa followed the apparent abandonment of villages in

An aerial view of Badger Springs Pueblo, at the edge of the Agua Fria River Canyon on Black Mesa.   [Courtesy of the Bureau of Land Management/photo by Joe Vogel]

the valleys and foothills to the south and west. Arrivals of families or other small groups of immigrants, from different places at different times, may be reflected in the physical and spatial patterns of pueblo architecture.

The masonry buildings, mostly one story tall, contained blocks of rectangular rooms constructed largely of unshaped or shaped basalt cobbles. Interior doorways connected rooms within room clusters. The lack of exterior doorways indicates that people entered the rooms from rooftop entrances that required the use of ladders. There were no kivas or other obvious ceremonial chambers, interior courtyards, or formal plazas. However, rocks were cleared from the surface around many of the structures—perhaps for use in construction—and some of these areas are bordered by stone walls. Many daily activities, such as cooking and tool making, likely took place in these cleared areas.

The architecture of the main room block at Pueblo la Plata typifies a generally haphazard approach to building. Starting with a room block that accounts for one-fifth of the pueblo's ultimate size, the builders added sets of rooms in at least six phases of construction, ending up with seventy rooms. The rooms varied in size and were rarely aligned next to each other to create shared corners. Within single phases of building, the residents constructed some walls from shaped slabs, others from unshaped cobbles, and still others from varying combinations of both. Current information is not precise enough to determine the lengths of time between the phases of construction. Nevertheless, these architectural patterns would indicate episodes of construction by a series of family groups or immigrants, rather than a centrally planned and coordinated effort.

The people of the Perry Mesa tradition cultivated maize, squash, and other crops. They also gathered and consumed wild plants of the desert and grasslands, including various grass seeds, edible weeds, cactus fruits, nuts, and wild barley. Hunters captured deer, pronghorn antelope, bighorn sheep, and rabbits. Agave plants, spiky succulents with tall flower stalks, were an important source of food and fibers. The ancient inhabitants roasted the carbohydrate-rich hearts and stalks of the plant for food and beverages, and they extracted fibers from the leaves to create basketry and other textile products.

The narrow canyons, rocky surfaces, and clay soils posed obstacles to agriculture. The canyon bottoms did not provide much space for farming along streams. Prehistoric farmers modified the natural landscape in order to capture and retain rainwater runoff and soil within plots of farmland. They cleared rocks and used them to build low walls and alignments to create check dams, systems of artificial terraces, and bordered gardens. Archaeologists have also identified areas

An aerial view of Pueblo la Plata on Perry Mesa.   [Courtesy of the Bureau of Land Management/photo by Joe Vogel]

devoted to the cultivation of agave plants. Since agave thrives in rocky areas, rock piles were created to enhance their growth. Clusters of agave plants still exist in these ancient fields.

THE PERRY MESA SETTLEMENT SYSTEM

Each primary community on Perry Mesa and Black Mesa contained one or more large room blocks, surrounded by smaller residential and special activity sites. Six of the eight major settlements were near the rims of deep canyons, while the other two were situated in the hilly zone at the eastern margin of Perry Mesa. Inside this nearly circular ring of communities, the interior areas of Perry Mesa appear to have been used mainly for farming, plant gathering, and hunting. Although site layouts and floor plans varied, the major settlements shared obvious similarities in architecture, subsistence, and material culture. With intervening distances ranging from 3 to 10 kilometers, most were within a day's walking distance of each other.

Proximity would have supported cooperation and interdependence among the villages. Their unique environmental settings provided access to different sets of resources and opportunities, such as agricultural land, wood, concentrations of wild plant foods, and trade routes. The villages could have shared harvests to compensate for crop failures in particular locations. The ties among communities may have been reinforced through social events, intermarriage, cooperation in defense, and routine exchanges of goods.

Archaeologists have identified a network of hilltop sites that could have supported a communication system among the villages. Experiments have shown that from the structures on these high points, people could have relayed messages using smoke or other means of signaling. Horseshoe Butte, a high point near the northern edge of Perry Mesa, was visible from all of the major villages and may have served as a primary point for relaying messages.

Rock art also was an important medium of communication. The most spectacular rock art sites are near the large communities, often in dramatic settings such as the cliffs below pueblos. Archaeologists can only speculate about the meanings of the symbols pecked into the black surfaces of the basalt rocks. Petroglyphs of the Perry Mesa tradition appear to share a distinctive style that is different from the rock art styles of surrounding areas.

Similarities among the villages' art, particularly in the repetition of symbols such as the dominant and nearly identical depictions of deer and bighorn sheep, appear to support the concept of a shared social identity. Yet there are striking differences among sites. For example, the abundant depictions of human figures at Pueblo Pato are virtually absent at Baby Canyon Pueblo, where the artists favored abstract designs that are rarely seen at Pueblo Pato. Such differences could reflect distinct village identities related to the various immigrant or kinship groups that comprised local populations. The traditional migration stories and symbols of Hopi clans could shed some light on this possibility.

An aerial view of Richinbar Pueblo on Black Mesa.   [Courtesy of the Bureau of Land Management/photo by Joe Vogel]

ECONOMIC AND SOCIAL RELATIONS BEYOND PERRY MESA

The residents of Perry Mesa obtained many items through trade networks that extended for hundreds of kilometers in all directions. They imported painted pottery, primarily Roosevelt Red Ware from the east and Jeddito Yellow Ware from the Hopi Mesas about 250 kilometers to the northeast. Obsidian, a shiny, volcanic glass used to make finely crafted tools, came from sources near present-day Flagstaff, about 130 kilometers to the north. Parrot bones observed at Baby Canyon Pueblo demonstrate the extension of trade networks south into Mexico. Other items received in trade included ornaments of turquoise and marine shell. What the Perry Mesa folk offered in return is unknown.

Defensive features of these settlements indicate that external relations were not entirely friendly. The architecture and locations of the villages seem designed to monitor and restrict access by outsiders. The builders constructed many settlements at the edges of steep canyons, where entrance ways were blocked by sheer slopes, rugged terrain, or piled stone walls. Many small structures, sometimes called forts, seem to have been lookouts established at strategic vantage points on hills and canyon rims.

Some archaeologists have compared the mesas to medieval castles designed for defense against aggressors. Difficulty of access, combined with a signaling network that functioned as an early-warning system, could have supported an effective defense during a period of conflict and shifting alliances. The southern edges of Perry Mesa and Black Mesa appear to have been more heavily fortified, indicating that the people expected attacks from the south.

Considering the backwoods character of Perry Mesa, where exotic items were imported rather than produced, it is difficult to imagine why anyone would want to attack its villages. One hypothesis is that war parties from the mesas raided and stole goods from the larger, more prosperous Hohokam settlements in the Salt River valley (present-day Phoenix), provoking retaliatory attacks in response. Dr. David Wilcox and his colleagues have proposed that the Perry Mesa tradition was part of a larger system of political alliances that linked clusters of Pueblo IV period sites in central and eastern Arizona. He has suggested that the Perry Mesa settlements participated in an alliance defined as the Verde Confederacy, which linked several clusters of settlements within the Verde River watershed. Perry Mesa would represent the southwestern outpost of such an alliance.

The people of the Perry Mesa tradition left their settlements by AD 1450. Their departure may have occurred gradually as individual families moved elsewhere over a number of decades. These events represent a local example of population changes and movements that were widespread in the Southwest between AD 1300 and 1450. Populations declined dramatically in many regions, while groups migrated over long distances and gathered into fewer and larger settlements. Archaeologists are studying the complex social, political, demographic, and environmental factors that may have caused these changes.

An example of rock art images at Baby Canyon Pueblo.   [Courtesy of the Bureau of Land Management/Joe Vogel]

Environmental changes may have contributed to the settlement and abandonment of Perry Mesa. Climatic reconstructions indicate that the period between AD 1250 and 1425 was relatively favorable for agricultural productivity in the Perry Mesa region. In general, drought years were less frequent and severe during this period. After AD 1425, longer and more extreme periods of dry and hot weather may have induced families to leave the mesas.

HISTORY OF RESEARCH

Perhaps due to the presence of spectacular sites in more accessible locations, early archaeological explorers largely ignored the ruins on Perry Mesa. James W. Simmons, a local amateur archaeologist, described Baby Canyon Pueblo in 1936 when he worked for the Federal Writer's Project, a division of the Work Projects Administration, during the Great Depression. The Museum of Northern Arizona documented many sites during the 1970s in surveys of alternative routes for electric transmission lines. From 1973 to 1975, Southern Illinois University and Prescott College conducted a large-scale research project called the Central Arizona Ecotone Project. The researchers compared settlement systems within three environmental zones, including a mesa-canyon complex that encompassed Perry Mesa. The project involved extensive surveys, limited excavations, and studies of hydrology and agricultural systems.

During the 1990s, the Bureau of Land Management and the Tonto National Forest conducted extensive site mapping in order to complete a site vandalism study and a comprehensive overview of Perry Mesa archaeology.

Gerald Robertson Jr., an avocational archaeologist who served as an army captain in the Vietnam War, recognized the

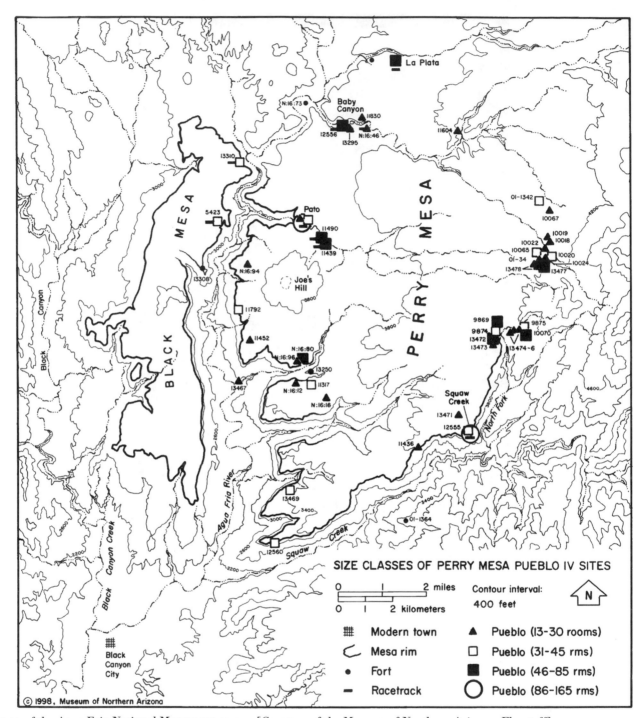

A map of the Agua Fria National Monument area.   [Courtesy of the Museum of Northern Arizona, Flagstaff]

defensive aspects of the Perry Mesa settlement system. With Dr. David Wilcox of the Museum of Northern Arizona and J. Scott Wood of the Tonto National Forest, he developed hypotheses relating to conflict, defense, alliances, and communication networks.

The designation of national monument sparked a resurgence of scientific research, beginning with a survey of 1,230 acres on Black Mesa. The Deer Valley Rock Art Center and the Arizona Archaeological Society have recorded many rock art sites, including the multitude of petroglyphs at Baby Canyon Pueblo. Dr. Katherine Spielmann, Dr. Keith Kintigh, and other researchers from Arizona State University began the Legacies on the Landscape project, which is examining the long-term environmental effects of prehistoric land uses.

Related studies include architectural mapping and analyses of agricultural fields and agave cultivation. The Museum of Northern Arizona and Northern Arizona University are completing a detailed study of the architecture, ceramics, and obsidian at Pueblo la Plata and other sites. The Center for Desert Archaeology has assisted this effort in conjunction with its large-scale study of late prehistoric communities and demographic changes throughout the Southwest.

VISITOR OPPORTUNITIES

Many sites in the Agua Fria National Monument are remote, and the rough roads require the use of high-clearance vehicles. There are no visitor centers. The Badger Springs Trail, which is very accessible from Interstate 17, offers an easy but scenic hike to the Agua Fria River Canyon, where visitors can view the Badger Springs rock art site. Visitors can also travel to Pueblo la Plata on Perry Mesa, where they can observe a large village and a defensive site called Silver Creek Fort. These sites will be the focus of future interpretive development.

Adventurous visitors can hike into backcountry areas to observe archaeological sites in natural settings that evoke a feeling of travel into the past. Maps and brochures are available at Bureau of Land Management offices in Arizona.

Further Reading: Agua Fria National Monument Web site, http:///www.az.blm.gov/aguafria/pmesa.htm; Ahlstrom, Richard V. N., and Heidi Roberts, *Prehistory of Perry Mesa: The Short-Lived Settlement of a Mesa-Canyon Complex in Central Arizona, ca. A.D. 1200–1400*, Arizona Archaeologist No. 28 (Phoenix: Arizona Archaeological Society, 1995); Huang, Jennifer K. K., *Petroglyphs of Baby Canyon Pueblo, Agua Fria National Monument, Arizona* (Phoenix, AZ: U.S. Bureau of Land Management, Phoenix District, 2005); Kuhn, Tom, "Ancient Ruins in the Stark Outback," *Arizona Highways* (November 2003): 40–43; North, Chris D., *Farmers of Central Arizona's Mesa-Canyon Complex: Archaeology Within and Adjacent to the Agua Fria National Monument*, Cultural Resources Report No. 02-339 (Phoenix, AZ: SWCA Environmental Consultants, 2002); Spoerl, Patricia M., and George J. Gumerman, eds., *Prehistoric Cultural Development in Central Arizona: Archaeology of the Upper New River Region*, Occasional Paper No. 5 (Carbondale: Southern Illinois University, Center for Archaeological Investigations,1984); Stone, Connie L., "The Perry Mesa Tradition in Central Arizona: Scientific Studies and Management Concerns," in *Archaeology in West-Central Arizona: Proceedings of the 1996 Arizona Archaeological Council Prescott Conference*, edited by Thomas N. Motsinger, Douglas R. Mitchell, and James M. McKie (Prescott, AZ: Sharlot Hall Museum Press, 2000), 205–214; Wilcox, David R., "Perry Mesa and Its World," *Plateau* (Spring/Summer 2005): 24–35; Wilcox, David R., Gerald Robertson Jr., and J. Scott Wood, "Perry Mesa, a Fourteenth-Century Gated Community in Central Arizona," *Plateau* (Summer 1999): 44–61; Wilcox, David R., Gerald Robertson Jr., and J. Scott Wood, "Organized for War: The Perry Mesa Settlement System and Its Central Arizona Neighbors," in *Deadly Landscapes: Case Studies in Prehistoric Southwestern Warfare*, edited by Glen E. Rice and Steven A. LeBlanc (Salt Lake City: University of Utah Press, 2001), 141–194.

Connie L. Stone

VERDE VALLEY SITES—TUZIGOOT AND MONTEZUMA CASTLE NATIONAL MONUMENTS

Central Arizona

Ancient History and Ways of Life in Central Arizona

The Verde River is one of Arizona's last perennial streams. It extends from the Chino valley, near modern Prescott, to its confluence with the Salt River, just north of Phoenix. The river is divided into upper, middle, and lower stretches. Each of these areas is rich in archaeological sites, but the history of research is sporadic and uneven. Some of the important research was done in the late nineteenth century, and only now are archaeologists developing a good understanding of the region's ancient history.

Most of what we know about the area derives from the middle stretch of the river—also the location of all of the reconstructed sites that are open to visitors. The area encompasses the modern towns of Sedona, Cottonwood, Clarkdale, and Camp Verde. Like much of central and southern Arizona, the middle Verde valley is hot and dry with desert vegetation, punctuated with juniper and pinyon pine at higher elevations and the linear oases of the river and creeks with their verdant vegetation.

The story of the Verde River valley is one of mixed and mingling cultures, rapidly shifting cultural boundaries, and changing ideas about cultural development. Its prehistory extends back into the Archaic period, although archaeologists know relatively little about this time (called the Dry Creek and Squaw Peak phases). It was once thought that when

Hohokam people from the Phoenix basin moved into the Verde valley, it was unoccupied. Now we know this is untrue. An indigenous culture that probably developed from Archaic roots occupied the valley during the Early Formative period, around AD 1–650.

Sometime around AD 750, during the early colonial period, the Hohokam left their homes in the Phoenix area and moved up the river valleys into promising areas. The Verde valley was one of these places. Its permanent water, rich soils, and suitability for diverse farming techniques were attractive to Hohokam farmers. They built settlements in the valley, constructing their pit houses and ceremonial facilities (called ball courts). They buried their dead in the traditional Hohokam cremation style. We lack a good understanding of how the local residents interacted with the Hohokam. Archaeologists label the Hohokam era in the Verde valley as the Hackberry, Cloverleaf, and Camp Verde phases.

By AD 1050 or so, rapid changes were taking place. The residents built aboveground masonry pueblos that differed strikingly from the pit houses of the Hohokam. Most of these were small hamlets ranging from two to twenty rooms. Instead of the red-on-buff and micaceous plain-ware (undecorated) pottery of the Hohokam era, potters made unpainted red and brown ware by the paddle-and-anvil method. In this technique, the potter makes thick coils of clay paste that will be formed into the pottery vessel, wraps the coils one atop the next into the rough shape of a bowl or other type of vessel, and literally pounds them together with a wooden paddle held on the outside and a stone or ceramic anvil held on the inside. Often this pottery was tempered with the volcanic materials characteristic of the Flagstaff region.

These changes in housing and pottery were sufficiently marked to suggest to Harold S. Colton, then director of the Museum of Northern Arizona, that this time represented a migration of Sinagua peoples from Flagstaff into the middle Verde valley. The word "Sinagua" means "without water" in Spanish and was given to the Flagstaff area because it lacked surface streams.

What did these changes mean? The most plausible explanation is that the Hohokam abandoned the area or were absorbed into the local population, who had developed masonry architecture and different ways of making containers and tools. This shift from pit house architecture to aboveground masonry took place in many parts of the Southwest around this time. Other archaeologists think that the Hohokam changed their culture radically to become the pueblo dwellers. Whichever explanation the reader may choose, there are archaeologists who also support the view.

The Honanki and Tuzigoot phases represent the era of pueblo builders in the Verde valley from AD 1150 until the region was abandoned around AD 1400–1450. Many of the pueblos built at this time were cliff dwellings tucked into the limestone, along with sandstone rockshelters marking the canyon lands bordering the valley. The so-called cavate lodges of this time typically

were small, one- or two-room dwellings built into small rockshelters. In the Tuzigoot phase, a process archaeologists call aggregation (or coalescence) brought people living in the small settlements together in large villages of 100 or more rooms.

Several sites in the middle Verde valley are open to visitors. These include Montezuma Castle, near modern Camp Verde, and Tuzigoot National Monument, near Clarkdale. Montezuma Castle National Monument includes two sites operated by the National Park Service: a well-preserved, twenty-room Sinagua cliff dwelling overlooking Beaver Creek, and Montezuma Well, located 11 miles from Montezuma Castle. Oddly, neither Montezuma Well nor Montezuma Castle had anything to do with Montezuma.

Montezuma Castle was built in the late AD 1300s or early 1400s. The monument was dedicated by President Theodore Roosevelt in 1906. Like Tuzigoot, it was excavated during the Depression years as a public-works project. A self-guided trail takes visitors to the five-story ruin, and a picnic area is located along the creek under ancient, huge Arizona sycamores. The visitors' center is open daily, in general from 8 am to 5 pm, although exact hours vary during the year. It offers exhibits and a bookstore.

Montezuma Well is a natural, spring-fed lake in a limestone sink. More than one and a half million gallons of water flow into the well every day. The water is highly carbonated and contains high levels of arsenic. At the outflow point, located on the east side of the well, water bubbles up through a cleft in the rock. This irresistible attraction drew Hohokam farmers during the eighth and ninth centuries—and later, the Sinagua residents. Farmers built irrigation ditches to carry water to their fields on the valley floor. Part of a prehistoric canal is preserved at the picnic ground, and portions of the original canal are still in use today. Pueblo rooms are built into ledges overlooking the lake. Like so many rare desert places where water flows and shines, this secret, shady oasis is a sacred place. Modern Yavapai and Apache Indians who live in the Camp Verde area link their origin story to this lake. Several Hopi clans also trace their roots to immigrants from the Montezuma Castle–Beaver Creek area. Clan members periodically return for religious ceremonies.

For information about both sites, write to Montezuma Castle National Monument, PO Box 219, Camp Verde, AZ 86322, or phone the visitors' center (928-567-3322) or the park headquarters (928-567-5276). The Web site address is http://www.nps.gov/moca.

Tuzigoot National Monument is located along U.S. 260. It is also managed by the National Park Service. This 110-room pueblo sits atop a hill overlooking the fields of the Verde River floodplain. It was occupied during the Tuzigoot phase (AD 1300 until abandonment) and represents the aggregation period. Tuzigoot, an Apache word meaning "crooked water" (a reference to nearby Peck Lake), was excavated in 1933 as a federal works project.

Byron Cummings, at that time head of the Department of Archaeology at the University of Arizona, envisioned excavation, restoration, and a public museum—one of the first public outreach projects in Arizona. The vision was realized when Tuzigoot was designated a national monument in 1939. Unfortunately, the reconstruction was not sound, and it became necessary to rebuild many rooms. Generally, Tuzigoot is open between 8 am and 5 pm; however, exact hours vary depending on the season. Exhibits and a bookstore are located in a stone building that dates to the Great Depression. To learn about visiting Tuzigoot, write to Tuzigoot National Monument, P.O. Box 219, Camp Verde, AZ, 86322, or phone 928-634-5564 or 928-567-5276. The Web site is http://www. nps.gov/tuzi.

Another exciting place to visit is the Honanki Heritage cliff dwelling and rock art site located near Sedona. Honanki, which means "Bear House," was first described by pioneer archaeologist Jesse Walter Fewkes in the late nineteenth century along with Palatki pueblo (more on that in a moment). Today, Honanki is managed by the U.S. Forest Service (Coconino National Forest). The site is open to the public seven days a week (closed Thanksgiving and Christmas). Call the Red Rock Ranger District at 928-282-4119 or 928-282-3854 before you go. Directions and further information can be found at http://www.fs.fed.us/r3/coconino/recreation/red_rock/honanki-ruins.shtml. Some local jeep tours operating out of Sedona include Honanki (but not the Palatki Heritage site) on some excursions.

The Palatki Heritage cliff dwelling and rock art site is located near Sedona, not far from Honanki, and also is managed by Coconino National Forest. The Hopi people link one of their migration stories to Palatkwapi, the place of red rocks, and some believe this refers to the red-rock country around Sedona. Palatki, which means "Red House," is open seven days a week (closed Thanksgiving and Christmas). A small visitors' center and bookstore are located a short distance from the parking lot. There are two trails at the site. One trail takes visitors to the cliff dwellings, and a second goes to the rock art alcoves. Reservations are required; call 928-282-3854 between 9:30 am and 3:30 pm seven days a week. Information is also available at the Red Rock Ranger District at 928-282-4119, Monday through Friday, 8:00 am to 4:30 pm, and at http://www.fs.fed.us/r3/coconino/recreation/red_rock/palatki-ruins.shtml.

Further Reading: Bostwick, Todd W., *Byron Cummings: Dean of Southwest Archaeology* (Tucson: University of Arizona Press, 2006); Colton, Harold S., *Black Sand: Prehistory in Northern Arizona* (Albuquerque: University of New Mexico Press, 1960); Jackson, Earl, and Sallie Pierce Van Valkenburgh, *Montezuma Castle Archaeology, Part 1: Excavations*, Technical Series No. 3 (Globe, AZ: Southwestern Monuments Association, 1954); Miller, Jimmy H., *The Life of Harold Sellers Colton: A Philadelphia Brahmin in Flagstaff* (Tsaile, AZ: Navajo Community College Press, 1966); Reid, Jefferson, and Stephanie Whittlesey, *The Archaeology of Ancient Arizona* (Tucson: University of Arizona Press, 1997); Whittlesey, Stephanie M., Richard Ciolek-Torrello, and Jeffrey H. Altschul, eds., *Vanishing River: Landscapes and Lives of the Lower Verde Valley: The Lower Verde Archaeological Project* (Tucson, AZ: SRI Press, 1998).

Stephanie M. Whittlesey

CLINE TERRACE PLATFORM MOUND AND TONTO NATIONAL MONUMENT

Roosevelt Lake Area, Central Arizona

Ancient Architecture, Ceremony, Function, and Symbolism

The Cline Terrace site (AD 1280 to 1400) was a Hohokam-style platform mound in the Tonto basin of central Arizona. Cline Terrace is one of the most thoroughly documented platform mounds in the Southwest. A modern excavation project, the Roosevelt Platform Mound Study, generated a large data set from the platform mound, as well as from three villages and two hamlet sites surrounding the mound. This data enabled detailed comparisons between a platform mound and the associated communities where most of the population lived. The three large villages and numerous hamlets were located within a 2- to 3-kilometer radius of the mound. At Cline Terrace, it has been possible for researchers to test alternative hypotheses about how platform mounds operated within the prehistoric society.

The Cline Terrace Platform Mound served a number of functions: as home to a small group of nine households, as a civic and ritual center for some fifty to seventy households living in surrounding communities, and quite possibly as a calendrical device used by the inhabitants to regulate their agricultural cycle. The mound was a center in which four different groups maintained their council chambers and where a few households resided. While the families living at the Cline Mound were accorded special recognition as elites, their authority was based on the conduct of ritual rather than economic and civic functions.

The Cline Terrace Platform Mound and its associated villages were located on Tonto Creek in the Tonto basin. The inhabitants used irrigated fields on the lower terraces and a few on the higher terraces to raise crops of corn, beans, squash, cotton, and native barley. These they augmented with the abundant wild plant foods available in the upland Sonoran Desert, including a variety of cactus fruits, tree legumes, wild greens, and the lower stem of the agave or century plant.

THE SALADO HORIZON AND HOHOKAM TRADITION IN THE TONTO BASIN

Archaeologists refer to the prehistoric ruins in the Tonto basin as both Hohokam and Salado, but these terms have different meanings. Hohokam is considered by archaeologists to be a tradition—a consistent set of cultural characteristics and traits that has great time depth and covers a single region. On the other hand, archaeologists consider Salado an example of a horizon—a set of cultural characteristics or traits that has a brief time depth but is found across multiple regions.

From about AD 100 to AD 1050, the populations living in the Tonto basin used Hohokam red-on-buff ceramics, the Hohokam style of architecture (pit houses), and Hohokam burial treatments (cremations). The culture history sequence for this period includes the Early Ceramic horizon (ca. AD 100–300) and the Snaketown, Gila Butte, Santa Cruz, and Sacaton phases (AD 650 to 1050). This sequence is identical to the comparable sequence found at archaeological sites in the lower Salt and middle Gila river valleys.

Around AD 1050, the people of the Tonto basin stopped trading for red-on-buff ceramics from the middle Gila River valley, obliging archaeologists to develop a sequence of local phase definitions specific to the Tonto basin. The people living in the Tonto basin after AD 1050 were of the same culture as those living there before AD 1050; they merely stopped trading red-on-buff pottery from the south and started trading black-on-white pottery from areas to the north. They continued to maintain contacts with other Hohokam populations living to the south and west, and they rapidly adopted the concept of the platform mound from the Hohokam in the period after A.D. 1250.

The Salado horizon crosscuts eight traditions of the desert Southwest and lasted from the late 1200s into the middle 1400s. Its characteristics include the appearance and use of Gila (Salado) polychrome and the enclosing of communities within walled compounds in those areas.

The Salado horizon lent a veneer of similarity to cultures across a wide area, but considerable variability remained in other aspects of these cultures. For instance, in the Tonto basin, the Salado horizon was associated with Hohokam platform mounds, while in southwestern New Mexico, it was associated with Mogollon Great Kivas.

Further complicating the usage of the term "Salado" is that early archaeologists used it in referring to a hypothesized population that purportedly originated in the Tonto basin and migrated from there into the Hohokam and other regions in the thirteenth century. With the accumulation of more data, however, archaeologists realized that the direction of the influence, and possibly of population movement, was the opposite. Archaeologists gradually changed the usage of the term to mean an archaeological-horizon style.

The population of the Tonto basin adopted the Hohokam architectural concept of the platform mound and began building their own at about AD 1280; it is possible that some Hohokam migrations also added to the population of the Tonto basin at that time. The situation in the middle thirteenth century was made even more complex as Sinagua, Mogollon, and Ancestral Pueblo (also known as Anasazi) migrants from the surrounding mountains also began moving into the Tonto basin.

While platform mounds were a Hohokam development, their existence reflects efficient and flexible political organizations that were capable of incorporating different populations into integrated territorial communities. These organizations were thus well suited for the multiple traditions that characterized the Tonto Basin after AD 1250. They served this function in the Hohokam region as well, where they provided a means for the Hohokam populations living on the irrigation canals to add other Hohokam groups who had been living in the surrounding desert and relying on non-irrigation agriculture.

THE ROOMS OF CLINE TERRACE MOUND

There were four general categories of rooms at the site: (1) rooms occupied year-round; (2) rooms occupied temporarily, possibly during multi-day ceremonies; (3) council chambers; and (4) rooms used to store ceremonial items and prepare for ceremonies.

Temporarily occupied rooms occurred in the outer plazas (e.g., plazas 20, 31, 95, 98, 18) of the site and were apparently used to shelter visitors who were dressed for the occasion in fine jewelry but were not concerned with processing or cooking food—probably because food for visitors was provided in the context of feasts. Four council chambers—rooms 58, 78, 93, and 137—were arranged around the perimeter of Plaza 45N and had substantially larger floor areas (45 ± 8 m²) than the residential rooms (22 ± 11 m²). Eight smaller rooms, also distributed around the edges of Plaza 45N, were used as storage and space for preparing for ceremonies.

Households at Cline Terrace

The households at Cline Terrace lived year-round in some of the rooms (category 1, listed above) located on top of the platform mound (with the exception of Room 137, a council chamber), and in plazas 45S and 159. Each household had two to three room suites. These suites included living quarters, where people sat and slept, and the floors were kept relatively free of artifacts; kitchens, where food was prepared, and grinding implements and storage vessels took up space on the floor; and store rooms, where extra supplies and surplus food were stored, and the floor was thoroughly covered by artifacts and granaries. In some households, the storage function was combined with the kitchen, thus reducing the number of rooms to two. The settlement as a whole had about nine households—six occupying rooms on top of the platform mound, two in Plaza 159, and one in Plaza 45S.

Many of the delegates to the council chambers in the Cline Mound compound came from the three large villages and additional smaller hamlets that were located within a 2- to 3-kilometer radius of the mound. The four council chambers at the platform mound were capable of seating more than 150 people—a figure much larger than the number of adults living at the mound itself.

Ranking of Households and Corporate Groups

What were the implications for households living on top of the platform mound? When the volume of the platform was included as part of the construction effort, rooms on top of the mound required ten times more material and effort to construct than rooms built at ground level. This means that about 43 percent of the energy cost to obtain materials and construct the 200 rooms in the dispersed settlements of the Cline complex was spent on 8 percent of the population living in the fourteen residential rooms on top of the mound.

The people who lived on the mound must have had considerable prestige within the larger community, as did the group that constructed its council chamber (Room 137) on the mound, to warrant this unequal expenditure of labor and materials on their rooms. In modern industrial societies, prestige is frequently linked to economic wealth and political power, but at the prehistoric Cline Terrace Platform Mound, prestige was based on ritual authority. This may seem odd, but it was characteristic of some pre-industrial societies.

ARCHITECTURE AS SYMBOL AT CLINE TERRACE

The Cline Terrace Mound was built in large part to be used as a centralized arena or stage for the holding of integrative ceremonies, and the architecture itself may have served as a symbol of the beliefs of the agricultural people who built and used the site.

In discussing the ritual drama of modern Pueblo societies in the American Southwest, Alfonso Ortiz (see, e.g., Ortiz 1972) described how key concepts of Pueblo worldview are frequently incorporated into ceremonies, either through the placement of participants or by the arrangement of architecture. Three of these concepts are (1) a tendency to move in a dominant centripetal or inward spatial orientation, related to oral traditions of migration routes; (2) a well-elaborated concept of the middle of the cosmos, usually equated with the current location of the people; and (3) an expression of dualism, of opposing parts that together form a whole.

These Puebloan concepts are expressed architecturally at Cline Terrace by (1) a counterclockwise circuit from the main entrance of the compound through the outer plazas to the center of the site; (2) the elaborate architectural emphasis placed on Plaza 45, located at the center of the site—the architectural analogue of the center of the cosmos; and (3) the special treatment given to a pair of L-shaped rooms (rooms 81 and 29) that form mirrored oppositions of each other.

The Counterclockwise Processional Route

The procession route began outside the southeastern compound wall of the site, entering through the wide gate in that compound wall into Plaza 13 and progressing from there through plazas 14, 18, 19, and 20, through a door in a high wall into Plaza 34, and finally over another high wall into the innermost plaza, Plaza 45.

The prehistoric people following this route sometimes carried pine boughs with them—which is how David Jacobs, the archaeologist who directed the excavation of the site, was able to identify the location of the route. Pollen samples were collected from different parts of the plazas, and the samples in the center of the plazas consistently had higher counts of pine pollen than the samples near the edges of the plaza, next to the walls. Since Cline Terrace is located on a valley floor in the desert, people at Cline Terrace would have had to hike 20 or so kilometers up into the surrounding mountains to find pine trees.

The walls separating the plazas may in some places have been low enough to step over, although a doorway in a high wall allowed passage from Plaza 20 into Plaza 34, and it is almost certain that at least the final wall between plazas 34 and 45 was crossed by ladders. The function of these divisions is not known.

The Central Ceremonial Plaza (Plaza 45)

The importance of Plaza 45 as an analogue for the center of creation was symbolized architecturally in several ways. It was surrounded on its perimeter by four large council chambers (features 78, 58, 93, and 137), where members of the community met for civic and ceremonial functions. There was also a spectacular tower (Feature 37) that extended out into the plaza and was faced on three sides with large, tabular blocks of white gypsum. Additionally, the northern and western faces of the platform mound bordering the processional route were also faced with tabular gypsum blocks; when polished, these surfaces would have been a startling white color in a world that was otherwise rendered in shades of brown. The tower had a second-story doorway looking out onto this innermost plaza, and on the winter solstice, sunset spectators in the plaza facing the tower could look through the doorway and see the sunset over the mountainous horizon behind the room (there was no rear wall to Room 37).

The dirt floor of the plaza itself was strewn with fragments of shell ornaments (called tinklers) made of cone-shaped shells that were strung into anklets or bracelets. Dancers wore these to make a rhythmic sound in time to their movements.

Sometime after the site was abandoned, the northeastern wall of the tower fell outward as a single unit onto the plaza floor, faithfully retaining the outline of the doorway and the linear arrangement of the gypsum slabs used as a facing on the tower. This plaza was the ceremonial center of the site; for the people who built the site, the plaza quite probably symbolized the center of their cosmos, with its alignments and divisions spatially linked.

Mirrored Dualism of Rooms 81 and 29

The two L-shaped rooms (features 81 and 29) are architectural expressions of dualism, another theme that Alfonso Ortiz (1972) identified as prominent in the worldview of Puebloan peoples in the Southwest. The interiors of both rooms were lined with white gypsum blocks—the only room interiors to be given such treatment—and each room was a tunnel or cave-like intrusion into the mass of the elevated platform mound. Only a few people probably ever glimpsed the interiors of these white-walled rooms, which were used for the storage of ceremonial items and perhaps as a place in which masked dancers prepared themselves and other items prior to a ceremony.

The entrance to Room 81 had been sealed off with an adobe wall before the site was abandoned, and within the room, archaeologists found pigment minerals, large *Laevicardium* shells (possibly used as dippers for serving the contents of the large ollas along the back wall of the room), obsidian flakes, miniature axes, and painted and plain-ware vessels concentrated around two stone-floor altars. One of the stone-floor altars is located at the back edge of the entry corridor to the room and is illuminated by the rising sun only at the time of the winter solstice sunrise.

Despite the architectural similarities between these two rooms, they were also mirror images of each other, similar to interlocking motifs commonly found on painted ceramic vessels. One room opened onto Plaza 45, the center of the site, while the other room opened onto Plaza 14, which was part of the procession route leading into the center of the site. The group using Room 29 may have had duties related to the procession, or perhaps they joined the procession at that point, while the people using Room 81 had duties involving the central Plaza 45, perhaps to receive those in the procession. The dualism of the rooms conveys the concept of two similar, but different entities—each with its own duties, but both needed for the performance of a ceremony that maintained the well-being of the community.

SUMMARY

The synchronization of agricultural activities, such as planting and harvesting of crops with the seasonal changes, is crucial to the success of any agricultural society. The construction and usage of the Cline Terrace Mound indicates it played a central role in the integration of the Salado agricultural population inhabiting the area. The architectural alignments and divisions of the platform mound site spatially link it to the land and sky; the contents of the rooms and plazas suggest the site served as the central integrative location for rituals associated with tracking important calendrical events.

VISITING PLATFORM MOUND SITES IN TONTO BASIN

Both the Cline Terrace Platform Mound (inquire locally about road conditions and crossing Tonto Creek) and the Schoolhouse Point Mound are accessible from Forest Service roads in the Tonto Basin; the USDA Forest Service Visitor Center is located along Highway 188, east of the blue arch bridge over the Roosevelt Dam and near the marina.

The Salado cliff dwelling at the Tonto National Monument, located in Tonto Basin 30 miles northwest of Globe, Arizona, on Highway 188, was contemporary with the platform mounds at both Cline Terrace and Schoolhouse Point. Formal tours of each mound are periodically available through the NPS Tonto National Monument. Drive time to Tonto Basin is approximately 2 to 2.5 hours from the Phoenix metro area and 3 to 3.5 hours from Tucson or Flagstaff.

It is against federal law to remove prehistoric artifacts from an archaeological site, even artifacts lying on the surface, and unauthorized excavations are even more damaging; please report any such activities you witness to the Tonto National Forest at the USDA visitors' center along Highway 188.

Further Reading: Archaeological Research Institute (curator of the Roosevelt Archaeological Project collections), Arizona State University Web site, http://archaeology.asu.edu; Jacobs, David, ed., *A Salado Platform Mound on Tonto Creek, Roosevelt Platform Mound Study, Report on the Cline Terrace Mound, Cline Terrace Complex*, Anthropological Field Studies, No. 36 (Tempe: Office of Cultural Resource Management, Department of Anthropology, Arizona State University, 1997); Oliver, Theodore J., "Warfare in Tonto Basin," in *Deadly Landscapes: Case Studies in Prehistoric Southwestern Warfare*, edited by Glen E. Rice and Steven A. LeBlanc (Salt Lake City: University of Utah Press, 2001), 195–217; Oliver, Theodore J., and David Jacobs, eds., *Salado Residential Settlements on Tonto Creek, Roosevelt Platform Mound Study, Report on the Cline Mesa Sites, Cline Terrace Complex*, Anthropological Field Studies, No. 38 (Tempe: Office of Cultural Resource Management, Department of Anthropology, Arizona State University, 1997); Ortiz, Alfonso, *The Tewa World: Space, Time, Being, and Becoming in a Pueblo Society* (Chicago: University of Chicago Press, 1972); Rice, Glen E., "Hohokam and Salado Segmentary Organization: The Evidence from the Roosevelt Platform Mound Study," in *Salado*, edited by Jeffrey S. Dean (Albuquerque: University of New Mexico Press, 2000), 143–166; Rice, Glen E., "Warfare and Massing in the Salt and Gila Basins," in *Deadly Landscapes: Case Studies in Prehistoric Southwestern Warfare*, edited by Glen E. Rice and Steven A. LeBlanc (Salt Lake City: University of Utah Press, 2001), 289–330;

Rice, Glen E., ed., *A Synthesis of Tonto Basin Prehistory: The Roosevelt Archaeology Studies, 1989 to 1998. Roosevelt Platform Mound Study*, Anthropological Field Studies, No. 41 (Tempe: Office of Cultural Resource Management, Department of Anthropology, Arizona State University, 1998); Simon, A. W., ed., *Salado Ceramics and Social Organization: Prehistoric Interactions in the Tonto Basin, The Roosevelt Archaeology Studies, 1989 to 1998, Roosevelt*

Platform Mound Study, Anthropological Field Studies, No. 40 (Tempe: Office of Cultural Resource Management, Department of Anthropology, Arizona State University, 1998); Simon, Arleyn W., and James H. Burton, eds., "Anthropological Interpretations from Archaeological Studies in the American Southwest," *Journal of Anthropological Research* 54 (1998).

Glen E. Rice, Arleyn W. Simon, and David Jacobs

THE MESA VERDE REGION

Southwestern Colorado
The Ebb and Flow of Ancient Settlement and Life

INTRODUCTION

The Mesa Verde region is among the most famous archaeological areas in the world. The region is named for Mesa Verde, a landform in southwestern Colorado where Mesa Verde National Park is located. Mesa Verde, which is a Spanish term that means "green table," is a small uplift where thousands of archaeological sites of ancestral Pueblo (also referred to as Anasazi) cultural affiliation are located. The most famous of these are the remarkably well-preserved cliff dwellings, including Cliff Palace, which is the largest known cliff dwelling in North America. Mesa Verde National Park, established in 1906, was one of America's first national parks, and it remains the nation's premier archaeological park. But the Mesa Verde uplift is only a small part of the larger region. The larger region is located primarily in southwestern Colorado and southeastern Utah, although it also extends into a small portion of northwestern New Mexico. This region has the highest recorded archaeological site density of anywhere in the United States.

DEFINITION OF THE REGION
AND SUB-REGIONS

Archaeologists sometimes refer to the Mesa Verde region as the "northern San Juan region." The region includes the area within which material remains are generally similar, and these Mesa Verde region remains are different in some respects from surrounding areas, for example, the Kayenta region to the southwest. The portion of the area most densely settled in pre-Hispanic times is called "the "central Mesa Verde sub-region" or sometimes "the Great Sage Plain." Finally, the area to the south, along the middle San Juan River in extreme northwestern New Mexico, is often referred to as a distinct sub-region: the Totah. *Totah* is a Navajo word that roughly translates as "between rivers," and the Totah region

is centered on the area where the Animas and La Plata rivers join the San Juan. The Totah is best known for two large sites, Salmon Ruins and Aztec Ruins.

THE HISTORY OF ANCIENT CULTURES

The Mesa Verde region has archaeological remains that date from the earliest times—the Paleoindian (earlier than 7500 BC) and Archaic (7500–1000 BC) periods—and from the historic period (best known from after AD 1776), when the area was occupied by Ute, Navajo, Anglo-Americans, and others. People who occupied the region during the Paleoindian and Archaic periods had a gathering and hunting subsistence economy, as did the Utes. Traditionally, Navajos had a mixed economy that included farming, hunting, and gathering. Settlers during the historic period relied primarily on farming and ranching along with a mix of other activities.

These early and late periods are important, but most archaeological sites (over 90 percent) in the Mesa Verde region date from between 1000 BC and AD 1285 and are associated with the ancestral Pueblo cultural tradition. The homeland of ancestral Pueblo people was a vast area that covered the southern portion of the Colorado Plateau and beyond. The Mesa Verde region is but one portion of this larger Pueblo homeland. As an archaeological culture, the Mesa Verde Pueblo people refers to the group who occupied the region from the time when maize (corn) farming was introduced until Pueblo people migrated from the region at about AD 1285.

Farmers ancestral to today's Pueblo people began farming maize in the Four Corners area around 1000 BC. Little is known about life in the Mesa Verde region for the first 700 years after the introduction of maize because few sites from this time period have been identified in the region. At about 300 BC many more sites were established in the area to the west (in southeastern Utah) and east (in the Animas River valley). In contrast, Pueblo

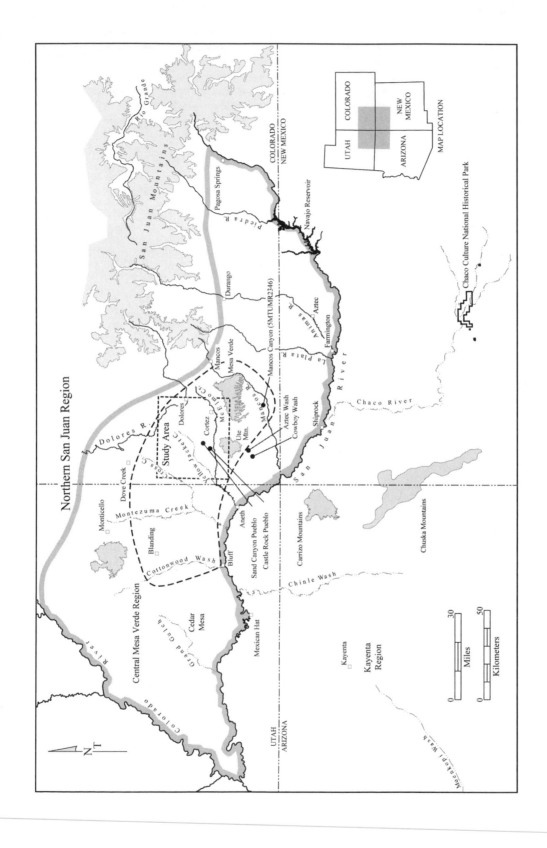

Map of the northern San Juan region showing the location of Mesa Verde, several other inportant ancient archaeological sites (filled circles), and modern towns (small dotted squares).   [Mark D. Varien]

Cliff Palace. [Mark D. Varien]

A historic photo of a portion of Spruce Tree House, probably dating to around 1907.   [Mark D. Varien]

people did not settle in great numbers on Mesa Verde or in the rest of central Mesa Verde region until about AD 600. It was at this time when many other types of artifacts and technologies made their first appearance or became more common, including pottery, the bow and arrow, domesticated turkeys, a more productive strain of corn called *mais de ocho,* and techniques for dry farming. These changes were accompanied by rapid population growth, and although population levels fluctuated over time, Pueblo people lived and farmed in the Mesa Verde region continuously from AD 600 until its depopulation around AD 1285. Pueblo people then moved south. Among the areas where they settled were the Rio Grande River valley and its tributaries, the Acoma and Zuni areas, the upper Little Colorado River drainage, and the Hopi mesas.

HISTORY OF ARCHAEOLOGICAL RESEARCH IN THE MESA VERDE REGION

The Mesa Verde region has played an important role in five important areas: (1) the development of American archaeology as a professionalized research discipline; (2) the expansion of Southwestern archaeology as a topic of broad interest to scholars and the general public; (3) the emergence of the historic preservation movement in America; (4) the

reconstruction of Pueblo history; and (5) the interpretation of human cultural evolution.

Manuel Rivera was the first Spanish explorer in southwestern Colorado in 1765. His visit was followed by the Dominguez-Vélez de Escalante expedition of 1776. Vélez de Escalante provided a description of an archaeological site near the Dolores River, and a site that fits that description is now known as Escalante Ruin.

The first thorough scientific documentation of archaeological sites in the Mesa Verde region was by William H. Holmes and William H. Jackson, who, as members of the Hayden Survey, visited the region between 1874 and 1877. Their publications, along with Jackson's photographs, served to draw national and international attention to the Pueblo sites of the region. Although they did not visit Mesa Verde proper, they documented many sites in other parts of the region, including many of the largest sites that date to the AD 1200s. Their work led to important pioneering research by others, including Morgan, Nordenskiold, Kidder, Morley, and Fewkes. But the event that did the most to bring widespread recognition to the region was the "discovery" of Cliff Palace on Mesa Verde in December 1888 by Richard Wetherill and Charlie Mason, ranchers from Mancos, Colorado (Ute Indians had earlier knowledge of Cliff Palace, but they did not make their knowledge public).

After this period of early exploration, research in the Mesa Verde region sought to develop taxonomies that classified the distribution of archaeological remains in time and space. Among others, this included the work of Jeançon, Morris, O'Bryan, and Roberts. This classificatory effort culminated in the Pecos Classification, an archaeological ordering of Southwestern pottery styles developed by A. V. Kidder in 1927 (Kidder 1962). Subsequent archaeologists sought to refine the Pecos Classification, including the documentation of important regional variation. Martin's work in the Ackmen-Lowry area, Brew's work on Alkali Ridge, and the work of Lancaster and others in Mesa Verde National Park was especially important in this regard. The 1970s ushered in a new era in archaeology: the beginning of salvage archaeology and cultural resource management. This was archaeology done to manage archaeological resources on federally owned lands, and it accounts for a significant portion of the archaeology conducted in the region between that time and the present, including the excavation of many sites and the rapid growth of the number of sites identified and recorded.

The Mesa Verde region has witnessed several of the largest archaeological projects conducted anywhere in the world: the Glen Canyon Project (1957–1963) in the far west; the Navajo Reservoir Project (1956–1964) along the San Juan-Piedra drainages in the far eastern portion of the region; the Wetherill Mesa Project (1958–1965) in Mesa Verde National Park; the Dolores Archaeological Program (DAP) (1978–1985) in the Dolores River valley; the Four Corners Archaeological Program (FCAP) (1983–1997); the Ute Mountain Ute Irrigated Lands Archaeological Project (UMUILAP) (1992–1996); the Animas–La Plata Archaeological Project (2002–2005); and a series of projects conducted by the Crow Canyon Archaeological Center (1983–present). Each of these projects has an impressive series of reports and other publications that have made the Mesa Verde region one of the most intensively studied areas in the world.

Among the most recent projects, the DAP focused on the mitigation of adverse effects, mainly destruction or disturbance, to significant archaeological sites impacted by the construction of the McPhee Dam and the filling of the reservoir; the FCAP and UMUILAP mitigated impacts to sites from the irrigation systems related to this reservoir. Together the DAP, FCAP, and UMUILAP constitute the largest archaeological project ever conducted in the United States. Their work resulted in many exemplary publications and in the construction of one of the region's most important facilities for public interpretation and the curation of collections: the Anasazi Heritage Center (AHC).

The Crow Canyon Archaeological Center was established in 1983. The center's original mission was to conduct multidisciplinary archaeological research in the context of education programs that directly involve the public in field and laboratory research. In the mid-1990s this mission was expanded to include American Indian participation in these research and education programs. Since 1983, Crow Canyon has conducted excavations at over twenty sites; implemented archaeological survey and environmental archaeology programs; created a variety of large archaeological databases, including information on over 9,000 sites in the region; developed innovative methods for reporting the results of its research on the Internet; involved over 75,000 students in its programs; and established a Native American advisory group to work with the center's staff to create educational curriculum, collaborate on research initiatives, and establish institutional policy on matters of concern to American Indians.

RESEARCH FINDINGS

Over 100 years of research have resulted in many important finds, including studies that examine the introduction and adoption of agriculture during the Basketmaker II period. This research indicates that the earliest evidence of agriculture was brought by people who migrated into the Mesa Verde region and influenced local hunter and gatherers who adopted this new subsistence strategy. The southern immigrants settled in the western portion of the region and are best known from archaeological research on Cedar Mesa, Utah. The eastern portion of the region was settled by local hunter-gatherers who adopted corn farming, once it was introduced, and this is best known from sites in the Animas River drainages and areas to the east of this river. By the late Basketmaker II period (300 BC–AD 400), people were heavily dependent on maize, as shown by studies of plant remains, human coprolites, and stable carbon isotope analysis of human bone.

Recent studies have reconstructed the population dynamics of the central Mesa Verde region. These show that there were very few people living in the region between AD 400 and 600, but population increased dramatically after this time. Between AD 600 and 1285, the population grew and declined in two cycles, one from 600 to 920 and the other from 920 to 1285. Both cycles began with low population density and ended with high population density. Both cycles began with dispersed settlement patterns where most people lived in small, single-family farmsteads; they ended with aggregated settlement patterns where most people lived in large villages. Both cycles were just over 300 years long. Finally, there was emigration from the region at the end of both cycles. The first left the area with a reduced population between AD 920 and 1060; the second left the region entirely depopulated.

Many immigrants moved into the Mesa Verde region during the Basketmaker III period (AD 600–725), and sites dating to this time period have been excavated in most parts of the region. This group set the stage for dramatic developments at the end of the first occupational cycle, especially the formation of large villages. The process of village formation began around AD 780 and ended a little over a century later. Most of these early villages had relatively short occupation spans. The primary construction materials were earth and timber, so they are not as well preserved or visually impressive as the villages constructed at the end of the second occupational cycle. The largest and best-known early villages are those excavated by the DAP in the Dolores River valley. The two largest, Grass Mesa and McPhee villages, were home to many hundreds of people, and they were therefore as large as any settlements found in the region during any period. Studies have shown that these villages formed in the context of people migrating into the Dolores River valley, so the villages were likely composed of people who came from varied places and backgrounds. Further, it has been shown that one mechanism for integrating these early villages was a ritual that included ceremonial feasting.

The Dolores villages were depopulated during a drought that plagued the region in the early AD 900s. Population remained low in most of the region throughout the tenth and into the eleventh centuries, although there are exceptions. Mesa Verde appears to maintain relatively high population levels at this time, and a few large villages have been documented in the Great Sage Plain. Population throughout the region expanded again around AD 1060. Population growth appears to be linked to the expansion of the Chacoan regional system into the Mesa Verde region. The two largest Chacoan sites outside of Chaco Canyon—Aztec Ruins and Salmon Ruins—were built between about AD 1080 and 1140. Both sites are located in the Totah sub-region, and they were almost certainly built by people from Chaco Canyon. Some interpret the construction of these buildings as a deliberate move by an elite leadership in Chaco Canyon who abandoned Chaco Canyon and eventually relocated their ceremonial center at Aztec. Chimney Rock Pueblo was also constructed in the far eastern portion of the Mesa Verde region at this time, and it too was likely constructed by people from Chaco Canyon.

Numerous smaller Chacoan sites are found elsewhere in the Mesa Verde region. At these sites the connections to Chaco Canyon are unclear and remain the subject of ongoing research. In addition, many of these sites remained occupied after AD 1140, when construction at Great House sites in Chaco Canyon came to an end. Instead, these sites in the Mesa Verde region became community centers that continued to grow in size during the twelfth and thirteenth centuries.

Population peaked in the Mesa Verde region during the mid-1200s, with the greatest population density occurring in the central part of the region. Estimating population is notoriously difficult, but it appears that there were at least 30,000 people living in the region around AD 1250. The population growth during this period was probably a combination of internal growth and immigration.

There were two important changes in settlement patterns during the thirteenth century. First, people moved the location of their residences from the mesa tops, where they were located next to the best soils for dry land farming, to the canyons, most of which were located at or near springs that supplied water for daily domestic activities. Second, more people moved from small farmsteads occupied by one or a few households into large, aggregated villages occupied by many households. The largest of these villages were Yellow Jacket, Sand Canyon, and Goodman Point pueblos; each of these was home to over 500 people. These three villages were part of a network of over sixty villages located throughout the central Mesa Verde region.

Recent research shows that the population peak during the AD 1200s was a time when agricultural production was, for the most part, below average. Below-average agricultural production was a result of colder temperatures, shorter growing seasons, and drier-than-normal conditions. Why did the population peak during a period of when the environment was deteriorating? It may be that conditions outside of the Mesa Verde region were even worse, and the region provided a refuge for Pueblo people during the thirteenth century.

These two changes in the settlement pattern—the shift in the location and size of settlements—anticipate the most dramatic change of all: the complete depopulation of the region. Recent studies have shown that population decline occurred on the periphery of the Mesa Verde region first, beginning during the early to middle 1200s. In contrast, population levels remained high in the central Mesa Verde region well into the 1270s. The latest tree ring cutting date from the Mesa Verde region is AD 1280. This suggests that the depopulation of the region was shortly thereafter. In general, the period between 1276 and 1285 was drier and colder than normal. There is also evidence of increased warfare during this decade. High population density, deteriorating climate, declining agricultural production, and increased warfare combined to create conditions that led Pueblo people to emigrate, leaving the area depopulated by about AD 1285.

Pueblo people from the Mesa Verde region likely migrated to various parts of the Southwest. It is clear that when they departed, people from the Mesa Verde region left behind many things that characterized their occupation of the area, including mugs, kiva jars, bone scrapers, small kivas, towers, D-shaped buildings, and the distinctive ground plan that was common to villages in the region. These items, which were a part of life in the Mesa Verde region, are not found in fourteenth-century Pueblo villages located elsewhere. But other lines of evidence—especially skeletal characteristics and the use of specific types of shrines to mark community boundaries—has demonstrated an especially strong connection between the Pueblo people who lived in the Mesa Verde region and pueblos in New Mexico where people speak the Tewa language. The modern Tewa villages are located along the section of the Rio Grande drainage centered on the contemporary town of Espanola, New Mexico.

MESA VERDE REGION AND PUBLIC ARCHAEOLOGY

Today the Mesa Verde region is home to several of the premier archaeological parks and monuments, with Mesa Verde National Park being the largest and most heavily visited area.

Besides Mesa Verde National Park, there are Aztec, Yucca House, Hovenweep, and Natural Bridges National Monuments, which are administered by the National Park Service. There is also Canyons of the Ancients National Monument (CANM), administered by the Bureau of Land Management (BLM); CANM is an area of over 164,000 acres with abundant archaeological resources. The Ute Mountain Ute Tribal Park is managed by the Ute Mountain Ute Tribe; it covers approximately 125,000 acres, and the tribe provides guided tours to many archaeological sites in that area. Other sites open for visitation include Chimney Rock, managed by the Forest Service, and Salmon Ruins, which is administered by the San Juan County (New Mexico) Museum Association. The Anasazi Heritage Center near Dolores, Colorado, is the primary administrative and interpretive facility for the CANM; it receives heavy use by researchers, is the primary curation facility for collections in southwestern Colorado, and provides several types of public interpretation. The Southwest Studies Center at Fort Lewis College near Durango Colorado and Edge of the Cedars State Park Museum in Blanding, Utah, also provide curation space, resources for research, and

interpretation to the public. The Crow Canyon Archaeological Center offers research and education programs on its campus near Cortez, Colorado, between March and November, and it offers educational travel programs throughout the year. All of these parks, monuments, and facilities are open to the public year-round.

Further Reading: Kidder, Alfred V., *An Introduction to the Study of Southwestern Archaeology* (New Haven, CT: Yale University Press, 1962); Lipe, William D., Mark D. Varien, and Richard H. Wilshusen, *Colorado Prehistory: A Context for the Southern Colorado River Basin* (Denver: Colorado Council of Professional Archaeologists, 1999); Lister, Florence C., *Troweling Through Time: The First Century of Mesa Verean Archaeology* (Albuquerque: University of New Mexico Press, 2004); Noble, David Grant, *The Mesa Verde World: Explorations in Ancestral Pueblo Archaeology* (Santa Fe, NM: School of American Research Press, 2006); Thompson, Ian, *The Towers of Hovenweep* (Mesa Verde, CO: Mesa Verde Museum Association, 1993); Varien, Mark D., and Richard H. Wilshusen, *Seeking the Center Place: Archaeology and Ancient Communities in the Mesa Verde Region* (Salt Lake City: University of Utah Press, 2002).

Mark D. Varien

MESA VERDE NATIONAL PARK

Southwest Colorado

History and Archaeology of an American Icon

Mesa Verde is an elevated flat table land located in the southwestern corner of Colorado, rising well above most of the rest of Montezuma County. Sloping to the south from a northern escarpment of over 8,000 feet, Mesa Verde is subdivided into a series of smaller finger-like mesas separated by deeply entrenched canyons that deliver intermittent water into Mancos Canyon, located farther south. On the top of the mesas, most vegetation consists of dense pinyon-juniper woodland with enclaves of sagebrush located in areas of deep soil and other brushy species in rocky areas, although plant growth over much of the Mesa has been impact by wildland fires occurring over the last century. These fires intensified between 1995 and 2005, prompting a decade of archaeological survey that discovered new sites and led to a better understanding of ancient land use patterns.

Much of the Mesa Verde is now part of Mesa Verde National Park, established in 1906 and closely tied to the passage of the Antiquities Act that same year. Pioneering excavations during the 1890s with the Richard Wetherill family of Mancos, Colorado, assisting Swedish archaeologist Gustaf

Nordenskiold had led to the removal of ceramic vessels and other artifacts to Europe, resulting in an outcry that supported passage of the act. Working under the auspices of the Smithsonian Institution and the Bureau of American Ethnology, J. W. Fewkes excavated many important archaeological sites in the park between 1907 and about 1920, including Cliff Palace, Spruce Tree House, Far View House, and several sites in what is now named Fewkes Canyon. His primary thrust was to open the sites for public interpretation and tourism, which often involved stabilization of the walls to prevent further collapse and enhance visitor safety.

Within Mesa Verde National Park, most of the over 4,000 archaeological sites can be dated to a period between AD 570 (Basketmaker II) and 1300 (Pueblo III). Of this number, about 600 are cliff dwellings, often very well preserved. The ancestral Puebloan residents of Mesa Verde built most of the cliff dwellings in shallow alcoves, using them between AD 1200 and 1300. Although there was an emigration from Mesa Verde near AD 1300, along with most of the rest of the Four Corners region, modern Native American descendants consider Mesa

Verde an important place where ancestral spirits dwell; thus social and religious ties remain strong.

Most of the remainder of the landform of Mesa Verde is part of the adjacent Ute Mountain Tribal Park, which includes areas adjacent to the Mancos River. A Ute Mountain Ute enterprise that focuses on tourism, the tribal park also contains many important and well-preserved cliff dwellings, including Eagle's Nest House, Two-Story House, and Lion House. An important open site is the unexcavated Kiva Point complex, which has a tri-walled structure and a Great Kiva, plus a compact block of rooms and kivas. This may show a connection with the Chacoan fluorescence. In any event, it is likely that Mesa Verde was accessed from the Mancos River corridor via the deep canyons from the Basketmaker III period onward. Although there has been some archaeological survey of the tribal park, the overall site population is unknown.

Returning to Mesa Verde National Park proper, the various elevated mesas and entrenched canyons have different characters as one considers them from east to west, which has impacted the nature of the archaeological sites. Broad, grassy valley bottoms with deep soils dominate in the eastern Prater and Morefield canyons. These two canyons were occupied for a long period, probably from about AD 700 to between 1100 and 1150. Although the Prater Canyon complex has not been studied, it is believed to be similar to the Morefield Canyon complex, partially excavated by the University of Colorado during the late 1960s. There is at least one Great Kiva, and a massive test trench extending from it exposed parts of many earlier or contemporaneous structures that show a spectrum of architectural and ceramic development lasting several centuries. There is also a reservoir that was in use over at least a century and was recently studied anew by engineer Kenneth R. Wright's paleo-hydrological team. Recent wildfires have impacted the entire Morefield Canyon area, exposing new sites and features.

The western part of the park contains broad mesa tops flanked by deeply entrenched canyons such as Soda, Cliff, Navajo, Long, and Rock canyons, dominated by sheer cliffs and alcoves. In contrast to the eastern part, there is generally little sediment in these canyons, but mesa tops still retain the deeper soil important to the agricultural groups that resided there. Two major finger mesas with dense distributions and high numbers of archaeological sites are Chapin and Wetherill mesas, and the canyons defining them are where most of Mesa Verde's famous cliff dwellings are located. Arthur H. Rohn consolidated survey information and supplemented fieldwork on Chapin Mesa, and Alden C. Hayes did the same for Wetherill. Both activities were part of the Wetherill Mesa Project, a major thrust to open that unit for visitation in the late 1950s and early 1960s, which also involved excavations at Mug House by Rohn and Long House by George S. Cattanach Jr., among others.

As part of a better-generalized knowledge base about the distribution of archaeological sites on each mesa top, Rohn and Hayes each found evidence for major communities or clusters of sites. Although these sites often lacked the tree ring dates that are used to pinpoint the time of cliff dwelling construction, most of the open (or non–cliff dwelling) sites contained ceramics that indicated they were earlier than the cliff dwellings, ranging in time from a little before AD 600 up through about 1150. By contrast, tree ring dates for the cliff dwellings almost always testify to construction at AD 1150 or later, and almost inevitably after AD 1200. The seemingly, but not certain, divergent temporal placements of the mesa top sites and the alcove sites has resulted in one enigma for Mesa Verde research—the potential contemporaneity of open and cliff dwelling sites. More precision about the chronology of mesa top settlements would aid evaluation of social, religious, and community relationships during the period after AD 1100. One example is hereditary land tenure and transfer as occupation of the landscape intensifies.

By linking survey with excavation data, Hayes studied the Badger House community on Wetherill Mesa. This site grouping ranges in time between AD 750 and 900. Overall, the architecture represents a transition from shallower pit houses to deeper ones, with a roughly contemporaneous focus on rows of rectangular surface rooms. Construction of surface rooms is quite eclectic, ranging from coursed mud with cobble hearting to mud with upright posts and often with upright slab bases. The amount of stone used in building walls increased over the years. An experimental period that is not always well dated, the Badger House community seems to have lasted longer than others in contemporaneously occupied areas. A key factor is that some of these sites were quite large, consisting of over thirty households.

FAR VIEW HOUSE AND THE FAR VIEW COMMUNITY

In his survey of Chapin Mesa, Rohn more intensively examined the Far View community first identified by J. W. Fewkes in the early 1900s. Rohn considered the Far View area to be part of the Pueblo II mesa top landscape ranging between AD 900 and 1150. Centered on Far View House but including between thirty and forty sites, this area is located a few miles north of the major cliff dwelling villages, where the escarpments are higher and alcoves are often larger. Later, the University of Colorado field schools working under the direction of Robert H. Lister, David A. Breternitz, and Jack E. Smith continued working this site grouping to better understand Pueblo II development, which seems to consist of small dispersed pueblos made from pecked and ground block construction that were grouped around one to three kivas and seemed to be the residences of successful lineages or clans.

However, there are additional important features of a few Far View sites that indicate that they probably integrated a large group of local residents. Within the community are larger sites with more elaboration in terms of public spaces and integrating architecture. These include circular towers, enclosed plazas, intramural kivas, and Chaco-style kivas with eight low pilasters and sub-floor ventilation systems. An example of a tower-kiva complex site with an enclosed plaza is Coyote Village, discovered in a dig by Smith. An unexcavated site almost identical to it is located close by. The community also includes a masonry-walled water impoundment, Far View Reservoir, formerly termed Mummy Lake. Previously studied by Breternitz and Smith, this structure and other reservoir systems scattered across the park were studied in the late 1990s by a multidisciplinary team headed by Kenneth R. Wright.

Considering these factors, the Far View community shows a potential connection to Chaco Canyon that is unusual on the Mesa Verde proper, even though the ceramics appear to have been produced locally. Far View House, a large mass of masonry at least two stories in height with a Chaco-style kiva as well as more typical Mesa Verde–style kivas, is seen as a potential Great House. Because the site has not yielded any tree ring dates and was excavated prior to development of tight ceramic sequencing, it is not known whether the site might also have been contemporaneous with the earliest of the cliff dwellings. Recent excavations in support of stabilization and preservation work show that Far View House was built over an existing structure that was filled with soil to create a construction pad. Coupled with high site densities, this fact suggests that the local populace somehow was incorporated into a more complicated social environment resulting either from internal population growth or more distant social or religious impetus.

MUG HOUSE

Excavated by Rohn as part of the Wetherill Mesa Project between 1959 and 1963, Mug House is a cliff dwelling of about 100 rooms and eight kivas, as well as a structure Rohn termed a *kihu*. Although like many cliff dwellings the tree ring dates include a smattering of earlier dates, perhaps from Basketmaker or earlier Puebloan structures dismantled to make room for the final village plan, Mug House was probably built after AD 1230. The main part of the village is on the floor of a compact alcove, but more rooms are located on a ledge above it.

In considering the architecture of Mug House, Rohn introduced the concept of room suites organized around courtyards, suggesting that each suite was occupied by a household. In a few cases, the courtyards entailed the use of kiva rooftop plazas. Furthermore, Rohn noted that the lower portion of the village was divided into what he termed two architectural "dual divisions," suspecting that they were used by social units called moieties. These assertions were based on the presence of a dividing wall that was part of normally constructed rooms but that would once have spatially separated the residents into two groups. In addition, each group had a circular structure in its half of the dwelling. This approach was novel for Mesa Verde sites that had been studied up to then.

Artifacts from Mug House include not only a large number of ceramics and stone tools but also a large number of plant parts and human coprolites (dried fecal material). These latter items allowed Rohn to examine the diet, manufacturing technology, and economy during the thirteenth century, making Mug House among the first cliff dwellings studied in this fashion.

LONG HOUSE

This alcove village seems to have served as the epicenter for Pueblo III activities on lower Wetherill Mesa. Excavated by George S. Cattanach Jr., also as part of the Wetherill Mesa Project, Long House includes about 150 rooms and twenty-one kivas, plus a large quadrilateral space that is an unroofed square Great Kiva. Cattanach also uses rooms grouped around kivas as the organizing architectural principle. Long House has three levels. There is an extensive main level divided into two major and approximately equally sized architectural blocks that flank the Great Kiva. Although most of the massive structures on the sides of the Great Kiva have fallen, a close study of the ghost lines that previously defined rooms reveals that a very high ledge above the Great Kiva could have been reached by a very short rooftop ladder. This area has a masonry wall around it with several "loopholes." The Great Kiva has a cliff behind it that leads up to an intermediate ledge housing a number of rooms and kivas. There are seeps in the area of the Great Kiva as well as on the intermediate ledge.

When Nordenskiold first encountered Long House, he noted burned human remains. Coupled with the high ledge of very difficult access and some remnants of burned buildings, he believed that the village had a defensive orientation and had been the scene of depredations and violence. Cattanach noted disarticulated skulls in one kiva. Recently, in a re-evaluation of tree ring dates, David Street proposed that the number of burned structures plus a relatively early construction date as cliff dwellings go, between AD 1150 and 1200, suggest that the village had been destroyed, perhaps somehow in relation to Chacoan incursions. Although an intriguing concept, this view would benefit from additional study at other cliff dwellings.

SPRUCE TREE HOUSE

One of the larger residential cliff dwellings at the park, Spruce Tree House is located in narrow Spruce Tree Canyon, found on Chapin Mesa. There is a reliable spring in the canyon's head. Spruce Tree House consists of about 150 rooms and about eight kivas, and was excavated by J. W. Fewkes. The ground plan forms a relatively symmetrical E-shape with two open courtyards separated by a central two-story room block. The courtyards contain kivas and are defined along the rear by two- or three-story rooms as well. The overall flavor that Fewkes depicted was one of symmetry and planned spatial use.

A recent, as-yet-unpublished study of the architecture by Joel M. Brisbin confirms Fewkes's observations but adds many new ones about social relationships within the village, which seems to have been built mostly between AD 1230 and

1250, although some level of building continued after that date. The central room block has elaborate decorated plaster, with additional ceramic-like designs incised into some of the stones. There is also a weaving room and tunnel connections to kivas in either plaza. This central location seems to have performed a pivotal role in village society or religion. Altogether, Brisbin sees evidence for between fifteen and twenty households, most often indicated by the presence of tau-shaped doorways opening onto the plazas. At the southern end are a series of living rooms without suites, suggesting the possibility of spaces to house temporary visitors. Brisbin's study should be completed sometime in 2008.

CLIFF PALACE

This most famous of the Mesa Verde cliff dwellings was excavated by J. W. Fewkes in the first decade of the twentieth century, when formal archaeological methods and techniques were only beginning to develop. Situated in an enormous alcove on the side of Cliff Canyon, the site includes twenty-three kivas and, Fewkes estimated, up to 200 enclosed rooms. The village also includes a circular tower, a four-story tower with interior painted plaster (the "painted tower"), and what Fewkes termed the speaker-chief's house. Situated prominently within the village, this latter building appears very unusual, with bi-chromatic plaster treatment. There is also a ledge that houses a series of low rooms.

In 1996 water seepage into the rear of Cliff Palace damaged the village, and Larry V. Nordby began a project to study the village more intensively, using some of the ideas developed by Rohn and other archaeologists working since the time of Fewkes. From the few tree ring dates remaining, Nordby found that although there is probably a still-buried or partially dismantled Basketmaker component at the site, much of it was built after AD 1240, and most of it postdated AD 1265, with public buildings probably added after AD 1270.

Applying the same ideas as were introduced by Rohn at Mug House, in addition to ideas about room usage and function, Nordby believed that there were about eighteen to twenty-five households at Cliff Palace, and almost the same number of kivas. Coupled with the fact that tau-shaped doorways were few and most doorways sealed from the exterior and probably were storage rooms, Nordby suggested that these households served a caretaker role for a larger group that came together periodically to carry out social or religious responsibilities at Cliff Palace. At least some of the kivas also served as residences.

Nordby also noted the presence of dual divisions at Cliff Palace, with a specialized surface room and intramural kiva-like rooms serving each of these two larger social units. As Rohn had noted at Mug House, there was a point at which it would have been necessary to walk to the front of the village to get into the other half. These two major groups coalesce at the speaker-chief structure, which actually includes Kiva Q with its bi-chromatic kiva plaster.

Cliff Palace is a Chapin Mesa structure similar to Long House, but it lacks a square great kiva. The analogous Chapin Mesa great kiva, Fire Temple, is located across Cliff Canyon in Fewkes Canyon, a very short distance to the southwest. On the rim above the confluence of Cliff and Fewkes canyons is Sun Temple, an open site that may have astronomical purpose and can be viewed from Cliff Palace's painted tower. It thus seems likely that Cliff Palace was part of a community of sites that included about fifty other cliff dwellings. Further work on these relationships continues.

OTHER SITES

Mesa Verde has been the scene of many other archaeological studies on various sites. Among these are other cliff dwellings such as Square Tower House, with its unusual "crow's nest" and Balcony House, which has very complex and difficult access that is offered as a paramount example of defensive architecture. Fewkes Canyon is home to an early residential village dating to about AD 1190, Oak Tree House. Other noteworthy sites include Big Juniper House and Two Raven House, both open villages that pre-date the cliff dwellings.

Further Reading: Cattanach, George S., Jr., *Long House, Mesa Verde National Park, Colorado*, Publications in Archeology No. 7-H, Wetherill Mesa Studies (Washington, DC: National Park Service, 1980); Fewkes, J. W., *Antiquities of Mesa Verde National Park: Spruce Tree House*, Bureau of American Ethnology Bulletin No. 41 (Washington, DC: Smithsonian Institution, 1909); Fewkes, J. W., *Antiquities of Mesa Verde National Park: Cliff Palace*, Bureau of American Ethnology Bulletin No. 51 (Washington, DC: Smithsonian Institution, 1911); Fiero, Kathleen, *Balcony House: A History of a Cliff Dwelling, Mesa Verde National Park, Colorado*, Archeological Research Series No. 8-A (Mesa Verde, CO: Mesa Verde Museum Association, 1999); Hayes, Alden C., *The Archeological Survey of Wetherill Mesa, Mesa Verde National Park, Colorado*, Archeological Research Series No. 7-A (Washington, DC: National Park Service, 1964); Hayes, Alden C., and J. A. Lancaster, *Badger House Community, Mesa Verde National Park, Colorado*, Archeological Research Series No. 7-E, Wetherill Mesa Studies (Washington, DC: National Park Service, 1975); Lister, Robert H., *Contributions to Mesa Verde Archaeology, III: Site 866 and the Cultural Sequence at Four Villages in the Far View Group, Mesa Verde National Park, Colorado*, Studies in Anthropology No. 12 (Boulder: University of Colorado, 1966); Nordby, Larry V., *Prelude to Tapestries in Stone: Understanding Cliff Palace Architecture*, Archeological Research Series, Architectural Studies No. 4 (Mesa Verde, CO: Mesa Verde Museum Association, 2001); Nordenskiold, Gustaf, *The Cliff Dwellers of Mesa Verde*, (Stockholm: P. A. Norstedt & Soners Forlag, 1893; reprint Mesa Verde, CO: Mesa Verde Museum Association, 2007); Rohn, Arthur H., *Mug House, Mesa Verde National Park, Colorado*, Archeological Research Series No. 7-D, Wetherill Mesa Studies (Washington, DC: National Park Service, 1971); Smith, Jack E., *Mesa Cliffs and Canyons: The University of Colorado Archaeological Survey of Mesa Verde National Park*, Mesa Verde Research Series, Paper No. 3 (Mesa Verde, CO: Mesa Verde Museum Association, 1987); Wright, Kenneth R., *The Water Mysteries of Mesa Verde* (Boulder, CO: Johnson Books, 2006).

Larry Nordby

SAND CANYON PUEBLO

Southwest Colorado

Ancient Life at an Agricultural Village

Sand Canyon Pueblo is the remains of an ancient Pueblo Indian village in southwestern Colorado. The village was home to ancestors of modern Pueblo people; the Pueblo nations of today are located approximately 200 miles (333 km) south of Sand Canyon Pueblo in New Mexico and Arizona. With more than 500 structures, the site is one of the largest (5.42 ac or 2.19 ha) and most archaeologically significant in the central Mesa Verde region. Tree ring dates indicate that occupation of the site began during the late AD 1240s or early 1250s and lasted until approximately AD 1280, at the end of the late Pueblo III period. The pueblo was one of the last villages constructed in the Mesa Verde region, and it was occupied until

the region was depopulated late in the thirteenth century. Sand Canyon Pueblo is one of the most intensively investigated sites from this time period in the modern era.

Ancestral Pueblo (also known as Anasazi) people have lived in the Four Corners area since about 1000 BC, when they began farming maize (corn) in the region. Little is known about the Pueblo occupation of the central Mesa Verde region for the first 700 years after the initial introduction of maize. About 300 BC, many more sites were established in the area to the west (in southeastern Utah) and east (in the Animas River valley). Pueblo people did not settle the area where Sand Canyon Pueblo would later be built until about AD 600;

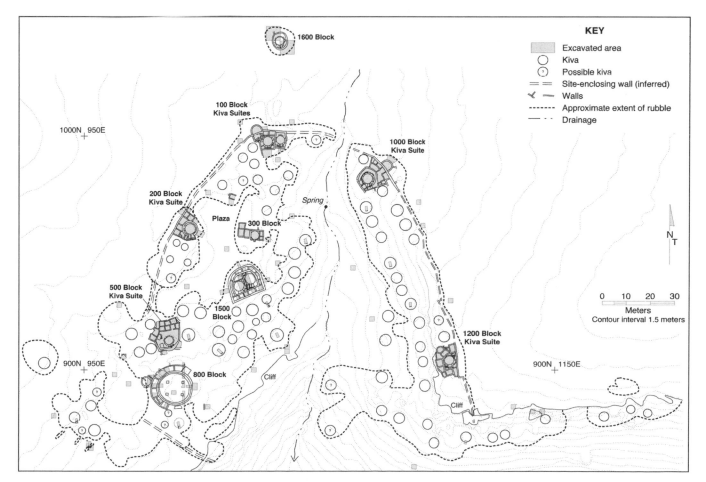

Plan of Sand Canyon Pueblo archaeological site, Canyons of the Ancients National Monument, Colorado, showing excavated structures and unexcavated areas.   [Mark D. Varien and Crow Canyon Archaeological Center]

An artist's rendition of Sand Canyon Pueblo as it may have appeared in its heyday.   [Mark D. Varien and Crow Canyon Archaeological Center]

they lived and farmed in this area until its depopulation around AD 1285. Pueblo people then moved south. Among the areas where they settled are the Rio Grande River valley and its tributaries, the Acoma and Zuni areas, the upper Little Colorado River drainage, and the Hopi mesas.

Sand Canyon Pueblo is situated around a spring at the head of a small tributary to Sand Canyon; this drainage cuts through Dakota Formation sandstone and divides the site into east and west areas. A gently rolling upland rises to the north, east, and west. The site itself wraps around the canyon rim and extends partly down the steep talus slope. At an elevation of 6,800 feet (2,073 m), Sand Canyon Pueblo is located near the top of the McElmo dome, an asymmetric structural uplift composed of a central dome and satellite anticlines. Sand Canyon is at the approximate center of the dome; the dome and its anticlines extend about 20 miles (33 km) east-west, and 10 miles (17 km) north-south. Because of the deep, eolian soils found there, the area around Sand Canyon Pueblo is one of the best dry-farming locales in southwestern Colorado and on the larger Colorado Plateau.

In partnership with the Bureau of Land Management (BLM), the Crow Canyon Archaeological Center conducted excavations

at Sand Canyon Pueblo from 1984 through 1989 and from 1991 through 1993. These excavations were supervised by Bruce Bradley; Kristin Kuckelman is the primary author and editor of the excavation report, which is published online at http://www.crowcanyon.org/publications/sand_canyon_pueblo. asp. In addition to this report, a series of journal articles and other publications examine the archaeology of Sand Canyon Pueblo, and these references can be found online at http://www.crowcanyon.org/research/research_bibliography.asp.

Sand Canyon Pueblo was one of the first sites reported in the region, with early published descriptions by T. Mitchell Prudden (1903) and Jesse Walter Fewkes (1919). The site was known then as Johnson Ruin, named for a family whose homestead was nearby. The first recordation of the site was in 1981, when it was designated 5MT765. Some stabilization was done at that time.

The first systematic site map was completed in 1983, and this map became the basis for the excavations conducted by Crow Canyon. These intensive excavations revealed that Sand Canyon Pueblo had an estimated 420 rooms, ninety kivas, and fourteen towers, as well as an enclosed plaza, a D-shaped bi-wall building, and a Great Kiva. Most of the structures are located within the arc of a wall that enclosed the site on the east, north, and west. Structures are present both above and below cliff faces, on talus slopes, and on boulders. Fourteen architectural blocks were defined, including two public buildings (a D-shaped structure and a Great Kiva). In addition, a large, generally level area in the west part of the site was defined as a plaza. The spring in the center of the site was the source of water for daily domestic activities.

Many important results have emerged from research at Sand Canyon Pueblo. Among these are studies of pottery and architecture that show the community living at the pueblo was integrated socially through rituals that included communal feasting. Public architecture in the village included a communal building (a Great Kiva), which was probably used by large numbers of people, and a building where access to ritual activity was more restricted (a D-shaped bi-wall structure).

Food remains from the site indicate that the subsistence economy virtually collapsed during the final years of occupation. This probably resulted in part from crop failures due to a series of drier-than-normal years that began in the mid-1270s and continued into the early 1280s. The subsistence data suggests that maize (corn) and turkey were the most common foods consumed during most of the occupation of the village. But these staples became scarce in the final years of occupation and wild resources—including foods obtained from a great distance from the pueblo—were utilized much more heavily.

Analysis of skeletal remains identified a male individual at Sand Canyon Pueblo who might have been a descendent of a person interred at Pueblo Bonito in Chaco Canyon during the early 1100s. The remains of the Pueblo Bonito individual were found among burials that were accompanied by abundant and spectacular grave goods, which has led to the interpretation that those individuals were among elite leaders of this impressive pueblo. Other skeletal anomalies link some of the residents of Sand Canyon Pueblo with people who lived on the Pajarito Plateau in northern New Mexico during the fourteenth century. This is striking evidence that some of the inhabitants of Sand Canyon Pueblo might have migrated southeast to that area. Finally, analysis of architecture and skeletal material indicates that conflict and violence occurred during the occupation of Sand Canyon Pueblo, and the occupation of the village ended as a result of a warfare event.

Located about 12 miles northwest of Cortez, Colorado, Sand Canyon Pueblo is now a part of Canyons of the Ancients National Monument, which is administered by the BLM. The site is open to the public for visitation. There is a beautiful walking trail and excellent interpretive signs, although the excavations have been backfilled and no standing architecture is visible. Those interested in learning more about the site also can visit the Anasazi Heritage Center for information.

Further Reading: Bradley, B. A., "Pitchers to Mugs: Chacoan Revival at Sand Canyon Pueblo," *Kiva* 61 (1996): 241–255; Kuckelman, Kristin A., ed., *The Archaeology of Sand Canyon Pueblo: Intensive Excavations at a Late Thirteenth-Century Village in Southwestern Colorado,* http://www.crowcanyon.org/sandcanyon (2003); Kuckelman, Kristin A., "The Depopulation of Sand Canyon Pueblo, a Thirteenth-Century Village in Southwestern Colorado," *American Antiquity* (in press); Ortman, Scott G., and Bruce A. Bradley, "Sand Canyon Pueblo: The Container in the Center," in *Seeking the Center Place: Archaeology and Ancient Communities in the Mesa Verde Region,* edited by M. D. Varien and R. H. Wilshusen (Salt Lake City: University of Utah Press, 2002), 41–78.

Mark D. Varien and Kristin A. Kuckelman

HOVENWEEP NATIONAL MONUMENT

Southwest Colorado

Ancient Pueblos and Dryland Farmers

Hovenweep National Monument was set aside to preserve and protect a unique set of Ancestral Pueblo (also known as Anasazi) canyon-head community complexes. These communities date between AD 1150 and 1350, also known as the Pueblo III period. Early historic period accounts of the sites reported well-preserved prehistoric masonry architecture composed of towers, multi-story living and storage rooms, and subterranean kivas. These sites were situated at the heads of many canyons containing springs or seeps that drain from Cajon Mesa southward toward the San Juan River. The well-preserved ruins were constructed with finely shaped and pecked masonry blocks of locally procured Dakota sandstone.

The monument consists of six units of various acreages. These units straddle the Colorado-Utah border in southwestern Colorado and southeastern Utah in the Four Corners area of the southwestern United States. The separated units of Hovenweep are located on Cajon mesa, which is part of an extensive flat area known as the Great Sage Plain. The mesa is broken up by numerous canyons and ridges that tend to create their own environments.

Archaeological evidence shows that the area surrounding Hovenweep has been occupied for the last 10,000 years, from the Paleoindian period (10,000–5500 BC) through the Pueblo III period (AD 1150–1350).

Photo of Square Tower structure and site, Hovenweep National Monument, Utah.   [Courtesy of Noreen Fritz and the National Park Service]

Hovenweep National Monument was created by presidential decree in 1923 upon recommendation by Jesse Walter Fewkes. The areas were designated a national monument in order to preserve and protect the ruins for the benefit of future generations of Americans. The National Park Service (NPS), Department of the Interior, was charged with the maintenance of the monument and its cultural resources. Thus the NPS has conducted and/or overseen the majority of the studies as well as the preservation of the resources.

THE SQUARE TOWER UNIT, UTAH

The largest unit of Hovenweep National Monument is the Square Tower unit, which contains the densest concentration of standing ancient architecture in the monument and is nearly 400 acres in size. Researchers believe the structures at Hovenweep were built around AD 1276 when water became scarce. These canyon-head communities were designed to protect the springs located beneath the canyon rims.

This unit is the location of the visitors' center and campground. Here visitors can proceed down a handicap-accessible walkway to an overlook of the sites in Little Ruin Canyon or continue on a 2-mile loop trail that winds around the head of the canyon. Near the canyon head is three-story Hovenweep Castle and Hovenweep House, and below the canyon rim on a detached boulder is the unit namesake, Square Tower. Other named sites within the canyon are Stronghold House, Eroded Boulder House, Twin Towers, Unit Type House, Tower Point, and Rimrock House. Directions to Hovenweep's outlying units can be obtained at the visitors' center. A four-wheel-drive vehicle is needed to access most of the outliers.

The Ancestral Pueblo (also referred to as Anasazi) inhabitants of Hovenweep practiced dry land farming along the mesa tops and adjacent to the spring-fed intermittent streams. Evidence of stone check dams and terraces along mesa-top drainages has been identified by previous archaeological investigations. Agriculture was supplemented by hunting small game and the raising of domestic turkeys. The talus slope below Hovenweep Castle contains a large amount of rubble that may represent farming terraces or additional collapsed and buried structures.

Architectural features known as "loopholes" are present in several of the walls of Hovenweep Castle. These are constructed features or portals in the walls of unknown function. Two loopholes in a room of Hovenweep Castle have astronomical significance—they mark the summer and winter solstices at sunset. It is speculated that loopholes are defensive in nature, but this has not been proven.

THE CAJON UNIT, UTAH

The detached unit of Cajon is located approximately 9 miles from Hovenweep's visitors' center. This unit is completely surrounded by the Navajo reservation, and Monument valley is visible in the distance. Remaining intact structures are two and three stories high and built directly on bedrock. These are situated around the head of a small canyon that drains to the southwest. A seep is located beneath the canyon overhang and was walled off by the Civilian Conservation Corps during the late 1930s or early 1940s to keep livestock from damaging the area around the spring. Cajon has been a part of Hovenweep National Monument from the time of its inception in 1923, and appears to have been a large habitation site. Many of the structures that originally stood on the south side of the canyon are visible as rubble mounds. In addition, several small masonry structures are preserved beneath the canyon rim where they have been protected from the elements. White painted pictographs can be observed beneath the rim, and grinding areas are present on the bedrock outside of the small structures. It is in this area that food processing likely took place, and the protected structures were probably used for storage.

Numerous loopholes are present in many of the standing walls at Cajon, particularly in Cajon Castle. Again, these loopholes may be of a defensive nature, used to monitor those approaching the site from various directions, some may have an astronomical or solar significance, or they may have been simply for ventilation.

THE HOLLY UNIT, COLORADO

The Holly site is located east of Hovenweep's visitors' center and across the Utah-Colorado state line. Another canyon-head community, the Holly site is situated at the head of Keeley Canyon and includes a large, two-story great house, a two-story tower built on a detached monolith in the canyon bottom, a "round-corner tower," several multi-room roomblocks, a rim dam, possible kiva depressions, and other archaeological features. There is no spring present at this unit but rather an intermittent drainage at the head of the canyon. For more intrepid visitors, a 4-mile hiking trail links Holly with the campground at the Square Tower unit. This trail crosses Bureau of Land Management property.

THE HACKBERRY OR HORSESHOE UNIT, COLORADO

This unit encompasses two separate canyon-head communities located less than half a mile from each other. These sites are contained within a 142-acre parcel. The Horseshoe site is the first one encountered when traversing the interpretive trail that begins at the access road. The site is located on the east spur of the west fork of Hackberry Canyon.

An isolated tower associated with the site is the first architectural feature encountered by visitors along the trail. The main site complex is located to the northeast at the canyon head. It consists of a horseshoe-shaped structure that opens toward the canyon. A large central room is surrounded by peripheral rooms. These rooms are connected to each other as well as to the central room. Below the canyon rim is an active seep, a masonry kiva constructed against the rock face that is protected by the overhang, and an adjacent storage room.

The Hackberry site is located at the head of Hackberry Canyon and is less than a quarter-mile walk from Horseshoe. The Hackberry group is one of the most impressive sites at

Hovenweep, consisting of a tower, a possible rim dam, roomblocks (rubble mounds), talus slope debris, kiva depressions (some of which may be tower-kiva complexes), and an alcove with a spring and cultural deposits. The structures were constructed with shaped and finely pecked sandstone blocks, wet-laid or dry-laid/mudded in a coursed pattern. Most of this large site is represented as rubble mounds, but the area that constitutes the whole site is quite impressive in its size.

THE CUTTHROAT GROUP, COLORADO

Cutthroat Castle is a large, late Pueblo III cluster of room blocks, towers, kiva depressions, and natural shelters clustered around a spring at the head of the lower west branch of Hovenweep Canyon, a major side drainage. The head of the canyon is relatively narrow and shallow such that the site extends from the sandstone rim-rock to the drainage bottom.

Cutthroat Castle consists of a compact tower complex that is bisected by the main drainage, which divides the site into eastern and western architectural blocks. Six towers are present, five of which are still standing. Fifteen pit structures (modern surface depressions that seem to indicate the locations of ancient semi-subterranean kivas) have been identified as well. Cutthroat Castle may represent a ceremonial center with very few residences. There may be adequate rubble present on the site to contain residential rooms.

THE GOODMAN POINT UNIT, COLORADO

The Goodman Point unit of Hovenweep National Monument is located northwest of Cortez, Colorado. This 143-acre unit is unique in the fact that it was set aside from homesteading in 1889 in order to preserve the extensive ruins, thus making Goodman Point the first prehistoric archaeological site protected by the U.S. government. There are no standing architectural remains at Goodman Point; however, the extent and scale of the masonry rubble mounds is impressive.

Goodman Point Pueblo is an extensive masonry pueblo site located on the west rim of Goodman Canyon. Juarez spring provides the focal point for the pueblo, possibly providing for the domestic water needs of the inhabitants. The site contains at least 111 kivas, thirteen roomblocks, several towers and bi-wall structural complexes, a great kiva, a dam, and a somewhat continuous village enclosing wall. Several of the roomblocks are multi-storied, making room counts somewhat difficult. The site was constructed and occupied for only a brief period of time, perhaps less than twenty years, between AD 1250 and 1280.

Further Reading: Crow Canyon Archaeological Center Web site, http://www.crowcanyon.org; Hovenweep, National Park Service Web site, http://www.nps.gov/hove; Thompson, Ian, *The Towers of Hovenweep* (Mesa Verde, CO: Mesa Verde Museum Association, 1993).

Noreen R. Fritz

CANYONS OF THE ANCIENTS NATIONAL MONUMENT

Southwest Colorado

Paleoindian to Historic Period Activities and Settlements

Located in the southwest corner of Colorado, Canyons of the Ancients National Monument sprawls a few miles northwest of Mesa Verde National Park across a landscape known as the Great Sage Plain. Tens of thousands of archaeological sites are contained within the monument's 164,000 acres, the highest site density documented in the United States.

A few sites provide evidence that the Paleoindians were here more than 8,000 years ago. Several dozen more sites include the remnants of the Archaic period hunter-gatherers who roamed the area until about 1500 BC and of the Basketmakers, who lived in subterranean shelters, called pit houses, from 1500 BC until about AD 750. More than 5,000 recorded sites are the result of intensive use by Ancestral Puebloan (also known as Anasazi) farmers who built and left behind small one- or two-roomed houses built near agricultural fields, modest-sized villages with several structures with 10–100 rooms each, and large dwellings with more than 100 rooms. Individual sites range in size from less than 1 acre to more than 10 acres. The

Ancestral Puebloans also built small cliff dwellings, Great Kivas, check dams and reservoirs to control and store water runoff, granaries, two- and three-story towers, and ancient roadways. They used large oblong trench kilns for firing pottery, and created shrines and rock art sites. Table 1 summarizes the archaeological record for this region.

From a distance, the Great Sage Plain looks like a featureless plateau but is actually incised by a dozen major canyons from 400 to 500 feet deep. Smaller side canyons further carve the plateau into a geologically complex landscape. Only three of these canyons have perennial water, although a few springs are tucked beneath the upper canyon rims and offer some relief in this dry, high desert environment. The canyons all drain into McElmo Creek, flowing westward along the southern monument boundary and emptying into the San Juan River in southeastern Utah.

The deep fertile soils of the uplands were, and still are, excellent farmland, but with only 12 inches of rainfall a year,

Table 1 Cultural Chronology for Southwest Colorado (adapted from Lipe, Varien, and Wilshusen 1999)

Dates	Periods	Distinctive Characteristics
A.D. 1300 to present	Ute	Mobile lifestyle based on seasonal rounds of hunting and gathering. Later farms in McElmo Canyon. Early sites represented by wickiups, rock art, and brown ware pottery.
A.D. 1300 to present	Navajo	Seasonal use of the area for livestock grazing and resource gathering. Hogans, sweat lodges, and distinctive pottery.
A.D. 1150–1300	Pueblo III	Large pueblos and/or "revisionist great houses" in some areas, dispersed pattern in others; high kiva to room ratios; cliff dwellings; towers; triwalls; corrugated gray and elaborate B/W pottery, plus red or orange pottery in some areas; abandonment of the Four Corners by 1300.
A.D. 900–1150	Pueblo II	Chacoan florescence; "Great Houses," Great Kivas, roads, etc. in many but not all regions; strong differences between Great Houses and surrounding "unit pueblos" composed of a kiva and small surface masonry room block; corrugated gray and elaborate B/W pottery, plus decorated red or orange types in some areas.
A.D. 750–900	Pueblo I	Large villages in some areas; unit pueblos of "proto-kiva" plus surface room block of jacal or crude masonry; Great Kivas; plain and neck-banded gray pottery with low frequencies of B/W and decorated red ware.
A.D. 500–750	Basketmaker III	Habitation in deep pithouses plus surface storage pits, cists or rooms; dispersed settlement with occasional small villages and occasional Great Kivas; plain gray pottery, small frequencies of B/W pottery; bow and arrow replaces atl atl; beans added to cultigens.
A.D. 50–500	Basketmaker II (late)	Habitation in shallow pithouses plus storage pits or cists; dispersed settlement with small low density villages in some areas; campsites important as well; no pottery; atl atl and dart; corn and squash but no beans; upland dry farming in addition to flood-plain farming.
1500 B.C.–A.D. 50	Basketmaker II (early)	Long-term seasonal use of caves for camping, storage, burial, rock art; San Juan anthropomorphic style pictographs and petroglyphs; camp and limited activity sites in open; no pottery; atl atl and dart; corn and squash but no beans; cultivation primarily floodplain or runoff based.
7000–1500 B.C.	Archaic	Subsistence based on hunting and gathering of wild foods; high mobility; low population density; shelters and open sites; atl atl and dart; no pottery.
8000–7000 B.C.	PaleoIndian	Big game hunting; high mobility; low population density; large, unfluted lanceolate projectile points; no pottery.

agriculture offered a marginal existence even in the best of times. Fields were cultivated in diverse environmental locations (e.g., uplands, benches, canyon bottoms, and slopes) to maximize the likelihood of successful crop production.

Native vegetation—pinyon, juniper, mountain mahogany, serviceberry, skunkbush sumac, drought-tolerant grasses, sage, Gambel oak, yucca, and prickly pear cactus—supplemented domesticated maize, beans, and squash and provided materials for home construction, fuel wood, clothing, and tools. Villagers raised domesticated turkeys and hunted rabbits and deer. Local clays were used to make bowls, storage jars, and mugs with intricate black and white designs. Unpainted gray vessels with corrugated exteriors as evidence of the coil technique used in their manufacture were used for cooking and for storing food supplies and water. Studies have demonstrated that local pottery was traded between villages, and some pottery was imported from Utah, Arizona, and New Mexico.

Within the monument, the Sand Canyon Archaeological District has sites representative of the mid to late Ancestral Puebloan occupation in the Pueblo II and Pueblo III time periods (AD 900–1300). Almost 1,400 sites are recorded in

this 14,500-acre area. Most sites in Sand Canyon and elsewhere are small pueblos with a few rooms, one- or two-room field houses, and limited activity or food and resource processing areas. Dozens of small cliff dwellings were built in natural shelters and have standing masonry walls.

Especially intriguing is the high concentration of pottery firing kilns on the mesa top above Sand Canyon. Over 200 kilns were recorded in a 2002 archaeological survey. These kilns were tightly clustered, usually within 350 meters of at least one other kiln. They are typically located on west or north-facing slopes and in or along shallow intermittent drainages on rocky slopes. Almost none are in agricultural soils, nor are they near habitation sites. Kiln locations may have been chosen for favorable airflow and fire control and because fuel wood was scarce near habitations. This also meant that unfired vessels had to be carried some distance from the place of manufacture (i.e., villages) to the kilns where they were fired. Given that each kiln would hold 12–30 or more vessels, between 5,400 and 6,600 vessels could have been fired during the Pueblo II and Pueblo III occupation. Overall, this reflects a significant investment in labor for kiln construction; for collection of clay and other ceramic manufacturing supplies; for

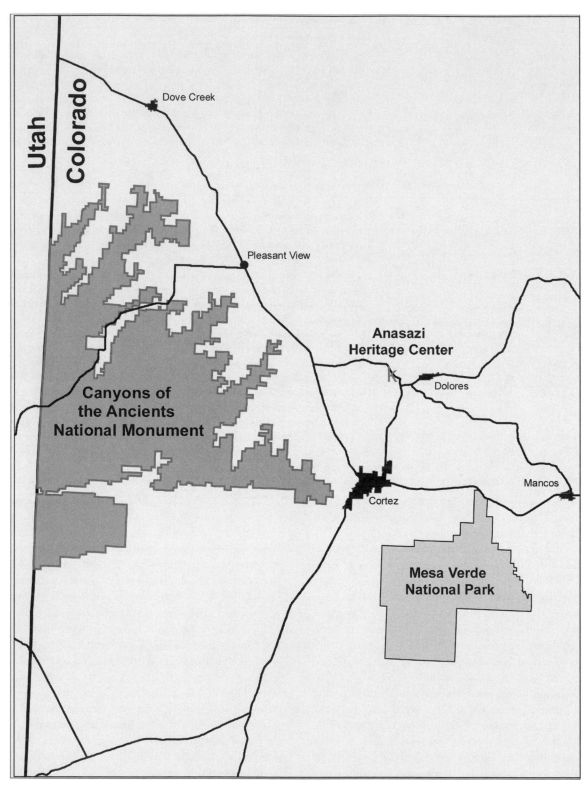

Utah

Colorado

Dove Creek

Pleasant View

Anasazi
Heritage Center

Dolores

Canyons of
the Ancients
National Monument

Cortez

Mancos

Mesa Verde
National Park

Vicinity map, Canyons of the Ancients National Monument.   [Courtesy of the Bureau of Land Management, Anasazi Heritage Center]

Cliff dwelling in the Sand Canyon vicinity.   [Courtesy of the Bureau of Land Management, Anasazi Heritage Center]

vessel manufacture and transport to the firing areas; and for gathering fuel wood and supplies for the actual firing.

Even more remarkable are the large habitation sites like Sand Canyon Pueblo, with 420 rooms and ninety kivas (subterranean rooms used for domestic and religious activities). Sand Canyon Pueblo, like other large late Pueblo III sites in the monument (and elsewhere in southwestern Colorado and southeastern Utah), is a "canyon-rim" community wrapped around the upper edge of a deep canyon and protecting a natural spring. Plazas, Great Kivas, and D-shaped structures were often incorporated into these large sites and served as places where villagers from the surrounding area could gather for ceremonies and community activities. Other common elements include north-south orientation, an enclosing wall, and a bilateral layout with two parts of the site separated by an ephemeral drainage. This site, one of about thirty-six in the monument, clearly demonstrates a shift from earlier dispersed settlements to population aggregation and a tendency to build larger habitation sites after AD 1200. Population was probably at its highest from 1200 to 1250, but tree ring dates indicate that some construction continued into the 1270s. Migration out of the area then accelerated, and by AD 1290 or 1300 the Ancestral Puebloans had moved south into northern New Mexico and Arizona.

Soon after the Ancestral Puebloans left, the Ute and Navajo took advantage of the diverse resources available on the mesa tops and in the canyon bottoms. Because of their nomadic lifestyle, there is little evidence left of their occupation except for remnants of brush shelters and forked-stick hogans.

The Canyons of the Ancients landscape has been a focal point of archaeological research for more than 125 years. Western photographer William Henry Jackson and the Hayden Survey, part of the U.S. Geological Survey, explored the area in 1874 and 1875 and produced the first photographs of ancient pueblos and towers. Just outside the Canyons of the Ancients boundary, Goodman Point was the first archaeological area in the United States set aside for protection. The first excavation in the area was conducted at Cannonball Pueblo by Sylvanus Morley of the Archaeological Institute of America in cooperation with the State University and State Historical Society of Colorado. Alfred Kidder, the "father of Southwestern archaeology," began his career surveying areas in the monument under the direction of Edgar Hewitt at Yale University. In the 1930s, Lowry Pueblo and nearby sites were excavated by Paul Martin, sponsored by the Chicago Field Museum. The 1960s saw the beginning of cultural resource management inventories and university-sponsored field schools. Investigation continues into the present with the innovative, landscape-based research

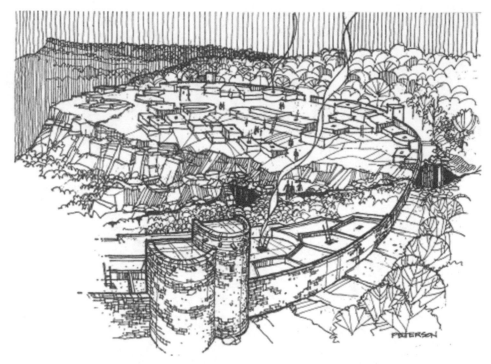

Artist's reconstruction of Sand Canyon Pueblo.   [Courtesy of the Bureau of Land Management, Anasazi Heritage Center]

Mesa Verde (Pueblo III) black-on-white mugs from Sand Canyon Pueblo.   [Courtesy of the Bureau of Land Management, Anasazi Heritage Center]

of Crow Canyon Archaeological Center and Washington State University. Throughout these expeditions, excavations, and surveys, thousands of artifacts, information, and photographs have been collected. These materials are an integral part of the resource and must be cared for in unison with the landscape.

Today, many Native Americans regard this place as their ancestral homeland. Contrary to the concept of abandonment, all ancestral places within the monument are considered a living part of Native American culture. Modern Native people maintain close ties to the spirits of ancestors who are buried and rest in peace on this landscape. Sites are visited and blessings made on a regular basis to "keep these places warm." Centuries-old oral traditions tell stories of migration, feast, famine, conflict, and comedy on this landscape, and shrines, traditional plant-gathering areas, sacred springs, and ponds of cattails are still regarded with great respect.

Public land users are attracted by the scenic beauty of the landscape; others specifically seek out ancient cultural sites and structures. Striking a balance between modern use of the landscape and the need for respect can only be achieved through education and interpretation. Site stewardship and healthy landscape programs, educational curriculum, student activities, and interpretive programs all provide opportunities to learn about and appreciate past cultures and the fragility of Canyons of the Ancients National Monument. Visitors to Canyons of the Ancients are encouraged to start at the Anasazi Heritage Center near Dolores, Colorado, where they can get an introduction to the monument and to the archaeology and history of southwest Colorado, as well as information about places to visit. Lowry Pueblo National Historic Landmark, Sand Canyon Pueblo, Painted Hand Pueblo, and the Sand Canyon Trail all have either trails or footpaths and interpretive signs or brochures available.

The monument's cultural resources reflect continuity in cultural traditions as well as adaptation to changing natural and social conditions. The longevity of human use—from the earliest hunter-gatherers to the more sedentary Ancestral Puebloan farmers and the multi-generational farming and ranching families of today—reflects the diversity and importance of this landscape.

Further Reading: Anasazi Heritage Center, Bureau of Land Management Web site, http://www.co.blm.gov/ahc/index.htm; Canyons of the Ancients National Monument, Bureau of Land Management Web site, http://www.co.blm.gov/canm/index.html; Cohn, Teresa, *Getting to Know Canyons of the Ancients National Monument* (Bozeman, MT: Watercourse, 2005); Crow Canyon Archaeological Center Web site, http://www.crowcanyon.org/; Fewkes, J. W., *Prehistoric Villages, Castles, and Towers of Southwestern Colorado*, Bureau of American Ethnology Bulletin No. 70 (Washington, DC: Smithsonian Institution, 1919); Glowacki, D. M., H. Neff, and M. D. Glascock, "An Initial Assessment of the Movement of Thirteenth Century Ceramic Vessels in the Mesa Verde Region," *Kiva* 63 (1998): 217–240; Horn, Jonathon C., *Landscape-Level History of the Canyons of the Ancients National Monument, Montezuma and Dolores Counties, Colorado*, Alpine Archaeological Consultants Inc. report submitted to the Bureau of Land Management (Dolores, CO: Canyons of the Ancients National Monument, 2004); Hovezak, T. D., L. M. Sesler, J. E. Fetterman, and L. Honeycutt, *The 2002 Canyons of the Ancients National Monument Survey, Montezuma County, Colorado*, Woods Canyon Archaeological Consultants Inc. report submitted to the Bureau of Land Management (Dolores, CO: Canyons of the Ancients National Monument, 2003); Kuckelman, K. A., ed., *The Archaeology of Castle Rock Pueblo: A Thirteenth Century Village in Southwestern Colorado*, Crow Canyon Archaeological Center, http://www.crowcanyon.org/castlerock; Lipe, W. D., M. D. Varien, and R. H. Wilshusen, eds., *Colorado Prehistory: A Context for the Southern Colorado River Basin* (Denver: Colorado Council of Professional Archaeologists, 1999); Ortman, S. G., D. M. Glowacki, M. J. Churchill, and K. A. Kuckelman, "Pattern and Variation in Northern San Juan Village Histories," *Kiva* 66(1) (2000): 123–146; Petersen, K. L., *Climate and the Dolores River Anasazi: A Paleoenvironmental Reconstruction from a 10,000 Year Pollen Record, La Plata Mountains, Colorado*, Anthropological Papers No. 113 (Salt Lake City: University of Utah, 1988); Varien, Mark D., *Sedentism and Mobility in a Social Landscape: Mesa Verde and Beyond* (Tucson: University of Arizona Press, 1999); Varien, Mark D., ed., *The Sand Canyon Archaeological Project: Site Testing*, CD-ROM version 1.0 (Cortez, CO: Crow Canyon Archaeological Center, 1999); Village Project Web site, http://www.wsu.edu/~village/.

LouAnn Jacobson

THE MARANA MOUND SITE

Tucson Basin, Southern Arizona

The Archaeology of an Ancient Hohokam Community

Just north of present-day Tucson, the Marana Mound site was one of the largest Hohokam villages in southern Arizona at AD 1250. With 800 to 1,200 inhabitants, it was a major center of the Early Classic period (AD 1150–1300). This center with an earthen platform mound was located in the midst of a multi-site "community," a Hohokam civic and territorial entity consisting of a cluster of related settlements and their surrounding land. The platform mound served as the foremost public building for all outlying settlements in the Marana community. Since the 1980s, researchers have explored the mound site and its associated community to investigate Classic period trends toward centralization and complexity in Hohokam political and economic organization.

Full-coverage survey delimited the 143-square-kilometer Marana community of dispersed hamlets and small villages stretching across the Tucson Basin between the Tortolita and Tucson mountains. Settlement of the Marana Mound site occurred within a context of population aggregation in the Tucson Basin near the beginning of the Classic period. A 10-kilometer canal from the Santa Cruz River supplied residents with domestic water. The mound center was not situated among long-established populations in the agriculturally most favorable Santa Cruz River and Tortolita Mountain edge locales, but rather in a new area lacking both irrigable land and prime opportunities for floodwater cultivation. On the driest slopes in the community, mound site inhabitants cultivated drought-adapted agave for food and fiber in extensive fields with linear stone alignments and rock piles. Due to locally limited agricultural potential, the large population of the mound site would have had a strong stake in a comprehensive and dependable system of exchange with groups living in nearby locations where agriculture was more easily pursued. Higher frequencies of exotic materials such as shell and obsidian, craft tools, and craft debris than at other sites in the community mark concentrated craft production at the mound cluster. Also indicative of exchange, its plant remains emphasize annual crops such as corn but relatively low occurrences of agricultural weeds.

The unusual preservation of the Marana Mound site in its entirety, undisturbed by urban development, farming, or extensive vandalism, affords a unique insight into the overall layout of a large Classic period center. The site covers over 3 square kilometers. Interpretations of site organization and structure are based on detailed mapping, systematic surface collection, extensive excavations in nine compounds, and test excavations in twenty-five associated trash mounds. A platform mound of moderate size was centrally placed within a dispersed distribution of thirty-five to forty compounds. The walled compounds were large by Hohokam standards, enclosing the structures of up to five or six households within areas as large as a modern football field. The compounds appear to have housed the members of persistent corporate groups with civic, ritual, and land-holding roles. Repeated remodeling and multiple floors in most rooms in all excavated compounds, tens of thousands of decorated ceramics indicating no occupations earlier or later than the Tanque Verde phase, and absolute radiocarbon, tree ring, and archaeomagnetic dates restricted to the 1200s suggest the general contemporaneity of compounds throughout the site.

Marana compound rooms were substantial structures. Calculated from a collapsed wall that fell into one of the larger structures, the floor-to-ceiling height was 9 feet. As one measure of investment in these structures, the builders regularly hauled pine and fir beams 50 kilometers from the Catalina Mountains. They carried large stones from distant sources to use as doorsteps and for other purposes. Similarly, the smaller stone pegs that bonded adjacent adobe courses in walls and the calcium carbonate added to adobe for strength had to be obtained upslope from the site.

Many rooms began as adobe-walled pit houses with floors recessed below ground level. As they were remodeled, a thick layer of clean earth fill was often placed over the existing floor as a base for a subsequent floor at a higher level. Assemblages with both intact and broken objects left on the older floor were covered and preserved by this fill layer. Several successive floors typically transformed the original pit house to a structure with its final floor near ground level. Floor assemblages (artifacts found during the archaeological excavations of these floor layers) contain numerous craft production tools and manufacturing wastes, usually indicating combined production of shell and stone ornaments, pottery, and cotton and agave textiles.

An excavation program has investigated the manner of mound construction and activities within its compound precinct that might reflect residence of elite leaders, communal ritual, or other public events. The wall of the compound surrounding the Marana platform mound was 75 centimeters wide and enclosed 2,500 square meters. Aside from the platform mound, its compound contained at least two specialized rooms, one over 100 square meters and among the largest in the Hohokam region, and a line of huge, shallow cooking pits along one side of the outer wall. The mound top supported four rooms in the residential size range that were further secluded by a high wall around the summit. Many large adobe mixing pits and multiple plaster coatings on the mound retaining wall show repeated refurbishing.

A trench through the mound revealed a massive adobe retaining wall over 1.5 meters wide around the perimeter that gave the mound a rectangular shape and vertical sides. This exceptionally thick retaining wall was necessary to hold over 1,500,000 kilograms of internal earthen fill. The mound incorporated one and possibly two pre-existing rooms within its mass, demonstrating that construction began after an initial interval of site occupation.

Residents left the Marana Mound site and the other settlements throughout its community soon after AD 1300, before Salado polychrome pottery appeared in the Tucson Basin at the advent of the Late Classic period. However, post-occupational deposits in the platform mound compound document periodic revisits to the ritual precincts of the former center. The significance of the Marana Mound site continues today as one of the best-preserved and most intensively studied examples of a major Hohokam settlement of classic times.

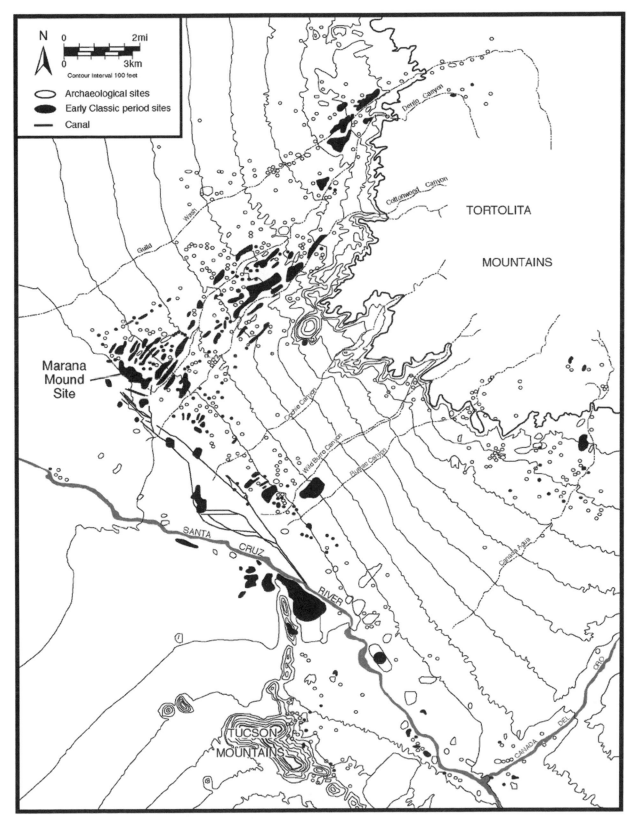

Location of the Marana Mound site near the center of the multi-site Marana community in the northern Tucson Basin.   [Paul R. Fish]

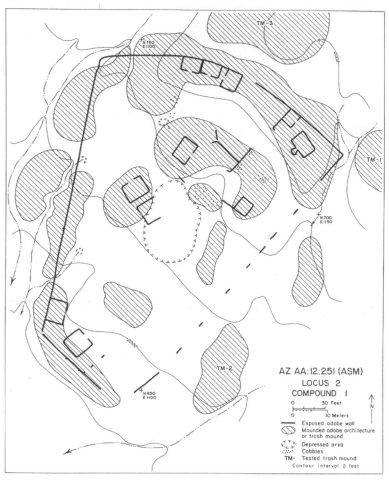

Outline of the wall of an adobe residential compound and a sample of excavated interior rooms at the Marana Mound site.   [Paul R. Fish]

Further Reading: Bayman, James M., "Shell Ornament Consumption in a Classic Hohokam Platform Mound Community Center," *Journal of Field Archaeology* 23 (1996): 403–418; Fish, Paul R., and Suzanne K. Fish, "The Marana Mound Site: Patterns of Social Differentiation in the Early Classic Period," in *The Hohokam Village Revisited*, edited by David E. Doyel, Suzanne K. Fish, and Paul R. Fish (Glenwood Springs, CO: American Association for the Advancement of Science, 2000), 245–271; Fish, Suzanne K., Paul R. Fish, and J. Madsen, *The Marana Community in the Hohokam World*, Anthropological Papers of the University of Arizona No. 56 (Tucson: University of Arizona Press, 1992).

Suzanne K. Fish, Paul R. Fish,
and James M. Bayman

PUEBLO GRANDE MUSEUM AND ARCHAEOLOGICAL PARK

Phoenix

Ancient Large Town in a Modern Metropolis

On the north bank of the Salt River in south central Arizona are the remains of a large prehistoric village occupied by the Hohokam culture for more than 1,000 years. Long abandoned when first mapped in the 1880s, this village was named Pueblo Grande (Large Town) by archaeologists, after its massive platform mound. Pueblo Grande was once more than 1 square kilometer in area and contained as many as 1,000 people.

Pueblo Grande platform mound in the thirteenth century, in an illustration by Michael Hampshire.   [Courtesy of Todd Bostwick]

Several famous archaeologists worked at the site while it was privately owned, including Adolph Bandelier, Frank Hamilton Cushing, Jesse Walter Fewkes, and Eric Schmidt. In an effort to save the site from destruction by local farmers, its central portion was donated by local citizens to the City of Phoenix in 1924. A municipal museum built by Odd Halseth in 1934 has since been expanded into a 100-acre archaeological park and museum. During the Great Depression, large-scale excavations took place under the supervision of Julian Hayden. In 1964 Pueblo Grande was declared a National Historic Landmark, and in 1999 the museum was accredited by the American Association of Museums.

Pueblo Grande was first settled in the fifth century AD, around the same time that an impressive series of canal systems were built by the Hohokam in the Phoenix region. Located at the headgates of several major canals at a bend in the Salt River, Pueblo Grande controlled the water that irrigated thousands of acres of farmland planted with maize, beans, squash, and cotton. Using only stone and wooden tools

as well as baskets, the Hohokam dug canals that were up to 9 meters wide and 3 meters deep. The earth that was removed was used to create earthen banks as high as 3 meters. Canals that originated at Pueblo Grande maintained a constant gradient over a distance of 3–10 kilometers and distributed river water to a network of secondary canals, a clear demonstration of ancient surveying skills. Pueblo Grande's strategic location allowed this village to become one of the leading administrative and religious centers in the Phoenix region.

For hundreds of years, the main type of residential structure at Pueblo Grande was the pit house, a semi-subterranean house built of wood, brush, and earth. Pit houses typically were clustered in groups, with most of the houses facing into a central courtyard. Large communal cooking ovens, called hornos, were placed outside the pit house clusters. Adjacent to groups of pit house clusters were cemeteries, most likely containing individuals who had once lived in the nearby pit houses. The patterned internal layout of Hohokam villages and their arrangement every 5 kilometers along the major canals suggest that the Hohokam practiced village planning.

In the twelfth century, the Hohokam began to live in above-ground adobe rooms, usually arranged in compounds of up to three dozen rooms. This change in domestic architecture may represent an increasing scarcity of wood, or it may reflect social changes within Hohokam society, perhaps similar to our modern gated communities.

At least two ball courts were constructed at Pueblo Grande, one of which was fully excavated in the 1950s and is currently one of the few that can be viewed by the public. Built in the eleventh century, this oval-shaped, subsurface ball court contained stone markers imbedded in its sloping plastered floor and open goals at each end of the court. The type of game played is unknown, but a stone ball the size of a modern-day baseball was found in the fill excavated from the court. After perhaps two centuries of use, the Hohokam abandoned the ball court and allowed it to fill with debris.

South of the ball court is a platform mound, one of the largest mounds ever built by the Hohokam. This structure started in the twelfth century as two small square mounds in the center of the village. Over the next 200 years the two mounds were expanded into a single rectangular mound nearly 4 meters high, not including the structures on top. Overall, its top was as big as a modern-day football field. The platform itself was constructed of rock-walled rectangular cells filled with earth and trash, the top of which was covered with plaster. Surrounding the entire platform mound was an adobe wall more than 2 meters high that restricted access to the mound.

The architecture on top of the platform mound is unique in several significant ways. There are many high walls and cumbersome patterns of access, with several rooms that have only rooftop entryways and unusual architectural spaces that are combined as units. The latter include large floor spaces; high rooms; narrow corridors; small, square rooms adjacent to larger spaces; adobe blocks, some with different colors of adobe; benches; and adobe stub walls and masonry columns in the middle of certain rooms that may have been altars. This unusual architecture combined with the presence of numerous ceremonial objects—red and green pigments, bone whistles, quartz crystals, and other ritual artifacts—suggest that the platform mound was used for ceremonial as well as administrative purposes.

North of the platform mound, the Hohokam built a "Big House," that is, a multi-story adobe tower similar to the one at Casa Grande Ruins National Monument in southern Arizona. Although the Pueblo Grande Big House no longer exists, it was recorded by Frank Hamilton Cushing in the 1880s. He noted that the building had three or four stories and was covered with a fine white plaster. Inside one of the rooms were etchings of a hunting scene and of a lightning symbol, reminiscent of Hohokam rock art located in nearby mountain canyons.

Because of its large size and long occupation, more than 2,000 human burials have been discovered at Pueblo Grande.

Careful study of these individuals has provided a wealth of information about the health and social status of the people who once lived in the village. Although there is no evidence for a state or chiefdom level of society, objects placed in the graves varied according to gender and age, suggesting some hierarchical ranking within the community.

Analysis by Douglass Mitchell of more than a dozen Classic period (AD 1150–1450) cemeteries revealed some interesting patterns. Overall, the graves of the youngest individuals—infants—contained the smallest number of ceramic vessels (about three per infant), with children's graves containing about four vessels each. Sometimes these vessels were turned upside down and placed on the child's chest. Adults also had around four vessels per grave. Curiously, some infant and child burials contained up to twelve or thirteen vessels each, similar to the maximum number of vessels for adult burials.

Adult burials tended to contain more ground-stone tools used for food processing—manos and metates—compared to those of infants and children. This was also true for spindle whorls, used for spinning fibers, and for bone awls, tools for basketry and leather working. The infrequent occurrence of utilitarian objects in the graves of infants and children indicates that they had not yet taken on adult social roles. Like adults, many of the children's burials were accompanied with jewelry ornaments in the form of various animals, including birds, snakes, lizards, or frogs, perhaps representing membership in certain lineage or social groups.

Some of the children's graves contained a number of high-status items, including copper bells imported from western Mexico, carved shell jewelry, and painted pottery vessels. A child burial on top of the platform mound had six shell bracelets on its left side, a flared-rim bowl, a scoop, black beads, and red pigment. An adolescent burial on the mound top contained offerings of maize, beans, a red jar, a scoop, a shell bracelet on its left side, and several olivella shells around its neck, probably a shell necklace. A child burial off the platform mound had five shell bracelets, a shell ring, a shell pendant, and three carved shell frogs.

A few of the adult burials also contained offerings that suggested the individuals held special status at Pueblo Grande, possibly as priests or shamans. None of these burials, however, were on top of the platform mound. A young male inhumation burial was accompanied with three ceramic bowls, a pitcher, a scoop, a projectile point, shell beads and needles, bone hairpins, several quartz crystals, red hematite, two pairs of eagle wings, and a pair of raven wings. A cremation burial contained several shell beads and broken bracelets, hundreds of stone beads, eleven obsidian nodules, more than a dozen quartz crystals, minerals, smoothed pebbles, three large pointed stones, a stone palette, a projectile point, and bird and lizard ornaments.

Quite a few Hohokam dog burials have been found at Pueblo Grande. These domesticated animals probably served as guard and hunting dogs; there is no evidence that they were used for food. Rather, faunal remains indicate that rabbits, deer, and mountain sheep were the preferred source of protein for the Hohokam. Interestingly, during the Classic period freshwater fish were added to the diet, perhaps a result of decreasing availability of game animals.

Pueblo Grande was well connected to other prehistoric cultures in the American Southwest. More than fifty different types of imported ceramics were found at the site, indicating trade with the Ancestral Pueblo (also known as Anasazi) and Prescott cultures to the north, the Mogollon and Mimbres to the east, Trincheras and Casas Grandes cultures to the south in present-day Mexico, and cultures to the west along the Colorado River. Marine shell was obtained from the Gulf of California, more than 250 kilometers from Pueblo Grande. In addition, obsidian (volcanic glass) artifacts at Pueblo Grande originated from at least ten different sources located in all directions from the village.

In the fifteenth century, before Columbus arrived in the New World, Pueblo Grande was abandoned, as were all the other Hohokam villages in the Phoenix region. The cause of this abandonment is debated, but a series of alternating floods and droughts that damaged their irrigation systems, combined with poor health and social unrest among the local populations, appear to have contributed to the collapse of the Hohokam culture. The Hohokam did not disappear, however, because the Piman-speaking (O'odham) Indians of southern Arizona claim to be their descendants. The O'odham have an agricultural lifestyle well adapted to the Sonoran Desert, and they call their ancestors the Huhugam.

Visit the Pueblo Grande Museum and Archaeological Park Web site (http://www.pueblogrande.com) for more information.

Further Reading: Abbot, David R., *Ceramics and Community Organization among the Hohokam* (Tucson: University of Arizona Press, 2000); Abbott, David R., ed., *Centuries of Decline during the Hohokam Classic Period at Pueblo Grande* (Tucson: University of Arizona Press, 2003); Andrews, John P., and Todd W. Bostwick, *Desert Farmers at the River's Edge: The Hohokam and Pueblo Grande* (Phoenix, AZ: Pueblo Grande Museum and Archaeological Park, 2000); Bostwick, Todd W., and Christian E. Downum, eds., *Archaeology of the Pueblo Grande Platform Mound and Surrounding Features*, Vol. 2: *Features of the Central Precinct of the Pueblo Grande Community*, Anthropological Papers No. 1 (Phoenix, AZ: Pueblo Grande Museum, 1994); Downum, Christian E., *Archaeology of the Pueblo Grande Platform Mound and Surrounding Features*, Vol. 4: *The Pueblo Grande Mound Compound*, Anthropological Papers No. 1 (Phoenix, AZ: Pueblo Grande Museum, 1998); Downum, Christian E., and Todd W. Bostwick, eds., *Archaeology of the Pueblo Grande Platform Mound and Surrounding Features*, Vol. 1: *Introduction to the Archival Project and History of Archaeological Research*, Anthropological Papers No. 1 (Phoenix, AZ: Pueblo Grande Museum, 1993); Foster, Michael S., ed., *The Pueblo Grande Project*, Vol. 4: *Material Culture*, Soil Systems Publications in Archaeology No. 20 (Phoenix, AZ: 1994); Mitchell, Douglas R., ed., *The Pueblo Grande Project*, Vol. 7: *An Analysis of Classic Period Mortuary Patterns*, Soil Systems Publications in Archaeology No. 20 (Phoenix, AZ: 1994); Van Gerven, Dennis P., and Susan Guise Sheridan, eds., *The Pueblo Grande Project*, Vol. 6: *The Bioethnography of a Classic Period Hohokam Population*, Soil Systems Publications in Archaeology No. 20 (Phoenix, AZ: 1994).

Todd W. Bostwick

SNAKETOWN AND OTHER SITES

Gila River Indian Reservation, Central Arizona
The Archaeology of Desert Farmers

Prehistoric agriculturalists of the Sonoran Desert recognized as the Hohokam lived and flourished in the middle Gila and Salt river valleys of Arizona for 1,000 years. These desert farmers constructed and maintained hundreds of miles of irrigation canals to water their crops of corn, beans, squash, cotton, and tobacco. Their adaptation to a desert environment and their unique cultural traits, such as red-on-buff pottery and ball courts, distinguish them from the Anasazi and Mogollon, the other major Southwestern cultural traditions.

Until quite recently, archaeologists' reconstruction of the cultural evolution of the Hohokam was based primarily on the large and well-reported site of Snaketown. A National Historic Landmark site, Snaketown is located on a terrace of the Gila River about 12 miles northwest of Sacaton, Arizona, on the Gila River Indian Reservation. The name Snaketown originates from the modern-day Akimel O'odham (River People), descendants of the Hohokam, who established a village in the same location in the 1870s and called their home *Skoaquick*—the "place of the snakes." The name of Snaketown was a good choice, unknown to the Akimel O'odham at the time, because excavations of the site revealed that the prehistoric inhabitants of Snaketown relied heavily on the use

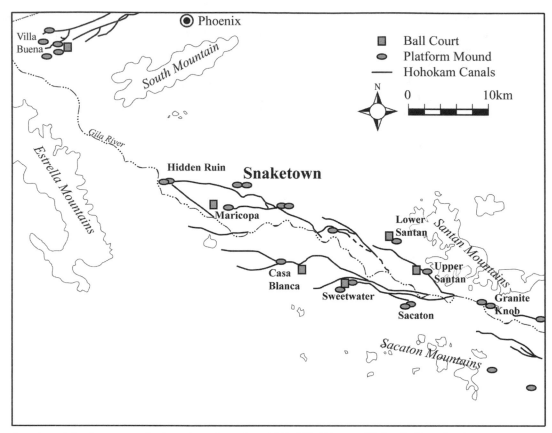

Map showing location of Snaketown and other sites along the middle Gila River.   [John C. Ravesloot]

of snake motifs in their art, as reflected in carved stone and shell artifacts and painted pottery.

Despite the importance and significance of the research conducted at Snaketown, this single-site focus or "type site" model fostered a view of Hohokam culture history that emphasized large sites that controlled smaller, lesser-developed groups who colonized areas peripheral to the Hohokam heartland. This core-periphery model of Hohokam culture was accentuated by the absence of excavation data from other large villages located outside of the Gila and Salt river valleys—the defined heartland of the Hohokam.

The distinctive Hohokam cultural pattern was first recognizable around the time of Christ, or AD 1. The major characteristics of the Hohokam culture include an integrated regional belief and ritual system, construction and maintenance of extensive canal irrigation systems, production of red-on-buff pottery, a cremation mortuary complex, long-term residential stability, a distinctive iconography, and the manufacture of exotic artifacts. The Hohokam also built monumental public architecture—earthen ball courts and platform mounds. The geographical extent of the Hohokam culture was greatest during the Sedentary period (AD 900–1200), when it covered roughly 65,000 square kilometers. A regional system of over 225 ball courts was gradually replaced during the

Classic period (AD 1200–1450) with over forty-five platform mounds. Sometime between AD 1350 and 1450, many of the sites located within the Gila and Salt river valleys were abandoned.

Two major large-scale archaeological excavations have been conducted at Snaketown. Gila Pueblo's excavations at Snaketown in 1934–35, organized and financed by Harold S. and Winifred J. Gladwin and directed by Emil W. Haury, provided the first comprehensive definition and chronological sequence for Hohokam culture. Gila Pueblo (in operation 1928–50) was a private archaeological institution located in Globe, Arizona. Three major chronological periods (Pioneer, Colonial, and Sedentary) possessing numerous 200-year phases were established on the basis of stratigraphic excavations at Snaketown, conducted in several of the site's larger trash mounds. A Classic period previously defined by archaeological investigations at the Casa Grande Ruins National Monument was not originally identified at Snaketown. In 1964–65, Haury returned to Snaketown in an attempt to reconfirm the original developmental sequence and to evaluate newly proposed schemes that had been introduced in the years since Gila Pueblo's first excavations of the site. Haury's 1960s studies also focused on gathering new data on Hohokam origins, Mesoamerican influences, and the Snaketown canal system. The 1960s fieldwork reaffirmed the original chronology developed in the 1930s but altered Haury's views about the origins of the Hohokam. Haury now believed that the origins of the Hohokam lie in migrants from Mexico who brought with them a well-developed water management technology. Archaeologists presently working in central Arizona, however, see an indigenous origin for the Hohokam culture.

Snaketown was one of the largest and likely the most important of the ball-court communities within the middle Gila River valley—what many archaeologists would refer to as a primary center. We now know that this site was the focal point of a regional ball-court system and a local irrigation community that was continuously inhabited from roughly AD 1–1100. Haury posited that the Hohokam selected the terrace above the Gila River to construct Snaketown because of the availability of fertile land to cultivate and water for drinking and crop nourishment. The Hohokam most likely also determined that its location on the highest terrace above the Gila River was a good place to settle because it had not flooded in recent memory. Snaketown proper, as defined by Gladwin and Haury, covered over 100 hectares by the Sacaton phase (AD 900). The site possessed two ball courts, multiple residential areas, and sixty trash mounds arranged in a concentric pattern around a central plaza. The trash mounds range from a height of 1 to 3 meters and a diameter of 10 to 30 meters. Their size was a reflection of the length of time they were used and the number of people who piled rubbish on them.

Providing population estimates for Hohokam sites is a difficult if not impossible exercise due to the site's open nature and absence of surface residential architecture. Hohokam archaeologists rely on the estimated number of pit houses present, number of persons per pit house, and pit-house use life (in years) to formulate site-specific and regional population estimates. In 1976 Haury estimated a peak population of 2,000 for Snaketown during the Sedentary period. In the intervening years, alternative estimates for Snaketown's population have ranged from a low of 350 to a high of 1,060 for the same period.

The large ball court excavated by Haury at Snaketown is unique for both its size and the height of its embankments. This oval-shaped ball court was formed by two parallel earthen embankments measuring 60 meters long, 2.5 meters high, and located 66 meters apart. Similar large courts have been documented at Hidden Ruin and Villa Buena. Twenty-eight ball courts have been recorded at fifteen sites located within the boundaries of the Gila River Indian Reservation along the middle Gila River. Most sites were found to possess a single small court, but nine were found to have had multiple courts. Ball courts fall into two general size groups: large and small. Large courts were oriented roughly east to west and constructed primarily during the Colonial and Sedentary periods. Small courts were constructed more often, over a longer time period, and were oriented north to south.

For decades, the commonly accepted view by archaeologists working in the Hohokam culture area was that the majority of the Snaketown settlement was abandoned at roughly AD 1100. A recently conducted large-scale archaeological survey of the middle Gila has revealed that the Snaketown settlement is much larger than the arbitrarily defined 100 hectares that constitute the National Historic Landmark site. The Snaketown community complex stretches for over 6 miles in length along the second terrace of the Gila River, with its widest point over 2 miles to the north of the river. Within this greatly expanded landscape, residential areas occupied during the Sedentary and Classic periods have been identified, as well as multitude of other types of cultural features including canals, trash mounds, and roasting pits. On the basis of this new survey data, it appears that rather than abandoning the site after AD 1100, populations inhabiting Snaketown, neighboring residential sites, and other ball-court communities located along the middle Gila River reorganized themselves into a small number of settlements possessing public architecture. The aggregation of populations into a number of fewer and larger settlements was a process that took place throughout the Southwest at this time. On the middle Gila, sites possessing public architecture were reduced from fifteen to six, and canal systems were consolidated. Multiple hypotheses have been proposed to explain this transition between the Sedentary and Classic periods, including warfare, disease, landscape change, droughts, flooding events that destroyed canal systems, and salting of fields resulting from centuries of over-irrigating.

Snaketown is recognized as an ancestral village and sacred site by modern Akimel O'odham (River People). The Gila River Indian community does not allow visitation to the site. In 2003 the community opened the Huhugam Heritage Center (http://www.huhugam.com), located at 4759 N. Maricopa Road in Chandler, Arizona, where artifacts recovered from the 1934–35 and 1964–65 excavations at Snaketown are curated. Visitors interested in learning more about Snaketown and Hohokam culture are encouraged to visit this center and the nearby Casa Grande Ruins National Monument.

Further Reading: Doyel, D. E., "Hohokam Cultural Evolution in the Phoenix Basin," in *Exploring the Hohokam: Prehistoric Desert Peoples of the American Southwest*, edited by George J. Gumerman (Albuquerque: University of New Mexico Press, 1991); Gladwin, Harold S., E. W. Haury, E. B. Sayles, and Nora Gladwin, *Excavations at Snaketown, Material Culture*, Medallion Papers No. 25 (Gila Pueblo, AZ: 1937); Haury, Emil, *The Hohokam: Desert Farmers and Craftsmen* (Tucson: University of Arizona Press, 1976); Ravesloot, John C., "Changing Views of Snaketown in an Expanded Landscape," in *The Hohokam Millennium*, edited by Suzanne K. Fish and Paul R. Fish (Santa Fe, NM: School of American Research Press, 2008); Waters, Michael, and John C. Ravesloot, "Landscape Changes and the Cultural Evolution of the Hohokam along the Middle Gila River and Other River Valleys in South-Central Arizona," *American Antiquity* 66 (2001): 285–299; Wells, E. Christian., Glen E. Rice, and John C. Ravesloot, "Peopling Landscapes between Villages in the Middle Gila River Valley of Central Arizona," *American Antiquity* 69 (2004): 627–652.

John C. Ravesloot

CASA GRANDE RUINS NATIONAL MONUMENT

Coolidge, South Central Arizona

An Ancient Community Center and American Archaeological Icon

Casa Grande Ruins National Monument consists of a large ancient Hohokam site along the southern bank of the Gila River, in the Sonoran Desert of south central Arizona. The monument is located in Coolidge, Arizona, which is about 55 miles south of the city of Phoenix and 70 miles north of the city of Tucson. The monument is administered by the National Park Service. In 1892 President Benjamin Harrison issued an executive order to legally protect the ruins; this was the first such federal preservation action in the United States. In 1918 President Woodrow Wilson proclaimed it a national monument. Today, Casa Grande Ruins National Monument covers 472.5 acres, and it has been slated for enlargement in the foreseeable future.

Casa Grande Ruins is most famous for its "Great House," a multi-story adobe building that the Hohokam constructed in a large walled compound during the Late Classic period (AD 1300–1450). The Great House had four stories, and at least eleven rooms were constructed within its massive outer walls. Several other rooms lie outside the Great House but within its compound (Compound A), which was the largest one at the settlement. To the amazement of archaeologists, the Hohokam used logs from pine trees to support the floors and the ceilings of the Great House. Hohokam laborers invested a great deal of time and energy to construct this building, since the closest pine trees were 50 miles from the site. To construct the walls of the Great House, the Hohokam added water to a mix of caliche and clay that was easily kneaded into adobe. Caliche occurs naturally in southwestern desert soils, and it consists of clay, sand, and calcium carbonate. However, the Hohokam did not make adobe bricks to construct their buildings (e.g., the Great House), as did some Ancestral Pueblo societies to the northeast. Instead, Hohokam artisans compressed adobe into walls that quickly dried in the desert sun. There is no evidence that wooden frames or molds were used to form the walls.

Scholars estimate that the Hohokam used about 2,800 tons of adobe to construct the Great House at Casa Grande. Scientific studies confirm that caliche is more abundant in the Great House than in any other Hohokam adobe building in south central Arizona. This study also indicates that adobe walls with large amounts of caliche are quite durable, which suggests that Hohokam at Casa Grande intended for the Great House to withstand the wear and tear of nature's elements; indeed, it is the only one that that is still standing today in Arizona. Once the walls and floors were constructed, they were evidently plastered and covered with several layers of paint. The color of the paint varied, including tan, pink, and dark red.

Archaeologists have long wondered why the Great House was made, since it was probably the largest building ever constructed in Hohokam society. Researchers have proposed a variety of ideas about its purpose, for example, that it was a chief's house, a religious temple, a storage granary, an astronomical observatory, or a defensive fort. Archaeologists who have studied the Great House believe that it was constructed rapidly by a powerful chief who mobilized a sizable labor force. Whether or not the Great House was constructed rapidly, it is a remarkable achievement for a pre-industrial society that lacked the wheel, draft animals, and a system of writing. The geometric symmetry of the Great House reflects Hohokam knowledge and skill in architecture and engineering.

Casa Grande Ruins National Monument also includes remains of fourteen walled compounds with plazas, single- and multi-story rooms, burial grounds, two platform mounds, and trash dumps. Ancient people at Casa Grande would have used the adobe buildings to house their families and for various activities such as food preparation, pottery making, marine shell ornament manufacture, storage of corn and other food, and perhaps religious services. The Hohokam also constructed and used a ball court at the settlement. Although such facilities were used for competitive games, other activities probably took place in their vicinity, including the exchange of food, pottery, and other goods. The second largest compound at the site (Compound B) included two large earthen platform mounds.

Burial styles at the site include both cremations and extended inhumations; examples of valuable burial goods include pottery vessels, marine shell ornaments, and obsidian. The Hohokam painted colorful (i.e., red, yellow, white, and black) murals inside the so-called Clan House at Casa Grande. According to Jesse W. Fewkes, the excavator of the Clan House, the mural images included geometric designs, birds, and other animals. The Clan House also had a sarcophagus (burial crypt) with an extended burial. A variety of offerings had been deposited with the burial, including arrowpoints and colorful pigments.

Irrigation canals for watering crops, such as maize and beans, also crosscut the site. The surface of the monument is littered with broken pottery vessels, stone tool debris, fragments of marine shell jewelry, oven stones, corn-grinding

Great House at Casa Grande Ruins National Monument. [Courtesy of Western Archeological and Conservation Center, the National Park Service]

implements (i.e., *manos* and *metates*), and many other kinds of artifacts.

HOHOKAM ECONOMY AND CULTURE

Although Hohokam artifacts have been found across much of southern Arizona and in Sonora, Mexico, their archaeological sites are concentrated near the confluence of the Salt and Gila rivers and along the Santa Cruz River. The Hohokam made a living by farming, gathering wild plants, and hunting game. Plant remains in archaeological sites reveal that ancient diets focused on domesticated plants such as maize, squash, beans, and agave, along with wild cactus fruit and seeds from grasses, shrubs, and trees. People in Hohokam society were aggregated into towns, villages, and farming settlements along the large streams and rivers in south central Arizona. Smaller groups of Hohokam also lived in outlying desert settlements where year-round water for human consumption and watering crops was relatively scarce.

Archaeologists divide Hohokam history into three major periods of time: the pre-Classic period (ca. AD 700–1200), Early Classic period (AD 1200–1300), and Late Classic period (AD 1300–1450). While the Hohokam are especially notable for their red-on-buff pottery, they also made red ware (and later) polychrome pottery containers. Hohokam red-on-buff pottery was made with clay that became beige (buff) in color as it was hardened through fire. This buff color contrasted with the red decorations that were painted on pottery jars and bowls before they were fired in open-air kilns of burning wood.

During the pre-Classic period, Hohokam families constructed their houses in shallow pits in the desert floor. Such pit houses offered insulation from hot days and cool evening temperatures. Hohokam people also built and used ball courts in most large villages during this period. Arizona archaeologists have discovered these ball courts as far north as the town of Flagstaff and as far south as the city of Tucson and its neighboring mountains. Researchers believe that these facilities, which are generally similar to ancient courts in Mesoamerica, were used for ball games that some people in Central America still play today. Interestingly, an ancient rubber ball was discovered near a ball court at Casa Grande Ruins National Monument.

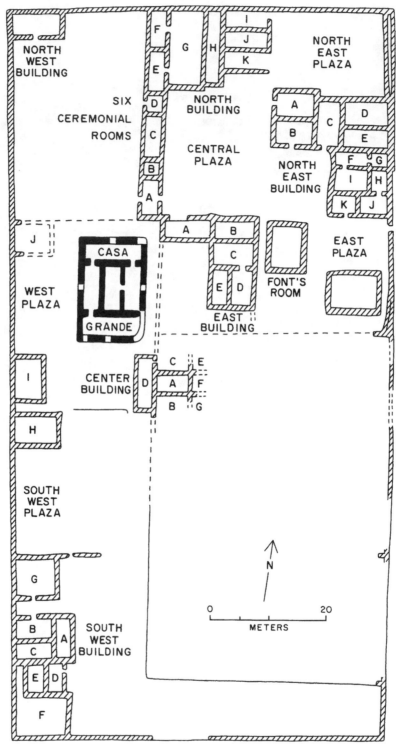

Plan of the Great House and its compound at Casa Grande Ruins National Monument.   [Adapted from Wilcox and Shenk (1977, 167)]

With the onset of the Early Classic period, Hohokam families constructed above-ground pueblo houses of adobe and/or stone; they also built platform mounds rather than ball courts. Archaeologists have long debated the functions of platform mounds in Hohokam society. Some archaeologists contend that the Hohokam used platform mounds as religious shrines, whereas other archaeologists argue that elite political leaders lived atop mounds with their families. Ancient Hohokam often left rare and exotic artifacts on their platform mounds. These special goods include quartz crystals, oddly shaped concretions, turquoise beads, polished stone ax heads, and pottery vessels that are shaped like plants with hallucinogenic properties, such as datura (jimson weed). The discovery of such artifacts supports the contention that mounds were used for religious and ceremonial activities. The rooms and building on top of some platform mounds often have items that could be used to prepare and consume meals, such as hearths, pottery bowls and jars, and manos and metates for grinding corn and seeds into flour. Human burials on many mounds, including men, women, and young children, reveal that elite families retained control of mounds for several generations. By the Late Classic period (AD 1300–1450), many Hohokam communities had enlarged their platform mounds. Only in a few large towns (e.g., Casa Grande, Los Muertos, and Pueblo Grande) did they construct monumental Great Houses.

ARCHAEOLOGICAL FINDINGS AT CASA GRANDE

In November 1694 Father Eusebio Francisco Kino and his Piman Indian guides observed the Great House at Casa Grande as they traveled to the Gila River valley. Kino held a religious mass inside the Great House as his awestruck companions left behind offerings of arrows, colorful feathers, and other valuable goods. Many archaeologists assume that the Hohokam had already abandoned Casa Grande when Kino visited the site; more than one early Spanish observer noted that it was (apparently) unoccupied in the late seventeenth century. The site remained unoccupied when it was visited in 1884 by Adolph Bandelier, a famed explorer and scholar.

The earliest archaeological studies at Casa Grande were conducted in the late nineteenth century and early twentieth century by employees of the Bureau of American Ethnology (then an agency of the Smithsonian Institution): Frank H. Cushing, Cosmos Mindeleff, and Jesse W. Fewkes. Although Jesse W. Fewkes conducted the most intensive excavations at the site in 1906, his work was undertaken before techniques of modern field archaeology (such as sieving or screening) were adopted across the Southwest. Fortunately, in 1927, the Gila Pueblo Foundation (under the direction of Harold Gladwin) conducted more systematic excavations at Casa Grande and neighboring sites to determine their ages. Shortly thereafter (in 1930 and 1931), Arthur Woodward and Irwin Hayden conducted additional scientific excavations at Casa Grande and neighboring locations under sponsorship from the Los Angeles Museum. Gladwin and his team of fieldworkers conducted careful excavations at Casa Grande, and its relative chronological age was refined with an analysis of decorated pottery.

Archaeological fieldwork in the nineteenth and twentieth centuries has unearthed a variety of rare artifacts from the site, such as shell-and-turquoise pendants, turquoise beads, wooden hoes and "swords," "charm stones" (natural pebbles with unusual shapes), red and yellow ocher, gourds, marine shell trumpets, quartz crystals, and charred textiles. Iron pyrite mirrors and copper bells imported from Mexico have also been excavated from Casa Grande. The discovery of spindle whorls reveals that the Hohokam made textiles at the settlement. Residents of Casa Grande engaged in far-flung trade networks to acquire non-local pottery and obsidian. This non-local pottery was acquired from Ancestral Puebloan societies in northern Arizona, west central New Mexico, and elsewhere in the greater Southwest. The Hohokam must have greatly valued this non-local pottery, because it was imported over great distances. The Hohokam at Casa Grande, like other southwestern societies, used black obsidian to manufacture exceptionally sharp tools, such as arrow points and knives. Geochemical studies confirm that obsidian at Casa Grande was imported across great distances in the Southwest: it originated from at least eight locations, including the Mexican state of Sonora, southwestern and northern Arizona, and west central New Mexico. The Hohokam surely valued obsidian, considering the effort they undertook to acquire it.

Several archaeologists after Gladwin undertook excavations at the monument during the remainder of the twentieth century with support or sponsorship by the Civil Works Administration, the National Park Service, and the Arizona State Museum. Most recent excavations just outside the monument indicate that Casa Grande's founders hailed from the neighboring village, which today is called the Grewe site. Together, Casa Grande and Grewe cover at least 2 square miles, making this one of the largest ancient residential complexes in the American Southwest.

The Great House overlooks one of the largest expanses of irrigable farmland in the valley, and it was located at the end of an ancient canal 32 kilometers long. Casa Grande's size and superb farming location suggests that it was a powerful economic and political center in Hohokam society. Archaeologists have also documented ten canal segments in the vicinity of the monument. Interestingly, the Hohokam constructed several other platform mound settlements along this canal and in desert areas in the greater vicinity of Casa Grande. Because it is the largest settlement in the area, and the only one with a Great House, archaeologists have speculated that Casa Grande was a preeminent political center in Hohokam society during the Late Classic period (AD 1300–1450).

Descendant communities of Casa Grande's inhabitants include the Pima Indians (also called Akimel O'odham). Members of these communities have a rich corpus of oral traditions about Casa Grande and its history, as well as many other archaeological sites in the Gila River valley. In 1775 the Spanish priest Pedro Font recorded some of these oral traditions at a Piman village near Casa Grande. According to Piman traditions, Casa Grande was the home of Chief Morning Green, a powerful ruler in Hohokam society. Chief Morning Green belonged to an elite class of Hohokam society: the so-called Jackrabbit Eaters. These oral traditions also chronicle an ancient class struggle in the Sonoran Desert when a Piman culture hero, Elder Brother, and his band of warriors, overthrew Chief Morning Green and burned Casa Grande.

Anecdotal reports that glass beads have been discovered at Casa Grande suggest that it was possibly still occupied shortly before (or after) the Spanish entered Arizona. Conceivably, descendants of the ancient Hohokam might have occupied Casa Grande and imported glass beads from Mexico shortly before the Spanish entered Arizona. Indeed, glass beads are present in the Casa Grande artifact collections that are housed at the Smithsonian Institution. Unfortunately, however, it is not clear whether these beads were actually excavated from Casa Grande or whether they were found elsewhere and simply added to the Casa Grande materials.

PUBLIC EDUCATION AT CASA GRANDE RUINS NATIONAL MONUMENT

Public outreach at Casa Grande Ruins National Monument has a rich and colorful history, especially during the 1920s, when a great deal of effort was undertaken to attract visitors. Notable among these efforts was the orchestration of fictional plays at the monument by the Arizona Pageantry Association between 1926 and 1930. The first pageant (in 1926) was a three-day production that involved a cast of 300 actors; it was attended by 13,000 people, who arrived in thousands of automobiles. The plays included fanciful reenactments of Spanish contact in the Southwest during the fifteenth century as well as events during subsequent centuries, including the arrival of Mormons.

Today, public outreach at Casa Grande Ruins National Monument is decidedly different in that it is more educational in nature. The monument is open to visitors between 8:00 am and 5:00 pm every day of the year, except for December 25. Visitors may take self-guided tours of the monument and its visitors' center, which includes a small museum and a gift shop, during normal operating hours. Guided tours are regularly scheduled from November through April, when visitor traffic is highest at the monument. The monument is wheelchair accessible. Summer daytime temperatures often exceed 100°F, and winter temperatures range from the 60s to the 80s.

Further Reading: Bayman, James M., "The Hohokam of Southwest North America," *Journal of World Prehistory* 15 (2001): 257–311; Bayman, James M., and M. Steven Shackley, "Dynamics of Hohokam Obsidian Circulation in the North American Southwest," *Antiquity* 73 (1999): 836–845; Casa Grande National Monument, National Park Service Web site, http://www.nps.gov/cagr/; Clemensen, A. Berle, "Casa Grande Ruins National Monument, Arizona: A Centennial History of the First Prehistoric Reserve, 1892–1992," National Park Service, http://www.nps.gov/archive/cagr/adhi/adhi.htm (1992); Fewkes, Jesse W., "Casa Grande, Arizona," in *Twenty-Eighth Annual Report of the Bureau of American Ethnology, 1906–1907* (Washington, DC: Bureau of American Ethnology, 1912), 25–179; Matero, Frank, "Lessons from the Great House: Condition and Treatment History as Prologue to Site Conservation and Management at Casa Grande Ruin National Monument," *Conservation and Management of Archaeological Sites* 3 (1999): 203–224; Shapiro, Jason S., "New Light on Old Adobe: A Space Syntax Analysis of the Casa Grande," *Kiva* 64 (1999): 419–446; Wilcox, David R., and Lynette O. Shenk, *The Architecture of Casa Grande and Its Interpretation*, Arizona State Museum Archaeological Series No. 115 (Tucson: University of Arizona, 1977).

James M. Bayman

HOHOKAM PLATFORM MOUNDS

Lower Salt River Valley, Phoenix Basin, Central Arizona
Platform Mound Archaeology and Architecture: AD 1250–1400

The prehistoric Hohokam people of central Arizona constructed platform mounds at more than 100 sites between AD 1250 and 1450. These were stage-like platforms 2–2.5 meters high on which the Hohokam built rooms to place them in higher and more prominent locations in comparison to other rooms in the surrounding community. Sometimes additional rooms were constructed around the base of the platform mound, and a wall was built at ground level to surround the platform mound and rooms inside a compound. Additional compounds and room blocks, each providing homes for two to thirty or more households, were scattered in the landscape surrounding the platform mound. Archaeologists refer to the platform mound and the surrounding residences together as a "settlement complex" or a "community complex." When agricultural fields are included, individual platform mound settlement complexes covered territories of 10–50 square kilometers or more. Platform mound settlement complexes are important examples of Native American polities (in this case small, self-governed territories) that flourished and declined in the American Southwest prior to the arrival of Columbus in the New World.

The minimum and sufficient architectural components of the Classic period platform mound are the association of the flat-topped, rectangular platform with two or more oversized (30 to 60 m²) public rooms used as council chambers for civic and ceremonial occasions. Frequently, platform mounds were also associated with residential rooms (12 to 22 m² in area), but residential rooms do not occur in all the platform mound compounds. It is only in the last two decades, with the excavation of a sufficient sample of platform mounds, that researchers have recognized the importance of the council chambers as necessary architectural components of platform mounds; previously emphasis had been given to the relationship between residential rooms and the platform mounds.

THE ARCHITECTURE OF PLATFORM MOUNDS

The Hohokam people exercised their engineering skills not only in the construction of their extensive canal systems but also in building platform mounds. The construction of a platform mound began with the raising of the exterior retaining wall to serve as the outside face of the mound and to contain the fill. Interior retaining walls were then constructed dividing the enclosed space into cells, and an architectural fill of dirt and cobbles was added to each cell. Sometimes individual fill episodes are visible in the stratigraphy of the cells, and some episodes were completed by placing a layer of flowers or cottonwood bark, possibly to commemorate the efforts of a particular work party. Finally, a cap of adobe plaster was added to the top to seal the cells, and rooms were built on top of the platform.

The interior retaining walls helped stabilize the lateral stress exerted by the mass of the fill on the exterior retaining wall, and even with this precaution the exterior walls of a platform mound could with the passage of time begin to buckle outward. In the worst of such cases additional buttress walls were constructed immediately adjacent to the exterior wall to enclose the leaning wall, and some platform mounds were enclosed in three to four exterior retaining walls added over the period of time that the platform mound was in use.

The retaining walls in the early platform mound at Las Colinas (pre–AD 1250), in what is now the city of Phoenix, did not form a rectangular grid but were instead built as a sequence of concentric circles about 1 meter apart and sharing a single center. One straight wall was constructed on a radius extending from the center of the mound outward, cutting perpendicularly through the concentric circles and extending beyond the face of the mound to a large public room. This configuration, resembling an umbilical cord linking the free-standing room physically to the center of the mound, is sufficiently unusual to have had some iconographic significance. Although the circular configuration of interior walls was dropped in subsequent mound construction, the notion of subdividing the interior space into cells persisted as an architecturally necessary component of the platforms.

THE DEVELOPMENT OF PLATFORM MOUNDS, AD 700–1250

The concept of a rectangular, flat-topped mound serving as a platform on which rooms were constructed developed slowly over several centuries in the lower Salt and middle Gila river valleys. The Hohokam practice of surrounding their larger villages with mounds of earth and refuse was well underway by the Snaketown phase (AD 700s), and the first architectural elaboration of a mound involved the application of a caliche (a natural lime material) plastered surface over a dome-shaped earthen mound, providing a compact floor elevated above the surface of the surrounding desert (Mound 40, Snaketown). By the Sacaton phase (AD 950–1150), Hohokam engineering had advanced to flat-topped mounds with sloping sides (Mound 16, Snaketown), followed shortly by the use of walls to provide a vertical face to the mound. By about AD 1200, council chambers were being constructed in the same precincts as flat-topped mounds, and by around AD 1250 the Hohokam had mastered the engineering principles necessary to build a mound stable enough to support big rooms (council chambers) on top of the platform (Mound 8, Las Colinas).

Once the architectural form of the Classic period platform mound had crystallized, the idea spread in less than fifty years throughout the rest of the Hohokam and parts of the Salado region. Such was the urgency of some communities to construct their own mounds that they used existing rooms for the cells of the mound, removing the roofs and filling the interiors of the rooms with dirt and cobbles (Pillar Platform Mound in Tonto Basin). This practice proved a boon to later archaeologists because it preserved fragile items that were buried inside the fill. Examples of preserved items include mud-plastered wicker granaries and at least two standing wattle-and-daub pit houses intentionally buried by the Hohokam inside platform mounds.

PLATFORM MOUNDS AS CENTRAL PLACES

The big nonresidential rooms or council chambers at platform mounds usually occur in sets of two or more; only the earliest of platform mounds may have had a single council chamber. A platform mound was thus a special place in which several corporate groups, each with access to a particular council chamber, symbolized their association into a larger corporate entity by building and sharing the platform mound, while at the same time retaining their own identity by maintaining separate council chambers.

At some platform mounds one or more big-room council chambers might be singled out for special treatment by being placed on top of the platform itself, whereas others were constructed at ground level around the base of the mound. Since a room constructed on top of the mound required about ten times more effort to build than a room at ground level (when the effort of constructing the platform is also included), this can be construed as a ranking of the groups with respect to each other. At other mounds the council chambers were all constructed at ground level around the base of the platform mounds, and at yet others all council chambers were placed on top of the mound.

Compound B of the Casa Grand Ruins National Monument enclosed two platform mounds of roughly comparable size, representing an amalgamation of lower-order units at not one but two levels of inclusiveness.

The council chambers were made of thick-walled, puddle adobe walls, whereas a series of residential rooms were constructed of post-reinforced walls. The southern platform mound was an association of four lower-level corporate groups with council chambers, and the northern platform mound was associated with two council chambers. If one refers to each corporate group as a segment of the community, the architecture of Compound B represents a hierarchical amalgamation of minor segments (with council chambers) into segments (with platform mounds), and of segments into major segments (with a walled compound). But the organization of the Casa Grande does not stop there. Compound A at the site also had a platform mound on which stood a three-story building (the Casa Grande itself) of eleven rooms (the top story was a single room), and although the floors collapsed in antiquity, these were probably also council chambers. In addition, there are other large rooms built at ground level that might have served as council chambers. The settlement of Casa Grande was a hierarchical amalgamation of at least seventeen council chambers (minor segments) grouped into three platform mounds (segments), then grouped into two platform-mound compounds (major segments), all of which was consolidated into the central place of a polity (a major-major segment).

Platform mounds functioned as central places for a social system based on segmentary principles of organization, and most of the population having vested interests in the council chambers actually lived not at the platform mound but rather in the compounds dispersed in the surrounding countryside. At Compound B the residential rooms (those made of thinner, post-supported walls) held only a small fraction of the population represented by the six council chambers, and probably housed caretakers assigned from each of the six groups to maintain a presence at their central place.

The activities conducted in the council chambers and plazas of the platform mounds were largely ritual in nature. Compared to the surrounding settlements, where the bulk of the population resided, platform mounds had greater densities of items used in ritual, but not objects in craft production or items obtained through trade. Items that tend to occur more commonly at platform mounds include *Olivella* shell beads, shell tinklers, pigment minerals, obsidian tools, and argillite and turquoise beads. Tabular knives used for harvesting the stem of the agave plant are also more common at platform mounds, indicating that the baked, carbohydrate-rich base of the agave stalk was used during the feeding of the populations gathered for ceremonial events at the platform mound.

Individuals living at the platform mounds did not control or oversee long-distance exchange. In quantitative archaeological comparisons of artifact assemblages in burned room contexts, platform mounds tend to have greater quantities of trade items such as shell, obsidian, and pigment minerals than neighboring residential settlements. However, the differences are small in terms of the overall amount and represent quantities that could be transported by a single person. There may have been little economic advantage gained in controlling the level of the ancient exchange. Although platform mounds did have more *Olivella* shell beads and shell tinklers, they did not have more shell bracelets, which occur in equal densities in the surrounding settlements and were obtained from the same distance as the *Olivella* beads and tinklers. The platform mounds contained greater quantities of some items because they were required for the performance of ceremonies, not because the mounds exercised control over long-distance exchange.

However, the emphasis on ritual at platform mounds does not preclude the potential importance of the mounds in providing an infrastructure for action in the civic and economic realms. The ritual events held at a common locality symbolized and reinforced the readiness of the lower-order segments to act in concert to pursue their collective objectives, as would be served in constructing and maintaining irrigation canals, dealing with other settlements in the equitable allocation of water, and fielding groups of warriors to meet military threats. Although platform mounds did not exist solely because of trade, it may well be that some platform mounds did serve as marketplaces for the exchange of ceramic vessels, cotton, or other commodities.

PLATFORM MOUNDS AS SOCIAL MECHANISMS OF INCLUSION

The Classic period (AD 1250–1450) was a time of change and population movement in the greater Southwest. The platform mounds were the social, religious, and political core of their extended communities. Migrants, even those from different ethnic and cultural backgrounds, could be allowed participation, and hence membership, in the platform mounds through communal feasting and ritual events. Social status within each community was determined primarily by access to land and water, and secondarily by providing services such as ceramic and other craft production, agricultural and construction labor, and joining in defense against outside advances from competing groups. As suggested by Arleyn Simon and

David Jacobs, the platform mound villages competed with each other for influence and control of territory and resources. By providing membership through fictive or ceremonial kinship to unrelated persons and groups, a platform mound community was able to rapidly add more members, thereby increasing its military capabilities as well as its ability to produce food and craft commodities. Thus the platform mound communities promoted the amalgamation of disparate groups into a cohesive social structure. This melding of cultural and ethnic traditions flourished for well over 200 years, until changing social and environmental forces brought about the dissolution and dispersal of these large communities.

WHERE TO SEE PLATFORM MOUNDS

Fortunately, two of the largest and most important Hohokam platform mound sites have been preserved and are open to visitors as public parks. In Phoenix, Arizona, the Pueblo Grande Museum includes the platform mound of the same name and has excellent indoor and outdoor exhibits. The city of Phoenix purchased the Pueblo Grande platform mound and a portion of the associated settlement complex in 1928, establishing it as a park and museum. Visitors are able to take a self-guided tour of the top of the platform mound along wheelchair-accessible trails and can walk out to a stabilized Hohokam ball court to the north of the platform mound. The outdoor exhibits include a somewhat scaled-down replica of a Hohokam compound (AD 1200 and 1400) along with replicas of Hohokam pit houses, which served as residences during earlier times (pre–AD 1200).

The Casa Grande Ruins National Monument is located in the city of Coolidge (and not, paradoxically, in the city of Casa Grande) about an hour's drive south of Phoenix. The monument includes an excellent museum exhibit, and visitors are allowed to walk freely through Compound A with the Big House, a multi-story building constructed on top of a platform mound. Unfortunately, the Big House was excavated in the early twentieth century, and the edges of the platform mound on which it stood were removed in the mistaken belief that they constituted collapsed rubble, so visitors no longer see the raised platform that surrounded the Big House. Special guided tours are provided at regular intervals to Compound B, where it is possible to see the two platform mounds and glimpse the walls of some of the council chambers. A large Hohokam ball court, better preserved than that at Pueblo Grande, can also be viewed on these tours. The site of Casa Grande covers about 3.9 square kilometers (1.5 mi^2), and only a portion of it has been preserved within the boundaries of the national monument.

Further Reading: Bostwick, Todd W., and Christian E. Downum, *Archaeology of the Pueblo Grande Platform Mound and Surrounding Features*, Vol. 2: *Features in the Central Precinct of the Pueblo Grande Community*, Pueblo Grande Museum Anthropological Papers No. 1 (Phoenix, AZ: City of Phoenix Parks, Recreation and Library Department, Pueblo Grande Museum, 1994); Haury, Emil W., *The Hohokam: Desert Farmers and Craftsmen* (Tucson: University of Arizona Press, 1976); Rice, Glen E., "War and Water: An Ecological Perspective on Hohokam Irrigation," *Kiva* 63 (1998): 263–301; Rice, Glen E., "Hohokam and Salado Segmentary Organization: The Evidence from the Roosevelt Platform Mound Study," in *Salado*, edited by Jeffrey S. Dean (Albuquerque: University of New Mexico Press, 2000), 143–166; A twelve-volume report on the Roosevelt Platform Mound Project, including data on five platform mounds and 129 associated settlements, is available through the Archaeological Research Institute, School of Human Evolution and Social Change, Arizona State University, Tempe, AZ 85287-2402 (Attention Dr. Arleyn Simon).

Glen E. Rice, Arleyn W. Simon, and Owen Lindauer

MIMBRES SITES AND SETTLEMENTS

Southwest New Mexico, Southeast Arizona, and Northwest Chihuahua, Mexico

Agricultural Villages and Remarkable Pottery

MIMBRES MOGOLLON HISTORY AND CULTURE

The Mimbres region is known for the spectacular black-on-white painted pottery made in southwestern New Mexico from the AD 900s to 1100s, featuring intimate depictions of scenes from spiritual and everyday life. Mimbres is part of a larger Mogollon tradition that spanned the Chihuahuan desert of the U.S. Southwest and northern Mexico but had a unique culture and history from AD 200 to about AD 1500. The Mimbres heartland centers on the Mimbres River valley and the valleys of the upper Gila River and its tributaries, but Mimbres Mogollon sites extended for about a 100-kilometer radius in all directions from the Mimbres valley: west to the Safford valley, north to the plains of San Augustin, east to the Rio Grande, and south into northern Mexico.

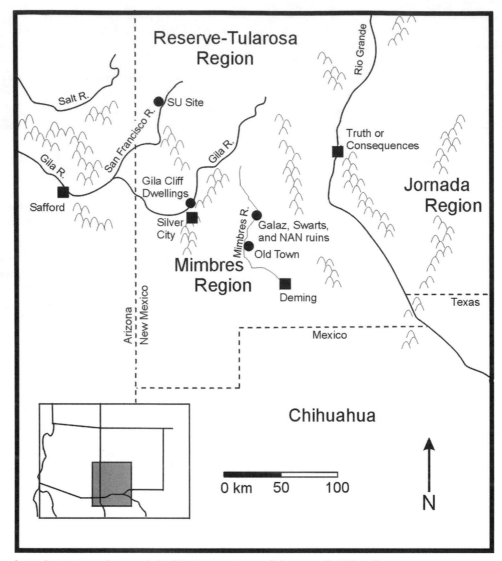

Important archaeological sites in and around the Mimbres region.   [Margaret C. Nelson]

Mimbres culture developed out of local hunting and gathering traditions; well before AD 1000, the start of the Classic period, people lived in farmsteads, hamlets, and small semi-agricultural villages along major drainages. Around AD 1000 a rapid transformation occurred in both architectural style and community structure, leading to a florescence of art and culture, the Classic Mimbres period, which lasted only a century. During the centuries following the Classic Mimbres period until AD 1450, populations were lower and people established a broad array of new interactions with regions to the east, north, west, and south. By the time of Spanish occupation, Apachean groups occupied the former Mimbres territory.

Archaeological research since the early 1970s has led not only to a better understanding of the cultural history of the area but has enriched the discipline of archaeology.

Archaeological data from the Mimbres Mogollon area has provided insights into important issues such as the relationship between sedentism and agricultural reliance, human impacts on the environment, and the study of architecture and floor artifacts to understand how structures and sites were used and then abandoned. The archaeological record in this area documents several dramatic episodes of change, when long periods of stability in land use and material culture are punctuated by abandonment or dispersal across sub-regions. These contrasting periods of stability and change take place under different levels of sedentism, agricultural reliance, and social cohesion, providing an excellent laboratory for developing archaeological theory and for understanding human strategies for addressing natural and social challenges in the environment.

Early Pit House Period, AD 200–600

The Early Pit House period marks the beginning of what archaeologists commonly consider the Mimbres Mogollon. Growing out of Late Archaic/Early Agricultural traditions, most Early Pit House period settlements represent a modest reduction in mobility and in reliance on hunted and gathered resources, with a concomitant increase in the use of agricultural products. Domestic and ritual architecture consisted of semi-subterranean structures with an above-ground superstructure of wooden posts, beams, and adobe, entered through ramp entryways. Early pit house settlements range from farmsteads to larger clusters of pit houses. Some intensively excavated sites, such as the SU site near Reserve, New Mexico, appear to include several contemporaneous pit houses with abundant below-floor storage pits and possible communal structures. Such large sites tend to be located in areas of high natural or agricultural resource productivity and may represent incipient, if short-term, village-level aggregations. Some of these larger sites continue to be occupied in subsequent Pit House period phases. Other Early Pit House sites have been found in upland areas away from major drainages, where conditions for agriculture are potentially more challenging. These tend to have few pit houses and no communal structures and may be seasonally occupied or special-use sites where hunting and gathering were emphasized. These smaller sites tend not to be reoccupied in subsequent phases of the Pit House period.

The spread of pit houses is roughly contemporaneous with the development of a coil-and-scrape pottery technology. Archaeologists hypothesize that the introduction of pottery, probably from Mexico, increased both storage and cooking efficiency of dried maize and beans. This promoted increased reliance on agriculture and greater commitment to residential permanence during the agricultural growing season. In spite of these changes, evidence from architecture, food grinding tools, and plant remains suggests that Early Pit House period populations were still fairly mobile, acquiring resources from different areas of the landscape on a seasonal basis. Most modern excavations in the area have not focused on Early Pit House remains, so there is limited information related to changes in subsistence and social interaction. Agriculture became more important over time, and the Mimbres Mogollon began building larger communities, not unlike the Neolithic shift to agriculture and sedentary village life in the Old World.

Late Pit House Period, AD 600–1000

In this period, population increased dramatically as evident in an increase in the number and size of settlements. During the Georgetown phase of the Late Pit House period (AD 600–725) people interacted more with others in the Hohokam region to the west than they had during the Early Pit House period. Shell bracelets, stone palettes, and a new red-slipped pottery technology are abundant on Georgetown phase sites. Evidence for agricultural technology during the

Georgetown phase has been discovered recently in several parts of the Mimbres Mogollon region. In the Safford valley at the western edge of the Mimbres region, Mimbres-affiliated pit house dwellers constructed and used substantial agave roasting pits, and may have built stone features for runoff or dry farming. By the AD 700s an irrigation canal was constructed leading water from the Mimbres River to the NAN Ranch ruin. These recent discoveries are promoting new understandings of early agricultural experimentation and investment.

The subsequent San Francisco and Three Circle phases continue trends established in the Georgetown phase of increasing population and investment of time and labor in agriculture. The relatively benign climate during these phases may have allowed production of some agricultural surplus and likely permitted higher population levels than during previous pit house phases. San Francisco and Three Circle pit houses appear to have been lived in longer than Georgetown phase pit houses, with more episodes of remodeling or replastering of floors indicating increased sedentism. The larger, more continuously occupied settlements have communal structures—exceptionally large pit houses with unique features such as extra hearths and unusual deposits of shell, bone, or other items interpreted as offerings. In many cases, communal structures at larger settlements were ritually "retired" by intentional burning and dismantling before a new communal structure was erected. Near the end of the Late Pit House period, a large number of these structures at different sites were burned within a very short time, which may signal a change in Mimbres social relationships. This dramatic pattern is one of a number of changes at the end of the Late Pit House and beginning of the Classic Mimbres period. Archaeologists continue to debate issues such as how abrupt this transition was and what the highly visible changes in material culture imply about shifts in social organization and interaction with outside groups.

Classic Mimbres Period, AD 1000–1130

From about AD 975 to 1025, residential architecture abruptly changed across the region. Semi-subterranean pit houses were abandoned in favor of rectangular surface rooms built of cobble masonry walls, joined together into pueblo-style room blocks. In many cases, these rooms and room blocks were built directly over the earlier pit houses, one of several lines of evidence showing regional population persistence as people continued to use the same village locations despite the change in architecture. Nevertheless, this change in architecture represents a radical reconfiguration of long-held cultural traditions regarding the use and configuration of household space and implies a reduction of household autonomy, privacy, and mobility relative to the more fluid and flexible pit house communities.

Classic Mimbres villages consist of one or more extended blocks of rooms, each ranging in size from two to several dozen individual rooms. Large, long-occupied Classic Mimbres villages of up to 200 rooms were located adjacent to wide floodplains, including well-known Mimbres valley sites such as the NAN Ranch Ruin, the Galaz Ruin, the Swarts Ruin, and Old Town. Smaller sites continued to be scattered along the valleys between villages as well as in upland areas. Facilities for community gatherings varied between villages and included walled courtyards between room blocks, unusually large surface rooms, and semi-subterranean rooms resembling kivas.

The shift to masonry pueblos occurred at about the same time that potters began to produce the famous Classic Mimbres black-on-white pottery, particularly bowls with striking naturalistic designs of people, animals, and mythical creatures, as well as geometric designs. Chemical analyses have demonstrated that production was widespread in villages throughout the Mimbres region rather than in a single site, locale, or valley. Some archaeologists associate certain bowl designs with specific villages; others suggest the work of individual painters can be identified. Despite the diversity of scenes represented on Mimbres Classic bowls and their widespread manufacture, the painted designs all follow specific design rules. In addition to the pottery, architectural styles are similarly homogeneous throughout the Mimbres Mogollon region.

Classic Mimbres village residents were more sedentary than during the Pit House periods, relying on farming of adjacent floodplains as well as more distant upland dry-farming fields for much of their food. Hunted and gathered foods remained an important supplement to their maize-based diets, and wild species were also important sources of building materials, fuel wood, and other resources. The large Classic period population may have negatively impacted the environment around their sites. Animal and plant remains from several sites indicate intense vegetation disturbance, and the wood used as construction material and as fuel wood along major valleys shows a reduction of riparian species by the early Classic period, indicating intensive use of cleared floodplain and arroyo-mouth lands for agriculture. This data also suggests that villagers traveled longer distances to acquire wood and to hunt large game in the Three Circle phase and the Classic period. The effects of these changes on land use and subsistence strategies before, during, and after the Mimbres Classic period are current topics of research and debate among archaeologists.

Postclassic Period, AD 1130–1300

The period after AD 1130 has been a problematic one for archaeological interpretation. Before this time, architecture and pottery styles were quite similar across the Mimbres Mogollon region. During the Postclassic period, however, areas within this larger region have very different settlement patterns and material culture. Archaeologists once thought that the end of large-scale Classic Mimbres black-on-white

pottery production around AD 1130 and depopulation of many large Mimbres valley villages meant the entire region was abandoned. More recent research indicates that this was a time of reorganization, as people in many areas adopted new ceramic styles indicating affiliations with neighboring groups rather than leaving the region.

Classic period pueblos excavated in the Mimbres valley have few if any tree ring cutting dates after the early AD 1100s, indicating little or no construction after the Classic period and a probable reduction in population in the mid- to late 1100s. Sporadic occupation of village sites by a much-reduced population characterizes Postclassic occupation in the Mimbres valley. This smaller population continued to use some Classic Mimbres black-on-white pottery but also incorporated newer pottery styles from areas to the south, including Chihuahua.

Outside the heartland of the Mimbres valley, in the San Francisco and Blue River valleys along the Arizona–New Mexico border, Classic occupation may continue after the Classic period with an influx of population, or at least pottery styles, from the Cibola (Tularosa) and White Mountain areas to the north. East of the Mimbres valley, residents of large Classic Mimbres villages dispersed into smaller, scattered hamlets. Some of these settlements were built around smaller, pre-existing Classic Mimbres structures, with new rooms added for incoming residents. Residents of these hamlets continued to use and make some older Mimbres-style pottery, but assemblages are dominated by diverse new styles characteristic of groups to the south and north. Maize continued as the primary staple, but fields were scattered along both primary and smaller side drainages and were no longer concentrated in the widest floodplain areas. In the desert regions south of the Mimbres valley, including northern Chihuahua, sites with significant amounts of Mimbres Classic black-on-white may have continued to be occupied, and these appear to be associated with a rising population at Casas Grandes, or Paquimé, although little excavation has been conducted at these Postclassic sites.

In the second half of this period, sites in the southern, desert areas of the region are characterized by adobe architecture and southern-style ceramics. These adobe room-blocks are often built on top of or adjacent to large Classic Mimbres villages. Plazas enclosed by adobe room-blocks constitute the only known communal spaces at most of these sites, although a few sites in the extreme southern portions of the region, close to Chihuahua, also have Paquimé-style ball courts. Ceramics, architecture, and the organization of space point to affiliation with contemporaneous cultural developments in Chihuahua. Although few sites from this period have been investigated using modern excavation practices, there is evidence that occupation persists in some southern sites after AD 1300. In the northern and western areas of the Mimbres Mogollon region, masonry pueblos and northern ceramic styles suggest that interaction with cultures to the north continued. Little is known about this time period in many areas, however. Some archaeologists suggest parts of the region were abandoned for a short time before the subsequent Cliff phase, while others argue that reduced populations remained throughout this time period.

Explaining the dramatic Postclassic period changes in settlement patterns and material culture promotes exciting debates among Mimbres Mogollon archaeologists and underscores the opportunity for new research in several areas. Although a brief period of reduced and more variable precipitation occurred from AD 1125 to 1150, it was shorter and less extreme than some earlier climatic shifts that did not cause cultural collapse. This climatic shift may have been problematic when combined with environmental impacts along floodplains near large Classic Mimbres villages and the demands of a greater regional population size. Finally, the extreme regional homogeneity in Classic Mimbres pottery and architecture may have been a sign of strict social controls used to bind residents of large villages together. The explosion of diversity characterizing the Postclassic periods may signal a shift toward a more flexible social environment. Research into all of these potential influences is ongoing, and archaeologists no longer see the Postclassic Mimbres as simply a cultural "collapse" or regional abandonment.

Cliff Phase, AD 1300–1450 or Later

Sites dating to this time period in the Mimbres Mogollon region have been identified along the Mimbres and Gila rivers and in the Mule Creek, Blue River, and San Francisco River areas north of the Gila. The sites, mostly small- to medium-sized villages of ten to seventy rooms (along with a few larger sites), consist primarily of single- or multi-story adobe room-blocks with supporting cobble foundations. Arrangements of adobe room-blocks and attached or freestanding adobe walls create central plaza areas. This pattern is similar to contemporaneous Cibola-affiliated sites to the north and northwest, Casas Grandes residential compounds to the south, and to Classic period Hohokam and Saladoan sites in the Tonto and Phoenix basins to the west. Salado polychromes are common in all of these sites and are one of the primary criteria for identifying Cliff phase components at sites in the Mimbres Mogollon region. These pan-regional architectural and ceramic similarities show links with a broad, southern southwest phenomenon that is called Salado. Like most regional variants of Salado, Cliff phase sites differ from Salado sites in the Tonto Basin, Arizona, heartland in characteristics such as architectural features, hearth form, and mortuary practices.

Three Cliff phase sites excavated in the upper Mimbres valley are relatively small and were apparently occupied for only part of this period, whereas larger villages to the west in the Gila area have evidence for longer occupations. Unfortunately, large contemporaneous sites in the lower Mimbres valley outside of Deming, New Mexico, were extensively vandalized in the 1970s, and no professional excavations were conducted there. Similarly, although there were once extensive excavations in larger Cliff phase sites as tourist attractions in some areas, professional excavations with published reports have examined only a handful of rooms at a few of these sites, providing scant evidence for settlement patterns and land use during the Cliff phase.

The occupations during and following the Cliff phase are ripe for research; there is still much to learn about population continuity with earlier phases, the nature of interaction between these sites, and the relationship with related Salado and Casas Grandes sites during the Cliff phase. Archaeologists still have no firm understanding of when the Cliff phase actually ends, so there are many unresolved questions about the ultimate depopulation of the area and the relationships among various cultural groups during the Spanish *entrada*.

MIMBRES SITES: DESTRUCTION AND PRESERVATION

The Classic Mimbres period is particularly well-known for its black-on-white pottery, and many of these beautiful pots are visible in museum collections around the country. Although this has sparked interest in Mimbres Mogollon archaeology, pottery sales in the art market have also led to the destruction of many sites by local amateur pothunters, and more recently by commercial looters. Virtually every large Classic Mimbres village in the Mimbres valley has been looted, and some have been completely destroyed by bulldozers, including the famous Galaz Ruin. In the summer of 2005, commercial looters bulldozed one of the few remaining Classic Mimbres villages on the Mimbres River. Fortunately, landowners have better-protected smaller sites and villages in less accessible areas, and archaeological research on both unlooted and partially preserved sites continues to address current issues and questions.

The Gila Cliff Dwellings National Monument north of Silver City, New Mexico, is a well-preserved example of a Postclassic period site just north of the Mimbres valley. The site was first recorded during Lieutenant George M. Wheeler's geographical survey of the western U.S. territories in 1874, and the first scientific description was written in 1884 by the well-known early American archaeologist Adolph F. Bandelier. A visitors' center provides interpretive displays, and a 1-mile trail winds through the prehistoric rooms built into shallow caves in the cliffs of a side canyon along the Gila River. No other Mimbres Mogollon sites currently have facilities for visitors. A number of U.S. museums preserve and display Mimbres Mogollon items; museums with particularly extensive collections include the Maxwell Museum in Albuquerque, New Mexico; the Western New Mexico University Museum in Silver City, New Mexico; and the Logan Museum in Beloit, Wisconsin.

Further Reading: Anyon, Roger, and Steven LeBlanc, *The Galaz Ruin: A Prehistoric Mimbres Village in Southwestern New Mexico* (Albuquerque: University of New Mexico Press, 1984); Brody, J. J., *Mimbres Painted Pottery* (Santa Fe, NM: School of American

Research Press, 2004); Gila Cliff Dwellings National Monument, National Park Service Web site, http://www.nps.gov/gicl/ (online September 2005); Hegmon, Michelle, "Recent Issues in the Archaeology of the Mimbres Region of the North American Southwest," *Journal of Archaeological Research* 10 (2002): 307–357; Lekson, Stephen H., *Archaeology of the Mimbres Region, Southwestern New Mexico, USA*, BAR International Series No. 1466 (Oxford: Archaeopress, 2006); Nelson, Margaret C., *Mimbres during the Twelfth Century: Abandonment, Continuity, and Reorganization* (Tucson: University of Arizona Press, 1999); Nelson, Margaret C., and Michelle Hegmon, eds., *Archaeology Southwest* 17(4) (2003): 1–12; Shafer, Harry J., *Mimbres Archaeology at the NAN Ranch Ruin* (Albuquerque: University of New Mexico Press, 2003).

Karen Gust Schollmeyer, Steve Swanson,
and Margaret C. Nelson

MIMBRES POTTERY AND ROCK ART SITES

Mimbres Valley, Southwest New Mexico, and Upper Gila River, Southeast Arizona

Classic Mimbres Art and Iconography

Archaeologists call one group of ancient farmers of southwestern New Mexico the Mimbres and, to a remarkable extent, the pictures they painted on relatively small pottery bowls are used to characterize and identify them. They are named for the narrow, oasis-like river valley that was their main population center, and they are considered a subdivision of a group of southern ancestors of the modern Puebloan people known as the Mogollon. The Mimbres pottery painting tradition, using red-brown or black paint on white surfaces, developed its unique qualities late in the AD 800s and reached maturity in the Mimbres valley, its major production center, during the Mimbres Classic period (ca. 975 to 1130–40). Mimbres-style pottery paintings were also made in villages along tributaries of the upper Gila River north and west of the Mimbres valley, and some may have been made as far south as northern Chihuahua, Mexico.

Drawings called petroglyphs that were pecked into or engraved on stone and that are stylistically and iconographically similar to Mimbres pottery paintings are also found clustered on various rock outcrops throughout the region. Archaeologists assume these to have been contemporaneous with the pottery and use them to further define the ecologically diverse area of rugged mountains and flat, arid deserts that was known to and used by the Mimbres people. Some petroglyph sites are situated on high places located not far from major villages, but most are farther away, near natural resource areas where food-gathering and hunting activities would have taken place. Some of these sites, including the volcanic boulders of Three Rivers in the Tularosa Basin east of the Rio Grande and small petroglyph locations in the high valleys of the Chiricahua Mountains of eastern Arizona, are more than 125 miles from the Mimbres valley. These may mark the eastern and western boundaries of the Mimbreño landscape.

By analogy with modern practices, and because many of these places are so far from home villages—and by habits of thought—the petroglyph artists are usually assumed to have been men. There are few sure indicators to demonstrate why any petroglyph images were made at any particular place or how they functioned, thus leaving few interpretive options. In the end, little more can be done than to state the obvious: some of the sites may have served as shrines or territorial markers, and all of the images interact with the natural landscape.

Far more is known about the painted pottery because much of it has been recovered under well-controlled archaeological conditions. Most was made locally by part-time artists who, by analogy with historic era Pueblo practices, are generally thought to have been women. Most were made as serving bowls and storage containers and were used in daily life and for feasting and other social rituals. Some are found at far distant places, especially in southeastern New Mexico, but it is not known whether these were gifts, trade items, or containers that once held more desirable objects. Most show evidence of the wear and tear of daily use, and great numbers of shards from accidentally broken vessels that once littered the remains of every Mimbres village testify to their mundane utility. Some vessels, including most whole ones that have been recovered in modern times, were removed from ordinary use and selected, for reasons that continue to elude investigators, to become mortuary offerings. These were usually sacrificed by having holes punched out of the bottom as they were buried with the honored dead.

Most Mimbres pottery paintings are non-figurative abstractions that suggest mountains, clouds, lightning, rain, and other natural phenomena, but a significant proportion represent humans, other animals, and fantastic beings, any of which may be shown interacting with any other. Many such pictures show the profile of a single animal whose body contains a single geometric emblem. These usually stand in a more or less static pose within a framed void. A substantial minority of figurative pictures are narratives that illustrate a range of activities from scenes of daily life to illustrations of what must have been a rich oral tradition. Similar iconography is found at petroglyph locations; however, the proportion of animal representations there is very much higher, and narrative pictures are far less common.

Profound differences between Classic period small-scale pottery paintings and large-scale petroglyphs are noted at the compositional level. Most petroglyphs are either framed by the rock faces on which they were made or not framed at all, and many give the impression of having been drawn without much consideration for other, nearby images. In contrast, paintings on pottery are nearly always highly structured compositions framed on the interior of a bowl. Non-figurative pictures are often segmented into four, three, or two equal units that circulate around a central void. Their complex symmetries are choreographed to circulate in, out, and around the central space of every composition, and each picture is held in precarious and delicate balance by the interplay of many different opposing forces.

The rhythmic and spatial illusions of these paintings depend as much upon manipulation of ambiguous inversions, especially positive-negative forms, as on more obvious patterning of symmetry and motif. The net effect is of highly stylized natural phenomena that are structured within a tense, multidimensional pictorial universe. They seem to express a worldview that is comfortable with the notion that ours is a dynamic universe of parallel oppositions where nothing is "whole" without its diametric opposite: male-female, life-death, above-below, dark-light. All of these dichotomies are in a constant state of transformation and transition that is visualized by an art that helps to maintain their tenuous balance.

Production of Mimbres art ended within about a generation of the time in the AD 1130s when most of their long-established villages were depopulated. After that time, archaeologists lose their ability to distinguish Mimbreño people from their neighbors, and by about AD 1200 it appears that even the memory of their art had been lost. Rediscovery began late in the nineteenth century, when some recently arrived Euro-American settlers began excavating at Mimbres villages to recover artifacts. By 1914 local collectors of Mimbres pottery paintings caught the interest of J. Walter Fewkes of the United States National Museum, and professional investigations began. The first published monograph on Mimbres art appeared that year, as did active acquisition by purchase and excavation of Mimbres painted pottery for anthropology museum collections. Within fifteen years, about 3,000 Mimbres pottery paintings had been acquired by American anthropology and university museums. By about 1935 most investigations had

ended, and archaeologists had sketched in a rough chronology and prehistory of the Mimbres. By then it was obvious that Mimbres populations had never been very large and that most of this remarkable art was the product of about six generations of artists, part-time specialists whose art was made primarily for use by people they knew in their daily lives.

Until late in the 1960s, Mimbres art largely remained the province of anthropology, and relatively few art collectors or art museums were interested in or even knew of it. By 1970, however, a sudden surge of interest by art collectors in Native American art soon turned Mimbres pottery paintings into a fine-art commodity, and a seemingly insatiable art market developed for it that is largely responsible for the mechanized looting that destroyed a large number of Mimbres villages during the last forty years of the twentieth century. In response, several institutions and archaeologists developed strategies to protect remaining sites, and through carefully controlled, conservation-minded excavations, they salvaged data from badly damaged sites, adding immensely to the once-limited knowledge about the Mimbres past and Mimbres art.

Ever since Mimbres paintings on pottery were introduced to the modern world, they have been characterized in many different ways: as archaeological artifacts, precious art objects, trivial decorations, statements of profound spiritual significance, emblems of ethnic identity, subjects of casual humor, and everything else imaginable. Archaeologists have learned to see them as they see most pictures: either as static, vertical images oriented on two-dimensional plane surfaces, or as potentially active ones, vertically oriented but on mobile, small-scale surfaces such as books. But Mimbres paintings fit neither of those models; instead, they are pictures placed on the interior walls of three-dimensional, mobile, portable, imperfect hemispheres. In their original settings they were placed on the ground or on a person's lap, below eye level in a world that had no distinguishable furniture. Each flatly painted picture is confined and defined by its framing lines without reference to a top or bottom—rather than created illusions of three-dimensional space, the paintings are *inside* such space and integral to it. Regardless of subject, each Mimbres painting on the walls of its three-dimensional container is a micro-universe, and its container is a stage on which a visual drama is played out.

Suspension of disbelief, metaphor, and illusion are at the heart of all drama. Mimbres paintings are famously ambiguous and transformational, loaded with visual puns and are never only documentary or decorative. When they are activated in their real-world space, they have a three-dimensional, dynamic reality. Only when they are immobilized and perceived as two-dimensional do they reasonably translate as static images, as logos, signs, symbols, icons. To see only the parts is to lose the drama of the whole, and when that happens, these paintings about ambiguity and transformation are themselves transformed into modern-day pictures of things.

Further Reading: Brody, J. J., *Mimbres Painted Pottery*, rev. ed. (Santa Fe, NM: School of American Research Press, 2004); Brody, J. J., and Rina Swentzell, *To Touch the Past: The Painted Pottery of the Mimbres People*, (New York: Hudson Hills Press, 1996); Fewkes, J. Walter, *The Mimbres: Art and Archaeology* (Albuquerque, NM: Awanyu, 1989); Hegmon, Michelle, "Recent Issues in the Archaeology of the Mimbres Region of the North American Southwest," *Journal of Archaeological Research* 10(4) (2002): 307–357; LeBlanc, Steven A., *The Mimbres People: Ancient Pueblo Painters of the American Southwest* (London: Thames and Hudson, 1983); Shafer, Harry J., *Mimbres Archaeology at the Nan Ranch Ruin* (Albuquerque: University of New Mexico Press, 2003).

J. J. Brody

SCHOOLHOUSE POINT MESA SITES

Roosevelt Lake, Tonto Basin, Central Arizona
The Salado Culture and Community

The Sonoran Desert in the Tonto basin where the Salt River and Tonto Creek meet is the heartland of what archaeologists call the Salado culture. What made the ancient inhabitants of the Tonto Basin of interest to archaeologists were the distinctive aspects of their culture that suggest a discontinuity from the earlier society. The Salado culture was more complex, grew rapidly, and included outsiders. Archaeologists use the term "Salado"—Spanish for "salt," in reference to the Salt River—to describe the culture that thrived between AD 1250 and 1450. It is associated primarily with the distinctive black, white, and red Salado polychrome pottery found at sites in the basin as well as across the southwestern region that was seen to represent this widespread cultural horizon. Questions of how this society was organized have been the focus of recent investigations. Scientific excavations during the last decade of the twentieth century in Arizona's Tonto basin have uncovered important clues to answering the questions about these people.

Although archaeologists have focused their attention on the Tonto basin for a little more than 100 years, it was only in the 1990s that a concentrated effort was made to investigate archaeological sites across the basin from the smallest to the largest. This effort was largely the result of construction to increase the height of the Theodore Roosevelt Dam and the level of the artificial lake it has created, as well as new development or reconstruction of highways there. In order to comply with environmental and historic preservation laws and regulations, archaeologists conducted a great number of investigations in advance of development. Planning for these studies led them to review, reconsider, and debate the interpretations of early investigations in the basin. Old ideas proposing that Salado culture resulted from an intrusion of outsiders were ripe for re-evaluation, and fresh ones were hatched.

SALADO CULTURE FROM THE PERSPECTIVE OF COMMUNITY

Archaeologists describe the ways of life of the people they study in terms of culture, the all-encompassing idea of the traditions held by a people. The focus here will be one aspect of culture—the social organization of the Salado in the Tonto basin. Social organization, how people organize themselves, can be studied archaeologically from the perspective of considering architectural spaces of a community in a landscape. Although the rules and actual groupings of Salado people are long gone, archaeologists can understand past social organization and other aspects of culture by comparing the location, size, arrangement, and composition of the remains of settlements or villages and their preserved archaeological features.

THE SALADO COMMUNITY ON SCHOOLHOUSE POINT

On the southern end of the Tonto basin, along the waters of the Salt River, is a peninsula of land known as Schoolhouse Point Mesa, for the small school that once was located there. The structure and arrangement of the community on Schoolhouse Point Mesa reflect the characteristics of five other, nearby communities in the basin that also overlook the Salt River. Like the other four villages nearby, the Schoolhouse Point community grew quickly starting around AD 1250, called the Roosevelt phase by archaeologists. But unlike the others, which were largely abandoned by AD 1350, the time marking the end of that phase, Schoolhouse Point Mesa continued to be occupied into the next phase, the Gila phase, until around AD 1450. The continuous occupation of this mesa through both phases provides a case study of the rapid growth, consolidation, and changing organization of a village over the period of time that defines the Salado.

The steep sides of Schoolhouse Mesa along with the Salt River and desert washes bound the settlements there and

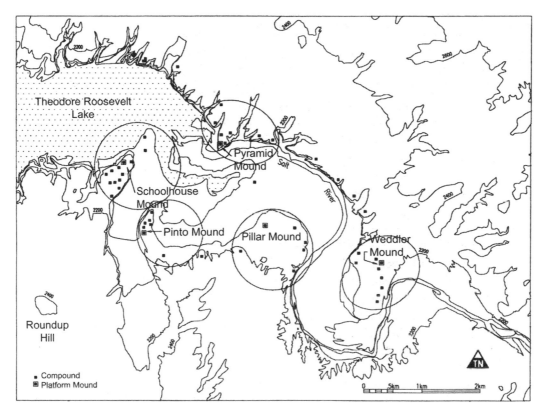

Five village-size clusters of sites on mesas of the Salt River.   [Owen Lindauer]

focused the interactions among the inhabitants that made them a community. This community is known from excavations of nineteen archaeological sites and additional information about unexcavated sites from archaeological surveys. Not surprisingly, most of the sites are concentrated on the northern end of the mesa, which is closest to the Salt River. Although dispersed, most sites are separated by less than 100 meters. The sites range in size and complexity from a year-round residential village that combined an architectural mound with scores of rooms, to briefly occupied locations used as places to grow or process food, whose remnants now are scatters of artifacts.

COMPONENTS OF A DISPERSED COMMUNITY

The preserved features of the Schoolhouse Point community consist of five basic archaeological site types. The first four types were residential: the compound, room block, platform mound, and room cluster. The last type, called a limited-activity site, was briefly occupied in order to conduct processing tasks.

A compound site consists of usually two to four rooms built within an enclosing compound wall that defined unroofed areas, which usually were subdivided further to form two or more plazas. The plaza areas contain small cemeteries as well as a variety of features that result from domestic cooking and processing activities, such as hearths, storage pits, and roasting

pits. Outside the compound walls were low-mounded trash areas and, at a few sites, large burned areas that resulted from large-scale repeated processing activities involving the roasting of plants for meals or long-term storage. Some compounds had little or no areas of trash and no roasting areas, an indication of real differences in activity among compounds. The implication is that the inhabitants of the mesa were interdependent, dividing different kinds of labor among themselves.

Compared with compounds, room block sites were uncommon, and only one is recorded on Schoolhouse Point. They have rooms arrayed such that they share a substantial number of common walls and the open space between the rooms is not enclosed by a compound wall. This distinctive organization of residential and shared unroofed space differs so much from that found in compounds that it is thought to signify that compounds were constructed and inhabited by Tonto basin outsiders who had socially integrated locally.

Platform mounds are artificially constructed flat-topped hills that were built only high enough for those on the platforms to see above the desert treetops. These sites likely served as special residences for the community and religious leaders who organized and orchestrated the interdependencies of the mesa community. The construction of platform mounds marks the beginning of the Roosevelt phase; these occur around Schoolhouse Point but not on the mesa itself. It was only after the others were abandoned early in the Gila phase that a

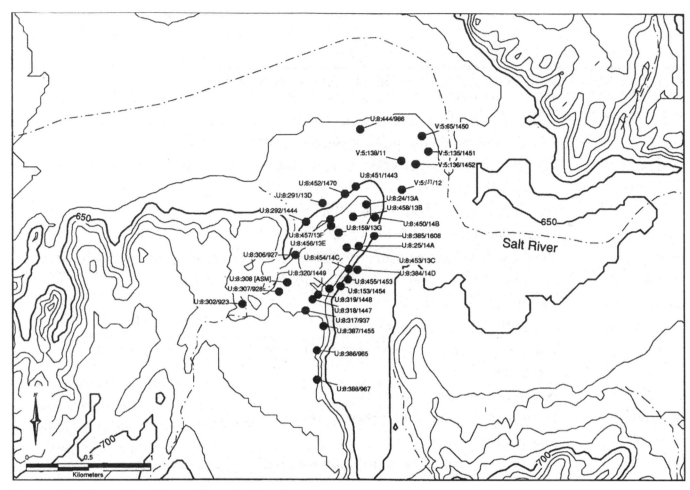

Sites on Schoolhouse Point Mesa.   [Owen Lindauer]

platform mound was built on the mesa. The single mound site on Schoolhouse Point is constructed of rooms arrayed in linear blocks with a substantial number of common walls. While incorporating many of the concepts of a room block site, it differs in having rooms built both at ground level and on artificially filled platforms. It also differs from the mounds dating to the Roosevelt phase in its lack of an enclosing compound wall. By this design the mound reflects both differences in the organization of residential and open space and continuities with architectural construction of the Roosevelt phase.

Room cluster sites consist of three to six structures built either at the surface or in shallow room-sized pits that surround or define a common space. None of these structures have common walls, and these sites also lack enclosing compound walls.

Limited-activity sites lack evidence of habitation and contain scatterings of artifacts believed to be discarded trash and roasting pits; these likely mark the locations of agricultural fields. Fields are preserved in traces of ephemeral structures and in piles of rocks and check dams that served to retain soil and moisture.

RESIDENTIAL CONTINUITY AND CHANGE IN THE SCHOOLHOUSE POINT COMMUNITY

People of the Tonto basin were farmers who lived in room cluster sites on the mesa for many years before the Roosevelt phase. These habitations were built in low pits that, by their number, indicate the mesa was lightly occupied. Elsewhere in the Tonto basin, early room cluster sites are widely dispersed in low concentrations that suggest by their distribution the earlier community was loosely integrated.

The Roosevelt phase marks a change in the number and distribution of sites on Schoolhouse Point Mesa. Most of the twenty-two sites built were compounds that were occupied year-round and indicate a dramatic population increase. The scattering of compounds, some with large rooms, large roasting areas, and granary storage facilities, indicates that the inhabitants of those compounds interacted and were perhaps interdependent. Many compounds have traces of earlier room cluster sites beneath their walls, suggesting growth of the local population, but the new construction is evidence that other populations moved to the mesa from within, and a few from outside the Tonto basin.

Many residences of this dispersed community were abandoned at the outset of the Gila phase, and residence on Schoolhouse Point Mesa was focused on a single, large, aggregated village. Surrounding the mesa, the four dispersed compound communities with their platform mounds were largely abandoned, which indicates that after AD 1350 there were fewer people in the eastern Tonto basin.

During the Roosevelt phase, one of the compounds on Schoolhouse Point was unusually large and had extensive associated trash mounds. It also housed unusually large storage facilities that could have supported periodic feasting, which made it a place where people played out their independencies through shared obligations and ceremonial events. Erratic Salt River stream flow during the Roosevelt-Gila phase transition likely led to conflicts because of the heavy reliance on irrigated fields, made more intense because the basin's population was then at its height. Conflict and a breakdown and reorganization of the society may largely explain the abandonment of the communities around Schoolhouse Point. People who remained concentrated in the settlement that became the Schoolhouse Point Mound in the very location of the unusually large Roosevelt phase compound. The number of people living on Schoolhouse Point in the Gila phase was about the same as the number living there during the earlier Roosevelt phase. Architectural details of the village there suggest Schoolhouse Point folk reorganized and persisted by both maintaining continuities with the past and making changes in their organization.

One important change was that the Schoolhouse Point Mound was an enormous storehouse where food surpluses were concentrated. The construction of the platforms served partly to restrict access to the central store rooms of the mound. Its combination of mound architecture, surplus food storage, and aggregated residential rooms allowed residence year-round, and it continued to be a place where the interdependencies among mesa residents played out. Food remains collected by archaeologists suggest that irrigation agriculture continued to be the primary subsistence strategy.

Eventually new problems arose in association with people living in an aggregated settlement who had an overreliance on canal irrigation for subsistence. Reconstruction of the prehistoric flows of the Salt River from the study of tree rings suggests that a succession of drought years were followed by devastating floods. Whereas once the extensive canals could have been rebuilt by a large local population, the depleted population along the Salt River of the mid-fifteenth century could not keep the canals functioning. Abandonment of the river-oriented villages probably occurred soon thereafter.

Further Reading: Dean, Jeffery S., *Salado* (Albuquerque: University of New Mexico Press, 2000); Lindauer, Owen, and John H. Blitz, "Higher Ground: The Archaeology of North American Platform Mounds," *Journal of Archaeological Research* 5(2) (1997): 169–207; Rice, Glen E., "Salado Horizon," in *Archaeology of Prehistoric Native America*, edited by Guy Gibbon (New York: Garland, 1998), 729–733; Rice, Glen E., and Charles Redman, "Platform Mounds of the Arizona Desert: An Experiment in Organizational Complexity," *Expedition* 35(1) (1993): 53–63.

Owen Lindauer

THE GRASSHOPPER AND POINT OF PINES SITES

Central Arizona Mountains

Defining and Investigating the Mogollon Cultural Tradition

Labeled on most contemporary maps of east central Arizona are two isolated mountain locations that were the scene of forty-five years of archaeological research and teaching by the University of Arizona Archaeological Field School. Point of Pines, a cattle station on the San Carlos Apache Reservation, designates a large fourteenth-century pueblo ruin and the immediate region investigated by the field school from 1946 through 1960. This investigation was established and directed by Emil W. Haury, with Edward B. Danson and Raymond H. Thompson also serving as directors. Similarly, Grasshopper, a summer cowboy camp and one-time trading post on the adjacent Fort Apache Reservation, is the locale of a large fourteenth-century pueblo ruin and a region explored by archaeologists for thirty years from 1963 to 1992. It was established and directed by Thompson (1963–65), who was succeeded by William A. Longacre (1966–78) and J. Jefferson Reid (1979–92).

POINT OF PINES PUEBLO

The Point of Pines region is an area of 175 square miles marked by pine and mixed evergreen woodland surrounding the Circle Prairie grassland. Elevations range around 6,000 feet with a growing season between 165 and 170 days and annual precipitation of 18–19 inches. A high water table was tapped prehistorically for shallow, walk-in wells. The concentration of resources in the area contributed to a long history of occupation extending from the Late Archaic Cienega Creek site to the small pueblos built atop Point of Pines Pueblo.

Point of Pines Pueblo (AZ W:10:50) is a large masonry ruin of over 800 ground-floor rooms surrounded by a half-dozen satellite ruins and three post-abandonment pueblos with twelve or more rooms on top. The total number of pueblo rooms in the vicinity occupied during at least part of the 1300s was between 1,600 and 2,000—the highest population density in the Arizona mountains during the Pinedale (AD 1265–1325) and Canyon Creek (AD 1325–1400) phases. Field school students excavated 111 masonry rooms, eleven pit houses, one Great Kiva, five small kivas, 248 burials, and 213 cremations. Two plazas were identified within the pueblo. Although the founding population may have included people from the nearby 335-room Turkey Creek Pueblo, Point of Pines Pueblo is best known as one of the strongest southwestern cases for a prehistoric migration. According to Jeffrey S. Dean, this initial migration—designated the Maverick Mountain phase (AD 1265–1300)—represents Anasazi (also known as Ancestral Puebloan) immigrants with Kayenta-Tusayan affiliations from the middle Little Colorado River region of the Colorado Plateau. Their presence is indicated by distinctive architectural features and local copies of Tsegi Orangeware polychrome designs, and it is accurately dated by tree rings or dendrochronology. Because their rooms were burned when some of their store rooms were stocked with corn and flour, and people were killed, Haury infers that the fires were set intentionally. After the fire and expulsion of the immigrants, a wall was built encircling the pueblo, presumably for defense. A Point of Pines phase (undated but estimated at AD 1400–50) is marked by locally made imitations of Four Mile Polychrome pottery and the occupation of small pueblos surrounding Point of Pines Pueblo prior to abandonment of the region.

Field school research at Point of Pines was pivotal to the controversy over the Mogollon culture and its conclusion. Haury defined the Mogollon culture in 1936 based on a 1931 survey in the mountains of east central Arizona and west central New Mexico and the excavation of two pit house villages discovered during that survey. Mogollon Village, on a bluff above the San Francisco River, was excavated in 1933, and Harris Village, on a terrace in the Mimbres River valley, in 1934. Identifying the Mogollon as a culture separate from and equivalent to the Anasazi and the Hohokam created a furor among the prominent archaeologists of the times. In an attempt to address the criticisms of the Mogollon concept, Haury first established a field school in the Forestdale valley of Arizona, which, although cut short by World War II, provided valuable excavation information on the Bluff and Bear pit house villages. This work extended the geographic range of the Mogollon and also pushed back the presence of pottery to around AD 200, long before the appearance of Anasazi pottery. After the war Haury moved the field school to Point of Pines, where the first major project was the Crooked Ridge pit house village, excavated and reported by Joe Ben Wheat. Two Pecos conferences held at Point of Pines in 1948 and 1951,

which brought Southwestern archaeologists to view the Mogollon evidence firsthand, combined with Wheat's synthesis of Mogollon culture and sites to put the controversy to rest by the late 1950s.

In addition to its critical role in charting the prehistory of the Arizona mountains, and especially the place of the Mogollon in that story, Point of Pines conjures up nostalgic memories of a special place that provided early field training to many of the prominent archaeologists of the last half of the twentieth century.

GRASSHOPPER PUEBLO

The Grasshopper region consists of a rugged plateau and adjacent steep canyons at the west end of the Fort Apache Reservation, bounded on the north by the Mogollon Rim and on the south by the Salt River. Vegetation ranges from western yellow pine above 6,000 feet—the elevation of Grasshopper Pueblo—to evergreen woodland, thick chaparral brush, and desert plants at the lower elevations of the Salt River at 3,000 feet. Ample annual precipitation of around 19 inches is constrained by a growing season of less than 140 days. Until the late AD 1200s the occupation of the Grasshopper region was sparse, probably seasonal, and limited to hunting and wild plant collecting. Over the thirty years of fieldwork at Grasshopper Pueblo, 103 rooms out of over 500 were excavated, and 672 burials were identified before all disturbances to human remains ceased in 1979 in accord with cultural values and norms of the White Mountain Apache.

Grasshopper Pueblo (AZ P:14:1), occupied from AD 1275 to 1400, was first settled by people of Mogollon culture affiliations but grew rapidly with the immigration of Anasazi from the Colorado Plateau as well as other ethnic groups. This social phenomenon of ethnic co-residence is supported at Grasshopper by chemical and design analysis of pottery as well as trace element analysis of tooth enamel. A small population at Grasshopper during the Great Drought (AD 1276–99) was joined by people from the nearby villages of Chodistaas and Grasshopper Spring around AD 1300, thus beginning a period of rapid population growth coinciding with high rainfall and agricultural productivity that lasted until between AD 1325 and 1330. It was during this period that the Grasshopper Mogollon became fully dependent on farming. Establishment of satellite communities brought more land under cultivation during a period of reduced rainfall that lasted until AD 1355 and initiated a gradual abandonment of Grasshopper Pueblo and the region. The latest tree ring date of AD 1373 or later is consistent with the estimated abandonment of the region by AD 1400.

The traditional mountain Mogollon subsistence strategy of hunting, wild plant gathering, and opportunistic, small-scale farming of corn, beans, and squash gave way rather quickly to full dependence on agriculture in response to the rapid regional population increase and the degradation of wild plant and animal resources. This rapid conversion to full dependence on agriculture is supported by several independent lines of evidence, including chemical analysis of diet indicators found in human bone.

Grasshopper society was organized into nuclear households, extended households sharing ritual structures, and male ceremonial societies from which community leaders were chosen. Households are recognized archaeologically by the distribution of artifacts and features associated with four recurrent domestic activities—habitation (food processing and consumption), storage (food, raw materials, and tools), manufacturing, and ritual—that define nine room types. These functional types are specialized and generalized habitation rooms; storage, storage-manufacturing, manufacturing, and special-purpose (food processing and manufacturing) rooms; ceremonial rooms; four small kivas; and one Great Kiva, which served the regional population. As is the case today among the Pueblo people of Arizona and New Mexico, three open plazas at Grasshopper were the scene of public rituals as well as areas of daily domestic activities. Four male ceremonial societies (restricted sodalities) are identified by artifacts included as part of the mortuary ritual. The most important was the Arrow Society, restricted to Mogollon males and probably similar to ethnographically recorded hunting and war societies among the historical Pueblos. Grasshopper society is interpreted as being similar to a generalized ethnographic model of Western Pueblo structure and organization characterized by a hierarchy of kinship relations, non-kinship-based ceremonial societies, ritual knowledge, and ceremonial performance.

Further Reading: Haury, Emil W., *Mogollon Culture in the Forestdale Valley, East-Central Arizona* (Tucson: University of Arizona Press, 1985); Haury, Emil W., *Point of Pines, Arizona: A History of the University of Arizona Archaeological Field School*, Anthropological Papers No. 50 (Tucson: University of Arizona Press, 1989); Lowell, Julie C., *Prehistoric Households at Turkey Creek Pueblo, Arizona*, Anthropological Papers No. 54 (Tucson: University of Arizona Press, 1991); Reid, J. Jefferson, and David E. Doyel, eds., *Emil W. Haury's Prehistory of the American Southwest* (Tucson: University of Arizona Press, 1986); Reid, Jefferson, and Stephanie Whittlesey, *Grasshopper Pueblo: A Story of Archaeology and Ancient Life* (Tucson: University of Arizona Press, 1999); Reid, Jefferson, and Stephanie Whittlesey, *Thirty Years into Yesterday: A History of Archaeology at Grasshopper Pueblo* (Tucson: University of Arizona Press, 2005); Riggs, Charles R., *The Architecture of Grasshopper Pueblo* (Salt Lake City: University of Utah Press, 2001); Wheat, Joe Ben, *Mogollon Culture Prior to A.D. 1000*, Memoirs of the American Anthropological Association No. 82, Memoirs of the Society for American Archaeology No. 10 (1955).

J. Jefferson Reid

HOMOL'OVI RUINS STATE PARK

Near Winslow, East Central Arizona
Ancestral Villages of the Hopi

Homolovi Ruins State Park was established in 1986 to protect important and unique villages ancestral to the Hopi Indians, whose present villages are only 60 miles north of the park. The villages protected within the park are Homol'ovi I, Homol'ovi II, Homol'ovi III, and Homol'ovi IV. Homol'ovi is a Hopi word translated as "place of (ovi) hills or buttes (homol)" and is the word used by the Hopi to describe the area where the park is located. The villages were first explored by the anthropologist Jesse Walter Fewkes, who had been visiting and studying the Hopi for several years in the 1890s on behalf of the Smithsonian Institution. His interest in tracing Hopi migrations led him to visit the Homol'ovi area at the urging of Hopi religious leaders. He spent the summer excavating in all but Homol'ovi IV, but he documented, named, and numbered the villages.

Due to their large sizes, proximity to the railroad (which helped establish the nearby town of Winslow in 1881), and proximity to Route 66, the Homol'ovi villages became subject to more and more intense vandalism as time went by. Finally, Hopi concerns and support of then Governor Bruce Babbitt enabled the creation of the Homolovi Ruins State Park to help protect and interpret the pueblos. The park opened in 1993 with a visitors' center and exhibits, paved roads, and trails to the two largest villages, Homol'ovi I and Homol'ovi II. From 1984 to 1999, archaeologists from Arizona State Museum, through the University of Arizona, excavated in all four villages.

HOMOL'OVI VILLAGES
The four villages within the park's boundaries were all settled between AD 1250 and 1400, principally by groups migrating down from Hopi Mesa villages 60 miles to the north. They were attracted to the area by the presence of the Little Colorado River, which drains over 26,000 square miles of the southern Colorado Plateau, mostly in Arizona but extending into west central New Mexico. This large drainage area enabled the stream to maintain perennial flows along much of its course, which were used by farmers who grew corn and squash starting at least 3,000 years ago. The situation in the Homol'ovi area was even more unusual. Due to large upstream springs in

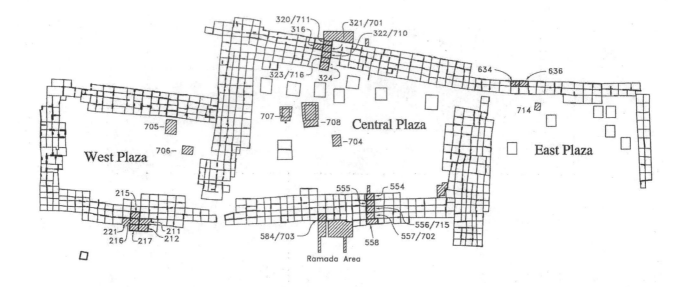

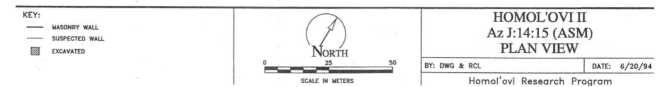

Plan view of Homol'ovi II.   [E. Charles Adams]

side drainages, the river actually flows year-round, providing water for personal and farming needs. The recovery of fish remains in the archaeological deposits of the villages indicates the year-round flow occurred while the villages were occupied. An additional bonus is the large floodplain of the river, which near the Homol'ovi villages is 2.5 miles wide. A persistent problem for the area is flooding, which historical records indicate occurs on average once every seven years. Major floods in ancient times, like those that occurred in 1993, 1995, and 2004, not only would have inundated any agricultural fields in the floodplain, but would also have caused the river to change course, which would have further threatened farming along the river. These challenges confronted historic period Mormon settlers who established two villages along the Little Colorado River near Homol'ovi I in 1876 and then, due to persistent flooding, gave up and moved by 1885.

The threat of flooding and the constant migration of the river are reasons archaeologists believe the Homol'ovi area was not more permanently and heavily settled before 1250. Prior to 1250, settlements were typically small villages of a few households that were likely occupied for only a few years or even seasonally. No local traditions of pottery manufacture are known for the Homol'ovi area, adding further evidence to the short-term or seasonal nature of these occupations, which began in the AD 600s and persisted into the early 1200s.

HOMOL'OVI I

At 1,100 rooms, Homol'ovi I is the second largest of the Homol'ovi area villages. It was established about AD 1290 on a small hill next to the floodplain, possibly by groups immigrating from Homol'ovi III and IV. At first it consisted of several linear blocks of rooms built by social, possibly kinship, groups, who then occupied them. Ceremonies were held in small subterranean structures, called kivas, which were used by small groups such as extended families or lineages. Exchange was far-ranging, with pottery traded from groups still living on the Hopi mesas to the north and with others living from 35 to 100 miles southeast, south, and southwest. However, a local tradition of black and white painted, orange-hued pottery was developed and also traded to nearby communities who did not have traditions of decorated pottery making. Cotton seeds are common in Homol'ovi I deposits. Archaeologists believe cotton was also an exchange item to communities located in surrounding mountains where cotton could not be grown. The village continued to grow slowly over the next fifty to seventy years, but a surge in building occurred around AD 1350 that saw the construction of a large plaza space enclosed on all sides by rooms in which large kivas were constructed. This seems to represent a shift in community organization and social power as public spaces probably housing ceremonies appeared in villages throughout the region at this time or even earlier. In addition, production of the local decorated pottery slowed or even ceased altogether, replaced by a yellow-hued imported pottery made in the Hopi mesa communities. Homol'ovi I continued to grow and prosper until about AD 1390, when a rapid abandonment took place, with villagers likely moving to join Hopi mesa villages. Homol'ovi I is open to the public with a campground about half a mile away.

HOMOL'OVI II

At 1,200 rooms, Homol'ovi II is the largest and latest of the Homol'ovi villages. Established about AD 1350 or possibly even later, it is located about 3 miles downstream from Homol'ovi I and sits atop a small mesa overlooking the Little Colorado River floodplain. The edges of the mesa and some of the surrounding buttes are covered with petroglyphs; most are contemporary with the village, whereas others are associated with use of the area going back thousands of years. A distinctive set of petroglyphs depict what are interpreted to be katsina faces that relate to the first appearance of katsina religion in the area. Homol'ovi II is distinct from the other villages in having three large plazas, two fully enclosed by rooms and one enclosed on three sides. Within each of the plazas many kivas were constructed. On the walls of one kiva are depicted dancing figures believed to be katsinas. Similarly styled figures were found on kiva walls in contemporary Hopi mesa villages that were excavated in the 1930s. Yet another kiva at Homol'ovi II had the topography of the region depicted on its walls, including the San Francisco Peaks, which are the highest mountains in Arizona and are located 60 miles west of Homol'ovi II. Today the Hopi believe that katsinas arrive in their villages through an opening in the top of the peaks. These kivas support the petroglyph evidence that katsina religion was brought to the area when Homol'ovi II arrived. The San Francisco Peaks painting suggested to a Hopi religious leader that the group responsible for observing the movements of the sun and setting the calendar for the village probably used the kiva.

The method of construction, layout of the village, and uniformity of the pottery all indicate Homol'ovi II was constructed rapidly and occupied a fairly brief period of time, especially compared to Homol'ovi I. Nearly 90 percent of its decorated pottery is yellow ware that compositional analyses have demonstrated was made at Hopi mesa villages. Thus, the builders and occupants of Homol'ovi II were almost certainly immigrants from Hopi mesa villages and apparently depended on trade with those villages for all of its pottery. A high frequency of cotton seeds and fibers in Homol'ovi II deposits suggests cotton was becoming more important in the exchange from the Homol'ovi area to its neighbors and, in particular, to Hopi mesa villages to acquire yellow pottery. The occupants of Homol'ovi II left their village about AD 1400, slightly later than Homol'ovi I,

and almost certainly returned to their communities on the Hopi mesas that they had left only a generation or two earlier. A paved road and trail takes visitors to Homol'ovi II, where a kiva and several rooms have been left open for interpretation.

HOMOL'OVI III AND IV

These smaller villages are located on the west side of the river, in contrast to Homol'ovi I and II on the east side. Homol'ovi III is not open to the public, but Homol'ovi IV can be visited with a permit and directions from the visitors' center. Homol'ovi IV has about 200 rooms and is the earliest of the Homol'ovi villages, founded about AD 1260 and occupied perhaps twenty-five years. It is unique in being built on the top and sides of a small butte that stands 50 feet high. The pueblo was built rapidly and is dominated by locally made orange-hued pottery that is stylistically identical to pottery being made at contemporary Hopi mesa villages. Many of these villages are also located on the top or sides of small buttes. Thus, it seems the founders of Homol'ovi IV likely came from the Hopi mesas as well. Archaeologists believe Hopi ancestors chose to settle the area in part to take advantage of riverine resources but also to keep control over these resources as immigration became more common in the region in the late AD 1200s. It seems most likely that rather than moving back to Hopi, the Homol'ovi IV occupants simply moved upstream about 3 miles and established Homol'ovi I, which was in an environmentally more favorable area.

At fifty rooms, Homol'ovi III is far and away the smallest of the four villages. Founded about AD 1290 and a contemporary of Homol'ovi I, the location of Homol'ovi III in the floodplain of the Little Colorado River doomed it to failure, much like the later Mormon settlements. Although originally occupied for only about twenty years before its occupants moved to Homol'ovi I, the village was later used seasonally first as a farm house occupied sporadically during the summer by individuals farming in the area, and later becoming a larger farming village. In this form, it was occupied for the entire summer by several families. Hopi and Zuni use farm houses and farming villages even today, although they are now occupied year-round.

Further Reading: Adams, E. Charles, *Homol'ovi: An Ancient Hopi Settlement Cluster* (Tucson: University of Arizona Press, 2002); Arizona State Museum Web site, http://www.statemuseum.arizona.edu/arch/arcprojs.shtml; Fewkes, Jesse Walter, "Two Summers' Work in Pueblo Ruins," in *Twenty-Second Annual Report of the Bureau of American Ethnology for 1899–1900* (Washington, DC: Smithsonian Institution, 1904), 3–196; Homolovi Ruins State Park Web site, http://www.pr.state.az.us/Parks/parkhtml/homolovi.html; Walker, William H., *Homol'ovi: A Cultural Crossroads* (Winslow: Arizona Archaeological Society, 1996).

E. Charles Adams

GALISTEO BASIN PUEBLOS

Northern Rio Grande Valley, New Mexico
Fourteenth- to Eighteenth-Century Pueblo Agricultural Communities

By the time the first Europeans settled in the northern Rio Grande valley, the Galisteo basin was among the most densely settled and geographically central regions of the Pueblo world. Large villages and extensive farmsteads had defined the landscape for almost 300 years, and much of the pottery used and traded throughout the Rio Grande came from within its boundaries. Within the span of a century, however, this region was virtually abandoned. Most of its villages and fields lay in ruin, and its former inhabitants had become refugees, settling in other Pueblo villages or founding new ones in more remote parts of the northern Southwest. This history of village settlement and growth, colonization and transformation, and ultimately depopulation and abandonment in many ways encapsulates the experience and heritage of much of the Rio Grande valley between AD 1300 and 1700. It is not surprising, then, that the Galisteo basin has been an important research focus from the very beginning of professional, scientific archaeology in the southwestern United States. The seminal work of Nels Nelson, in particular, has an important role in the history of American archaeology. Today the Galisteo basin is the subject of extraordinary federal legislation that identifies and protects prominent archaeological sites through a partnership between state and federal agencies, tribal governments, local communities, nongovernmental organizations, and private landowners.

Like any area with a long and complex history of human occupation, the Galisteo basin has been defined from a number of geographic and cultural perspectives. From a topographic viewpoint, the Galisteo basin is a broad, eroded lowland that formed in the shadows of the Rocky Mountains over the past 60 million years. It is bounded by mountainous uplands to the east and west and high plateaus on north and south. The Rio Galisteo and its tributaries flow from the Sangre de Cristo Range of the Rocky Mountains westward through the Santo Domingo basin to the Rio Grande valley. Seven large late prehistoric Pueblo settlements are located within this lowland. Several more villages are located in the immediately surrounding areas: the Santa Fe Plateau to the north, the Santo Domingo and Hagan basins to the west, and the saddle between the Sandia and Ortiz mountains to the southwest. The Galisteo basin, enlarged to include sites such as San Marcos and La Cienega on the Santa Fe Plateau, was consistently recognized by the Spanish as a distinctive province on the basis of linguistic and geographic criteria. This expanded definition provides the basis of most archaeological

discussions. The dominant language of the Galisteo basin as identified by the Spanish was Tano, a language very closely related to Tewa and other languages spoken in contemporary Pueblo communities. Other languages were spoken as well, however, including Keres at San Marcos. Recently, the Galisteo Basin Archaeological Sites Protection Act has expanded the geographic scale of the basin even further to include twenty-four prominent sites along the Rio Galisteo and surrounding areas.

However its boundaries are defined, humans have occupied this region since the end of the last Ice Age. Although there is some evidence of short-term use of the area as early as 8,000 years ago, prior to the thirteenth century AD human occupation of the Galisteo basin was relatively sparse and short-term with no permanent settlement. Evidence of campsites in the form of hearths and concentrations of discarded chipped-stone tools, animal bones, and charcoal suggests that small, seasonally mobile groups traversed the area while hunting or collecting plant and mineral resources. Year-round occupation of the Rio Grande valley and Santa Fe Plateau seems to have preceded that of the Galisteo basin, but by about AD 1200, small agricultural communities began to be established in the eastern part of the basin. The period from about AD 1200 to 1325 (known as the Coalition period to archaeologists working in the Rio Grande valley) is characterized by an increase in the number of village sites, an expansion in the geographic range of these sites, and wide variation in architecture and material culture. This period begins with the development of locally manufactured carbon-painted whiteware ceramics and ends with the inception of Rio Grande Glazewares. Early thirteenth-century settlements in the Galisteo basin include both subterranean (pit house) and above-ground (Pueblo) architecture clustered around water sources appropriate to small-scale runoff-fed and dry farming. After about AD 1250, however, the establishment of large, permanent villages constructed of masonry and mud brick (adobe) signaled a new era of immigration, population growth, and intensified farming activity. Many of the occupants of these newly founded villages are believed to have been recent Ancestral Puebloan (also known as Anasazi) migrants from the Colorado Plateau, because that region underwent large-scale abandonments during the thirteenth century. Some of the most famous and long-lived sites in the basin were founded in this period, including San Lazaro Pueblo and Pueblo Largo, while others, such as Burnt Corn Pueblo, were short-lived.

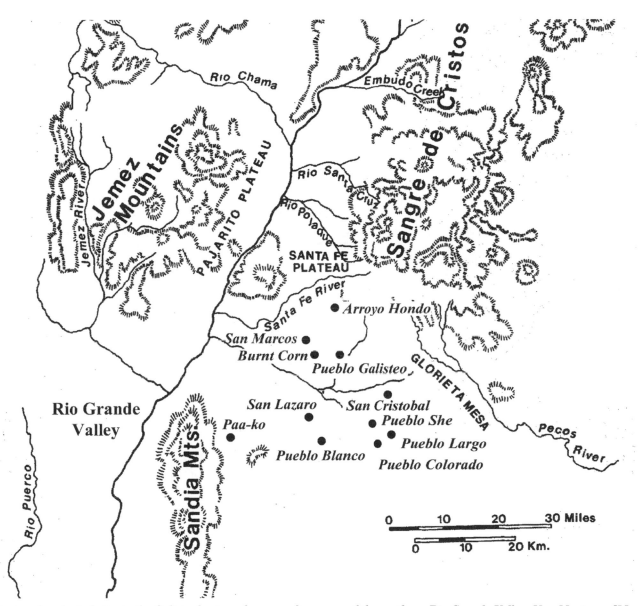

Important archaeological sites in the Galisteo basin and surrounding areas of the northern Rio Grande Valley, New Mexico. [Mark T. Lycett]

The founding and growth of large settlements continued into the fourteenth century, the beginnings of a period known by archaeologists as the Rio Grande Classic. The early Classic period (ca. AD 1300–1425) is characterized by shifts in the location and form of residential settlement as well as changes in the organization of land use. Many very large villages were founded and occupied in this region during this time period, including Paa-ko, San Cristóbal, and Arroyo Hondo. During this period, red pottery with a lead-glaze paint became predominant in the region, many villages increased dramatically in size, and many more were abandoned. Settlements began to concentrate on floodplains and tributaries of major drainages. At the same time as these very large aggregated villages began to develop, the number and variety of small farmsteads,

campsites, agricultural fields, rock art panels, and shrines increased. New agricultural technologies, including large runoff-fed reservoirs, terraces, and elaborated field systems, appear throughout the landscape. By this time, the Galisteo basin supported a thriving population and a complex farming and foraging economy. Although the overall population of the basin continued to grow throughout this period, the population history of individual villages is more complex, with many episodes of growth, decline, temporary abandonment, and reoccupation in even the largest communities. Many of the largest villages in the region, including Arroyo Hondo and Paa-ko, were finally deserted by the middle of the fifteenth century AD.

The region was then dominated by eight large population centers: Galisteo, San Cristóbal, San Lazaro, Pueblo Largo,

Pueblo Shé, Pueblo Colorado, and Pueblo Blanco along the Rio Galisteo, and San Marcos on the Santa Fe Plateau. These villages were large, compact, adobe and masonry buildings joined into room blocks and organized around central plazas with semi-subterranean chambers (kivas) important in ceremonial and ritual practices. Some grew to more than 1,800 rooms in size and may have had populations ranging from a few hundred to more than a thousand people. New styles of glaze-painted ceramics became common during the AD 1400s, with yellow-white and multicolored, or polychrome, vessels replacing the redwares of the previous century. Communities in the Galisteo basin and nearby areas became among the most important producers of these ceramics, and their wares were exchanged widely throughout the northern Rio Grande valley. The most important source of lead mineral for glaze paints was located in the Cerillos Hills near San Marcos Pueblo. This mining district was also an important source of turquoise, copper ore, and iron minerals. Although these minerals had been mined for hundreds of years, the growing importance of lead-based glaze paint in ceramic production may have lent them a new significance. These mineral resources would come under new scrutiny with the arrival of Spanish colonists in the succeeding century.

The expansion of New Spain first encompassed the Galisteo basin during the Vásquez de Coronado expedition of AD 1540–42. A series of exploratory expeditions, or *entradas*, between AD 1581 and 1590 brought Pueblo groups into increasing contact with Europeans, ending in the first permanent colonization of New Mexico in AD 1598. Spanish settlement in the seventeenth century led for the first time to direct and regular involvement of Pueblo populations in European colonial administrative and economic systems. Santa Fe was the most important center of colonial settlement, but by the middle of the seventeenth century many colonists had established small ranches and farmsteads in outlying areas like the Galisteo basin.

The Franciscan missions were perhaps the single most dominant social, political, and economic power in the New Mexico colony at this time. The local administrative unit of missionization was the *doctrina*, consisting of a central mission settlement with one or more resident Franciscans, a permanent church, a *convento* (friar's residence and workrooms) and associated facilities, and its *visitas*, nearby smaller settlements lacking resident friars and with only a limited range of mission structures and facilities. These institutions were always situated within existing Pueblo settlements. In addition to their role in religious and cultural indoctrination, the missions were the single most important centers of economic production and controlled the colony's only regular long-distance transportation and supply system.

Of the eight large settlements within the Galisteo basin, four survived into the seventeenth century. Missions were established at Galisteo and San Lazaro between AD 1610 and 1613, at San Cristóbal in 1621, and at San Marcos in the 1630s. A missionary was resident at San Cristóbal in the 1620s, but by mid-century both San Lazaro and San Cristóbal had become *visitas* of Galisteo. Galisteo was the earliest and longest-occupied mission site. Other villages that had been abandoned in the previous century were reoccupied as missions, including La Cienega, a *visita* of San Marcos, and Paa-ko, a small, outlying *visita* that was renamed San Pedro.

San Cristóbal, a well-documented site where Nelson excavated 239 rooms in 1912, exemplifies the life history of these communities in the seventeenth century. This settlement includes nineteen room blocks, eleven plaza areas, eight middens, and many associated features, including the mission complex, rockshelters, a large shrine, corrals, and two reservoirs. Soon after the mission period began, the village was reorganized, with newly refurbished room blocks covering a small area of the pre-colonial site. The church and *convento*, although large and visually impressive, were segregated from the settlement as a whole. New domestic animals, plants, and European tools first became available to the inhabitants of San Cristóbal during this period. However, many new burdens, including introduced infectious diseases, also arrived with the colonists. The population of this community fell throughout the seventeenth century, until the site was finally abandoned at the time of the Pueblo Revolt in AD 1680.

The mission of San Pedro, or Paa-ko, is one of a small number of *visitas* with a long history of well-documented research. Located on the eastern slope of the Sandia Mountains to the southwest of the Galisteo basin, this village was much smaller in scale and more politically and geographically peripheral than San Cristóbal during the colonial period. The site includes more than twenty room blocks arranged in eight plaza groups; however, the colonial period settlement was confined to a single plaza group of four small, single-story house blocks. Like San Cristóbal, the population of this village dwindled throughout the seventeenth century, and the settlement was abandoned prior to AD 1680. New structures built during the mission period include a reservoir, corrals, a small chapel situated within the seventeenth-century plaza, and, more surprisingly, a metalworking facility. A terraced hill slope built in the first half of the seventeenth century was used for copper and lead smelting, iron working, and other, similar activities. Both Spanish and Puebloan techniques were used in the design and manufacture of these facilities. Metal has been recovered from the seventeenth-century missions at the sites of Abo Mission and Quarai, in the Salinas district; from San Marcos, San Lazaro, and San Cristóbal in the Galisteo basin; and from the Zuni site of Hawikuh and the Hopi site of Awatovi; however, only San Marcos and Paa-ko show any evidence of metal production.

The Spaniards were expelled from the colony in the Pueblo Revolt of 1680, only to return twelve years later. This period of violent indigenous resistance and colonial suppression witnessed historically unprecedented displacement, disruption, and realignment of Pueblo society. Following the Pueblo Revolt, remaining Pueblo settlements in the Galisteo basin were abandoned in favor of the former colonial settings of Santa Fe and La Cañada in the Española basin. With the return of the Spaniards in 1692, the former inhabitants of the Galisteo basin and Santa Fe Plateau were forced from their new settlements and dispersed to a number of other areas, including Laguna and First Mesa at Hopi. In 1706 Governor Cuervo y Valdes resettled the pueblo of Galisteo with ninety Tano speakers who had been resident at Tesuque Pueblo. This resettled community never prospered. The report of Fray Dominguez, a Franciscan visitor in 1776, notes the "ruinous condition" of the architecture and the "deplorable poverty" of the people. Dominguez describes a community on the verge of abandoning their village and lands. This abandonment would come to pass in the wake of the AD 1780–81 smallpox epidemic, when the mission records were transferred and the last occupants moved on, ending nearly 600 years of continuous occupation of the Galisteo basin by Pueblo communities.

At the same time, the colonial government encouraged the creation of "buffer communities" on the frontier between the Rio Grande valley and the Great Plains. New communities of Hispanic and *Genízaro* (or displaced Native American) settlers were established to the east of the Sandia Mountains and within the Galisteo basin during the second half of the eighteenth century.

NELS NELSON AND THE HISTORY OF RESEARCH IN THE GALISTEO BASIN

Although Adolph Bandelier visited most of the important sites in the Galisteo basin in the nineteenth century, the history of scientific research in the region begins with Nels C. Nelson. Between 1912 and 1917, Nelson undertook an ambitious research program for the American Museum of Natural History. Nelson set out to establish a chronological framework for the Puebloan Southwest and trace the historical roots of modern Pueblo villages. The most notable aspect of this program was Nelson's excavation of several large, late prehistoric or contact period habitation sites in the Galisteo basin. Following an initial six-week reconnaissance that took note of more than 115 sites, Nelson chose the historically Tano-speaking settlement cluster as the basis for his chronological framework. His excavations focused primarily on San Cristóbal but included Galisteo, San Lazaro, Pueblo Largo, Pueblo Colorado, Pueblo Blanco, and Pueblo Shé. Between 1914 and 1916, Nelson extended his excavations to large prehistoric and historic sites located in areas adjacent to the Galisteo basin, including Paa-ko and San Marcos. In 1914 Nelson returned to San Cristóbal

to excavate the stratigraphic block that provided the data for *Chronology of the Tano Ruins*. Nelson's publication of this seminal paper set the groundwork for the incorporation of stratigraphic methods into studies of chronology and culture history in New World archaeology.

Since Nelson's time, work on this region has been limited compared to other areas of the northern Southwest. This research, much of it very recent, has focused on the initial settlement of the Galisteo basin and the mission sites of the colonial period.

THE GALISTEO BASIN ARCHAEOLOGICAL SITES PROTECTION ACT

The Galisteo Basin Archaeological Sites Protection Act was enacted in 2004 to provide for the protection, preservation, and interpretation of significant archaeological sites in the Galisteo Basin. The act identifies twenty-four sites, including pueblos, rock art panels, and Spanish colonial settlements. Unlike other protected sites in the southwestern United States, the Galisteo basin sites are located primarily on private land, requiring a new and inclusive framework for public and private cooperation. The preservation of these sites requires a diverse partnership of federal and local agencies, Native American tribal governments, landowners, developers, researchers, and historic preservation advocacy groups. At present, most of the sites covered by the act are closed to the public; however, occasional guided tours of selected sites are offered through organizations and agencies active in the preservation effort. For up-to-date information on visiting and preservation and research in the area, consult the Galisteo Basin Archaeology Web site.

Further Reading: Adams, E. B., and A. Chavez, eds., *The Missions of New Mexico 1776: A Description by Fray Francisco Atanasio Dominguez with Other Contemporary Documents* (Albuquerque: University of New Mexico Press, 1956); Lambert, M. F., *Paa-ko: Archaeological Chronicle of an Indian Village in North Central New Mexico*, Monograph No. 19 (Santa Fe, NM: School of American Research, 1954); Lycett, M. T., "Transformations of Place: Occupational History and Differential Persistence in 17th Century New Mexico," in *Archaeologies of the Pueblo Revolt: Identity, Meaning, and Renewal in the Pueblo World*, edited by Robert Preucel (Albuquerque: University of New Mexico Press, 2002), 61–74; Lycett, M. T., and N. H. Thomas, "Pueblo Indian Adaptations of Spanish Metallurgy," in *The Encyclopedia of the History of Science, Technology and Medicine in Non-Western Cultures*, edited by Helaine Selin (Dordrecht: Kluwer Academic, 2008); National Park Service and Bureau of Land Management, *Galisteo Basin Archaeology*, http://galisteoarcheology.org/home.php; Nelson, N. C., *Pueblo Ruins of the Galisteo Basin, New Mexico*, Anthropological Papers No. 15(1) (New York: American Museum of Natural History, 1914); Snead, J. E., "Ancestral Pueblo Settlement Dynamics: Landscape, Scale, and Context in the Burnt Corn Community," *Kiva* 69 (2004): 242–270.

Mark T. Lycett

PECOS NATIONAL HISTORICAL PARK

North Central New Mexico
Ancient and Historic Crossroads of Uplands and Plains

OVERVIEW

Quiet now except for the wind and the sounds of tourists, the nearly 7,000 acres of Pecos National Historical Park have witnessed human activity for centuries. More than a record of a single people, Pecos National Historical Park witnessed myriad clashes of the New World with the Old, of differing ideologies and social organization, and of technology. It was the birthplace of modern Southwestern archaeology, as A. V. Kidder married science with stratigraphy (layers in the earth) to understand the development of Pueblo culture through broken and discarded artifacts. A. O. Shepard, focusing on the nature of clay and paint instead of just vessel form, started a quiet revolution in the understanding of the origins of ancient pottery that continues to unfold today. The dust has settled, and descendants of the Pueblo and Hispano players still live nearby, sharing a common heritage and bond with Pecos Pueblo. Pecos National Historical Park is, indeed, a place where the past is present.

THE CREATORS OF THE ANCIENT AND HISTORIC SITES AT PECOS NATIONAL HISTORICAL PARK

Human use of the area within the Pecos National Historical Park spans many centuries. Hundreds of generations of nomadic families left behind spear points of chipped stone, clusters of burned rocks that encircled long-ago fires, and stones used to grind small seeds for food. By the ninth century, their temporary camps and brush shelters were replaced by pit houses, which were substantial family dwellings set in deep circular pits with roofs supported by upright logs and thatched with branches, reeds, and a final covering of earth. The pit house dwellers were the first farmers in the Pecos area and grew corn, beans, and squash and gathered wild plants for fruit, condiments, dye, and medicine, although they continued to hunt wild game. By the twelfth century, extended families came to build multi-story houses known as pueblos on the surface of the ground, and cotton, used for food and clothing, was added to the crops in farm fields.

The archaeological remains of these people's lives can be difficult for the untrained eye to see, and as a result public interpretation at Pecos National Historical Park focuses on the ancient architecture of pueblo villages that were built from the twelfth century onward. Forked Lightning Pueblo, for example, was constructed in the twelfth and thirteenth centuries. The ruins of several other multi-room pueblos remain

from the thirteenth century, including Arrowhead Ruin and the first constructions that became Pecos Pueblo. But sometime after AD 1325, only Pecos Pueblo remained occupied to command the landscape then as now, and it is Pecos Pueblo about which the most is known today.

Pecos Pueblo is situated on a narrow ridge at the imaginary edge between the Rio Grande valley and the southern high plains, between settled farmers and nomads, potters and bison hunters. Built in the early fourteenth century over earlier ruins, Pecos Pueblo became a regional power in the fifteenth century as hundreds of farm families came and built contiguous rooms onto the pueblo that reached as high as five stories in places. Buffalo-hunting traders from the southern high plains came to exchange meat and hides for maize and pottery in a relationship with Pecos Pueblo farmers that had started 100 years before Columbus. Two hundred years later, the pueblo and its commerce greatly impressed the Spanish explorer Coronado, the first European to see the city in 1540.

Beginning in 1598, Pecos Pueblo labor was harnessed by Don Juan de Oñate and his settlers, livestock, and Franciscan priests to build the massive adobe Spanish colonial religious and secular buildings so visible at the park today. Viewed both as souls to be saved by conversion to Catholicism and as labor to be used to produce tribute and Spanish crops, the Pueblo people at Pecos and elsewhere bided their time as their resentments grew and their numbers plummeted. In 1680 Pueblo peoples speaking a variety of languages across northern New Mexico joined together in a revolt against the Spanish, said to have started at San Juan Pueblo (now Ohkay Owingeh Pueblo, north of Española). The occupants of Pecos Pueblo joined in. Death and destruction ruled the land as Pueblo refugees fled the unrest and the Spanish were driven south of the Rio Grande into modern-day Mexico. The Spanish reconquest in 1692 resulted in a more respectful co-existence as politics and governance changed in response to the stunning revolt.

The years passed and Pecos Pueblo continued as a mission outpost of Catholic Spain and a major trading center with Plains groups, while population numbers continued a silent downward spiral from death by disease and raids by Comanches and Apaches. By the 1780s, Pecos Pueblo was occupied by fewer than 300 people. In 1821 Mexico achieved its independence from Spain, and the Santa Fe Trail, carrying trade goods between St. Louis and Santa Fe, passed by a Pecos Pueblo that was almost a ghost town. New Mexico was occupied by U.S. forces under General Kearney in 1846 and became a territory of the United States two years later. New Mexico became a state in 1912. Largely spared resettlement by land-hungry Americans, New Mexico's Native peoples today occupy their ancestral homelands as they engage in Western civilization on their own terms. Pecos Pueblo became a New Mexico state park in 1935 and a national monument in 1965.

ARCHAEOLOGY AT PECOS NATIONAL HISTORICAL PARK

Site Layout

Pecos Pueblo (North Pueblo) dates to the fourteenth century and by AD 1600 comprised at least 600 rooms in separate block-like buildings that were four to five stories high in places, constructed much like apartment buildings today. Suites of rooms in the masonry room blocks were occupied by individual families. The room blocks themselves surrounded large open spaces (plazas), which were multipurpose areas for community work spaces and special-purpose kivas (pit structures). Kivas were also built outside the pueblo.

The huge open rectangle of North Pueblo suggests to archaeologists that the pueblo was designed in advance and constructed all at once. A Spanish observer in 1540 remarked that covered corridors or galleries ran around the village at the second-story level, making it possible to move all around the pueblo without descending to the plaza level.

The South Pueblo dates somewhat later than the North Pueblo, has a complicated construction history, and might have been inhabited by Spanish sympathizers at Pecos Pueblo. Mostly unexcavated, it was multi-storied but probably not as tall as Pecos Pueblo (North Pueblo).

The Mission of Our Lady of the Angels of Porciuncula, constructed in 1717, was built over the foundations of the earlier mission of the same name, which was built in 1625 but destroyed during the Pueblo Revolt. The foundations of the 1625 church—22 feet thick in places—still can be seen in the interior of the standing ruins from 1717, showing that the two buildings were oriented 180 degrees from each other. The priests' quarters (convento) adjoined the 1625 church on the left side of the sanctuary, whereas they adjoined the 1717 sanctuary on the right.

The convento served many purposes for the priests and populace of Pecos Pueblo. It encompassed small, dark rooms used for sleeping quarters, cooking, dining, workshops, and storerooms as well as a stone-floored corral and a rainwater collection system that drained into a cistern.

Alfred Vincent Kidder and Early American Archaeology at Pecos

Alfred Vincent Kidder, an American archaeologist interested in correlating changes in southwestern cultural history, began his excavations at Pecos Pueblo in 1915 knowing two things: (1) pottery technology and decoration change over time, and (2) the bottom layer of an archaeological site is the oldest and each layer above the bottom is progressively younger. Until radiocarbon dating was invented in 1950, no one could determine whether one kind of pottery fragment (shard) was relatively older or younger than any other. Which kind of decoration or way of making a pot came first? Kidder hoped that careful archaeological excavation and detailed stratigraphic recording would demonstrate the exact sequence of older to younger kinds of shards. If it worked out, this "relative dating" would, for the first time, allow an archaeologist to understand from broken pottery when an archaeological site was occupied.

Kidder chose to excavate at Pecos Pueblo for several reasons. Occupations at the pueblo were known to have extended from at least AD 1540 until its abandonment in 1838, meaning that written records existed and interviews with descendants could fill in details about what was found. Deep trash deposits had been created by centuries of occupation at the pueblo and could be expected to yield material resulting from successive centuries. Finally, the position Pecos Pueblo held as a trading center meant that excavated artifacts from Plains groups could be compared with archaeological and ethnographic work then proceeding among cultures to the east and thereby dated, at least in a relative fashion.

Kidder's work at Pecos Pueblo demonstrated that evidence of culture change is preserved in stratigraphic deposits and that careful excavation, detailed recording, systematic collection, and analysis can provide insights into what and how such change occurs. Stratigraphy, pottery sequences, and dendrochronology underpin Southwestern archaeology to this day.

Kidder's work at Pecos Pueblo lasted twelve field seasons. Insight into the visibility of ancestral Puebloan sites was gained inadvertently when he realized that his field camp had been built squarely on top of Forked Lightning Pueblo four years earlier. More than 100 rooms were eventually excavated by Kidder, who learned that the evidence of even long occupations in sizable adobe pueblos can essentially disappear. This means that more chapters in the story of past human activity in the Pecos National Historical Park are likely to be preserved, even if unseen at present.

Anna Osler Shepard and Pioneering Ceramic Analysis

Working as a young archaeologist with Kidder was Anna Osler Shepard, one of the women pioneers of archaeology. As was expected of women at the time, Shepard worked primarily in the laboratory, in her case categorizing broken pottery. Bucking the belief of the day that every Pueblo woman made her own pots, Shepard studied pottery shards from Pecos Pueblo in literally microscopic detail. Far from confirming the accepted belief, Shepard demonstrated that different kinds of pottery were made using clays, tempering agents, or paints that were foreign to the area around Pecos Pueblo. The pottery could not have been made by Pecos Pueblo women but instead had to have been made in other Pueblo communities, some hundreds of miles away. This imported pottery was evidence of trade networks whose existence had not even been suspected according to the dominant thinking of the day. Shepard's unusually technical work and contrary conclusions were largely ignored by twentieth-century archaeologists. Long after her death, her findings are being rediscovered and used by increasing numbers of archaeologists today.

The Pecos Conference

In 1927 Kidder initiated an annual meeting of archaeologists to discuss the exciting findings of his, and others', work and to develop a classification system to recognize the cultural development of Southwestern peoples. Known as the Pecos Classification, Kidder's chronology—the first historical reconstruction in the Southwest—was born of careful correlation of site stratigraphy and pottery types. In its original form, the Pecos Classification recognized the following cultural stages:

- Basketmaker II: Families of farmers use *atl atl* (spear thrower) but lack pottery.
- Basketmaker III: Groups of farmers and potters build pit houses or slab houses and use the bow-and-arrow.
- Pueblo I: Farmers and potters build above-ground dwellings of contiguous rectangular rooms.
- Pueblo II: Farmers and potters live in small villages of above-ground dwellings.
- Pueblo III: Farmers, potters, artists, and craftspeople live in large towns of above-ground dwellings.
- Pueblo IV: Farmers, potters, artists, and craftspeople live in a few very large towns of above-ground dwellings while parts of the Pueblo world are abandoned.
- Pueblo V: Spanish explorers use the term "pueblo" upon seeing the very large multi-story communities built during Pueblo IV, and their inhabitants become "Pueblo Indians."

Each time period or cultural stage is associated with particular kinds of pottery, other artifacts, and details of architectural construction. Working at the same time as Kidder, the astronomer A. E. Douglass was exploring the use of tree rings to determine when an ancient construction timber had been cut. Eventually, in 1929, dendrochronology, as the science came to be known, was able to tie occupations at Pecos and other pueblos to calendar dates.

The Pecos Classification, still a useful shorthand for pre-Columbian cultural development in the northern Southwest, has been modified by later workers to apply to other parts of New Mexico, Arizona, and elsewhere. As new techniques to date archaeological sites are developed, the relative dates of various types of pottery are refined and tightened.

Archaeologists continue to meet at the annual Pecos conference, as the meeting came to be called, to this day.

Continuity with Living Descendants of Pecos Pueblo

The people who built the Pecos Pueblo in the early fourteenth century had been joined by other Natives, the Spanish, and then other Europeans. Having survived centuries of Spanish colonization, disease, raids, and changing political alliances, the last seventeen Pecos Pueblo survivors left in 1838 to join Towa-speaking relatives at Jemez Pueblo some 80 miles west. The Jemez people still recognize Pecos Pueblo as a living part of their heritage, although it appears abandoned to non-Native eyes. Descendants of Pecos Pueblo return and gather at the great adobe church on August 10 each year to commemorate the anniversary of the beginning of the revolt of 1680.

VISITING PECOS NATIONAL HISTORICAL PARK

A short thirty-minute drive north on Interstate 25 from Santa Fe, New Mexico, Pecos National Historical Park lies at a pass in the foothills of the Sangre de Cristo Mountains. The ruins of the Spanish Colonial church can be glimpsed from the highway, but they are only the tip of the iceberg of human history in the area.

Several architectural remains are interpreted for the public:

- The North Pueblo contains more than 600 rooms in a building that towered four to five stories high. It was built and occupied from the early fourteenth century until 1828. The unexcavated mounds at the site are at the level of about the second story.
- The South Pueblo might have been a separate community whose inhabitants were more closely allied with the Spanish. Once multi-storied, the village housed families whose homes had rooms upstairs as well as down. Roof entries protected lower rooms from unauthorized entry. South Pueblo is largely unexcavated.
- The first church, the Mission of Our Lady of the Angels of Porciuncula, was constructed in 1625 but destroyed during the Pueblo Revolt. Its massive foundations are visible inside the sanctuary of the still-extant ruins of the 1717 church.
- The huge ruins of the adobe 1717 Mission of Our Lady of the Angels of Porciuncula are still standing along with the ruins of the *convento*, whose rooms housed the priests and various mission activities. The small dark rooms of the *convento* were arranged around a central flagstone patio. Rooms were used as sleeping quarters, kitchen, dining room, workrooms, and store rooms. A drain in the patio dates to the earlier seventeenth-century mission church and carried water running off the sloped roofs to a cistern at the other end of the *convento*. A stone-floored corral was built onto the edge of the *convento*.

- A kiva (underground ceremonial structure) associated with the standing mission ruins is thought to have been built after the 1680 revolt as a show of defiance and later filled in with dirt by returning Spanish friars in 1692. More recent evidence suggests that the kiva could have been constructed by the Franciscans decades earlier to facilitate conversion of the Pecos Pueblo populace and perhaps buried when it was no longer needed.
- Ruts from the wheels of wagons traveling the Santa Fe Trail west from St. Louis can be seen within the park. They are tangible remains of the famous commerce begun in the fourteenth century between the Puebloan Southwest and the prairies that endured into the nineteenth century.
- The Battle of Glorieta Pass, a decisive Civil War battle dubbed the "Gettysburg of the West," took place in 1861 within the current park's boundaries.
- Finally, the Forked Lightning Ranch, also in the park, started out as a dude ranch and became the home of actress Greer Garson in the twentieth century.

Further Reading: Bishop, Ronald L., and Frederick W. Lange, eds., *The Ceramic Legacy of Anna O. Shepard* (Boulder: University Press of Colorado, 1991); Cordell, Linda S., *Ancient Pueblo Peoples* (Washington, DC: Smithsonian Books, 1994); Kessel, John L., *Kiva, Cross, and Crown: The Pecos Indians and New Mexico, 1540–1840* (Washington, DC: Government Printing Office, 1979); Kessel, John L., *The Presence of the Past: Pecos Pueblo*, Annual Bulletin of the School of American Research Exploration (Santa Fe, NM: School of American Research, 1981), 12–14; Kessel, John L., *The Gateway Pueblo of Pecos: Spaniards and Indians in Colonial New Mexico* (Washington, DC: Smithsonian Institution Press, 1988); Kidder, Alfred Vincent, *An Introduction to the Study of Southwestern Archaeology with a Preliminary Account of the Excavations at Pecos* (New Haven, CT: Yale University Press for Phillips Academy, 1924); Levine, Frances, *Our Prayers Are in This Place: Pecos Pueblo Identify through the Centuries* (Albuquerque: University of New Mexico Press, 1999); Scheick, Cherie, Pecos National Monument National Register of Historic Places registration form, on file at the National Register of Historic Places (Washington, DC: National Park Service, 1991).

Glenna Dean

SALINAS PUEBLO MISSIONS NATIONAL MONUMENT

Mountainair, Central New Mexico

Adaptation and Change: 1200–1700 in Central New Mexico

In AD 1540, the Coronado expedition entered what is now the state of New Mexico and visited a number of Pueblo villages in and around the Rio Grande valley. Returning to Mexico the following year, the success of this foray opened the door for further exploration and, ultimately, in AD 1598, colonization and missionization of this region. Franciscan friars established missions directly in Pueblo villages up and down the Rio Grande area and among Pueblo populations further to the west, such as at Acoma, Hopi, and Zuni. Many of these villages continue to be occupied today. Others, however, were abandoned and thus became archaeological sites that contain important records of this early time of contact and missionization. The Salinas province contains several such sites, the three most important of which are protected within Salinas Pueblo Missions National Monument.

The Salinas province is situated in central New Mexico, east of the Rio Grande and the Manzanos Mountains. Its location provided ready access to the southern plains of eastern New Mexico and the Texas panhandle, as well as to extensive salt lakes, which were important sources of this mineral for the Pueblos of the Rio Grande. Archaeological sites in the region provide diverse kinds of material evidence concerning inter-pueblo exchange, intercultural relations between Pueblo and Plains peoples, and the Pueblo experience of Spanish colonization. These sites are spatially divided into two clusters— one to the northwest along the eastern flanks of the Manzanos Mountains, and the other to the southeast on the eastern side of Chupadero Mesa. The southeastern cluster was distinguished by the Spaniards with the term "Jumanos," which appears to refer to the trade relations that these villages had with Plains hunter-gatherers.

People hunted and gathered across the Salinas area for many thousands of years. Salinas Paleoindian and Archaic period occupations were concentrated particularly along the shores of Pleistocene lakes in the Estancia basin. Because these hunter-gatherers were few in number and highly mobile, their archaeological record is sparse, and relatively little is known about them. Sometime in the AD 800s–900s, based on ceramic dating, Salinas hunter-gatherers added the cultivation of corn to their food patterns and established more permanent habitations on the landscape in areas that were suitable for farming. They lived in round, semi-subterranean

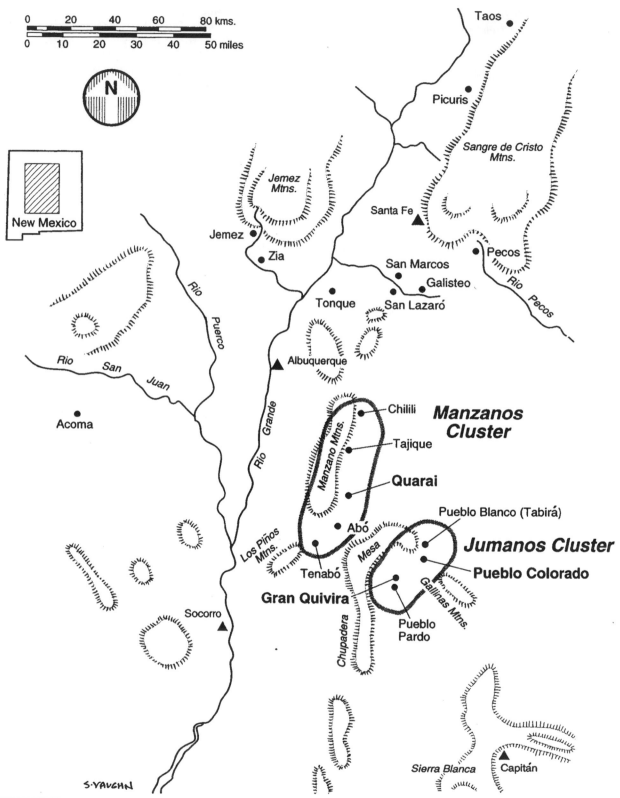

A map of the upper Rio Grande area showing sites described in this essay, other ancient, historic, and present-day Pueblo towns (filled circles), and modern cities (filled triangles).   [Katherine A. Spielmann]

Chupadero Black-on-White jar.   [Katherine A. Spielmann. Courtesy of Salinas Pueblo Missions NM]

pit structures. These farmers made pottery, including brown-ware jars for cooking and storage, white-slipped jars painted with black geometric designs (Chupadero Black-on-White) for carrying and storing water, and small bowls for serving food. They imported grayware and black-on-white ceramics from further to the west. Pit houses remained the primary form of habitation for the next three centuries. Compared with other regions in the Southwest, pit house occupation extends much later in time in the Salinas area in particular and the Rio Grande region in general, possibly because hunting and gathering remained an important component of people's subsistence for a longer period of time in this sparsely populated area.

In the 1100s some Salinas residents began to build surface jacal structures—room blocks constructed of upright stone slab bases and pole-and-thatch walls and roof—although others continued to build and live in pit structures. Initially, the jacals were as dispersed as the pit structure settlements had been. In the late 1100s to early 1200s, however, people began to aggregate into larger settlements, some as large as 200 to 300 rooms. Further construction in the late 1200s and 1300s at these same villages was of more permanent masonry walls.

This concentration of Salinas people into larger, longer-lasting villages may have occurred in response large-scale changes to the southwestern social landscape. In the AD 1200s, to the west of the Salinas province the Ancestral Puebloan (also known as Anasazi) world was changing dramatically, as thousands of Ancestral Puebloan people who had been living in the Four Corners region migrated into the Rio Grande valley and established settlements from the Socorro area on the south to the Chama valley on the north. In the Jumanos area of the Salinas province stone masonry room blocks often enclosed a central plaza, presenting an unbroken wall to the outside. There is no record of actual violence from these early masonry villages, but there seems to have been a concern for defense at this time. Enclosed pueblos may have also reinforced a sense of community identity and solidarity. At the Gran Quivira unit of Salinas Pueblo Missions National Monument there is both a quadrangular (Mound 21) and a circular (lower Mound 7) early masonry pueblo.

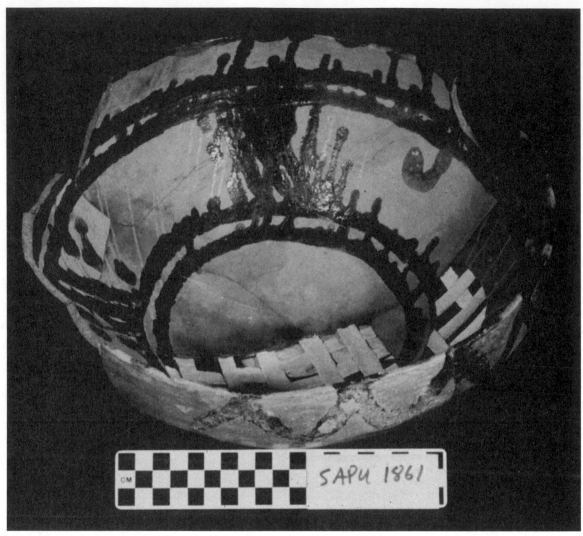

Photo of a Glazeware bowl, note the characteristic decoration using dark glaze paint.   [Katherine A. Spielmann. Courtesy of Salinas Pueblo Missions NM]

The massive Ancestral Puebloan migrations of the 1200s to early 1300s brought about marked changes in Pueblo ritual activities across the Southwest, including the development of a new ritual system, the Southwestern Cult. This cult was associated with the manufacture and use of red-slipped bowls and jars, which were decorated with new iconography. In the Rio Grande area, including Salinas, potters used both red and yellow slips on these new ceramics and made the decorations with dark glaze paints. Thus Rio Grande archaeologists call this new ceramic tradition Glazeware. Glazeware iconography focused in particular on bird (probably parrot) imagery. Glazeware bowl sizes were much bigger than the black-on-white bowls had been, suggesting that communal feasting was a component of the new ritual system.

In the early 1400s, the inhabitants of the now populous Rio Grande region moved from pueblos of a few hundred rooms into very large pueblos of several hundred rooms, which housed several hundred to a thousand or more people. Many of these villages occur in clusters, suggesting some level of pan-village organization, such as a confederacy or polity, in which villages are allied with one another for economic, ritual, and/or social exchanges. Residents of the Salinas area participated in this trend, creating clusters of large villages in both the Manzanos and Jumanos portions of the region. It is these large villages that the Spaniards encountered in 1540 and missionized in the 1600s.

These large, long-lived sites include the stone ruins of the pueblo room blocks, numerous semi-subterranean ritual structures called kivas, and very deep, dense trash deposits. The trash contains hundreds of thousands of pot shards, as well as stone flakes and projectile points, small pieces of obsidian from the Jemez Mountains, broken manos and metates for corn grinding, animal bone, and charred plant remains such as corn cobs, kernels, and pinyon nut shells. Abo, and possibly Tenabo, residents began to make Glazeware for use throughout the Salinas province, although significant

Top view of Tabira Black-on-White jar showing elaborate decoration from Gran Quivira.   [Katherine A. Spielmann. Courtesy of Salinas Pueblo Missions NM]

quantities of glaze-decorated ceramics continued to be imported.

The province was abandoned in its entirety in the 1670s due to drought, famine, and Apache raiding. Ethnohistorical accounts and Pueblo traditions indicate that those Salinas residents who survived the famine moved west to the Rio Grande and joined their Tiwa-speaking relatives at Sandia and Isleta.

PLAINS-PUEBLO RELATIONS

Castaneda, chronicler of Coronado's 1540–42 expedition to New Mexico, mentions groups of Plains hunters visiting eastern border pueblos to trade. The items involved in the exchange included bison meat, fat, and hides from the Plains and corn, squash, cotton blankets, and ceramics from the

Pueblos. Plains bands would often camp for several months near the pueblo of their trading partners. Artifacts from the Salinas pueblos indicate that this trade had a long history in the eastern Pueblo area.

Located on the eastern border of the Pueblo world, villagers in the Salinas province were well situated to interact with Plains bison-hunting peoples. The Pueblos of the Jumanos cluster, in particular, took advantage of their frontier location. Plains artifacts excavated from the trash mounds at Gran Quivira include beveled knives made of Alibates dolomite from the Texas panhandle and shell pendants made of a Plains species of shell. Bison bone is also found in the Gran Quivira trash. The fact that these bones are primarily ribs suggests that the products of bison hunts were transported long distances. Hunters would have dried most of the meat for ease of transport and left the heaviest and bulkiest bones, such as leg bones and the pelvis, at the kill site. Both people and German shepherd–size dogs would have transported these goods to the pueblos from the southern plains.

The stratigraphy and datable artifacts, such as decorated ceramics, in the trash middens at Gran Quivira indicate that people had inhabited this large Pueblo village for roughly 100 years before trade relations were established with Plains hunters. During that time Gran Quivirans relied primarily on local antelope and rabbits as their meat source. With the arrival of populations who were probably ancestral Athabascans on the southern plains in the 1400s, however, the opportunity for exchange developed at the same time as local antelope were becoming scarce due to hunting pressures. It is in the mid-1400s Gran Quivira trash that the Plains artifacts first appear.

Plains trade continued into the historic period, but the amount of Plains material in the Gran Quivira trash decreased, probably due to Spanish interference in Plains-Pueblo trade. This interference, including the taking of Apache children as slaves, likely led to a pattern of raiding and trading on the part of the Apaches in the 1600s.

Plains hunters traded for corn, cotton blankets, and ceramics. Although remains of the first two do not frequently survive in the archaeological record, shards of Pueblo Glazeware have been found at many Plains hunter-gatherer sites. The paste of these shards, in particular the type of crushed rock that the clay was tempered with, allows the identification of the manufacturing village. Ceramic evidence for Plains trade specifically with Salinas pueblos has been retrieved from hunter-gatherer camps of the 1400s and 1500s in Blanco Canyon in the Texas panhandle.

MISSIONIZATION AND ITS AFTERMATH

The villages of Abo and Quarai were missionized by 1629, whereas Gran Quivira was missionized briefly in the late 1620s and then abandoned by its friar. There was then no resident friar at Gran Quivira until 1660. Colonization dramatically changed Salinas Pueblo lives. Spanish missionaries and colonists alike made demands on Pueblo labor and products, and the missionaries sought to eradicate Pueblo religion and replace it with Catholicism. Evidence for these diverse activities is visible in the archaeological and bioarchaeological records from the Salinas area.

Eradication of Pueblo religion is most evident in the burning of seven seventeenth-century kivas at Gran Quivira, probably in the 1660s in response to orders from the friar in charge of the New Mexican missions, Fray Alonso Posada. It is also evident in marked changes in the iconography on pottery of the 1600s. Post-colonial Glazeware was produced at two of the missionized pueblos, Abo and Quarai, where Spanish friars were in residence. Potters in these villages simplified their designs so that the Southwestern Cult iconography was not evident. At Gran Quivira, where there was no

resident friar until the 1600s, potters who made the black-on-white jars markedly elaborated the iconography on their pots, depicting ritual garments, paraphernalia, katsinas, and gods. This elaboration may have been one means of maintaining and teaching Pueblo ritual knowledge where missionaries were not present, and under conditions in which ritual specialists were being imprisoned or otherwise punished by Spanish authorities.

Spanish demands on the labor of Salinas Pueblo peoples are evident from bioarchaeological information from Gran Quivira. Burials excavated and later reburied from this village provide osteological information related to repetitive tasks performed by Gran Quivirans living before and after Spanish missionization of the area. Analyses of the muscle attachment sites on human remains document a marked increase in burden bearing on the part of adult men. This is corroborated by Spanish documents that discuss Salinas people transporting loads of salt, corn, and pinyon nuts between villages in the Salinas area to villages on the Rio Grande, to Santa Fe, and even as far as the silver mines in northern Mexico. Adult women appear to have increased the amount of effort spent on corn grinding. In addition, older women increased their labor after colonization, probably to process hides, which were paid in tribute to Spaniards.

Archaeological excavations have also documented postcontact dietary change in the Salinas province. Pueblos incorporated Spanish domestic animals into their diets and consumed less local game. At Quarai, Pueblo residents consumed a fair quantity of sheep, although not as much as the friars themselves. Sheep were the primary stock raised by Salinas friars. At Gran Quivira, however, sheep are rare due to the insufficiency of surface water near this village. Instead, cattle are the primary domestic animal in post-colonial Gran Quivira trash deposits. Gran Quivirans likely obtained these animals "on the hoof," because cattle were an important export commodity from New Mexico and were not even well represented in friars' diets of the time.

SALINAS PUEBLO MISSIONS NATIONAL MONUMENT

Salinas Pueblo Missions National Monument protects the remains of three large missionized Pueblo villages: Gran Quivira, Abo, and Quarai. Abo and Quarai are situated in the Manzanos cluster of pueblos. Gran Quivira is part of the Jumanos cluster. Each site contains several plazas surrounded by pueblo room blocks and a large masonry church with attached living quarters for the friars and their assistants.

The churches and living quarters at all three sites were excavated in the 1930s and have been stabilized. Self-guided trails at all three sites lead visitors around portions of the pueblo villages, into the massive churches, and through the friars' living quarters. Small portions of the Pueblo room blocks at Abo and Quarai have been excavated and stabilized for visitor viewing. At Gran Quivira the largest of the twenty-one room blocks at the site, Mound 7, portions of several other room blocks, and several kivas have been excavated and stabilized; these are accessible to the public. The park headquarters in Mountainair provides an introductory film and small museum. Small museums at Quarai and Gran Quivira house informative exhibits of artifacts from excavations at these sites and provide background on the culture history of the area.

Further Reading: Chamberlin, Matthew A., "Aggregation and Social Identity in Salinas: Landscape Formation in the Coalition-Classic (A.D. 1250–1350) Transition," paper presented at the annual meeting of the Society for American Archaeology, Denver, March 2002; Graves, William M., "Power, Autonomy, and Inequality in Rio Grande Puebloan Society, A.D. 1300–1672," Ph.D. diss. (Arizona State University, , 2002); Hayes, Alden, Jon N. Young, and A. H. Warren, *Excavation of Mound 7*, Publications in Archeology No. 16 (Washington, DC: National Park Service, 1981); Leonard, Kathryn, "Directionality and Exclusivity of Plains-Pueblo Exchange during the Protohistoric Period (A.D. 1450–1700)," master's thesis (Arizona State University, 2000);

Rautman, Alison, "Resource Variability, Risk, and the Structure of Social Networks: An Example from the Prehistoric Southwest," *American Antiquity* 58 (1993): 403–424; Rautman, Alison, "Population Aggregation, Community Organization, and Plaza-Oriented Pueblos in the American Southwest," *Journal of Field Archaeology* 27 (2000): 271–283; Spielmann, Katherine A., "Colonists, Hunters and Farmers: Plains-Pueblo Interaction in the Seventeenth Century," in *Columbian Consequences, Volume 1*, edited by David Hurst Thomas (Washington, DC: Smithsonian Institution Press, 1989), 101–113; Spielmann, Katherine A., "Clustered Confederacies: Sociopolitical Organization in the Protohistoric Rio Grande," in *The Ancient Southwestern Community: Models and Methods for the Study of Prehistoric Social Organization*, edited by W. Wills and R. Leonard (Albuquerque: University of New Mexico Press, 1994), 45–54; Spielmann, Katherine A., Tiffany Clark, Suzanne K. Fish, Diane Hawkey, Katharine Rainey, and Margaret Schoeninger, ". . . Being Weary, They Had Rebelled": Pueblo Subsistence and Labor under Spanish Colonization," *Journal of Anthropological Archaeology* (in press); Tainter, Joseph A., and Frances Levine, *Cultural Resources Overview: Central New Mexico* (Albuquerque, NM: USDA Forest Service, 1987).

Katherine A. Spielmann

THE PAQUIMÉ (CASAS GRANDES) SITE

Northwestern Chihuahua, Mexico

A Link between the Puebloan Southwest and Mesoamerica

Paquimé (or Casas Grandes), dating from AD 1200 to 1450, long has been recognized as one of the most important and elaborate prehistoric communities in the American Southwest and northern Mexico. The site's extensive residential architecture is of the Pueblo style that is well known from the Southwest. Also present is ritual architecture that is not characteristic of the Pueblo world, including flat-topped earthen mounds and ball courts. Both of these were important elements in the ritual of central and western Mexico, or northern Mesoamerica. Paquimé contains large quantities of trade goods from regions to the north and south, and it is seen as a link between the Pueblo cultures of the Southwest and the more complex societies of Mesoamerica. Finally, a large surrounding area was influenced by the community.

Cultural development in northwestern Chihuahua began with Paleoindian and Archaic hunter-gatherers. By about AD 300, small villages of semi-subterranean pit houses were relying increasingly on farming. By AD 1200, pit houses had been replaced by the clusters of surface rooms known as pueblos. Pueblo people were more numerous and more agricultural than their pit house predecessors. This way of life existed until AD 1450 or 1475, when much of the region was abandoned by farmers. There are no indigenous people in the region that can be linked to the ancient builders of Paquimé.

Paquimé is a cluster of room blocks, platform mounds, ball courts, and other facilities covering about 36 hectares. It lies at the headwaters of the Casas Grandes River, where there is both dependable water and good valley floor farming land. The 2,000 rooms of the community mostly are concentrated in a large, central room block, parts of which rise to three stories. These rooms are unusually large, averaging 27 square meters; average room area is less than 10 square meters in the rest of the Pueblo world. Walls at all sites in Chihuahua were built by packing successive layers of damp earth between horizontal wooden forms. The normal thickness of these walls is 20–40 centimeters. At Paquimé, all walls were 90–110 centimeters thick, even in the single-story room blocks. Lastly, some of the rooms at Paquimé were of elaborate shapes, with ten to eighteen walls. Such rooms are almost unknown at neighboring sites. The architecture of Paquimé, then, is much more elaborate than that of its neighbors. It has been suggested that this represents an "architecture of power," or a symbolic statement of the preeminence and grandeur of the community.

Map of the Paquimé (Casas Grandes) site loaction within the wider Southwest region. [Michael E. Whalen]

The site's Mesoamerican-derived ritual architecture is equally notable. There are eleven platform mounds, which were common loci for ritual activities in Mesoamerica. Paquimé also has two large ball courts, or sunken I-shaped fields on which the ancient Mesoamericans played a ball game that was an important part of their ritual system. This concentration of ritual architecture has no equal at any other known contemporary site in the Southwest or in northwestern Mexico, and some archaeologists see Paquimé as a pilgrimage center and a seat of supernatural power for surrounding populations.

Long-distance exchange was a second source of the community's power. Trade was characteristic of all prehistoric Pueblo cultures, but Paquimé raised this activity to an unprecedented level. One room at the site, for example, contained more than 4.5 million small sea shells that were imported from the Gulf of California, which lies to the southwest in Mexico. The skeletons of some 350 macaws and other parrots were found at Paquimé, as were the cages in which they were kept. Areas to the south, in Mexico, are the only sources for these birds. Copper ornaments were brought to

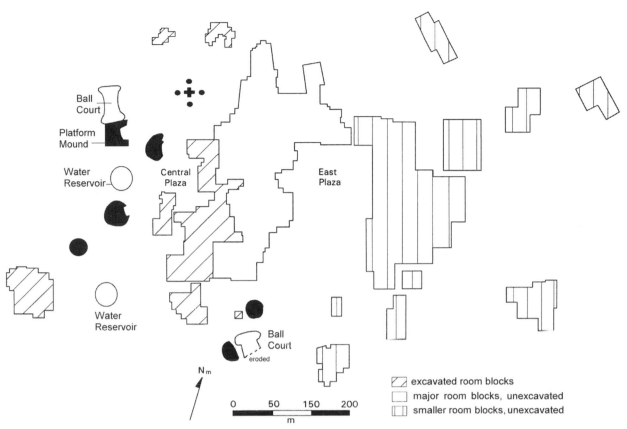

Ball Court

Platform Mound

Water Reservoir

Central Plaza

East Plaza

Water Reservoir

Ball Court
eroded

N m

0   50   150   200
m

⬚ excavated room blocks
☐ major room blocks, unexcavated
▥ smaller room blocks, unexcavated

Plan showing the site of Paquimé (Casas Grandes) showing the major architectural components. Only about ten percent of the site has been excavated by archaeologists. [Michael E. Whalen]

Paquimé from their places of origin in western Mexico. Trade with the Pueblo societies to the north also is evident. Hundreds of ceramic vessels of many types were imported from all across the southern part of the Southwest, and pottery from Paquimé was traded into these areas. Also brought to Paquimé was turquoise, a prized raw material from mines in the Southwest.

Much of the traded material likely was used in special circumstances. Parrots and their feathers were important in the ritual of Pueblo peoples. Ornaments of shell, turquoise, and copper are what archaeologists term "prestige goods," or expensive elaborate items used by the elite people of society to display and emphasize their privileged status. Certainly, the exotic material that flowed into Paquimé made it one of the wealthiest communities in the prehistoric Pueblo world.

Although all agree that Paquimé stood out dramatically from its contemporaries, there has been much debate about exactly what kind of place it was. Since the late 1800s, the majority of archaeologists stressed the strong resemblance and probable developmental links between Paquimé and the Pueblo communities of the Southwest. The Mesoamerican-style ritual architecture was recognized, but it was seen as a minor component of the community's identity.

This widely held perspective was altered radically by the Joint Casas Grandes Project, begun in 1958 by the American archaeologist Charles C. Di Peso and Eduardo Contreras of Mexico's National Institute of Anthropology and History (INAH). Three years of intensive excavation provided a huge body of data on Paquimé, and this was the basis of a completely new interpretation of the site. Di Peso maintained that Paquimé was established on the edge of the Southwest by *Pochteca*, or traveling merchants from Mesoamerica, with the aim of controlling trade between the two regions. The Pochteca organized local populations to build Paquimé, and they imported Mesoamerican ritual architecture, along with the associated ceremonial concepts and symbols, to support and legitimize their authority over the locals. Paquimé thus was seen as a development that was not indigenous to its region. In the intervening years, many have strongly criticized the Pochteca model, but some still contend that significant developmental stimuli came from Mesoamerica.

Others have taken a different position, maintaining that Paquimé developed entirely from local antecedents, without impetus from Mesoamerica. This argument sees Paquimé as occupying a favorable ecological position that allowed it to prosper and grow beyond its neighbors. Emerging elite people at Paquimé used their increasing wealth to import some elements of ritual and some prestige goods from the more developed societies of northwestern Mesoamerica. Ethnographic and prehistoric contexts all over the world show that this is a common strategy by which aspiring people or groups gain and enhance social power. In this view, Paquimé is one of prehistoric North America's few examples of indigenous complex society development. Its origin is only one of many interpretive questions surrounding the community. The ways it maintained social control and the nature and extent of its influence over its near and distant neighbors are additional issues that continue to be debated.

Paquimé has been designated a World Heritage Site by the United Nations Educational, Scientific, and Cultural Organization (UNESCO). The excavated areas are open to the public every day except Monday, and trails lead visitors through the ruins. Beside the site is the Museum of Northern Cultures. Many of the artifacts from Paquimé and neighboring sites are on display, and the exhibits are arranged to tell the story of

cultural development in the region. Paquimé is about 5 miles from the town of New Casas Grandes, Chihuahua. Both are accessible from the United States by paved roads that are suitable for all types of vehicles. Be sure to consult a Mexican consulate or a travel guide for information on border crossing requirements.

Further Reading: Di Peso, Charles C., *Casas Grandes, a Fallen Trading Center of the Gran Chichimeca*, Vols. 1–3 (Dragoon and Flagstaff, AZ: Amerind Foundation and Northland Press, 1974); Van Pool, Christina S., and Todd L. Van Pool, *Signs of the Casas Grandes Shamans* (Salt Lake City: University of Utah Press, 2007); Whalen, Michael E., and Paul E. Minnis, *Casas Grandes and Its Hinterland: Prehistoric Regional Organization in Northwest Mexico* (Tucson: University of Arizona Press, 2001).

Michael E. Whalen and Paul E. Minnis

LOWER PECOS RIVER ROCK ART AND ARCHAEOLOGICAL SITES

Southwestern Texas

Amistad National Recreation Area and Other Sites

THE LOWER PECOS RIVER CANYON LANDS

Amistad National Recreation Area is located in the heartland of a roughly 100-square-mile area that archaeologists call the Lower Pecos River Canyon Lands, or simply the Lower Pecos region. In this rugged part of southwest Texas and northeastern Mexico, where the deep canyons of the Devils and Pecos rivers enter the Rio Grande along the Mexican border, Native American prehistory existed roughly 12,000 years ago and continued to exist in various forms up until the nineteenth century. In addition to having some of North America's oldest-dated and best-preserved archaeological deposits, the region also possesses internationally recognized prehistoric rock art sites. The post-contact history of the area is little known in the literature but includes key events, places, and individuals significant in the settlement of much of western Texas.

Over 2,000 documented archaeological sites exist on the U.S. side of the Rio Grande. There are three National Register Historical Districts, with one site listing collectively 183 sites at a national level of significance, while an equal number (or more) are yet to be nominated. The most common site types include rockshelters, deeply stratified river terrace sites, rock art sites, and upland sites. Together, these offer an unparalleled opportunity for scientists of all types to study North American prehistory, and they are the reason the Lower

Pecos region may be the most intensively and extensively researched geographic area in Texas.

The Lower Pecos Canyon Lands are formed from Cretaceous period limestone that over millions of years have been deeply carved and bisected by three major river valleys and literally hundreds of intervening side canyons and drainages. Wind, water, and time have created countless caves, rockshelters, and cliff overhangs in canyon walls, which can in certain sections rise more than 200 feet above the river bottoms. These types of geological features, which were heavily utilized by prehistoric cultures, are collectively referred to as rockshelters by archaeologists.

This semi-arid region receives less than 12 inches of rain annually. Biologists attribute the region's incredible biological diversity to geography; the area is topographically situated at the convergence of the Balcones, Chihuahuan, and Tamaulipan biotic provinces. Each biotic zone has a unique suite of plants and animals based on minor variations in regional climate, geology, and rainfall. Prehistoric peoples early on discovered this oasis of biotic diversity and developed technologies to exploit seasonal abundances of both plants and animals. The semi-arid climate over the past 5,000–6,000 years provides the ideal environmental conditions for the preservation of organic materials in rockshelter deposits. The extraordinary preservation of organic materials linked to human activities, such as food and plant remains, human feces, human burials, and artifacts (including, sandals, basketry, textiles, wooden and bone artifacts), and cordage provides current researchers an unparalleled opportunity for the study of everyday life ways of ancient North American cultures.

Archaeological research in the region began in the 1930s and continues to the present. The earliest excavations were conducted by relic hunters as well as by museums and academic institutions such as the Smithsonian, Gila Pueblo, and the Witte Museum. These organizations targeted rockshelter sites; their main purpose was the collection of artifacts, burials, and other items of general interest for museum exhibits, with little interest in identifying the people who had produced them. Decades later, academic research began to focus on chronological relationships among archaeological sites and cultures, identifying changes over time in artifact styles, and understanding regional subsistence patterns. By the time Lake Amistad was constructed in the late 1950s, the focus of archaeological interest was much more scientific and utilized a multidisciplinary approach. Researchers focused on all classes of artifacts, the first-time regional application of radiocarbon dating, the refinement of projectile-point chronologies, systematic rock art documentation, the scientific analysis of plant and animals remains, studies of human health and mortuary patterns, and the development of paleoclimactic models.

The National Park Service (NPS) sponsored much of the pre-inundation archaeological research for Lake Amistad from 1958–70. In cooperation with the University of Texas at Austin, the NPS published the results from over twenty major excavations (none from the Mexican side of the Rio Grande) at sites such as Devils Mouth, Javelina Bluffs, Damp Cave, Centipede Cave, Mosquito Cave, Devils Rock Shelter, Arenosa Rock Shelter, Doss site, Cueva Quebrada, Coon Tail Spin Rock Shelter, Parida Cave, Fate Bell Shelter, Eagle Cave, Bonfire Rock Shelter, Zopilote Cave, Nopal Terrace, and Perry Calk site. Collectively, this research from over 300 different sites produced a museum collection estimated to contain at least 1.4 million artifacts, of which about 680,000 specimens have been cataloged into an NPS database. Today, the collection is curated at the Texas Archeological Research Laboratory (TARL) at the University of Texas at Austin and managed by Amistad National Recreation Area. It is available to researchers by appointment with TARL staff. The TARL library contains at least nineteen master's theses and doctoral dissertations that focus, at least in part, on the NPS collections from Lake Amistad.

Decades of archaeological research demonstrate that rockshelters were used as general habitation sites, burial sites, and the locales for shamanic (or religious) activities by countless generations of Native American groups. Sites with deeply stratified perishable artifacts, that is, those with multiple layers of organic artifacts that are the byproducts of human activities, demonstrate that rockshelters served as the primary loci for everyday life. River and stream terrace sites reveal the extent to which canyon land and riverine resources were exploited, while upland sites adjacent to the canyon lands seem to be more narrowly focused on hunting, the procurement of plant foods, and the gathering of materials necessary for making tools, clothing, and items essential to daily life.

CULTURE HISTORY

Archaeologists in the American southwest generally divide regional prehistory into smaller units of time known as "periods." A geographic region's "culture history" usually consists of four general periods: Paleoindian, Archaic, late prehistoric, and historic. Each period is distinct and is based on the archaeological evidences for the presence or widespread usage of specific technologies (e.g., the bow and arrow, pottery, or the domestication of plants or animals), differences in subsistence or economic strategies, and settlement patterns (the spatial distribution of sites). The general dates for each period are derived from radiocarbon dating of organic materials in archaeological deposits. By dating multiple samples from different sites across a broad area, archaeologists are able to provide a general beginning and ending date for each period within a regional culture history. A single radiocarbon date works well to determine the age of a single burial or ancient campfire pit. However, a single date from a single site provides a tenuous basis for making regional characterizations about any specific type of mortuary practice, subsistence activity, hunting technique, or settlement pattern.

PALEOINDIAN PERIOD (12,500–7000 BC, OR 8,500–14,500 YEARS AGO)

The first people arrived in the Lower Pecos region at the end of the last Ice Age, about 12,000 years ago. They are known in archaeological literature as Paleoindians, but archaeologists have no way of knowing what they actually called themselves. Their world was one of vast grassland savannahs and pine forests filled with Pleistocene animals such as saber-toothed cats, ground sloth, mammoth, bison, tapir, camels, and the giant armadillo. The most common type of artifact attributable to this period is the chipped-stone projectile point, also known as a spear or dart point. Archaeologists have defined a limited number of specific types (or styles) of Paleoindian points, including Folsom, Angostura, Golondrina, and Plainview. Although some collectors and looters claim to have found Clovis points, these findings have yet to be documented by professional archaeologists. Paleoindian projectile points are distinctive in shape from later cultural periods in that they all lack a definable stem, all are usually parallel-sided with basal grinding, some have a distinctive flute or channel-flake removal, and all have a general outline that is lanceolate or lozenge shaped.

Although Paleoindian sites are rare, the archaeological evidence from Bonfire Rock Shelter, the Devils Mouth Site,

Arenosa Rock Shelter, and Cueva Quebrada suggest the earliest cultures developed a reliance on the hunting of now-extinct animals such as the mammoth and giant bison (*Bison antiquus* or *occidentalas*). At Bonfire Rock Shelter near Langtry, Texas, ancient hunters may have organized in small groups to stampede herds of several hundred bison over a cliff to their death below in a rockshelter. Excavated from more than 15 feet below the modern rockshelter floor, Bone Bed II at this site has been radiocarbon-dated to 9300 BC and represents the earliest dated example in North America of the bison-jump technique of hunting. Although little is known about the everyday life of Paleoindians, recent excavations at the Gault site in central Texas are shedding new light on the life ways of these early settlers in Texas.

ARCHAIC PERIOD (7000–1500 BC OR 1,200–8,500 YEARS AGO)

The Ice Age environment with the associated plants and animals in this region was rapidly disappearing about 8,500 years ago as the climate gradually became warmer and drier. At Hinds Cave near the Pecos River and at Baker Cave on a tributary off the Devils River, xeric (desert-adapted) plants have been found in archaeological deposits dating to around 7000 BC. Today's well-known plants, such as prickly pear, sotol, lechugilla, and agave, were well established by 4000 BC. As the Holocene (modern) environment developed, so did new economic strategies, artifact types, and the specialized subsistence patterns that are now feeding an ever-increasing regional population. The archaeological evidence suggests that during this period, there was a shift away from a reliance on big game and herd animal hunting toward a small game hunting and plant gathering way of life. People appear to have exploited a wider range of both animal and plant resources, used more regularly ground stone artifacts for processing plant materials, and increased their reliance on aquatic riverine resources as well as on the use of earth ovens to cook plant materials.

The Archaic period lasted nearly 6,000 years and is generally further broken down into Early, Middle, and Late Archaic; the distinctions will not be differentiated here. Archaeologists believe that Archaic peoples, in comparison to Paleoindians, literally tried to eat everything that did not sicken or kill them. They exploited every niche of the ecosystem. This type of subsistence pattern, known as broad-spectrum hunting and gathering, appears to have continued with only minor technological innovations and limited geographic expansions and contractions up through the later prehistoric period and probably until the coming of the first Europeans in the late sixteenth century.

Fired-cracked limestone rock features and "earth oven" remains are among the most common site types for the Archaic period. Earth ovens, often referred to as sotol pits or fire-cracked rock middens, are shallow, excavated pits that were filled with wood, rocks, and plant materials and then covered with earth. Cooking this way allowed the food (often sotol or lechugilla bulbs) to cook for extended periods of time. Recent replicative studies indicate that earth oven cooking reduces complex starches to simple sugars, thus improving the digestibility (and taste) of both sotol and lechugilla bulbs. Gone were the stemless Paleoindian projectile point styles, replaced over the following thousands of years of the Archaic period by an ever-increasing variety of side- and corner-notched types and varieties of stemmed points. At Conejo Rock Shelter, a wide variety of basketry types and woven plant artifacts shed light on everyday living activities. Recent research on the ichthyofauna (fish remains) from Arenosa Rock Shelter indicates a wide variety of fish were utilized during the Archaic, including sturgeon, drum, and catfish. Microscopic evidences on catfish bones reveals the fish were filleted (rather than cut up as steaks) after the muscles controlling the spines were disabled by a precise cut utilizing a small flint tool.

The basic social unit for these Archaic cultures may have consisted of what cultural anthropologists call the extended family unit (husband, wife, children, grandparents, children's wives) of up to about twenty-five people. These people grew no plants or crops, domesticated no animals, buried their dead with a limited variety of grave goods, and did not live in any permanent structures. They probably moved frequently within the larger region to take advantage of seasonal geographical abundances in the fruiting cycles of plants and migratory patterns of animals, birds, and fish. The region's many dry rockshelters provided them with refuge from environmental extremes. There is little archaeological evidence from which to infer that any regular trade networks existed between the Lower Pecos peoples and adjoining culture areas in the United States or northern Mexico. The answers to such questions as to who these people were, what languages they spoke, and what names they bore will probably never be uncovered by an archaeologist's trowel.

LATE PREHISTORIC (AD 1000–1500, OR 500–1,000 YEARS AGO)

The late prehistoric period is defined by artifacts associated with the introduction of the bow and arrow, the appearance of wikiup rings, and the presence of pottery in the archaeological record. Evidence from Arenosa Rock Shelter demonstrates that around AD 650 the use of the bow and arrow had spread southward, out of northern Texas and New Mexico, down into the Lower Pecos region. Arrow point styles, such as Scallorn and the later Perdiz types, replace the larger spear and dart points of the Archaic period as the new technology of the bow replaced the use of spears and the *atl atl*. The presence of metal arrow points is still just a rumor among collectors; there are no known sites documented by archaeologists.

The appearance of wikiup rings (circular features consisting of multiple stones) suggests the use of brush shelters, tepees, or wikiups in upland areas. At the Infierno Camp site, over 100 tepee and wikiup features have been documented by archaeologists. During a regional drought in the late 1990s, which dramatically lowered Lake Amistad, three recently exposed sites were documented adjacent to the Rio Grande that included wikiup features, ceramics, and arrow points. There are also several other late prehistoric period sites that include the remains of modern bison, infrequent visitors to the region, which were apparently driven southward from the Great Plains by extreme continental weather patterns in the late fall and winter. A preference for earth-oven cooking technology and a general use of riverine and canyon land resources continued into the late prehistoric period.

Evidence of low-fired earthenware ceramics vessels made from local clays appears in some archaeological sites. The ceramic type, known as Leon Plain, is more common to southern Texas, with the Lower Pecos region representing the extreme northwest extent of this pottery tradition. At a terrace site below Amistad dam on the Rio Grande, archaeologists obtained a radiocarbon date (Beta 108178) of about 660 ± 50 years ago (or AD 1290), for a stratigraphic zone containing a ceramic shard. Leon Plain is distinctive in its manufacture because the makers added crushed, and sometimes burnt, pieces of animal bone as temper to the clay before firing in open pits. Typically lacking any kind of surface decoration, there are only a few vessel forms known for this ceramic type, which has been found as far south as the Texas gulf coast.

HISTORIC PERIOD (AD 1590–PRESENT, OR 500 YEARS AGO TO THE PRESENT)

Historians, anthropologists, and archaeologists are quick to point out that there is very little substantive ethnological or historical information concerning any Native American groups at or after European contact (1590). The Apache, and later the Comanche, are known to have frequented the region in the seventeenth, eighteenth, and nineteenth centuries. Researchers believe that other nomadic and horse-mounted groups certainly traversed the region but were misidentified or stereotyped by the Spanish and other explorers as being simply Apache or Comanche. Archaeologists have yet to identify a site with artifacts attributable to any specific historic Native American group. The best evidences for post-contact groups are rock art sites and historic documents. At present, there are no federally recognized Native American groups claiming the Lower Pecos Canyon Lands as sacred lands, as ancestral homeland, or as the locus for traditional activities.

History, in the European sense of time, begins in the region in 1590 with Gaspar Castano de Sosa's journey from Monclova, Mexico, to the Pecos Pueblo (east of present Santa Fe, New Mexico). De Sosa's expedition journal refers to the region as *despoblado*, or unpopulated. Although a bountiful region to indigenous cultures, it lacked the natural prerequisites for Spanish colonization—readily available forests, areas for growing crops, accessible mineral deposits such as gold or silver, and settled Native American groups requiring Christian salvation. Nearly eighty years after de Sosa's bleak description of the region, the Spanish did establish a mission on the southern periphery of the area, but it was more for launching punitive military attacks than for Christianizing indigenous peoples. Located on the San Diego River, adjacent to the Rio Grande and modern-day Mexican town of Jimenez, the Spanish settlement of Agua Verde lasted only from 1773 to 1780.

There are few documents and even fewer archaeological sites in the region that represent the historic period. From the sixteenth century to 1821, the present-day Lower Pecos region belonged to Spain. Mexico was granted independence from Spain in 1821, and with the 1846 Treaty of Guadalupe Hidalgo, Mexico ceded the land between the Nueces River and the Rio Grande to the Republic of Texas, which, in 1847, became the twenty-eighth state to join the United States. But despite statehood, there were no real economic, social, or demographic changes in the broader region until after the Civil War in the late 1860s.

With statehood, the U.S. Army Bureau of Topographic Engineers began an intensive program to identify potential locations for military posts and commercial transportation links between existing cities and the Gulf of Mexico. In 1848 alone, there were seven major topographic expeditions in the state; the Whiting-Smith Expedition (1849) and Neighbors-Ford Expedition (1849) traversed the Lower Pecos region. These two surveys led to the establishment of a military and commercial route that became known as the San Antonio–El Paso Road. From 1850 to 1883, this wagon-train road through the region was the single most important transportation route west of San Antonio and figures prominently in the larger development of western Texas. By 1854, Camp Blake was established at the confluence of the Devils River and the Rio Grande; Fort Clark was established to the east, with Camp Hudson (on the Devils River) and Fort Lancaster (on the Pecos) established to the north in an effort to protect commerce and the wagon trains of newly arrived emigrants from Texas's gulf coast traveling west along the San Antonio–El Paso Road.

In 1874 Lieutenant John L. Bullis and three Seminole Negro-Indian scouts on routine patrol from Fort Clark ambushed a group of "Indians" trailing what appeared to be stolen horses near the mouth of the Pecos River at the Rio Grande. After dismounting and an initial skirmish on foot, Bullis and his scouts were outflanked, necessitating a hasty retreat; the lieutenant's horse was shot from under him in the process. Scouts Pompey Factor and John Ward and trumpeter Isaac Payne made a daring rescue of the downed Bullis while under heavy fire. Months later, all three scouts were awarded the Congressional Medal of Honor for their heroism. Several sources claim that the 1874 Bullis Skirmish represents the largest number of awarded Medals of Honor for a single incident in the American West. All three scouts are buried in the Seminole Scout cemetery adjacent to Fort Clark in present-day Bracketville, Texas.

By 1875, the U.S. Army and a detachment of scouts completed the first engineered wagon trail across the Pecos River near the Rio Grande. Portions of the eastern river approach are still visible in the brush below the road used to launch boats at the National Park Service facility on the Pecos River. Known as Bullis Trail, this crossing was a vital link for military patrols west of the Pecos and was plotted on military topographic maps until the 1920s. By 1925, the first automobile bridge was constructed nearby. The bridge was destroyed by flooding and repaired several times before being replaced in 1958 by what is known today as the Pecos High Bridge on U.S. Highway 90—said to be the tallest highway bridge in Texas.

In the early 1880s Val Verde County, Texas, was at the center of construction for the first southern transcontinental railroad. In 1881–82, more than 4,000 laborers including Germans, Italians, Mexicans, blacks, and Chinese were building grades and laying track between the new towns of Shumla and Del Rio. Workers were quartered and provisioned in temporary camps erected by the railroad and entrepreneurs, which included Roy Bean's site of Vinegarron, east of Langtry, Texas. The West of Pecos Railroad National Register District provides some of the only systematic documentation available on the railroad campsites and the ethnic diversity of workers that is obvious in the archaeological remains.

On January 12, 1883, east and west sections of the Southern Pacific route were joined with a silver spike amid much fanfare at a location on the Rio Grande about 1 mile north of the confluence with the Pecos River. A stationhouse was built between Tunnel No. 1 (the first railroad tunnel in Texas) and the fair-weather bridge, 40 feet above the river, in the canyon bottom at the mouth of the Pecos River. The station was called Painted Caves, named for the prehistoric pictographs in two nearby rockshelters. Today, Painted Caves Station is known as Parida Cave and is managed by the National Park Service as an interpretive site for visitors to Lake Amistad.

The Phoenix Bridge Company, in 1892, replaced the original railroad bridge at the Pecos–Rio Grande confluence with an engineering marvel known as the Pecos Viaduct Bridge. The company published a limited-edition book on the project, with over thirty sepia photographs, which is now available online (http://bridges.lib.lehigh.edu/books/book1631.html). Situated about 5 miles up river from the original 1883 bridge, the Viaduct Bridge was 322 feet, 10¾ inches (90 meters) above the Pecos River bottom. It is said to have been the tallest bridge in the United States at the time and the third tallest bridge in the world. This bridge served as a vital link for commerce between the west coast and gulf coast ports until it was replaced in 1948 by a more substantial structure, which today continues to carry freight and Amtrak passengers over the deep chasm of the Pecos River. The concrete footers for the Viaduct Bridge are all that remain today and are hazards to boaters on the river at times of low water.

With the coming of the railroad to southwest Texas, Val Verde County was carved out of two adjoining counties, and the small town of Del Rio was made the county seat in 1885. The Southern Pacific Railroad used the town as its regional headquarters for commerce and included a roundhouse for redirecting locomotives. The railroad brought a major wave of European settlers to southwest Texas as small towns such as Pumpville, Double Tanks, Loma Alta, Comstock, Langtry, and Shumla sprang up adjacent to the tracks. Judge Roy Bean, "Law West of the Pecos," set up his barroom (the Jersey Lily) and courthouse in Langtry, Texas. The sheep and goat ranching industries expanded rapidly as the railroad brought an economic prosperity to the entire region that continued through the Great Depression, almost until World War II.

ROCK ART

The region is internationally known in the literature for its prehistoric rock art, which includes both petroglyph and pictograph sites. Petroglyphs are designs that have been carved, scratched, or pecked into rock surfaces, whereas pictographs are painted images on rockshelter walls. Petroglyph sites are few—less than ten have been documented. Most are found on boulders and rocks, and they occur in V-shaped and U-shaped forms of manufacture. The Lewis Canyon Petroglyph site has long been a fascinating enigma. It has nearly 1,000 individual designs spread out across several acres of exposed bedrock adjacent to the Pecos River and may represent a phenomenon associated with cultures north of the region. Among the more than 350 documented pictograph sites, researchers have defined four prehistoric styles for the region: the Pecos River, Bold Line Geometric, Red Linear, and Red Monochrome styles. Each style is defined by a similar cluster of attributes, including size, color, motifs (or designs), relative location on rockshelter walls, and, to some degree, topographic setting.

The oldest of the pictograph styles is the Pecos River, which is found at over 225 different sites and is best known for the huge (up to 4 meters tall) anthropomorphic (human) figures painted in several different colors. At Rattlesnake Canyon, Panther Cave, Jefferson Davis site (also known as the White Shaman site), Black Cave, Fate Bell Rock Shelter, Cedar Springs, Mystic Shelter, Halo Shelter, Satan Canyon, Indian Cliffs, Leaping Panthers site, and dozens of other sites known only by their state of Texas site numbers, pictographs cover hundreds of feet of rockshelter walls. Many of the anthropomorphic images are depicted with an object in the right hand, which researchers have interpreted to be an *atl atl* (spear thrower), indicative of the Archaic period. The application of radiocarbon dating to pictograph pigment, although still considered an experimental technique, has been used on over a dozen samples of paint from this style at several archaeological sites and reveals an age of around 4,000 years (consistent with an Archaic period date), with some samples dating older or younger.

The Red Linear style is diminutive in size (10 cm or less), compared with the Pecos River style, but is also considered to date to the Archaic period. More than a dozen sites exist where motifs are always painted in solid red lines; these images include depictions of animals and stick figures involved in group activities and are infrequent design elements in the Pecos River style. Sites with this style of pictograph are often found in small, remote, and isolated rockshelters rather than in the huge rockshelters geographically situated at the confluences of tributaries and side canyons with major river valleys.

Another style, known as the Bold Line Geometric, is vividly portrayed at Parida Cave as well as at an adjacent site on the Rio Grande, and is believed by some to date to the late prehistoric period. This style is defined by the use of straight lines at varying angles and zoomorphic figures (animals and insects) with sharply bent limbs that are usually less than 1 meter high. A common motif is a pattern often referred to as a diamond, net, or checkerboard design.

The fourth prehistoric style, identified at over fifteen sites, is known as the Red Monochrome style and features red-painted, life-like depictions of animals (rabbits, deer, turtles, and cat fish) as well as people (sexual dimorphism is evident with both male and female depictions) that are up to 2 meters tall. Also common are red handprints created by placing a hand on the wall and spraying liquid paint (from the mouth or through a tube), creating a stenciled outline of the hand and part of the forearm. This style is best represented at the Painted Canyon site. Humans are frequently depicted holding a bow and arrow in one hand, which indicates the late prehistoric period.

The four styles of prehistoric pictographs are generally believed by researchers to be among the very few remaining tangible artifacts that can be used to infer shamanic or religious activities. "Shaman" is an anthropological term applied to a specific type of religious practitioner among hunter-gatherer societies who, through rituals and ceremonial activities, attempts to control the supernatural forces governing both the natural and spiritual world to the benefit of all societal members. Documented by ethnographers worldwide among various cultures, shamanic rituals and attendant ceremonies (including rock art) include activities related to hunting magic, supplication, initiation rituals, mystical creatures, and representations of out-of-body or other mental experiences.

As such, the rock art is a symbolic representation of the various cognitive processes, once articulated through a now-extinct language, for the ancient societies that long ago produced them. Despite substantial research by such individuals as A. T. Jackson, Forrest Kirkland, David Gebhard, Terence Greider, and Solveig Turpin, the true meanings and societal functions of the pictographs within their original cultural contexts have died with the passing of these ancient societies. Recently, however, new studies published by Carolyn Boyd offer compelling arguments on the meanings, purpose, and functions of this ancient imagery.

While fewer in number, research indicates that there are at least fifteen documented historic period pictograph and petroglyph sites in the region. These sites necessarily date to sometime after the arrival of the first Europeans in Texas (1528), because they include depictions of the horse, buildings, guns, uniformed men, domesticated cattle, sabers, and other trappings of European origin. Sites on the U.S. side of the Rio Grande include Myers Springs, Ringbit Shelter, Dolan Springs, Live Oak Hole, Caballero Shelter, Hussie Myers, Missionary Shelter, and Vaquero Shelter; and those in Mexico include Arroyos de los Indios and El Caido. Such sites collectively provide a narrow but unique insight into post-contact groups in the region.

There appear to be at least four styles, or time periods, evident in the imagery at historic period pictograph sites. Each time period is relatively short and difficult to define in terms of absolute dates, but it can generally be characterized by the near political or geographical dominance of one cultural group (with a distinctive material culture) over one or several other semi-identifiable groups. The short-term dominance over, and later extinction of, indigenous Native American groups in the region by the Spanish, by successive waves of southern plains groups, by Anglo-European settlers, and by Republic of Texas and U.S. Army personnel all occurred in just over 300 years. But each culture left a distinctive mark on the region, although some are more recognizable than others.

PUBLIC EDUCATION AND ACCESS

Unlike most other regions in western United States, here there is very little federal, state, or public land in the Lower Pecos region. The vast majority of rock art sites and historic sites in the Lower Pecos River Canyon Lands are on private property and are therefore not open to public visitation. The National Park Service manages Lake Amistad as Amistad National Recreation Area (http://www.nps.gov/amis) and operates a visitor information center with bookstore, theater, and regional information. The park provides boat docks and interpretive developments at Panther Cave and Parida Cave. Seminole Canyon State Park and Historical Site (http://www.tpwd.state.tx.us/park/seminole) is open year-round; has a recreational-vehicle campground, interpretive center, and bookstore; and offers guided tours to several rock art and historic sites. The Rock Art Foundation, a private organization, operates the Galloway White Shaman Preserve (http://www.rockart.org) adjacent to the Pecos River on U.S. Highway 90 and offers seasonal tours to some of the region's most famous rock art sites by special arrangement with property owners.

The Texas Department of Transportation operates the Judge Roy Bean Visitor Center (http://www.dot.state.tx.us/travel) in Langtry, Texas, and features historic railroad exhibits, the reconstructed remains of Roy Bean's Jersey Lily saloon, and a short nature walk with over 100 native plants. Historic Fort Clark, located in Bracketville, Texas, has many original structures from the late nineteenth century and reconstructed buildings with a museum, and it is open to the public (http://www.fortclark.com). The Whitehead Memorial Museum in Del Rio, Texas, contains numerous exhibits on topics such as the Southern Pacific Railroad, Seminole Scouts, Judge Roy Bean, Native Americans, and local history (http://www.whitehead-museum.com). The Witte Museum (http://www.wittemuseum.org) in San Antonio has the most extensive museum exhibit on the Lower Pecos that is available to the general public. There are multiple exhibits of artifacts from their 1930s archaeological expeditions to the region as well as exhibits from later museum-sponsored excavations at Baker Cave in 1980s.

There are many Web-based digital resources on the Lower Pecos River Canyon Lands that are easily found through the use of Internet search engines. The best single Web site is http://www.texasbeyondhistory.net/pecos. This Web-based project is a collaborative effort among more than a dozen state, federal, and academic institutions and includes digital exhibits, instructor resources, student resources, suggested readings, and links to additional Web sites.

Further Reading: Acker, G. Elaine, *Life in a Rockshelter: Prehistoric Indians of the Lower Pecos* (Dallas, TX: Hendrick-Long, 1996); Boyd, Carolyn, *Rock Art of the Lower Pecos* (College Station: Texas A&M University Press, 2003); Jackson, A. T., *Picture Writing of Texas Indians*, Publication No. 3809 (Austin: University of Texas, 1938); Kavanagh, Thomas W., *The Comanche: A History 1705–1875* (Lincoln: University of Nebraska Press, 1996); Kirkland, Forest, and W. W. Newcomb, *Rock Art of Texas Indians*, 2nd ed. (Austin: University of Texas Press, 1999); Newcomb, W. W., *The Indians of Texas: From Prehistory to Modern Times* (Austin: University of Texas Press, 1984); Nunly, Parker, *A Field Guide to Archeological Sites of Texas* (Austin: Texas Monthly Press, 1989); Perttula, Timothy K., ed., *The Prehistory of Texas* (College Station: Texas A&M University of Press, 2004); Shafer, Harry J., *Ancient Texans: Rock Art Along the Lower Pecos* (Austin: Texas Monthly Press, 1986); Skiles, Jack R., *Judge Roy Bean Country* (Lubbock: Texas Tech University Press, 1989); Terrell, John Upton, *Apache Chronicle: The Story of the People* (New York: World, 1972); Turner, Ellen Sue, and Thomas R. Hester, *A Field Guide to Stone Artifacts of Texas Indians* (Austin: Texas Monthly Press, 1989); Turpin, Solveig, *Papers on Lower Pecos Prehistory*, Texas Archaeological Research Laboratory Studies in Archeology No. 8 (Austin: University of Texas, 1991); Zintgraff, Jim, and Solveig Turpin, *Pecos River Rock Art: A Photographic Essay* (San Antonio: Sandy McPhearson, 1991).

Joseph H. Labadie

EL CAMINO REAL NATIONAL HISTORICAL TRAIL AND RELATED SITES

Central New Mexico

First Long-Distance Route Established by Europeans in America

The Camino Real was the first long-distance route established by Europeans in the Western Hemisphere. It extended some 1,600 miles from near Mexico City to near Santa Fe, New Mexico, and was officially in use from AD 1598 (when Don Juan de Oñate established its northern extension) until around AD 1880 (when its utility was diminished by the construction of the railroad). The Camino Real was important, and has historic significance today, because it brought people with extraordinarily different cultural traditions into contact. The linkage of these diverse people, broadly defined as European and American yet exhibiting much greater cultural diversity than this bifurcation suggests, had a profound impact on New Mexican history and heritage.

The entire Camino Real can be usefully envisaged as an archaeological site. Although it might appear counterintuitive to treat a 1,600-mile trail as a single site, doing so makes sense when one considers the ultimate goals of archaeological research. Traditionally, archaeological sites are thought to have limited spatial extent and clear boundaries. Yet sites are more usefully defined in functional than in spatial terms. The entire Camino Real was a functional entity. Thinking about it in a functional way thus allows for a better understanding of its historical context and significance.

The impact of the Camino Real on Mexican and New Mexican history has been profound. Even a cursory visit to museums and monuments along its route provides convincing evidence of this fact. In Santa Fe, near the northern terminus of the trail, exhibits at any of the four museums that make up the Museums of New Mexico system (the Palace of the Governors, the Museum of International Folk Art, the Museum of Fine Arts, and the Museum of Indian Arts and Culture/Laboratory of Anthropology) reflect the importance of the Camino Real on the area's history and heritage. And in Las Cruces, near the southern end of the trails journey through the state, the New Mexico Farm and Ranch Heritage Museum does the same, most notably in its permanent exhibit of historic farming and ranching activities carried out by various immigrant groups through the centuries.

Between the two, just south of Socorro, stands the pinnacle of recognition of Camino Real significance, the El Camino Real Heritage Center. There, visitors can immerse themselves in the history and importance of the trail by viewing exhibits, performances, and other offerings. The center is an appropriate and long-overdue tribute to this history.

Archaeologists have learned many details from the various projects conducted at Camino Real. What is reported here is based on more than a decade of archaeological investigations by this author along the Camino Real in southern New Mexico at the following locations: the Paraje de San Diego (a "paraje" is a campsite), 30 miles north of Las Cruces, New Mexico; a nearly 35-mile corridor of the Camino Real from Las Cruces to El Paso; a 7-mile segment of the trail along the Camino Real that crosses the Chihuahuan Desert Rangeland Research Center (CDRRC) of New Mexico State University; the village of Dona Ana, just south of the CDRRC and located on the Camino Real, first as one of the original parajes and later as a village along its route; and historic Fort Fillmore, occupied from 1851 until 1862 and located just south of Las Cruces.

THE CAMINO REAL WAS A TRAIL

When the Camino Real was conceptualized as an archaeological site, archaeologists realized that it exhibited certain distinctive and, at times, unexpected characteristics. One of the more surprising was that the Camino Real was a trail, not a road.

It is widely thought that all long-distance routes created by complex societies are *roads*, the products of purposeful and considerable construction efforts with resulting architecture that often defies the natural landscape and requires great effort to create and great effort to remove. Roads, and the particular routes roads take, are relatively permanent phenomena. They persist even when their original functions or their original cultural contexts fade away.

Formal roads are often distinguished from *trails*. The latter are simply the products of use rather than purposeful construction. Trails exhibit little or no architecture and adjust to the landscape rather than impose themselves upon it. Trails are easily altered, moved, or even removed (often simply as a result of disuse). Roads are persistent entities even when the larger cultural context changes, whereas trails are responsive to such changes—themselves changing form, moving from place to place, or disappearing completely in reaction to shifting cultural realities.

Roads are often associated with complex societies, especially predatory colonial empires motivated by a desire to control various hinterlands through symbolic, economic, political, or military coercion. Empires build roads into new territories in order to effectively exert power within them. Trails occur in all societies, but they are most prominent among those exhibiting band and tribal levels of complexity.

The Camino Real was the product of an archetypal colonial empire. Yet, quite remarkably, it exhibited all of the characteristics of an archetypal trail. Throughout New Mexico, indeed along most of its entire route, the Camino Real exhibited little architecture, being nothing more than a trodden dirt path. Additionally, people who traveled the Camino rarely found themselves defying environmental conditions, but rather adjusting to them as best they could. Remarkably, southern New Mexico was not (and is not) a permissive environment. Numerous natural obstacles along with the generally harsh and water-starved conditions were anything but permissive. Surely, the natural surroundings would have encouraged the creation of a formal road if the Spanish authorities deemed it appropriate. For whatever reasons, they did not. The Camino Real remained a trail and never became a formal road, despite the cultural complexity and predatory ambitions of the Spanish Empire. The resulting physical characteristics of the Camino Real have had profound impacts on its precise location and degree of preservation in the archaeological record today, as well as on an archaeologist's ability to locate relatively well-preserved remnants of it.

SUBSEQUENT TRANSPORTATION ROUTES

The Camino Real persisted as a trail for nearly three centuries. A true road finally dislodged it, but not until the late nineteenth century. The culprit was the railroad, which of course was (and is) a road in the context of the trail/road dichotomy considered here.

The New Mexico portion of the Atchison, Topeka, and Santa Fe railroad was completed in the early 1880s. Vehicular routes and highways, also true roads, were constructed subsequently. These included New Mexico State Route 1, U.S. Highway 85, and Interstate 25. The transition from Camino Real to interstate was ultimately dramatic yet incremental as the years unfolded.

All of these roads generally followed the route of the Camino Real, but none of them have followed it exactly. The roads could be located where the Camino Real could not, because roads can overcome environmental constraints; trails cannot. So although these various routes are adjacent to one another, because they go through and to the same places, their exact locations are not identical. Roads are also spatially "locked" in place once they are constructed. Trails are not; their exact locations move easily from time to time, precisely because they need to respond to environmental contingencies. Put simply, roads can be initially located in a greater variety of places, but once established they cannot be easily moved in response to changing conditions. Trails have fewer options to begin with, but these remain viable throughout their existence. All these facts worked to increase the archaeological preservation of old trails, including the Camino Real.

The most convincing evidence supporting this conclusion comes from a 2002 survey of the Camino Real between Las Cruces and El Paso. Before this fieldwork, most scholars assumed that all remnants of this trail segment would be found under the present-day railroad tracks and/or New Mexico Highway 478–Texas Highway 20. The results of the 2002 fieldwork bring that assumption into question. Intriguing archival and archaeological data, including a 1907 survey of the Camino Real from Las Cruces to the Texas border conducted by then County Surveyor C. L. Post, show the route (or perhaps one of several alternative routes) well to the east of the railroad tracks and the highway from Mesquite to Anthony. This data raised hopes of finding segments of the Camino Real accessible for further study.

The 2002 field survey was conducted over a roughly rectilinear area of 35 × 5 miles within which it was known the Camino Real was located. This area was subdivided into survey units of roughly 1 × 2 miles. Field crews were assigned survey units to explore as much of this as was possible on private property that is developed and rather densely populated. Crew members recorded landscape characteristics, current land use, and archaeological resources visible on the surface. At the same time, numerous archives were searched for information on the precise location of the Camino Real in the project area, its use and condition up until the present, and details regarding property ownership. It was during this archival search that C. L. Post's 1907 survey of the trail was discovered.

Survey crews identified and recorded seven prehistoric sites, twenty-four historical sites, and two multi-component (i.e., prehistoric and historic) sites. Of greater significance for this project, it is believed that at least three segments of the Camino Real itself were identified. These segments are linear depressions 3–5 meters wide and approximately 80–300 meters long. Their north-south orientation is the direction once taken by the trail, and they almost always run through relatively dense desert scrub yet contain very little plant life. These characteristics are similar to vast stretches of the Camino Real identified in undeveloped desert throughout northern Mexico and New Mexico where identification is incontrovertible.

Bolstering the interpretation that these features are indeed segments of the Camino Real is the fact that two of them are contiguous to archaeological sites dating to the use of the trail (AD 1598–ca. 1880). In one case, the trail segment is associated with a relatively large site

(25,000–30,000 m^2) containing several very dense concentrations of historical artifacts and what appear to be several structural remains. These materials and related archival information make this locale especially interesting and potentially significant.

The trail segment and site in question are found in the village of Vinton, Texas, and might be the remains of the paraje commonly known as La Salinera, which was the first paraje north of El Paso and a place where the Camino Real crossed the Rio Grande. While identified in contemporary documents and on maps, La Salinera has not previously been described archaeologically. Archaeologists hope to conduct limited excavations at this locale sometime in the future to determine whether such identification is correct.

Parajes were established roughly every 10 miles along the Camino Real. They were not final destinations, although they were visited repeatedly for nearly 300 years as groups of people moved up and down the trail. Few of the material manifestations of permanent or even long-term occupation were ever constructed at these places. The archaeological record of them is the result of complex formation processes that cause them to be ephemeral and sometimes inscrutable. The resulting archaeological sites tend to be obscure, difficult to find, and very difficult to study (as discussed later).

La Salinera might be somewhat different, however. This particular paraje was located at the upper of two fords across the Rio Grande to the immediate north of El Paso. The paraje at the lower ford, named La Salineta, was the more commonly used through the centuries. It was the site of several failed attempts to bridge the river and is well known as the place where nearly 2,000 refugees who fled the Pueblo Revolt remained for almost two months (September and October, AD 1680). Still, La Salinera, just a few miles north of La Salineta, was and is significant. Its greatest archaeological significance is that it was a place where groups of people traveling the Camino Real would wait, sometimes for substantial periods of time, until conditions allowed the river to be crossed safely. As a result, the archaeological record at this paraje might be more extensive and diverse relative to what might be found at many of the other parajes along the trail.

DIFFICULTIES

The Camino Real and related sites are difficult to study archaeologically. The promise of rewarding archaeological research along the Camino Real is tempered by the challenges it presents. As discussed previously, the Camino Real was a trail and not a road. The fortunate outcome is that portions of it and some related sites have been preserved for study. The unfortunate outcome is that there is nothing very obvious to be seen in the archaeological record and archaeological observation and recording are most demanding.

The best example of this challenge is found at the Paraje de San Diego. Initial surface inspection of the site revealed no obvious concentrations of material culture or features. Instead, a low-density scatter of artifacts was observed across the entire site area (160 × 200 m), indicative of repeated, short-term occupation.

Given these conditions, archaeologists emphasized strategies for site survey and sampling that would best reveal an extensive but obscure collection of cultural materials. Every other unit 20 × 20 meters on a grid covering the entire 200 × 160 meter site area was surface-collected. Several transects 1 meter wide running north-south across the site at 40-meter intervals were shovel-scraped. A metal detector survey was conducted over most of the site, and sixty-four units of varying dimensions were excavated. These units were located across the site both randomly and in areas of perceived high investigative potential.

Paraje de San Diego was discovered to contain archaeological materials spanning the entire historical period during which the Camino Real was in use. There is also a prehistoric component consisting of lithics (stone tools) and several features (facilities such as hearths or storage pits created by people as part of their activities at a site), expanding the temporal range a good number of centuries into the more distant past. Still, the site is obscure, primarily because it was occupied repeatedly but only for short periods of time throughout its long existence, which has made archaeological investigation challenging and interpretation somewhat uncertain. Yet the investigation, which was sufficiently intensive and lengthy to allow researchers to observe, record, and map the widespread, scattered remains, was fruitful largely because the obscurity of the site has enhanced site preservation and integrity.

The work might be difficult, but it is not impossible. More important, the site holds tremendous potential not only for scholars but also for others who can appreciate its significance, especially those who live near or travel along the route of the Camino Real. The uniqueness of the trail, in addition to the history of transport along it and adjacent to it in more recent times, maximize the potential for heritage tourism development. The trail is preserved because subsequent roads did not follow its exact path and obliterate it. At the same time, it is accessible to potential tourists because these roads are adjacent to it, going through and to the same places.

HERITAGE TOURISM AND ECONOMIC DEVELOPMENT

The potential for heritage tourism and economic development along the Camino Real is great. Opportunities exist throughout southern New Mexico for developing cultural or heritage tourism and educational outreach programs related to the Camino Real and regional history. These opportunities might be greatest in the southern portion of the trail in the village of Vinton, but they exist everywhere along the trail.

Heritage tourism and outreach provide cultural enrichment, which is important but not the only advantage.

Fortunately, developing heritage tourism and outreach also results in economic enrichment, a very real need in the economically deprived communities of the Mesilla valley. It is both reasonable and appropriate to take advantage of Vinton's historic resources in order to bolster the local economy.

Vinton will never be a major tourist destination, but it could easily be a place people visit while touring the region, which is full of related points of interest. Transforming the archaeological remains of La Salinera into an attraction worth stopping for will require careful planning so that the interests of various stakeholders are not jeopardized. For scholars, the greatest interest is in maintaining the integrity of the resource while presenting an authentic and accurate representation of the past. This interest can be satisfied while the economic needs and social concerns of everyone else are also met.

CONCLUSIONS

The Camino Real was a trail, not a road. It was not formally constructed and it exhibited little associated architecture, lacked permanence, and was adjusted to local environmental conditions when necessary. Subsequent north-south transportation routes in New Mexico were roads, not trails. These included the railroad, New Mexico Route 1, U.S. Highway 85, and Interstate 25. Such roads are permanent architectural features spatially locked in place that often defy environmental conditions and constraints. Thus, although the Camino Real and later roads go through and to the same places, archaeological preservation and access to the original trail is good because the roads never followed the exact trail.

Although it is difficult to study obscure and ephemeral archaeological sites such as trails, the potential for research is high. In the case of the Camino Real there is the additional potential to develop heritage tourism in places such as Vinton, Texas. Those who live in and near these deprived communities stand to benefit economically when heritage tourism efforts are realized.

Further Reading: Marshall, M. P., *El Camino Real de Tierra Adentro: An Archaeological Investigation*, unpublished manuscript on file (Santa Fe, NM: Office of Cultural Affairs, Historic Preservation Division, , 1990); Moorhead, M. L., *New Mexico's Royal Road: Trade and Travel on the Chihuahua Trail* (Norman: University of Oklahoma Press, 1958); National Park Service/Bureau of Land Management, *El Camino Real de Tierra Adentro National Historic Trail: Draft Comprehensive Management Plan/Environmental Impact Statement* (Santa Fe, NM: National Park Service/Bureau of Land Management, 2002); Staski, E., "Change and Inertia on the Frontier: Archaeology at the Paraje de San Diego, Camino Real, in Southern New Mexico," *International Journal of Historical Archaeology* 2(1) (1998): 21–44; Staski, E., "An Archaeological Survey of El Camino Real de Tierra Adentro, Las Cruces–El Paso," *International Journal of Historical Archaeology* 8(4) (2004): 231–245; Trombold, C. D., ed., *Ancient Road Networks and Settlement Hierarchies in the New World* (Cambridge: Cambridge University Press, 1991).

Edward Staski

TUMACACORI NATIONAL HISTORICAL PARK

Santa Cruz River Valley, Southern Arizona

The Archaeology and Architecture of Spanish Colonial Missions

Tumacacori National Historical Park (NHP) is located in the fertile Santa Cruz River valley, which stretches from northern Mexico into southern Arizona. The park, located 48 miles south of Tucson, Arizona, and 12 miles north of the U.S.-Mexico border, lies in an area that has been occupied for at least 12,000 years. There are over 4,000 archaeological sites in the Santa Cruz watershed. Archaeological sites within the Santa Cruz River valley include prehistoric sites, historic Pima-Papago and Apache sites, Spanish colonial sites, and Anglo ranching and mining sites.

Tumacacori NHP comprises three Spanish mission sites: Calabasas, Guevavi, and Tumacacori. At each site Spanish colonial mission churches and their associated ruins are protected, preserved, and interpreted by the National Park Service. Calabasas is located 9 miles south of Tumacacori, and Guevavi is located 3 miles south of Calabasas near Nogales, Arizona. Tumacacori NHP has great significance as one of the oldest outposts of European colonialism in the United States. Tumacacori, Calabasas, and Guevavi were economically and religiously connected settlements.

In 1691 Father Eusebio Kino arrived in what was to become southern Arizona to begin establishing mission settlements. The first Spanish missions in Arizona were operated by the Jesuit Order of the Roman Catholic Church. The goals of the Spanish mission system were to create a self-sufficient community, convert local Indians to the Catholic religion, and generate revenue for Spain.

The Spanish colonial system divided missions into two classes: the *cabecera*, or head mission, where priests lived; and *visitas*, where a priest would visit but did not usually reside. Cabeceras typically had churches, but churches were built at visitas only if there was extra time and money. Both types of missions were established at Indian villages. The mission grounds were an institutionalized landscape with a highly defined spatial pattern that divided and separated land for religious use, priest quarters, specialized work areas, Christianized Indian quarters, mission agricultural/livestock lands, orchards, and irrigation ditches (*acequias*).

The mission Indian population was mostly local O'odham Indians. Of the distinct O'odham groups identified by the Spanish, most mission Indians were Sobaipuri, Papagos, and other Pimas. The Sobaipuri were Upper Piman Indians that lived along the Santa Cruz and San Pedro rivers. Some Sobaipuri were relocated from the San Pedro valley to the Santa Cruz valley by the Spanish in the eighteenth century. As a distinct group the Sobaipuri are difficult to trace archaeologically. The Papago are linguistically related to the Pimans, and historically there are few differences between the two groups. Native settlements consisted of large villages of mud and brush houses and numerous smaller scattered villages and extended family habitations. One of the unfortunate results of Spanish colonization was the 50–60 percent reduction of native populations due to infectious diseases such as smallpox and measles. Disease often spread in waves ahead of the Spaniards, decimating native villages before the Spaniards arrived.

Indian knowledge of the Spanish missionaries preceded Father Kino's arrival by decades. In January 1691 a delegation from an Indian village requested that Father Kino visit the village of Tumacacori. The Spanish renamed this Indian village San Cayetano de Tumacacori. The village was located on the east side of the Santa Cruz River, opposite the present site of San Jose de Tumacacori. Unfortunately, the original site of San Cayetano de Tumacacori has not been located. It is difficult to identify the site archaeologically because there were many villages in the area during the time of Kino's arrival. Many archaeologists claim to know the location of the original site of San Cayetano de Tumacacori, but today the site remains elusive and difficult to identify.

Small adobe mission churches and adobe residences for priests were constructed at Tumacacori, Guevavi, and Calabasas. Before the twentieth century, adobe—mud mixed with sand and sometimes straw—was the most common construction material in the desert parts of the southwestern United States. Prior to Spanish arrival, structures were built by adding handfuls of mud until walls were formed. The Spanish introduced wooden frames for making sun-dried mud bricks, called *adobes*. Besides adobe frames, the Spanish also introduced new agricultural products, livestock, and the Roman Catholic religion. Local inhabitants previously relied on corn, beans, squash, wild plant gathering, and hunting. With the addition of wheat, fruit trees, and livestock, the subsistence strategies and general lifeways of native peoples changed, resulting in the unique mix of Native American and Spanish cultures seen today.

SAN JOSE DE TUMACACORI MISSION SITE, TUMACACORI, ARIZONA

In November 1751 the Pima Indians of southern Arizona revolted against the Spanish colonial oppression. Luis Oacpicagigua, a Spanish-appointed captain general of the

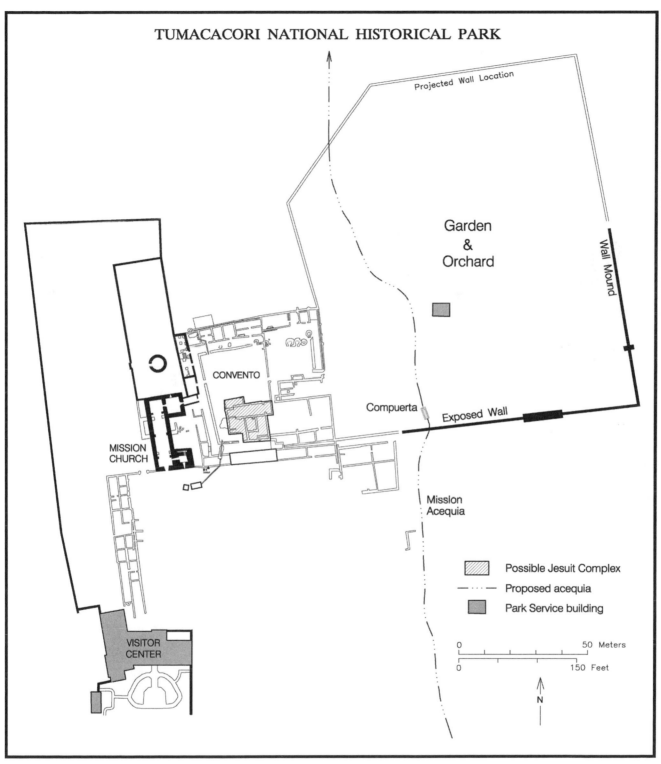

A map of the San Jose de Tumacacori Mission site, Tumacacori National Historical Park. [Courtesy of the National Park Service/Jeremy M. Moss]

Photograph of San Jose de Tumacacori mission church. [Courtesy of the National Park Service/Jeremy M. Moss]

Pima, led a group of Pima Indians against the Spanish. Sixty-four years of Jesuit and Spanish presence had fundamentally changed native social, political, and religious organization, and had instituted a growing dependence on introduced non-native goods.

The Pima Revolt of 1751 is a landmark event in the history of Spanish-Indian relations in southern Arizona. It resulted in the consolidation of Indian and Spanish populations. The Tumacacori Indian population was moved to the west side of the river to the present location of park headquarters, and a presidio, or military post, was established at Tubac just 4 miles north of Tumacacori. With the establishment of the new Tumacacori, the settlements' patron saint was changed and the site renamed San Jose de Tumacacori.

By 1757 a small adobe church measuring 60 × 20 feet was built at Tumacacori. The foundations of this church were discovered in 1934 when National Park Service archaeologist Paul Beaubien excavated at Tumacacori. All foundations were made of large river cobbles, and the walls were adobe bricks covered with lime plaster. In 1767 the Jesuit Order was expelled from the New World by the king of Spain due to accusations of greed and corruption, as well as the Jesuits growing influence and weighty demands. The Franciscan Order took over the missions formerly run by the Jesuits in 1773, and Tumacacori was designated a cabecera, or main mission.

Tumacacori reached its architectural and religious zenith between the 1780s and 1828. Construction of the large Franciscan church began sometime between 1799 and 1802. The church was designed by architects from Spain, but the newly converted Pima and Papago Indians were the builders of the mission churches. The church was dedicated in 1822, but the two-story bell tower was never completed, and construction continued intermittently until the last padres departed in 1841. The lengthy construction time was due to a lack of funds and difficulties keeping a large labor force at the mission.

Paul Beaubien's excavations are the most extensive archaeological investigations at Tumacacori (1934–35). After Beaubien, small-scale excavations were carried out periodically, mostly associated with stabilization/preservation efforts and exposing features for interpretation. Beaubien's excavations revealed construction sequences of the Franciscan church, the priest quarters (convento), the room blocks housing newly converted Indians, and various domestic features. Beaubien's goal was to uncover all wall outlines and features outside of the Franciscan church so they could be mapped. Therefore, he only collected rare artifacts and did not screen the fill removed from rooms. Most of the rooms Beaubien excavated had previously been disturbed by treasure hunters looking for rumored Spanish gold and silver. Treasure hunting has resulted in severe damage to the archaeological integrity of missions in the Southwest.

Christmas Eve luminarias at San Jose de Tumacacori.   [Courtesy of the National Park Service/Jeremy M. Moss]

There were two separate architectural elements associated with the mission church: the priest quarters, with their associated work areas, and the quarters for newly converted Indians. The Franciscan convento, located near the east side of the church, formed a square and had a central plaza. Convento rooms were connected through a series of hallways that may have had arched columns. Work areas in the convento consisted of a bakery, a grain milling room, and three large metal smelting ovens called *vasos*. An open drain led from two square cisterns in front of the church through the convento, possibly continuing to the mission orchard. The function of the drain and cisterns is debated, but the drain was probably part of an open sewage system, similar to those used in ancient Rome. Just to the north of the convento are the remains of a lime kiln used to heat limestone that was processed into lime plaster. The plaster was used as a protective cover over the adobe brick walls.

The Indian quarters were less uniform and ornamental than the rooms in the convento. They were rectangular room blocks that extended to the south from the front of the church. There was a square enclosing wall that created a large open space or plaza where activities took place in front of the church.

Beaubien's excavations also revealed that the church design had been altered during construction. Originally, the church was to be cruciform. Beaubien uncovered the wall foundations for the east and west wings that were to form the cross shape. Due to a lack of funds, the church design was modified into one long corridor, or nave, that led to the sacristy and main altar. The sacristy has painted plasters that are highly iconographic and rarely preserved.

Throughout the life of the mission, Apache attacks were a constant threat. The Apaches were one of the main factors influencing the continuity of settlement at the missions in southern Arizona. San Jose de Tumacacori was abandoned during the harsh winter of 1848. No priests had visited in seven years, and there was no military to protect the Indian population from Apache raiding. As the last Pima and Papago Indians fled Tumacacori, some of the church's statues and religious items were collected and taken to San Xavier del Bac for safe keeping. Some of these religious objects can be seen in the park visitors' center.

CALABAZAS MISSION SITE, RIO RICO, ARIZONA

The complex archaeological remains of Calabazas attest to its long, diverse cultural history. Sometime during the 1750s the Jesuit Order founded Calabazas at the Indian village of Toacuquita. Calabazas was a visita of Guevavi, and a church was completed in 1756. The following years brought turmoil in the form of disease epidemics and intense Apache raiding. By 1773 a small Franciscan church was completed and a cemetery established. Four years later the church and associated houses were burned by Apaches. The site was abandoned in 1786 and reoccupied in 1807, when the Jesuit adobe church was repaired by local Pimans under the supervision of Franciscan priests. The site served as the headquarters of a large cattle ranch serving the cabecera of San Jose de Tumacacori until 1830, when it was once again attacked and burned during an Apache raid. Calabazas was reoccupied as the *hacienda* of the governor of Sonora in 1844. The site served as the headquarters for two early U.S. Army posts in the 1850s and 1860s.

The remains of Calabazas consist of eroded portions of the church measuring 60 × 13 feet. The remains of the adobe church are surrounded by a square stone-wall foundation. No definite remains of the cemetery or of the Piman village have been located; however, small stone foundations discovered in a 1979 archaeological survey may be the remains of the Piman village. The adobe church was modified and reused in the 1850s, and a block of adobe and masonry rooms were constructed, forming a square that incorporated the old church. The ruins of the adobe church stand 7–10 feet high and are presently preserved by a metal shelter.

GUEVAVI MISSION SITE, NOGALES, ARIZONA

Guevavi is significant because it is one of a few pure Jesuit sites with no later Franciscan intrusions or disturbances. Father Kino designated Guevavi as a cabecera in 1701 with Tumacacori as one of its visitas. At that time a small church was built. A larger adobe church was constructed by 1751. The church measures 80 × 20 feet. A circular tower 20 feet in diameter is attached to the southeast corner of the church, probably as a watchtower. Excavations in 1992 show the church interior was plastered and stained red along the bottom of walls. This same red stain was found in rooms at Tumacacori that date to the Jesuit Period (1691–1767). Convento rooms were attached to the Guevavi mission church, forming a square with a central plaza, or open space. Guevavi became a visita of Tumacacori prior to 1770, and it was completely abandoned by 1775. By 1926 nothing was left of Guevavi except a few fragments of walls and eroded trash mounds. Both Guevavi and Calabasas were difficult locations to defend from Apache attacks. They were both isolated from the military fort at Tubac, Arizona, and were constantly threatened.

Today small portions of the adobe mission church are preserved, and Guevavi is considered one of the oldest remnants of the Jesuit Order in the United States. Guevavi is surrounded by sites dating from the Late Archaic period (2000 BC–AD 200) to historic times. Habitation sites dating to the late nineteenth and early twentieth centuries are most common, suggesting that the area surrounding the Guevavi mission was a major focus of occupation during this time.

PUBLIC OUTREACH AND INTERPRETATION AT TUMACACORI NHP

One of the goals of the park is to extend a message of preservation through environmental and cultural education. The park has school programs that are conducted at the park site as well as programs brought to local and regional schools. In addition, staff members give lectures at local community events. The visitors' center has a small museum with interpretive exhibits, and a trail leads visitors through the mission church, convento, and cemetery of San Jose de Tumacacori. The Juan Bautista de Anza Historic Trail starts near the visitors' center and extends along the Santa Cruz River for 4 miles to the Tubac Presidio State Park. It also leads south to the town of Rio Rico, Arizona.

Throughout the year the park hosts cultural events that celebrate local traditions and provide educational opportunities to the public. The park hosts an annual fiesta that brings together local musicians, folk dancers, poets, scholars, and food and craft vendors. The event takes place during the first weekend of December. It is a celebration of the unique cultural diversity of the region and provides an excellent opportunity to educate the public about aspects of Mexican American and Native American cultures. In addition, every Christmas Eve the mission church is donned with *luminarias*, which are candle lanterns. Luminarias are placed on the exterior and in the interior of the church, creating a luminous glowing church. This event is a local tradition that is practiced throughout the southwestern United States. With special-use permits, church masses and weddings are held in the main mission church.

The main mission church of San Jose de Tumacacori can be visited from 8:00 am to 5:00 pm every day of the year except Thanksgiving and Christmas. Guevavi and Calabazas are not open to the public. Tours of the sites are conducted during different times of the year. Interested parties should contact the park visitors' center at (520) 398-2341. Living history tours and lecture tours are conducted daily. The best time to visit the park is in the winter months.

Further Reading: Beaubien, Paul, *Excavations at Tumacacori, 1934*, Southwest Monuments Special Report No. 15 (Tumacacori, AZ: National Park Service, 1937); Burton, Jeffery F., *Remnants of Adobe and Stone: The Surface Archaeology of the Guevavi and Calabazas Units, Tumacacori National Historical Park, Arizona*, Publications in Anthropology No. 59 (Tucson, AZ: Western Archaeological and Conservation Center, National Park Service, 1992); Burton, Jeffery F., *San Miguel de Guevavi: The Archaeology of an Eighteenth Century Jesuit Mission on the Rim of Christendom*, Publications in Anthropology No. 57 (Tucson, AZ: Western Archaeological and Conservation Center, National Park Service, 1992); Dobyns, Henry F., *The Pima-Maricopa* (New York: Chelsea House, 1989); Fontana, Bernard L., James E. Officer, and Mardith Schuetz-Miller, eds., *The Pimeria Alta: Missions and More* (Tucson: Southwest Mission Research Center, Arizona State Museum, University of Arizona, 1996); Horton, Tonia W., "Tumacacori National Historical Park Cultural Landscape Documentation Study," unpublished manuscript on file at Tumacacori National Historical Park (Tumacacori, AZ:, 1998); Kessell, John L., *Mission of Sorrows: Jesuit Guevavi and the Pimas, 1691–1767* (Tucson: University of Arizona Press, 1970); Kessell, John L., *Franciscan Tumacacori 1767–1848: A Documentary History* (San Francisco, CA: National Park Service, Western Regional Office, 1972); Kessell, John L., *Spain in the Southwest: A Narrative History of Colonial New Mexico, Arizona, Texas, and California* (Norman: University of Oklahoma Press, 2002); Matson, Daniel S., and Bernard L. Fontana, *Before Rebellion: Letters and Reports of Jacobo Sedelmayr, S. J.* (Tucson: Arizona Historical Society, 1996); Ortiz, Alfonzo, ed., *Handbook of North American Indians*, Vol. 10: *Southwest* (Washington, DC: Smithsonian Institution, 1983); Rothman, Hal, *America's National Monuments: The Politics of Preservation*, 2nd ed. (Lawrence: University Press of Kansas, 1989); Shenk, Lynette O., *San Jose de Tumacacori: An Archaeological Synthesis and Research Design* (Tucson: Arizona State Museum, University of Arizona, 1976); Underhill, Ruth M., *The Papago and Pima Indians of Arizona*, 2nd ed. (Palmer Lake, CO: Filter Press, 2000).

Jeremy M. Moss

THE ALAMO, SAN ANTONIO MISSIONS NATIONAL HISTORICAL PARK, AND OTHER SITES

San Antonio Region, Texas
Spanish Colonial Settlement in the San Antonio River Valley

The headwaters of the San Antonio River with the springs and creeks flowing into it represent a natural gathering place for animals, people, and diverse flora. There is evidence of Native American occupation and exploitation of the rich resources dating back to the Paleoindian period. As the Spanish expanded their empire northward, rumors of this oasis of riverine resources sparked their interest in the area. The first Spaniards to reach Texas soil discovered the mouth of the Rio Grande in 1519. Alvar Nunez Cabeza de Vaca, who had been shipwrecked and captured by the Karankawa, a coastal Texas tribe, accidentally became the first Spaniard to witness the San Antonio River valley in the 1530s when he was accompanying a migratory group of Native Americans. He later wrote of the beauty and bounty of the river valley. The Spanish were not worried about their claim on these lands until the late 1600s, when French explorer Robert LaSalle established the short-lived Fort St. Louis and made claim to this area for France. The Spanish named Domingo Teran as the governor of this new territory of "Tejas." In 1691 he reached the headwaters of the San Antonio River and named it San Antonio de Padua in honor of Saint Anthony of Padua, Italy.

It was several decades after this visit in 1718 that the interim governor of Coahuila, Don Martin de Alarcon, was given the authority to establish a mission and presidio at San Antonio. The missions of Texas were established by the Franciscans, who sent out missionaries from the Colleges of Querétaro and Zacatecas. The purpose of the missions was to secure the land for Spain, convert the native tribes to Catholicism, and make them into good Spanish citizens, familiar with Spanish ways of farming, ranching, and village life.

The native tribes in the San Antonio River valley at the time of the establishment of the missions were small bands of hunter-gatherers who harvested the resources of the river and the land. They traveled from as far as the coast in their seasonal migrations and traded with one another for marine shell, stone for grinding and cutting tools, and other natural resources. The language of these groups is not known, but anthropologists collectively call them Coahuiltecans.

In the San Antonio River valley, particularly the headwaters of the river, there was an intense focus of Spanish occupation in the eighteenth century. Within this area the villa de Bexar, the presidio of San Antonio, and five missions were established. The mission was a compound that provided housing for the Native Indians, housing for the friars, a small military contingency, workshops, grain storage, and a chapel or church. Each mission had its own irrigation ditch system (*acequias*) with a dam and farm fields (*labores*). The missions also had a few thousand acres of designated ranchland for their livestock. The village also had personal residences, a church, and places of business. There is some evidence of pre-mission Spanish colonial campsites along the river as well.

DOWNTOWN SAN ANTONIO
San Antonio de Valero (the Alamo)
San Antonio de Valero was established in 1718 by Friar Antonio Olivares of the College of Querétaro. Shortly after the official establishment of the mission, the Presidio de Bexar and the Villa de Bejar were established. Mission San Antonio de Valero was never completely finished during the mission period. In 1794 the mission turned over the lands and their operation to the Native Indians who were living there (secularization). The various buildings of the mission were used for different purposes, and by 1836 it was used as a fort to protect against the invasion of Santa Ana's army from Mexico during the fight for Texas's independence. The façade of the church that is so famous today was completed in the 1840s, when the U.S. Army used it for storage. By the turn of the twentieth century most of the compound for the mission was gone, and care of the Alamo was turned over to the Daughters of the Republic of Texas. They restored some of the barracks/Indian quarters and maintain a compound surrounded by modern San Antonio buildings. A portion of the irrigation ditch, or acequia, for Mission San Antonio de Valero is preserved as a modern concrete channel on the Alamo grounds. Across the street from the Alamo there is a small sidewalk exhibit that shows a portion of the wall of the original compound as it was excavated.

Spanish Governor's Palace
In addition to Mission San Antonio de Valero, the main plaza preserves the Military Plaza of the Presidio de Bexar. At 105 Military Plaza the Spanish Governor's Palace still stands. This structure was completed in 1749 and housed the captain of the presidio. This National Historic Landmark was purchased by the city in 1928 and restored by architect Harvey P. Smith, who also restored Mission San José y San Miguel de

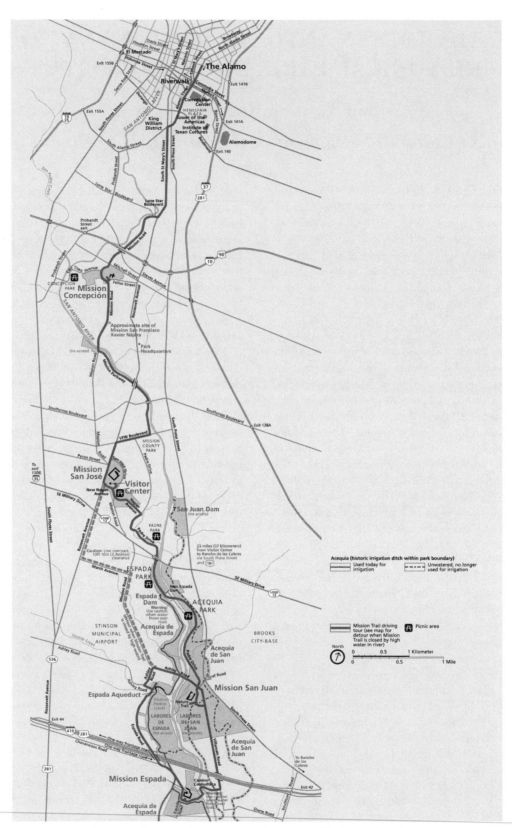

Map showing the locations of the Alamo and sites within San Antonio Missions National Historical Park. [Courtesy of the National Park Service]

Mission San José, also known as the Queen of the Missions, was established in 1720 and moved to its present location by 1721. [Susan Snow]

Aguayo. The city maintains it as a museum that is open to the public.

San Fernando Cathedral

Also located along main plaza is San Fernando Cathedral. It was the first parish church in Texas. Construction began in 1738 and was completed in 1749. Although there have been additions through the years, the original walls form the sanctuary today. A new restoration was recently completed with the addition of a museum attached to the cathedral. Archaeological investigations prior to construction revealed midden deposits related to the presidio occupation in this area. The church is still an active parish, and visitors can attend mass and tour the facility.

NORTH OF DOWNTOWN SAN ANTONIO

San Pedro Springs

San Pedro Park is located across from San Antonio College just north of downtown San Antonio. Mission San Antonio de Valero was first located west of the springs, then moved to the east side for better farmland, and moved to its current location in 1724. King Philip V of Spain declared the springs and the land surrounding them to be public land in 1729, making this one of the oldest public parks in the United States. The San Pedro acequia was established in the 1730s, and a remnant of this acequia can still be seen today. By the early 1990s the springs were almost dry due to pumping from the Edwards Aquifer. A restoration project was begun in 1998 and completed in 2000. There is a walking trail along the San Pedro acequia remnant, and a small stone building dating to sometime in the Spanish colonial period still stands.

Brackenridge Park

Just below the headwaters of the San Antonio River and east of San Pedro Springs is Brackenridge Park. The San Antonio River runs through the modern park and has not been as intensively modified as the portions further downstream. The Alamo Madre (main) ditch ran east, carrying water back to the farm fields of Mission San Antonio de Valero. The ditch left the river opposite the back side of the current Witte Museum on the east side of Brackenridge Park. On the west side of the river today is the San Antonio Zoo. In 1776 the Upper Labor (field) ditch for Valero was in this area, and remnants are visible within the zoo.

San Antonio Springs

Just north of Brackenridge Park lies the San Antonio Springs, which are the headwaters of the San Antonio River. These springs are located on the property of the University of the Incarnate Word. Due to pumping from the Edwards Aquifer, these springs have little water flow today unless there are extremely heavy rains. In 1996 the dam that diverted water to the Upper Labor ditch was found just below Hildebrand Avenue between Brackenridge Park and the San Antonio Springs.

SAN ANTONIO MISSIONS NATIONAL HISTORICAL PARK

San Antonio Missions National Historical Park was established by an act of Congress signed by President Carter in 1978. The park preserves and interprets the largest single concentration of Spanish colonial resources in the United

States. It includes the four southern missions of San Antonio—Mission Nuestra Señora de la Purisma Concepción, Mission San José y San Miguel de Aguayo, Mission San Juan Capistrano, and Mission San Francisco de la Espada—as well as the farm fields of missions San Juan and Espada, the San Juan and Espada acequias, the San Juan and Espada dams, the Espada aqueduct, and Rancho de las Cabras, which is the only extant mission ranch site.

Mission San José y San Miguel de Aguayo

Mission San José, also known as the Queen of the Missions, was established in 1720 and moved to its present location by 1721. It was founded by Friar Antonio Margil, president of the Zacatecan missionaries. Mission San José was the largest and most populous of any of the San Antonio missions. At its peak, over 300 Native Americans lived in the Indian quarter's walls. By the early 1920s, however, the site had been secularized for over 100 years, and most of the stone for the Indian quarters had been used for other buildings. The only standing structures were the church and the granary, with some visible ruin walls and newer buildings built out of the rubble. The San Antonio Conservation Society purchased the granary and began restorations in 1928. At the same time, the bell tower of the church collapsed for the second time. Through the Works Project Administration, architect Harvey P. Smith restored the compound, and it became a National Historic Site in 1941. During the restoration, a subterranean stone feature was discovered. This turned out to be a grist mill that was built in 1794 to grind wheat for the mission friars. In 2001 this mill was restored to working condition, and visitors can observe an interpretive ranger in period costume running the mill. The mill sits on a small remnant of the San José acequia.

Mission Nuestra Señora de la Purisma Concepción

In 1731 pressures from the French and hostile Indians in East Texas forced three missions to move westward to the San Antonio River. These missions were Mission Nuestra Señora de la Purisma Concepción, Mission San José de las Nazonis (now called Mission San Juan Capistrano), and Mission San Francisco de los Neches (now called Mission San Francisco de la Espada). Mission Concepción is located between Missions San Antonio de Valero and San José on the east side of the river. It was located at what may have been the second site for Mission San José in 1720 as well as what may have been the site of Mission San Xavier de Nàjera in 1722. The Mission Concepción compound quickly fell subject to urban growth after complete secularization in 1810. The church itself was used by the military during the Battle of Concepción during the Texas Revolution as well as later to house General John J. Pershing's troops during the U.S. Army's 1916 campaign to retaliate for Pancho Villa's cross-border attack in New Mexico. Only the church, the convento, and the limestone quarry for the mission remain visible today.

Extensive archaeological investigations were undertaken in 1972, 1980–81, and 2000–06 to investigate the nature of the compound. Mission Concepción is a National Historic Landmark and is the oldest unreconstructed church in the United States. It also contains the largest collection of Spanish colonial frescoes. The interior frescoes include those in the "Eye of God" room as well as in the church and sacristy. Archaeological evidence of the pre–Mission Concepción Spanish colonial occupation at the site has been found in the area behind the convento. Recent architectural investigations of the church structure indicate that the windows are placed to allow the sun to illuminate the altar on certain feast days. In 2005 the Archdiocese of San Antonio restored an original eighteenth-century painting to its location in the front of the church. All of these remarkable features are open to visitors year-round, with interpretive staff and wayside exhibits available for more information.

Mission San Juan Capistrano

Mission San Juan Capistrano compound is located south of Mission San José. The compound consists of the church and convento and ruins of the Indian quarters and exterior walls. There is also a structure built in 1850 from the remains of the Indian quarters. Both Mission San Juan and Mission Espada remain in a more rural setting than the northerly missions. The local community retains strong ties to these missions, and there are still residents in the area that remember living in the 1850 structure. As with the other four missions in the park, it has an active parish. The site was extensively excavated from 1968 to 1972 by the Witte Museum. These excavations provide the greatest detail about daily life in the missions through the large amount of ceramics, animal bone, and other artifacts that were recovered. A remnant of the original San Antonio River prior to channelization in the 1950s–70s has been preserved at the mission, and visitors can walk a trail along the remnant.

San Juan Acequia and Dam

The San Juan acequia runs south of the compound but originates farther north along the San Antonio River. During the channelization of the river, the original San Juan dam was cut off from the river, and water ceased to flow in the acequia. This caused the many farmers that were still utilizing the acequia in the 1970s to lose productivity. A pump system was developed to return water to the acequia, and the park has been working to repair damage to the acequia caused by urban development and runoff in order to restore the water to the acequia and the farmlands.

San Juan Farmlands (Labores)

The original farmlands for the mission are within park boundaries and, between Espada and San Juan, cover over 200 acres. The San Juan acequia runs across the San Juan farmlands, with lateral ditches off of the acequia still visible on the fields. Long-term plans include a demonstration farm using Spanish colonial techniques and crops.

Mission Espada

Mission Espada is the southernmost mission of San Antonio. The compound itself was occupied until the 1950s, with Indian quarters modified into small houses. Remnants of these houses as well as the church and convento are extant today. Ruins of an earlier church and granary are also visible just above the surface. As at all of the missions, wheelchair-accessible sidewalks allow visitors to walk around the compound. East of the compound in the woods along the original San Antonio River channel were a series of lime kilns that provided mortar for the construction of this mission.

Espada Aqueduct, Dam, and Acequia

The Espada acequia is unique because it is the oldest continuously running ditch in the United States. It is managed through a cooperative ditch company, and farmers near Mission Espada still exercise their water rights for irrigating their fields. About 1 mile north of the Espada compound, the Espada dam is preserved, and water is diverted from a small remnant channel of the San Antonio River into the Espada acequia. Downstream of the dam, the acequia crosses Piedras Creek. The Spanish missionaries built an impressive aqueduct to carry the acequia water over the creek. This aqueduct remains today and is a National Historic Landmark. When the San Antonio River was channelized, a special effort was made to protect the aqueduct from flood waters. Not far from the aqueduct, some prehistoric sites have been identified on either side of this original river channel as well as an early Spanish colonial site that may represent early Spanish explorers or Native Americans who were trading for Spanish/Mexican goods.

Rancho de las Cabras

Mission Espada is also unique because its ranch was located farther from the compound than any of the other ranches. For this reason, Rancho de las Cabras, located outside of the town of Floresville, 25 miles south of Mission Espada, was constructed of sandstone and adobe rather than the more typical jacal structures, which have left very little trace in the archaeological record. Rancho de las Cabras is located above the confluence of the San Antonio River and Picosa Creek. It represents a unique picture of Spanish colonial life because it has not been continuously occupied. The ranch was occupied from 1760 to 1810 and then abandoned except for cattle grazing, hunting, and occasional picnicking by locals. The site has great potential for intact archaeological remains. The National Park Service acquired the site in 1990 and provides tours monthly.

CONCLUSIONS

The Spanish colonial time period in the San Antonio River valley was a period of great change. Within a relatively short period of time, 1718–1810, missionaries came to the area, brought together various bands from around south Texas, and taught the natives Spanish customs; these customs merged with traditional ways to form the Tejano culture of south Texas today. Fortunately, a good deal of that story has been preserved by various partners in preservation in San Antonio: the San Antonio Conservation Society, the City of San Antonio, the San Antonio River Authority, the Archdiocese of San Antonio, and the National Park Service. Today visitors can experience Spanish colonial San Antonio by visiting these sites, which have been preserved for generations to come.

Further Reading: Center for Archaeological Research, University of Texas at San Antonio Web site, http://car.utsa.edu (online January 2007); Eckhart, Greg, *San Antonio Springs, San Pedro Springs*, Edwards Aquifer Web site, http://www.edwardsaquifer.net (online January 2007); Fontana, Bernard L., *Entrada: The Legacy of Spain and Mexico in the United States* (Tucson, AZ: Southwest Parks and Monuments Association, 1994); Habig, Marion A., *The Alamo Chain of Missions*, rev. ed. (Chicago: Franciscan Herald Press, 1976; reprint Livingston, TX: Pioneer Enterprises, 1997); *Handbook of Texas Online*, http://www.tsha.utexas.edu/handbook/online (online January 2007); Quirarte, Jacinto, *The Art and Architecture of the Texas Missions* (Austin: University of Texas Press, 2002); San Antonio Missions National Historical Park Web site, http://www.nps.gov/saan.

Susan Snow

PALO ALTO BATTLEFIELD NATIONAL HISTORIC SITE

Near Brownsville, Southern Texas

An Archaeological Account of a Mexican War Battle

"To the victor go the spoils," asserts the old proverb. Indeed, it is an axiom of warfare that the possessions of the vanquished become the booty of the victor. And who is likely to win the corollary prize, the right to interpret the conflict for future generations? The victor, of course. Yet due to an ironic fluke of historical oversight, Mexico, the losing nation at Palo Alto, won a sort of revisionist version of battle events—at least in the history books.

Palo Alto battlefield is the site of the first major engagement between the forces of Mexico and the United States

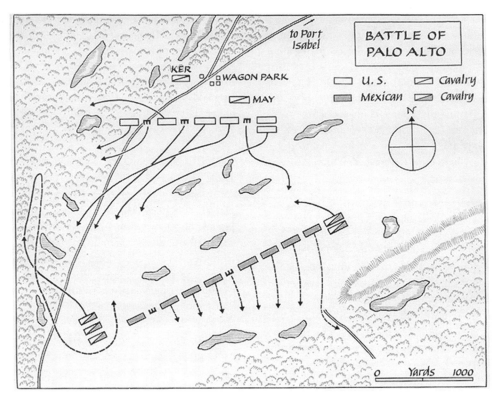

A map of the battle of Palo Alto.   [Courtesy of *Archaeology* Magazine/AIA. Based on research described in Haecker 1994 and 1996]

during the U.S.-Mexican War of 1846–48. The May 8, 1846, battle was the first between the United States and a foreign power since the War of 1812. For a new generation of professional officers, including Ulysses S. Grant, George G. Meade, and James Longstreet, the battle provided the first major test. For Mexico, the outcome of this battle meant loss of sovereignty over its northern frontier. Ultimately, Mexico's defeat in this war meant losing approximately half of its land. The United States won a vast region that became a prize of contention between the North and the South, between the forces of slavery and anti-slavery, a struggle that led inexorably to a greater conflict, the Civil War.

Under the administration of President James K. Polk (1845–49), the United States sought to persuade Mexico to sell lands for U.S. westward expansion. This persuasion included steady diplomatic and economic pressure. The strategy of "graduated pressure" was conceived in an atmosphere characterized by ignorance of Mexican domestic politics. Since the loss of the province of Texas, no Mexican government dared discuss the voluntary surrender of additional land to the United States for fear of being overthrown. Polk's diplomatic onslaughts convinced various Mexican leaders that their aggressive northern neighbor was attempting to annex their country. Mexico severed diplomatic relations with the United States following its annexation of Texas in February 1845.

Polk's aggressive diplomacy included military threats. In May 1845 Polk ordered General Zachary Taylor to move 1,500 regular troops to Corpus Christi, Texas, 140 miles north of the newly established Rio Grande border. During the succeeding months the camp increased in size to approximately 4,300 men, about half of the entire regular U.S. land forces. When the diplomatic pressures ultimately failed, Polk, in January 1846, ordered Taylor to move his troops to the Rio Grande. Taylor led 2,800 men to the northern bank of the river, where they built a star-shaped earthen fort, named Fort Texas, located opposite the Mexican town of Matamoros.

Mexican forces, led by General Mariano Arista, secretly attempted to surround the fort and thus trap the poorly provisioned U.S. army inside. Taylor, however, learned of this stratagem just in time. On May 1 Taylor led 2,300 men to his supply base some 20 miles away, leaving 500 men to defend the fort. Arista's first plan had failed; now he had to destroy the U.S. army in the open. Arista positioned his army at a road fork, within a broad, open plain surrounded by a jungle-like forest of mesquite trees. This area was named Palo Alto.

On May 8 Taylor's relief force of 2,250 men and 300 supply wagons was blocked by a force of some 6,000 Mexicans. Arista was confident his numerical superiority would prevent Taylor's much smaller force from relieving the Fort Texas, now under siege.

BATTLE of PALO ALTO.
CHARGE OF CAPTMAY'S DRAGOONS,
in which Genl La Vega was taken prisoner.

A historical depiction of the battle of Palo Alto.   [Library of Congress]

Arista arranged his army to form a trap for an infantry attack either across the plain or down the road that bisected Palo Alto. In either case, Mexican cavalry could envelop the attackers. The formation's weakness was the length of the double line of Mexican troops; this formation absorbed all available men, with no reserves to contain a breakthrough or counterattack. Also, because the antiquated Mexican artillery was difficult to shift on the battlefield, Arista could not significantly rearrange his batteries once these were placed in position.

Taylor ordered his infantry to advance in columns across the plain, whereupon the Mexican artillery opened the contest. After experiencing some artillery-related casualties, the American infantry halted while its horse artillery of 6-pounder and 12-pounder guns and howitzers quickly wheeled forward to within a few hundred yards of the Mexican battle line. They then opened fire with rapid and precise destructiveness. Two 18-pounder siege guns contributed to the decimation of the Mexican infantry. The Americans concentrated their fire on the Mexican left flank guarding the road. The Mexican 4-pounder and 8-pounder guns lacked the maneuverability and range needed to counter their enemy's rapidly deployed field batteries. Flanking attempts by Mexican cavalry were invariably repulsed, while entire ranks of largely stationary Mexican infantry were mowed down by solid and sustained cannon fire.

The four-hour battle ended with the collapse and rout of the entire Mexican battle line. At least 400 Mexican soldiers had been killed, with well over a thousand wounded. Total U.S. losses were 9 killed and 49 wounded. The following morning Arista's demoralized army retreated to a more defensible position at Resaca de la Palma, a marshy area 7 miles south of Palo Alto, where they were reinforced by fresh troops. Taylor's army, in hot pursuit, struck again, driving the Mexicans back across the Rio Grande. The siege was lifted; Taylor's smaller force had won the day.

In June 1992 Congress passed the Palo Alto Battlefield National Historic Site Act, which recognized the significance of the engagement in American history and in the U.S.-Mexican War as a whole. In so doing, it authorized the National Park Service to conduct an archaeological survey of the battlefield to sample the area for battle-related artifacts and archaeological features. The primary goal of this survey was to determine the approximate location of the Mexican and American battle lines.

Historical interpretation of the battle of Palo Alto depends on battle maps made at the time of the conflict, or soon thereafter, that illustrate the placement of military units and their various tactical maneuvers. Archival research conducted prior to fieldwork resulted in the discovery of a sketch map showing the order of battle of Palo Alto. The map was produced by a Captain Jean Berlandier, one of General Arista's staff officers. Berlandier's map formed the basis of a battle map published by the Mexican government a few months after the event. For over 100 years after its publication Berlandier's map, and its English translation variant published in the United States, were used by various historians when they wrote about this battle. Unfortunately, for whatever reason, U.S. topographical engineers on Taylor's staff did not prepare official battle maps of Palo Alto and Resaca de la Palma as they did for all the rest of the major battles south of the Rio Grande. Several contemporary American battle maps of Palo Alto were produced based on accounts from unknown sources.

Berlandier's map shows the initial phase of the battle as two opposing parallel battle lines about a mile apart, along an east-west axis. The Mexican line is shown as 1.5 miles long and consisting of the First, Fourth, Sixth, and Tenth Line Regiments interspersed by artillery. Both flanks were guarded by cavalry. The Fourth Line Regiment, supported by cavalry and artillery, formed the Mexican left flank and blocked the road where it forked. This map also shows the final phase of the battle as an aggressive advance of the Mexican battle line, with the Fourth acting as a stationary "hinge" for the advancing regiments. As the hinge, the Fourth was a non-moving target. In fact, several battle accounts describe this regiment as having suffered the brunt of U.S. artillery.

Comparisons of eyewitness descriptions of specific topographic features with those found on the battlefield today provided archaeologists with several correlations. These natural and man-made features were then used to select promising areas for archaeological study. Thus, it was possible to locate the approximate area where the Fourth once stood. Within that area archaeologists expected to find concentrations of Mexican-related artifacts, including the numbered insignia of this regiment, intermixed with U.S. round shot, shrapnel, and canister shot. Once the exact position of the Fourth Regiment was found, archaeologists believed it would be a relatively simple task to identify the remainder of the Mexican battle line.

During the first field season in 1992 archaeologists recovered hundreds of artifacts. The southern half of the battlefield produced most of these, including fragments of Mexican muskets, uniform accouterments, and personal items intermixed with U.S. shrapnel and shot. American and Mexican canister shot, cannonballs, and shrapnel were intermixed within the central, no-man's-land portion of the battlefield. The northern part of the battlefield produced few U.S.-related artifacts, presumably because there had been relatively few U.S. casualties.

Yet of all these artifacts, none came from the location where archaeologists expected to find strong evidence of the Mexican Fourth, that is, near the road fork where it had been stationed. At about 1,000 feet east of this location archaeologists discovered a concentration of Mexican-related artifacts, including numbered insignia representing all four Mexican line regiments. Suspicion arose that Berlandier's portrayal of certain battle events might not be entirely accurate.

Research continued up to the initiation of the second field season in 1993. This research located several unofficial battle maps that had been executed by American officers who had fought at Palo Alto, but that had been overlooked in earlier historical research about the battle. On certain tactical issues, such as the orders of battle for both armies, the American maps agreed with Berlandier's map. However, it was also obvious that the American officers' recollections were radically different from Berlandier's map with regard to what had transpired toward the close of battle.

Recall that Berlandier's map shows the Mexican Fourth as the steadfast hinge for the three advancing Mexican regiments. The opposing American version, however, shows the Mexican Fourth well to the east and away from the road. The main goal of the second archaeological field season was to determine which of the two map version was correct. Archaeologists now sampled the area where, according to the American maps, the Mexican army stood during the final hours of battle. It was hoped that, within this location, an artifact pattern would be discovered that would indicate the orientation of the Mexican battle line. In fact, this evidence was found. One survey unit 700 by 500 feet contained a broad band of Mexican-related artifacts that extended about 500 feet along a north-south axis, up to the opposite edges of the survey unit. Here was conclusive evidence that the Mexican army was facing almost due west, not north, during the final hours of the battle.

Contrary to what Berlandier had indicated on his battle map, the consensus was that the Mexican left flank was forced away from the road shortly after the battle began. The U.S. army advanced down the road, and then formed a battle line that faced east. The eastward re-deployment of the Mexican left flank, which included its Fourth Line Regiment, impinged upon the steadfast Mexican center. With their battle line now dangerously compressed, the Mexican army offered an even better target for U.S. artillery. Although compacted and its morale probably shaken, the Mexican army was, at least for a while, a cohesive fighting force, as indicated by the linear patterning of artifacts. According to the researchers, the final collapse and rout of the Mexican army is reflected by the aforementioned admixture of regimental insignia found in another, nearby sample unit.

To the north and east of this artifact concentration archaeologists discovered additional Mexican-related artifacts, albeit more widely dispersed. This artifact deposition reflects a rapid deployment of Mexican troops over a short period of time. In fact, both Mexican and American battle accounts describe such a charge by the Mexican army's right flank. This tactic was a final, desperate attempt to get around the American left flank and destroy the lightly defended wagon train parked in the rear. The charge was a brave but costly failure: whole units of Mexican infantry were mowed down by enfilade fire from American artillery. Units broken by this cannon fire collapsed onto the already compressed Mexican left flank, causing even greater confusion. Shortly thereafter, the Mexican army retreated in disorder from the battlefield.

Why should there be discrepancies between Mexican and American battle maps? Granted, the "fog of battle" will result in some misinterpretations, but there may be an additional explanation. It is suspected that Berlandier's original sketch map was an attempt to put the best face on an otherwise ignominious defeat. It was perhaps preferable to explain the heavy Mexican casualties as the result of a bold, final attack rather than the result of poorly used troops slaughtered by the superior artillery of an outnumbered enemy. This sketch map almost certainly was presented by Arista in his own defense at the court of inquiry, convened a few weeks after the battle. The court found Arista innocent of charges of incompetence, and so Berlandier's sketch map soon metamorphosed into a government document of impeccable credentials. Later historians, when conducting their research regarding this first battle of a half-forgotten war, perforce used the official Mexican map of the battle of Palo Alto, and thereby perpetuated the error. The accurate historical documents—obscure battle maps printed in period newspapers, post-battle propaganda handbills, and unpublished letters written by American eyewitnesses—were tucked away in obscure American archives. However, a source of unbiased data, the archaeological record of the battle, with careful collection, recording, and analysis, has enabled us to finally provide the correct historical interpretation.

Further Reading: Bauer, K. Jack, *The Mexican War, 1846–1848* (Lincoln: University of Nebraska Press, 1974); Fox, Anne A., *Archaeological Investigations in Alamo Plaza, San Antonio, Bexar County, Texas, 1988 and 1989*, Center for Archaeological Research Report No. 205 (San Antonio: University of Texas, 1992); Haecker, Charles M., "The Guns of Palo Alto," *Archaeology* (May/June 1996):48–53; Haecker, Charles M., *A Thunder of Cannon: Archaeology of the Mexican-American War Battlefield of Palo Alto*, Professional Paper No. 52 (Santa Fe, NM: National Park Service, Southwest Regional Office, 1994); Haecker, Charles M., and Jeffrey J. Mauck, *On the Prairie of Palo Alto: Historical Archaeology of the U.S.-Mexican War Battlefield* (College Station: Texas A & M University Press, 1997); Henderson, Timothy J.. *Glorious Defeat: Mexico and Its War with the United States* (New York: Farrar, Straus and Giroux, 2007); Houston, Donald E., "The Role of Artillery in the Mexican War," *Journal of the West* 11 (April 1972): 173–184; Kendall, G. Wilkins, and Lawrence D. Cress, *Dispatches From the Mexican War* (Norman: University of Oklahoma Press, 1999); Smith, George W., and Charles Judah, eds., *Chronicles of the Gringos: The U.S. Army in the Mexican War, 1846–1848* (Albuquerque: University of New Mexico Press, 1968).

Charles M. Haecker

MID- AND LATE-NINETEENTH-CENTURY MILITARY SITES

Arizona, New Mexico, and Texas
The Archaeology of Historic Battlefields and Forts

In the afternoon of August 18, 1846, the advance guard of the Army of the West, under the command of Colonel Stephen Watts Kearney, peacefully entered Santa Fe, the Mexican capital town of New Mexico. Five days later American troops began constructing Fort Marcy, an earthen star fort strategically placed on a hill and overlooking the heart of the town. Completed a year later, the fort was a reminder to all—both friend and foe—as to who was now in charge in this new American territory. In 1995 archaeologists excavated portions of the site of Fort Marcy and made a surprising discovery: there was no physical evidence to indicate the fort was ever occupied. Ironically, the first American fort built in the Southwest functioned as an empty threat (Snow and Kammer 1996).

All other American forts built in Arizona, New Mexico, and west Texas were definitely utilized. With cessation of the Mexican War in 1848 the United States Army found itself charged with protecting hundreds of thousands of square miles of newly acquired territory. The vast expanse and rugged, parched nature of the Southwest placed serious constraints on military operations in terms of mobility, supply, and communication. In response to these strategic concerns the military in the 1850s initiated a program of constructing a network of forts, supplemented by sub-posts and semi-permanent camps at particularly critical points. This strategy ultimately led to pacification of the region toward the close of the 1880s, but at a great cost in lives and treasure.

The military's primary adversaries in the Southwest were tribes of Apaches, a people well adapted to their environment whose warriors were notorious for their ferocity. Troops battle-hardened by the Mexican War had never campaigned against Indians as elusive as the Apaches and were unprepared for the swift movements necessary to bring them to bay (Watt 2002). Frontier forces underestimating the Apaches' mastery of guerrilla warfare paid dearly for this mistake, as evidenced by the battle of Cieneguilla.

BATTLE OF CIENEGUILLA
During the fall and winter of 1854 hostile bands of Jicarilla Apaches attacked emigrant trains on the Santa Fe Trail in northeastern New Mexico. Companies of United States

Iron arrow points, excavated at Mescalero Apache encampments dating to the period 1855–1885 located within the military reservation of Fort Stanton, New Mexico. During this period between 300–500 Apache men, women, and children lived within this military reservation on a peaceful basis. Many of the Apache warriors provided their services to Fort Stanton as scouts and provisioners of wild game in exchange for manufactured goods and the right for their people to scavenge for useable objects deposited in the fort dumps. The arrow points were manufactured from segments of barrel hoop.   [Photo © 2007 Joseph Arcure]

Dragoons were ordered to halt these depredations and determine the locations of all of the Jicarilla bands, both peaceful and hostile. First Dragoons Captain John Davidson received a scouting report that a Jicarilla band had set up camp in the rugged foothills near Picuris Pueblo. Davidson did not know if this particular band was hostile or not; nonetheless, he decided to attack their camp. During the early morning of March 30, 1854, Davidson and his sixty-man command quietly advanced toward the ridge on which the Jicarilla camp was located. The Apaches, however, were aware of the dragoons' approach and had prepared a surprise of their own. Upon reaching the base of the ridge, Davidson ordered his men to dismount. Their horses, guarded by fifteen men,

stayed at the ridge base while the larger detail advanced upslope toward the waiting Apaches. After a brief but fierce fight the Apaches retreated down the opposite side of the ridge. The dragoons' self-congratulations ended, however, when they discovered that the horse guard was under attack. Forced to retreat, Davidson had his men form a defensive ring around their horses. For the next two hours the dragoons suffered aggressive attacks by over 100 warriors, who held high ground on three sides. Finally, Davidson ordered his men to gallop through a gauntlet of arrows and rifle balls and regroup at the top of a nearby ridge. They gained the ridge top only to find another group of warriors arrayed before them. With ammunition supplies now low, Davidson's desperate command scrambled down the opposite slope and escaped total destruction. They left behind the bodies of twenty-two of their comrades (Bennett 1948; Taylor 1969). Two years later the military conducted a court of inquiry to determine how and why such a defeat could have happened. Based on testimonies by several of his men, Davidson was found innocent of charges of cowardice and incompetence; in fact, he was commended by the court for his "gallantry and bravery."

In 2002 and 2003 U.S. Forest Service archaeologists conducted a metal detector survey to determine the location and complexity of the battle and associated Apache camp. Once it was discovered, the site produced a wealth of information regarding pre–Civil War dragoon tactics, Apache counter-tactics, and the material culture found within an Apache camp from the 1850s. Based on material evidence found at the battle site, archaeologists concluded that the sequence and intensity of battle events largely occurred as noted by Davidson in his own defense. Other findings suggest that the accusations that Davidson was an incompetent tactician were correct (Johnson 2007).

FORT STANTON

A frontier military post in territorial New Mexico from 1855 to 1896, Fort Stanton is the only intact New Mexico fort built before the Civil War and one of the Southwest's most significant and best-preserved forts. The fort was established within the traditional home range of the Mescalero Apaches with the intent of curbing their raids throughout New Mexico, west Texas, and northern Mexico. Burned and abandoned when a Confederate army invaded New Mexico in 1861, Fort Stanton was briefly occupied by the Confederates. After their defeat in New Mexico, the fort was re-established in 1862 as part of a Union Army campaign to round up the Mescaleros and place them on Bosque Redondo Indian Reservation along with the Navajo Indians. When decommissioned by the Army in 1896, Fort Stanton became a Merchant Marine tubercular hospital. During the 1930s a portion of the military reservation was reserved for use by a Civilian Conservation Corps (CCC) camp. In 1941 the then-abandoned CCC camp was expanded and modified to accommodate an internment camp for German merchant seamen; this was the first American internment camp of the war.

Although long valued as a place of great historical significance, Fort Stanton was not considered an important archaeological resource until 2004. In that year the National Park Service, in partnership with the state of New Mexico and the Bureau of Land Management, initiated a multi-year archaeology survey and testing program focused on identifying military, civilian, and Apache sites within the 24,000-acre military reservation. As of 2007 project members have identified intact refuse dumps associated with the 1855–96 military period; they also located the post firing range, a brewery dating to about 1880, and twelve Apache encampments that date to between 1855 and 1880. Project members also conducted a mapping and testing program within the World War

II German internment camp. To date, the Fort Stanton Archaeology Project has provided insights into the day-to-day lives and interactions of soldiers and civilians on an isolated frontier post, of Apache bands who chose to live in close proximity to the fort for certain benefits otherwise unobtainable by them, of tubercular patients and those who tended to their needs, and of German prisoners of war who made adaptations to their surroundings in order to cope with their confinement (Haecker 2007).

APACHE PASS BATTLEFIELD

By the eve of the Civil War the Chiricahua Apache conflict in Arizona had reached a crisis. Army posts were too widely scattered and poorly manned to pose a significant threat to raiding Apaches, who roamed virtually unrestricted over the entire region. Finally, by the spring of 1861, the withdrawal of federal troops in Arizona to eastern theaters of the Civil War presented Apache chiefs Mangas Coloradas and Cochise an opportunity to annihilate all remaining intruders. They assembled an arsenal of firearms and strengthened alliances with other Apache bands. In early July 1862 warriors prepared Apache Pass in southeastern Arizona as a place of ambush for the troop formations who funneled through it. They constructed stone breastworks having overlapping fields of fire and overlooking the only spring within the pass. At the western approach the chiefs positioned warriors whose duty was to prevent soldiers from escaping once the attack began. If their scheme worked, all trapped soldiers would die from either gunfire or thirst.

On the morning of July 15 a weary, thirsty column of ninety-six California Volunteers, with two mountain howitzers, entered the western end of Apache Pass. The chiefs intended to initiate their surprise when all of the soldiers were contained inside the pass; however, some warriors fired prematurely at the rear guard, which signaled the other Apaches to open fire. The parched soldiers were unable to dislodge the Apaches from their masked positions; even explosive cannonballs fired from their howitzers had no effect. The battle raged through the night, with Apache sharpshooters keeping desperate soldiers away from the spring. The situation changed the next morning when the soldiers received reinforcements. Screened by flank skirmishers, the howitzer battery advanced toward the spring and periodically fired at elevated positions. Finally, soldiers charged upslope to take high ground—only to discover that their tormenters had melted away. The two chiefs realized success was now impossible, so no value remained in continuing the fight (McChristian 2005).

The soldiers' retelling of the battle turned the event into a struggle of epic proportions. Newspapers reported as many as 800 Apaches being at the battle, armed with state-of-the-art Sharps carbines, rifled muskets, and revolvers. The official report stated that the howitzer fire was accurate, and many Apaches had been killed during the battle (Fountain 1962, 34–35). Apache versions understated the incident, claiming the soldiers killed few warriors (Ball 1970, 46). Questions about the battle's intensity and complexity have been archaeologically investigated: What varieties of firearms did the Apaches use? Did the Apaches construct breastworks? Approximately how many Apaches participated in the battle? Was artillery fire as intense and accurate as described by the soldiers? National Park Service archaeologists conducted a metal detector survey of Apache Pass. Their findings indicated that most of the battle took place in the vicinity of the spring. Apache-fired bullets found in and around the soldiers' position represented only 4 percent of the total bullet count, and the Apache bullets indicated that the warriors possessed a mix of military and nonmilitary firearms of varying firepower. Conversely, the firepower of the soldiers was superior to that of the Apaches, suggesting that the Apaches neither significantly outnumbered the soldiers nor were uniformly armed with quality weapons. The amount of cannonball shrapnel was sparse on high ground that had been targeted by the artillerymen, but shrapnel could be found well beyond the confines of Apache Pass. These findings suggest that the howitzers were fired less often and with less accuracy than as reported by the soldiers and later historians (Haecker 2001).

PINE SPRINGS "BUFFALO SOLDIERS" BASE CAMP

In 1867 the Army re-established its presence in west Texas by stationing the newly formed Ninth Cavalry regiment at forts Davis and Concho, and at ancillary sub-posts. All of the enlisted men of the Ninth were African American; their officers were white. For the next nine years this regiment conducted patrols; pursued marauding Apaches, Comanches, and Mexican bandits; and established semi-permanent camps at major water sources. One of these water sources was Pine Springs, located on the eastern slopes of the Guadalupe Mountains and what is now Guadalupe Mountains National Park. Pine Springs Camp was established in 1870. Typically, one troop out of twenty or so men protected the base camp with its supplies while another troop patrolled through the mountains, looking for sign of hostile bands of Apaches. In 1875 the Ninth Cavalry transferred to Fort Stanton, whereupon the Tenth Cavalry—the other African American cavalry regiment—took over its duties. In 1879–81 Pine Springs Camp became a major point of operations for patrols that combed the Guadalupe Mountains for any sign of Apache Chief Victorio's band. The Apache War was effectively over by the end of 1881, and Pine Springs was finally abandoned by the military (Haecker 2004; Leckie and Leckie 2003).

The Pine Springs site was archaeologically recorded in 1970 by the Texas Archaeological Society. The field team described and mapped 21 hearths in alignment, and collected several surface artifacts. These surface indicants suggest that the camp was limited to a three-acre area centered on the hearth alignment, and it was concluded that the site had been severely impacted by illicit relic collecting. In 2004, 2005, and 2006 the National Park Service, in partnership with the Howard

University Anthropology Department and the Mescalero Apache Tribe, conducted an archaeology field school program at Pine Springs. Results indicate that the camp is largely intact and actually comprises over 60 acres, it holds an array of features greater in number and variety than was initially interpreted, there is evidence of an Apache encampment whose occupants may have occupied the site when military forces were absent, and scatterings of cartridge cases and fired bullets suggest an Apache-Cavalry battle also took place at Pine Springs about 1870 (Fox and Scott 1991; King and Haecker 2007).

Further Reading: Ball, Eve, *In the Days of Victorio: Recollections of a Warm Springs Apache* (Tucson: University of Arizona Press, 1970); Bennett, James A., *Forts and Forays: A Dragoon in New Mexico 1850–1856* (Albuquerque: University of New Mexico Press, 1948); Fountain, Albert J., "The Battle of Apache Pass," in *Arizona Cavalcade: The Turbulent Times*, edited by Joseph Miller (New York: Hastings House, 1962), 31–35; Fox, Richard A., and Douglas D. Scott, "The Post–Civil War Battlefield Pattern," *Historical Archaeology* 25(2) (1991): 90–103; Haecker, Charles M., "A Well-Laid Trap: Artifact Pattern Analysis of an Apache Ambush Site, Apache Pass, Arizona," paper presented at the 34th Conference on Historical and Underwater Archaeology, Long Beach, CA (paper on file and available from the author, National Park Service, Santa Fe, NM) (2001); Haecker, Charles M., "Historical and Archaeological Investigations of Apache War Sites, Guadalupe Mountains National Park, in *The Guadalupe Mountains Symposium, Proceedings of the 25th Anniversary Conference on Research and Resources Management in Guadalupe Mountains National Park*, edited by Fred Armstrong and K. Keller Lynn (Washington, DC: National Park Service, 2004), 183–192; Haecker, Charles M., "Archaeology of Institutional Solitude, Fort Stanton, New Mexico," book manuscript on file with the author (Santa Fe, NM: National Park Service, 2007); Johnson, David M., "Apache Victory against the U.S. Dragoons, the Battle of Cieneguilla, New Mexico," in *Fields of Conflict: Battlefield Archaeology from the Roman Empire to the Korean War*, Vol. 2: *Nineteenth and Twentieth Century Fields of Conflict*, edited by Douglas Scott, Lawrence Babits, and Charles Haecker (Westport, CT: Praeger Security International, 2007), 235–254; King, Eleanor M., and Charles M. Haecker, "Emancipation on the Frontier: Buffalo Soldiers, Apaches, and the Battle over Land in the Southwest," paper presented at Society for Historical Archaeology, Albuquerque, NM, January 12 (paper on file with the author, Howard University Anthropology Department, Washington, DC) (2007); Leckie, William H., and Shirley A. Leckie, *The Buffalo Soldiers: A Narrative of the Black Cavalry in the West* (Norman: University of Oklahoma Press, 2003); McChristian, Douglas C., *Fort Bowie, Arizona, Combat Post of the Southwest, 1858–1894* (Norman: University of Oklahoma Press, 2005); Snow, Cordelia T., and David Kammer, *"Not Occupied . . . Since the Peace": The 1995 Archaeological and Historical Investigations at Historic Fort Marcy, Santa Fe, New Mexico*, Archaeological Records Management System (ARMS), NMCRIS No. 49311 (Santa Fe, NM: Laboratory of Anthropology, 1996); Taylor, Morris F., "Campaigns against the Jicarilla Apache," *New Mexico Historical Review* XLIV(4) (1969): 269–292; Watt, Robert N., "Raiders of a Lost Art? Apache War and Society," *Small Wars & Insurgencies* 13(3) (2002): 1–28.

Charles M. Haecker

THE PALACE OF THE GOVERNORS

Historic Plaza, Santa Fe, New Mexico
The Archaeology and Architecture of the Oldest Public Building

The Palace of the Governors is one of the oldest continuously occupied public buildings in the United States. Since its construction in 1610 by Governor Don Pedro de Peralta, the palace has housed governors from Spain, Mexico, and the territorial United States, along with Pueblo Indians, the United States military, and, since the turn of the twentieth-century, the Museum of New Mexico. The Palace of the Governors was central to the Pueblo Revolt of 1680, when Pueblo Indians and allies joined to expel the Spanish from New Mexico; this event is considered by some to be the first American Revolution. Now a quadrangle of buildings 260 feet long and 115 feet wide with an open-air courtyard, the Palace of the Governors has undergone many structural changes during 395 years of use. Its polyethnic past, urban location, and long history mark the Palace of the Governors as a unique symbol of the United States' diverse cultural heritage.

The Palace of the Governors was part of a changing constellation of buildings located north of historic Santa Fe plaza. It served as government offices, a military post, and the home of designated governors and their families until 1908, except during the Pueblo Rebellion from 1680 to 1692, when Pueblo Indians and allies occupied it. From 1610 to 1821 (Spanish colonial period) fifty Spanish governors served typically two- to four-year terms and lived at the Palace of the Governors. It was primarily a residence and government building with grounds that contained a garden, fields, orchards, storage buildings, and military barracks. Ditches or *acequias* brought water from a nearby spring and swamp for household and agricultural use. Large-scale irrigation supported cultivation of Old World plants, such as wheat, barley, hops, fruit trees, and grapes, and New World corn, beans, squash, cotton, and tobacco. Domesticated cattle, sheep, goats, pigs, and horses served as draft and food animals and a source of economic prosperity, while wild game supplemented a protein-rich diet. Wool and cotton products, game including buffalo, pinyon (pine) nuts, and occasionally pottery were traded with northern Mexico through the governor and a small number of merchants.

During the Mexican period (1821–46) fourteen governors oversaw important social and economic changes brought by opening of the Santa Fe Trail from Independence, Missouri. Although the Santa Fe Trail trade increased access to manufactured goods, the regional economy remained agrarian. Americans seeking opportunity renewed interest in control and ownership of large tracts of land and natural resources, as some of the largest land grants were made during this time. The governor collected tariffs on goods from the United States before they were sent to Mexico. Described as derelict or in disrepair, the palace was intermittently occupied by the governor but was more commonly used to store goods and livestock or for business transactions. Wagons off-loaded merchandise at the plaza, where there was a brisk trade in local and imported goods and foodstuffs.

The United States Army of the West entered Santa Fe and occupied the Palace of the Governors in 1846, marking the beginning of New Mexico's Territorial period (1846–1912). By 1850, a territorial governor with other territorial officials and the legislature occupied the palace until 1909. Twenty-two territorial governors presided over a state that was rich in natural resources and land but was plagued by land-rush problems that displaced and disrupted lives of the multiethnic traditional peoples. In 1879 completion of the Atchison, Topeka, and Santa Fe Railway connected New Mexico to the national economy, bringing goods and people on a previously unparalleled scale.

Incidental, salvage, and scientific archaeological studies at the Palace of the Governors span the last 140 years. Newspapers report the finding of a Spanish forge during an 1867 renovation and the 1884 unearthing of human skeletons suggested to be the remains of seventy Indians executed during Don Diego de Vargas's 1692 reconquest. Before 1970, small-scale room investigations yielded limited architectural information consisting of cobble foundations capped by one or two courses of adobe bricks. From 1974 to 1975, Museum of New Mexico archaeologists and volunteers led by Cordelia T. Snow excavated most of three rooms and a hallway exposing building foundations and adobe floors as well as many storage and refuse pits containing over 75,000 artifacts from the 1600s and early 1700s. Pueblo Revolt period modification of palace rooms was suggested by large Spanish-style rooms that were subdivided into smaller residential and storage rooms. From 2002 to 2004 excavations were conducted by the New Mexico Office of Archaeological Studies immediately north of, but within, the historical Palace of the Governors grounds. Excavations recovered 800,000 artifacts and revealed extensive Spanish colonial and American territorial cobble foundations, a cobble-lined orchard or garden irrigation ditch, refuse-filled pits, roasting and outdoor cooking features, a probable butchering facility, and adobe-material borrow pits as well as 1880s construction of a small-scale assayer's building, furnace, and refuse pits.

Today the Palace of the Governors is an architectural amalgamation of Pueblo, Spanish, and American architectural styles. Many questions remain about changes in the size, floor plan, and organization of activities, especially for the Spanish colonial period. Maps for all periods provide limited information, and only two exist from the Spanish colonial period. Translated Spanish documents depict a rambling, mostly one-story adobe brick building with few windows containing residences, meeting rooms, storehouses, and courtyards, but they provide no actual measurements or floor plan. Beneath the modern palace, cobble foundations and wall stubs suggest a flexible Spanish colonial floor plan. Specialized and mundane activities are suggested by the side-by-side occurrence of ornately patterned adobe brick floors and simple compacted dirt floors from the seventeenth century. North of the palace, archaeologists have exposed east-west cobble building foundations that were 40–90 meters long and divided into rectangular rooms 8–12 meters long by 6 meters wide. These rooms had dirt floors, and adobe corner fireplaces defined courtyard and work spaces as they rose and fell. Few buildings were depicted on the Spanish colonial or early territorial maps. Many episodes of remodeling are evident from abundant fire-reddened adobe from ovens and fireplaces; unburned adobe, lime, gypsum, or adobe plaster traces from building walls; and mica or selenite sheets from windows. The Spanish colonial palace dimension and construction history is best known from its archaeological evidence, since map and documentary sources provided limited and disparate details.

Soon after the Army of the West arrived in 1846, the palace was characterized as ample in size and habitable, measuring 350 feet long and consisting of twenty rooms. This description may apply to the palace as it stood within the dilapidated presidio during the late Spanish and Mexican periods. Between 1846 and 1868, rooms and buildings were remodeled to fit more eastern architectural tastes of central fireplaces, wood floors, and glazed windows, as indicated by window glass, framing nails, and calcimine wall plaster coatings. Between 1866 and 1869, the palace was reduced to its modern length of 260 feet to accommodate Lincoln and Washington Avenues as north-south boulevards to a new federal courthouse and oval. Behind the palace, store rooms, water closets, and sheds partly enclosed an outdoor courtyard. Excavation showed that these buildings were built on top of earlier foundations. Spanish, Mexican, and remodeled territorial period buildings north of the palace were razed and replaced by Fort Marcy Military Reservation houses and facilities. Some of these buildings still stand, including the post commandant's house (the Hewett House), and officers' houses on Grant Avenue.

After 1880 the palace was outfitted with modern conveniences, including electricity and asphalt roofing steam heating. Copper wiring, electric light bulb fragments, and tar and gravel are intermingled with abundant kitchen debris, glass ink wells, Japanese ink pots, champagne and beer bottles, and medicinal bottles from the eastern United States, Canada, and Europe in massive refuse pits behind the Palace of the Governors.

The Palace of the Governors is operated by the Museum of New Mexico as a history museum. It has period rooms displaying, describing, and interpreting different aspects of Spanish colonial, Mexican, and American life in New Mexico during 298 years of governors and their administrations. Other rooms house exhibits on people, places, and experiences of New Mexico, such as the Segesser hide paintings, Jewish pioneers, and Spanish colonial lifeways. A print shop has numerous historic presses, and the Fray Angelico Chavez library and photographic archive offers extensive research materials and images on New Mexico and southwestern history. At the Palace of the Governors visitors experience New Mexico's historic past through architecture and artifacts, while digging deeper they can learn about the personal histories that make Santa Fe and New Mexico unique within the United States.

Further Reading: Kessell, John L., *Kiva, Cross, and Crown: The Pecos Indians and New Mexico, 1540–1940* (Tucson, AZ: Southwestern Parks and Monuments Association, 1995); Moorhead, Max L., "Rebuilding the Presidio of Santa Fe, 1789–1791," *New Mexico Historical Review* XLIX (1974): 123–142; Noble, David G., ed., *Santa Fe: History of an Ancient City* (Santa Fe, NM: School of American Research Press, 1989); Shishkin, J. K., *The Palace of the Governors* (Santa Fe: Museum of New Mexico, 1972).

Stephen S. Post

Great Basin/Plateau Region

KEY FOR GREAT BASIN/PLATEAU REGIONAL MAP

1. Death Valley National Park: Harmony Borax Works and Keane Wonder Mine
2. Willow Spring
3. Gypsum Cave
4. Tule Springs
5. Zion National Park
6. Carson Sink-Stillwater Marsh sites
7. The Grimes Point Archaeological Area, Spirit Cave, and Hidden Cave
8. Monitor Valley: Gatecliff Shelter, Triple T Shelter, Hickison Summit, and Alta Toquima Village
9. Defiance House
10. Anasazi State Park
11. Danger Cave
12. Fremont Indian State Park
13. Fort Rock Cave
14. Gold Hill, Limpy Creek, Marial, and Windom
15. Roadcut (Five Mile Rapids)
16. Kennewick
17. Marmes Rockshelter
18. Mt. Rainier sites
19. Cascade Pass
20. Newhalem Rockshelter
21. Nez Perce National Historic Park
22. Whitman Mission National Historic Site
23. Fort Spokane
24. Spokane House
25. St. Paul's Mission
26. Fort Okanogan
27. Donner Party sites
28. Fort Churchill
29. Fort Simcoe
30. Virginia City
31. Barkerville
32. Lovelock Cave and Humbolt Cave
33. Hogup Cave
34. Bonneville Estates Rockshelter
35. Grapevine Wash
36. Valley of Fire State Park
37. Lost City
38. Lake Mead National Recreation Area
39. Red Cliffs
40. Capitol Reef National Park
41. Nine Mile Canyon
42. Great Salt Lakes caves
43. Wizard's Beach, Pyramid Lake
44. Cowboy Cave
45. Paisley 5 Mile Point Caves
46. Catlow and Roaring Springs Caves
47. Connley Caves
48. Paulina Lake, Newberry Volcanic National Monument
49. Carlon and Boulder Village
50. Wilson Butte Cave
51. Tonopah Lakebed sites
52. Kettle Falls
53. Hatwai
54. Dietz
55. Umatilla
56. Wildcat Canyon
57. Mack Canyon
58. Lake Wallula and Strawberry Island
59. Hanford Reach
60. East Wenatchee Clovis Cache
61. Keatley Creek
62. Parowan, Evans Mound, and Median Village
63. Massacre Lake
64. Pahranagat Lake and Mt. Irish Archaeological District
65. Lagomarsino Canyon
66. Dirty Shame Rockshelter

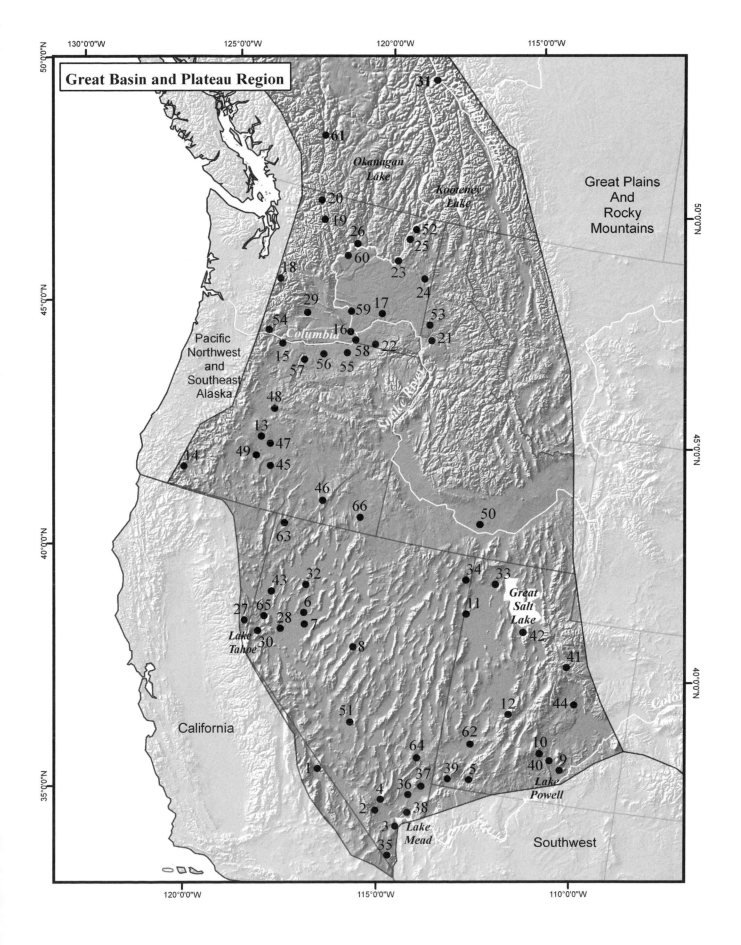

INTRODUCTION

This section of *Archaeology in America* includes essays about archaeological sites in the Great Basin and Plateau region of North America. The Great Basin comprises the southern portion of the region. The Plateau, basically the drainage of the Columbia River in Idaho, Oregon, Washington, and adjacent portions of Canada, constitutes the northern part. The region is bounded on the east by the Rocky Mountains, roughly from south central Utah to the western border of Wyoming and northward along the western border of Montana. The southern boundary runs roughly from southwestern Utah to the southern California desert. Along the west side of the region are the Sierra Nevada Mountains and foothills in the south and the Cascade Mountains in the north. The northern boundary is roughly the northern extent of the Columbia River.

None of the rivers that begin flowing within the Great Basin drain to the ocean. In its eastern half, the Great Salt Lake is a remnant of a larger ancient lake, Lake Bonneville, which at its largest extent covered 50,000 square kilometers of the Basin. In the western part of the Basin, Pyramid and Walker lakes are the remains of another large ancient lake, Lake Lahontan, which once covered about 22,000 square kilometers. There are also other, smaller lakes and wetlands throughout the otherwise arid Basin. The shores of the pluvial (i.e., caused or supplied mainly by rainfall) lakes and wetlands were the locations of human activities and settlements from earliest times to the historic period (e.g., the essays on the Grimes Point Archaeological Area, Carson Sink–Stillwater Marsh sites, Humboldt Cave, Lovelock Cave, and Wizard Beach sites).

The Plateau is a large area drained by the Columbia River and its tributaries. The western portion of the Plateau, in the rain shadow of the Cascade Mountains, receives limited rainfall. The dominant landscape feature of the Plateau is the Columbia River channel, which winds its way from southern Canada, down the center of Washington State, and then westward, serving as the border between Washington and Oregon, to the Pacific Ocean.

The ingenuity of humans in adapting to difficult environments is displayed in the cultural systems of the ancient inhabitants of the Great Basin and Plateau region. Living under natural environmental constraints, ancient inhabitants of the region managed to thrive (e.g., the essays on Monitor Valley sites, Hogup Cave, Danger Cave, Fremont State Park sites, Cascade Pass, and Newhalem Rockshelter). A rich artistic record documents these cultural adaptations (e.g., the essays on rock art styles of the Great Basin and Plateau, Red Rock Canyon petroglyphs, and mountain petroglyphs of Monitor Valley).

Around its southern margin, the Great Basin–Plateau region includes sites linked to cultural traditions of the Southwest. In southern Nevada and southwest and south central Utah are sites associated with the Ancestral Pueblo or Anasazi cultures (e.g., Virgin and Muddy Rivers sites, Defiance House site).

Along the western border of the Great Basin and Plateau region, there is a transition from the relatively flat and very arid plains or desert environments to the Sierra Nevada mountains in the south and the Cascade range in the north. In the southwestern corner, we have made the boundary of the Great Basin confirm roughly to the eastern border of California, however, careful readers will note that our introductory essay extends the Great Basin into the Mojave Desert of southern California. These regional boundaries are somewhat flexible. We have included specific site essays from the desert portions of southeastern California in the California section of the West Coast volume (volume 4) of this encyclopedia.

Historic period events, patterns, and archaeological sites in the Great Basin–Plateau region also are represented in the essays in this section. Exploration sites, historic settlements and industrial sites, and sites linked to conflicts between Euro-Americans and Indians during the nineteenth century are included.

We have focused these essays on the most important and interesting archaeological sites and topics in the Great Basin–Plateau region. Readers can learn more about these sites, and others as well, by using the sources of information and references in the last section of each essay. Many of the sites can be visited as part of national, state, or local public parks.

The Great Basin–Plateau section of *Archaeology in America* includes six general essays on topics that cover ancient or historic time periods. These general essays are followed by twenty-two essays on specific archaeological sites or about archaeological sites in a particular region. These more specific essays are arranged roughly geographically beginning in the southern Great Basin, moving northward and ending in the Plateau.

ENTRIES FOR THE GREAT BASIN/PLATEAU REGION

INTRODUCING THE ARCHAEOLOGY OF THE GREAT BASIN AND PLATEAU

The areas discussed herein are the adjoining physiographic Great Basin and Columbia Plateau regions. The historic Columbia Plateau and Great Basin culture areas, as defined by anthropologists (d'Azevedo 1986; Walker 1998), are much larger, extending into or across adjacent physiographic areas. The physiographic Basin-Plateau region covers over 580,000 square kilometers. The Plateau section is bounded on the east by the Rocky Mountains, on the west by the Cascade Mountains, and on the north by the Okanogan Highlands. The regions merge in the High Lava Plains of south central Oregon. The Great Basin section is bounded on the west by the Sierra Nevada and on the east by the Wasatch Mountains and the Colorado Plateau; on the south it merges into the Sonoran Desert section of the Basin and Range physiographic province.

The Great Basin, covering about 290,000 square kilometers, is an area of internal drainage; no rivers originating therein drain to the ocean. There are 150 individual basins, or valleys, separated by160 north-south-trending mountain ranges. Ranges and valleys vary from 50 to 350 kilometers long. During the Pleistocene epoch many valleys were filled with pluvial lakes (lakes formed and refreshed mainly by precipitation), some of great size. Lake Bonneville at its maximum covered 50,000 square kilometers and was 330 meters deep. Its remnant is the Great Salt Lake in Utah. Lake Lahontan covered about 22,000 square kilometers and was 230 meters deep. Its remnants are Pyramid and Walker lakes in western Nevada. There were over 100 other, smaller pluvial lakes. The shores of the pluvial lakes and their successor remnant lakes were important places for the occupants of the Great Basin from earliest times until the twentieth century.

The Columbia Plateau is a vast basaltic lava plain, also about 290,000 square kilometers in extent. It is drained by the Columbia River and some of its tributaries. The northern and western sections are covered by windblown loess and water-deposited sediments. The latter derive from periodic catastrophic outflows of Glacial Lake Missoula during the late Ice Age, which carved deep coulees and scablands into and across the landscape.

The Basin-Plateau region has two major biogeographic divisions: the high desert, north of 36 degrees north latitude, with valley floors lying at 1,000–1,840 meters in elevation, and the low desert to the south, with valley floors 800 meters and below in elevation, including Death Valley, which is 100 meters below sea level at its lowest point. Both divisions have characteristic biomes containing vertical successions of temperature- and moisture-sensitive ecological zones of plant and animal communities from the floors of plains or valleys to mountaintops. Both regions have arid to semi-arid climates.

HISTORY OF ARCHAEOLOGICAL RESEARCH

Systematic archaeological work in the Plateau began with surveys of petroglyph (rock art) sites in the 1920s, followed by archaeological site surveys and excavations in the early 1930s. Major hydroelectric dam construction began on the Columbia River and its tributaries in the 1930s, which led to large-scale salvage archaeology surveys and excavations that continued into the 1970s. After World War II, archaeology programs were established at state universities in Washington, Oregon, and Idaho. State-wide surveys and salvage archaeology programs carried out in conjunction with federal agencies have continued and expanded to the present time.

In the Great Basin, "mound sites" of the later-named Fremont cultures began to be excavated and reported in the mid-1890s. The first scientific excavations of Fremont sites were conducted by the U.S. National Museum from 1915 to 1920. During the 1930s, various cave sites around the Great Salt Lake were excavated, as were additional Fremont sites in western Utah.

Lovelock Cave in north central Nevada was excavated in 1912 (and again in the 1920s), initiating a long period of excavation of Great Basin cave and rockshelter sites that continues into the twenty-first century. Some sites, such as Danger and Hogup caves in western Utah, the Bonneville Estates Rockshelter in eastern Nevada, Wilson Butte Cave in Idaho, and the complex of Fort Rock and nearby caves in Oregon, contain nearly continuous depositional records of human occupation, some extending over 10,000 years and possibly more. Research at Marmes Rockshelter and at other sites in the Plateau demonstrates a similar time depth, although no one site has contained a complete stratigraphic record. Radiocarbon dating done during the 1970s also disproved earlier reports that humans occupied Gypsum Cave near Las Vegas, Nevada, at the same time as Ice Age giant sloths. The sloth remains dated to over 12,000 years ago; the artifacts proved to be only about 3,000 years old. There is also no valid scientific evidence proving that the Calico site in the Mojave Desert of southeastern California is in fact an archaeological site. The reputed "artifacts" from the site are not of human manufacture but rather are the result of natural geological processes. Major Great Basin archaeological research programs are ongoing at state universities and museums in Nevada, Oregon, California, Utah, and Idaho.

FIRST PEOPLING OF THE BASIN AND PLATEAU
The cultural histories of the Great Basin and Columbia Plateau can be characterized as general hunter-gatherer lifeways, with some regional semi-sedentism, extending over some ten millennia. The semi-sedentary lifeways were made possible by a relative abundance of wild plants, animals, and fish in parts of the Plateau and, in Utah and western Colorado, by the exploitation of domesticated plants. A basic cultural-chronological framework in both regions has been worked out through stratigraphic and radiocarbon analyses of many sites in both regions (see Table 1).

PALEOARCHAIC TIMES
The first humans entered the Great Basin–Columbia Plateau region about 12,000 years ago, possibly as early as 13,000 years ago. Widely scattered surface finds of Clovis points suggest that Paleoindian peoples, as they are called in the Great Plains and elsewhere, briefly explored or passed through the area. Elsewhere in North America, Paleoindian artifact assemblages are associated with late Ice Age megafauna, such as mastodons, mammoths, horses, and camelids. There are no demonstrated stratigraphic relationships of Clovis or other early lithic complexes (discussed later) with such fauna in the Basin or Plateau.

The exception is the East Wenatchee Clovis Cache site in Douglas County, Washington. The cache contained fourteen beautifully flaked classic Clovis projectile points, each 20–23 centimeters long, together with other finely flaked stone tools, and thirteen bone rods made on mammoth limb bones, one of them engraved. Similar caches, but without bone rods, have been found in Utah, Colorado, and Montana, the latter associated with a burial. The cached points are much larger than those from megafauna kill sites in the Great Plains, Southwest, and Mexico and are regarded as ceremonial.

All other Clovis points that have been reported to date are surface finds, for example, the Dietz site in Oregon, the Tonopah Lakebed sites in south central Nevada, and scattered

occurrences elsewhere. The technology used to make Clovis points and associated tools differs significantly from that used to produce other early tools found on the surface or in stratigraphic contexts—for example, the Mojave lakes complexes—throughout the Basin and Plateau. This suggests the latter were made and used by peoples who differed from the Clovis folk. Because of the uncertainty of a Paleoindian occupation, archaeologists use the term "Paleoarchaic" to refer to the first cultures of the area, extending from possibly 12,000 to about 8,000 years ago.

In the Great Basin the initial focus was on the plant, bird, fish, and mammal resources found in wetlands around the pluvial lakes, as well as upland plants and animals, seasonally available rodents, elk, deer, and mountain sheep. In the Plateau, people generally followed an annual round focusing on fishery resources during the upriver runs of anadromous fish, especially salmon species and steelhead trout, taking uplands game animals, and a collecting a variety of seed and root plants during other seasons. The root plant camas (*Camassia quamash*) was of particular importance. In some areas of present-day Oregon, Washington, and Idaho, camas grounds hundreds of hectares in extent were annually exploited by groups collecting the camas tuber, some coming from far distances. Roasting pits up to 2 meters in diameter and 1.5 meters deep, in which the camas was cooked to make it edible, occur in numerous archaeological contexts across the Plateau from at least the Middle Archaic period until the present.

The early peoples brought with them, and further developed over time, expert knowledge of stone and bone tool technologies. They also were experts at finely made textile manufacture—nets, bags, mats, sandals, and baskets—using various fibrous plants available in local areas. Fishing technologies evolved over time, especially on the Plateau, drained by the Columbia River system. There was widespread trade for high-grade obsidian or chert tool stone from various sources in both regions, as well as for shells and other valuables from the Pacific coast.

Although seemingly simple, the stone, bone, and fiber technologies were in fact quite sophisticated, portable, and well adapted to hunter-gatherer lifeways. Lithic technologies changed over time. One change was a shift from slender, lanceolate spear points to triangular notched forms. This shift and other technological developments mark the beginning of the Early Archaic period.

MIDDLE ARCHAIC
Many archaeologists mark the end of the Early Archaic at about 4,800–5,000 years ago, the time of eruption of Mount Mazama, a huge volcanic upsurge that created Crater Lake in Oregon and spread a layer of volcanic ash across a large area of western North America. The ash is found as a distinctive layer in numerous stratigraphic geomorphological and archaeological contexts, providing a convenient recognizable

Table 1   Generalized Basin-Plateau Culture Chronology

Late Archaic	2,000 to 200 years ago
Middle Archaic	5,000 to 2,000 years ago
Early Archaic	8,000 to 5,000 years ago
Paleoarchaic	ca. 12,000 to 8,000 years ago

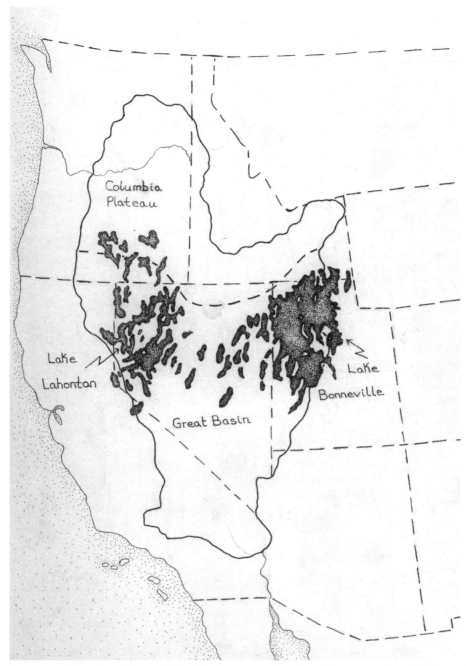

Outline map showing the extent of the Great Basin, Columbia Plateau, and major Pleistocene pluvial lakes.   [Don D. Fowler]

time marker for the region—the onset of Middle Archaic times. Newer forms of notched triangular projectile points and knives appear during this period. The way of life in the Great Basin continued to be a generalized hunter-gatherer pattern focused on plant and animal resources available to local groups making an annual round through the vertical succession of ecological zones from valley floors and the upper reaches of mountain ranges. In riverine areas and areas with permanent lakes, water bird and fish resources were seasonally important. Middle and Late Archaic tool complexes are well demonstrated in collections from Hogup Cave, the Great Salt Lake caves, Gatecliff Shelter, Hidden Cave, and Dirty Shame Rockshelter and from hundreds of surface sites.

For an undetermined period around 4,000 years ago there was a burial complex, that is, a distinctive pattern in the way the dead were buried that was centered on the Snake River Plain in western Idaho. Deceased persons were buried in shallow graves with large, finely chipped obsidian "turkey

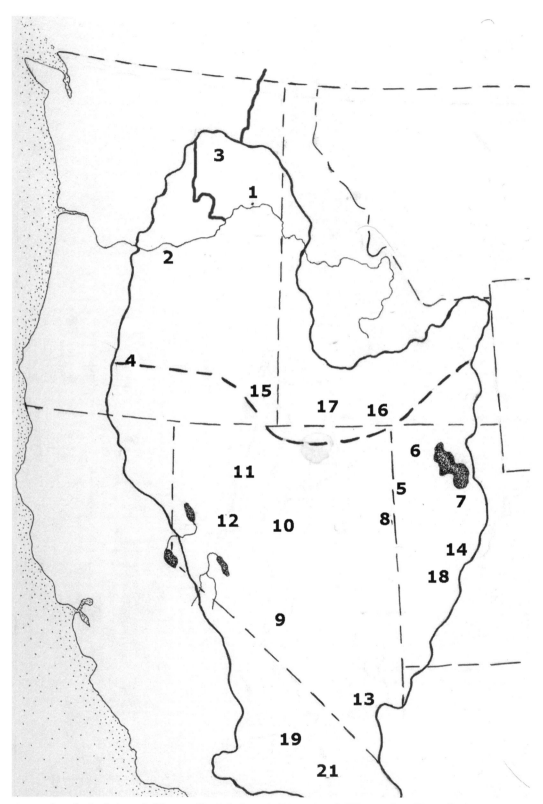

Locations of major archaeological sites: *1*, Marmes Rockshelter; *2*, Dietz site; *3*, Wenatachee Clovis Cache; *4*, Fort Rock, Connolly, Cougar Mountain, Paisley Cave complex; *5*, Danger Cave; *6*, Hogup Cave; *7*, Great Salt Lake caves; *8*, Bonneville Estates Rockshelter; *9*, Tonopah Lakebed sites; *10*, Gatecliff Shelter; *11*, Lovelock Cave; *12*, Hidden Cave; *13*, Gypsum Cave; *14*, Cowboy Cave; *15*, Dirty Shame Rockshelter; *16*, Wilson Butte Cave; *17*, Idaho Burial Complex; *18*, Fremont sites; *19*, Mojave Lakes sites; *20*, Crater Lake; *21*, Calico site.   [Don D. Fowler]

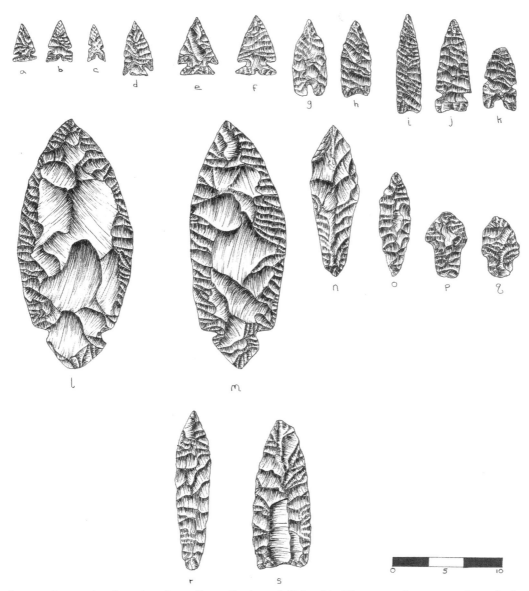

Characteristic time-marker projectile points from Great Basin and Columbia Plateau regions: *a–c*, Late Archaic; *d–f*, Middle Archaic; *g–k*, *n–q*, Early Archaic; *r, s*, Paleoarchaic; *l, m*, Idaho Archaic Burial Complex cache blades. *Scale: d*, length 3.8 cm; *l*, length 16 cm. *Sources: a–k, n–s*, d'Azevedo (1987, 118–119); *l, m*, Pavesic (1985).   [Don D. Fowler]

tail" blades up to 19 centimeters long, as well as olivella shells (imported from the Pacific Coast) and various other "ritual" objects such as stone pipes.

LATE ARCHAIC

The bow and arrow reached the Great Basin–Columbia Plateau region about 2,500 years ago, and this event marks the beginning of the Late Archaic period, which continued until the advent of Euro-Americans in the eighteenth century. The introduction resulted in a major reduction in the size of projectile points. Large stemmed or triangular-shaped points work well on spears propelled by an *atl atl*, or spear thrower,

but not on arrows. *Atl atl*–propelled spears have a hafted projectile point designed to detach from the socketed end of a spear shaft when it hits a target. The shaft must then be recovered and fitted with a new hafted point before it can be used again. Numerous arrows can be launched at prey in the same amount of time from a stationary point. The bow and arrow made the taking of game animals from rodent size up to elk, as well as birds, much easier.

There was an increased reliance on a variety of wild seeds for food in the Great Basin region after about 3,000 years ago, as new textile forms—seed beaters, gathering baskets, and parching trays—were developed for gathering and processing them. Some archaeologists suggest that this new technology, together with the bow and arrow, allowed the ancestral Numic-speaking peoples to expand from the Mojave Desert region across the Great Basin and beyond (discussed later). Sophisticated textile manufacturing continued in the Late Archaic period, including long nets over 100 meters used to snare rabbits driven into them by groups of hunters as well as finely made fishing nets and large nets for snaring water birds. In western Nevada about 2,000 years ago, the occupants of Lovelock Cave and adjacent areas made very realistic decoys from tule rushes covered with feathers of ducks and geese.

PLATEAU SEMI-SEDENTISM

Pit houses began to be constructed in the Columbia Plateau about 6,500 years ago. The houses were based on a circular plan, were up to 4 meters or slightly larger in diameter and up to 1 meter deep, and had an above-ground earth-covered pole and mat superstructure. First built as widely scattered individual units, they later aggregated into small villages, often along or adjacent to watercourses. Aggregated villages (ten or more houses) were common in some parts of the Plateau by 3,000 years ago. Circular pit houses were the norm by 2,500 years ago, but some villages also contained rectangular longhouses built over a rectangular pit, perhaps an influence from the adjacent northwest coast. Whatever the house form, a semi-sedentary lifestyle continued—people moved annually from villages to temporary encampments to exploit specific plant, animal, or fish resources. Fish, animal flesh, roots, and seeds were all dried and stored for winter consumption. The use of circular pit houses extended into the northern Great Basin to just below the present-day Nevada-Oregon border between about 3,000 and 4,000 years ago but did not continue after that time.

GREAT BASIN SEMI-SEDENTISM

By about 3,000 years ago, corn (maize), squash, and, later, bean horticulture was introduced into the cultures of the Southwest, making possible a pattern of semi-sedentary living that included circular pit houses and pottery manufacture. Knowledge of some horticultural practices spread from locations in the Southwest and were taken up by various hunter-gatherer groups in what is present-day Utah and western Colorado by about 2,000 years ago. By about 1,300 years ago some of those groups were living in settled pit house villages and making both utilitarian and decorated pottery. Some groups seem to have been almost fully sedentary; most, however, were part-time farmers and part-time hunter-gatherers. Collectively, these varied groups are called the Fremont peoples, named for type sites along the Fremont River in eastern Utah. Some of the villages grew to a relatively large size, perhaps 200–300 people, in particularly favorable areas along the western and eastern fronts of the Wasatch Plateau in Utah. Some villages had irrigation systems that tapped streams emerging from the mountainous plateau.

The Fremont peoples developed distinctive cultural features, including a unique style of coiled basketry, a moccasin style that incorporated the dew claws of deer or mountain sheep on the heels, an art style used in rock art and on small clay figurines that depicted trapezoidal human forms with necklaces and distinctive hairstyles, and utilitarian gray pottery as well as gray bowls painted with black geometric designs. The Fremont folk also made sophisticated snare traps, rabbit nets, and fur and leather clothing, including mittens. It is unclear who the Fremont folk were or what happened to them. The culture continued to exist until about 600 years ago but then is no longer seen in the archaeological record. The people may have moved eastward onto the high plains or been incorporated into the culture of the expanding Numic peoples, or both. Some archaeologists have suggested that the Fremont folk were the ancestors of the Apachean peoples (ancestors of the historic Navajo and the various Apache tribes) present on the western high plains when the Spanish arrived after 1540.

By about 1,000 years ago, or perhaps a few hundred years earlier, Numic-speaking peoples (the linguistic ancestors of the Northern Paiute, Southern Paiute, Ute, Shoshone, and Comanche populations of historic times) began a rapid expansion into the Great Basin from a homeland centered in the Mojave Desert region of southeastern California. By the mid-1600s, the Spanish in New Mexico were encountering Ute groups in the southern Rocky Mountains. By 1700, as the fur trade expanded across the high plains, into the Rockies, and on into the Basin-Plateau region, the Numic peoples were in place—all across the Great Basin, in southern and central Idaho, Wyoming, and Colorado and, as the Comanche, into the central and southern high plains. The only non-Numic populations in the Great Basin were the Washo people, whose territory had centered on Lake Tahoe and the adjacent Sierra Nevada for several millennia. The Numic peoples seem to have displaced ancestral Klamath and other groups in the northwestern section of the Basin.

The early Euro-American explorers of the Columbia Plateau encountered speakers of both the Sahaptin and Salishan language families, whose ancestors had been there since at least Middle Archaic times, if not earlier. In both regions, the tribal peoples—Washo, Numic, Sahaptin, Salishan, Klamath, and others—were heirs of sophisticated cultural traditions, developed and improved over ten millennia and more, and were well adapted to the varied and changing arid to semi-arid environments of the Great Basin and Columbia Plateau.

Further Reading: d'Azevedo, Warren L., ed., *Handbook of North American Indians*, Vol. 11: *Great Basin* (Washington, DC: Smithsonian Institution, 1986); Fowler, Don D., and Catherine S. Fowler, eds., *Great Basin Archaeology* (Santa Fe, NM: SAR Press, 2008); Fowler, Don D., and David Koch, "The Great Basin," in *Reference Handbook on the Deserts of North America*, edited by Gordon L. Bender (Westport, CT: Greenwood Press, 1982); Graf, Kelly, and David

Schmidt, eds., *Paleoindian or Paleoarchaic: Great Basin Human Ecology at the Pleistocene-Holocene Transition* (Salt Lake City: University of Utah Press, 2007); Madsen, David B., and David Rhode, *Across the West. Human Population Movement and the Expansion of the Numa* (Salt Lake City: University of Utah Press, 1994); Pavesic, Max, "Cache Blades and Turkey Tails: Piecing Together the Western Idaho Archaic Burial Complex," in *Stone Tool Analysis. Essays in Honor of Don E. Crabtree*, edited by M. G. Plew,

J. C. Woods, and M. G. Pavesic (Albuquerque: University of New Mexico Press, 1985), 55–89; Prentiss, William C., and Ian Kuijt, *Complex Hunter-Gatherers: Evolution and Organization of Prehistoric Communities on the Plateau of Western North America* (Salt Lake City: University of Utah Press, 2004); Walker, Deward E., Jr., ed., *Handbook of North American Indians*, Vol. 12: *Plateau* (Washington, DC: Smithsonian Institution, 1998).

Don D. Fowler

PREHISTORIC SETTLEMENT PATTERNS OF THE GREAT BASIN AND COLUMBIA PLATEAU

THE EVOLUTION OF VILLAGE SETTLEMENT PATTERNS

Village social patterns emerged in the interior West only after populations increased and more sedentary communities developed between 4000 and 2000 BC. Sedentary life depended on technological innovations and family adaptations based on fishing and the management of plant resources and big game populations. Throughout much of the Columbia Plateau and some parts of the Great Basin, larger more permanent settlement were supported by harvesting and storing large quantities of fish. Within the northern Rockies and eastern Great Basin, family bands remained highly mobile over hundreds of generations. However, between AD 1000 and 1400, horticultural communities also developed across the southern, eastern and central Great Basin.

Beginning about 4000 BC in the Columbia Plateau and northern Great Basin, people were constructing deep pit houses. The houses were often circular or oval and ranged from under 3 meters to over 30 meters in diameter. Some small to medium-size houses were roughly square. Above ground, the structures consisted of a pole framework covered by timber and earth or tule mats. Many generations occupied a variety of these types of semi-subterranean homes during the next six millennia. The depth and size of houses, their internal structure and activity areas, and the number of houses per settlement varied through time from region to region.

Plateau cultural traditions expanded widely throughout the Columbia and Snake River basins and into the higher tributaries of the Cascade Mountains and the northern Rockies. Early traditions in the north and south, affiliated with different language families, were based on subsistence economies that included root propagation and fire-managed big game habitats combined with fishing and freshwater mussel gathering. Many of the tools during these ancient times were made

of stone. Two general manufacturing techniques were used—grinding or flaking—to shape the tool. Ground-stone tools included hand-milling stones, edge-ground cobbles, pestles, hopper mortar bases (smooth stones with surface concavities within which grains, seeds, nuts, or roots were placed and ground using stone pestles), mauls, and clubs. Flaked stone tools included cobble choppers and notched cobble net sinkers, scrapers, knives, and large and small corner- and base-notched arrow points. After 1000 BC sites contain more examples of figurine carving in both stone and bone. Textiles, baskets, sandals, and cordage are seldom preserved in archaeological sites, but finds of these items in dry rockshelters match historic examples and prove the great importance and antiquity of these crafts, as well as the wide range of tools and equipment used by these ancient Americans.

Some early year-round settlements no doubt occurred along major river corridors; however, no sizable pit house features or larger settlements are known to pre-date 2000 BC. Winter communities were established to provide access to both fish, such as salmon runs, and fall and winter big game ranges. The varieties of salmon and the timing of their runs varied between rivers and sections of rivers. Prime settlement locations also gave access to early spring roots. In general, such locations were found on stretches of river that also provided easy access to upper-elevation meadows and conifer forests. After 2000 BC some settlements increased in size near major fishing locations, at the confluences of rivers and major tributaries, and on larger islands. These settlements dramatically changed about AD 500 and then again with the adoption of the horse between AD 1750 and 1850.

Beginning about 4000 BC in the lake basins of the northern Great Basin people were constructing deep pit houses much like those in the Columbia Plateau. Settlements developed around lakeside wetlands. Fishing and hunting of shore birds and waterfowl especially attracted communities to these areas. There are general similarities in all types of flaked-stone and ground-stone artifacts found across the Columbia Plateau and Great Basin. Great Basin sites also yield extraordinary examples of equipment and tools made from wood, hide, and textile work, and pottery appeared by AD 1000.

After 2000 BC population density increased along the riparian corridors of the middle and upper Snake River and within most of the wet basins in the northern and western Great Basin. However, across much of the Great Basin mobile family bands heavily relied on upland areas for roots, grasses, small and big game, and pinyon pine nuts. By AD 1000 maize, a variety referred to as Fremont Dent by scientists, began to be used in the region. This variety of maize may have resulted from selective adaptation by ancient farmers and, along with beans and squash, supported a variety of farming societies. These settlers are known collectively as the Fremont peoples. Climate conditions either improved the productivity of maize gardens or lowered the productivity of grass and marsh seeds to the point that maize gardens were necessary and farming spread as far northward as the Snake River plain. The adoption of ceramics for cooking and storage also led to greater reliance on the agricultural crops.

The specific ethnic and linguistic affiliations of the Fremont peoples are still debated, along with ideas regarding the amount of in-migration of farmers and the absorption or replacement of earlier foraging groups. Wherever full-time farming developed, significant societal changes occurred. Settlements increased in size, and families and communities became more structured. More permanent settlements included stone and adobe structures and storage features. However, these settlements could not be supported over the course of more than a few centuries. Within the more unique setting of the Owens valley at the foot of the Sierra Nevada in eastern California, systems of irrigation were created and used for semi-cultivated plants, such as spikerush and grassnuts.

POPULATION GROWTH AND MIGRATION

By the AD 1800s, in the Plateau region, interior Salish-speaking people (and related peoples such as the Kootenai) occupied the mountains and foothills of inland British Columbia, Idaho, and Washington. The remainder of the Columbia and Snake river basins, as well as the Klamath River basin of southern Oregon, were settled by Sahaptin speakers, or people speaking related languages (Penutian language family).

Most archaeologists working in the Plateau assume that the historical geographic pattern resulted from earlier population movements. It is inferred that Salish peoples expanded south and east in the middle and upper Columbia River basin, while Sahaptin peoples spread north and east into the middle Columbia and Snake river basins. The exact times and the relative rates of these movements are debated, but significant population expansions associated with intensification of salmon fishing were under way by 3000 BC. An alternative model of in situ development of cultural differentiation also is

possible. However, this explanation postulates differential adoption of language and technologies by an early ancestral population that would have been culturally homogeneous. This hypothetical explanation requires further development and ultimately would have to be confirmed through the study of ancient skeletal collections, including analysis of ancient DNA. What is known currently about the distribution of the genetic marker haplogroup A suggests that a prehistoric population intrusion from the subarctic and coastal region occurred on the Columbia Plateau in prehistoric times. Overall, mitochondrial DNA (mtDNA) patterns in the Northwest suggest significant amounts of gene flow among northwest coast, Columbia Plateau, and Great Basin populations.

The presence of Athabascan-speaking communities in the Rocky Mountains is relatively easily understood given the origins of these peoples in the boreal regions of Canada and Alaska. However, the historical movements of these Athabascan speakers to the more isolated communities of the lower Columbia and lower Klamath are more difficult to trace. Movements of these peoples through the Plateau or down the Pacific coast probably occurred between 2000 and 1000 BC. Still, the specific histories of these migrations are not well understood even in comparison to the longer-range migrations of Athabascan groups down along the Continental Divide into the Colorado and Arkansas river basins.

Except in the area of the White Mountains and Owens Lake, at the time of contact with Europeans and Euro-Americans most of the Great Basin was occupied by smaller communities of family bands, all of whom spoke one or more varieties of Numic (Ute, Paiute, and Shoshone). Specific language affiliations of early Great Basin peoples, including the Fremont, remain unknown. The distribution of ancient mtDNA haplogroups of the Great Basin is most similar to those of some of the historic inhabitants of California. This data suggests that the early and widespread settlers of the Great Basin contracted westward into the Sierras and were replaced by ancestral Numic. At present there is general consensus that several waves of populations probably moved through the Great Basin between 3000 BC and AD 1000. According to this consensus, the distinct trajectories of the last human populations to enter the Great Basin before the reintroduction of the horse by Spanish colonists during the early historic period best explain the historic distribution of Northern and Southern Paiute speakers in the western and northwestern areas of the Great Basin, and the several Shoshone dialects of the eastern and northeastern Great Basin and northern Rockies. The historical distributions of different languages and dialects have been used to hypothesize associated population movements.

The possible periods and rates of expansion of Uto-Aztecan, Numic-speaking peoples throughout the Great Basin, although modeled with sophisticated computer simulations, are still much debated. Seven divisions of Numic language are identified within the Great Basin. Western Numic is divided into

Northern Paiute and Mono. From south to north the Central Numic is divided into Kawiisu, Panamint, and Shoshone. The Southern Numic speakers are represented by the Ute.

Glottochronological (i.e., related to the historical study of languages) evidence suggests that Uto-Aztecan speakers originated in the greater Southwest and northern Mexico and spread northward into the northern Great Basin and northern Rockies as early as 500 BC, again about AD 1000, and still again with the adoption of the horse as early as 1600. The adaptive advantages that made these expansions possible include the bow and arrow, seed-gathering technologies, horticulture and/or pottery (assuming the Fremont were Numic speakers), and the horse. South of the Great Basin, early Pueblo societies developed by 1000 BC, but these maize farmers also experienced regional disruption and migration by 1200 BC. Populations in the southern and eastern areas of the Great Basin interacted with related Pueblo people, especially Uto-Aztecan speaking groups such as the people who were ancestral Hopi.

The Northern Paiutes gained opportunities presented by warming climate and expanded into the upper Klamath basin and the Deschutes River basin, and moved more deeply into the Blue Mountains of northeast Oregon. The Northern Shoshone moved into the Salmon River Mountains and into the Lemhi and Beaverhead ranges of Idaho and Montana. Evidence also suggests pre-horse Numic occupation of the Wind River range and the Yellowstone-Teton Plateau. These are the ancestral populations of Sacagawea (the indispensable young Indian woman who accompanied the Lewis and Clark expedition) and her kin among the Lemhi Shoshone. Trade and intermarriage were common among these more northern Numic peoples. Numic settlers were the targets of slave raids by villagers from the lower middle Columbia River area, where communities were more ranked and slave labor supplemented the accumulation of surplus stores of salmon. After adoption of the horse, hostilities with Plateau people no doubt increased.

PLATEAU CULTURE

The Plateau culture area includes the southern Columbia Plateau (middle Columbia and Snake rivers); the northern Plateau (Fraser, Thompson, and upper Columbia rivers), and the eastern Plateau (Kootenai, Pend d'Oreille, Clearwater, Salmon, and middle Snake rivers). Some seventeen groups of peoples are divided between the Salish speakers in the north and Sahaptin speakers in the south.

As early as AD 1300 or 1400 villages of the southern Plateau were composed of extended families living in conical and oval mat-covered lodges. Winter hamlets and villages were occupied by a few dozen to as many as 600 or more people. Later, use of horses provided greater physical and social mobility and contributed to the general dispersal of people and winter settlements. Also, the needs of extensive herds of horses for seasonal pasturage meant less permanent settlements. Although significant numbers of horses were present

by 1800, the fuller adoption of the horse and related patterns of social mobility probably developed after 1800. Thus, these major social changes may have also been caused by epidemic diseases and depopulation.

Historic winter households were established as part of riverine hamlets and villages, and they depended on stocks of stored salmon and harvested wild roots. Intermarriage among different social groups residing throughout the Plateau facilitated the movement of people between different resource areas in winter as well as in other seasons. Spring and summer were times for gatherings of large numbers of people for trading and celebrating first salmon, first roots, and first fruits. By the 1800s, spring and summer gatherings in uplands with prime root and pasture grounds sometimes included 3,000 or more people living in semi-dispersed lodges.

Winter lodges were up to 30 meters long and 10 meters wide. Superstructures of poles covered with thatch and mats were built over shallowly dug depressions, and hearths were placed along the middle of the floors. Some accounts suggest that pit houses may have still been in use for storing foods. Sweat lodges and menstrual houses are also well documented. Archaeological and historic records establish the use of cemeteries near villages.

In the northern Plateau large extended families grew. Social ranking with economic, political, and social differentiation developed within and between these families. Such social changes were especially well represented along the middle and upper Fraser River, where pit houses grew to over 30 meters in diameter and some villages may have grown to include as many as 1,000 occupants. However, such factors as population pressures, conflicts, and downturns in salmon runs caused the disaggregation of these villages by AD 1300. Another possibility is that epidemic diseases may have vectored through both the northern and southern areas of the Columbia Plateau as early as this time. It is hypothesized that disease introduced by European contact halved populations in the 1700s, as they did again in the early 1880s.

Historically, the area was occupied by peoples speaking different Salish languages, as well as by the Nicola Eyak, Athabascan speakers, and Kootenai (distantly related with the Salish). Alexander MacKenzie and Alexander Ross were among the first to explore interior British Columbia and describe settlements along the uppermost stretches of the Columbia River and the Fraser River. Communities located along the rivers and lakes above the major falls that blocked salmon runs depended on a broad spectrum of plants and animals, but the more westerly Salish and Kootenai people also crossed and re-crossed the northern Rockies, in both fall and winter, to hunt bison on the northern plains of present-day Alberta and Montana.

Most all of the Fraser River and its tributaries and higher-elevation lakes have bear, salmon runs, or resident salmon. Here, within the steep terrain of mountain canyons and valleys, permanent villages developed and task groups from corporate families ventured out from the village home bases to conduct deer and mountain sheep drives and gather wild roots, berries, and pine nuts. Giveaway events and feasts (akin to the coastal potlatch ceremonies) marked the status of elite families and reinforced their mutual obligations and social contracts. Distinct ethnic groups probably never organized as territory-based chiefdoms, but some villages were large and powerful. Families "held," or included, slaves, and communities practiced slave raiding. Communities and different ethnic groups also engaged in more general violent conflict to steal provisions of stored salmon and other trade goods, and sometimes they took control of productive fishing sites.

By AD 1000, Salish and Sahaptin population expansion resulted in areas of co-utilization along the middle Columbia and adjacent uplands. Here defensive sites, some with stone walls, house pits, or both, are located on isolated mesa tops. These steep mesas, with their high cliff walls and steep talus slopes, were created earlier during the late Pleistocene, when floods from glacial Lake Missoula channeled the basalt lands, also know as scablands, of the central Columbia basin. Limited but clear evidence of community conflict and murder exists in the form of several sets of human remains with arrow wounds, and one site includes a mass grave of partially cremated victims.

Lewis and Clark explored the Snake and Columbia rivers (1804–06) and described many settlements, most with mat lodges and at least one with a pit house. Other traders and explorers in the first half of the 1800s included Alexander Ross and Paul Cane. Many settlements are identified in early accounts and historic period ethnographies with native place names associated with features of the land or river, known resources, or social historical or mythological events. With the exception of Kettle Falls on the upper Columbia River, population densities were higher along the middle Columbia and the lower Snake rivers, and still higher along the lower middle Columbia River approaching Cellio Falls and the Dalles. Populations were dense enough to sustain more complex social and political organizations, for example, emergent chiefdoms, also referred to as trans-egalitarian societies. The term "chiefdom" broadly refers to a wide range of types of societies organized with leaders and councils who established political authority through family ties and achieved social status. The term "trans-egalitarian" is used to describe a society in which social ranking is in part determined by inheritance within powerful families, and family-controlled slaves may make up the lowest social rank.

Late prehistoric period mortuary customs and the distribution of grave goods in burials that have been excavated and analyzed, including native copper and marine shells, suggest relatively equal status between men and women. Patterns of burial offerings indicate that in some areas status differentiation of individuals existed from childhood. These patterns probably represent inherited social rank within powerful families. Cremation practices and communal ossuaries are also common in both the late prehistoric and protohistoric periods. The lack of grave goods associated with these types of burial patterns probably obscures the full extent of achieved wealth and/or inherited status. In fact, it may be that these communal burial rituals for the dead were meant to ameliorate social inequalities between groups who were differentiated by status in life.

No Plateau society survived the pervasive disruptions of European colonization, and by the mid-1800s many families had been forced to move by the pressure of Euro-American settlement in the region to the Nez Perce Reservation on the Clearwater River, the Yakama Reservation on the Yakima River, and the Colville and Spokane reservations, which straddle the upper Columbia in Washington State. Today all of these nations still actively manage their resources and practice the gathering, fishing, and hunting rights reserved for ceded lands and reservation areas.

NORTHERN AND SOUTHERN PLATEAU SETTLEMENT

By 6000 BC seasonal subsistence was based upon salmon fishing and big game hunting using *atl atl* technology. One interpretation proposes that fishing peoples expanded up the Fraser River and replaced or absorbed earlier occupants. The alternative is that cultural traditions evolved in place with a gradual development of larger pit house villages. Abundant salmon and deer were critical resources for denser populations; however, a broad spectrum of fish and shellfish, small game, and plants also were utilized. After 4500 BC, intensification of fishing and the storage of salmon may have developed in response to a combination of population growth and improved salmon spawning. Improved salmon runs and increased spawning are attributed to the cooler and moister conditions that prevailed between 4500 and 2500 BC.

Interpretations of southern Plateau settlement have placed varying emphasis on several different factors that might have led to winter sedentism by 3000 BC: migration of Salish speakers into the Columbia River basin, social investment in areas central to multiple resource exploitation, resource and social exchange, improvements in salmon spawning, innovative fishing technology, human population growth, storage technology, and intensification of root gathering, root storage, and root propagation. Many researchers are now willing to acknowledge that combinations of most of these factors were at work, and they recognize that the ecology of distinct regions in the Plateau produced highly variable settlement patterns.

From the start of settlement studies by archaeologists, it was recognized that changes in types of pit houses and trends in the increased sizes of houses and settlements would be hard to summarize. For example, radiocarbon dates from the Hatwai site revealed four different episodes of house construction between 3500 BC and AD 1700 (i.e., 250–5,500 years ago). Each of these episodes was punctuated by abandonment in favor of more mobile residence patterns.

More recent synthesis of settlement changes recognizes two major periods and modes of economic and social organization. The first period, Pit House I, developed between 4,500 and 3,800 years ago (2500 BC and 1800 BC). The second, Pit House II, developed by 3,100 to 2,200 years ago (1100 BC and 200 BC). This period lasted until 300 or 250 years ago (AD 1600) and therefore includes greater regional variability through time.

Pit House I subsistence was characterized by forager-like strategies. Subsistence during Pit House II followed a more collector-like strategy. Foragers and collectors practice plant gathering, fishing, and hunting on a continuum of mobility that ranges from daily and weekly movements to seasonal or annual movements. Foragers tend to move more often between widely dispersed resource locations. Collectors may move in small task forces back and forth from a central settlement to various distant resource locations.

Period I pit houses exhibit very little refuse around house rims, and deposits on living floors are thin. During Pit House I greater moisture was available, and temperatures remained warm. After 2900 BC available moisture remained high, but temperatures cooled. Settlements during the cooler and moister period between 1600 and 500 BC (3,600 and 2,500 years ago) are characterized by small hamlets and villages with fewer than ten houses, central-based collector strategies, and salmon storage. Village size increased in select areas, but house size decreased. Villages with between ten and fifty pit houses appeared during the start of Pit House II. Examples of these changes in settlements between the two Pit House periods are found at the Dalles, Umatilla, Wildcat Canyon, Mack's Canyon, Strawberry Island at the confluence of the Snake and Columbia rivers, and the Vallican site on the upper Columbia.

After the fixed-forager pattern was replaced by the collector strategy, about 1600 BC, house features range from 5 to 12 meters in diameter, although much larger examples (17–22 m) are known from the Fraser and upper Columbia areas. Smaller groups of mobile foragers living in hamlets begin to settle larger, more centralized villages to construct houses for larger extended families. These families organized to collect resources and process and stored them in their more permanent villages.

A decline in human populations on the Columbia Plateau is hypothesized between 300 BC and AD 200 (ca. 2,300 and 1,800 years ago). This time is also marked by the introduction of the bow and arrow, evidence of violence, and the growth of larger "gateway" settlements. These new types of settlements are characterized by large, multi-family, corporate-group households. This community organization permitted simultaneous harvesting and production of a wide variety of foods and items for use and exchange. Large corporate households at the Keatley Creek Village site emerged only after about AD 400. Small hamlets and villages containing mid-size to smaller houses (less than 14 m) are also represented at several

sites: Alpowai, Lyons Ferry Fish Hatchery, site 45DO372, Knight Creek, Harper Ranch, and Curr. Most pit houses at these sites have thin floors and relatively little refuse. A large variety of sites on upland plains and river terraces contain evidence of intense and repeated use. These sites were used to stage hunts for elk, deer, sheep, and bison, as well as for root gathering and roasting.

In some areas Pit House II appears to have arrived "full-blown"—that is, without any evidence of an earlier, Pit House I occupation—and may have spread as part of a Salish population expansion from the Canadian Plateau and/or the northwest coast. Populations and pit-house settlements grew in situ or expanded up or down major river corridors. Regardless of the exact demographic process, corporate households from permanent villages were able to out-compete less organized communities. The more complex collectors developed ranked leadership positions and expanded resource territories and exchange in response to drought-induced resource stress and population decline between AD 200 and 700. However, in the select areas where these adaptations emerged, they were ultimately discontinued as climatic conditions became more unstable during the Little Ice Age, AD 800 to 1350.

As early as AD 1200 (about 700 to 800 years ago) catastrophic landslides dammed the Columbia River near the Dalles to a height of over 100 feet. A complex of four landslides, known as the Cascade Landslides, cover 14 square miles, and at one or more times these slides must have disrupted salmon runs on the Columbia River above the Dalles. A more recent slide, known as the Bonneville Slide, may have impacted the river as recently as 450 or even 200 years ago. The Fraser River was also blocked by one or more massive rockslides in the Lillooet area roughly 1,000 to 1,100 years ago. This catastrophe is, at a minimum, responsible for the local abandonment of several large villages in upriver vicinities.

Only a few villages regrouped after AD 1300 or 1400, and if these communities were not already experiencing mass mortality, they were soon to be devastated by epidemic diseases precipitated by contact with European explorers and traders and with Euro-American settlers. Some evidence exists for epidemic-related population declines along the upper middle Columbia River between AD 1520 and 1540. If epidemics were causing this type of depopulation, then the diseases responsible would have spread rapidly from southern Spanish contacts some 200 years prior to regular coastal and overland trade contacts.

GREAT BASIN CULTURE

The Great Basin culture area covers five major geographic provinces. The northern Great Basin is composed of several large internally drained basins, including the Harney, Warner, Albert-Chewaucan, Fort Rock, and Klamath basins. The western Great Basin includes Pyramid Lake, Walker River and Lake, and the Humbolt River-Carson Sink region. The central

Great Basin incorporates the upper Humboldt River, Reese River, and Monitor valley. The eastern Great Basin comprises of the Great Salt Lake basin, the Wasatch Range, and Green River basin, including the Uinta basin. Ten groups are divided between the Ute, Paiute, and Shoshone peoples, all of whom are Numic speakers (a major branch of the Uto-Aztecan language family), except the Washoe of the Lake Tahoe region.

Permanent or large villages were rarely maintained during the historic period, except where groups associated with white settlements. Agriculture was not generally sustainable, and native plant and animal resources were, for the most part, widely dispersed in different habitats. Seasonal gatherings of family bands rarely exceeded 100 people. Wickiups (small, round, dome-shaped, often temporary structures) were constructed of limbs and brush and covered with hide and grass. Each house was used by a small nuclear family, or part of a family. Windbreaks and shades were used to protect living and working places in and around family wickiups. Some houses were built over shallow depressions, and others might have low surrounding rock walls. Most cooking was done outdoors, and seed and nut crops were sometimes stored in one or two small storage pits adjacent to houses.

Family bands would come together in winter to live in or near pinyon pine forests or to conduct communal hunts for antelope and rabbits. Spring and summer gatherings were possible in areas with fish spawns. Base camps of all seasons have cached metates and manos for seed and nut processing. The systems of irrigation for semi-cultivated plants, such as spikerush and grassnuts, developed by the Owens Valley Paiute deserve special consideration.

In 1842 John C. Fremont explored the northern Great Basin and observed that the lower basins were occupied by Northern Paiute and that the Klamath inhabited the Cascades foothills. The Northern Paiute, Klamath, and Modoc occupied the Klamath basin. Loosely associated Northern Paiute bands spread into the northern basins as part of one of more waves of Numic expansion. The Klamath and Modoc were longer-term residents of the basins and are probably descendents of peoples who were once widely spread throughout the Great Basin and Columbia Plateau. By the time of contact, the Northern Paiute fully occupied the Warner Valley region and shared areas with the Klamath. The Modoc and Klamath people may have spoken a separate branch of Sahaptin or shared a distinct dialect of Lutuami, a Penutian language.

Paiute and Shoshone microbands were composed of family groups, and these groups were in turn affiliated with spring and fall macrobands, which were often named according to the resource areas they exploited (e.g., Root Eaters, Salmon Eaters, Ground-Hog Eaters, Elk Eaters, Mountain Sheep Eaters). This practice of geographic naming facilitated temporary partnerships of mobile bands and probably guided exogamous marriages. Seasonal gatherings among the Western Shoshoni were known as fandangos. In the northern Great Basin small settlements, with two or more single-pole conical houses, were set up for the longer winter season, and then larger gatherings would develop for spring fishing, bird hunting, and root harvesting.

GREAT BASIN SETTLEMENT

Historic Numic populations were never dense, but larger populations seem to have grown in areas with more productive pine forests. Here stores of winter food could be gathered and families could disperse to hunt deer and mountain sheep. Most Numic peoples remained hunters and gatherers into the late 1800s, when Mormon contact and American military actions disrupted their traditional subsistence rounds. They often moved to new homes two or three times in one season. Apart from their extensive use of seed grasses, they are most known for their harvests of pinyon pine nuts. Forests of pinyon pine are located only at higher elevations with moderate precipitation. Cones are produced each fall by October. Production of pine cones can vary greatly from year to year and limit harvests. The production of cones with high nut content is thought to follow the five- to ten-year cycles created by climatic patterns affecting vegetation growth throughout the desert west.

At least within the northern and western Great Basin archaeological evidence suggests very different settlement patterns prevailed during earlier periods of time. Within the Surprise Valley of northeast California, relatively large pit houses were constructed by 4500 BC; however, after 2500 BC lighter-build homes and wickiups replaced pit houses. Hunting patterns shifted from big game to smaller mammals and waterfowl. Along the eastern Sierra in places such as Owens Valley, heavy utilization of pinyon nut developed by AD 200 or 300, and settlements began to include up to a dozen or more substantial structures as well as milling stones and ceramic vessels (i.e., Owens Valley Brownware). About AD 1000 in both the Toquima Range and the White Mountains, seasonal hunting and intensive plant gathering were staged from residence sites, with house features located at surprisingly high altitudes.

The significance of rivers, wet basins, and lakes for long-term settlement tended to be overlooked by many early anthropologists and archaeologists who were interested in Numic adaptations to desert basins and high arid mountain ranges. In fact, the rivers and wetlands were critical to people throughout much of the Great Basin for many millennia. Fishing was most common in rivers connected to larger lakes where spawning fish could be netted, trapped in baskets, or speared. Tui chub (*Gila bicolor*) is the most common fish found in archaeological sites throughout the Great Basin. This chub, a large minnow, was taken in the summer when it spawned in the shallows. A diversity of lakes and rivers also supported a variety of sucker (including the boney sucker called *cui-ui*), pikeminnow, trout, and sculpin. Suckers reach a size of 18 inches and can weigh over 5 pounds. They actively spawn in February, when they school in shallow flows of cold spring water, but spawning extends from January through June.

Pyramid Lake and Walker Lake in west central Nevada sustain large runs of black-spotted cutthroat trout and *cui-ui*. Kokanee (land-locked salmon) still run out of Lake Tahoe from September through November. Analysis of ancient human feces from Lovelock Cave in the Cason Sink also in west central Nevada show that from 2500 BC on, people depended heavily on chub and sucker, as well as seeds of bulrush, cattail, and various water weeds and grasses. More than thirty-six species of shorebird and waterfowl are represented in the assemblages of bird bone and egg shells from Stillwater Marsh. The Carson Lake and Stillwater Marsh environs were a hub of settlement activities from as early as 3000 BC; however, after AD 500 this settlement probably included growing numbers of Numic speakers. Between AD 600 and 1200 small pit houses were present and people appear to have been more reliant on wetland resources

The Klamath occupied upper Klamath Lake, Klamath Marsh, and the Williamson and Sprague rivers in southern Oregon. The Lost River region Modoc settled south central Oregon and north central California. Both peoples inhabited permanent winter villages near lakes and marshes and more temporary spring-summer villages (fishing and root gathering). Modoc settlements included several lakeside pit houses, which tended to be smaller and deeper than other pit houses. Klamath settlements might comprise dozens of lodges, some up to 12 meters in diameter, spaced along a river. Sucker fishing began in March, and in June root harvesting began in higher uplands. A second sucker run started in August, and fall berry gathering and game hunting (e.g., deer, elk, mountain sheep, and bear) followed. Locating settlements between uplands and lower wetlands provided logistic advantages for collecting and storing foods from both resource areas, as well as local use of winter cattails, fish, waterfowl, and mammals.

The development of moister climate between 1600 BC and AD 1000 resulted in increased sedentism and denser populations. Some local populations moved in from neighboring regions. Climate changes, population growth, and fish and root storage led to spring and winter sedentism in upland and lowland villages. In the Fort Rock, Lake Abert, Warner Valley, and Harney basin, arid uplands and low wetlands settings supported annual subsistence rounds of settlers. In the lower Klamath basin, Knight Island was built up of basalt and earth by pit house villagers as early as 3600 BC. During this period there was a dramatic increase in fishing (Tui chub) and the use of ground stones, as well as in the use of pits for storing foods. Greater artifact diversity also reflects increased sedentism and exchange.

Through much of the northeastern Great Basin pit houses were abandoned around 1100 BC, when wetland marshes began to dry up and residents adopted more mobile lifestyles and built lighter houses and shelters. Villages were probably not reestablished adjacent to marshlands in areas such as Fort Rock due to intensified use of uplands roots. Colder, pro-tracted winters and cooler, longer springs may have forced people to move into the Fort Rock basin. This crowding may then have necessitated more intensive use and storage of seeds and fish.

Clusters of radiocarbon dates from sites that had large storage pits containing Northern Side-notch projectile points with foliate and Elko points suggest a period of winter stress between 3600 and 3000 BC. Another cluster of dates suggest that between 1800 and 1500 BC increased precipitation may have drowned marshes and displaced settlements. The resulting shift to more permanent settlements is marked by a greater reliance on roots harvested during wetter springs and summers. Root crops were among the first fresh foods to be gathered once winter stores were fully depleted. Ground-stone tools associated with processing plant foods increased dramatically.

In the Diamond Swamp region, areas such as Dunn and McCoy creeks were occupied by larger groups with pit houses between 1500 BC and AD 1000, when greater precipitation improved the productivity of marshes and juniper grasslands. Starting about 1000 BC, settlers were again heavily dependent on wetlands resources, and a dual settlement system developed among the Klamath and Modoc. Beginning about AD 500 upland settlements included many stone-ringed houses and talus pit storage features. This settlement pattern spread throughout the majority of basins and valleys of this region. Also at this time megalithic stone structures were built at Carlon Village in the Fort Rock basin.

The majority of basin settlements were disrupted by drought conditions about 900 years ago and again between 300 and 500 years ago. The effects of this drought, and/or depopulation due to epidemic diseases, could have caused the retraction of Klamath and Modoc peoples. Such events no doubt favored the expanding Numic populations. Desert Side-notched and Cottonwood Triangular projectile points and wickiup features mark their expansion beginning by AD 1400. Thus, oral history and archaeological evidence suggest that Penutian speakers probably moved into the desert basins as wetlands became more productive, but they later moved to the more western and southern basins and river drainages as conditions became warmer and drier and pulled Northern Paiutes into the northern Great Basin.

Between 500 BC and AD 500 the inhabitants of the central Wasatch Plateau in what is now central Utah began growing maize and other cultivated plants. These people who archaeologists refer to as Fremont shifted between hunting and gathering and gardening from season to season and from year to year. They no doubt spoke several dialects, if not distinct languages (Uto-Aztecan, proto-Numic, and/or Athabascan). Gardening and thin-walled gray pottery spread outward from this region. By AD 750, settled villages developed in the heartland that included pit houses with timber and mud-plastered roofs and above-ground granaries. Farming in some areas probably included limited use of irrigation. Overall favorable climatic conditions developed between AD 700 and 1250, and the Fremont prevailed. Their neighbors, the Pueblo people, also flourished during this time. Settlement within the area now designated as the Grand Staircase–Escalante National Monument and the Henry Mountains evidence trade intermarriage with Pueblo groups. Between AD 1250 and 1500, decreased precipitation probably prohibited farming, and the protohistoric ancestors of the Ute, Paiute, and Shoshoni peoples may have replaced or absorbed the Fremont farming families.

Archaeologists in the 1970s and 1980s typically thought of Fremont villages as consisting of several pit houses with combinations of families totaling less than thirty residents. However, in the 1990s larger population centers were identified that probably represent settlements with thirty to forty households within Clear Canyon. As many as fifty households may have occupied Nawthis Village, and here as at other sites (Baker, Garrison, and Round Springs) above-ground room blocks of jacal construction (mud and pole structures), as well has settlement mounds in the Parowan Valley (Evans Mound and Median Village), suggest larger settlements.

In and around the Great Salt Lake basin, between AD 400 and 1350 the earliest Fremont sites were still temporary hunting camps lacking permanent structures, or hamlets composed of relatively semi-permanent houses. Later households occupied more substantial pit houses, and pottery appeared along with maize, but horticulture never seems to have been the mainstay of these settlers. At the Willard site at least fifty mounds contain evidence of multiple, superimposed households (pit houses and adobe surface structures). Above-ground storage features were in use and house plans change from round to square about AD 1500. The Knoll and Levee sites also contain both round and square houses. Jacal houses were constructed at the Levee, Bear River, and Injun Creek sites.

In the Uinta basin, Fremont settlements disappeared by AD 1000. In west central Utah in the Sevier basin large, extensive adobe villages appeared, but over 80 percent of settlements included only a few pit houses and roughly built adobe storage structures. In the Parowan valley of southwestern Utah, between AD 1100 and 1250 corrugated pottery and four-walled pit houses appeared. Trade and influence connected these settlers to the Pueblo peoples. East of the Wasatch Plateau, San Rafael Fremont sites are also characterized by a few pit houses and storage structures; however, homes were built of stone masonry and had plastered interior walls and slab-floor fire pits. Sites containing evidence of permanent habitation are often located on low ridges or knolls easily accessible to freshwater and arable land. Several local varieties of pottery were developed, and Pueblo trade pottery appeared from Mesa Verde and the Kayenta area.

The spread of maize farming probably developed out of existing traditions of wild grass collecting and was made possible due to increased rainfall that made gardens easier to cultivate and maintain. The spread of maize must have involved significant levels of population expansion and outside contact and trade. Along with these factors, genetic improvements were made in varieties of maize, such as Fremont Dent corn. It is most probable that increased moisture improved conditions for farming and grass collecting during this period. However, another possibility is that periodic shortages of grasses during droughts required maize gardens. In this scenario it would be the return of improved grass production that precluded the need for gardening.

Oxygen isotope values, based on analyses of human skeletons from several Fremont settlements along with dozens of Great Salt Lake wetland burials, have been compared to isotope values for other maize-farming people of the Pueblo area. This data along with tree ring and pollen data strongly support the hypothesis that climatic deterioration caused crop losses that led the majority of Fremont families to abandon farming. Later, in the early historic period, Numic peoples developed maize horticulture within the southern Great Basin as an adaptation to disruptions to the native plant communities and the seed-gathering cycle caused by Euro-American settlement and related patterns of overgrazing.

Further Reading: Aikens, M. C., "Adaptive Strategies and Environmental Change in the Great Basin and Its Peripheries as Determinants in the Migrations of Numic Speaking Peoples," in *Across the West, Human Population Movement and the Expansion of the Numa*, edited by David B. Madsen and David Rhode (Salt Lake City: University of Utah Press, 1994), 35–43; Aikens, M. C., and D. L. Jenkins, eds., *Archaeological Researches in the Northern Great Basin: Fort Rock Archaeology Since Cressman* (Anthropological Papers No. 50, Eugene: University of Oregon, 1994); Brenner, Joan, and Steven Leavitt, "Climate and Diet in Fremont Prehistory: Economic Variability and Abandonment of Maize Agriculture in the Great Salt Lake Basin," *American Antiquity* 67(3) (2002): 453–485; D'Azevedo, Warren, ed., *Handbook of North American Indians*, Vol. 11: *Great Basin* (Washington, DC: Smithsonian Institution Press, 1986); Hemphill, Brian, and C. S. Larsen, eds., *Prehistoric Lifeways in the Great Basin Wetlands: Bioarchaeological Reconstruction and Interpretation* (Salt Lake City: University of Utah Press, 2000); Jenkins, D. L., *University of Oregon Field School Northern Great Basin Prehistory Project Research Design* (2000), http://www.obsidianlab. com/pdf/fort_rock_research.pdf; Kaestle, F. A., and D. G. Smith, "Ancient Mitochondrial DNA Evidence for Prehistoric Population Movement: The Numic Expansion," *American Journal of Physical Anthropology* 115 (2001): 1–12; Madsen D. B., and S. R. Simms, "The Fremont Complex: A Behavioral Perspective," *Journal of World Prehistory* 3(12) (1998): 255–336; Malhi, R. S., K. Brece, B. Shook, F. Kaestle, J. Chatters, S. Hackenberger, and D. Smith, "Patterns of mtDNA Diversity in Northwestern North America," *Human Biology* 76(1) (2004): 33–54; Prentiss, W. C., J. Chatters, M. Lenert, D. Clarke, and R. O'Boyle, "The Archaeology of the Plateau of Northwestern North America during the Late Prehistoric Period (3500–200 BP): Evolution of Hunting and Gathering Societies," *Journal of World Prehistory* 19(1) (2005): 47–118; Walker, Deward, ed., *Handbook of North American Indians*, Vol. 12: *Plateau* (Washington, DC: Smithsonian Institution Press, 1998).

Steven Hackenberger

HISTORIC EARLY EURO-AMERICAN EXPLORATION AND TRADING IN THE GREAT BASIN AND PLATEAU

The period from 1776 to 1840 was a time of early exploration by Europeans and Euro-Americans in the vast interior of western North America, including the Great Basin and Plateau regions. These areas were among the last to be traversed by non-Natives, but during this time people came into them from all directions. This was an important time for first encounters with the region's Native Americans, although some Native people were already aware of the presence of foreigners in surrounding areas. This was also an important period for many first exchanges of non-Native material items for Native information and goods. This was a period of minor and a few major changes in lifeways for the indigenous peoples, changes that would soon multiply as more Euro-Americans established themselves permanently in their regions.

Most first contacts occurred in places and along pathways that were already in use for millennia. The Great Basin and Columbia Plateau, like most regions in the Americas before contact, included vast networks of natural and human-made trails in use long before the arrival of these latest visitors, pathways with long histories of travel and trade within and beyond regional borders. These pathways linked important centers of tribal and inter-tribal interaction as well as local places. Many became important centers for post-contact gathering and later settlement often for the same reasons they were chosen by indigenous peoples (i.e., food, water, fuel). The pathways of the past have since become highways and freeways connecting places and peoples in even broader systems of contact and commerce today.

PREHISTORIC AND HISTORIC NATIVE AMERICAN TRAVEL AND TRADE

Numerous archaeological sites in both the Great Basin and Plateau contain nonperishable and a few perishable exotic artifacts and raw materials that suggest contact and interaction of peoples over hundreds of miles as well as over many millennia. Included in the artifacts for the Great Basin are marine shells and beads (clamshell, olivella, haliotis, dentalium), tool stones (especially obsidians, some cherts), pigments, salt, turquoise, and a few textiles. Sites such as Lovelock, Danger, Gypsum, Cougar Mountain, and Wilson Butte caves are among hundreds of Great Basin sites suggesting trade in these items at least by Middle Archaic times (approximately 5,000–2,000 years ago). Many are along major river corridors, such as the Humboldt, Snake, and Colorado, that served as avenues of travel. Major passes in the Sierra Nevada on the west and in the long chain of the Rocky Mountains on the east connect to these routes as additional

sites with exotic goods near and along them attest. In the Plateau, the vast Columbia River trading network, with its linkages to the Fraser and its tributaries, brought similar exotic items including diverse marine shells (especially haliotis and dentalium), shell beads, whale bone, nephrite, copper, obsidian, and other items to and from the northwest coast and the interior also at least by Middle Archaic times. Sites reflecting such trade include Fivemile Rapids, Wakemap Mound, Marmes, Kettle Falls, and others in the Columbia River drainage; Scowlitz in the Middle Fraser and Lytton; Nicola Lake and Spences Bridge on the upper Fraser; and numerous others. Major centers of exchange along the Columbia, still very active at contact, included the Dalles and Celilo Falls in present-day Oregon, Kettle Falls in Washington, and the Lower Fraser Fishery and Kamloops Lake in British Columbia. Perishable items including pine nuts, baskets, and rabbit skin blankets from the Great Basin as well as favored salmon pemmican, dried roots and berries, and baskets from the Plateau undoubtedly moved in prehistoric times as well.

Even geographic areas that might be considered impediments to travel, such as the deeply dissected Colorado River canyons or the desiccated Mojave Desert did not block trade from the south and southeast into and from the Great Basin. There were at least four major routes across the Mojave east to west from the Colorado River to the California coast linked by springs, potholes, and other small water sources. These were in use by at least the Middle Archaic and saw additional activity during Ancestral Puebloan (also known as Anasazi) times, as scatterings of Puebloan potshards and other items along their lengths attest. They continued to be vital links historically, including for early European travelers.

Items of inter-tribal trade documented ethnographically include many of the same nonperishable items along with a much longer list of perishables not likely to be recovered archaeologically. Marine shells, tool stones, turquoise, salt, whale bone, and textiles continued to be traded along with hides and hide clothing, rabbit skin blankets, weapons and tools (bows, arrows, knives, axes, adzes, pestles, mortars), pigments, numerous foodstuffs (particularly dried fish, roots, berries, pine nuts), fibers, additional and specific textiles (baskets, nets, raw materials for them), dogs, and slaves, in some areas. Some of these were scarce commodities that other groups needed; others were prestige or status items; and yet others were surplus products that were redistributed in both regions. Slave raiding involved the Klamath and other groups in the Plateau, and principally the Ute in the Great Basin. Each preyed on weaker groups in their areas (Achomawi and

Atsugewi for the Klamath; Southern Paiute and Western Shoshone for the Ute). These activities intensified once horses were introduced into the region (from mid-1600s to 1700s, depending on sub-area) and European and Euro-American markets opened (discussed later).

Along with slaves and other commodities, horses themselves became a primary focus for trafficking. Both perishable and nonperishable goods could be transported in greater and heavier quantities by horses than by individuals on foot with pack baskets or carrying nets. The horse also opened up new transportation routes, although traders were still limited by requirements for water and feed for their animals, especially in the Great Basin. Networks easily incorporated links to the Plains, Southwest, Pacific Northwest, and California through the Ute, Comanche, Navajo, Wind River Shoshone, Crow, Nez Perce, Flathead, Salish, and other groups who had yet wider contacts and could serve as middlemen for and beyond their local regions. Trading centers became more important, although most had been significant before the arrival and spread of the horse. The most important trading centers were Humboldt Sink, Pyramid Lake, Walker Lake, Utah Lake, Las Vegas Valley, Owens Valley, Birch Creek Valley, Camas Prairie, Jackson Hole, Wind River Basin, Colorado Springs, and other locations along the front range of the Rockies as well as the Dalles, Celilo Falls, mouth of the Snake River, Salmon Falls, Kettle Falls, southern Okanogan Valley, Deschutes River, Klamath Lakes, and Klamath Falls. Some were sites of seasonal festivals that attracted people to share in the abundance of a local resource (e.g., camas, berries, pine nuts, salmon, whitefish). Others were major traditional meeting points for inter-tribal gatherings (the Dalles, Oregon; Shoshone Rendezvous, southwestern Wyoming; Lower Fraser Fishery, British Columbia) that now attracted horse travelers in addition to European and Euro-American traders and trappers.

EURO-AMERICAN EXPLORATION AND NATIVE INTERACTION

Historical accounts document the importance of established Native American pathways to successful exploration and passage through the Great Basin and Plateau. Major and minor trails are commonly mentioned in the diaries and journals of early explorers, trappers, and even the first non-Native settlers to come into the region. Most early expeditions were led by Native American guides, sometimes reluctantly or in exchange for some desired items of trade, such as horses, metal knives or projectile points, brass or iron kettles, hatchets, glass beads, mirrors, trade cloth, and later guns and ammunition.

In 1776 the Franciscan priest Francisco Garcés with Juan Bautista de Anza (the younger) traversed the Mojave Desert from the Colorado River west to the Los Angeles basin by following one of the established routes of the Mojave Trail system. He is the first European to record contact with the

Chemehuevi of the Great Basin and to describe their location, distribution, and dress. Fellow Franciscan priests Francisco Atanasio Domíngues and Silvestre Vélez de Escalante, in the same year, made a large circuit from Santa Fe north through what would become southern Colorado, west into Utah through a major pass in Wasatch Range near Utah Lake, south along that range into southern Utah, and finally traversing present-day northern Arizona and crossing the Colorado River to return to Santa Fe. The Franciscans hoped to link the Spanish settlements on the upper Rio Grande with those of southern California, but they were defeated. They were guided by Native Americans of different tribes at various points in their journey. They described Utes, who were already in possession of many Spanish goods, mounted on fast horses in Colorado. Some Utes in Utah west of the Wasatch Range were also mounted, but others were not, and the influences of Spanish trade seemed minimal. The Southern Paiutes in southern Utah and northern Arizona did not have horses, but they were anxious to obtain red cloth from their party, leading the priests to believe that they knew that the Spanish were present to the south. Southern Paiutes offered turquoise and shells to trade, and they had blue cloth likely traded from the Hopi.

By at least 1813, slave trafficking had intensified in the central and southern Great Basin, and it would last for the next forty years. Principal traffickers were Utes, Navajos, Spanish, and, after 1821, Mexicans from the northern Southwest as well as at least some early American trappers from the north and east. By the early 1830s, the Old Spanish Trail was operating from Santa Fe to Los Angeles (including across the northern Mojave Desert), following part of the route Domínguez and Escalante had pioneered but now rerouted to allow for passage of more animals and wagons. Items that moved along the trail included horses, mules, blankets, and metal objects of various kinds as well as Southern Paiute and Western Shoshone slaves, who were sold in the settlements around Santa Fe and Los Angeles and far south into Mexico. Slave raiding likely decimated Southern Paiute populations in certain areas, particularly parts of southwestern Utah from the 1820s to 1840s, and seems to have caused significant population relocations away from the avenues of heaviest traffic. Introduced diseases were another likely factor in population reductions in the region.

By the 1770s, northern and southern Plateau peoples had already felt some impacts of contact with French, British, Russians, and Spanish fur merchants operating along the Pacific Coast as well as to some degree inland. Southern Plateau tribes had horses by the early part of the 1700s, and thus travel to and from these areas and the northern plains had already been facilitated. Smallpox reached the interior by this time, or within a decade of it, from coastal sources or from northern plains sources and caused significant population losses. Trade goods had reached many groups, and intergroup conflicts had already changed some territories and alliances, with more conflicts to come.

In 1805–06 with the expedition of captains Meriwether Lewis and William Clark through the northern Great Basin and southern Plateau, additional information comes to light on indigenous trade, as well as existing non-Native contacts. In addition to Sacajawea, a Northern Shoshone girl who helped guide the expedition into the country of her people along trails established by them previously for trade and hunting on the plains, the expedition called upon several other Native Americans to help them find trails from the upper Missouri across the Rocky Mountains and down the Columbia River. When they contacted the Shoshone west of the Missouri, the Shoshones told them that they were already trading for horses, mules, cloth, metal beads, and shells with the Spanish. They also had obtained a few guns. Farther west, Lewis and Clark visited the important trading centers at the Dalles and Celilo Falls on the Columbia, noting that these centers had been receiving seasonal calls (and goods) from American and British traders and/or their middlemen from the Pacific coast since at least 1792. They saw copper kettles, Spanish coins, blue beads, and many additional western trade items. Russian and Spanish ships, also involved in the fur trade, were operating in northern coastal waters at least twenty years earlier.

Exploration into the interior by fur traders and trappers, either as individuals or in small or large parties, opened up additional sources of trade, especially in the northern and eastern Great Basin and much of the Plateau. The North West Company and Hudson's Bay Company opened permanent posts for the fur trade in various locations along the Fraser River and the Columbia River between 1806 and 1825 (Forts St. James, St. George, Chilcotin, Thompson, Kamloops, Okanagan, Colville, Kootenay, Walla Walla, etc.). Initially the posts were largely set up to trade furs taken by Native Americans. Later, non-Native and eastern Indian trappers (i.e., Hawai'ians and Iroquois) entered into direct competition with local people, and severe conflicts ensued. Continued trade ultimately put guns and ammunition into the hands of most Plateau groups. This tipped the balance in both trading and power relationships among a number of groups in those decades and with their neighbors (e.g., the Blackfoot), that is, until missionization, the military, and non-Indian expansion and settlement in their regions forced additional accommodations.

As company trapping parties of the Hudson's Bay Company began to move farther south from the Plateau and independent company (Rocky Mountain Fur Company) American trappers came east over the Rockies in the early 1820s, they too found groups in the northern Great Basin already in possession of European trade goods. For example, Peter Skeen Ogden (Hudson's Bay Company), working the waters of the Humboldt River in Nevada for beaver and river otter between 1824 and 1830 came across Shoshones and Northern Paiutes with horses, metal knives, and guns. Jeddediah Smith, an independent American, noted in his journals of trips made from New Mexico through Utah to California and then back to Utah across the central Great Basin (1826–30) that not only were the Utes of Colorado and Utah in possession of Spanish guns and frequenting trading fairs at Taos in the northern Southwest (which they had been doing for some decades by then), but also the Southern Paiutes of central and southern Utah had iron knives and kettles and the Northern Paiutes at Walker Lake in the interior of the Great Basin had buffalo robes, knives, and Spanish blankets. Western Shoshones and Gosiutes were fearful of him and his party, but Bannocks near the Great Salt Lake were eager to trade.

Although records are sparse and data is inconclusive, introduced diseases had undoubtedly taken a toll among Native Americans even in the deep interior Great Basin by this time. Some diseases likely spread through earlier trading networks; others through indigenous trading centers now incorporated into the fur trading and supply "rendezvous" system. The American rendezvous system operated largely at sites in Utah and Wyoming from 1825 to 1840 (supplanting the indigenous Shoshone Rendezvous) and attracted mounted and pedestrian groups from the Great Basin, Plateau, Plains, and parts of the Southwest. Supply lines moved furs eastward and brought additional goods of all types westward, along with liquor and more guns and ammunition. Most of the fur trade waned in the 1840s because of a decline in pelts and the price of beaver in eastern and European markets. In many areas, especially the more fragile environments of the Great Basin, beaver and river otter were "trapped out," and ecological damage from increased subsistence hunting and grazing stock was already evident. By the early 1840s, a few additional expeditions (John C. Frémont through various parts of the Great Basin; Charles Wilkes, Father Pierre John de Smet in the Plateau) documented additional evidence of the effects of some seventy years of contact in the two regions. They witnessed already changed attitudes and relationships between Native Americans and Euro-Americans. By this time, there had been dozens of hostile encounters in the regions between trappers, traders, and others. So that what started with initial curiosity and more or less friendly intergroup activities had increasingly turned cautious and hostile. Missionaries and immigrants were already traversing the Oregon Trail, some Plateau trading posts had become settlements, and the mass overland migrations to California, Oregon, Utah, and Idaho were about to begin. Native Americans were increasingly involved in encounters involving permanent settlements, with more and more people and subsistence patterns forever altered from those of trade and exploration.

Further Reading: Euler, Robert C., *Southern Paiute Ethnohistory*, University of Utah Anthropological Papers No. 78, Glen Canyon Series No. 28 (Salt Lake City: University of Utah Press, 1966); Malouf, Carling J., and John M. Findlay, "Euro-American Impact Before 1870," in *Handbook of North American Indians*, Vol. 11: *Great Basin*, edited by Warren L. d'Azevedo (Washington, DC: Smithsonian Institution, 1986), 499–516; Ray, Arthur J., "The Hudson's Bay

Company," in *Handbook of North American Indians*, Vol. 4: *History of Indian-White Relations*, edited by Wilcomb E. Washburn (Washington, DC: Smithsonian Institution, 1988), 335–350; Stern, Theodore, "Columbia River Trade Network," in *Handbook of North American Indians*, Vol. 12: *Plateau*, edited by Deward F. Walker (Washington, DC: Smithsonian Institution, 1998), 641–652; Swagerty, William R., "Indian Trade in the Trans-Mississippi West to 1870,"

in *Handbook of North American Indians*, Vol. 4: *History of Indian-White Relations*, edited by Wilcomb E. Washburn (Washington, DC: Smithsonian Institution, 1988), 351–374; Walker, Deward F., and Roderick Sprague, "History Until 1846," in *Handbook of North American Indians*, Vol. 12: *Plateau*, edited by Deward F. Walker (Washington, DC: Smithsonian Institution, 1998), 138–148.

Catherine S. Fowler

ROCK ART STYLES AND SITES IN THE GREAT BASIN

Rock art is a common archaeological monument throughout the Great Basin and Colorado Plateau regions of western North America. "Rock art" is widely used and recognized as a general term for all forms of intentional, culturally meaningful, markings (Bednarik 2001, 31–32) that are made on bedrock, cliff-faces, and cave ceilings and walls, as well as other modifications of the natural landscape, such as geoglyphs (or rock alignments). Rock art comprises two principal forms, petroglyphs (engravings, etchings, and scratchings) and pictographs (paintings). Petroglyphs are the most common form of rock art; pictographs may have once been more frequent but are less likely to survive in exposed environments, which is why they tend to be concentrated in rockshelters, caves, and other protected landscape contexts.

Because of the difficulty in scientifically dating petroglyphs, the lack of chronological resolution in the data has led to generalized theories to account for rock art's cultural functions and meanings. Rock art is often a highly visible monument form, its use life extends well beyond the act of its creation—such imagery would have attracted interest and provoked cultural responses from those that subsequently encountered it (Bradley 2000; Quinlan and Woody 2003). Most rock art sites represent a palimpsest of visual imagery— it is often only possible to identify phases of production rather than specific episodes. Sites that exhibit multiple generations of production, such as the Massacre Lake site in northwestern Nevada (Woody 1996), indicate that rock art was made, modified, or enhanced as a continuous process during long periods. Accordingly, interpretation of the social dimensions of rock art can only detect the broad trends in its past uses.

Great Basin and Plateau rock art attracted interest from early Euro-American explorers and settlers. The earliest academic studies of the region's rock art date from the mid-nineteenth century (e.g., Schoolcraft 1851–57); however, the first general survey of the region's rock art was made by Garrick Mallery as part of his broader study of Native American systems of visual communication (Mallery 1886, 1893). The first systematic study of Great Basin rock art was made by Julian Steward (1929), who synthesized data for the region,

characterized its content and styles, and outlined their distribution. Steward also identified the important research theme of the balance between schematic and naturalistic imagery in rock art assemblages as a characteristic of stylistic variation. Steward's work was built upon by the important and highly influential work of Robert Heizer and Martin Baumhoff (1962), which refined Steward's style definitions, outlined a general chronology of styles, and presented the first theorized interpretation of Great Basin rock art functions and meanings. Although criticized by more recent authors (e.g., Hedges 1982), no one has yet provided a universally accepted replacement to Heizer and Baumhoff's classification, and their style classes still minimally shape researchers' general terminology and chronology.

STYLES

Great Basin and Plateau style definitions traditionally are based on a combination of method of execution and then a consideration of motif types or themes portrayed. The supposedly oldest style is "Pit-and-Groove," or cupules, which is widely distributed in the western United States. It comprises circular depressions, usually a few centimeters wide and deep, seemingly made randomly on boulders (Grant 1967, 27; Heizer and Baumhoff 1962, 209). The style is assumed to be of great antiquity because in other parts of the world, particularly India, cupules appear to be among the oldest known styles of rock art. The apparent antiquity of this style in the Great Basin is highlighted by the Grimes Point site in western Nevada, where cupules on basalt boulders have completely revarnished and are indistinguishable from the rock's natural patina. Some of the art at this site may be 8,000 years old or older (Alanah Woody, personal communication, 2004). Cupules sometimes co-occur with other rock art styles, but are often the only type of rock art present.

The two most common petroglyph abstract styles are curvilinear and rectilinear (Heizer and Baumhoff 1962), which are regarded by some researchers as components of the Basin and Range tradition (Woody 2000), drawing attention to the wide spatial and temporal distribution of these "styles" that extend far outside the Great Basin culture area. The curvilinear style is defined by the predominance of circular forms (circles, concentric circles, connected circles, etc.), curvilinear meanders, and sinusoidal lines (Heizer and Baumhoff 1962). The rectilinear style is composed of linear motifs and elements that are organized in a linear fashion, such as rows of dots, grids, rectangles, squares, triangles, lines, and cross-hatching (Heizer and Baumhoff 1962). Rectilinear and curvilinear styles frequently co-occur at Great Basin rock art sites and are widespread throughout the region (Schaafsma 1986) and beyond. These two styles are the predominant type of rock art in the western Great Basin, specifically Nevada, and seem to always accompany other rock art styles in the region (Woody 2000). The relative dates assigned to these styles by Heizer and Baumhoff (approximately 3,500–150 years ago) can no longer be supported, but, in the absence of scientific dating, the chronology of these styles can only be said to span the entire period of rock art production in the region (i.e., from as early as 10,000 years ago until the late prehistoric period). Basin and Range tradition rectilinear and curvilinear elements are strongly associated with Archaic hunter-gatherer cultures in the desert west. However, these elements are also present in styles associated with Fremont and Ancestral Puebloan (also known as Anasazi) groups, although they are not as prominent.

The oldest petroglyph style that has been scientifically dated is the Great Basin Carved Abstract style (Cannon and Ricks 1986; Ricks and Cannon 1993). This style can be regarded as a variant of Basin and Range tradition rectilinear and curvilinear elements. The style was first identified at the Long Lake site in southern Oregon by Mary Ricks and Bill Cannon; its currently known distribution is restricted to southern Oregon and the northernmost part of northern Nevada (see Cannon and Ricks 2007). The style takes the form of very deeply engraved motifs with wide lines that form intricate, tightly packed designs with little white space. These designs incorporate curvilinear and rectilinear elements, and dots; however, they are substantially different from the rectilinear and curvilinear styles as defined by Heizer and Baumhoff, primarily in the depth and width of lines (Ricks and Cannon 1993, 94). The style is known to be at least 6,850 years old because a panel of this rock art style at Long Lake was found covered with ash from the eruption of Mt. Mazama (Ricks and Cannon 1993, 94).

The other major abstract petroglyph style is the Scratched style and comprises incised lines made using a sharp stone tool. Typical elements in this style include dense cross-hatching, squares, rectangles, and circles with lines radiating from them (Schaafsma 1986, 217). This style is widely distributed throughout the Great Basin but is rarely the predominant style at any site. It has been assumed to much more recent, dating from 1,000 years ago to the ethnohistoric period (Heizer and Baumhoff 1962). Bettinger and Baumhoff (1982) argued that Scratched style rock art is associated with the dispersal of Numic peoples across the Great Basin, noting that Scratched style art, particularly in the western Great Basin, often is superimposed on other styles of rock art. They explained this as an attempt by Numic groups to obliterate earlier, pre-Numic rock art (1982). However, Ritter (1994) has noted that some Scratched style art may be as old as the Middle Archaic, because old specimens of this style are can be hard to discern (1994, 60–61).

Most defined representational styles are distinctive treatments of anthropomorphs and zoomorphs. Representational styles also distinguish Colorado Plateau rock art styles from Great Basin styles, because they display a greater emphasis on representational forms. Distinctive anthropomorph styles in the southwestern Basin and Colorado Plateau are associated with Fremont and Ancestral Puebloan cultures—horticultural cultures with a distinctive material culture that developed from around 1,500 years ago until 750 years ago. Plateau rock art styles have been described thoroughly by Schaafsma, whose works are seminal on this subject (Schaafsma 1971, 1980, 1986).

The Great Basin Representational as defined by Heizer and Baumhoff (1962) comprises schematic anthropomorphs (stick figures) and naturalistic zoomorphs. This style largely shares the spatial distribution of Basin and Range abstract motifs. Examples of this style are better regarded as highly localized stylistic treatments of a widespread symbolic theme. They lack the stylistic unity and spatiotemporal definition of the representational styles outlined next.

The Coso style is restricted to the Coso Range of eastern California and its massive rock art sites in the China Lake area. Coso style rock art is typified by its emphasis on representational imagery, principally life-sized (and larger) bighorn sheep motifs that have boat-shaped bodies and elaborate, patterned-body anthropomorphs that are rectangular and often have headgear (Grant et al. 1968). Bighorn sheep and elaborate anthropomorphs are prominent in this art, which is characterized as dominated by representational forms but is accompanied by Basin and Range tradition abstract elements. Estimates of the age of the Coso style vary greatly, ranging from 9,000 years ago to the ethnohistoric period (Whitley 1998c, 162) to 3,000–1,000 years ago (Grant et al. 1968). The fame of this style is such that it has led to the misperception that bighorn sheep motifs are the characteristic motif of Great Basin rock art. This style is associated with Archaic hunter-gatherers and Numic peoples.

Sharing some formal similarities to Coso style patterned-body anthropomorphs is the Pahranagat style, which is restricted to the Pahranagat valley area of eastern Nevada (Schaafsma 1986, 218). Any similarities between anthropomorphs of the Pahranagat and Coso styles are largely the result of the symbolic treatment of the same subject—clothed anthropomorphs—as the differences between the two are generally striking. The Pahranagat style was defined from the Pahranagat Lake site and sites in the Mt. Irish Archaeological

District (Heizer and Hester 1974; Stoney 1992). The Pahranagat style is composed of two anthropomorph types: a patterned-body figure and the Pahranagat figure. The patterned-body anthropomorph has a rectangular shape, no head, a fringe between stick legs, short arms that sometimes hold an *atl atl*, and various internal geometric designs. "Blanket" figures, also part of this style, may be schematic variations of this patterned-body anthropomorph but sometimes lack limbs. Pahranagat figures have solid pecked bodies, are either rectangular or oval in shape, have large eyes, and have a line protruding from their head. These anthropomorph types often co-occur and are associated with other representational elements, usually naturalist depictions of bighorn sheep. Pahranagat style rock art is associated with campsites and resource areas and is dated to 1,500–200 years ago (William White, personal communication, 2006). The cultural affiliations of this distinctive, localized style are unclear.

In eastern Nevada and western Utah distinctive anthropomorph styles are strongly associated with Fremont and Ancestral Puebloan cultures. Executed as petroglyphs and as paintings, these styles are characterized by stylized trapezoidal and triangular anthropomorphs, often portrayed with elaborate headgear, horns, or jewelry. Some are strikingly similar to distinctive anthropomorphic figurines that are an important part of Fremont material culture. Part of this Fremont and Kayenta style rock art includes square-shaped bighorn sheep motifs (Schaafsma 1986, 217).

Colorado Plateau rock art styles are characterized by their emphasis on distinctive, stylized anthropomorph forms that are associated with Fremont horticultural groups. Although Basin and Range tradition motifs are present, these are not prominent and are assumed to be the work of preceding Archaic hunter-gatherers and late prehistoric Numic groups. Perhaps the most arresting style in this region is the Barrier Canyon style, which is largely found along western tributaries of the Green River in central and eastern Utah and in the White River drainage. The style is dominated by a very distinctive anthropomorph form—an elongated, tapering figure painted in dark red that has a stylized head, large eyes, and minimal or no limbs (Schaafsma 1980). The appearance of these figures, particularly those at the Barrier Canyon type site, is often described as "spectral," because they are arranged "hovering" in rows (Schaafsma 1986, 223).

Fremont-style anthropomorphs similar to those found in the eastern Great Basin complement the region's Classic Vernal and San Rafael styles, which are important components of Plateau Fremont rock art. The Classic Vernal style is characterized by large, elaborately decorated anthropomorphs that dominate Fremont rock art assemblages in northeastern Utah. They have trapezoidal bodies and splayed limbs and fingers (when these are depicted), and wear elaborate headgear and jewelry (armbands, necklaces, earrings, etc.). Various types of animals are often associated with this style (Schaafsma 1980, 171, 175). The San Rafael style also includes elaborate,

heavily decorated anthropomorphs, but bighorn sheep are also an important element. These are portrayed with square or crescent bodies, sometimes incorporated in apparent hunting scenes (Shaafsma 1986, 223). An important element of Fremont styles in both the eastern Great Basin and the Plateau is the shield-bearer figure. These anthropomorphic figures include shields that often completely obscure their body; the shields are often decorated with geometric motifs. Shield designs are also a characteristic of Kayenta rock art.

FUNCTION AND MEANING

The issues of rock art function and meaning have played an important role in Great Basin rock art research since the publication of Heizer and Baumhoff's (1962) *Prehistoric Rock Art of Nevada and Eastern California*. Heizer and Baumhoff modified hunting-magic interpretations of European Paleolithic cave art (e.g., Begouen 1929; Breuil 1952; Reinach 1903) to Great Basin archaeological contexts. Hunting-magic theory interprets rock art as having been made and used in the context of rituals intended to ensure hunting success, increase numbers of game animals, or symbolically treat prized or feared animals.

Heizer and Baumhoff's (1962) interpretation of the Lagomarsino Canyon petroglyph site in northwestern Nevada exemplifies their hunting-magic approach. Lagomarsino is a large site dominated by Basin and Range tradition abstract forms, where naturalistic zoomorphs and anthropomorphs are rare (Quinlan and Woody 2001). Heizer and Baumhoff's interpretation highlighted the site's favorable environment, hunting-related features, and hunting themes in the art. A substantial rock wall crosses through the western half of the site and was interpreted as a game drive fence, indicating that hunting was an important part of the site's function. Imagery of bighorn sheep and putative pinyon cones was cited as evidence that the rock art was associated with practices and beliefs focused on increasing the fecundity of critical resources (Heizer and Baumhoff 1962, 290–291).

Although Lagomarsino comprises several thousand rock art panels, each composed of numerous elements, Heizer and Baumhoff's interpretation cites only the specific imagery of three motifs (including a bighorn sheep motif and the putative pinyon cones), largely ignoring the site's Basin and Range tradition abstract motifs (Quinlan and Woody 2001, 213). This was a problem repeated in their discussions of other sites (Whitley 1998c, 135–136). One can also question why an art intended to increase the numbers of critical resources portrays only one or two types of game animals (bighorn sheep and deer) and rarely depicts seeds, roots, or small mammals, resources known from ethnohistoric and archaeological data to have been critical to economic reproduction in the Great Basin (Fowler 1986; Steward 1938).

The presence of hunting-related archaeology is also overemphasized. Lagomarsino's rock wall, which Heizer and Baumhoff (1962, 291) believed was a game division fence, runs for several miles and is probably neither prehistoric nor connected with hunting; more likely it marks a mining claim or is associated with ranching (Quinlan and Woody 2001, 213). Other researchers have noted that Heizer and Baumhoff's approach generally ignores settlement archaeology at other rock art sites, a criticism that also applies to proponents of the more recent shamanistic approach (see discussion in Quinlan 2007a). If site contexts and associated archaeology are used to define informing contexts for interpretation, then all on-site activities indicated by archaeological data should be considered in interpretation (Bradley 2000; Quinlan 2007b; Quinlan and Woody 2003). Despite these problems with Heizer and Baumhoff's hunting-magic approach, it remains popular with some archaeologists and has prompted important research on the relationship between rock art sites and their natural environments (e.g., Gilreath 1999; Matheny et al. 1997; Nissen 1982, 1995).

Since the 1970s Great Basin rock art has increasingly been interpreted in terms of its relationship to prehistoric and ethnohistoric shamanistic practices. Proponents argue that much North American rock art imagery portrays mental imagery (entoptic phenomena) experienced during shamanistic trance states (Blackburn 1977; Hedges 1976, 1985). Geometric motifs are identified as representations of entoptic phenomena, and figurative compositions are interpreted as depictions of shamanistic rituals, or at least are associated with them because they apparently incorporate elemental entoptic forms (Lewis-Williams and Dowson 1988, 205). In addition, the content of rock art imagery is explored for the expression of common shamanic themes. Avian imagery has been interpreted as a metaphor of shamanic soul flight or the transmogrification of shamans into birds (e.g., Hedges 1985; Schaafsma 1994). Ethnographic descriptions likening trance states to dying have led to images of death (e.g., hunting scenes, anthropomorphs falling) being interpreted as visual metaphors for entering trance states (e.g., Lewis-Williams 1982, 1997).

The shamanistic approach in the Great Basin is exemplified by David Whitley's interpretations of the Coso Range (Whitley 1992, 1994, 1998c). Whitley has argued that Coso rock art was made by male shamans to record imagery experienced during trance states. Rock art sites were perceived as places were power could be acquired and, therefore, also functioned as vision quest locales. Because a shaman's spirit helper contacted him during trance, giving the shaman instructions and various powers, some art also depicts spirit helpers. In the Coso Range, bighorn sheep motifs were interpreted by Whitley as the specific spirit helper of rain shamans. Scenes of bighorn sheep apparently being hunted by anthropomorphs are interpreted as metaphors of shamanic trance because they portray dying. The elaborate patterned-body anthropomorphs are argued to incorporate unique geometric motifs; hence, these are interpreted as portrayals of shamans wearing clothing decorated with designs of entoptic

phenomena experienced during trance (1998c). Some Coso anthropomorphs have "bird-claw feet and whirlwind faces," which are interpreted by Whitley as visual metaphors of trance (1998c, 157). Because rock art sites are envisioned as vision quest locales, they are interpreted as being some distance from settlement or domestic activity areas and would only have been visited by shamans (Whitley 1998a).

In common with hunting magic, the shamanistic approach is challenged by the evidence of domestic archaeology in association with rock art. If rock art locales are remote vision quest locales, then why is settlement archaeology so near to it? Whenever domestic artifacts are directly associated with rock art, it is argued that the artifacts were used at different times and that rock art was purposely put there to exert male spiritual dominance over women's mundane daily activities (e.g., Whitley 1998b; Whitley 1998c), an argument reflecting the androcentric bias of some contemporary archaeologists rather than that of prehistoric groups (Cannon and Woody 2007). The readings of certain rock art imagery as expressing shamanic themes is highly speculative and is largely based on representational imagery. Abstract imagery is cited to establish a precedent for a trance-based explanation of a corpus of rock art (because it is assumed to encode entoptic phenomena), but thereafter it is largely ignored. As Robert Layton (2000) has pointed out, if rock art portrays shamanic spirit helpers, then why is such a limited range of animals portrayed in the art? Also, the shamanistic approach is not that solidly based in regional ethnography or the anthropology of religion, because it relies on metaphoric reinterpretations of ethnohistoric accounts that support alternative readings (see discussion in Francfort and Hamayon 2001).

CONCLUSION

It has become increasingly apparent, particularly in the Great Basin, that the relationship between rock art and settlement archaeology has been under-reported and misinterpreted (see discussion in Cannon and Ricks 1986; Green 1987; Quinlan 2007a; Quinlan and Woody 2003). Across much of the Great Basin, rock art sites are closely associated with the residues of past domestic activities—such as middens, ground stone, lithic scatters, house rings, milling slicks, and ground stone—that are not normally taken into consideration by either hunting-magic or shamanistic approaches. This has fostered the misperception that rock art somehow is distinct from the routines of daily life. As the relationship between rock art and the settled landscape becomes better understood, it will be possible to outline how rock art was used in daily social life. Rock art is a symbolic resource that people would have referenced in interpreting the theories of being that structure social life. Rock art remains a living cultural resource—contemporary public and academic interest in it indicates its continuing power to excite the imagination, and it retains a powerful cultural resonance for Native American peoples, its traditional custodians.

Further Reading: Bednarik, Robert G., *Rock Art Science: The Scientific Study of Palaeoart*, International Federation of Rock Art Organizations, Vol. 1 (Turnhout, Belgium: Brepols, 2001); Begouen, Henri, "The Magic Origin of Prehistoric Art," *Antiquity* 3 (1929): 5–19; Bettinger, Robert L., and Martin A. Baumhoff, "The Numic Spread: Great Basin Cultures in Competition," *American Antiquity* 47 (1982): 485–503; Blackburn, Thomas C., "Biopsychological Aspects of Chumash Rock Art," *Journal of California and Great Basin Anthropology* 4(1) (1977): 88–94; Bradley, Richard, *An Archaeology of Natural Places* (London: Routledge, 2000); Breuil, Henri, *Quatre Cents Siècles d'Art Pariétal* (Montignac, France: Centre D'Études et de Documentation Préhistoriques, 1952); Cannon, William J., and Mary Ricks, "The Lake County Oregon Rock Art Inventory: Implications for Prehistoric Settlement and Land Use Patterns," in *Contributions to the Archaeology of Oregon 1983–1986*, edited by Kenneth M. Ames, Department of Anthropology and University Foundation Occasional Papers No. 3 (Salem: Portland State University and Association of Oregon Archaeologists, 1986), 1–22; Cannon, William J., and Mary Ricks, "Contexts in the Analysis of Rock Art: Rock Art and Settlement in the Warner Valley Area, Oregon," in *Great Basin Rock Art: Archaeological Perspectives*, edited by Angus R. Quinlan (Reno: University of Nevada Press, 2007), 107–125; Cannon, William J., and Alanah Woody, "Towards a Gender Inclusive View of Rock Art in the Northern Great Basin," in *Great Basin Rock Art: Archaeological Perspectives*, edited by Angus R. Quinlan (Reno: University of Nevada Press, 2007), 37–51; Fowler, Catherine S., "Subsistence," in *Handbook of North American Indians*, Vol. 11: *Great Basin*, edited by Warren L. d'Azevedo, (Washington, DC: Smithsonian Institution, 1986), 64–97; Francfort, Henri-Paul, and Roberte N. Hamayon, eds., *Bibliotheca Shamanistica*, Vol. 10: *The Concept of Shamanism: Uses and Abuses*, edited by Mihály Hoppál (Budapest: Akadémiai Kiadó, 2001); Gilreath, Amy J., "The Archaeology and Petroglyphs of the Coso Rock Art Landmark," in *American Indian Rock Art*, Vol. 25, edited by Steven M. Freers (Tucson, AZ: American Rock Art Research Association, 1999), 33–44; Grant, Campbell, *Rock Art of the American Indian* (Dillon, CO: Vista Books, 1967); Grant, Campbell, James W. Baird, and Kenneth Pringle, *Rock Drawings of the Coso Range: An Ancient Sheep-Hunting Cult Pictured in Desert Rock Carvings* (China Lake, CA: Maturango Museum, 1968); Green, Eileen M., "A Cultural Ecological Approach to the Rock Art of Southern Nevada," unpublished master's thesis (University of Nevada, Las Vegas, Department of Anthropology, 1987); Hedges, Ken, "Southern California Rock Art as Shamanic Art," in *American Indian Rock Art*, Vol. 2, edited by Kay Sutherland (El Paso, TX: American Rock Art Research Association, 1976), 126–138; Hedges, Ken, "Great Basin Rock Art Styles: A Revisionist View," in *American Indian Rock Art*, Vols. 7 and 8, edited by Frank G. Bock (El Toro, CA: American Rock Art Research Association, 1982), 205–211; Hedges, Ken, "Rock Art Portrayals of Shamanic Transformation and Magical Flight, in *Rock Art Papers*, Vol. 2, edited by Ken Hedges, San Diego Museum Papers No. 18 (San Diego: Museum of Man, 1985), 83–94; Heizer, Robert F., and Martin A. Baumhoff, *Prehistoric Rock Art of Nevada and Eastern California* (Berkeley: University of California Press, 1962); Heizer, Robert F., and Thomas R. Hester, "Two Petroglyph Sites in Lincoln County, Nevada," in *Four Great Basin Petroglyph Studies*, Contributions of the University of California Archaeological Research Facility No. 20 (Berkeley: University of California, Department of Anthropology, 1974), 1–52; Layton, Robert, "Shamanism, Totemism and Rock Art: *Les Chamanes de la Préhistoire* in the Context of Rock Art Research," *Cambridge Archaeological Journal* 10(1) (2000): 169–186; Lewis-Williams, J. David, "The Economic and Social Context of Southern San Rock Art," *Current Anthropology* 23 (1982): 429–449; Lewis-Williams, J. David, "Agency, Art and Altered Consciousness: A Motif in French (Quercy) Upper Palaeolithic Parietal Art," *Antiquity* 71 (1997): 810–830; Lewis-Williams, J. David, and Thomas A. Dowson, "The Signs of All Times: Entoptic Phenomena in Upper Palaeolithic Art," *Current Anthropology* 29(2) (1988): 201–245; Mallery, Garrick, "Pictographs of the North American Indians: A Preliminary Paper," in *4th Annual Report of the Bureau of American Ethnology for the Years 1882–1883* (Washington, DC: Bureau of American Ethnology, 1886), 3–256; Mallery, Garrick, "Picture-Writing of the American Indians," in *10th Annual Report of the Bureau of American Ethnology for the Years 1888–1889* (Washington, DC: Bureau of American Ethnology, 1893), 3–822; Matheny, Ray T., Thomas S. Smith, and Deanne G. Matheny, "Animal Ethology Reflected in the Rock Art of Nine Mile Canyon, Utah," *Journal of California and Great Basin Anthropology* 19(1) (1997): 70–103; Nissen, Karen M., "Images from the Past: An Analysis of Six Western Great Basin Petroglyph Sites," unpublished Ph.D. diss. (University of California, Berkeley, Department of Anthropology, 1982); Nissen, Karen M., "Pray for Signs? Petroglyph Research in the Western Great Basin, North America," in *Rock Art Studies in the Americas: Papers from the Darwin Rock Art Congress*, edited by Jack Steinbring, Oxbow Monograph No. 45 (Oxford: Oxbow Books, 1995), 67–75; Quinlan, Angus R., ed., *Great Basin Rock Art: Archaeological Perspectives* (Reno: University of Nevada Press, 2007a); Quinlan, Angus R., "Integrating Rock Art with Archaeology: Symbolic Culture as Archaeology," in *Great Basin Rock Art: Archaeological Perspectives*, edited by Angus R. Quinlan (Reno: University of Nevada Press, 2007b), 1–8; Quinlan, Angus R., and Alanah Woody, "Marking Time at Lagomarsino: The Competing Perspectives of Rock Art Studies," in *American Indian Rock Art*, Vol. 27, edited by Steven M. Freers and Alanah Woody (Tucson, AZ: American Rock Art Research Association, 2001), 211–220; Quinlan, Angus R., and Alanah Woody, "Marks of Distinction: Rock Art and Ethnic Identification in the Great Basin," *American Antiquity* 68(2) (2003): 372–390; Reinach, S., "L'art et la magie à propos des peintures et des gravures de l'âge de rennes," *L'Anthropologie* XIV (1903): 257–266; Ricks, Mary F., and William J. Cannon, "A Preliminary Report on the Lake County, Oregon, Rock Art Inventory: A Data Base for Rock Art Research," in *American Indian Rock Art*, Vol. 12, edited by William D. Hyder (San Miguel, CA: American Rock Art Research Association, 1993), 93–106; Ritter, Eric W., "Scratched Rock Art Complexes in the Desert West: Symbols for Socio-Religious Communication," in *New Light on Old Art: Recent Advances in Hunter-Gatherer Rock Art Research*, edited by David S. Whitley and Lawrence L. Loendorf (Los Angeles: University of California, Institute of Archaeology, 1994), 51–66; Schaafsma, Polly, *The Rock Art of Utah: from the Donald Scott Collection*, Papers of the Peabody Museum of Archaeology and Ethnology, Vol. 65 (Cambridge, MA: Harvard University, 1971); Schaafsma, Polly, *Rock Art of the Southwest*, School of American Research Southwest Indian Arts Series (Santa Fe and Albuquerque: University of New Mexico Press, 1980); Schaafsma, Polly, "Rock Art," in *Handbook of North American Indians*, Vol. 11: *Great Basin*, edited by Warren L. d'Azevedo,

(Washington, DC: Smithsonian Institution, 1986), 215–226; Schaafsma, Polly, "Trance and Transformation in the Canyons: Shamanism and Early Rock Art on the Colorado Plateau," in *Shamanism and Rock Art in North America*, edited by Solveig Turpin, Special Publication No. 1 (San Antonio, TX: Rock Art Foundation, 1994), 45–71; Schoolcraft, Henry R., *Historical and Statistical Information Respecting the History, Condition and Prospects of the Indian Tribes of the United States: Collected and Prepared under the Direction of the Bureau of Indian Affairs per Act of Congress of March 3rd 1847*, 6 vols. (Philadelphia: Lippincott, Grambo, 1851–57); Steward, Julian H., *Petroglyphs of California and Adjoining States*, Publications in American Archaeology and Ethnology 24(2) (Berkeley: University of California, 1929), 47–238; Steward, Julian H., *Basin-Plateau Aboriginal Sociopolitical Groups*, Bureau of American Ethnology Bulletin No. 120 (Washington, DC: Smithsonian Institution, 1938); Stoney, Stephen A., "Anthropomorphic Symbolism in Southern Nevada: A Study in Cultural Diversity," in *Rock Art Papers*, Vol. 9, edited by Ken Hedges, San Diego Museum Papers No. 28 (San Diego: Museum of Man, 1992), 57–66; Whitley, David S., "Shamanism and Rock Art in Far Western North America," *Cambridge Archaeological Journal* 2(1) (1992): 89–113; Whitley,

David S., "Shamanism, Natural Modeling and the Rock Art of Far Western North American Hunter Gatherers," in *Shamanism and Rock Art in North America*, edited by Solveig A. Turpin, Special Publication No. 1 (San Antonio, TX: Rock Art Foundation, 1994), 1–43; Whitley, David S., "Finding Rain in the Desert: Landscape, Gender, and Far Western North American Rock-Art," in *The Archaeology of Rock-Art*, edited by Christopher Chippindale and Paul S. C. Taçon (Cambridge: Cambridge University Press, 1998a), 11–29; Whitley, David S., *Following the Shaman's Path: A Walking Guide to Little Petroglyph Canyon, Coso Range, California* (Ridgecrest, CA: Maturango Press, 1998b); "Meaning and Metaphor in the Coso Petroglyphs: Understanding Great Basin Rock Art," in *Coso Rock Art: A New Perspective*, edited by Elva Younkin (Ridgecrest, CA: Maturango Press, 1998c), 109–174; Woody, Alanah, *Layer by Layer: A Multigenerational Analysis of the Massacre Lake Rock Art Site*, Department of Anthropology Technical Report No. 97-1 (Reno: University of Nevada, 1996); Woody, Alanah, "How to Do Things with Petroglyphs: The Power of Place in Nevada, USA," unpublished Ph.D. diss. (University of Southampton, Department of Archaeology, 2000).

Angus R. Quinlan

ROCK ART STYLES AND SITES ON THE COLUMBIA PLATEAU

More than any other region of North America, the Columbia Plateau is characterized by long-term cultural stability and homogeneity that is clearly reflected in both its rock art and archaeological record. Based on a hunting and fishing economy for the past 8,000 years, Plateau culture is best known from large permanent villages that served as trading centers at Kettle Falls, the Dalles, and the lower Fraser River. Long-distance trade, the immigration of Chinookan-speaking tribes in the late prehistoric period, and the arrival of the first Europeans were the only factors that provided significant modification to this long-term homogeneity. Throughout the region, however, similarities of tools, houses, and material culture items demonstrate that for the last 5,000 years Columbia Plateau people had a cultural system remarkably similar to that characteristic of the area's ethnographically known groups.

This cultural homogeneity provides one of the region's primary strengths for studying rock art. Plateau ethnohistoric and ethnographic reports contain North America's most detailed ethnographic information about pictographs and petroglyphs—in a record that spans more than 100 years. This information can be directly related to nearly all aspects of the thousands of carvings and paintings scattered across the

region. The tribal elders' words recorded in some of these reports bring to life the forgotten dreams of the Columbia Plateau.

The Columbia Plateau is the large intermontane basin lying between the Cascade and Rocky Mountain ranges in the northwestern corner of the United States and far southwestern Canada. Drained primarily by the Fraser, Columbia, and lower Snake rivers, the region has been shaped by immense Miocene age basalt flows, Pleistocene glaciers, and the catastrophic outflows of ancient Lakes Bonneville and Missoula.

The northern Plateau is heavily forested with dense stands of fir and pine that cover steep mountain ranges separating deep valleys containing swift-flowing rivers or deep, narrow lakes dammed behind glacial moraines. The central and southern Plateau is an arid basin formed by basalt flows more than 10 million years old. In the basin center lie the channeled scablands—prehistoric landscapes cut by immense floods from glacial Lake Missoula, which occupied the mountain valleys of western Montana and emptied repeatedly between 12,000 and 20,000 years ago.

Along these river valleys, lake shores, and canyon walls there are thousands of miles of basalt, limestone, and granite cliffs and innumerable boulders that provide surfaces on which ancient artists carved and painted one North America's most homogeneous rock art traditions.

Columbia Plateau people were hunter-gatherers and fishermen who shared basic themes of religion, subsistence, and warfare across more than twenty tribes from six language families. Most groups occupied seasonal riverine villages, usually situated at key fishing stations along major rivers. Groups traveling away from villages, and those living in the Rocky Mountain valleys, lived in mat lodges or skin tepees, which could be easily set up and transported. All of these groups lived in autonomous villages or bands to whom members gave their allegiance and from whom they received their identity. Village or band membership was remarkably fluid, and intermarriage between groups was common. "Chiefs" were almost always men who occupied a hereditary position and "governed" through charismatic leadership and group consensus.

The Columbia Plateau economy was based primarily on salmon fishing, but hunters killed deer, mountain sheep, mountain goats, and other big game, and women dug roots and picked berries. Groups living near the Rockies made regular buffalo-hunting expeditions to the plains. With the arrival of the horse in the early 1700s, many groups became more Plains-like, and warfare became more important as a source of men's social identity.

Columbia Plateau religion centered on the personal vision quest, and the role of the guardian spirit was greater here than anywhere else in North America. Nearly all men and women obtained a spirit helper at puberty to assist in various aspects of life. Often undertaken at a rock art site, the vision provided the supplicant with a supernatural helper in the form of a bird or other animal, celestial being, or even a plant. Rock art was often made to commemorate successful visions.

Shamans—both men and women—were religious specialists in Columbia Plateau culture. Usually they possessed multiple spirit helpers (obtained by the same vision quest) and used them to care for the dead, predict the future, control weather and game, and cause and cure disease. Numerous ethnographic references document that shamans made and used rock art in their rituals.

TRADITIONS AND STYLES

Columbia Plateau rock art includes three traditions—the widespread Columbia Plateau tradition, the Columbia River Conventionalized style of the Northwest Coast tradition, and a Biographic tradition that was associated with warfare and horse raiding that developed in the historic period. Columbia Plateau tradition rock art is classified into six regional styles and a seventh scratched style that is widespread across the southern half of the region.

Plateau tradition rock art includes both petroglyphs and pictographs. Most petroglyphs are pecked, but incised or scratched images characterize one style. These scratched petroglyphs are most often clusters of apparently random scratches or series of small nicks that create scalloped or serrated edges on angular cliff corners. Pecked petroglyphs are most common in the western Columbia Plateau.

Pictographs are mostly red, although white, yellow, black, and green examples also occur. The Yakima Polychrome style is characterized by spectacular red and white painted circles, arcs, and faces, but polychromes are rare in other styles. Most pictographs were finger-painted, but others were applied with brushes or drawn with lumps of raw ochre or ochre crayons.

Columbia Plateau tradition rock art emphasizes human and animal figures, spirit beings, geometric motifs, and tally marks, all of which occur as both pictographs and petroglyphs. Most images are small and drawn in secluded places, indicating that they were a private personal art.

Humans are almost always simple stick figures with arms, legs, and a dot or open circle for a head. Hands, feet, and genitals are rarely shown. Only a few dozen examples from the entire region hold or use weapons, and almost no other material culture items are shown. Overall these humans are drawn more simply than anywhere else in North America. Frequently these simple humans are juxtaposed with an animal, a group of tally marks, an overhead rayed arc, or a cluster of dots, or they are enclosed in a circle. Such juxtaposed compositions are identified in ethnographic accounts as vision quest records.

Spirit beings are humanoid figures that include extra appendages or attributes that are obviously unreal. These spirit beings are much simpler than those characteristic of the Columbia River Conventionalized style.

Like humans, most animals are simple stick or block-body figures. Although more than twenty species are identified, most recognizable animals are in hunting scenes. Animals drawn in vision quest compositions appear in their role as guardian spirit helpers, juxtaposed with a human or geometric figure or shown encircled by a painted line, surrounded by dots, or surmounted by a rayed arc. Most of these animals are specifically unidentifiable because a person's spirit helper was kept secret.

Geometric motifs include rayed arcs, tally marks, dots, zigzags, crosses, circles, ladders, and curvilinear and rectilinear line abstracts. Some of these may indicate stars, the moon, or the sun—a powerful guardian spirit sought in vision quests. Concentric polychrome red and white arcs common as Yakima Polychrome images may represent rainbows. Geometric motifs are often juxtaposed with humans or animals in vision quest compositions.

Rayed arcs—upward arching lines with upward pointing rays—are often situated just above, or attached to, a human's head, but others are drawn alone, and a few surmount animal figures. Occasionally, two and three rayed arcs are stacked one above the other. Archaeological and ethnographic research has shown that rayed arcs symbolized guardian spirit power, hence their frequent inclusion in vision quest compositions.

Tally marks occur throughout the Columbia Plateau. Occurring primarily as horizontally oriented series of short, evenly spaced vertical lines, they exist as groups numbering from two to more than twenty. Ethnographic informants identify them as representing the number of visits to a site, days spent there, spirit helpers obtained, or steps in prescribed rituals. A few sites in the eastern part of the region are nothing but tallies, sometimes totaling more than 100 marks.

Five of the seven currently defined Columbia Plateau tradition styles are variants of a widespread, homogeneous theme. These are geographically based and distinguished primarily by the frequency and/or occurrence of characteristic motifs. In contrast, the Yakima Polychrome style is both geographically and thematically distinguishable. Although this style includes the typical rayed arcs and some Columbia Plateau–style stick figures, it has numerous other more elaborate motifs, including rayed arc faces, four-pointed stars, polychrome "rainbow" arcs, and highly stylized spirit beings. Most of these images are fantastic red and white bichrome paintings, although some are painted only in white, and a few are petroglyphs.

Northwest Coast art is represented in the Columbia Plateau by the Columbia River Conventionalized style, localized along the lower Columbia River and its major tributaries in the territory occupied historically by Chinookan-speaking tribes who moved in from the southern Northwest Coast. Composed primarily of fantastic spirit beings and elaborate animals, these images are predominantly petroglyphs, although some pictographs are known.

These spirit figures emphasize faces with large, staring concentric-circle eyes. Often these spirit beings are bizarrely abbreviated or include stylized zoomorphic or anthropomorphic attributes, although they clearly do not represent real people or animals. Mouths, teeth, and facial features are often exaggerated, and multiple heads, X-ray-style bodies showing internal organs or skeletal elements, and extra or missing limbs are common. Lower Columbia River rock art spirit beings include Spedis Owl, Thunderbird, Land Monster, Cannibal Woman, Swallowing Monster, and Tsagiglalal (She Who Watches), all of whom can be identified from ethnographic sources.

In contrast to the small vision quest images intended for personal use that characterize Columbia Plateau tradition art, Columbia River Conventionalized style motifs are mostly large, prominently displayed images clearly intended for public audiences.

Biographic tradition rock art is scattered across the southern and eastern parts of the region and appears to be related to Plains Biographic imagery found more commonly to the east. Only recently recognized, more Columbia Plateau sites are likely to be found in the future. So far, this Biographic art includes finger-painted and fine-line pictographs and scratched petroglyphs. Humans include shield-bearing warriors (although lacking the elaborate shield heraldry characteristic of Plains examples) and stick figures, usually arranged in combat, horse-raiding, or buffalo-hunting scenes.

Horses and bison are the only animals so far noted. Three stick-figure humans are drawn in one scene with horse tracks or "hit marks" stacked overhead to document coups. Hand prints are used at another site, apparently for the same purpose. Weapons are common and include spears, clubs, shields, guns, and bows and arrows.

In contrast to the simple juxtaposed Columbia Plateau vision quest compositions, Biographic images are composed into action scenes. Although most of these are significantly simpler than Plains Biographic compositions, some include track sequences, postures, horse tack, and costume elements nearly identical to Plains scenes. One drawing relates horsemen to a group of pedestrian shield bearers by using sequences of human and horse tracks. A scene in Hells Canyon shows a mounted warrior spearing a pedestrian warrior, and another near Flathead Lake shows a man holding the halter of a horse that has a rider. All of these humans have scalp-lock hairstyles. Shield-bearing warriors at four sites are arrayed in hand-to-hand combat.

DATING

Columbia Plateau tradition rock art was quite long lived. Some images date as far back as the Archaic period, based on archaeological context at two sites, atl atls drawn at two other sites, and images of an Archaic period projectile point type painted at another. The maximum age is unknown, but images more than 7,000 years old have been found at two sites. Columbia Plateau tradition art continued throughout prehistory, and the fact that several Columbia Plateau styles were still drawn in historic times is demonstrated by detailed ethnographic references, sometimes to specific sites, found throughout the region.

Comparison with dated portable art objects and the known time frame for the immigration of Chinookan-speaking coastal people into the lower Columbia River region demonstrates that Yakima Polychrome and Columbia River Conventionalized styles could have begun only in the last 1,000 years.

Columbia Plateau Biographic art dates exclusively to the late prehistoric and historic periods—the last 400 years. Fighting shield-bearing warriors carrying large body shields probably predate the introduction of the horse in the early 1700s, but a dozen scenes have horses that confidently date them after AD 1700, and a group of guns at an Idaho site must post-date about AD 1800.

FUNCTION AND MEANING

Columbia Plateau tradition art functioned in vision quest and shamanic rituals, mortuary practices, and hunting magic. The ethnographic record demonstrates that the primary motive for most Columbia Plateau tradition art was the personal vision quest. Done by both men and women, this ritual quest was often commemorated by painting or carving rock art, and many groups specifically chose rock art sites as vision locations. The art itself shows frequent vision quest symbolism including small juxtaposed compositions of humans, animals, geometric designs, rayed arcs, or tally marks—all used to show a person obtaining or possessing spirit power.

Ethnographic sources also document that Columbia Plateau shamans made and used rock art. Shamans underwent the same vision quest as laymen, but as specialists in all things spiritual, they visited the supernatural world more frequently and usually had several spirit helpers. They were thus more familiar with the pantheon of spirit beings than anyone else, so it is likely that the fanciful rock art spirit beings were drawn by shamans.

Additionally, strong ethnographic references associate some rock art with shamans' curing and burial rituals. Columbia River Conventionalized Tsagiglalal images and Yakima Polychrome–style rayed arc faces, circles, and rainbow arcs are situated at cemeteries and talus cremation sites all along the lower Columbia River. One ethnographic reference relates a known Yakima Polychrome painting to a known shaman effecting a cure in about 1900.

Columbia Plateau rock art was also done to invoke hunting magic. Ethnographic references to this practice and Columbia Plateau rock art scenes illustrating both individual and communal hunting (portrayed with exacting detail and realism) indicate the use of rock art for this type of sympathetic magic.

Columbia River Conventionalized style art was mostly of shamanic provenience. The types of figures, their public placement, the multiple images of known supernatural beings (e.g., Tsagiglalal, Spedis Owl, Swallowing Monster, Land Monster), and the conventionalized skeletal imagery all point to knowledgeable shamans as the artists.

Columbia Plateau Biographic tradition art functioned to record a man's warfare and hunting prowess so he could validate his position as an important man in his group. The rock art images are similar in structure and symbolism to Plains Biographic art and resemble ledger drawings and robe paintings done by famous Columbia Plateau warriors for just such purposes. Biographic rock art sites in the eastern Columbia Plateau were drawn by warrior artists from tribes such as the Flathead, Nez Perce, Cayuse, and Shoshone, all of whom participated in the historic period Plains warfare and status acquisition system.

In summary, archaeological and ethnographic research indicates five major functions for Columbia Plateau rock art. Given the vision quest as a unifying force in Columbia Plateau religion, however, it is not surprising that all of these rock art functions interrelate to some extent. There is no clear distinction between laymen's and shamans' vision quest imagery, and shamans routinely used mortuary rock art in their curing and death rituals. Likewise, hunting power was acquired through the vision quest, so hunting-magic scenes can be painted at the same rock art sites. Further, a warrior wanting to record his coups might also chose a well-known rock art site, since these places would attract both secular and supernatural audiences. Thus, a Columbia Plateau rock art site might contain images related to any of these aspects of the supernatural world, and many of the larger, more complex sites have images that served multiple purposes.

Further Reading: Keyser, James D., *Indian Rock Art of the Columbia Plateau* (Seattle: University of Washington Press, 1992); Keyser, James D., and George Poetschat, "The Canvas as Art: Landscape Analysis of the Rock-Art Panel," in *The Figured Landscapes of Rock-Art: Looking at Pictures in Place*, edited by Christopher Chippindale and George Nash (Cambridge, UK: Cambridge University Press, 2004), 118–130; Keyser, James D., George Poetschat, and Michael W. Taylor, eds., *Talking with the Past: The Ethnography of Rock Art*, Oregon Archaeological Society Publication No. 16 (Portland: Oregon Archaeological Society, 2006).

James D. Keyser

HISTORIC SETTLEMENTS AND INDUSTRIAL SITES OF THE GREAT BASIN AND PLATEAU

Historic period archaeological sites, many agricultural and industrial, are found throughout the American Great Basin and Plateau. Some of the sites are as early as the eighteenth century, but most date to the nineteenth and twentieth centuries. They include agricultural farmsteads and ranches, villages and towns, work camps, sawmills and charcoal kilns, mines and mills, water conveyance and storage systems, transportation networks, military and government establishments, and exploration sites and trails. Historical settlements and industrial sites in the region are found along rivers, in north-south trending valleys and basins, and in or around metallic or mineralized geological formations. Geographically, the Plateau covers the high mountainous and forested region of the Pacific Northwest between the Rocky Mountains on the east, the Cascade Range on the west, the upper reaches of the Columbia River on the north, and the Salmon River on the south. It encompasses northern Idaho, northwestern Montana, western Oregon, and eastern Washington in the United States, and the Canadian provinces of southern British Columbia and southwestern Alberta. The Great Basin is an arid region that includes north-south trending mountain ranges and closed basins between the Rocky Mountains on the east and the Sierra Nevada Mountains on the west; it extends over the states of Nevada, Utah, southeastern California, southeastern Oregon, southern Idaho, western Colorado, and northwestern Arizona.

EXPLORATION

Historic period archaeological sites, trails, and places mark the European and Euro-American exploration and early settlement of the region. Spanish explorers crossed the southern Great Basin in the eighteenth century. Juan Maria de Rivera explored the eastern region of what later became the Old Spanish Trail in 1765 and reached the Colorado River at Moab, Utah. Expeditions led by three Franciscan missionaries traveled from the Spanish colonial town of Santa Fe, New Mexico, through the Great Basin in 1776. Early in the year, Father Francisco Tomás Hermenegildo Garcés and Juan Bautista de Anza led a party across the very southern tip of the region. Fathers Francisco Atanasio Dominguez and Silvestre Vélez de Escalante also explored the area later in the same year in an unsuccessful effort to find a route from Santa Fe to Monterey, the Spanish capital of Alta California; they crossed the Uinta Basin and the Wasatch Mountains in Utah before returning to Santa Fe. Later explorations in the area established what American explorer John Fremont named the Old Spanish Trail in 1844; the trail extended from Santa Fe to Los Angeles, crossed the southern Great Basin through Utah and Nevada, and was used regularly from the 1820s into the 1850s as a trade route. Russian, Spanish, and English exploration took place along the Pacific coast as early as the 1700s. From 1804 to 1806, the American government expedition led by Meriwether Lewis and William Clark traveled from St. Louis on the Mississippi River to their winter camp at Fort Clatsop on the Oregon Pacific coast and left traces on the Plateau. They include the sites of Camp Disappointment, the northernmost Lewis and Clark campsite, now on the Blackfeet Reservation in Montana; the Lolo Trail in the Bitterroot Mountains of Montana and Idaho; and sites along the Columbia River.

FUR TRADE

The fur trade played a key role in the earliest exploration and historical settlement of the region. Fur trade settlements were the early focus of archaeological studies on the Plateau. Major excavations took place at Fort George and Fort Dunvegan in Alberta and at Fort St. James and Fort Langley in British Columbia; all involved restorations and reconstructions for public interpretation. John Jacob Astor's Pacific Fur Company established the fur trading post of Fort Astoria on the Oregon coast, which became the earliest American settlement in the Pacific Northwest, in 1811. In 1825 the Hudson's Bay Company established an administrative post and supply depot at Fort Vancouver in 1825. Fort Vancouver served as the principal distribution center for commodities to fur trade, agricultural, and industrial settlements throughout the Pacific Northwest from 1829 to 1849; the post received its last shipment of goods from England in 1853. The fort served as the first terminus of the Oregon Trail; it is now a National Historic Site managed by the National Park Service. The U.S. Army established another Fort Vancouver (later renamed Vancouver Barracks) just north of the trading post in 1849 as the first American military post in the Pacific Northwest and continued operations there until the twentieth century. In 1833 the Hudson's Bay Company established Fort Nisqually as the first European settlement on Puget Sound, which emerged as a principal trading center in the Pacific Northwest and later became a large agricultural enterprise; now it is the site of a living history museum in Tacoma, Washington. The company established Fort Boise in 1834 in southwestern Idaho and in 1837 acquired Fort Hall 300 hundred miles to the east. During the same time period, the Hudson's Bay Company sent out trapping brigades from Fort Vancouver down the "Siskiyou Trail" into northern California. Fur trappers, first with the American Astoria expedition and then with England's North West Company, traveled through the northern Great Basin in the Snake River area in the 1810s. Trappers for the Rocky Mountain Fur Company worked within the northern Great Basin in the 1820s. Jedediah Smith and Peter Skene Ogden explored the region in the same decade. In 1845 Miles Goodyear established Fort Buenaventura, the first Euro-American settlement in the Great Basin, on the Ogden River; the next year it was purchased by Mormon settlers and eventually renamed Ogden. The fort has been reconstructed and is now a Weber County park.

EMIGRATION AND EARLY HISTORIC SETTLEMENT

Several emigrant trails cross the region and are associated with historical sites such as campsites, trash scatters, graves, and abandoned wagons. They include the famous Oregon-California Trail, which opened in 1841 with the Bartleson-Bidwell party, and subsidiaries such as the Applegate-Lassen Trail in the northern Great Basin. More than 300,000 people used the trail network between 1841 and 1865. Perhaps the best known of these is the Donner party, whose journey ended in tragedy near Truckee, California, in the Sierra Nevada Mountains during the winter of 1846–1847. Archaeological research on the Donner party has been conducted at the sites of the two winter camps in the mountains and at a site of wagons abandoned by the party in the Great Salt Lake Desert.

Another famous emigrant party entering the Great Basin on the Oregon-California Trail were the Mormons (members of the Church of Jesus Christ of Latter-Day Saints), the first Euro-American group to intentionally establish settlements in the Great Basin. Brigham Young led the pioneer party into the Great Salt Lake valley in 1847, along a trail through the Wasatch Mountains created the year before by the Donner party, and founded the settlement of Salt Lake City. By 1850 the Mormon community had established cooperative farm-villages at Bountiful, Ogden, Tooele, Provo, and Manti in what is now the state of Utah. Early Mormon settlements typically were forts with log cabins laid out in a square. Planned settlements of farmers and tradesmen were patterned after Joseph Smith's "City of Zion," with grid layout, central residential area, and farmsteads on the periphery. Mormon settlers established about 500 settlements in Utah and neighboring states by 1900. In Nevada the settlements included Genoa in Carson Valley, Franktown in Washoe Valley, Mormon Fort in Las Vegas Valley, and St. Joseph in Moapa Valley, a site of extensive archaeological research. Elsewhere in the region, Mormon settlers established a farming settlement at Franklin, the earliest historical townsite in Idaho, in northern Cache Valley in the spring of 1860. Some buildings remain standing, including the Hatch House and Franklin Cooperative Mercantile Building. And in Montana, Mormons established a settlement at Lemhi Pass, one of the Lewis and Clark campsites, in 1855 and named it Fort Limhi; it is now a National Historic Landmark just west of Dillon.

The rapid increase of mining in the 1860s and 1870s throughout the Great Basin and Plateau greatly increased military hostilities between whites and Indians in the region, resulting in the establishment of military forts, reservations, and Indian agencies throughout the region. Archaeological studies have taken place at many sites of military forts, including Fort Churchill in Nevada and Fort Simcoe in the Washington Cascades, and have involved restorations and reconstructions. In western Canada archaeological excavations of North West Mounted Police posts flourished in the 1970s and also involved numerous restorations and reconstructions. Historic settlements on Indian reservations are found at Fort McDermitt, Fort Hall, Colville, Spokane, Coeur d'Alene, Flathead, Yakama, Nez Perce, Warm Springs, and Klamath.

INDUSTRIAL SITES

Many historical sites throughout the Great Basin and Plateau are associated with extractive industries, especially the mining of metals such as gold, silver, and copper, but also the mining or harvesting of coal, salt, borax, and wood. Industrial landscapes and sites in the region are marked by archaeological and architectural remnants of underground and open-pit lode and placer mines, mine waste rock dumps, placer tailings, mine shafts and adits, mill tailings, dredges and hydraulic operations, hoisting works, work

camps and towns, smelters and concentration mills, tramways, hoisting works, charcoal kilns, and sawmills. Several gold and silver mining "rushes" with population booms and busts in isolated geographical islands took place during the nineteenth and the early twentieth centuries. The California gold rush in 1849, while mostly outside the region, marked the beginning of a series of mining rushes into the Plateau and the Great Basin that continued until the first decade of the 1900s. On the Plateau, mining rushes took place in British Columbia, first in 1858–1860 on the Fraser River and then in 1862 in the Cariboo region. A mining settlement system centered on the boomtown of Barkerville emerged and has been the site of extensive archaeological research. Another gold rush took place in the Rocky Mountains, beginning in 1862 with the discovery of placer gold at Bannack in southwestern Montana and followed in 1863 by another discovery in Alder Gulch; the ensuing rush and mining settlement system centered on the boomtown of Virginia City, Montana. Southern Idaho witnessed another gold rush in the 1860s and became the precious metals mining center of the area for the next two decades. It began in the Clearwater region and expanded to the Florence Basin and the Boise Basin. Pierce is a townsite in the Clearwater River area that dates to late 1860–early 1861 and is associated with earliest gold rush to the Nez Perce Reservation; the Pierce courthouse remains standing at the site. Silver City in Idaho's Owyhee Mountains was founded in 1863 and boomed shortly thereafter as a silver mining district second in production only to Nevada's Comstock Lode in the 1860s and 1870s. Elsewhere on the Plateau, archaeological studies have been done on Chinese placer mining sites in the Oregon Siskiyou Mountains.

Archaeological sites associated with extractive industries, especially gold and silver mining, also abound in the Great Basin. Mormon emigrants traveling on the California Trail discovered placer gold on the Carson River near the present town of Dayton, Nevada, in 1850 and stimulated prospecting in the nearby Virginia Range, which led to the discovery of the famous Comstock Lode in 1859. The mining camp that followed in the 1860s centered on the town of Virginia City and grew into an urban corridor that included the neighboring settlements of Gold Hill, Silver City, and Dayton in Gold Canyon. Comstock mining from the 1860s to the early twentieth century left behind an industrial landscape that includes not only the deep hardrock mines of the Virginia Range but also mills and placer mines on the Carson River; sawmills, wood camps, and flumes in the Carson Range and the Lake Tahoe basin; agricultural settlements in the Carson Valley, Washoe Valley, and the Truckee Meadows; and the Virginia and Truckee Railroad, extending from Virginia City to the Central Pacific railhead at Reno. Other gold and silver rushes targeted the Great Basin in the following decades and established mining settlement systems and industrial sites centered on boomtowns or smaller mining camps throughout the area. In Nevada they include the Reese River and Treasure Hill rushes in the 1860s; Osceola, Tuscarora, Pioche, Candelaria, and Eureka in the 1870s and 1880s; and Tonopah and Goldfield in the first decade of the twentieth century. Elsewhere, gold and silver mining in Utah began in 1863 and established extensive mining settlement systems and industrial sites in the 1870s and 1880s at Stockton, Ophir, Mercur, Park City, Frisco, Tintic, and Silver Reef.

Mining of other metals and minerals also left behind a significant industrial landscape in the Great Basin and Plateau. Copper mining was a key player in the region. The settlement of Butte in southwestern Montana emerged in the 1880s as the center of copper mining in the region and continued to be one throughout the twentieth century. Daniel Jackling created the first open-pit copper mine in Utah's Bingham Canyon in the early 1900s. The Guggenheim family and the Nevada Consolidated Copper Company, and later the Kennecott Copper Company, established a large open-pit copper mining and smelting operation close to Ely, Nevada, in the first decade of the 1900s and it continued until the 1970s. Their operation included the company towns of McGill, Ruth, and Kimberly; outlying satellite settlements such as Reipetown and Steptoe City; open-pit mines and smelters; and railroads. Coal mining was another significant industrial activity in some parts of the Great Basin and Plateau. In Utah coal mining and company towns appeared in Carbon County in the early 1900s. Archaeological studies of coal mining towns in the Rocky Mountains have taken place in southwestern Alberta at the sites of Lille, Passburg, and Pocohantas. The wood industry is also well represented by archaeological sites in the region. They include the archaeological and architectural remains of sawmills, flumes, work camps, oxen trails and railroads, and tramways. Wood industry sites also include kilns used to produce charcoal; numerous examples are found in southwestern Montana and at the site of the Ward charcoal ovens, near Ely, Nevada.

TRANSPORTATION AND COMMUNICATION NETWORKS

Many historic period sites in the Great Basin and Plateau reflect transportation and communication networks associated with overland stage and freight, pony express, railroad, and telegraph operations. The earliest overland stage and freight lines in the region appeared in the 1850s and lasted until the early 1900s. John Butterfield and Ben Holladay established the earliest stage operations in the region in the early 1860s; Wells Fargo acquired Holladay's operation in 1866 and was the key player afterward. Rock Creek Station in south central Idaho, which was a campsite on the Oregon Trail in the 1840s, is a good example; Ben Holladay constructed a stage station at the site in the 1860s, and a settlement emerged nearby as a social and transportation service center. Several buildings remain standing, including the Rock Creek Store, China House, and Stricker Home. Railroads

were constructed in the region from the late 1860s to the first decade of the twentieth century and are associated with a great variety of archaeological sites, which include construction and section camps, track systems, water towers, bridges, and engine houses. Among others, the railroads include the Central Pacific and Union Pacific, which crossed the region after joining at Promontory Summit, Utah, on May 10, 1869; the Great Northern, Montana, and Utah and Northern Pacific; the Carson and Colorado and Virginia and Truckee; and the Oregon Short Line. The Pony Express delivered mail along the "Central Overland" route, which crossed Utah and Nevada, in 1860–1861; several pony express sites with still-standing buildings and structures have been excavated and can be visited (e.g., Cold Springs and Sand Springs in Nevada). Other communication systems are represented in the archaeological record of the historic period. They include sites of the Transcontinental Telegraph system, which was completed in 1861, and the Deseret Telegraph, which connected Salt Lake City with outlying Mormon settlements in the 1860s.

AGRICULTURE AND RANCHING

Many historic settlements in the region reflect agriculture and ranching. Mormon settlers established farm-villages and other agricultural settlements as early as the late 1840s. Homesteading of public lands after 1862, and especially during the first two decades of the twentieth century, greatly increased farming activity. The construction of federal irrigation projects, such as the Newlands Project in western Nevada in the early 1900s, further contributed to the expansion of farmsteads. Cattle ranching expanded throughout the Great Basin and the Plateau in the last half of the nineteenth century. Ranches tended to be distributed on the level floors of inland basins near water sources such as springs and streams. Native Americans often worked as ranch hands and lived in houses and settlements on the ranches.

Further Reading: Adams, William H., *Silcott, Washington: Ethnoarchaeology of a Rural American Community*, Laboratory of Anthropology Reports of Investigation, No. 54 (Pullman: Washington State University, 1977); Dixon, Kelly, *Boomtown Saloons: Archaeology and History in Virginia City* (Reno: University of Nevada Press, 2005); Hardesty, Donald L., "Archaeology and the Chinese Experience in Nevada," in *Ethnic Oasis: The Chinese in the Black Hills*, edited by Liping Zhu and Rose Estep Fosha (Pierre: South Dakota State Historical Society Press, 2004), 69–85; Hardesty, Donald L., *The Archaeology of the Donner Party* (Reno: University of Nevada Press, 2006); Hattori, Eugene M., *Northern Paiutes on the Comstock: Archaeology and Ethnohistory of an American Indian Population in Virginia City, Nevada*, Occasional Paper No. 2 (Carson City: Nevada State Museum, 1975); Malouf, Carling, and John M. Findlay, "Euro-American Impact before 1870," in *Handbook of North American Indians*, Vol. 11: *Great Basin*, edited by Warren d'Azevedo (Washington, DC: Smithsonian Institution, 1986), 499–516.

Donald L. Hardesty

DEATH VALLEY NATIONAL PARK

Death Valley, Eastern California and Nevada
Ancient and Historic Sites in Death Valley National Park

Death Valley National Park covers nearly 3.4 million acres, and ranges in elevation from 282 feet below sea level at Badwater to 11,000 feet above sea level at the summit of Telescope Peak. This range in elevation gives rise to a widely varying landscape, and the Native peoples here in the past lived a relatively nomadic existence. There is therefore little in the way of built architecture, and the artifacts archaeologists find at prehistoric sites are more in keeping with those used by hunters and gatherers than by people who live sedentary lives. The climate and remoteness of the valley had a significant effect on people living there in historic times as well. Because mining figures prominently in the more recent history of the valley, success in overcoming obstacles associated with transportation, funding, and supply had almost as much to do with the success of different mining operations as did the extent of the mineral wealth in any claim.

THE PREHISTORIC PERIOD

Some of the earliest archaeological sites date to 7000–5000 BC, a time when the waters of Lake Manly covered a portion of the valley floor. Early inhabitants camped along the lake shore, but also stayed near springs and other sources of water. Features at the sites tend to be hearths, stacked-rock hunting blinds, cleared circles, and rock mounds. Few of these ancient sites have been found within the boundaries of the park, and all known examples are below 5,000 feet in elevation, an indicator that the cooler temperatures of the time made the valley bottom more hospitable year-round compared with conditions now.

Between 5,000 and 1,500 years ago, temperatures warmed and the inland lakes in the region dried up. As the environment changed, people altered the way they made their living off the land. Archaeologists find places where people lived in rockshelters and on mesas, as well as quarries where the raw material to make chipped-stone tools was gathered.

Still later, stones used for grinding (called metates and manos) and mashing (stone pestles used with mortars of stone or wood) became common. These were used to process plant foods such as grass seeds, mesquite pods, and pinyon nuts. At the same time, tools such as choppers and scrapers, used for processing large game such as desert bighorn sheep, were used less frequently than in the past. Archaeologists find campsites with artifact scatters; cleared circles of different sizes that are signs of round brush shelters, storage caches, sweat lodges, and hearths; rock mounds; and rock alignments in geometric and abstract shapes. Evidence of trade with Ancestral Puebloan (also known as Anasazi) people from the Southwest has been found in the form of pieces of Southwestern ceramics.

By the time Euro-Americans first came to the area in 1849, Native peoples living in Death Valley had started making pottery and coiled and twined baskets that served as water jugs, burden baskets, and winnowing trays. They made increasing use of dunefields in the valley bottom for camping and gathering mesquite pods. Glass beads arrived in the area by trade before actual Euro-American people did; the beads were made in Italy and were blue, white and blue, red and white, and yellow.

Remains of the prehistoric inhabitants of the park are scanty, since most shelters were simple and made of brush, and have not survived to the present. Other sites consist simply of scatters of artifacts or a few circles of stone, making it challenging to imagine what the campsites were like. Few are open to the public. One exception is a group of prehistoric petroglyphs near a spring in Titus Canyon, which is open to high-clearance vehicles.

THE HISTORIC PERIOD

Three different indigenous groups were living in Death Valley in the 1800s and early 1900s. The part of the valley southeast of Furnace Creek was used by Southern Paiute, the Kawaiisu occupied the extreme south end of the valley and the southern end of the Panamint Range, and the Shoshone lived in the northern part of the valley and the Cottonwood and Grapevine mountains. Members of the modern Timbisha tribe are considered the descendants of the Shoshone; a group of them still live at Furnace Creek. All three groups participated in active trade with neighbors in surrounding territories.

While each group spoke a language slightly different from the others, they all engaged in similar subsistence practices and settlement patterns, and had similar social structures. Groups supported themselves by hunting and gathering a wide range of animals and plants, following a seasonal round and moving to different areas as different resources became available. As contact with Euro-Americans increased, however, some Native Americans chose to work as day laborers or engage in small-scale horticulture, growing crops to sell. Some worked as ranch hands at Greenland Ranch, as laborers for Harmony and Eagle Borax Works, as woodcutters for the Wildrose charcoal kilns, as guides or scouts for miners, as laborers for the construction of Scotty's Castle, and in the

A cluster of cleared stone circles are all that remain of two brush shelters and a hearth from prehistoric times.   [Emily J. Brown]

mines. Though somewhat difficult to reach, the remains of Hungry Bill's Ranch in Johnson Canyon provide visitors with an experience of a historic native farm.

The earliest Euro-American use of the area was in the south of the park, as groups of traders, trappers, and horse thieves used routes there as an alternative to the Old Spanish Trail. One of these routes was taken by groups of 49ers on their way west from Salt Lake City to the Sierra Nevada Mountains, and it was one such group that gave the valley its name, despite the fact that only one of their party actually perished there. Some 49ers noted ore on their way through the valley, and these vague recollections gave rise to fables of mineral deposits of unimaginable value, such as the Lost Breyfogle Mine and the Gunsight Lode. Such tales inspired many prospecting expeditions throughout Death Valley and the surrounding areas once the search for mineral wealth

spread beyond the Sierra Nevada Mountains, though none of the subjects of such legends were ever definitively relocated. Early miners exploited the valley's deposits of gold, antimony, copper, lead, zinc, silver, and tungsten.

While there are thousands of prospecting pits and mine sites within the park, few were the sources of true financial success on the part of the owners and investors. The Keane Wonder Mine, on the west slope of the Funeral Mountains, is one exception. The remains of the mill are open to visitors, who can also hike up to the mines above. Leadfield, in contrast, was the site of a classic boom and bust town that lasted only two years. The story of Leadfield is replete with allegations of fraud and slander, and outrageous promotional devices. The townsite is along the scenic Titus Canyon drive in the northeast part of the park, and can be reached with a high-clearance vehicle.

An example of the historic cabins found at some of the mine sites in the park. Many miners slept in tents, but wooden cabins were built at the more successful mining operations.   [Emily J. Brown]

While many miners lived in the boomtowns that sprang up near successful strikes of ore and worked in mines owned by more wealthy investors, others chose to live and work alone. Some, such as Pete Aguereberry, spent much of their lives working independently on their own claims. Aguereberry's cabin and his Eureka Mine can be seen from the road to the Aguereberry Point overlook off the road through Emigrant Canyon in the Panamint Mountains.

As more infrastructure in the form of roads and railroads was built in the region, bulkier minerals such as borax, salt, and talc became viable business ventures. Transportation out of the valley to the nearest railroad was still challenging, however. The twenty-mule team wagons used to haul Death Valley's borax are one well-known example of a creative solution to this problem. One of the wagon trains is on display just outside Furnace Creek at the site of the Harmony Borax Works. Eagle Borax Works was the site of the first commercial borax operation in the Death Valley, and the site can be visited via the West Side Road.

Despite such efforts, all but the most successful attempts at mining in the area petered out by the late 1920s, and some entrepreneurs in the region turned to tourism. The same railroad lines that supported the mining industry brought tourists to the area. Visitors were able to stay at Stovepipe Wells and Furnace Creek, and Death Valley was established as a National Monument in 1933. The monument was host to groups of Civilian Conservation Corps workers during the Great Depression. These men graded roads and built buildings, trails, and an airstrip. Some examples of historic CCC-built facilities can be seen at Texas Springs Campground and the old ranger station on Highway 190 between Stovepipe Wells and Towne Pass.

Further Reading: Greene, Linda, and John Latschar, *A History of Mining in Death Valley National Monument*, Vol. I, Pts. I and II (Denver: National Park Service, 1981); Lingenfelter, Richard E., *Death Valley and the Amargosa: A Land of Illusion* (Berkeley: University of California Press, 1989); Stewart, Julian H., "Linguistic Distributions and Political Groups of the Great Basin Shoshoneans," *American Anthropologist* n.s. 39 (October–December 1937): 625–634; Wallace, William J., *Death Valley National Monument's Prehistoric Past: An Archaeological Overview* (Tucson, AZ: National Park Service, 1977).

Emily J. Brown

THE WILLOW SPRING SITE

Red Rock Canyon National Conservation Area, Southeastern Nevada

Adaptations to an Arid Environment, Pictographs and Petroglyphs

In 1990 congress established the Red Rock Canyon National Conservation Area near Las Vegas to conserve the spectacular landscape of the Keystone Thrust, a landform that is generally referred to as the Red Rock Escarpment. Included in this protected area, in addition to its extraordinarily colorful geologic sandstone formations, were a large number of archaeological sites, among them the Willow Spring site.

When viewed from its rim, Willow Spring, a thousand feet below, seems a fertile haven of life. This riparian spring environment attracted deer, small mammals, and in the higher reaches desert bighorn sheep. Aside from its use for hunting, the archaeological evidence indicates the site was occupied during late spring, when yucca could be harvested, as well as during the fall, when pinyon nut levels were high. In an arid environment that has the characteristics of the Colorado Plateau, Mojave Desert, and Great Basin, where food resources were patchy and subject to cycles of plenty and scarcity, it is hardly surprising that this site has given shelter and sustenance to human beings for over a thousand years, perhaps longer.

The Willow Spring site was first recorded at the relative late date of 1939, while Dr. Mark Harrington was director of the Civilian Conservation Corps excavations at Boulder Dam. This rugged and inhospitable region was penetrated by a few white explorers, pioneers, surveyors, and miners and was left largely unsettled until recent times. Subsequently, no further archaeological research was carried out until the 1970s, when a number of major archaeological surveys of the Red Rock area were completed. These surveys revealed the presence of numerous sites in many of the shallow rock alcoves in the sandstone cliffs that facilitated habitation, possibly from about 3000 BC to the ethnographic present. Recorded sites included the adjoining Lost Creek site, which, like Willow Spring, has roasting pits, rock art, rockshelters, and perhaps the remains of brush structures that were constructed in the shaded, protected canyon. Despite recent disturbances, small-site complexes like Willow Spring and Lost Creek have survived in relatively good condition and provide important information on the settlement and subsistence strategies of the area's prehistoric occupants. Considered together, the Lost Creek and Willow Spring sites are one of the best and most accessible examples of small-site complexes in the region.

Regular use of Willow Spring may have begun as early as 5,000 years ago. The earliest artifact reported in the Red Rock area, a Gypsum Cave–like projectile point, was found nearby at Red Springs and suggests early lakeshore dwellers from the Death Valley area and Archaic nomadic groups from the east visited the Red Rock area. Though no direct evidence of this Late Archaic presence has been found yet at the Willow Spring site, certainly beginning around AD 900 Ancestral Puebloans and Paiutes camped in the canyon.

Artifacts found during surveys and limited excavations indicate all of the area's inhabitants practiced a lifestyle that emphasized simple opportunistic horticulture during good years, with more hunting and gathering when crops were sparse. Even where farming economies did take hold in the major river valleys to the east, everyone relied heavily on the game and wild plant foods of the Red Rock and Las Vegas valley. The dispersed small rock mounds and sheer number of large roasting pits near well-watered areas attest to seasonal movements that coincided with crop cultivation and food processing. Not unlike similar forms of horticulture found in the Southwest, these rock mounds were constructed around many plant species, particularly agaves and yuccas, to encourage growth by keeping the ground moist. Plants that also provided nutrition to people included the seeds from Indian rice-grass and members of the chenopod family, mesquite and screwbean pods, and scrub oak acorns.

The roasting pits were peculiar to the region, however. These were circular pits dug several feet into the ground, where flensed agave bulbs were placed below a fire and limestone rocks. These rocks were used as heat conductors because they contain trapped water vapor. But after they burned they no longer functioned efficiently. As a result, each time new foods were roasted, fresh limestone was required. With repeated use, the discarded rock around the pit could build up to over 10 to 15 feet in diameter and several feet high.

Although the Willow Spring site is best known for its pictograph panel of five human handprints, which are rare in the area, the site has six roasting pits, which are textbook examples of the roasting pits in southern Nevada. These features demonstrate the use of the site over many generations, enough to build up associated middens (trash mounds) with depths over 2 to 3 feet. Ceramic types from the middens include brownwares, both plain and corrugated, and decorative wares (black on white), demonstrating that Ancestral Puebloan peoples entered the area from the east between 1,000 and 1,500 years ago, as did Paiute people from the upper Colorado River. Curiously, no diagnostic artifacts attributable to the Patayan people from the Arizona Strip area, known to have visited the Las Vegas Valley, have been found. These were contemporaneous archaeological cultures. But the artifactual remains suggest that almost exclusively Paiutes and Ancestral Puebloans (also known as Anasazi) used the Willow Spring site, possibly in a symbiotic relationship. This pattern continued until the general Ancestral Puebloan abandonment of the region around AD 1150, presumably after which the Paiute people intensively exploited the resources of the canyon.

These Ancestral Puebloans were related to the communities that lived to the east along the Muddy and Virgin rivers. They were a ceramic-making, agricultural people who took advantage of the naturally occurring resources in the Las Vegas valley and the surrounding mountains to relieve population pressure in the Muddy and Virgin river valleys and control trade to the east and west. It is believed that the Virgin River Ancestral Puebloans traded turquoise, salt, cotton, Pacific Ocean shell, and other goods with people in California, and as far east as Chaco Canyon in New Mexico. Their diagnostic artifacts include grayware, black-on-white ceramics, Rose Spring projectile points, generalized cutting/scraping tools, and grinding implements.

It is unclear whether Ancestral Puebloans and Paiutes actually lived side by side in the Las Vegas valley area. The origins of the Paiute are uncertain, and most theories fall into one of two camps. Some believe the Paiute, a Numic-speaking people, originated in southern California and migrated north and east from their homeland about 1,000 years ago. Other archaeologists believe that the Paiute are descendants of Pinto-Gypsum Archaic inhabitants of the region who interacted with the Virgin River Ancestral Puebloans and the Patayan before the region was abandoned.

This controversy is rooted in a major problem that underscores research in the region. A substantial portion of the archaeological record derives from observations of surface artifacts and features, many which are difficult to date due to a lack of diagnostic artifacts, as well as stratigraphically mixed radiocarbon dates that seem to conflict with the temporal placement of associated datable artifacts. Nonetheless, it is apparent the Paiute were horticulturalists, at least on a part-time basis, who preserved a highly successful subsistence strategy that emphasized wild resources. They made brownware ceramics and crafted Desert Side-notch style projectile points, and were the earliest people that Euro-American explorers and settlers encountered when they entered southern Nevada.

Whether Paiute culture emerged from an Archaic base adopting many Southwestern traits from the Ancestral Puebloan region of the Southwest, or migrated from their homeland as Numic-speakers expanded from the west, remains unresolved. Many of the most significant questions about the region relate to research that may be conducted in the Red Rock area, such as defining the chronology in terms of whether there was use and occupation of the area as early as 3000 BC, and whether exploitation was indeed confined to the Ancestral Puebloans and Paiutes. Because there are few instances where reliable radiocarbon dates have demonstrated an overlap between Rose Spring and Desert Side-notched projectile points, a date of about AD 1100 is used as an approximate beginning date for Paiute use of the Red Rock area.

It has been reported that an avocational archaeologist partially excavated the site in the 1960s. Later in the decade the site was incorporated into a picnic area. Two roasting pits on the west part of the site were nearly leveled for picnic tables and an outdoor toilet was placed in another roasting pit. Attempts to proactively manage the intense recreational use of the Willow Spring site have been relatively successful. As a result of recreational climbing near the shelter handprints, cactus was planted at the base of the pictograph panel and a barrier fence was constructed in front of the shelter and the large roasting pit. Defacement from rock climbing stopped in the area. Current efforts are under way to connect the various elements of the site complex, perhaps by boardwalk, and to turn the site into an interpretive exhibit-in-place. Many of the most significant questions about the region may be closely tied to research, both archaeological and environmental, that will be conducted before the development of this infrastructure.

The Red Rock Canyon National Conservation Area was set aside as a recreational area and geologic preserve. Administered by the Bureau of Land Management, it is located about 15 miles west of Las Vegas on State Highway 159. Within the

Conservation Area a 13-mile paved scenic loop leads to Willow Spring, where the Willow Spring site can be reached easily by foot. The Lost Creek trail begins at the Willow Spring parking area and terminates at the Lost Creek parking area, about a mile from Willow Spring. A short distance from Willow Spring on the Lost Creek trail is the Petroglyph Site, which also has rock art dating probably from AD 900 to 1200. Together these three sites should be viewed as part of the same small-site complex, even though they were not originally recorded this way. Red Spring and Brownstone Canyon are other small-site complexes located in the immediate vicinity and can be visited with a little time and effort. None of these sites is actively interpreted. Volunteers and staff at the visitors' center can give specific directions to any of these areas and will no doubt caution visitors regarding the fragility of and need to preserve these sites for the future.

Further Reading: Beck, Charlotte, ed., *Models for the Millennium: Great Basin Anthropology Today* (Salt Lake City: University of Utah Press 1999); Hester, Thomas R., *Chronological Ordering of Great Basin Prehistory* (Berkeley: University of California, 1973); Rafferty, Kevin, *Cultural Resources Overview of the Las Vegas Valley*, Nevada BLM Cultural Resource Publications, Technical Report No. 13 (1984), www.nv.blm.gov/cultural/reports/reports.htm; Warren, Claude N., "Pinto Points and Problems in Mojave Desert Archaeology," in *Anthropological Papers in Memory of Earl H. Swanson, Jr.*, edited by L. B. Harten, C. N. Warren, and D. R. Tuohy (Pocatello: Idaho State Museum of Natural History, 1980), 67–76.

Mark A. Boatwright

VALLEY OF FIRE, GRAPEVINE WASH, GYPSUM CAVE, AND LAKE MEAD NATIONAL RECREATION AREA

Near Las Vegas, Southeastern Nevada
Archaeological Sites in the Las Vegas Area

Las Vegas is near the western limit of the Colorado River drainage basin. In the 1930s Boulder Dam (now known as Hoover Dam) was built across the narrows in Black Canyon gorge, impounding the river and forming Lake Mead. Two more dams form smaller lakes downstream and diminish the river to a trickle by the time it reaches the Gulf of California, 200 miles to the south.

A variety of cultures have occupied southern Nevada at different periods in the past, resulting in an archaeological record that varies from mixed deposits at re-occupied sites, to single-period sites with blended characteristics of diverse groups, to distinct and discrete sites resulting from brief use by only one group. Prior to 1,500 years ago, local prehistoric practices and sites in southern Nevada were similar to those of Archaic hunter-gatherers throughout the Great Basin and Mojave Desert. Beginning around 1,800 years ago, this became the northwest frontier of ancestral Puebloan groups, agriculturalists living on the only permanent waterways in the area. Prolonged drought was a significant cause of the Puebloan retraction around 800 years ago. Far more subtle Patayan influences originating from western Arizona and the lower Colorado River appeared locally beginning 1,500 years ago and persisting until about 500 years ago. The Patayan practiced floodplain farming when adjacent to the Colorado River, but employed conventional hunting and gathering practices when in adjacent desert settings. Buffware pottery and medium to small, triangular arrow tips (Saratoga Spring and Cottonwood) are ascribed to these ancestral Yuman people. Numic-speaking Southern Paiute reside here today. Brownware pottery and Desert Side-notched arrow tips, which first appeared here around 600 years ago, are associated with the ancestral Paiute.

Much of the local tool stone throughout prehistory was procured from chert nodules eroding from Permian gray limestone formations. Geological islands of younger, Jurassic period Aztec sandstone provided a great number of small rockshelters and overhangs that were inhabited by prehistoric populations. Natural basins (*tenajas*) in the sandstone collect rainfall and were an important, albeit short-lived and episodic, source of water in the vast, dry landscape that extends out from the few flowing streams. Rock art tends to occur in the red rock formations at places such as Valley of Fire

GYPSUM CAVE

Gypsum Cave, 6 miles east of Las Vegas, is a five-chambered solution cave that extends 50 meters into the side of a limestone mountain. For a twelve-month period between January 1930 and 1931, Mark R. Harrington of the Southwest Museum, assisted by a small crew of Native Americans, thoroughly dug over most of the cave, yielding an extraordinary

An example of Great Basin Rectilinear style petroglyphs, including rectangular, shield-like patterns and vertical lines of diamonds that typify the petroglyphs found in Grapevine Canyon. [Amy J. Gilreath]

collection of terminal Pleistocene paleontological specimens and Holocene archaeological remains. Harrington reported Gypsum Cave as a location where "so many finds, scattered about the cave under widely varying conditions" proved that now-extinct mammals (especially ground sloth) and humans once co-existed in the Great Basin. In 1970 radiocarbon dating of wooden *atl atl* shaft parts from the cave established that the archaeological material and the Pleistocene megafauna were not contemporaneous, and so not genuinely associated. The wooden hunting gear is generally 2,000 to 4,000 years old, while the beds of sloth dung and remains of extinct camels, horses, and sloth are now firmly dated at more than 14,000 years old.

When Harrington reported his findings, his primary concern was with one item: possible evidence for "early man" in North America. Though the "early" age of the site has since been discredited, Harrington was in the vanguard, using interdisciplinary scientific studies to interpret the cave and its deposits. He gave considerable attention to stratigraphy and the vertical distribution of tools within the different strata, and he collaborated with paleontologists and botanists to identify the animal and plant remains preserved in the dry cave.

Re-excavation of Room 1, directed in 2004 by geoarchaeologist Dr. D. Craig Young of Far Western Anthropological Research Group, reaffirmed the presence of 1.8 meters of intact, vertically stratified deposits more than 13,000 years old at the bottom, and 1,000 years old at the top. The strata containing discarded tools and other detritus from human occupation were confined to the upper 0.7 meters, dating to less than 5,000 years old.

LAKE MEAD NATIONAL RECREATION AREA

From 1935 to 1941, the rising waters of Lake Mead, especially the Overton Arm, inundated most Virgin Anasazi (also known as Ancestral Puebloan) villages and field camps along the Virgin and Muddy rivers. Most studies of affiliated sites were prompted by dam construction. Consequently, most information about this culture is a product of 1930s research, as are the most impressive collections of pottery, milling tools, and jewelry, in museums such as the state-run Lost City Museum in Overton.

A few pit house villages have been identified and studied, such as the Black Dog Mesa site complex near Moapa, which attests to a Basketmaker presence (2,000 to 1,200 years ago). The number of sites and presumably the population level of Ancestral Puebloans increased gradually until 1,050 years ago, when a sudden spurt occurred during the Pueblo II period (1,000 to 800 years ago). At this peak, corn, beans, squash, and cotton were under cultivation along the floodplains of the Virgin and Muddy rivers, the only ones with year-round flows. By this time, villages had assumed a fairly regular layout, with a row of three to five surface storage units built in an arching or rectangular row partly encircling a courtyard, and a few habitation rooms set nearby.

These courtyard units were placed on the lip of the high terraces overlooking the adjacent floodplain and fields. In contrast to their relatives' villages to the east and southeast in Arizona, no kivas are associated with the Virgin Branch settlements.

VALLEY OF FIRE STATE PARK

The rock art pecked into the red sandstone formations that give this park its name provides good evidence of the different cultures that have occupied southern Nevada throughout the past. Each has left its mark on the cliffs, resulting in the designs that a visitor sees today. At Atlatl Rock, the namesake design is a 1.0-meter-long, detailed drawing of the paddleboard used to launch dart-tipped spears, the mainstay hunting weapon used throughout the desert west until 1,500 years ago. More recent designs of human figures, corn or agave stalks, birds, footprints and handprints, lively bighorn sheep, and large, stylized plus signs were made by Virgin Branch Anasazi, who lived and farmed along the few dependable rivers. More recent designs left by ancestors of the Southern Paiute who live here today are also present, most notably in the form of simple, stiff human (stick) figures, smaller bighorn sheep in a perfunctory style, and simple concentric circles. The younger rock art is most evident along the short hike to nearby Mouse's Tank.

GRAPEVINE WASH PETROGLYPHS

The rock art in Grapevine Canyon is stylistically very different from that in the red rock country to the north, further underscoring the diversity of prehistoric people in this region. Instead of the representational designs that characterize the Virgin Branch rock art, rectangular, shield-like patterns and vertical lines of diamonds typify the petroglyphs attributed to the Patayan culture, ancestors of Yuman groups. The Patayan culture inhabited the lower Colorado River and the adjacent desert to the south and west. The distribution of the rock art tradition suggests they occupied the lower desert persistently for perhaps the last 2,000 years.

Further Reading: Fowler, Donald D., and David M. Madsen, "Prehistory of the Southeastern Area," in *Handbook of North American Indians*, Vol. 11: *Great Basin*, edited by Warren L. d'Azevedo (Washington, DC: Smithsonian Institution, 1986), 173–182; Harrington, Mark. R., *Gypsum Cave, Nevada: Report of the Second Sessions Expedition*, Southwest Museum Papers, No. 8 (Los Angeles: Southwest Museum, 1933); Lyneis, Margaret, "The Virgin Anasazi, Far Western Puebloans," *Journal of World Prehistory* 9 (1995): 199–241; Warren, Claude, and Robert H. Crabtree, "Prehistory of the Southwestern Area," in *Handbook of North American Indians*, Vol. 11: *Great Basin*, edited by Warren L. d'Azevedo (Washington, DC: Smithsonian Institution, 1986), 183–193; Whitley, David S., *A Guide to Rock Art Sites, Southern California and Southern Nevada* (Missoula, MO: Mountain Press, 1996).

Amy J. Gilreath

THE TULE SPRINGS SITE

Clark County, Southeastern Nevada
A Chapter in the Historic Search for the Earliest Americans

Finding and dating the earliest evidence for the appearance of people in the New World is an enduring challenge for American archaeology. The Tule Springs site in Clark County has played a significant role in this effort.

In 1933 George Gaylord Simpson of the American Museum of Natural History announced the recovery of a human-made obsidian flake in apparent association with charcoal and remains of extinct horse, bison, and camel recovered from the wall of Tule Spring Wash. This was not long after J. D. Figgins had demonstrated the stratigraphic association of fluted projectile points and extinct bison at Folsom, New Mexico, in 1926. Figgins's discovery firmly established the Pleistocene presence of people in the New World.

In the following years, Mark Raymond Harrington and Ruth DeEtte Simpson of the Southwest Museum, Los Angeles, undertook small-scale explorations at Tule Springs. They found other bone deposits with what looked like charcoal, and some possible tools. Williard F. Libby was pioneering radiocarbon dating, and in 1954 Harrington sent him a sample that combined material from the American Museum of Natural History's locality and a second one excavated by Harrington. The sample dated to older than 23,800 years ago, firmly in Late Pleistocene times. A year later Simpson found a stone tool, a scraper, at a locality with apparent charcoal that was dated even earlier, older than 28,000 years ago.

These tantalizing finds were the basis for the Tule Springs expedition, a four-month, large-scale investigation beginning the fall of 1962. It was a joint venture of the Nevada State Museum and the Southwest Museum under the direction of Richard Shutler. Even now, the project is remarkable for the scale of its exposures and the integrated use of radiocarbon dating. Libby's radiocarbon laboratory at UCLA provided radiocarbon dates with a one-week turnaround.

The Tule Springs archaeological and paleontological locality is a stretch of wash about four-tenths of a mile long, generally east of Tule Springs, now Floyd Lamb State Park. The wash has cut into Late Pleistocene and recent deposits, exposing sediments that range from about 7,000 to more than 40,000 years ago. It was originally known as a paleontological locality for finds of Late Pleistocene mammals weathering out-of the wash channel walls.

The 1962–63 excavations focused on the Late Pleistocene deposits. Huge exposures, 15 feet or more in depth, in 7,000 linear feet of bulldozer trenches opened large areas for investigations. The project was strongly interdisciplinary, with the geological and chronological studies of C. Vance Haynes as its anchor. Paleontological and pollen studies filled out the

picture of the past environments. Archaeologists followed the bulldozers as they carefully cut through the sediments, watching for the appearance of bone, charcoal, or tools. These exposures yielded no further evidence of people in Late Pleistocene times, however.

To understand the claims from the Harrington-Simpson investigations, the project opened new, larger exposures at several localities. Investigators learned that charcoal-like material from the Late Pleistocene deposits was organic material formed in stream channels. Reddish and yellowish iron oxides formed below the channels appeared to be the result of heat, and in cross section with the dark, organic material had given the appearance of fire hearths. This organic material provided good dating of the stream channels but did not reflect human activity. The project also determined that the stone scraper Simpson found had come into secondary association with organic materials dated to 28,000 years ago. The expedition had documented an extensive post-Pleistocene artifact assemblage on the surface of the area. The scraper was part of that assemblage, and it had had been undercut by erosion and rolled down the side of the wash into contact with earlier sediments.

Additional trenches revealed new exposures of terminal Pleistocene deposits. Here the project personnel discovered a stone scraper, five chipped-stone flakes, a piece of modified bone, and a caliche object thought to be a large bead. All these artifacts came from deposits dating 10,000 to 12,000 years ago.

Today, no new sites with evidence for people in the New World prior to 13,500 years ago have been found. The earliest discoveries cluster in the range of 10,000 to 12,500 years ago. The Tule Springs expedition's evaluation of the apparently promising claims for evidence dating 20,000 to 30,000 years ago was an important step in focusing subsequent investigations on this narrower time period.

Further Reading: Floyd Lamb State Park Web site, http://parks. nv.gov/fl.htm; Harrington, Mark Raymond, and Ruth DeEtte Simpson, *Tule Springs, Nevada, with Other Evidences of Pleistocene Man in North America*, Southwest Museum Papers, No. 18 (Los Angeles: Southwest Museum, 1961); Simpson, George G., "A Nevada Fauna of Pleistocene Type and Its Probable Association with Man," *American Museum Novitiates* 667 (1933): 1–10; Waters, Michael R., and Thomas W. Stafford Jr., "Redefining the Age of Clovis: Implications for the Peopling of the Americas," *Science* 315 (2007): 1122–1126; Wormington, H. M., and Dorothy Ellis, *Pleistocene Studies in Southern Nevada*, Nevada State Museum Anthropological Papers, No. 13 (Carson City: Nevada State Museum, 1967).

Margeret M. Lyneis

VIRGIN AND MUDDY RIVER SITES, LOST CITY, AND ZION NATIONAL PARK SITES

Southern Nevada and Southwestern Utah

The Virgin Anasazi of the Far West

Only in the 1920s did we learn that prehistoric Pueblo peoples lived as far west as southern Nevada. Pueblo sites to the east, including the cliff dwellings at Mesa Verde, began to be explored in the late 1800s. The subtler remains in southwest Utah, northwest Arizona, and southern Nevada demonstrate Ancestral Puebloan (also known as Anasazi) occupation beginning just after AD 1 and continuing into the early 1200s. These people are sometimes called the Virgin Anasazi.

Most of this area is low-elevation desert with scant rainfall. Overton, Nevada, at 1,270 feet above sea level, receives less than 4 inches of rainfall in an average year. These farming people were dependent on the waters of the Muddy and Virgin rivers to sustain their crops. The Muddy River originates from warm springs in the upper Moapa valley and flows year-round. The headwaters of the Virgin River are on the Colorado Plateau east of Zion National Park. In spring it carries the runoff from melting snow, and in the late summer monsoonal rains fill it once again.

Early farming was carried out on the rivers' floodplains by Late Basketmaker II people. They lived in pit houses and sometimes constructed slab-lined and grass-lined pits in nearby rockshelters to protect their harvests of maize and squash. The styles of their basketry and sandals are very similar to those make by Basketmaker people to the east, suggesting that settlers from the Colorado Plateau founded the Pueblo occupation of this area.

As elsewhere in the Southwest, two technological changes occurred around AD 500: the addition of the bow and arrow, replacing the *atl atl*; and the beginning of pottery making. Gradually, pit houses gave way to habitation rooms built on the surface of the ground, and attached storage rooms replaced storage cists.

They did not live in villages. Instead, one or several families, probably related, formed residence groups. Their housing included several habitation rooms with hearths, and smaller store rooms typically attached to the habitation rooms in a curve. This small grouping of structures usually formed a courtyard opening to the south. Such residence groups were scattered along the margins of the Muddy and Virgin rivers. Investigations along the Muddy River near Overton and Logandale, Nevada, suggest that these residence groups relocated frequently, perhaps to take advantage of floodplain changes resulting from the changing course of the river and occasional floods. Situated far from the horizontally bedded sandstones of the Colorado Plateau, people along the Muddy and lower Virgin rivers built their homes from adobe, incorporating stone as available, or wattle and daub.

They continued to raise maize and squash, and added beans to their crops. Cotton was also grown. Sites along the Muddy River show that rabbits, desert tortoise, and other small animals provided much of their meat. Along the Virgin River near the Mormon and Virgin mountains, bighorn and deer were also consumed. Gathered foods including mesquite beans and amaranth also supplemented their crops.

The Muddy River people also had access to two special resources. They mined salt near the mouth of the juncture of the Muddy and Virgin rivers, now drowned by Lake Mead. They also mined turquoise near Boulder City.

The residents along the Muddy and Virgin rivers maintained continuing social, economic, and exchange networks with the Anasazi people on the Colorado Plateau. Much of their plain, corrugated, and black-on-white pottery was made by people living north of the western Grand Canyon. Black-on-red and polychrome pottery made in southeastern Utah and northeastern Arizona came to them in smaller quantities. Shell beads from the coast of California and from southern Arizona evidence contacts in other directions.

After the early 1200s residential sites were no longer occupied, and new ones were not built. When Europeans entered the area, it was occupied by Southern Paiutes.

LOST CITY

Residents of Overton, Nevada, first brought southern Nevada's Pueblo sites to the notice of the governor, James Scrugham. He dispatched Mark R. Harrington of the Museum of the American Indian, Heye Foundation, New York, to southern Nevada to examine ruins and Pueblo pottery in 1924. Harrington returned in 1925 and 1926, excavating forty-four residences closely packed on two narrow fingers of a ridge overlooking the floodplain of the Muddy River. His discoveries created great excitement, culminating in a pageant in April 1926. Although Harrington named the site Pueblo Grande de Nevada, the press called it and adjoining sites Lost City. More recently, the particular area of Harrington's 1925–26 excavations has been called Main Ridge.

Main Ridge is the exception to the generally scattered locations of Pueblo residential groups of the area. About 50 to 100 people lived there for a short time, perhaps not much more than a generation, just after AD 1050. Nowhere else are residence groups crowded so close together.

Harrington excavated forty-five burials at Main Ridge, the largest single-site burial population for the region. All had varied quantities of associations, most commonly pottery. Traces of baskets and cotton textiles were found, and some burials included shell or turquoise ornaments, dogs or puppies, and remains of maize, squash, and screwbeans.

Lost City and many other sites were inundated by the rising waters of Lake Mead. The Lost City Museum in Overton, Nevada, features information and artifacts, including pottery, from the prehistoric and historic occupations along the Muddy River, and photographs of the Civilian Conservation Corps excavations prior to the closing of Hoover Dam. Also featured there are a Basketmaker pit house and a Pueblo residential unit reconstructed on original foundations.

RED CLIFFS, UTAH

Late Basketmaker II and Pueblo occupation extended northward up the Virgin River through the St. George Basin in southwestern Utah, into Zion National Park, and on to the Colorado Plateau to the east.

The Red Cliffs site, near Leeds at Red Cliffs BLM Recreation Area, is open for visitation. Exhibited there are slab-lined cists and rooms. Red Cliffs was reused and its structures augmented over a period of 200 years or so, about AD 850.

Red Cliffs is situated on a ridge on the southeast flank of the Pine Valley Mountains at an elevation of about 3,260 feet above sea level. It is at a distance from the Virgin River, but overlooks Leeds Creek, a perennial stream. Its location is not ideal for farming, but gave access to diverse plant and animal resources on the surrounding slopes.

ZION NATIONAL PARK, UTAH

In Zion National Park, Late Basketmaker II occupations occurred in the canyons and its rockshelters. As elsewhere, about AD 500 these people moved to open sites to live in family-size residences. They adopted the bow and arrow, and began making pottery. On the adjoining plateau to the east, rainfall was sometimes sufficient for dry farming. About AD 900 many residential units were established where good soils provided patches of suitable land. Parowan Fremont people, whose settlements were in the vicinity of Cedar City and Parowan, also used the upland part of Zion National Park for hunting.

Further Reading: Harrington, M. R., "A Primitive Pueblo City in Nevada," *American Anthropologist* 29 (1927): 262–277; Lyneis, M. M., *The Main Ridge Community at Lost City: Virgin Anasazi Architecture, Ceramics and Burials*, Anthropological Papers, No. 117 (Salt Lake City: University of Utah, 1992); Lyneis, Margaret M., "The Virgin Anasazi, Far Western Puebloans," *Journal of World Prehistory* 9 (1995): 199–241; Schroeder, A. H., *Archaeology of Zion Park*, Anthropological Papers, No. 22 (Salt Lake City: University of Utah, 1955); Red Cliffs Recreation Site Web site, Utah Bureau of Land Management, www.ut.blm.gov/stgeorge_fo/sgfored_cliffs.html (online April 2007); Zion National Park Web site, www.nps.gov/zion/historyculture/people.htm (online April 2007).

Margaret M. Lyneis

CARSON SINK–STILLWATER MARSH SITES, HUMBOLDT AND LOVELOCK CAVES, AND THE WIZARD'S BEACH SITE

Western Nevada

Ancient Life around Wetlands in the Arid West

CARSON SINK–STILLWATER MARSH SITES

About 60 miles east of Reno, Nevada, lies a vast desert, the Carson Sink. To early pioneers it was the dreaded "forty-mile desert," a hot stretch of sand dunes that claimed many of their wagons and livestock. But just to the east of the California Trail lay many acres of wetlands that provided a livelihood for Native Americans for thousands of years.

Evidence from the nearby Spirit Cave site suggests that these wetlands, known today as Stillwater Marsh, provided food and shelter to people since at least 9,400 years ago. These hunters and gatherers lived in small villages, in temporary homes made from cattail and bulrush reeds. They gathered

duck eggs and freshwater mussels, and the seeds and tubers of cattail, bulrush, sago pondweed, and water plantain. Some families gathered various greens, bulbs, and tubers in the foothills of the Stillwater Mountains that form the eastern edge of the Carson Sink. Beginning about 1,500 years ago, pinyon pine trees appeared in the mountains, and their nuts were gathered in the fall. Prior to that date, men probably hunted rodents and bighorn sheep in the mountains, and jackrabbits and antelope on the valley floor. In the marsh, people used hooks and lines, dip and gill nets, or baskets to harvest various species of fish, a small chub in particular. Archaeologists have recovered some of this equipment, made of cordage and other perishable materials, from surrounding cave sites such as Lovelock, Humboldt, Spirit and Hidden caves.

Until the 1980s, much of what we knew of the archaeology of the Carson Sink and Stillwater Marsh came from these caves. Interestingly, those caves seemed to have been used most intensely prior to 1,500 years ago, and they were used not as living places, but as places to cache gear. This suggests that hunters and gatherers lived near the wetlands, but periodically left for extended periods, caching their gear in the dry caves until their return.

In the 1980s, however, archaeologists conducted surface surveys of the Carson Sink and Stillwater Marsh, as well as of the Stillwater Mountains. During this time, heavy winter precipitation created a 40-mile-wide lake in the northern Carson Sink, and flooded the Stillwater Marsh. As the waters receded in 1986, the waves exposed dozens of archaeological sites and hundreds of human skeletal remains.

The sites uncovered in the marsh area contained many shallow pit houses and pits, and the charred remains of meals, including bulrush and cattail seeds, and the remains of small mammals, especially rodents, mussels, and chub. Missing were any remains of pinyon pine nuts, and rare were the bones of large mammals. Radiocarbon dates on the sites and the burials suggest that most of the occupation dates to 1,400–700 years ago. Pinyon may be missing because it was not present in the adjacent mountains in economically useful quantities, but also because gathering it was not worth the effort given what the marsh had to offer in the fall. The wetland sites began to be used when the Carson Sink contained much water, in part because of increased precipitation, but mostly because the Walker River, which today runs into Walker Lake, appears to have cut a new channel and run for a while into the Carson Sink. Wetlands use by ancient occupants picked up after 1,000 years ago, when the western United States witnessed a severe, centuries-long dry spell known as the Medieval Climatic Warming. This drought did not destroy the marsh, which receives most of its water from snowpack in the Sierra Nevadas, and made it a better foraging alternative than the surrounding desert and uplands. At the same time that the marsh sites were occupied, caves sites in the uplands show a change. Prior to 1,500 years ago, the caves were used by residential groups, for extended times and for a variety of purposes. After this time, when occupation focused on the wetlands, the caves were used primarily as hunting camps. Game was probably killed and butchered in these caves, and dried meat carried the 30 kilometers back to the wetland villages.

The human remains exposed by the flooding were studied with the permission of the local Paiute and Shoshone peoples, and subsequently buried in a subterranean concrete vault on U.S. Fish and Wildlife property. These remains reveal people who lived physically demanding but nutritionally adequate lives. Men did more walking than women; this suggests that men traveled farther afield, into the mountains, to hunt, whereas women did more labor that affected their lower backs, such as carrying children while foraging and processing seeds on grinding stones. They had few cavities, though their teeth were heavily worn from the grit in their diet, and they were of average height. Chemical analysis of the bones shows that some people ate a lot of meat, while others ate less (but this does not represent a simple change over time or a difference between men's and women's diets); as the charred plants remains also suggested, pinyon was not eaten.

Use of the wetlands ceased about 700 years ago, about the time that the Numic peoples, direct ancestors of the Paiute and Shoshone, probably migrated into the region. While there is still some question of when the direct ancestors of the modern Native American inhabitants of the region appeared in the Carson Sink, there is reason to think that they arrived late in prehistory (though well before the Europeans). Basketry made prior to about 700 years ago, is more closely related to California styles than to the style of basketry made by the Paiute and Shoshone at the time of European contact. And genetic analyses of the human remains suggest that those people who were buried in the marsh are more closely related to some California Native Americans, notably speakers of the Penutian language family, than to speakers of the Numic languages.

HUMBOLDT CAVE

Like nearby Lovelock Cave, Humboldt Cave, excavated in the 1930s by Robert Heizer, overlooks the Humboldt Sink. A long, narrow tunnel, this site, like others in the region, was primarily used to cache gear. Some of these caches contain clearly usable tools, such as duck decoys and stone arrow points, while others contain an odd assortment of items, similar to those spare nuts and bolts that we all stash in our home workshops. For example, one cache included a mass of pitch with tule strands, a buckskin wrapping, and cord made from dogbane bark. This cave was also used in the distant past, as suggested by a single radiocarbon date of 1,953 years ago, although one cache contained historic goods, such as flour sacks. A notable aspect of the artifact assemblage is that the site contained some 2,000 pieces of basketry representing more than 400 baskets.

LOVELOCK CAVE

Lovelock Cave was the first major site excavated in the Great Basin. First excavated in 1912, and again in the 1920s and 1960s, Lovelock Cave overlooks the Humboldt Sink, north of the Carson Sink–Stillwater Marsh area. Like other caves in the region, such as Hidden Cave and Humboldt Cave, Lovelock Cave was not used as a camp. Instead, people used it as a safe deposit box, storing tools and food in more than forty basketry-lined pits; the dead were also buried there. For example, someone cached twelve duck decoys, beautifully fabricated from tule reeds and feathers, beneath a false basketry bottom.

Still usable today, they are more than 2,000 years old. Another pit contained 126 dried chub. In another was a basket-maker's tool kit, including two bone awls and a bundle of willow splints, all in a folded fox skin pouch and wrapped in a Canada goose skin. The site was primarily used prior to 1,500 years ago. During this time, people probably used the nearby wetlands in the Humboldt Sink as one stop on a seasonal round, and they stored the things they would not need in the cave.

WIZARD'S BEACH

At this site, which lies on the shores of Pyramid Lake in western Nevada, archaeologists found a set of human skeletal remains some 9,225 years old. Along with similarly ancient human remains, these gave us a new vision of how the Western Hemisphere was first colonized. The earliest human skulls from North and South America often are strikingly different in shape from the skulls of later Native Americans, being longer and narrower, with less pronounced cheekbones and more pronounced noses. These skulls are more similar to those of ancient peoples of southeast Asia, or the ancient inhabitants of Japan (whose descendants today are known as the Ainu). On the other hand, there are also some sites containing ancient skulls that look a lot like those of later Native Americans, and Wizards Beach is one of these. This pattern of variation in human skull shape suggests that the earliest

occupants of the New World may have come in not one, but several migratory waves.

Further Reading: Fowler, Catherine S., *In the Shadow of Fox Peak: An Ethnography of the Cattail-Eater Northern Paiute People of Stillwater Marsh*, Cultural Resource Series, No. 5 (Portland, OR: U.S. Fish and Wildlife Service, Region 1, 1992); Heizer, Robert F., and Alex D. Krieger, *The Archaeology of Humboldt Cave, Churchill County, Nevada*, Publications in American Archaeology and Ethnology, No. 47 (University of California, 1956); Heizer, Robert F., and Lyle K. Napton, *Archaeology and the Prehistoric Great Basin Lacustrine Subsistence Regime as Seen from Lovelock Cave, Nevada*, Contributions of the Archaeological Research Facility, No. 10 (University of California, 1970); Kelly, Robert L., *Prehistory of the Carson Desert and Stillwater Mountains: Environment, Mobility and Subsistence in a Great Basin Wetland*, Anthropological Papers, No. 123 (Salt Lake City: University of Utah, 2001); Larsen, Clark S., and Robert L. Kelly, *Bioarchaeology of the Stillwater Marsh: Prehistoric Human Adaptation in the Western Great Basin*, Anthropological Papers, No. 77 (New York: American Museum of Natural History, 1995); Loud, Llewelyn L., and Mark R. Harrington, *Lovelock Cave*, Publications in American Archaeology and Ethnology, No. 25 (University of California, 1929); Powell, J. F., *The First Americans: Race, Evolution, and the Origin of Native Americans* (Cambridge: Cambridge University Press, 2005); Thomas, David Hurst, *The Archaeology of Hidden Cave, Nevada*, Anthropological Papers, No. 61 (New York: American Museum of Natural History, 1985).

Robert Kelly

THE GRIMES POINT ARCHAEOLOGICAL AREA, HIDDEN CAVE, AND SPIRIT CAVE

Western Nevada

Ancient Rock Art, Cache Caves, and Burials

The levels of ancient Lake Lahontan have fluctuated widely over the last 10,000 years, and the vast desert lake has sometimes dried up completely. During the past several thousand years, Lake Lahontan has reappeared periodically in the Grimes Point area (due east of Fallon, Nevada). The lake and its marshy surrounds attracted a range of plants and animals, and Native Americans visited Grimes Point at least 8,000 years ago.

The Grimes Point Petroglyph Trail preserves hundreds of petroglyphs (ancient rock art) carved on the massive basalt boulders along the margins of Lake Lahontan. The oldest glyphs are conical pits pecked into the boulders, with occasional lines connecting the pits. Glyphs in this ancient style, covered with a smooth, glassy patina, are frequently overlain by a more recent, curvilinear style consisting of circles, snakes, wavy lines, and similar elements.

HIDDEN CAVE

Hidden Cave overlooks the Carson Desert, immediately to the north of Grimes Point. The cave itself was formed about 21,000 years ago, when the waves of rising Lake Lahontan gouged out a huge cavity beneath the tufa-cemented gravels in the Stillwater Range, overlooking central Nevada's now-arid Carson Desert. The floor of this cavern was alternatively flooded and exposed until shortly after 10,000 years ago. About 6,900 years ago, the Mazama volcanic ash (from the catastrophic volcanic explosion that created what is now Crater Lake in Oregon) washed into Hidden Cave. During brief intervals in the Holocene, Native American groups visited Hidden Cave, leaving behind a well-stratified, well-preserved archaeological record. Natural and cultural deposits continued to accumulate inside until the cave entrance became

Crew from the American Museum of Natural History excavating inside Hidden Cave in 1979. Note the quartz-halogen lighting and use of surgical masks to minimize the dust hazard.   [David Hurst Thomas]

choked with a debris cone. Hidden Cave was rediscovered in the 1920s, and teams of archaeologists excavated there in the 1940s, 1950s, and late 1970s.

Even today the entrance to Hidden Cave is difficult to find (hence the name). Anyone who crawls 15 feet inside the cave is engulfed in disorienting darkness; but with suitable lighting the visitor discovers that the cavern is huge, about 150 feet long and 95 feet wide—room enough for three regulation-size basketball courts. The roof rises 20 feet above the cave floor. The interior of Hidden Cave is pitch-black, and walking across the surface raises suffocating clouds of dust.

Working at Hidden Cave was no picnic, as three generations of archaeologists can attest. During the summer of 1940, S.M. Wheeler (archaeologist for the Nevada State Highway Commission) and Georgetta Wheeler conducted the first scientific excavations at Hidden Cave. Occasionally assisted by men from the local Civilian Conservation Corps, the Wheelers usually worked alone through the summer of 1940. Bedeviled by blinding dust inside the cave, the Wheelers breathed through a variety of masks and bandanas. They tried both carbide and electrical lighting to purge the cave's darkness, but no solution was particularly effective.

Ten years passed before geologists Roger Morrison arranged for two University of California graduate students, Gordon Grosscup and Norman Linnaeus Roust, to resume digging at Hidden Cave in 1951. The two received financial support from the U.S. Geological Survey through the University of California to work with Morrison while he studied the Pleistocene and recent geology of the Carson Basin, helping him date some of the more recent formations. When they first visited Hidden Cave, Wheeler's iron gate was in place, but it was silted in and could not be opened. Pothunters had burrowed in alongside the gate.

The American Museum of Natural History excavated at Hidden Cave in 1979 and 1980, under the direction of David Hurst Thomas. As it turns out, the hassles of digging inside Hidden Cave offers lessons useful for understanding how Hidden Cave functioned in the prehistoric past. Whatever people did at Hidden Cave 4,000 years ago, they obviously never lived there. Hunter-gatherers live only at places carefully selected to satisfy minimal conditions of human life: accessible food, water, and firewood; relatively level ground, adequate shelter; and acceptable levels of heat and light. Hidden Cave came up short on nearly all counts.

So if people did not live inside Hidden Cave, what were they doing there? Most of the cultural materials inside Hidden Cave were left there between about 5,000 and 3,200 years ago. Analysis of plant and animal remains shows that Native American people used Hidden Cave from spring through fall, and most intensively during the summer, when the cave's cool interior provided a temporary respite from the searing desert heat.

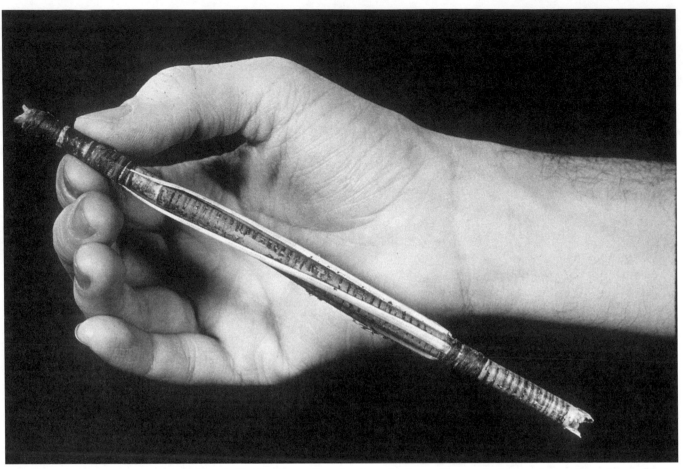

Butt end of a cane arrow shaft found inside Hidden Cave. Note the three feather quills attached in a spiral with cordage, and also the parallel brown and light green lines that decorate the arrow shaft.   [David Hurst Thomas]

The various excavations have shown that the archaeological deposits of Hidden Cave were riddled with dozens of ancient storage pits, most of them emptied of their contents millennia before archaeologists got there. During pre-contact times, the site was used mostly to temporarily store personal gear and, to a lesser extent, food supplies. Only occasionally did people camp inside, and, once in a great while, deceased were buried inside.

Archaeologist Lewis Binford made the useful distinction between "active" and "passive" artifacts. An active tool is one that is currently and regularly involved in everyday activities. Tools become passive when they fall out of synch with daily reality. Passive gear is only seasonally important, but it must be stored and cared for just the same, always ready to be upgraded to active duty.

Flat, abrasive grinding stones, for instance, are used to process hulled crops such as pine nuts. But pinyon nuts can be harvested only in the fall, so bulky grinding stones are cached in the pinyon groves, ready for the next fall's harvest (i.e., these grinding stones are "passive" for ten months every year). Similarly, squirrels and chipmunks hibernate during the winter, so the deadfall snares used to capture them become passive for several months a year. The more seasonally specific the tool kit and the higher the group's mobility, the higher the proportion of artifacts that pass between the active and passive states.

Hidden Cave contained hundreds of passive artifacts, often clustered around the cache pits in which they once may have been stored. Projectile points (dart tips and arrowheads), for instance, are common finds in archaeological sites of the desert West. But archaeologists usually find only broken discards. Not so at Hidden Cave. More than 80 percent of the hundreds of projectile points were unbroken and fully serviceable. These points had been heavily utilized—mostly as projectiles, but also as scrapers, knives, and drills. More than one-third had been resharpened in anticipation of future use. This was not discarded garbage; these passive artifacts were ready to be retrieved when the time was right. Like the modern attic, Hidden Cave was a place to keep valuables safe but not underfoot.

At least five people were buried inside Hidden Cave, and part of the artifact assemblage can be explained as grave furniture subsequently dispersed both laterally and vertically by rodent activity, scavenging carnivores, or excavation. The presence of burials might seem to contradict the storage/ warehouse hypothesis, but actually the two activities are not so dissimilar. Most grave goods are placed there to assist a deceased person in the afterlife. As such, burial caches reflect the deliberate placement of key items into storage for subsequent use by somebody. So viewed, grave furniture is another cache of passive gear.

Hidden Cave displays advance planning against a dynamic if sometimes hostile environment. This well-known locale was visited for a millennium and perhaps much longer. At times, Hidden Cave was a prehistoric attic where people hid tools to be retrieved later, a pantry where temporarily abundant food items were stashed for future need, and also a cache where loved ones were buried and equipped with the supplies necessary to cope with the afterlife.

SPIRIT CAVE

Spirit Cave, located almost adjacent to Hidden Cave, was also excavated in 1940 by S. M. and Georgetta Wheeler. The wave-cut cave is a west-facing, dry rockshelter about 25 feet wide and 15 feet deep.

The Wheelers located a quarter-circle of stones on the surface of Spirit Cave and, excavating inside, discovered a large, finely twined mat containing a few human bones (which they called Burial 1). Immediately below was a grave pit containing Burial 2, consisting of another large tule mat wrapped around a burial bundle. Based on comparisons with other excavations in the Fallon area and Lovelock Cave (to the north), the Wheelers concluded that Burial 2 was a young adult male who had been interred within the last 1,500 to 2,000 years. During subsequent excavations, the Wheelers also recovered two twined tule bags containing human cremations.

Subsequent radiometric analysis by the staff of the Nevada State Museum (Carson City) determined that the Spirit Cave remains are considerably older than originally believed. Human hair and matting from Burial 2 dates to a mean age of $9,415 \pm 25$ radiocarbon years ago. Several additional radiocarbon dates on Spirit Cave materials are also older than 9,000 radiocarbon years.

The Spirit Cave matting is among the oldest known textiles from western North America. The shroud around Burial 2, a warp-face plain weave, is extraordinarily fine, tight, and uniform, perhaps woven on an upright frame. The care and precision of manufacture suggests that the textiles may have been constructed specifically as mortuary shrouds.

In recent years, the burials from Spirit Cave been the subject of a repatriation dispute between the Fallon Paiute-Shoshone Tribe (representing all Northern Paiute tribal governments, who claim cultural affiliation to the remains) and the Bureau of Land Management (which claims the remains are unaffiliated with any modern Indian tribe).

Tours of the Grimes Point Archaeological Area and Hidden Cave begin at the Churchill County Museum in Fallon, Nevada. Following the trail to Hidden Cave, visitors will see petroglyphs and other sites with signs providing interpretation. Hidden Cave is today part of the Grimes Point Archaeological Area. The Churchill County Museum and the Bureau of Land Management co-sponsor guided expeditions inside Hidden Cave. These days no one has to crawl their way inside. Bureau of Land Management engineers have provided a passage so that visitors barely have to bend over to get inside.

Further Reading: Elston, Robert G., "Prehistory of the Western Area," in *Handbook of North American Indians*, Vol. 11: *Great Basin*, edited by Warren L. d'Azevedo (Washington, DC: Smithsonian Institution Press, 1986), 135–148; Fowler, Catherine S., Eugene M. Hattori, and Amy J. Dansie, "Ancient Matting from Spirit Cave, Nevada: Technical Implications," in *Beyond Cloth and Cordage: Archaeological Textile Research in the Americas*, edited by Penelope B. Drooker and Laurie D. Webster (Salt Lake City: University of Utah Press, 2000), 119–139; Heizer, Robert F., and Martin A. Baumhoff, *Prehistoric Rock Art of Nevada and Eastern California* (Berkeley: University of California Press, 1962); Shaafsma, Polly, "Rock Art," in *Handbook of North American Indians*, Vol. 11: *Great Basin*, edited by Warren L. d'Azevedo (Washington, DC: Smithsonian Institution Press, 1986), 215–226; Thomas, David Hurst, *The Archaeology of Hidden Cave, Nevada*, Anthropological Papers, No. 61 (New York: American Museum of Natural History, 1985).

David Hurst Thomas

MONITOR VALLEY

Central Nevada

Rockshelters, an Alpine Village Site, and Mountain Petroglyphs

Throughout the historic period, Monitor Valley (central Nevada) was occupied by Western Shoshone people, and their foraging ancestors lived here for millennia. The valley floor, which lies at 2,070 meters (6,790 ft), is covered by sagebrush flats and Monitor Lake, a shallow, sulfurous, alkaline playa lake. To the west is the Toquima Range, a block-fault mountain mass that tops out at Mt. Jefferson (11,949 ft, 3,642 m). The Monitor Range flanks the eastern margin of Monitor

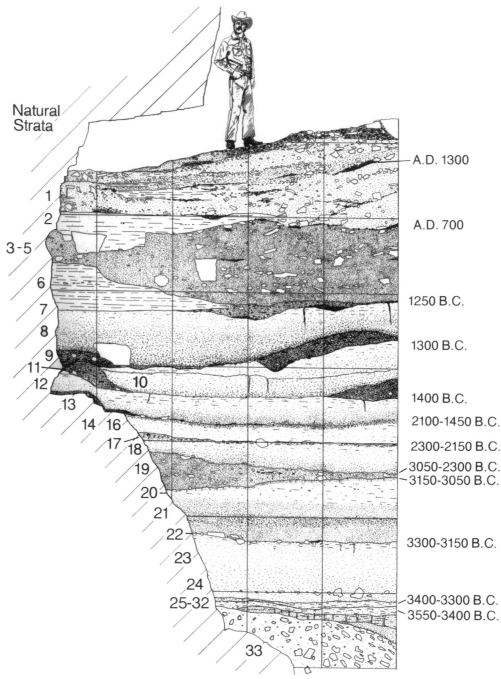

Natural
Strata

1
2
3-5
6
7
8
9
11
12
13
14 16
17 18
19
20
21
22
23
24
25-32
10
33

A.D. 1300
A.D. 700
1250 B.C.
1300 B.C.
1400 B.C.
2100-1450 B.C.
2300-2150 B.C.
3050-2300 B.C.
3150-3050 B.C.
3300-3150 B.C.
3400-3300 B.C.
3550-3400 B.C.

The master stratigraphic profile for Gatecliff Shelter (central Nevada). The standing figure is exactly 6 feet (1.8 m) tall, and the grid system is metric. Only the upper thirty-three (of the fifty-six) stratigraphic units are evident in this cross section.   [David Hurst Thomas]

Valley. Throughout the 1970s and 1980s, the American Museum of Natural History (New York) conducted extensive archaeological excavations and reconnaissance throughout the Great Basin uplands of central Nevada, including Monitor Valley.

GATECLIFF SHELTER

Gatecliff Shelter is the best-known archaeological site in Monitor Valley. The deepest archaeological cave or rockshelter in the Americas, Gatecliff contained more than 10 meters of extraordinarily well-stratified deposits, divided into fifty-six

Archaeological field crew excavating at the Terrace Midden of Alta Toquima Village (central Nevada). This site is located at 11,000 feet above sea level, and the remains of several prehistoric house foundations are evident in this picture.   [David Hurst Thomas]

distinct geological strata and sixteen cultural horizons. Most of this stratigraphic column was deposited by sediment-laden and extremely turbulent water, filtered from debris flows upslope and upcanyon. Primary chronological controls were derived from a sequence of forty-seven radiocarbon dates that span the last 7,000 years. The basal layer also contained a lens of 6,900-year-old volcanic ash, blown in from the explosion of Mt. Mazama, more than 600 kilometers to the northwest (at Crater Lake, Oregon). Evidence indicates that the first human usage of Gatecliff Shelter occurred about 5,500 years ago, and the most intensive periods of utilization took place during the last 3,200 years.

The Gatecliff Shelter excavations produced more than 400 projectile points that can be classified into distinct diagnostic styles, recovered in tight stratigraphic context. This assemblage allowed a refinement of the cultural chronology for the central Great Basin. Gatecliff also contained more than 400 incised limestone slabs. Although similar finds have been made elsewhere, this is the largest concentration of such artifacts in the New World. Significant parallels exist between this portable rock art and the wall art painted inside Gatecliff and elsewhere in the Great Basin. More than 51,000 animal bones were recovered through careful sifting of the deposits; more than 90 percent of these (by weight) came from bighorn sheep, a major target for these high-altitude hunters.

The pattern of artifact and ecofact distribution at Gatecliff is heavily size-sorted, with the smaller debris defining a distinctive "drop zone" in the rear, most sheltered part of the site. The larger items were found in an equally distinctive "toss zone" across the exposed apron of the site.

Three dozen hearths occurred on the various living surfaces inside Gatecliff Shelter. These features defined a distinctive "hearthline" approximately 4 meters from the rear cave wall, suggesting that they were deliberately situated to create a relatively warm and smoke-free work area. The rear wall effectively served as a passive heat sink, enabling visitors to warm the inner part of this south-facing shelter with a relatively small fire.

Male subsistence and tool repair activities dominate the archaeological record at Gatecliff Shelter, with only extremely limited evidence for female activities. Gatecliff Shelter was probably a short-term field camp, visited mostly by single-sex task groups working some distance from their base camp, although it is possible that small groups occasionally used Gatecliff as a residential base.

TRIPLE T SHELTER

An extensive randomized and systematic archaeological survey was conducted throughout the Monitor Valley to situate Gatecliff Shelter within its regional context. A dozen additional sites were also excavated in Monitor Valley, including Triple T Shelter (26Ny345), a small alcove in West Northumberland Canyon, about 12 kilometers (7.5 mi) west of Gatecliff Shelter. The Triple T stratigraphic column, more than 6 meters deep, is supported by thirteen radiocarbon dates. Taken together, Gatecliff and Triple T shelters provide an important stratigraphic and chronological baseline for the central Great Basin.

The Triple T artifact assemblage shows a superabundance of weapons, with small portions of domestic equipment and ceremonial items. The intrasite pattern shows heavy reliance on energy efficiency. The southern aspect maximizes solar input during the day and heat retention at night. Overall hearth technology and within-site positioning further enhanced the natural heat sink effect. Hearth positioning and debris disposal in the upper strata demonstrate that the enclosed reason zone functioned both as a sheltered workshop and a nocturnal sleep area. Triple T Shelter also has a disproportionate number of shallow-pit and rock-filled hearths, generally becoming larger toward the center, with the shallow-pit hearths constructed well inside the dripline, toward the rear and sides.

HICKISON SUMMIT

At the Hickison Summit rock art site (26La9), located at the northern end of Monitor Valley, petroglyphs are common along the narrow pass dividing the Toquima and Simpson Park ranges (through which game frequently migrate between the high summer ground of the Simpson Park Range and lower wintering grounds of Big Smoky Valley). Deep pits, some lightly scratched hatches and crosshatches, and an angular edge with several deep notches occur on a tuff outcrop that partly blocks the passageway through the saddle. Other panels of pecked petroglyphs (some enhanced with red ocher) appear along the eastern flanking cliff.

The rock art at Hickison Summit was first recorded by a field party from the University of California (Berkeley) in 1958. The obvious association between petroglyphs and potential game ambush features suggested to Robert Heizer and Martin Baumhoff the hypothesis that Nevada rock art functioned, in part, in a magical or ritual context involved with hunting large game.

ALTA TOQUIMA VILLAGE

Alta Toquima Village (26Ny920) is an unusual alpine settlement overlooking Monitor Valley. This site—located atop Mt. Jefferson, the highest peak in the Toquima Range—is a huge, table-like plateau that varies in elevation from about 10,000 feet (3,048 m) to 11,949 feet (3,642 m). Located almost exactly 11,000 feet (3,352 m) above sea level, Alta Toquima is located on an isolated spur along the tableland. Apparently this area had escaped the attention of artifact collectors (because when American Museum crews first encountered this site, the surface was littered with hundreds of complete artifacts). The site contains thirty-one rock house foundations, eighteen of which were excavated by the American Museum of Natural History in 1981 and 1983.

The chronology of Alta Toquima is anchored in a suite of forty radiocarbon dates on charcoal recovered during the American Museum excavations. More than 600 time-diagnostic projectile points were recovered by surface collection and stratigraphic excavation, which also produced a large sample of Shoshonean ceramics and more than fifty grinding stones.

A distinctive terrace midden fringes the eastern (downhill) margin of Alta Toquima. Buried beneath approximately 20 centimeters of colluvial and slopewash debris lie four black refuse middens, in places approaching 25 centimeters in thickness. The earliest radiocarbon date from the terrace midden is approximately 1130–830 BC. This is the oldest known occupation of Alta Toquima; stratigraphic, chronometric, and typological studies demonstrate that deposits here span the last 3,000 years. Despite the overall steepness, the terrace midden is probably the most desirable living space at Alta Toquima, providing adequate protection from the prevailing westerly winds, plus immediate access to water, firewood, and construction materials for houses. Moreover, the limber pine itself could have provided significant food resources during the late summer and early fall.

Roughly half the Alta Toquima houses were initially occupied between about AD 100 and 750. The occupation of Alta Toquima appears to have ceased during the ninth and tenth centuries AD. Then, shortly after AD 1000, occupation of Alta Toquima picked up once again, with several houses occupied and reoccupied, the site usage lasting into the late pre-contact and protohistoric periods.

Further Reading: Thomas, David Hurst, "How to Classify the Projectile Points from Monitor Valley, Nevada," *Journal of California and Great Basin Anthropology* 3(1) (1981): 7–43; Thomas, David Hurst, *The 1981 Alta Toquima Village Project: A Preliminary Report.* Technical Report Series, No. 27 (Tahoe, NM; Desert Research Institute, Social Sciences Center, 1982); Thomas, David Hurst, *The Archaeology of Monitor Valley: 1. Epistemology*, Anthropological Papers, No. 58 (New York: American Museum of Natural History, 1983); Thomas, David Hurst, *The Archaeology of Monitor Valley: 2. Gatecliff Shelter*, Anthropological Papers, No. 59 (New York: American Museum of Natural History, 1983); Thomas, David Hurst, *The Archaeology of Monitor Valley: 3. Survey and Additional Excavations*, Anthropological Papers, No. 66 (New York: American Museum of Natural History, 1988), 131–633.

David Hurst Thomas

DEFIANCE HOUSE AND OTHER ANCIENT AND HISTORIC SITES

Glen Canyon National Recreation Area, Utah

Ancient and Historic Cultural Adaptations in Glen Canyon

High on the overhanging cliff wall, three large painted figures brandish shields and clubs. Meant to be seen by anyone coming up the canyon, they are what gave the site its name: Defiance House. Below the figures are well-preserved structures dating to the mid- to late thirteenth century AD—three rooms, several storage structures, and a roofed kiva (partially underground room used both for living and for religious rituals). In front of the buildings, a low wall of stacked boulders gives further indication of the site's defensive posture. The National Park Service has stabilized the structures and has built a trail up the steep slope below the site.

Defiance House was named, mapped, and excavated in 1959 by a University of Utah crew under the author's direction. The work was part of the Glen Canyon Archaeological Project, designed to record archaeological evidence before the site was destroyed or otherwise affected by the filling of Lake Powell, which now stretches for nearly 186 miles behind

the Glen Canyon Dam. The site is in Forgotten Canyon, which now forms a small eastern arm of the lake. In 1959 the excavators hiked 3 miles upcanyon from their boat landing on the Colorado River and climbed to the site. It had been visited seven years earlier by intrepid canyon explorers Harry Aleson, Dick Sprang, and Dudy Thomas, who called it "Three Warrior Ruin."

Defiance House is one of many small "cliff dwellings" and other sites that record the lives of the Ancestral Pueblo (also known as Anasazi) people in the Glen Canyon region just before the whole Four Corners area (Four Corners is the area where the states of Colorado, Utah, New Mexico, and Arizona meet) was depopulated near the end of the thirteenth century AD. These people were farmers, growing maize, beans, squash, and cotton on small patches of alluvial (stream-deposited) soil in the narrow but well-watered canyons. The Glen Canyon region is very hot, dry, and low-lying by Four

Defiance House.   [Courtesy of the National Park Service]

Corners standards, so dry farming on the open benches and mesas between the canyons was generally impossible. However, those areas gave the canyon dwellers opportunities to hunt bighorn sheep, deer, and rabbits; to collect many wild plants useful as food or medicine; or to gather raw materials for making clothing, containers, and tools.

The defensive character of Defiance House is echoed by other thirteenth-century sites in the Glen Canyon National Recreation Area (GCNRA), and indeed by contemporaneous sites across the whole Four Corners area. This was a time of frequent conflict, evidently among the area's many Puebloan communities. In better-watered and more fertile parts of the Four Corners, people grouped together at this time in large villages of up to several hundred inhabitants; but this was not an option in the Glen Canyon area, where the scattered settlements each consisted of just one or a few families, as at Defiance House. Here the primary mode of defense was a difficult-to-access location high above the canyon floor.

Defiance House represents only one episode in the Glen Canyon area's long—though sporadic—history of human

occupation. Visitors to the 1.25 million–acre GCNRA often encounter rock art images, or series of "Moki steps" (hand- and toe-hold trails) that record Native American occupation at various times over thousands of years. A few Paleoindian projectile points have been found near Glen Canyon, indicating occasional visits by the earliest inhabitants of the Southwest, from about 10,000 to 6000 BC. Use of the area increased during the Archaic period (6000–500 BC), as documented by small campsites and hunting-gathering stations, and by particular styles of rock art. Small bands of foragers left these traces as they ranged seasonally over huge areas, using their sophisticated knowledge of natural history to exploit many wild plant and animal species.

By 500 BC, or perhaps even earlier, corn was being grown in the area. Maize was domesticated far to the south in Mexico and was borrowed by local foragers, initially to supplement their wild food diet. Other early farmers probably came in as migrants from growing agricultural settlements to the south. The resulting "Basketmaker II" culture is well represented in the Glen Canyon area between about

These pictographs of men brandishing clubs and shields led to the naming of the site Defiance House.   [Courtesy of the National Park Service]

500 BC and 500 AD. Several natural shelters and open sites have yielded Basketmaker II artifacts, storage pits, and shallow pit houses, and this period's characteristic broad-shouldered anthropomorphs can be seen in rock art panels here and there. Basketmaker sites occur in several parts of the Four Corners area, and this culture gave rise to the later Puebloans.

Between about 500 and 1000 AD, the Glen Canyon region saw relatively little occupation, but in the eleventh century small groups of Pueblo farmers began to move in from more populous surrounding regions. This was a time when summer rainfall was generally reliable over the region. In the north-western part of the GCNRA, there also is evidence of the Fremont culture—people who practiced a mixed farming-foraging economy.

After the thirteenth century AD, Puebloans ceased to live in the Glen Canyon region, but finds of distinctive yellow-ware potsherds indicate that people from the Hopi Pueblos to the south continued to visit—perhaps to hunt, trade with foragers, or visit ancestral shrines. Sometime after the thirteenth century, foragers related to the Paiute and Ute people of today

began to use the area. Because they were few in number and highly mobile, their archaeological record is sparse. Navajo people also occupied the southeastern portion of the Glen Canyon area in the nineteenth century. Today the Navajo reservation abuts the GCNRA to the south.

In the 1770s an expedition led by the Spanish friars Dominguez and Escalante crossed the Glen Canyon while returning to Santa Fe after an unsuccessful effort to find a route to California. The "Crossing of the Fathers" is now submerged under Lake Powell's Padre Bay. In 1869 the famed explorer and scientist John Wesley Powell named the Glen Canyon during his daring trip down the Colorado River. In the winter of 1879–80, over 200 Mormon settlers crossed the river after lowering their wagons through the "Hole in the Rock," a short, steep canyon still visible upstream from the Escalante River. After an extremely arduous five-month trip, they founded the town of Bluff on the San Juan River.

Grazing began in the Glen Canyon area in the late nine-teenth century, though it was less productive than on higher, better-watered ranges. The early Texas-based cattle outfits were rapidly replaced by Mormon ranchers from Bluff. The 1890s and early decades of the twentieth century saw many largely unsuccessful gold-mining ventures, a few traces of which are still visible. During the "uranium boom" of the late 1940s and 1950s, prospectors bulldozed many primitive roads into the rugged Glen Canyon area and established a few mines. Recreational use increased in the 1950s, as large military surplus rafts facilitated both private and commercial river-running through the canyons of the Colorado River system. Even so, visitation numbered in the few hundreds or at most a few thousand people annually before the Glen Canyon Dam was completed in 1963.

Today, of course, Lake Powell attracts hundreds of thousands of boaters and other recreationists. Insights into the Glen Canyon area's long and varied human history are available to these visitors, if they learn how to recognize and appreciate the traces of that history. These traces are also very fragile, so visitors must step cautiously to ensure that these mementos of history can be enjoyed by future generations as well.

Further Reading: Crampton, C. Gregory, *Ghosts of Glen Canyon: History beneath Lake Powell*, rev. ed. (St. George, UT: Publishers Place, 1994); Geib, Phil R., *Glen Canyon Revisited* (Salt Lake City: University of Utah Press, 1996); Jennings, Jesse D., *Glen Canyon: An Archaeological Summary* (Salt Lake City: University of Utah Press, 1998); Lipe, William D., "Anasazi Communities in the Red Rock Plateau, Southeastern Utah," in *Reconstructing Prehistoric Pueblo Societies*, edited by W. A. Longacre (Albuquerque: University of New Mexico Press, 1970), 84–139; Lipe, William D., F. W. Sharrock, D. S. Dibble, and K. M. Anderson, *1959 Excavations, Glen Canyon Area* (Salt Lake City: University of Utah Press, 1960); Martin, Russell, *A Story That Stands Like a Dam: Glen Canyon and the Struggle for the Soul of the West* (New York: Henry Holt, 1989); Powell, John Wesley, *Down the Colorado. John Wesley Powell. Diary of the First Trip through the Grand Canyon* (New York: E.P. Dutton, 1969).

William D. Lipe

SITES IN ANASAZI STATE PARK AND CAPITOL REEF NATIONAL PARK

South Central Utah

Sites of the Fremont and Anasazi Cultural Traditions

Capitol Reef National Park, encompassing some 75 miles of the Waterpocket Fold, is known for its geological features and Fremont Indian archaeology. Twenty miles west of Capitol Reef is Anasazi State Park, where Anasazi (also known as Ancestral Puebloan) Indians lived in a mountainside pueblo above the fold. In this region, for a short time, the Fremont and Anasazi interacted. But to appreciate the human history of the two parks, one must first understand the remarkable landscape they share.

THE WATERPOCKET FOLD

"Angle Rock" and "Jagged Rock" are what the Navajo of old called the steep, tilted sandstone spine that runs the length of Capitol Reef National Park. Today's geologists call it a monocline: a great wrinkle of rock formed by geological forces that pinched the earth's crust and buckled the landscape. That fold has since weathered into a colorful complex of cliffs, "capitol" domes, and undulating slickrock. It is incised with slot canyons, carved into fanciful formations, and dimpled with catchwater basins—the "waterpockets" that give the fold its name.

The Waterpocket Fold spans nearly 100 miles between Thousand Lakes Mountain (near Bicknell, Utah) to the north and the Colorado River to the south. It is a natural corridor for travelers moving north and south between the Arizona deserts and Utah's high plateaus. But along its length the Waterpocket Fold is a serious obstacle, like a reef in the ocean, to those traveling east or west. People and animals can most readily cross the "reef" by following one of several streams, such as the Fremont River, that have cut gorges through the escarpment. Archaeological evidence shows that people have been traveling those routes—and camping, hunting, and trading in the area—for thousands of years.

They picked a hard place to earn a living. Elevations along the Waterpocket Fold range from 4,000 to 11,000 feet, which means the crop growing season is short and winters are cold. Capitol Reef gets about 7 inches of rainfall annually, and only a few streams and some of the deeper waterpockets provide water year-round. Land suitable for farming is limited; reliable wild food sources are concentrated in small patches scattered over large areas. It is a rugged, remote, and fearsome country. Despite those challenges, people came.

The Waterpocket Fold and strike valley at Capitol Reef National Park. [Courtesy of the National Park Service]

PEOPLING OF CAPITOL REEF

Within the area now encompassed by the national park, the earliest firm evidence for human occupation is a fire hearth dating to about 7,500 years ago. At that time, hunter-gatherers were exploiting a wide range of plants and animals. Their tool kit included darts and throwing sticks (called *atl atls*) for hunting, and grinding stones for milling nuts and grass seeds. People lived in small, highly mobile family groups that ranged over large areas, camping in pinyon-juniper woodlands and taking shelter in alcoves. They moved seasonally from resource to resource, hunting mountain sheep, ground squirrels, and other game and harvesting pinyon nuts, cactus, ricegrass, and native fruits. This strategy defines a broad-based, generalist lifeway called the Archaic. Archaeologists working at Capitol Reef in the 1990s found plentiful evidence that Archaic groups used the area continuously over a span of about 6,000 years.

Archaic-age sites (7,500 to 2,400 years old) and Archaic-style dart points are found mostly in Capitol Reef's highlands—benches, mesas, domes, and flats over 7,000 feet in elevation. Human activity shifted to the lower valleys as populations grew, and a cultural transition began to emerge. This shift, evolving over 600 years, coincides with the appearance of maize (corn) in the area. Archaeologists recovered maize pollen and corn cupules in sites dating to 2,000 years ago, suggesting that the people of Capitol Reef were already beginning to dabble in farming. Archaic culture teetered at a prehistoric tipping point.

Then important changes happened quickly. First came the earliest solid evidence for agriculture at Capitol Reef: a corn-cob radiocarbon-dated to AD 250–300, followed closely by more corn dates from other sites. Domesticated plants and farming techniques developed in Mexico then take root. Next lightweight, finely crafted arrowheads appear. Bow-and-arrow technology, diffusing southward from northern Canada, has arrived. Next come ceramics—fire-hardened clay pottery—which, together with farming, suggest that people are adopting a somewhat more settled lifeway. This combination of traits characterizes the Formative period, when several well-known prehistoric cultures blossomed in the Southwest. One of those cultures was first identified along Capitol Reef's Fremont River.

THE FREMONT RIVER CULTURE

When archaeologist Noel Morss surveyed the Fremont River area in 1928–29, researchers already had a good understanding of the Formative pueblo culture known as Anasazi. Classic

Brigham Young University students documenting a common site type at Capitol Reef.   [Courtesy of the National Park Service]

Anasazi culture of the Four Corners region (where the corners of Utah, Colorado, New Mexico, and Arizona meet) is characterized by several key traits. For example, these Ancestral Puebloan people cultivated maize, beans, and squash and used grinding stones (manos and metates) to mill their corn into flour. They constructed pueblo villages with underground ceremonial rooms (kivas), wove fine baskets, and created pottery with delicate, intricate designs. But as one moves out from the core Anasazi culture area—say, toward the Waterpocket Fold—some of those customary traits vanish and entirely new characteristics appear.

Morss went to south central Utah to investigate those variations at the edges of Anasazi land. In his Fremont River sites, he found some customary Puebloan traits but he also observed some important differences. Based on those differences, Morss defined a "distinctive culture," which he named Fremont. Like the Puebloans, the Fremont grew maize, beans, and squash, and used manos and metates to grind their corn. But the Fremont River people lived in caves and shallow pit houses, and they built no kivas. Their pottery was mostly plain grayware, and they wove their own style of basketry. The Fremont wore unusual leather moccasins rather than the plant fiber sandals favored by Puebloans. They made distinctive

clay figurines and developed a rock art style featuring trapezoidal, horned human figures.

It is known that a highly variable Fremont archaeological complex occurred throughout Utah. The Southwestern influence seems strongest among the Fremont of southern Utah, where the Waterpocket Fold provided a corridor for people, goods, and ideas moving up from Arizona. Farther north, Fremont culture took on more Plains culture characteristics. Capitol Reef, as it turns out, is on the southern periphery of the Fremont culture area that it helped define.

Distinctive Fremont cultural traits emerged at Capitol Reef sometime between AD 500 and 900 and disappeared by 1300. Fremont sites in the park are mostly scattered along drainages, where farmland and irrigation water were available. "Villages" are small, single-family farmsteads consisting of just two or three pit houses, generally on a rise overlooking farmland. Fremont farmers built hidden granaries, tucked into rock crevices, to keep their food stores safe. They also hunted mountain sheep, antelope, rabbit, and ground squirrel, and collected pinyon nuts, cactus, and a wide variety of seeds, berries, and roots.

And they interacted with the nearby Anasazi, whose ceramic tradewares are found in Fremont sites in the central and southern parts of Capitol Reef National Park. A few Anasazi occupation sites occur in the south end of the park (possibly a cultural transition zone) and west of the Waterpocket Fold.

ANASAZI STATE PARK

Just 20 miles from Capitol Reef lies one of the largest Anasazi villages west of the Colorado River: Coombs Village, at Anasazi State Park in Boulder, Utah. Noel Morss excavated there as well, and he identified the site as a Puebloan outpost with Anasazi pottery.

Later excavations at the state park uncovered the remains of more than 100 masonry structures and jacal (mud and stick) pit houses, which sheltered up to 200 people. The Coombs Village people grew maize and squash (and probably beans), and hunted muledeer, mountain sheep, and smaller game. Archaeologists recovered numerous pottery items, including a small amount of Fremont-style ceramics suggesting that this village traded with its neighbors.

People lived at the pueblo for just seventy-five years, AD 1160 to 1235. Then the village burned to the ground and the site was abandoned. Over the next forty years people began abandoning other Anasazi villages and Fremont sites all over the region, evidently emigrating south. Researchers initially blamed the widespread abandonment on a long dry spell, but modern climatological studies indicate that the "Great Drought" was not severe enough to cause regional evacuation on that scale. Whatever their reasons for leaving, the Anasazi and Fremont people did not altogether disappear. Their descendants are the modern Pueblo Indians who live in the Southwest today.

LATER OCCUPATIONS

After AD 1300, solid archaeological evidence for a human presence at Capitol Reef consists of a few late prehistoric brownware pottery shards and two radiocarbon dates placing people in the area at about AD 1500 and again at 1600. These may indicate the arrival of the ancestors of Southern Paiute and/or Ute people, who occupied the region in historic times. Mormon pioneers began homesteading the area, one of the last places in the United States to be settled, in the 1870s.

VISITING THE PARKS

Fremont artifacts are exhibited at Capitol Reef National Park's visitors' center, and visitors can stop at a pull-off on Utah Highway 24 (1 mile east of the visitors' center) to view a series of Fremont rock art panels. A self-guided tour along the Hickman Bridge Trail, east of the rock art pull-off, takes hikers past a hidden granary and the remains of a Fremont pit house. And, of course, visitors can freely hike and explore Capitol Reef's 241,904 acres of mesas, deserts, and drainages.

For a stunning bird's-eye view across part of the Waterpocket Fold, pause at the Larb Hollow overlook and other viewpoints on Utah Highway 12 between Capitol Reef National Park and Anasazi State Park.

At Anasazi State Park, on Utah Highway 12 in Boulder, visitors can walk among the ruins of Anasazi dwellings and visit a reconstructed jacal pit house. The combined visitors' center/museum offers excellent archaeological and interactive exhibits about the area and its peoples. The site is listed on the National Register of Historic Places.

Further Reading: Janetski, Joel C., Lee Kreutzer, Richard K. Talbot, L. D. Richens, and Shane A. Baker, *Life on the Edge: Archaeology in Capitol Reef National Park*, Museum of Peoples and Cultures Occasional Paper No. 11 (Provo, UT: Brigham Young University, 2005); Lister, Robert C., and Florence Lister, *The Coombs Site, Part III*, Anthropological Papers, No. 41 (Salt Lake City: University of Utah, 1961); Madsen, David B., *Exploring the Fremont* (Salt Lake City, UT: Museum of Natural History, 1989); Morss, Noel, *The Ancient Cultures of the Fremont River in Utah: Report on the Explorations Under the Claflin-Emerson Fund, 1928–29*, Papers of the Peabody Museum of American Archaeology and Ethnology, Vol. XIL, No. 5 (Cambridge, MA: Harvard University, 1931).

Lee Ann Kreutzer

HOGUP CAVE AND DANGER CAVE

Northwestern Utah

The Desert Culture Tradition of the Great Basin

People have lived in the Great Basin of western North America for at least 11,000 years. Centered on Nevada and western Utah, the region extends into the dry parts of southeastern Oregon, southern Idaho, and eastern California. So called because no rivers reach the sea from its vast area of interior drainage, the Great Basin is a high, cool desert with hot summers and snowy winters. East and west it is bounded by the Rocky Mountains and Sierra-Cascades; to the north is the Columbia Plateau of Oregon and Washington, and to the south the Colorado River. Its distinctive basin and range topography alternates between valley floors at 4,000 to 5,000 feet elevation and mountain ridges as high as 13,000 feet, providing varied habitats that support a diverse population of plants and animals. Native occupants responded to the Great Basin landscape by developing a highly mobile hunting-gathering way of life. They tended to winter around lakes and marshes in the valley bottoms and ranged widely during the warmer seasons in the thickets, woodlands, and shrubby terrain of progressively higher elevations.

Archaeological excavations at Danger Cave brought into focus the long-lived "Desert Culture" tradition that Great Basin peoples developed in early Holocene times and sustained into the early twentieth century. The site lies on the Utah-Nevada border 120 miles directly west of Salt Lake City, at the base of a low range of hills that faces the Bonneville Salt Flats. This famous automobile race course was made on the perfectly smooth and level floor of Ice Age Lake Bonneville, which occupied much of western Utah at its peak, about 16,000 years ago, and then shrank steadily to nearly the level of the Great Salt Lake, its modern remnant, by about 12,000 years ago. Research at Hogup Cave, east of the salt flats near the edge of the modern lake, supports and broadens the picture from Danger Cave. Together the two sites give a rich and detailed picture of the long-lived Desert Culture pattern. Artifacts of all kinds, as well as plant remains and animal bones, were preserved by the thousands in well-stratified and extremely dry deposits up to 14 feet deep in places.

Some of the first people to camp at Danger Cave built a small fire on a clean sandy floor left as a late stage of the drying lake dropped below the cave mouth. Radiocarbon dates on charcoal from that hearth place the event at about 10,300 years ago, at which time a large shallow lake probably covered the flats in front of the cave. The earliest carbon-14 date from Hogup Cave is 8,800 years ago, a time when marshland grew around a seep spring on the old lake margin below the site. Deep deposits and a consistent ladder of radiocarbon dates from the two caves that currently number five to six dozen show that people returned often to both sites over the ensuing millennia. They were consistent waypoints in hunting-gathering "walkabouts" that brought small communal groups to various places where they could camp for a few days or weeks while harvesting local plants and animals for food and craft materials. Both sites were regular parts of the regional residents' lives, but people surely visited many other places in addition to the caves during their annual cycles. That Danger and Hogup caves usually hosted only periodic and short-term, albeit repetitive visits is clearly shown by the finely stratified deposits. At Hogup Cave the brevity and periodicity of human visits are also indicated by the many thin but continuous layers of bat droppings to be seen in the cave profiles, which accumulated on exposed surfaces during seasons when people were not around to trample and roil the cave floor.

Many seasonal economic events were recorded again and again in the cave stratigraphy. Especially at Hogup Cave the excavation profiles showed many thin but widespread layers of chaff, which people threshed from the seeds of the *Allenrolfea occidentalis* (pickleweed) that grows along the salty margins of old lakebeds and is ripe for harvesting in late summer. Seed remains of several kinds were abundant at both caves, as were fragments of the milling stones used to grind them into meal. Other thin and repetitive layers clearly seen at Hogup Cave consisted of the distinctively hollow hair of the pronghorn antelope, whose hides were evidently processed there. Written accounts of the historic period tell that Native groups killed pronghorn in some numbers during drive hunts. These were held in any given locality only at considerable intervals, so that herds might regenerate themselves between kills. Similar periodic drives were used to harvest jackrabbits. A complete net 4 feet wide and 140 feet long, made of milkweed and Indian hemp fibers spun into cordage, was found at Hogup Cave. It was of a type used historically to encircle and trap jackrabbits after long drives that brought them together by the hundreds. Fragments of knotted cordage from such netting were found throughout the cave deposits, as was jackrabbit bone, indicating that rabbit drives were practiced in the cave vicinity over thousands of years.

As is true of pronghorn hunts as well, a rabbit drive yielded not only food, but also hides for clothing and other manufactures. Large robes or blankets were made by twisting together strands of skin with the fur still attached, made in turn by cutting individual rabbit hides spiral fashion into long continuous strips. Two large fragments of such robes, and nearly 150 fragmentary strips of skin, were found from bottom to top of the Hogup Cave deposits. Native people throughout the Great Basin still make such robes today as heritage art.

The two caves additionally yielded evidence of many other kinds of manufactures. Trays and containers of basketry woven from split willow and other plant materials, mats made of bulrushes twined together with plant fiber cordage, bags of woven plant fibers or cut and sewn animal hide, carrying nets of plant fiber cordage, parts of wooden bows and cane arrows, bowstrings of sinew, spear throwers (*atl atls*) and darts, feather fletching for darts or arrows, and flaked stone knives, scrapers, drills, dart points and arrow points represent only a partial accounting of the many practical items that people carried with them or made during their sojourns at the caves.

Artifacts from the caves were almost entirely tools or practical items, but occasional specimens were clearly symbolic, reflecting social and spiritual aspects of Desert Culture life. A few beads made of *Olivella biplicata* shell from the Pacific coast show that Danger and Hogup caves lay within an ambit of long-distance exchange that is well documented from various sites across the Great Basin and goes back almost to the beginning of Holocene times. Disc and tubular beads of stone and shell were also found at both sites. Hogup cave additionally yielded small stones with incised designs, necklaces or bracelets made of perforated elk teeth, painted splinters of bone, and small figures that combined heads made of twisted plant fiber, horns made of bone splinters or porcupine quills, and bodies made of a bird feather.

A few fragments of grayware pottery appeared in the latest levels of both sites. Danger Cave yielded a single trace of Indian corn, and Hogup Cave about three dozen grains. These items—and hide moccasins of a very distinctive style at Hogup Cave—indicate occasional visits to the caves by people of the Fremont Culture. These horticulturists lived throughout most of Utah north of the Puebloan agricultural zone between roughly 1,500 and 600 years ago, but never penetrated significantly into the more arid central Great Basin. A few shards of brownware pottery identified with the ethnographically known Gosiute and Shoshoni peoples of the same vicinity were also found at both caves. The horticultural Fremont lifeway abruptly ceased throughout its former range about 500 years ago, but the long-established Great Basin Desert Culture way of life that had preceded it, and continued to exist alongside it, lived on into modern times. The Shoshoni, Gosiute, and Ute peoples who greeted the first Euro-American colonists in the late 1700s and early 1800s were exemplars of this ancient tradition, and they remain today as the aboriginal Native occupants of the region. It seems likely that some Fremont horticulturists followed the Puebloans who bordered them on the south as they retreated into central Arizona and New Mexico, where rainfall remained sufficient to support farmers. Others no doubt opted to remain and amalgamate with the Desert Culture hunting-gathering people who had always lived nearby.

Further Reading: Aikens, C. Melvin, *Hogup Cave*, Anthropological Papers, No. 93 (Salt Lake City: University of Utah, 1970); Beck, Charlotte, ed., *Models for the Millennium: Great Basin Anthropology Today* (Salt Lake City: University of Utah Press, 1999); Grayson, Donald K., *The Desert's Past: A Natural Prehistory of the Great Basin* (New York: Smithsonian Institution Press, 1993); Jennings, Jesse D., *Danger Cave*, Anthropological Papers, No. 27 (also released as Society for American Archaeology Memoir 14) (Salt Lake City: University of Utah, 1957); Madsen, David B., and David Rhode, eds., *Across the West: Human Population Movement and the Expansion of the Numa* (Salt Lake City: University of Utah Press, 1994).

C. Melvin Aikens

FREMONT INDIAN STATE PARK

Southwest Utah

Investigating and Describing the Fremont Culture

Fremont Indian State Park was established to house and display the archaeological collections resulting from the excavation by the Museum of Peoples and Cultures, Brigham Young University, of Five Finger Ridge and associated sites in advance of the construction of Interstate Highway 70. The museum displays include interpretive videos, a scale model of Five Finger Ridge, an excellent array of Fremont diagnostic artifacts, and a presentation of late prehistoric and ethnographic material culture. Twelve interpretive trails facilitate viewing of an impressive set of pictograph and petroglyph panels.

Since Noel Morss first defined the Fremont culture in 1931 based on his fieldwork along the Fremont River of south central Utah, its geographical extent has been expanded to cover the entire state of Utah north of the better-defined Anasazi and Western Anasazi areas, which lie primarily south of the Colorado River in the east and the Virgin River in the west, respectively. The material culture of the Fremont area is highly variable from region to region. Habitation sites range from isolated pit structures to hamlets and large sedentary villages. Typical artifacts include grayware ceramics, unique basketry, a variety of diagnostic arrow points, and distinctive anthropomorphic clay figurines. The latter bear a strong resemblance to human depictions in the abundant rock art frequently associated with Fremont archaeological sites. Subsistence was based on maize agriculture, supplemented by hunting and gathering. The largest villages are located in southwestern Utah, one of which is Five Finger Ridge. The Fremont culture, as a recognizable prehistoric entity, spanned the period from AD 500 to 1300. However, the regional variant of central and southwestern Utah, termed the Parowan Fremont by Jack Marwitt, began several centuries later than in other Fremont regions. The terminal occupation date of all Fremont regions corresponds with the final abandonment of the Anasazi area following a protracted Colorado Plateau drought. The ultimate fate of the Fremont people remains unresolved.

The origin of the Fremont culture is a subject of debate among scholars. In Noel Morss's original definition, the Fremont people were thought to have practiced a Puebloan culture on the northern periphery of the Anasazi area. The generally held opinion was that the Fremont presence resulted from a northward population movement of Anasazi farmers, whose material culture was modified through time as a result of adaptation to changing environmental and societal

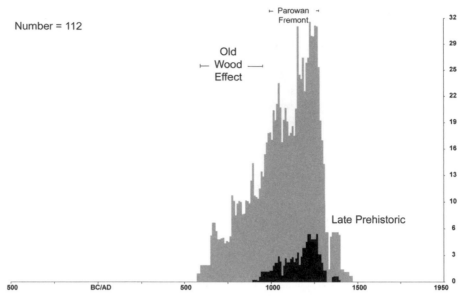

Histogram of tree-ring corrected radiocarbon dates for the southwestern Utah Parowan Fremont sites. Black bars refer to dates on high-credibility annuals. Gray bars refer to undifferentiated charcoal dates.   [Michael S. Berry]

conditions. Decades later, when it became clear from excavation of deeply stratified sites that the region had been occupied for at least 10,000 years, another theory evolved. Due in large measure to the work of Jesse D. Jennings and his students at the University of Utah, the concept of in situ development of the Fremont from an indigenous Archaic hunter-gatherer foundation became the predominant view. Predictably, that theory is now being challenged and the debate continues, supported by increasingly sophisticated analytic techniques including accelerator mass spectrometer (AMS) dating, mitochondrial DNA, and stable isotope analysis. This is an exciting time in North American archaeology in general and Fremont studies in particular as these new techniques are applied to long-standing theoretical questions and make possible the formulation of more powerful explanatory models.

Significant sites in the Clear Creek vicinity include Five Finger Ridge, Cave of 100 Hands, Sheep Shelter, North Cedars Cave, Trail Mountain Rockshelter, Coyote Granary, Falling Man Granary, Icicle Bench, Radford Roost, Lott's Farm, and forty-three rock art sites. This suite of sites constitutes a major contribution to our understanding of Parowan Fremont and Late Archaic prehistory.

Five Finger Ridge is by far the most important site in the Clear Creek area. The site was located on a high knoll 5 kilometers from the mouth of Clear Creek Canyon. It has subsequently been destroyed to provide fill material for the construction of Interstate 70. Eighty-one structures were excavated, including pit structures, surface structures, and granaries. Pit structures ranged from semicircular to rectangular with lateral ventilator shafts, typical of the late Fremont structures in southwestern Utah. The granaries are constructed of

coarse adobe and frequently divided into two compartments. This is reminiscent of the traditional Hopi practice of maintaining a two-year supply of maize as a buffer against low-yield agricultural years. Ceramics include Sevier Gray, Sevier Black-on-Gray, Snake Valley Black-on-Gray, Sevier Corrugated, Snake Valley Corrugated, and a variety of subtypes. The decorated grayware bowls are stylistically similar to the Sosi-Dogozhi Black-on-White ceramics in the Kayenta Anasazi region during the Pueblo II era. Corrugated grayware specimens are also similar to contemporaneous Anasazi ceramics. Projectile points include Parowan Basil-Notched as well as side- and corner-notched varieties. In addition, the artifact collection included ground-stone specimens unique to the Fremont culture, stone balls, and the Utah-type metate.

Chronometric dating of the site is based on sixty-two radiocarbon dates, forty-one archaeomagnetic dates, nine tree ring dates, and sixteen obsidian hydration dates. The original investigators relied primarily on the carbon-14 dates and conclude that the majority of site occupation occurred in the thirteenth century AD while acknowledging that the chronometric data is equivocal.

We have a picture of the patterns of occupation, but it is not all that clear, nor is it conclusive. One of the reasons is that many of the ^{14}C ages [i.e., radiocarbon dates] from structures were taken from wood charcoal from roof beams and posts, hearths, and from pooled samples on or near floors. . . . In essence, the old wood inside beams, posts, and any timbers give charcoal from these woods a high probability of assaying much older than the actual date of a building or hearth. This is what appears to have happened with a majority of ^{14}C ages from Five Finger Ridge. A series of radiocarbon ages assayed on corn from the structures would be much more useful. Some future researcher will undoubtedly see to this. (Talbot et al. 2000, 205)

The authors refer to the well-known problem of sample selection for radiocarbon (^{14}C) dating. Annual plants and other short-lived organics are to be preferred for this purpose over charcoal, which can yield misleading results due to both "built-in bias" and the use of old wood in hearths. This is a problem common to many areas of the Southwest that can readily be resolved through reliance on AMS dating of small samples such as seeds, maize cupules, and other types of samples that relate to the actual event in question. The difficulty we face is not merely poor sample selection at Five Finger Ridge, but a large corpus of ^{14}C data from southwestern Utah analyzed prior to the advent of AMS dating.

The charcoal dates reach back as far as AD 600 and are systematically a few centuries earlier than the more credible dates on samples from annual plants. The actual onset of Parowan Fremont in general—based on the dated annuals—is approximately AD 850, and, as mentioned above, occupation terminated at AD 1300. Five Finger Ridge may have been occupied as early as AD 1100 as indicated by the few tree ring samples analyzed, while most of the radiocarbon dates fall in the 1200s. Additional radiocarbon dates on carbon samples from annual plants might be carried out in order to resolve chronological issues for this important site. This is especially significant for pinpointing the abandonment to determine if it correlates with independently known climatic records of drought.

The other sheltered and domestic architectural sites yielded interesting information, but nothing approaching the sheer bulk of data recovered from Five Finger Ridge. They also are subject to the same difficulties regarding precise dating of the occupations due to ^{14}C sample selection. The most significant remaining archaeological phenomena are the spectacular rock art panels to which visitors have ample access via the many well-maintained trails. There are 43 rock art sites containing 677 panels. Anthropomorphs, zoomorphs, abstract figures, and geometric figures occur in vast profusion, executed in the form of both petroglyphs and pictographs. While it is inherently difficult to associate rock art temporally or culturally to the village and cave sites in the area, the intrinsic artistic value of the panels is undeniably beyond measure.

The Fremont Indian State Park is located 21 miles southwest of Richfield on Interstate 70 in southwest Utah. Fishing, hiking, camping, and picnicking are available. Tent sites and RV trailer sites are available. Additional details are available at http://www.utah.com/stateparks/fremont.htm.

Further Reading: Baker, Shane A., and Scott E. Billat, *Rock Art of the Clear Creek Canyon in Central Utah*, Occasional Paper No. 6 (Provo, UT: Brigham Young University, Museum of Peoples and Cultures, 1999); Janetski, Joel C., *Archaeology of Clear Creek Canyon* (Provo, UT: Brigham Young University, Museum of Peoples and Cultures, 1998); Jennings, Jesse D., *Prehistory of Utah and the Eastern Great Basin*, Anthropological Papers, No. 98 (Salt Lake City: University of Utah, 1978); Marwitt, John P., *Median Village and Fremont Culture Regional Variation*, Anthropological Papers, No. 95 (Salt Lake City: University of Utah, 1970); Morss, Noel, *The Ancient Culture of the Fremont River in Utah*, Papers of the Peabody Museum of American Archaeology and Ethnology, Vol. 12, No. 2 (Cambridge, MA: Harvard University, 1931); Talbot, Richard K., Lane D. Richins, James D. Wilde, Joel C. Janetski, and Deborah E. Newman, *Excavations at Five Finger Ridge, Clear Creek Canyon, Central Utah*, Occasional Paper No. 5 (Provo, UT: Brigham Young University, Museum of Peoples and Cultures, 2000).

Michael S. Berry

FORT ROCK CAVE, DIRTY SHAME ROCKSHELTER, NEWBERRY CRATER, AND OTHER SITES

South Central Oregon

12,000 Years of Changing Human Adaptations

The northern Great Basin of central Oregon is best known for the ancient archaeological deposits and amazingly well-preserved perishable artifacts (sandals, baskets, cordage, nets, threads, and *atl atls*) found in the dry caves of the region. Deep, cold-water lakes covered most of the basin and valley floors of the Great Basin (that portion of Oregon, Nevada, California, and Utah that does not drain to the Pacific Ocean) throughout the Late Pleistocene. Numerous caves in Oregon, wave-carved by huge lakes from pockets of soft volcanic rock in cliffs above valley floors at the height of the Pleistocene, were exposed for human occupation as the deep waters receded from high stands some 16,000 to

18,000 years ago. Biotically rich warm-water marshes, surrounded by expansive grasslands, were generally well established by about 12,000 BC. These new ecological niches were extremely productive, supporting dense populations of fish; waterfowl; large mammals such as bison, camels, horses, deer, mountain sheep, and pronghorn; and small animals like jackrabbit, cottontails, and squirrels. The environment that the first human colonists encountered in this region was much cooler, wetter, and more productive than the deserts of today. The weather and ecosystems changed throughout the last 14,000 or more years in which humans have been in this area, and the number of people living on the landscape increased. People had to adapt to accommodate these changes. Tracking those adaptations across time, space, and the landscape is an exciting process.

FORT ROCK CAVE, FORT ROCK, OREGON

The first human inhabitants arrived in the northern Great Basin sometime before 12,000 BC. Radiocarbon dating of a hearth excavated in rounded lakeshore gravels in the floor of Fort Rock Cave suggests that people may have occupied the site by 13,800 BC. However, there is only a very tiny tool assemblage associated with this hearth, and what there is looks much like the assemblage of the following cultural stage, including Western Stemmed points, scrapers, bifaces, and a mano (hand stone for grinding seeds). This possibly younger assemblage suggests that the charcoal dated from this hearth may have originated with old driftwood left by the lake in the back of the cave as it dried up, and that the date obtained from this old wood may be older than the first human occupation of the cave. The next, undisputed occupation of the cave occurred about 10,000 BC.

Fort Rock Cave is best known for the seventy-five sandals made of twisted sagebrush bark cords recovered by Luther Cressman—the "Father of Oregon Archaeology"—in 1938. These sandals have a toe flap that protects the front of the foot and helps to secure the sandal (along with lacing) tightly to the foot. This toe flap makes Fort Rock sandals distinctive from all other sandal types. Fort Rock sandals have recently been radiocarbon-dated to between 8000 and 7000 BC. Why so many of them have been found in this one site, when they are seldom found elsewhere, remains a mystery.

PAISLEY 5 MILE POINT CAVES, SUMMER LAKE BASIN, OREGON

The oldest securely dated site in the region is the Paisley 5 Mile Point Caves site located about 50 miles south of Fort Rock in the Summer Lake basin. Here, in a number of caves looking out over a broad, sandy plain that was once the bottom of pluvial Winter Lake, evidence was found of human occupations 14,300 years old (12,300 BC). Dried human feces (called coprolites) and tiny sewing threads made of tightly twisted animal sinew, processed grass, and Indian

hemp are found among the bones of camelids (probably *Camelops*), horses, bison, waterfowl, fish, and pikas (a small rabbit-like rodent now found only at much higher elevations). Ancient human DNA recovered from the feces clearly indicates that the occupants were the ancestors of Native Americans residing in the region today. The ancient site occupants had consumed bison meat, rosehips, and other plant materials before defecating in the caves. However, they did not stay long at the site and left only a few broken stone tools and flakes behind.

Some 1,300 years later (11,000 BC) the site was occupied again. This time people came more frequently and stayed longer, leaving more stone tools (points, knives, scrapers, and cores), stone chips, bone tools, bone food scraps, and perishable materials including feces, sagebrush rope, threads, cordage, and wooden pegs. Most stone tools are obsidian and have been dated by the obsidian hydration method. Obsidian hydration dating calculates the age of artifacts by measuring the thickness of the rind (in microns) formed by the adsorption of molecular H_2O by the stone after it was last chipped. At the Paisley Caves, the results of these measurements clearly support the radiocarbon dates, indicating that the caves were occupied at about 12,300 BC, abandoned, and occupied again at about 11,000 to 10,000 BC. The site continued to be used off and on until the historic period.

CATLOW AND ROARING SPRINGS CAVES, CATLOW VALLEY, OREGON

The presence of extinct Pleistocene animal bones (horse) mixed with human bones and stone artifacts in lake gravels at the bottom of Catlow Cave suggests that it may have been occupied as early as the Paisley Caves. However, the evidence has not been firmly established at this site. Though human bones were found in lakeshore gravels at the bottom of Catlow Cave, there was no way at the time (pre–radiocarbon dating) to prove that the disturbed bones were the same age as the gravels; they may simply have been mixed in with them by humans or animals digging in the cave deposits at a later date. The Catlow and Roaring Springs caves remain famous as the first Great Basin sites investigated by Cressman in his 1930s quest to prove that people had occupied the Oregon deserts during the Late Pleistocene, and are best known for the assemblages of wonderfully preserved baskets, sandals, cordage, bulrush matting, and *atl atls* (throwing boards) he found there. While some of these have been dated by the radiocarbon technique, they are all much younger than the Pleistocene.

CONNLEY CAVES, SILVER LAKE, OREGON

The Connley Caves, located in the Fort Basin about 10 miles south of the village of Fort Rock, are situated at the base of the Connley Hills about a mile north of Paulina Marsh. The Connley Caves are most famous as the type site from which the Western Pluvial Lakes tradition was defined. Here, in deposits dated between 11,000 and 6000 BC, an assemblage of tools and bones was found that seemed to reflect a strong subsistence focus on lacustrine resources (primarily ducks and geese) combined with grasslands resources such as bison, rabbits, and sage hens. By 6000 BC the marshes on which this subsistence strategy depended had begun to dry out. Native American lifeways changed to a more transient form of existence in which people visited sites in the marshes for very brief periods of time, and seldom camped in the caves located at somewhat higher elevations surrounding the valley floor.

The eruption of Mount Mazama (the collapsed volcanic caldera in which modern-day Crater Lake formed) at about 5600 BC spread volcanic ash across central Oregon, forming an excellent horizon marker in the stratigraphic deposits at many archaeological sites. In lowland settings, this ash was quickly re-deposited by the wind, settling into sand dunes and sand sheets draped across much of the northern Great Basin landscape.

PAULINA LAKE SITE, NEWBERRY VOLCANO NATIONAL MONUMENT, OREGON

At the Paulina Lake site, inside the Newberry Volcano caldera some 25 miles northwest of Fort Rock, Mt. Mazama ash deeply buried the charred remains of a small wickiup built of lodgepole pines about 7500 BC. This site, located next to the lake outlet at an elevation of 6,300 feet, was undoubtedly occupied during the summer since the area is often subjected to snow for much of the remainder of the year. Tracing rare elements found in obsidian artifacts at sites allows scientists to identify from which quarries the raw tool stones were collected. This process of obsidian sourcing indicates that the people who occupied the Paulina Lake site before Mt. Mazama erupted had recently come from the Fort Rock Basin, bringing obsidian tools with them made from sources located there and from locations even farther to the south and west. Blood protein analysis of stone tools indicates that the site occupants butchered bison, elk, and bear outside the wickiup. They processed rabbit inside the house, where the pollen of lomatiums (edible roots) was also found. The associated tool assemblage, including projectile points, knives, girdled stones, abraders, scrapers, and other tools, is relatively complex, suggesting that people performed many different kinds of tasks. Here, as at the Connley Caves, between 6500 and 5500 BC site occupations changed from longer-term stays, during which a broad range of hunting, collecting, processing, and manufacturing activities were conducted, to shorter stays characterized by intensive hunting and the production of stone projectile points and knives used in hunting and the processing of meat.

The Connley and other caves of the region were seldom occupied between 5600 and about 3600 BC, which is not to say that the region was abandoned. Ongoing research has documented the occupation of the sand dunes surrounding the marshes of the region during this period, indicating that changing lifestyles involving different settlement and subsistence patterns had taken Native Americans out of the caves during that portion of the year that they had previously occupied them (late fall, winter, and spring?) and into the dunes and other portions of the environment in early post-Mt. Mazama times.

FORT ROCK, CHRISTMAS VALLEY, AND SILVER LAKE SUBBASINS, FORT ROCK BASIN, OREGON

The caves began to be occupied again on a more frequent basis about the same time (ca. 4000–3600 BC) that the first houses and large storage pits (1–2 m in diameter) were built along the edges of ponds and channels in the Fort Rock marshes. The vast number of sites, including Bergen, Big M, and DJ Ranch, provide strong evidence that populations had increased dramatically. This may have initially been caused by people moving away from unusually deep snows or flooded marshes in surrounding basins and coming to the Fort Rock basin, where snows are seldom deep and the lay of the land is such that marshes do not usually get damaged by excessive flooding. Complex artifact assemblages—including shell and stone beads imported from southern California and northern Mexico; bone artifact kits including fancy spoons, spatulas, awls, net-shuttles, gaming pieces, and polished beads and tubes; smoking pipes of stone, bone, and clay; and groups of well-made stone balls, manos, metates, pestles, mortars, and mauls—all attest to an increasing length of stay in small family hamlets (usually only two to three houses at each location) out in the marshes of the Fort Rock basin and increasing social interactions. Supporting the development of these new settlements and social patterns were practices such as fishing for tui chubs (large minnows); the hunting of rabbit, deer, and waterfowl; and the intensive collection of small seeds such as bulrush, goosefoot, grass, and wada.

Between 2000 and 1500 BC upland root crops came to be more important than they had been previously. Changing weather patterns may have increased spring root crop reliability and length of annual availability, allowing human populations to steadily increase as winter survival rates improved. By 1000 BC the Fort Rock marshes, which continued to be exploited for important foods and materials on a seasonal (predominantly summer) basis, were no longer the location of choice for most winter houses. Instead, small winter villages and hamlets were generally built on low ridges at the base of foothills nearer the root grounds but still adjacent to the marshes, from which important resources were harvested also.

CARLON AND BOULDER VILLAGE SITES, SILVER LAKE, OREGON

Occasionally, as at the Carlon Village site near Silver Lake, the inhabitants built very impressive homes out of huge boulders weighing more than a ton each. Charcoal found inside these stone foundations indicates that the superstructures were made of lodgepole pine hauled from mountain ridges more than a mile away. The roof and walls were covered with sheaves of coarse grass and bulrush matting. These large stone circles—most are 7 meters or more in diameter and probably housed at least two families—undoubtedly indicate a higher degree of social standing among some residents. Like mansions everywhere, these houses are believed to be testament to the substance and social stature of owners capable of mobilizing workforces of skilled laborers. These people moved extremely heavy stones into position and then placed wedge-shaped stones under them to make them stand on end, forming the lower portion of the wall against which the lodgepole pine superstructure leaned. In at least one instance, they also placed a large boulder atop two smaller boulders to form an imposing billboard, decorating it with pictographs (designs painted on the surface) and petroglyphs (designs pecked into the surface with a hammer stone). These villages were clearly occupied by a culture (Klamath/Modoc?) with a somewhat higher degree of social complexity than is normally attributed to predominantly egalitarian Great Basin societies such as the Paiutes and Shoshones.

In the upland root grounds, some 1,000 feet or more above the basin floor, is the Boulder Village site, a seasonally (spring) occupied village located in a huge boulder field. Although 125 house foundations built of small boulders, and at least 48 well-made storage pits, have been found at this site, there is little evidence that it was occupied very long during any single year. There are very few bone and shell items of personal adornment (beads or pendants), and most functional artifacts are undecorated and shaped only to the minimal degree needed to make them functionally efficient. This indicates that the sites were used very briefly each year, probably during the spring root collecting season. The houses and artifacts were left at the site as the occupants moved to the next available food source each spring.

Northern Paiutes were visiting the Boulder Village site by the mid-1850s and claim the Fort Rock basin as their ceded land to this day. Tree ring analysis indicates that a small wickiup, some 4 meters in diameter, was made from junipers cut with an axe or hatchet in 1854. Glass beads and an iron knife blade were recovered from inside the circle of charcoal left after the house burned. While this must have been hard on the inhabitants, it was good for archaeology. Besides the stone, glass, and iron artifacts found inside the house were the remains of a mound of seeds and dried roots that had been charred in the fire, preserving the food remains for later discovery, analysis, and identification. These food items, though found together, were harvested from both the upland root grounds and lowland seed fields and during different seasons of the year (spring and summer), indicating a certain level of preservation,

transport, and storage of food items that do not normally occur together on the landscape.

THE SITES

Most of the sites listed here are located on public properties managed by the Bureau of Land Management (BLM), the Oregon State Park system, or the National Parks system. Fort Rock Cave can be visited by scheduling a site tour during the tourist season with Oregon State Parks personnel stationed in LaPine. This famous site is well worth the effort required to obtain a tour. Healthy visitors normally walk about a quarter mile into the site along a good but primitive dirt road. Disabled visitors are taken to the site in State Parks vehicles. The Paulina Lake site is located at the "Y" in the road next to the outlet of the lake. The road to the marina and cabins crosses the site to the north (left) while the main road continues east across the site past the Paulina Lake campground and on to East Lake. The site is buried beneath more than a meter of yellow Mt. Mazama volcanic cinders, but visiting the location and walking along the lakeshore is a good way to get a feel for what life next to the lake must have been like 10,000 years ago. The Connley Caves, Paisley 5 Mile Point Caves, Catlow Cave, Bergen, Big M, and Boulder Village sites are all located on public lands managed by the BLM. The locations of these sites are not readily disclosed to the public as a measure of site protection from vandalism. The Roaring Springs Cave and Carlon Village sites are located on private property.

Further Reading: Aikens, C. Melvin, and Dennis L. Jenkins, eds., *Archaeological Researches in the Northern Great Basin: Fort Rock Archaeology since Cressman*, Anthropological Papers, No. 50 (Eugene: University of Oregon, 1994); Bedwell, Stephen F., *Fort Rock Basin: Prehistory and Environment* (Eugene: University of Oregon Books, 1973); Connolly, Thomas J., *Newberry Crater: A Ten-Thousand-Year Record of Human Occupation and Environmental Change in the Basin-Plateau Borderlands*, Anthropological Papers, No. 121 (Salt Lake City: University of Utah, 1999); Cressman, Luther S., *Archaeological Researches in the Northern Great Basin*, Publication No. 538 (Washington, DC: Carnegie Institution, 1942); Cressman, Luther S., Howel Williams, and Alex D. Krieger, *Early Man in Oregon: Archaeological Studies in the Northern Great Basin*, Studies in Anthropology, Monograph No. 3 (Eugene: University of Oregon, 1940); d'Azevedo, Warren L., ed., *Handbook of North American Indians*, Vol. 11: *Great Basin* (Washington, DC: Smithsonian Institution, 1986); Jenkins, Dennis L., Thomas J. Connolly, and C. Melvin Aikens, eds., *Early and Middle Holocene Archaeology of the Northern Great Basin*, Anthropological Papers, No. 62 (Eugene: University of Oregon, 2004); Spier, Leslie, *Klamath Ethnography*, Publications in American Archaeology and Ethnology, No. 30 (Berkeley: University of California, 1930); Wingard, George F., *Carlon Village: Land, Water, Subsistence, and Sedentism in the Northern Great Basin* Anthropological Papers, No. 57 (Eugene: University of Oregon, 2001).

Dennis L. Jenkins

GOLD HILL, BORDER VILLAGE, WINDOM, AND OTHER SITES

Southwest Oregon

Ancient Life in the Klamath and Southern Cascade Mountains

The mountainous region of southwest Oregon is unique; here the Klamath Mountains—the remains of ancient seashores uplifted through plate tectonics—reach from the Pacific Ocean to the interior to meet the Cascade Range, a much younger mountain chain formed by ongoing volcanic activity that has created high, snowcapped mountain peaks and calderas such as Mt. Shasta, Mt. McLoughlin, and Crater Lake. Southwest Oregon is a region of transitions; it lies at the southern boundary of the Pacific Northwest rain coast, and the coastal mountains and alpine areas of the region are covered with rich pine, fir, and cedar forests interspersed with meadows rich in berries, camas, and other plant resources. The Rogue, Klamath, Coquille, and other rivers are home to rich seasonal runs of salmon—the staple resource of the Native American people of the region. However, the extensive oak prairies and hot summers bespeak the region's similarities to the drier regions of the interior valleys of California and the desert regions to the south and east.

People have lived in southwest Oregon for at least 10,000 years. The presence of Paleoindian spear points similar in characteristics to those found elsewhere in the Americas attests to human use of the region at the end of the ice ages, and shell middens—piles of shells and bones left over from ancient meals—have been identified on the southern Oregon coast that date to over 8,000 years ago. Since that time, many different people speaking many different languages have migrated into the region. When English-speaking American pioneers first arrived in the 1840s, they encountered Indian people who spoke diverse dialects of Athabascan, Penutian, and Hokan tongues.

Despite their diverse origins, the indigenous inhabitants of the region all shared an appreciation for their mountainous and relatively isolated home. For over 10,000 years Indian people remained gatherers, hunters, and fishers of the bounty of the land, relying on acorns, berries, camas, salmon, elk, and deer. They followed a cultural ecology predicated on mobility; living in permanent villages located adjacent to coastal estuaries or salmon-rich rivers, households traveled seasonally for a variety of social, economic, or spiritual reasons. Despite long-term continuity in cultural practices, archaeological and ethnographic evidence suggests that, like their neighbors in coastal California or elsewhere on the northwest coast, the social lives of the Indian people of the southwestern mountains of

Oregon became more complex over the last 2,000 years. The Indian people encountered by the first European explorers and settlers lived in a society where the differential accumulation of wealth and social power was common, and particularly rich chiefs and their families presided over large and relatively populous villages.

The archaeology of the southwestern mountains of Oregon has long been of interest to scholars. Professional archaeological research began in the region in the 1930s and accelerated after the 1960s as large-scale dams were built on the Rogue, Applegate, and other rivers of the region. Many villages, campsites, and other archaeological sites were and continue to be investigated within the context of public undertakings by the Department of Transportation, the Army Corp of Engineers, the Forest Service, the U.S. Fish and Wildlife Service, the Bureau of Land Management, and other public agencies.

GOLD HILL SITE

The Gold Hill site, located on a terrace overlooking the Rogue River, is among the most significant cultural places in the southwestern mountains of Oregon. Local residents initially identified the site, and beginning in 1930 Luther Cressman of the University of Oregon spent three field seasons excavating a cemetery of at least thirty-nine burials. These bodies were interred on their left side, head to the south, facing west, with the legs flexed against the chest. Grave goods included finely made obsidian bifaces, projectile points, broken mortars and pestles, schist and steatite tobacco pipes, and shell and pine nut beads. Based on the styles of spear and arrow points, the site likely dates to within the last 2,000 years.

The Gold Hill site remains the only well-studied cemetery in the region, and Cressman's work emphasizes several important points about the Native American people of the area. The Takelma and Athabascan people had a complex society that included social inequalities, as emphasized by the differential distribution of grave goods at the site—almost all of the shell and pine nut beads, for example, were recovered from the grave of a single eight-year-old child. Likewise, the obsidian blades were differentially distributed and were recovered in pairs from some but not all of the burials. These blades are finely made, slightly waisted bifaces up to 12 inches long. Based on their delicacy and the exceptional craftsmanship employed in their

The Rogue River canyon in the mountains of southwest Oregon. [Southern Oregon University Laboratory of Anthropology/Mark Tveskov]

manufacture, they almost certainly served as ceremonial items that emphasized social power and standing. The local importance of extra-regional social networks is reflected in the fact that the obsidian would have been traded or obtained from sources at least 100 miles to the east of the Cascade Range.

THE MARIAL SITE

The Native American people who interred their ancestors in the Gold Hill cemetery were the descendants of at least 10,000 years of occupation of the southwestern mountains of Oregon. Unfortunately for archaeologists, dramatic geological processes make accessing the material remains of the earliest inhabitants of the region difficult; mountainside terraces erode into steep river bottoms, often burying older sites under dozens of feet of sediment, and along the coast periodic earthquakes and rapid erosion bury or destroy ancient surfaces. Nonetheless, a handful of occupations dating to the earliest years of human use of the region have been found, and the Marial site is perhaps the most significant of these.

The Marial site is located in the precipitous gorge that separates the lower Rogue River estuary from the interior Rogue River valley. The site lies at the confluence of the Rogue

River and Mule Creek, both of which are home to large runs of salmon on a seasonal basis. A quiet pool bracketed by rapids—an ideal salmon fishing area—is located immediately adjacent to the site. Extensive archaeological excavations carried out in the 1980s by Oregon State University archaeologist Richard Ross and his students uncovered over 15 feet of finely stratified cultural materials, and radiocarbon dates on these layers demonstrate that the site was in use almost continuously from 9,000 years ago until almost the historic period. Cultural material from the site included numerous but highly fragmentary pieces of animal and fish bone, charred hazelnut fragments, and large numbers of spear, dart, and arrow points. As at the Gold Hill site, imported obsidian was also found.

THE LIMPY CREEK SITE

The Marial site emphasizes the long duration of human use of the interior mountains of southwest Oregon. For thousands of the years, the way of life of the Indian people of the region was stable, characterized by relatively low population densities and fishing, gathering, and hunting ecology. Over the last 3,000 years, however, this way of life was augmented by the use of permanent riverside villages from which salmon were

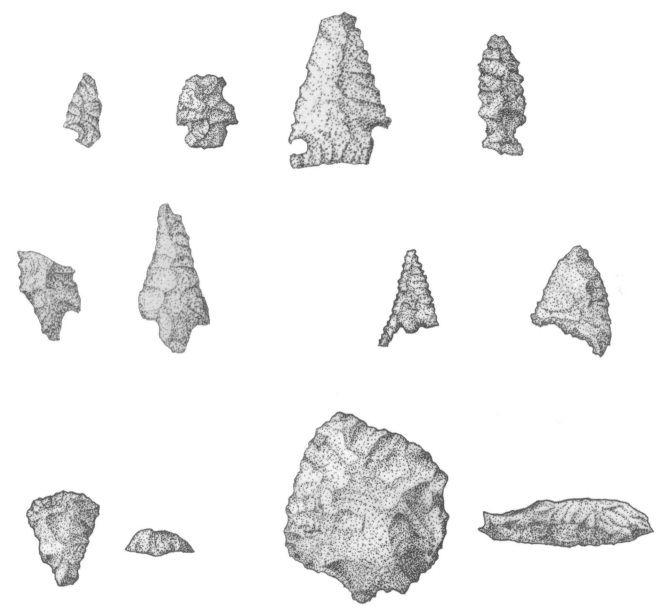

Chipped-stone tools from seasonal campsites in the Cascade Range of southwest Oregon.   [Illustrated by Celia-Moret Ferguson, Southern Oregon University Laboratory of Anthropology]

mass-harvested and stored, the emergence of elaborate wealth accumulation and exchange along with social inequality, and perhaps higher population densities. The reason for this transformation, a local manifestation of a larger pattern of cultural change occurring at this time up and down the west coast of North America, remains unknown, but increasing populations and the immigration of Athabascan- and Hokan-speaking peoples into the region after 2,000 years ago might have been catalysts.

Permanent architecture in the form of semi-subterranean houses, elaborate material culture, and intensified salmon fishing are all hallmarks of the late prehistoric cultures of the region and are found at village sites located sites across the region. Excavations at the Limpy Creek site in the 1990s by archaeologists from the Oregon State Museum of Anthropology recovered a rich assemblage of artifacts and features, including slate pendants, a steatite lamp, woodworking tools, and the remains of a semi-subterranean domestic structure that contained a well-made stone hearth. While the tools found at the site suggest that the inhabitants were hunting and gathering, salmon fishing was clearly one of the most important activities. The Limpy Creek site is located adjacent to the Rogue River just downstream from its confluence with the Applegate River, and the immediate site setting is clearly ideal for salmon fishing; the quiet pool below the site, to this day, is considered ideal "holding water" for salmon as they rest before ascending a long stretch of rapids just upstream. Numerous artifacts relating to fishing were recovered, including dozens of stone net weights that, according to Native American oral traditions from the region, were used to weight down the leading edge of large seine nets used to catch salmon. Although fish remains are usually too delicate to survive long in the acidic soils of southwest Oregon, the careful examination of sediment samples from the midden (trash dump) at the site yielded hundreds of almost microscopic fragments of salmon bone. Radiocarbon dates indicate that the Limpy Creek Site was first occupied within the last 1,000 years, and the presence of glass beads, iron horse tack, an 1838 U.S. dime, and other artifacts of European manufacture suggest that it was not finally abandoned until the mid-nineteenth century.

THE WINDOM SITE

The archaeological record of the southwestern mountains of Oregon indicates that for millennia, Indian people of the region followed a way of life that was predicated on an intimate relationship with and an intense understanding of the dynamics of the regional landscape. While permanent villages located on major rivers anchored their settlement patterns, their cultural ecology included the use of many resources besides salmon; elk, deer, and bear hunting were important activities, as was the gathering of acorns, camas (a starchy bulb), and many other plant species. Harvesting these resources required families to move on a seasonal basis to upland locations, and to employ techniques such as landscape burning to foster their productivity. The upland hills and mountain slopes of southwest Oregon yield numerous remains of these seasonal campsites and open meadows created during these activities.

One such site is the Windom site, one of several seasonal encampments excavated in recent years by archaeologists from Southern Oregon University. Located on a mountainside terrace, the site overlooks a meadow that is a relic of an ancient, fire-managed landscape. For generations, Indian people burned this landscape, maintaining a fertile, open meadow ideal for the growth of a few large, acorn-rich oak trees and stands of camas, tarweed, and other economically important species. The Windom site itself is exceptionally rich in cultural material, and projectile points and other evidence suggest that the site was used for at least 2,000 years and perhaps as long as 8,000 years. Like many of these upland sites, these remains were deposited on a seasonal basis, as families visited the location year after year to gather plant resources and hunt big game. Such upland landscapes were carefully maintained over generations by Indian people, and likely were important not only for economic reasons but also in fostering a sense of ancestral biography and tenure in a given place.

Further Reading: Aikens, Mel, *Archaeology of Oregon* (Portland, OR: U.S. Department of the Interior, Bureau of Land Management, 1994); Cressman, Luther S., "Aboriginal Burials in Southwestern Oregon," *American Anthropologist* 35 (1933): 116–130; Cressman, Luther S., *Contributions to the Archaeology of Oregon: Final Report on the Gold Hill Burial Site*, University of Oregon Studies in Anthropology (Eugene: University of Oregon, 1933); O'Neill, Brian M., and Mark Tveskov, *The Limpy Creek Site: A Contact Period Fishing Camp on the Rogue River, Southwestern Oregon*, University of Oregon Anthropological Papers (Eugene: University of Oregon, 2007); Tveskov, Mark A., and Amie Cohen, *The Archaeology of the Western Cascades of Southwest Oregon*, Southern Oregon University Research Report 2006-2 (Ashland: Southern Oregon University, 2006).

Mark Tveskov

LOWER COLUMBIA RIVER SITES:
FIVE MILE RAPIDS TO McNARY DAM

Northern Oregon and Southern Washington State
Ancient Habitation along the Columbia River

The Columbia River flows from the Canadian Rockies to the Pacific Ocean, winding for 1,300 miles through four mountain ranges. The 90-mile stretch between Five Mile Rapids and McNary Dam is part of the mid-Columbia River, which flows through the southern plateau. That area features rolling plains incised by steep-walled drainages and fringed by mountains.

The Cascade Mountains rise just west of Five Mile Rapids, separating the plateau from the northwest coast.

At the time of European contact, Sahaptin-speaking peoples lived along the mid-Columbia River. The western Columbia River Sahaptins, living between Five Mile Rapids and McNary Dam, identified with village communities rather

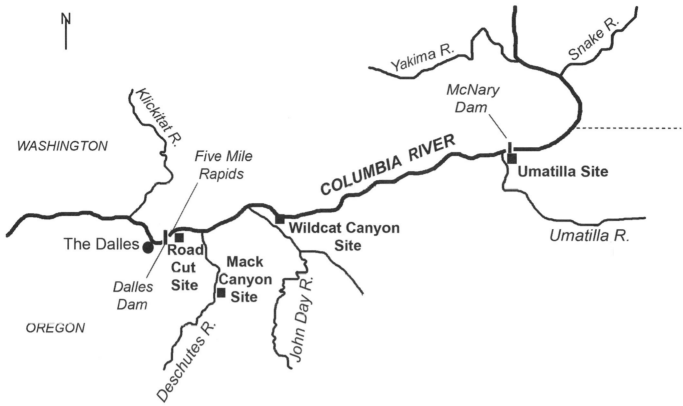

This map of the Columbia River shows geographic features and archaeological sites mentioned in the text.   [Elizabeth Sobel]

than any larger cultural group. Consequently, familiar names of cultural groups, for example, Tenino and Umatilla, stem from village names.

The Native economy was based on fishing, gathering, hunting, and trading. Staples included fish, roots, and berries. Fishing and trade were especially important because the area from Five Mile Rapids to Celilo Falls was among the most productive fisheries and active Native trade centers in indigenous North America. The inhabitants spent winters in pit houses and mat lodges within villages along the Columbia and its tributaries. During the warmer seasons, they dwelt in small mat lodges when hunting and gathering in the mountains.

The area between Five Mile Rapids and McNary Dam contains scores of archaeological sites. These sites bare remains of diverse features, including pit houses, mat lodges, hearths, ovens, storage pits, burials, rock art (carvings and paintings), refuse dumps, and stone alignments. The sites also contain animal bone, botanical remains (roots, seeds, wood), and artifacts of stone, bone, antler, shell, and plant fiber. Native sites dating to the time since European contact often yield European manufactures such as iron nails, brass buttons, and glass beads.

The archaeological findings indicate humans have inhabited the area for at least 12,000 years. Such early occupation is evidenced by surface finds of Clovis points, flaked-stone spear points made across much of North America during the Paleoindian period, between 13,500 and 12,000 years ago. From the Paleoindian period until about 3,000 years ago, the people living and traveling along the mid–Columbia River were highly mobile hunters and gatherers. By 2,500 years ago they had become more sedentary, as reflected by remains of villages and cemeteries. Archaeological materials from 2,500 to 250 years ago display an increased emphasis on fish, edible roots and tubers, long-distance trade, wealth, and social status. Remains from this period also evidence technological changes, including a shift from the *atl atl* (spear thrower) to the bow and arrow.

More recent archaeological sites, dating to the last 250 years, evidence changes relating to European contact. These changes include acquisition of European goods, adoption of the horse, and a resulting increase in trade and travel. At archaeological sites, these developments are reflected by the presence of European trade goods, greater quantities of Native trade goods, an increase in remains of mobile dwellings (mat lodges), and a decrease in remains of more permanent dwellings (pit houses). In addition, cremation pits with remains of many individuals may result from the widespread Native population declines that resulted from Old World diseases.

In the 1850s, the U.S. government placed most western Columbia River Sahaptins in the Confederated Tribes of

This photograph shows archaeological salmon bones embedded in deposits at the Roadcut site.   [Photograph by L. Virginia Butler]

Warm Springs, Confederated Tribes of the Umatilla Indian Reservation, and Confederated Tribes and Bands of the Yakama Nation, and forcibly moved them to reservations. Today many descendants live on and visit their ancestral lands along the Columbia River.

The public can learn about mid–Columbia River archaeology by visiting sites and museums in Washington and Oregon. Interpretive facilities in Washington include the Columbia Hills State Park in Dallesport, Columbia River Gorge Interpretive Center Museum in Stevenson, Maryhill Museum of Art in Goldendale, and Yakama Nation Museum in Toppenish. Facilities in Oregon include the Columbia River Discovery Center in The Dalles, Museum at Warm Springs, Museum of Natural and Cultural History at the University of Oregon in Eugene, Portland Art Museum, and Tmastslikt Cultural Institute in Pendleton.

Interpretive facilities shed light on four archaeological sites that are particularly important to our understanding of human heritage in the western mid–Columbia River valley: Roadcut, Mack Canyon, Wildcat Canyon, and Umatilla.

ROADCUT SITE, NORTH CENTRAL OREGON

The Roadcut site, also known as the Five Mile Rapids site, provides the strongest evidence of early, intensive salmon harvesting in the Pacific Northwest. In addition, along with several nearby sites, the Roadcut site evidences 9,000 years of human occupation along the Columbia River.

The Roadcut site is located in Oregon, on the south bank of the Columbia River, 5 miles east of the city of The Dalles. At the time of European contact, this area was inhabited by Sahaptin-speaking Tenino people. Like other Columbia River peoples, the Tenino had a subsistence economy based on fishing, gathering, hunting, and trading. Fishing and trading were especially important, as Tenino territory bordered a stretch of the Columbia called the Long Narrows by Lewis and Clark and Five Mile Rapids by later Euro-Americans. Before it was flooded by The Dalles Dam reservoir in 1957, this stretch was one of the most productive salmon fisheries in North America. The Tenino made use of this abundance, harvesting salmon for subsistence and export. The Roadcut site sheds light on the antiquity of these practices.

The Roadcut site was excavated in the 1950s by Luther Cressman of the University of Oregon and in 1993 by Virginia L. Butler of Portland State University. The excavations yielded remains of ancient daily activities between 9,300 and 5,000 years ago. Native peoples probably used the Roadcut site until after Euro-American arrival, given the excavation of historic artifacts from other archaeological sites in the area. However, twentieth-century development on the Roadcut site destroyed sediments deposited there over the last 5,000 years, precluding any definite conclusions about activity on the site during the past five millennia. Remains excavated from the site include animal bones, tools, tool-making byproducts, and sculptures of stone, bone, and antler. An absence of house remains may indicate that inhabitants typically used the site on a short-term basis.

One of the more important finds from this site is the roughly 250,000 salmon bones deposited between 9,300 and 8,000 years ago. Several researchers have suggested that natural processes such as water flow deposited these fish bones at the Roadcut site. However, Butler's investigation shows clearly that human fishing accounts for the fish bones. No other sites in the Pacific Northwest contain such a high quantity of salmon bones from such an early time period. Consequently, these bones provide the best evidence of regular salmon fishing by 9,300 years ago in the region.

Artifacts from the Roadcut site are on exhibit at the Museum of Natural and Cultural History at the University of Oregon in Eugene.

MACK CANYON SITE, NORTH CENTRAL OREGON

The Mack Canyon site reflects human activity from nearly 7,000 years ago to at least 250 years ago, when Euro-American activity began in the area. The site is located in Oregon, along the Deschutes River, 20 miles south of the Columbia River and 13 miles east of the modern city of The Dalles. At the time of Euro-American contact, the Mack Canyon site lay within the territory of the Tenino, a Sahaptin-speaking people with a subsistence economy based on fishing, gathering, hunting, and trading.

University of Oregon archaeologists conducted fieldwork at the Mack Canyon site in the 1960s. The archaeologists identified twenty-nine depressions on the ground surface. Excavation into three depressions revealed that they are remains of pit houses occupied between 2,000 and 250 years ago. Like historical Plateau pithouses, the ancient pithouses had a central floor surrounded by an elevated bench. The ancient dwellings were probably occupied in winter and perhaps also in warmer seasons.

Bones reveal that site inhabitants consumed various animals, including bighorn sheep, rabbit, fish, and freshwater mussel. Grinding stones indicate that residents ground plant foods such as roots and seeds. The site yielded other stone artifacts, including arrow points, scraping tools, knives, drills, and flakes (byproducts of tool manufacture). Bone artifacts include awls, beads, and one harpoon fragment.

The public can learn more by visiting the Mack Canyon site, which lies on public land managed by the U.S. Bureau of Land Management. A kiosk beside the site interprets its contents and significance. The Museum of Natural and Cultural History at the University of Oregon curates artifacts from the site.

WILDCAT CANYON SITE, NORTH CENTRAL OREGON

Wildcat Canyon is one of the most extensively studied archaeological sites containing both village and cemetery remains along the mid–Columbia River. The site lies on the south

bank of the Columbia River, several miles upstream from the John Day River mouth and 40 miles upstream from the modern city of The Dalles. At the time of Euro-American contact, the Wildcat Canyon site lay within the territory of the Sahaptin-speaking Tenino people. Like other Columbia River peoples, the Tenino had a subsistence economy based on fishing, gathering, hunting, and trading.

University of Oregon archaeologists conducted field work at Wildcat Canyon in the 1950s and 1960s. These investigations suggest that people inhabited the site between 9,000 and at least 250 years ago. From about 9,000 to 2,500 years ago, human activity consisted of occasional visits by small groups.

Later occupants were more sedentary, as evidenced by remains of at least six houses—most likely pit houses—dating between 2,500 and 1,000 years ago. These houses were probably occupied during winter and maybe in warmer seasons as well. Animal bones, arrow points, milling stones, net sinkers, and other excavated items indicate that residents subsisted on fish, shellfish, plants, and terrestrial mammals such as deer and antelope. Bone harpoon parts may reflect the pursuit of not only large fish, but also seals and sea lions available downstream near The Dalles. Site residents engaged in long-distance trade, indicated by obsidian (glassy volcanic stone), marine shell, and other artifacts of nonlocal origin.

Deposits dating between 2,500 and 1,000 years ago also held remains of nine dogs that were intentionally buried, perhaps during rituals. In addition, these deposits contained about eighty human burials. Remains of several human individuals displayed flattened foreheads, indicating intentional cranial modification during infancy. This modification may reflect a particular social status; historically, cranial modification was a mark of high status in northwest coast societies.

The period from 1,000 to 250 years ago at Wildcat Canyon is poorly understood because modern development disturbed remains from this period prior to archaeological excavation. However, glass beads, sheet copper, and other Euro-American trade goods recovered from the site reflect Native use until at least 250 years ago, when Euro-Americans began entering the area.

Artifacts from the Wildcat Canyon site are on exhibit at the Museum of Natural and Cultural History at the University of Oregon in Eugene.

UMATILLA SITE, NORTHEAST OREGON

The Umatilla site is one of the most extensively excavated—and plundered—archaeological sites along the mid–Columbia River. The site evidences human occupation from at least 7,000 years ago through the mid-twentieth century. Prehistoric materials include remains of a large village and cemetery. Historic materials include remains of Umatilla Landing, a Euro-American gold rush settlement begun in 1860.

The site is located on the south bank of the Columbia River, between McNary Dam and the modern town of

Umatilla, 90 miles upstream from the city of The Dalles. At the time of Euro-American contact, the site lay in the territory of the Umatilla people. Like other Plateau peoples, the Umatilla had a subsistence economy based on fishing, hunting, gathering, and trading.

During the twentieth century, looters destroyed and took many archaeological remains at the Umatilla site. Some looters were so intent on plundering the site that they dug tunnel systems in order to gain access. Despite this damage, some information about the site was recovered in the 1960s and 1970s through excavations by the University of Oregon, University of Idaho, Mid-Columbia Archaeological Society, Washington State University, and archaeological consulting firms under contract with the Army Corps of Engineers. The professional investigations revealed three major periods of human activity. The first period, from at least 7,000 to 2,500 years ago, consisted of multiple short-term occupations. The second period, from about 2,500 to 150 years ago, was characterized by more sedentary habitation, indicated by remains of more than 30 houses and 220 burials. Earlier houses were built over deep pits and had raised benches whereas later houses were built over shallow pits and had no benches; this change may reflect a shift from pit houses to mat lodges, and perhaps a change in site use from winter village

to fishing camp. Artifacts of stone, bone, and antler reflect hunting, grinding of plant foods, tool manufacture, and trade. Bones of salmon, rabbit, deer, elk, bighorn sheep, and antelope suggest residents harvested resources not only in the immediate vicinity but also in the more distant mountains. The third period, from AD 1860 to the 1960s, witnessed the founding and development of Umatilla Landing. Although most residents were Euro-American, the presence of Indians is indicated by historical records and artifacts such as flaked-glass tools.

Artifacts from the Umatilla site are curated by the Confederated Tribes of the Umatilla Indian Reservation at the Tmastslikt Cultural Institute.

Further Reading: Aikens, C. Melvin, *Archaeology of Oregon* (Portland, OR: U.S. Bureau of Land Management, 1993); Butler, V. L., and J. E. O'Connor, "9000 years of Fishing on the Columbia River, North America," *Quaternary Research* 62 (2004): 1–8; Keyser, James D., *Indian Rock Art of the Columbia Plateau* (Seattle: University of Washington Press, 1992); Confederated Tribes of the Umatilla Indian Reservation Web site, www.umatilla.nsn.us (online May 2007); Confederated Tribes of Warm Springs Web site, www.warmsprings.com/Warmsprings/Tribal_Community/History_ Culture (online May 2007).

Elizabeth Sobel

MIDDLE COLUMBIA RIVER SITES: LAKE WALLULA TO PRIEST RAPIDS

Southeastern Washington State

Kennewick Man Site and Hanford Reach Sites

The complex geological record of catastrophic flooding at the end of the glacial period provides the backdrop for the semi-arid landscape surrounding the Lake Wallula to Priest Rapids section of the Columbia River. The river bisects southeastern Washington for more than 100 river miles before it turns and flows westerly to McNary Dam, at the state boundary between Washington and Oregon.

Lake Wallula, the expansive reservoir behind the dam, was created by construction of McNary Dam in the early 1950s. The lake is approximately 61 miles long at 340 feet mean sea level, expanding from the dam upriver approximately 8 miles north of Richland, Washington. The lake inundated many significant archaeological sites and large areas of land near the Walla Walla River and Snake River confluences. Prehistoric and historic archaeological sites are present above the current lake shoreline, but urban

expansion, barge facilities, recreation areas, and agricultural expansion have all taken a toll on this irreplaceable resource, leaving few untouched archaeological sites in remote and undeveloped areas surrounding the reservoir.

Hanford Reach, the last free-flowing segment of the Columbia River, flows from Priest Rapids Dam into the northern boundary of Lake Wallula. The U.S. Department of Energy's 586-square-mile Hanford Site straddles much of the reach from Vantage to its southern boundary north of Richland, Washington. Public access to the Hanford site has been limited since federal land acquisition in 1943. The closure has meant that within site boundaries, archaeological resources have not been as heavily impacted by construction or by extensive urban or agricultural development as have other archaeological sites in the region and surrounding areas. Lake Wallula and the Hanford Reach area have been of interest to many visitors since captains Lewis and Clark and members of their party passed through the area in 1805 and 1806. The maps and descriptions they created provide some of the first documentation of Indian villages along the Snake River to the confluence and down the Columbia River.

Reservoir and dam construction coalesced with scientific archaeological interest in the early to mid-1900s. Early research on the Hanford Reach Wahluke site was conducted by Herbert Krieger in the 1920s. The Smithsonian Institution's River Basin Surveys program recorded archaeological sites in the Lake Wallula–McNary Reservoir area from 1947 to 1952. More systematic surveys and testing took place in subsequent years as federal agencies undertook archaeological studies around the lake and the Hanford Reach shorelines. Prehistoric archaeological sites dating from the early Holocene to the ethnographic period were recorded and described as pit house villages, temporary campsites, fishing stations, butchering sites, plant processing locations, quarries, vision quests, caches, trail systems, hunting blinds, and cemeteries/burials. Archaeological sites associated with the historic period, such as farmsteads and associated agricultural features, irrigation systems and canals, wells and cisterns, dumps and trash scatters, river crossings, trails and roads, and former town sites, were also recorded. As a result of these studies, a long and continued pattern began to emerge of human habitation and use near river shorelines, at confluences, and on islands—particularly in the Hanford Reach, where the archaeological record is relatively pristine.

LAKE WALLULA

Franklin Fenenga and Clarence E. Smith Jr. of the Smithsonian Institution's River Basin Surveys surveyed the Columbia River shoreline and islands before the land was inundated. Their pioneering fieldwork ended as Lake Wallula rose behind the newly constructed McNary Dam. In 1975 the new shoreline around the lake was surveyed to record visible archaeological sites, evaluate their condition, and describe impacts associated with erosion or vandalism. Subsequent to this, test excavations were conducted at Strawberry Island, where approximately 130 house pit depressions were noted, many oriented in a linear fashion along the north and south sides of the island. The island's previous inhabitants had relied on salmon fishing, as shown by recovered fish remains and notched net sinkers; processed plants with ground-stone tools; and extracted marrow or grease from fragmented bone. Controlled intensive surveys were conducted in 1981 and 1982 on islands and along the lake's northernmost shoreline, and again in 1999 along much of the entire shoreline.

KENNEWICK MAN

The earliest reported physical evidence of human habitation along this stretch of the Columbia River dates to approximately 9,000 years ago, as evidenced by skeletal remains discovered by recreationalists in 1996 near Kennewick, Washington. The nearly complete skeletal remains, known colloquially as "Kennewick Man" or "Ancient One," were found in the shoreline shallows of Lake Wallula, on the outskirts of Kennewick, Washington. The U.S. Army Corps of Engineers, land managers for the discovery location, followed the Native American Graves Protection and Repatriation Act process and published a newspaper notice that the skeletal remains were Native American and culturally affiliated with five Indian tribes. The published decision, although later rescinded, was followed by a legal controversy that endured for nearly a decade as several scientists, Indian tribes, and agency representatives confronted tough issues in federal court. These ancient skeletal remains have been the subject of a series of scientific studies by academic, museum, and government scientists to document the remains and provide information necessary to resolve the legal dispute. A total of five radiocarbon dates were taken from samples extracted from the skeletal remains. These dates and previous skeletal analysis suggest that the remains are those of a middle-aged male who was alive approximately 8,000 to 9,000 years ago. The great age of the remains became central to the legal opinion by Judge Gould, United States Court of Appeals for the Ninth Circuit, that the Kennewick Man remains are not ancestral to modern Native Americans. Following this decision, the remains were investigated further by a scientific team, including the plaintiffs in the legal case, who had petitioned the federal court for the right to examine the remains when they were first discovered. The remains are curated at the Burke Museum, University of Washington, Seattle.

Visitors to Lake Wallula can stay at any of several parks, launch boats at improved sites, or enjoy walks through wildlife refuges and habitat management units. Sites are protected by soil and vegetation or may be capped with riprap to reduce impacts from waves and reservoir operations. A visitors' center, located at Ice Harbor Dam, provides interpretive displays of the surrounding area and fish viewing windows.

HANFORD REACH

The Hanford Reach retains some of the richest archaeological resource areas in this portion of the Columbia River. Well-preserved sites from the prehistoric, contact, and historic periods are represented in large pit house villages, open campsites, spirit quests, hunting camps and blinds, game drives, quarries, and fishing stations. Six archaeological districts and three archaeological sites are listed in the National Register of Historic Places; many others have been found to be eligible for listing there. In prehistoric and early historic times, this portion of the Columbia River was populated by Native Americans of various tribal affiliations. Evidence of their presence is buried in extensive archaeological deposits on the shores and terraces near the river. Historic archaeological sites also abound, representing early settlement and agricultural developments, roads, and town building activities of the pre–Manhattan Project era. The Manhattan Project era is well represented by the built environment. Archaeological sites associated with this period include historic dumps, construction camps, and other, similar features. Historic archaeological military sites associated with the Cold War era are located away from the river corridor at former anti-aircraft artillery sites and four NIKE missile installations.

Leaf-shaped artifacts thought to date from 8,000 to approximately 4,000 years ago have been recovered from Hanford Reach archaeological sites. The climate during this period is thought to have been drier than today. Between 4,000 and 3,400 years ago inhabitants lived along the Columbia River. They consumed fish, small animals, roots, and seeds. From 3,400 to 2,000 years ago local climates became somewhat drier, with inhabitants continuing to live along the river and traveling to the uplands for seasonal hunting and root gathering activities. After 2,000 years ago people became more sedentary, living in large villages with plant gathering sites, fishing stations, hunting camps, and storage features located nearby.

LOCKE ISLAND

Locke Island is a large island located in the Hanford Reach portion of Columbia River about 30 miles north of Richland, Washington. The island is listed in the National Register of Historic Places as the Locke Island Archaeological District. The island contains numerous cultural layers and features suggesting a long history of occupation and use. Radiocarbon samples taken from cultural features exposed when high water eroded the eastern shoreline in 1996 and 1997 suggest that people were on the island from approximately 200 to at least 2,000 years ago. A deeply buried but undated cultural layer, situated as much as 4 meters below the island's surface, indicates that human occupation of the island may pre-date 2,000 years ago.

The Hanford Reach can be visited or toured by boat for a spectacular view of the shrub-steppe landscape. Visitors can view interpretative displays at the Columbia River Exhibition at the History, Science, and Technology Museum in Richland, Washington. Access to the Hanford Site is limited to site personnel and employees.

Further Reading: Ames, Kenneth M., Don E. Dumond, Jerry R. Galm, and Rick Minor, "Prehistory of the Southern Plateau," in *Handbook of North American Indians*, Vol. 12: *Plateau*, edited by Deward E. Walker Jr. (Washington, DC: Smithsonian Institution, 1998), 103–119; *Bonnichsen et al. v. United States et al.*, 1997 F. Supp. 614, 618 (Dist. Or.), 2002 F. Supp. 2d 1116 (Dist. Or.), 2004 Ninth Circuit Court of Appeals, No. 02–35996, 2004 U.S. App.; Chatters, James C., "The Recovery and First Analysis of an Early Holocene Human," *American Antiquity* 65 (2000): 291–316; Downey, Roger, *Riddle of the Bones: Politics, Science, Race, and the Story of Kennewick Man* (New York: Springer-Verlag, 2000); Hanford History Web site, Department of Energy, www.hanford.gov/doe/history/ (online May 2007); National Park Service, *Kennewick Man*, www.nps.gov/archeology/kennewick/ (online May 2007); Nickens, P. R., B.N. Bjornstad, N.A Cadoret, and M.K. Wright, *Monitoring Bank Erosion at the Locke Island Archaeological National Register District: Summary of 1996/1997 Field Activities*, PNNL-11970 (Richland, WA: Pacific Northwest National Laboratory, 1998). Schalk, R. F., *The 1978 and 1979 Excavations at Strawberry Island in the McNary Reservoir*, Project Report 19 (Pullman: Washington State University, Laboratory of Archaeology and History, 1983).

Mona Wright

MARMES ROCKSHELTER

Snake River, Southeastern Washington State
Archaeology before Dam Construction Finds Ancient Burials

Marmes Rockshelter is one of the more important archaeological sites in Washington State and the Pacific Northwest, not only because of the archaeological information it was found to possess, but also because of the attention it generated toward American archaeology. The political and administrative events associated with the discovery of Late Pleistocene/Early Holocene human skeletal remains in the Marmes site encapsulated, perhaps even incited, the transition in archaeological studies that played out in the 1970s, following passage of the National Historic Preservation Act of 1966. That transition led to the current era of archaeological studies, epitomized by cultural resources management approaches, and driven by federal government mandates to preserve archaeological materials and information and to seek greater public involvement in the management process.

The Marmes Rockshelter site (45FR50) is located in the southern Columbia River basin within the lower Palouse River canyon about 2.5 kilometers north of its confluence with the Snake River. The site is currently inundated by a reservoir. Although called Marmes Rockshelter, the site

Topography of the lower Palouse River canyon with Marmes Rockshelter in right foreground. View is to the northwest.   [Negative from 45FR50 archive, Museum of Anthropology, Washington State University]

contains two distinct landforms: a modest-size rockshelter in basalt bedrock and an area of Palouse River floodplain in front of the rockshelter. From the Palouse River mouth at the Snake River to a point approximately 10 kilometers north marked by Palouse Falls, the canyon is a striking representation of the impact of the late-glacial-era catastrophic flooding that created the scablands of the Columbia Basin. The walls of the canyon are generally exposed basalt bedrock and talus slopes rising up to 220 meters above the Palouse River floodplain.

The Marmes Rockshelter site was excavated between 1962 and 1964, and again in 1968 by archaeologists from Washington State University (WSU), prior to the site's inundation by the backwaters of Lower Monumental Dam. Construction of the dam, already under way when the archaeological project began, was expected to be completed within five years. WSU was to investigate some of the eighty archaeological sites along the lower Snake River that would be inundated by the reservoir formed behind the dam, including the Marmes Rockshelter.

Marmes Rockshelter was approximately 12 meters wide by 8 meters deep with a 1-meter-tall berm along the dripline when excavations began. Richard Daugherty, an archaeology professor, directed excavations while Roald Fryxell

conducted the geological and stratigraphic studies. Both Daugherty and Fryxell were believers in the then new idea of conducting interdisciplinary investigations into prehistory. Fryxell was keenly interested in the details of the Marmes site's stratigraphy, not only for providing a basic relative cultural chronology but also for assessing landscape evolution, paleoclimate, and human adaptation on the Columbia Plateau (Hicks 2004).

During the 1962–64 field seasons, excavations were confined to the rockshelter, and sediment was dry-screened through 6-millimeter ($^1/_4$-in.) wire mesh. In 1962 seventeen 5-foot-square units were excavated to a depth of about 1.5 meters over the course of ten weeks. The excavators recovered between 700 and 800 artifacts and 11 burials. During these excavations, materials found in the rockshelter were keyed to eight stratigraphic layers designated with Roman numerals I to VIII from bottom to top that Fryxell believed indicated a time depth of perhaps 10,000 years at the site (Fryxell and Daugherty 1962). Human remains became a focus of the Marmes Rockshelter investigations within two weeks of the initiation of excavations at the site in 1962. Three of the burials located that year were found under volcanic ash from Mount Mazama, which erupted around 6,730 years ago. These

View of the floodplain area from above the rockshelter, looking south down the 1965 bulldozer trench. Excavators and tractor are removing overburden above the Marmes horizon sediment layer.   [Courtesy of Ruth Kirk]

very early burials were unique in the region and called special attention to the site.

Cultural pit features dominated the later prehistoric period uppermost layers and were recognized as intrusive into earlier deposits, resulting in varying degrees of mixing of sediment and cultural materials. These pit features likely represented use of the rockshelter predominantly for storage, as has been found in other rockshelters throughout the Palouse River canyon, but a few were burial features (Rice 1969). The mixing of sediment and cultural materials in the upper stratum made interpretation of these features difficult.

A local media sensation was created by the recovery of the deepest human skeletons, which in 1962 were thought to be around 7,000 to 8,000 years old and therefore quite rare. But national attention was not brought to the project until an article in *Natural History* (Grosso 1967, 38–43) described the results of the first three years work at the rockshelter. By that time, three seasons of excavation in the rockshelter had been conducted and cultural deposits spanning at least 10,000 years were recognized. However, investigation of the site was considered completed by then, and the extensive excavations were thought to have recovered all of the human remains and enough archaeological materials and other data to fully analyze and interpret the rockshelter's cultural use. In addition, WSU needed to move on to investigate other sites among the eighty that also would be inundated by the planned reservoir. WSU, like most university archaeology programs at the time, had minimal funding, and facilities and contracts such as the one with the NPS provided a way to collect data

for advanced-degree students. Reporting of archaeological projects often took the form of student theses or dissertations.

Because of the disturbance to the upper strata in the rockshelter, it was decided in 1964 to shovel out areas of the upper strata; Daugherty and Fryxell, the principal investigators, were certain that 1964 would be the last season for excavation in Marmes, and investigating the lower strata was of greater interest to the chronologically (cultural-historically) focused study. What was particularly desired was the continued refinement of the understanding of rockshelter stratigraphy, which could then be applied at other sites to be excavated in the next few years, ahead of reservoir inundation. To that end, Fryxell returned to the site in 1965 with an idea to trace the stratigraphy recorded for the rockshelter out onto the adjacent floodplain, exposing a complete profile from the present to terminal Ice Age floods dating to 13,000 years ago. He thought this would allow more reliable correlation with open sites being excavated at different parts of the lower Snake River drainage. A bulldozer was used to excavate a trench through the berm at the mouth of the rockshelter, down the talus slope in front, and into the floodplain. At a depth of about 4 meters below the surface of the floodplain, they encountered a dark concentration containing a few bone fragments, which Gustafson later identified as elk and human (Fryxell et al. 1968a, 1968b).

Fryxell and his students revisited the site often over the next two years to study the stratigraphic profile and to attempt to find more remains in situ in the trench wall. Finally, in April 1968, they discovered more fragments of both elk and human bone in situ in the trench wall. A carbon-14 date of 10,750 + 100 years[1] had been obtained from shell recovered from the earliest cultural stratum in the rockshelter (Fryxell et al. 1968a). Tracing the deposits outward onto the floodplain, Fryxell demonstrated that the human remains were among the oldest yet discovered in North America. Subsequent radiocarbon dating placed the age of these remains at about 10,000 years (Fryxell et al. 1968a, 1968b; Sheppard et al. 1987).

The timing was fortuitous, as Daugherty had just been appointed by President Lyndon Johnson to the newly created National Advisory Council on Historic Preservation, the membership of which included the Secretary of the Interior, the Secretary of Agriculture, the Secretary of Housing and Urban Development, and the U.S. Attorney General, among others. Being in this political circle allowed Daugherty access to an important audience to announce the discovery of these oldest human remains, an announcement made in a meeting in Washington, D.C., with Senator Warren Magnuson, head of the Senate Appropriations Committee, the Director of the National Science Foundation, the Chief of the U.S. Army Corps of Engineers, and the Director of the National Park Service. The outcome of the meeting was that the Corps of Engineers transferred emergency salvage funds to the National Park Service for a major excavation effort at the Marmes site (Daugherty 2003).

The second excavation began in May 1968 and continued through February 1969, despite one of the coldest winters on record. Faced with the knowledge that in less than eight months the site would be flooded by water impounded behind the dam, Daugherty and Fryxell elected to sacrifice the upper deposits, most of which were removed by bulldozer. In the rockshelter, sediments above the Mount Mazama ash layer (Unit IV) were removed by a bulldozer or were shoveled out.

Numerous A horizons were discerned in the floodplain strata on which the site's residents had left their remains. Each of the A horizons may have been exposed only a few tens of years, but long enough for soil development to begin. Fryxell named the two uppermost incipient A horizons the Marmes horizon; it was in the Marmes horizon that the elk and human bone feature had been found. Below this was a layer of sterile alluvial silts and then three more A horizons, dubbed the Harrison horizon. Artifacts and charred animal bones were found in both horizons, but only the Marmes horizon contained human bone fragments. All hand-excavated sediment from the floodplain area was passed through 1-millimeter plastic netting in a water screen to collect cultural as well as microfloral and faunal material. The use of this fine mesh for screening resulted in the recovery of much smaller cultural items by comparison with the rockshelter excavations. Over 10,000 cubic feet of sediment was excavated at the Marmes site in 1968 (Fryxell and Keel 1969).

A great deal of attention was dedicated to trying to identify features or associated cultural materials in the floodplain area of the site in 1968. This was certainly in response to the desire to associate the human remains found in the floodplain with cultural deposits of equal antiquity. It is clear from the field notes that the floodplain excavations began with great expectations and excitement at the prospect of finding very old cultural material, probably fueled in part by the media attention directed at the project. Together with a continuous stream of visitors to the site throughout the summer, this lent an air of excited purposefulness to the work, which is evident in the excavators' notes—a feeling that cutting-edge science was occurring. This sense of purposefulness is clear in the field records, which indicate that fifty-two "Special Features" were defined based on just ninety-six artifacts found in place (rather than in the screens).

The momentum to produce a final report that presented all of the results and conclusions of the investigations at the Marmes site dissipated with Fryxell's death in a 1974 car accident. Recently, however, the USACE funded a major effort to complete analysis of the collection and produce a final report (Hicks 2004). This study involved analysis and interpretation of the 30-year old collection and its associated records and interprets the cultural uses of both the rockshelter and floodplain areas of the Marmes site and the relationship between them.

The final report study obtained eight new dates from charcoal and organic materials in the collection that, along with twenty-six previous radiocarbon dates and two volcanic tephra deposits, confirms the dating of the eight stratigraphic levels assigned by Fryxell (Fryxell and Daugherty 1962). One of the dates extends the earliest date of use of the site back to 11,230 years ago, and cultural material is found from the earliest dated deposits to the historic era at the Marmes site. The earliest date was obtained from a swan bone recovered in 1968, lying directly on ponded glacial flood sediments at the base of excavations in the rockshelter. The ponded sediments include volcanic ash believed to be from the Glacier Peak eruption that dates to virtually the same date (11,250 years ago; Johnson et al. 1994). Interestingly, this early date overlaps with the time period of the Richey Roberts Clovis Cache site (Mehringer and Foit 1990), a cache of Clovis points and other tools located 180 kilometers northwest of the Marmes site. However, with the exception of bone rods in both assemblages, there is little similarity between the two sites' collections, the Richey Roberts site being a cache rather than a habitation site.

Numerous cultural features were documented in the rockshelter, including twenty-five storage pit features and ninety-eight fire-related features such as hearths or firepits (Hicks 2004). With regard to the initial period of occupation of the site (Stratum I) there is a striking contrast in feature types between the rockshelter and the floodplain areas. The floodplain contains no fire-related features but otherwise

---

[1]All radiocarbon results are presented as uncalibrated radiocarbon years unless otherwise noted.

appears to represent an occupational use area where lithic reduction and butchering occurred; all cooking and other domestic activities that used fire occurred inside the rockshelter or off-site. This separation of activities between the two areas of the site appears to continue for the rest of the site's history, as the floodplain portion of the site sees relatively little use after the Marmes horizon. While this conclusion reflects the lack of excavation of post–Marmes horizon floodplain strata, observations of the project staff clearly indicate that any cultural materials in the floodplain did not approach the rockshelter materials in quantity or diversity (Hicks 2004, 375).

Within the rockshelter, the overall number of features increases greatly from the early to the late stratigraphic units. There is a gradual horizontal movement of cultural features from the front of the rockshelter in the earliest strata toward the interior of the rockshelter through time, which likely reflects the expansion of the cavern through erosion as well as the growth of the dripline berm at the front of the rockshelter. Prior to the period associated with Stratum VII, most of the features found in the rockshelter (other than burials) are fire-related features and likely represent activities connected with occupation of the rockshelter (cooking and warming), perhaps in tandem with resource processing (food preservation by drying or smoking, heat-treating rocks). Bone and shell were observed in most fire-related features in all stratigraphic units. Stone tools are most numerous in Strata II, VI, and VII features, but Stratum III features have a high incidence of projectile points or point fragments (Hicks 2004, 377).

Stratum VII has many fire-related features but also includes numerous storage pits that may have been burned in the process of preparation for re-use (Hicks 2004, 376; Hicks and Morgenstein 1994). Many more storage features likely were present in the rockshelter than the records indicate, given that the upper strata remaining in the rockshelter were shoveled out at the beginning of the 1968 field season. The great increase in this feature type from Stratum VI to VII probably reflects an increase in collector-like activity, which, following the predominant model of settlement and subsistence for the Interior Plateau in late prehistory, includes intensive collection, processing, and storage of food resources for later consumption (Ames and Marshall 1980; Ames et al. 1998).

That Marmes Rockshelter was used for storage is no surprise, as all of the large rockshelters in the Palouse Canyon area exhibit such features, and rockshelter pits maintain much cooler temperatures than the outside air, the temperature decreasing with depth. In addition, rockshelter sediments exhibit relatively high humidity compared with the open air (Hicks and Morgenstein 1994). In fact, rockshelters appear to be good locations for the storage of organics not because they are dry, but because they are cool and have relatively low temperature and humidity flux through the annual cycle (Hicks 1995, 83–84). Storage pit features were constructed to take advantage of these conditions, with bundles of stored foods raised above the rock floor on a platform of sticks and covered by layers of matting fragments and layers of grasses (Hicks and Morgenstein 1994). Rockshelters with prominent berms along the dripline were probably especially desirable because these features reduce the air exchange between the rockshelter cavity and the exterior.

HUMAN REMAINS

A minimum of thirty-six individuals are represented by the human remains features observed at the Marmes site, including twenty-six in the rockshelter, a minimum of six individuals in a cremation hearth in Stratum I/II (Krantz 1979), and four individuals represented mostly by skull fragments from the Marmes horizon in the floodplain (Hicks 2004, 377). The latter were found to date to approximately 9,800 years ago, whereas the cremation hearth dates to approximately 9,400 years ago and indicates some level of socio-religious structure at the time of earliest occupation of the site that at least extended to treatment of the dead (Hicks 2004, 410). The rest of the rockshelter remains are found in Strata III, V, and VII but only fourteen human remains concentrations could be confidently described as burials or interments (Hicks 2004, 140).

Placement of grave goods with burials at Marmes Rockshelter begins in Stratum III, but instead of the dentalia shell commonly found in late prehistoric burials in the Plateau, olivella shell from the Pacific Ocean was found in most. Stone tools (especially projectile points) also were common in the burials, beginning with the earliest confirmed burials in pits (Stratum III). Red ocher, in two cases as a blanket of the powder 1–2 centimeters thick, becomes a common burial inclusion by Stratum V, along with large numbers of olivella shell beads; various stone, bone, and antler formed tools; and hackberry and chokecherry seeds. Stone flakes and ornaments such as bear teeth occur in some Stratum V burials. The two Stratum VII burials, which date to the late prehistoric period, also reflect Sprague's (2000) burial pattern, with the continued presence of stone tools, olivella shell beads, and other cultural items (Hicks 2004, 379–380).

ASSEMBLAGE

The stone tool assemblage from the Marmes site confirms the general outline of Leonhardy and Rice's (1970) model of a cultural-historical sequence for the lower Snake River region. Projectile points of styles recognized to span the entire 10,000-year cultural chronology were recovered from the Marmes site and correlate well with the dated stratigraphic sequence. The stone tool and debitage collection reflects a habitation site where people performed a wide range of domestic tasks. The stone materials represent tool manufacturing and maintenance (of stone tools and tools of hard organic materials such as bone, antler, and wood), food procurement (projectile points, bola stones, possible net weights), and processing of food and other materials, probably including hides and fiber.

The artifact distribution data suggests very intensive occupations during the Cascade phase, from about 7,900 to about 6,200 years ago, and again during the Harder phase, from about 1,600 to about 700 years ago. Projectile points are most abundant in the Cascade (Strata II and III), and Harder (Stratum VII) phase sub-assemblages. Stone flake tools, choppers, hammerstones, and scrapers are also most abundant in these strata. The high frequencies of the butchery or animal processing tools and faunal remains found in these strata suggest intensive hunting activities during these periods (Hicks 2004, 380).

Over half of the bone tools were recovered from the earliest strata, including all of the bone pins and eyed needles. The presence of sewing and hide-working tools, such as needles and awls, suggests that family groups occupied the floodplain and rockshelter. Artifacts such as bone tubes and pendants also suggest Marmes inhabitants wore tailored hide clothing, and likely decorated their dress as well. Bone pins may have been worn in clothing, and perhaps even in hair (Hicks 2004, 382).

Faunal remains analysis found significant differences between the rockshelter and the floodplain, both in the number of different species represented and in the condition of the remains. Exotic taxa long extinct from the Plateau (e.g., arctic fox, pine marten) were present in the floodplain deposits but not in the rockshelter, correlating to the immediate post-glacial period, when the climate was colder and the vegetation more typical of northern Canadian vegetation zones today. Large mammal bones (e.g., deer, pronghorn, and elk), with evidence of butchery, were common in the rockshelter deposits. Fish bone analysis found relatively few salmon bones but a high representation of small fish species. This may be a result of field sampling methods or a reflection of the particular activities for which the site was used at different times correlated with fluctuations in river environments near the site. Shellfish species trends at the Marmes site follow the trends in the river environment, alternating between species that favor rocky versus sandy stream bottoms.

The combination of all the activities indicated by the artifacts and resources in the site's deposits characterize a residential camp; the lithic assemblage suggests the site was used for habitation, the most complex site type with the highest diversity of tool types. The evolution of technologies over the span of use of the Marmes site appears to be deliberate and conservative. While there are differences between successive occupations, they are gradual and incremental; what distinguishes one period from another is simply the relative frequency of certain artifact types and traits.

In the first several millennia of the use of the Marmes site it appears to have been a tethered mobile foraging settlement and subsistence strategy (after Binford 1980). The earliest date obtained by this study (11,230 years ago) sets a new limiting date for the latest that landforms at this elevation became available for human use. All other, similar elevations in the lower Snake River drainage would have become available at this time as well, and if people found and began to use Marmes Rockshelter at this time they likely were exploring and foraging over much of the Snake River bottomlands. The newly exposed landforms, draped with fine-grained, lake-deposited sediments, would have been a relatively productive environment for plant proliferation. The newly exposed soils would have been seeded by the adjacent plant communities, perhaps with a few exotic plants introduced from the upper reaches of the river during flood events. The climate at this time was much cooler than at present, and the relatively protected river bottom may have quickly become one of the more biologically diverse areas in the Plateau region. Animals and humans alike probably made use of the landforms and plant communities that developed as quickly as they became established (Hicks 2004, 406).

The hypothesized transition from foraging to logistical collecting (Ames and Marshall 1980; Binford 1980) for the Interior Plateau settlement and subsistence strategy, beginning roughly in the mid-Holocene, is not well reflected in the Marmes site. The use of the site as a base camp for foragers appears to continue into late prehistory until the rockshelter became a focus for storage, a mark of the logistical collecting strategy, but even then the site's assemblage continues to display a wider diversity of tools than is commonly associated with short-term base camps. Resource processing is indicated in most of the strata at the Marmes site and appears to have been the focus of at least some activity at the site by both foragers and collectors. The location of the site in the vicinity of several kinds of higher-volume food resources (e.g., shellfish, large mammals) probably favored the initial forager use of the site and also contributed to its persistent use well into the period hypothesized for a logistical collector strategy. At the same time, material densities at the Marmes site are not high enough to support continuous, year-round occupation during the time period associated with any of the strata or cultural phases; the assemblages represent palimpsests of multiple periods of use during each period. In addition, continuous use by tethered foragers may mean a three-week stay once each year (Hicks 2004, 395).

Despite its diverse and often dense cultural deposits, the Marmes site would have served as just one part of the area's residents' seasonal round that included the vicinity of the Palouse River canyon. Over ninety prehistoric cultural sites had been recorded in the area of the Palouse River canyon and the confluence of the Palouse and Snake Rivers, where

Marmes Rockshelter is located. Thirteen of these have had cultural materials radiocarbon dated, but none exhibit cultural use as far back as the early cultural strata in Marmes Rockshelter.

Considering social explanations for the continued appearance of habitation-related assemblages into the late prehistoric period, one could posit that group members may have been excluded from the larger group at times and resided in the rockshelter. Other rockshelters in the Palouse River canyon do not have such a collection of tools and debitage as does Marmes Rockshelter, but Marmes is the closest rockshelter to the two late prehistoric residential sites. Use of the site for burials apparently did not preclude its use for other activities, given that the rockshelter saw considerable use for storage and activities associated with the many fire hearths, so short-term residence also may have occurred (Hicks 2004, 419–420).

The Marmes site residents also interacted with other regional inhabitants, as evidenced by the presence of exotic stone (e.g., obsidian and petrified wood) and marine shells not available in the nearby environment. These materials have technological applications and are not used for subsistence consumption; the use of shell as decorative items has social motivations. Obsidian is prominent in exchange networks in the Plateau with most of the obsidian found in archaeological sites from sources located in south central Oregon, southern Idaho, and in British Columbia. These sources are widely used not only because of their high-quality stone, but also because they are major sources with high quantities of accessible stone (Hicks 2004:400).

All four sources of the obsidian items identified at Marmes are located in upland settings southeast of the Marmes site in eastern Oregon and western Idaho. Three of these are at short distances up primary tributary rivers that join the Snake River, but these materials probably did not reach Marmes by the most direct route—down the Snake River—because of the barrier to water travel represented by Hell's Canyon. A long history (at least 9,700 years) of travel to and/or trade for these materials is indicated, which may, in turn, indicate one of the directions that the Marmes site occupants traveled in the part of the annual round not spent at the site. Olivella shells are found in all of the rockshelter's strata (a span of at least 9,700 years) and are strongly associated with human remains features, although not necessarily with burials. The nearest source of olivella shell is the Pacific coast, roughly 500 kilometers west, indicating long-standing trade networks to the west as well (Hicks 2004, 401, 403).

All of the aspects of the Marmes site described above make it an archaeological site of singular importance to the Plateau archaeological record. In retrospect, the site's political importance is also clear. Science, public interest, and politics converged at Marmes Rockshelter. Cultural preservation is an issue everyone can rally behind. Washington State's congressional delegation had supported passage of the National Historic Preservation Act, and Marmes provided vindication. Public appreciation of Senator Magnuson's support for Marmes strengthened support of archaeology and historic preservation in general, and that favorably affected additional historic preservation legislation that followed. Magnuson called Marmes "a landmark precedent in our nation's responsibility to its own heritage, which will be felt for decades to come" (Daugherty 2004).

Further Reading: Ames, K. M., D. E. Dumond, J. R. Galm, and R. Minor, "Prehistory of the Southern Plateau," in *Handbook of North American Indians*, Vol. 12: *Plateau*, edited by Deward E. Walker Jr. (Washington, D.C Smithsonian Institution, 1998), 103–119; Ames, K. M., and A. G. Marshall, "Villages, Demography and Subsistence Intensification on the Southern Columbia Plateau," *North American Archaeologist* 2(1) (1980): 25–52; Binford, L. R., "Willow Smoke and Dog's Tails: Hunter-Gatherer Settlement Systems and Archaeological Site Formation," *American Antiquity* 45 (1980): 4–20; Daugherty, R. D., "Preface," in *Marmes Rockshelter: A Final Report on 11,000 Years of Cultural Use*, edited by B. A Hicks (Pullman: Washington State University Press, 2004), xiii–xv; Fryxell, R., T. Bielicki, R. Daugherty, C. Gustafson, H. Irwin, B. Keel, and G. Krantz, "Human Skeletal Material and Artifacts from Sediments of Pinedale (Wisconsin) Glacial Age in Southeastern Washington, United States," in *Proceedings VIIIth International Congress of Anthropological and Ethnological Sciences*, Vol. 3: *Ethnology and Archaeology* (1968a), 176–181; Fryxell, R., T. Bielicki, R. Daugherty, C. Gustafson, H. Irwin, and B. Keel, "A Human Skeleton from Sediments of Mid-Pinedale Age in Southeastern Washington," *American Antiquity* 33(4) (1968b): 511–514; Fryxell, R., and R. D. Daugherty, *Interim Report: Archeological Salvage in the Lower Monumental Reservoir, Washington*, Reports of Investigations, No. 21 (Pullman: Washington State University, Laboratory of Archeology and Geochronology, 1962); Fryxell, R., and B. Keel, *Emergency Salvage Excavations for the Recovery of Early Human Remains and Related Scientific Material from the Marmes Rockshelter Archaeological Site, Southeastern Washington, May 3-December 15, 1968*, report to the U.S. Army Corps of Engineers, Walla Walla District (Pullman: Washington State University, Laboratory of Anthropology, 1969); Grosso, G. H., "Cave Life on the Palouse," *Natural History* (February 1967): 38–43; Hicks, B. A., *Marmes Rockshelter: A Final Report on 11,000 Years of Cultural Use* (Pullman: WSU Press, 2004); Krantz, G., "Oldest Human Remains from the Marmes Site," *Northwest Anthropological Research Notes* 13(2) (1979): 159–174; Leonhardy, F. C., and D. Rice, "A Proposed Cultural Typology for the Lower Snake River Region, Southeastern Washington," *Northwest Anthropological Research Notes* 4(1) (1970): 1–29; Mehringer, P. J., and F. Foit Jr., "Volcanic Ash Dating of the Clovis Cache at East Wenatchee, Washington," *National Geographic Research* 6(4) (1990): 495–503; Rice, D., *Preliminary Report, Marmes Rockshelter Archaeological Site, Southern Columbia Plateau*, Report to the National Park Service, San Francisco (Pullman: Washington State University, Laboratory of Anthropology, 1969); Sheppard, J., P. E. Wigand, C. Gustafson, and M. Rubin, "A Reevaluation of the Marmes Rockshelter Radiocarbon Chronology," *American Antiquity* 52(1) (1987): 118–125.

Brent A. Hicks

MT. RAINIER SITES

East Central Washington State

Ancient and Historic Period Sites in the Cascade Mountains

Mount Rainier is the highest and most massive of the strato-volcanoes that dot the Cascade Range in western Washington and Oregon. At 14,411 feet, it rises over 6,000 feet above the older, more weathered Cascade peaks, visually dominating the region for almost hundred miles on all sides. Mount Rainier's snowcapped crest, subalpine meadows, and forested slopes have attracted explorers and tourists since the mid-1800s. In 1899 Mount Rainier became the fifth park in the national parks system. It remains a modern-day icon for the greater Pacific Northwest region.

Long before its historical story began, Indian people came to Mount Rainier, or *Takhoma* (Sahaptin for "the mountain"), for a variety of purposes. The archaeological record of their presence, in the form of chipped-stone tools and debris, indicates widespread use of its upper-elevation forest fringe and its subalpine to alpine meadow habitats. Archaeological tests suggest that human use began at least 7,500 and perhaps as many as 9,000 years ago when the mountain became free of Late Pleistocene glacial ice. Available information testifies to *Takhoma*'s long-standing importance to Indian people living in the nearby heavily forested western Cascade lowlands; as well as those residing on the drier eastern Cascade slopes and adjacent plains.

MOUNT RAINIER'S ARCHAEOLOGICAL HISTORY

The first ethnographic and archaeological surveys at Mount Rainier took place in 1963 under the direction of Allan H. Smith and Richard H. Daugherty with Washington State University. Smith and Daugherty hoped that interviewing Yakama, Nisqually, Puyallup, and Muckleshoot tribal elders as to their recollected uses of the mountain would provide insight into the probable distribution of archaeological sites. Despite repeated references to mountain activities—particularly huckleberry gathering and hunting in old burns and subalpine parklands—their subsequent survey identified only two archaeological locations: a sheltered rock overhang with chipped-stone debris on the northeast side of the mountain, and a single isolated projectile point on its southern flank. Test excavations at the rockshelter produced additional stone tools, fire-cracked rock, and the remains of deer and mountain goat hunted in nearby subalpine and alpine meadows and consumed at the shelter.

Despite these results, Mount Rainier's archaeological record remained largely unknown until the mid-1990s. Indeed, many people, including professional archaeologists,

incorrectly believed that Mount Rainier was too high and too remote to have been of much use to people residing in salmon-dependent valley floor villages (upstream obstacles prevented salmon from reaching all but the lowest of *Takhoma*'s mountain rivers in appreciable numbers). Believing that mountain landscapes were unimportant to pre-contact people, many archaeologists simply failed to look for sites in high-elevation places.

Recognition of Mount Rainier's archaeological record improved in the 1990s when the National Park Service contracted a second archeological survey and hired the park's first staff archaeologist. The survey involved extensive new reconnaissance in varied locations and environmental zones on the mountain. It increased the number of formally documented pre-contact sites and isolated artifacts to forty, including those found in 1963 and several recorded in the intervening years. The sudden jump in site count, combined with finds in the Pacific Northwest's two other mountain parks (North Cascades and Olympic) and on National Forest lands, drew attention to the long-standing presence of Indian people in montane wilderness environments. The project report also provided ecologically based arguments as to why Mount Rainier, and other high-elevation mountain landscapes, was important to pre-contact people.

Since the mid-1990s, park archaeologists have expanded the archaeological count to 79 pre-contact Native American sites and isolated artifacts, 123 historic-period properties, and 13 sites with both. There is no doubt that the count will rise further as survey efforts continue. We now know that Mount Rainier, once thought to be too logistically challenging to have been of significant use to indigenous people, played an important seasonal role in their subsistence and settlement systems for thousands of years. Mount Rainier's historical and precontact archaeological records also indicate that these properties are diverse in character and patterned in their distribution across the landscape.

MOUNT RAINIER HISTORICAL ARCHAEOLOGY

The oldest historic-period archaeological sites at Mount Rainier date to 1850s exploration and climbing excursions. By the late 1800s Mount Rainier's popularity was increasing with climbers and other visitors searching for less arduous, but still adventurous, experiences. Promoters developed trails, wagon roads, campgrounds, lodging, and spa facilities to appeal to these people. The mountain also attracted loggers

Mt. Rainier.   [National Park Service]

Excavations at Paradise Camp.   [Greg C. Burtchard]

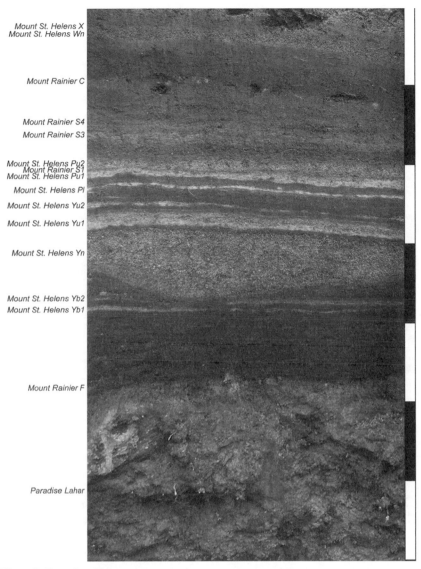

Mount St. Helens X
Mount St. Helens Wn

Mount Rainier C

Mount Rainier S4
Mount Rainier S3

Mount St. Helens Pu2
Mount Rainier S1
Mount St. Helens Pu1

Mount St. Helens Pl

Mount St. Helens Yu2

Mount St. Helens Yu1

Mount St. Helens Yn

Mount St. Helens Yb2
Mount St. Helens Yb1

Mount Rainier F

Paradise Lahar

Volcanic stratigraphy.   [Greg C. Burtchard]

and miners hoping to capitalize on natural resources that they believed could be found on, or under, its heavily forested slopes. Archaeological remains of roadbeds and trails, springboard stumps, survey marker trees, mine adits and mining gear, wells, trash dumps, isolated tools, and much more attest to these early ventures. Understandably, most historical sites are located where forest or mineral resources were expected to be found, and where mineral springs, scenic views, and proximity to growing Tacoma and Seattle population centers supplied recreation opportunities to hardy tourists.

After 1899, when Mount Rainier became a national park, dominant use shifted to development of Park Service infrastructure and to nationally promoted tourism served by rail lines and automobiles. The early 1900s archaeological record contains remains of historical lodge foundations, Park Service camps, watchtowers, communication lines, abandoned trails, Civilian Conservation Corps crew camps, and, of course, numerous trash dumps and isolated lost tools that span the park's development period. The park maintains records of these historical, as well as pre-contact, archaeological properties, on a global information system (GIS)–compatible database, and monitors them periodically to guard against vandalism and deterioration.

MOUNT RAINIER PRE-CONTACT ARCHAEOLOGY

Three aspects of Mount Rainier's pre-contact archaeological record warrant special consideration: its representation in vertically stratified deposits, its tendency toward environmentally patterned distribution, and its functional variation between archaeological sites.

Chipped-stone artifacts from one of the hunting and butchering camps found in a variety of higher-elevation settings. [Greg C. Burtchard]

Vertical Stratification

Mount Rainier's repeated volcanic episodes preserve much of its archaeological record in 1–2-meter-deep layered deposits. In many places excavators encounter a series of volcanic layers dating from 150 to over 9,000 years old. Buried soils containing pre-contact archaeological remains, sandwiched between these volcanic layers, span most of the ice-free Holocene epoch during which human beings could have used the mountain.

Mount Rainier's vertically stratified deposits are important because they provide opportunities to search for the earliest use of the mountain and to examine changes in use patterns through time. When archaeologists find cultural materials in buried soil layers, they can place them in time relative to the volcanic events above and below. Using these techniques, independently confirmed by radiocarbon dating, park archaeologists have demonstrated conclusively that indigenous people were using the mountain by at least 7,500 years ago. We expect the archaeological record of the earliest use of the mountain to be pushed back further as excavation research continues.

Environmentally Patterned Site Distribution

Mount Rainier's pre-contact archaeological record also is patterned in its relation to its environmental zones. Especially important are subalpine and alpine zones between about 5,000 and 7,000 feet. Late snowmelt at this elevation inhibits dense tree growth, promoting instead patchy tree stands interspersed with open meadows in subalpine parklands, and treeless alpine tundra higher up. These zones contain over 90 percent of Mount Rainier's documented pre-contact sites and isolates.

The pre-contact human presence in subalpine and alpine settings was due largely to enhanced forage available during the mountain's snow-free season. Upper-elevation meadows provided, with minimal human intervention, the largest and most productive habitats available in the late summer, when substantial numbers of elk, deer, bear, grouse, mountain goat, marmot, huckleberries, edible corms and bulbs, and other economically useful products could be found there. The fact that subalpine and alpine ecozones contain most of the mountain's archaeological properties reflects the economic importance of those resources to people residing in the vicinity of the mountain over a long period of time.

Functional Site Variation

Mount Rainier's pre-contact archaeological sites, while dominated by clustered associations of chipped-stone artifacts, are not all alike. Park archaeologists recognize at least ten distinct site types, reflecting different sets of pre-contact activities. These include residential base camps, limited-task field camps, single-event hunting locations, butchering sites, tool-stone quarries, stacked rock and talus pit locations, culturally modified trees, plant processing locations, trails, and isolated lost artifacts. To date, archaeologists have recorded all but one of these types by virtue of variation in environmental setting, artifact density, tool type, and tool-stone material. Because the remaining site type—plant processing—has been found in the form of huckleberry drying trenches south of the mountain, and because huckleberries were an important resource in the early historic period, archaeologists expect to find these features on Mount Rainier as well.

The largest, most complex archaeological sites are residential base camps located at the upper forest to lower subalpine margin. This setting was spared all but the most severe mountain storms while providing access to higher, more productive hunting and gathering grounds. Plausibly, these places served as mixed age and gender locations from which other, more specialized hunting and gathering tasks were launched.

More task-specific hunting and butchering camps are found in a variety of higher-elevation settings. Some of these sites—especially those in rockshelters such as the one documented in 1963— provided short-term storm refuge. Other sites on sun- and weather-exposed ridges afforded access to game and provided the exposure needed to dry meat. Such sites typically are difficult to see because of low artifact count, often with fewer than ten surface-exposed items. Subsurface testing typically produces a higher count, but compared to base camps, the total number and variety of tools remains small.

Stacked rock features consist of vertically stacked stones that form low columns or, occasionally, elongated mounds. Talus pits are depressions in rock rubble fields created by removing rocks and stacking them around the margin. Stacked rock features may have served as route markers, hunting blinds, or perhaps ceremonial vision quest markers. Talus pit features probably served as temporary food storage or hunting blinds. However, these rock features seldom contain artifacts, making functional and temporal inferences difficult.

Tool-stone quarries also tend to occur in upper-elevation settings because the best exposures of fine-grained tool-stone are found there. Angular shattered rock and flaked-stone debris created when the stone was first removed dominates the artifact selection found at these places.

Trails and modified, usually bark-peeled, trees are less confined to upland settings. In pre-contact times, trails were not the well-defined, permanent paths that we know today. Only a late 1800s trail used by Yakama people to cross the Cascade crest to Mount Rainier remains visible. Other routes followed river valleys and ridge crests to the mountain and back. We infer the existence of these routes more by their proximity to known low-elevation villages, and by alignments of isolated artifacts and campsites, than by physical trail scars per se.

In addition to upland sites, certain lowland trees and other plants provided valuable medicines, wood, and fiber. Western red cedar, arguably the most valuable of the trees, grows in low, moist river valley settings on Mount Rainier. Archaeologists record the rectangular and inverted-V scars created by removing bark from the trees. While the life span of these trees limits us to a roughly 1,000-year range, there is little doubt that use of these materials extended well into ancient times.

Finally, we know that people cannot use any place for long periods of time without losing things. Isolated finds—most often broken projectile points, bifacially worked tools, or lone stone flakes—probably represent off-target shots, projectile points taken away by unretrieved game, dropped tools, or one-time use of a particular place. Archaeologists record these to improve the general picture of widespread landscape use and to maintain the possibility that the location may be converted to a more substantial site at a later date when subsurface testing is possible.

MOUNT RAINIER ARCHAEOLOGY: A FINAL WORD

Mount Rainier's archaeological record makes it clear that, for thousands of years, the mountain has played an important role in the lives of Indian people living in its vicinity along western and eastern margins of the Washington Cascades. The mountain attracted people to it largely by virtue of the productive plant and animal communities that could be found in its subalpine and alpine habitats during its brief summer season. Native American use of the mountain continued into historical times, and indeed continues to this day. After 1850, however, use shifted toward the activities of explorers, adventurers, tourists and the National Park Service. The archaeological record of both pre-contact and historical uses provides information vital to understanding the relationship between the mountain and human beings since people first ventured onto its slopes.

Further Reading: Binford, Lewis R., *In Pursuit of the Past: Decoding the Archaeological Record* (Berkeley: University of California Press, 2002); Burtchard, Greg C., *Environment, Prehistory and Archaeology of Mount Rainier National Park, Washington* (Honolulu: International Archaeological Research Institute, 1998), www.nps.gov/archive/mora/ncrd/archaeology/index.htm (online 2007); Catton, Theodore, *Wonderland, An Administrative History of Mount Rainier National Park* (Seattle: National Park Service, Columbia Cascades System Support Office, 1996), www.nps.gov/archive/mora/adhi/adhi.htm (online 2007); Smith, Allan H., *Takhoma, Ethnography of Mount Rainier National Park* (Pullman: Washington State University Press, 2006).

Greg C. Burtchard

THE CASCADE PASS SITE

North Cascades National Park, Central Washington State
9,000 Years of Use of a Mountain Pass

Storm-borne Pacific westerlies stream across the imposing northern Cascades Range in North Cascades National Park, where a low saddle has formed along this highest and most glaciated segment of the range's crest. Cascade Pass funnels winds east to the dry interior Columbia Plateau after their ascent from rainforest lowlands of the northwest coast. Archaeological excavations at the pass uncovered a 9,000-year record of use in the form of campfire hearths associated with tool stone technologies. The findings reaffirm indigenous Salish elder oral histories and numerous ethnohistoric references asserting the traditional importance of the pass as a trans-Cascade route. Currently, Cascade Pass is the only site on the range crest having successive cultural occupation zones preserved underneath distinctive volcanic dust layers, in direct association with a precise radiocarbon chronology. Indigenous use of the pass shifted around 4,000 years ago, corresponding in time with a region-wide change to larger, more permanent villages and more intensive subsistence practices. The pass today rewards hikers with unmatched scenery and other wilderness values that attract and enrich visitor experiences.

Salish Indian cultures of western and eastern Washington trace their ancestry to people who colonized the land after the melting of Ice Age glaciers, roughly 14,500 years ago. The discovery of early-dated artifacts made from marine animals found in some eastern Washington archaeological sites suggests an early onset of travel and trade between marine-oriented populations along the coast and the riverine-oriented peoples of the arid interior. Because these distinct cultural and geographic areas are linked by the navigable Columbia River, few have asked what overland travel would have been like for people in the Early Holocene (all of the last 12,000 years or so), particularly in the challenging topography presented at places like Cascade Pass. Long before the first recorded non-Indian crossing in AD 1814, bands of Chelan and Entiat people, speakers of Interior Salish, hunted, fished, and resided along the Columbia River and into the mountain valley watersheds that bear these names today, crossing the crest at Cascade Pass, among others. On the west side, bands of coast Salish people were adapted not only to the diverse and highly productive marine and lower river valleys, but also to some of the upriver, mountainous environments. One such band, the Miskaiwhu, maintained permanent villages along the upper Skagit and lower Cascade rivers, and is one of several west-side bands who traditionally used Cascade Pass for trading, hunting, and gathering east of the

crest. Until the National Park Service's archaeological investigations at the pass in 2005, its long history of human visitation remained hidden. Beyond simply acquiring scientific evidence consistent with Salish oral traditions, Cascade Pass speaks broadly to the early development of cultural practices and strategies adapted to the demands of rugged mountain travel by northwest coast and Plateau peoples.

Barely 100 yards wide at its lowest point (5,400 feet above mean sea level [amsl]), Cascade Pass formed where a now-retreated glacier gouged a deep saddle into the otherwise rocky alpine spires and summits of the ridge crest, which today support small alpine glaciers. After melting away, the glacier left a rolling topography strewn with granitic rocks mixed with sterile, gravelly sands. By 10,000 years ago, soils had begun to form under a grass, shrub, and herb meadow community. In the ensuing millennia, successive layers of fine volcanic dust (ash) ejected from Cascade volcanoes buried the uneven glacial topography, helping to thicken the soil and create the level, lush meadows seen today. The volcanic ash also buried and preserved subtle clues left by the first people to use the pass.

After Congress created the North Cascades National Park Service Complex in 1968, park staff nurtured the native re-vegetation program begun earlier by the U.S. Forest Service. The need for subalpine plant re-establishment at the pass vicinity followed a period of increased use, then overuse, from overnight camping by hikers and horse parties. In the denuded tent sites and in muddy wallows, stone artifacts occasionally appeared that previously were obscured by native plant cover. A team of archaeologists from Western Washington University inventoried the Cascade Pass Site (45CH221) in 1977 after recording few visible artifacts on soils having questionable depth and preservation potential. In 1986 the park archaeologist began periodic monitoring visits to assess threats to the site's integrity; occasionally, artifacts from the disturbed surface were found, including a small, perfectly clear chunk of quartz crystal, its faces covered by parallel grooves left after the removal of tiny, razor blade–like "microblades." The park's archaeological overview (1986) recommended a significance assessment of the site using excavation techniques that minimize effects to the subalpine vegetation. In 1988 Congress formally designated roughly 93 percent of the park complex as the Stephen Mather Wilderness, which includes Cascade Pass. The first archaeological excavations at the pass took place in 2005, but even before this, deeply gullied trail segments revealed the accumulated layers of volcanic ash and soils.

Evidence gathered in the first three seasons of excavation indicates that people used the pass recurrently over the last 9,000 years or so. Remarkably well-stratified soil profiles, nearly 3 feet deep, preserve a record of human activities. Dark soil at the bottom of one excavation marked the ground walked on by the first people; it contained campfire charcoal and stone tools, mostly microblades. This soil is buried by a thick, light-colored layer of fine volcanic ash deposited from an eruption of Mount Mazama 7,650 years ago; the crater from this eruption forms today's Crater Lake, Oregon, in the national park of the same name. The eruption had little effect on human use of the pass, based on the presence of later campfires associated with more artifacts built directly on top of the Mazama layer; this occupation is 7,500 years old. Another, much closer volcano, Glacier Peak, erupted 5,800 years ago and deposited the white, double-banded layer halfway up profile. Shortly afterward, yet another, thicker campfire hearth was built and used until 3,800 years ago, when it was buried under a sandy ash ejected from a major eruption of Mount St. Helens, one of the most active Cascade volcanoes in Washington State. Both the Mount Mazama and Mount St. Helens ash layers (7,650 and 3,800 year ago, respectively) are widespread in the Pacific Northwest. Above the Mount St. Helens layer, a prepared basin-shaped campfire pit with a corner-notched dart point was dated as 2,000 years old. Altogether, five separate cultural zones were identified, sandwiched between identified volcanic ash layers. The abundant campfire charcoal yielded eight accurate radiocarbon ages that corroborated the ages previously assigned to the volcanic ash layers.

The identification of such a long, well-dated cultural sequence imparts great significance to Cascade Pass. Preliminary analyses reveal that site occupants brought pre-made stone tools with them to the pass, but that they also quarried locally gathered tool stone, including perfectly formed quartz crystals. Knowledge of the source locations of several tool stone varieties used at the pass leads to the inference that people arrived from lowland areas on both sides of the mountains. Hozomeen chert, for example, one of the most distinctive and well studied of these tool stone types, links Cascade Pass to people who lived in the Skagit River valley west and north of the pass.

An important observation is that quartz crystal tools dominate the two earliest components (spanning 9,000 to 7,500 years ago). Quartz crystal and Hozomeen chert together account for 70–84 percent of the artifacts in these components. But after 3,800 years ago, other tool stone varieties (mostly from eastern Washington) dominate while quartz crystal and Hozomeen chert drop to about 11 percent or less in the two youngest components. This pattern signals a change in use of the pass corresponding to a region-wide shift in subsistence "intensification," characterized by increased populations, larger and more permanent settlements, and more intensive use of subsistence resources than in earlier times. Thus, data from Cascade Pass supports a region-wide cultural development that previously had been detected only from lowland archaeological investigations. Somewhat surprisingly, artifacts considered to have high trade or prestige value in the region-wide exchange system, such as obsidian and steatite (talc), have yet to be found at the pass.

The reasons for an early emphasis at the pass on use of quartz crystals for manufacturing microblades and other tools remain a mystery. Microblade technology has been practiced for at least 14,000 radiocarbon years in northern North America and is linked to even earlier microblade sites in northeast Asia. Although this might suggest a direct cultural link with Old World technologies, it may simply be, as some archaeologists have suggested, that using microblades maximizes the total amount of cutting edge that can be created from a piece of stone, helping to minimize the volume and weight of tool stone carried on overland treks. Whatever the explanation, we know with certainty that some northwest coast and Plateau groups maintained long traditions of mountain travel.

Today, a summer day-hike trip from Marblemount to Cascade Pass and back takes six to eight hours, including driving time (keep in mind that for most of the previous 9,000 years, this rough overland trek required four days just to get to the pass). Snow avalanches guard winter approaches to the pass, which lies buried under many feet of corniced snow.

Currently, Cascade Pass experiences the highest visitation within the Stephen Mather Wilderness. A trailhead parking area is accessed via a 24-mile gravel road; it is important to first check in at the NPS information center in Marblemount, Washington, for updated road and trail conditions. Several new interpretive signs at the trailhead describe the historic, natural, and scenic values of Cascade Pass. A low-gradient trail built across precipitous slopes gains 1,800 feet elevation over the 3.7 miles to the pass. Due to abrupt and unexpected weather changes, visitors should bring raingear, extra clothes, water, and trail food. To prevent the trampling of native vegetation, overnight camping is permitted in several nearby campsites only. From the pass, visitors can continue hiking up Sahale Arm for even more spectacular views, or they can follow a trail down into Stehekin Valley, following an ancient travel route east to Lake Chelan.

Further Reading: Collins, June M., *Valley of the Spirits* (Seattle: University of Washington Press, 1974); Kirk, Ruth, and Richard D. Daugherty, *Archaeology in Washington* (Seattle: University of Washington Press, 2007); Mierendorf, Robert R., "Who Walks on the Ground," in *Impressions of the North Cascades*, edited by John C. Miles (Seattle: The Mountaineers, 1996), 39–53; Mierendorf, Robert R., *An Updated Summary Statement of the Archeology of the North Cascades National Park Service Complex*, ww.nps.gov/archive/noca/archeology1.htm (online May 1998); Mierendorf, Robert R., Franklin F. Foit Jr., and Monika Nill, "Earth, Wind, Fire, and Stone at Cascade Pass: Preliminary Archeology and Geochronology," in "Abstracts: The 59th Annual Northwest Anthropological Conference, March 29–April 1, Seattle," *Journal of Northwest Anthropology* 40(2) (2006): 273.

Robert R. Mierendorf

THE NEWHALEM ROCKSHELTER SITE

North Cascades National Park, Northwest Washington State
An Ancient and Historic Hunting and Food Processing Site

The marine climate of the Pacific Ocean pushes itself inland, far up the glaciated valleys that descend the western slopes of the Cascade Range in today's North Cascades National Park Service Complex. Newhalem Rockshelter, a cabin-sized boulder, hides under the thick canopy of the conifer rainforest. For 1,500 years the ancestors of today's Skagit River tribes came to the rockshelter to butcher mountain goats and cook the meat along with other animal foods brought down from the surrounding alpine meadows. Old-growth forest woody debris combines with breathtakingly steep terrain to effectively hide most archaeological remains. Under such conditions, public access to sites is limited. Newhalem Rockshelter offers an educational alternative through a self-guided tour along a handicapped-accessible trail, ending in close-up views of the rockshelter floor and the surrounding forest. The canopy-level viewing deck also overlooks nearby Newhalem Creek, whose rushing mountain waters echo from the rockshelter walls. Texts, photographs, and drawings on several panels explore the different values and meanings of the shelter through indigenous, scientific, and interpretive viewpoints.

In the 1850s this portion of the Skagit River valley was the permanent homeland of the most interior of upper Skagit Indian bands, the Miskaiwhu. Their permanent winter villages, consisting of cedar plank longhouses, lined the banks of the Skagit River all the way upstream to Newhalem. This place name is from northern Puget Sound coast Salish, the language spoken by Skagit people. "Newhalem" derives from *daxwáylib*, referring to "thread" or "rope," and is variously interpreted as relating to the traditional use of snares for capturing mountain goats on the adjacent slopes and to the procurement of goat wool. Newhalem was a good place to fish for salmon and trout, it was the head of canoe routes, and its position below the 10-mile-long Skagit Gorge made it a good place to wind-dry salmon.

Newhalem Rockshelter hides in the shade of a closed-canopy cedar and hemlock forest, along Newhalem Creek, less than a half mile upstream from the creek's junction with the Skagit River. The projecting boulder covers a dry floor area 7 by 4 meters. The soil under the floor, to a depth of 80 centimeters, revealed two cultural zones defined by a high density of artifacts. The lower zone radiocarbon-dated to around 1,500–1,200 years ago and the upper to 280–260 years ago. Both cultural zones reflect a set of hunting-associated activities, including butchering of animals, cooking and preserving of meat and other foods, and repairing of gear. The range of artifact types found under the floor includes side-notched and stemmed arrow points and other stone tools; abundant stone flaking debris; ground-stone tools; fragmented mammal bones, some identified as mountain goat; fish bones; worked bone points; and marine shell. Hearth charcoal is abundant, especially in the upper component. At least two small, bowl-shaped cooking pits were discovered intact under the shelter floor.

The majority of stone artifacts consist of broken flakes and small pressure flakes removed during the resharpening and repair of bifacial tool edges; there is little evidence for manufacturing at the site of other than that of simple flake tools and flaked arrow points. Fifteen arrow points from the site exhibit small triangular blades and prominent shoulders formed by either corner or side notches; both notching styles are typical of upper Skagit River valley sites from the last 2,000 years, the period when bow-and-arrow technology appeared and saw widespread adoption.

Obsidian artifacts reveal that the rockshelter inhabitants utilized quality tool stone from distant sources to make their hunting tools. An assemblage of obsidian points, tools, and flaking debris ($n = 21$) from the site were geochemically correlated with the Whitewater Ridge and Obsidian Cliffs quarries in Oregon, indicating that Skagit people 2,000 years ago actively participated in the extensive regional exchange network. Some of the obsidian artifacts came from mysterious, presently unknown source areas, and the geochemical data suggests that at least five distinct sources remain to be discovered.

The rockshelter inhabitants, we now know, also participated in and perpetuated an ancient Skagit River tradition of reliance on Hozomeen chert, a distinctive tool stone found only in the northern Cascade Range of Washington and British Columbia. Upstream of Newhalem Rockshelter, this gray, flinty rock was quarried from numerous bedrock outcrops for at least 8,500 years, and its earliest use in the range has been dated at earlier than 9,000 years ago.

The rich assemblage of preserved animal remains shows that the inhabitants subsisted on a wide range of local fauna. Although mountain goat remains are rare in archaeological sites in the western United States, they are relatively abundant in the rockshelter deposits and serve to, among other things, reaffirm Skagit peoples' oral traditions and the linkage of the indigenous place name Newhalem with its origin in the ecology of this local mountain landscape.

Rockshelter inhabitants maintained social relationships with other indigenous bands, some of whom lived along saltwater, distant at least 50 miles from Newhalem. Two *Dentalium* shell

The dense forest outside the North Cascades National Park visitors' center in Newhalem.　[Robert R. Mierendorf]

A stunning view in the North Cascades National Park in Washington.　[Courtesy of the National Park Service]

fragments recovered from the site deposits offer supporting evidence for this. *Dentalium* occurs naturally along the Pacific coast, where it was collected from the sea floor. Pacific Northwest populations highly valued *Dentalium* for use as decorative beads and as a type of indigenous currency.

From a more general viewpoint, Newhalem rockshelter embodies the important qualities that archaeological sites contribute to furthering our understanding of native histories, especially where such histories are incomplete and poorly understood. The site data clearly addresses research problems relating to regional exchange networks, cultural chronology, chipped- and ground-stone technologies, and procurement and use of local faunal resources from lowland to subalpine mountain zones. The site also embodies cultural values important to the heritage, traditional beliefs and customs, and oral histories of Skagit River Indian bands. These site values and the information they contribute, furthermore, illuminate what has only recently become apparent—that northwest coast anthropology has historically failed to recognize the extent to which some interior coast Salish bands became mountain-oriented and, in so doing, adopted settlement and subsistence practices that depart significantly from their lowland, saltwater counterparts.

Newhalem Rockshelter is open to public visitation year-round. It is located near the park's Newhalem visitors' center, and directions to it can be obtained from NPS information staff at the visitors' center or at NPS information offices in Sedro Woolley and Marblemount, Washington. A small parking area near the trailhead signboard includes handicapped parking; the trail to the rockshelter is 1,000 feet long.

The interpretive panels were designed by National Park Service staff, including Ryan Keahu Booth, who is also of Upper Skagit descent. Roger Fernandez, a Salish artist, educator, and storyteller from Seattle, prepared the panel's sketches. For accuracy, Roger consulted with Taqʷšəblu (Vi Hilbert), a highly respected Upper Skagit Indian linguist, teacher, native Lushootseed speaker, and tribal elder.

Further Reading: Collins, June M., *Valley of the Spirits* (Seattle: University of Washington Press, 1974); Lane, Robert B., and Barbara Lane, "Indians and Indian Fisheries of the Skagit River System," in *Skagit Salmon Study*, Vol. 1: *Archeological Background, Mid-Project Report* (Sedro Woolley, WA: Upper Skagit Indian Tribe, 1977); Mierendorf, Robert R., *Chert Procurement in the Upper Skagit River Valley of the Northern Cascade Range, Ross Lake National Recreation Area, Washington*, Technical Report NPS/PNRNOCA/CRTR-93-001 (Sedro Woolley, WA: North Cascades National Park Service Complex, 1993); Mierendorf, Robert R., *An Updated Summary Statement of the Archeology of the North Cascades National Park Service Complex*, www.nps.gov/archive/noca/archeology1.htm (online May 1998); Suttles, Wayne, and Barbara Lane, "Southern Coast Salish," in *Handbook of North American Indians*, Vol. 7: *Northwest Coast*, edited by Wayne Suttles (Washington, DC: Smithsonian Institution Press, 1990), 485–502.

Robert R. Mierendorf

NEZ PERCE NATIONAL HISTORIC PARK

Idaho, Oregon, Montana, Washington
Nez Perce Sites and Sites of the Nez Perce War of 1877

Nez Perce National Historic Park was established in 1965 and it is unique in being the only national park associated with a single Native American tribe, the Nez Perce (or *Nimiipuu* in the Nez Perce language). The park is headquartered on the Nez Perce Indian Reservation at Spalding, Idaho, with the majority of the park consisting of small, widely scattered federal and private land holdings associated with sites of cultural and historical significance. The original twenty-four sites in north central Idaho have been expanded to thirty-eight located across Washington, Oregon, and Montana. The park is also associated with the 1,170-mile Nez Perce National Historic Trail, which follows the route of the Nez Perce War of 1877 from northeastern Oregon across Idaho and Wyoming into north central Montana and the 3,700-mile Lewis and Clark National Trail.

Archaeological investigations began in the vicinity of the park in the early 1960s, but no comprehensive programs have occurred and most excavations have been limited to brief investigations necessitated by construction and development. However, archaeologists have encountered prehistoric components at several Nez Perce cultural and historic sites that illustrate the antecedents of the ethnographic pattern. Based on archaeological investigations at sites within the park, as well as at adjacent locations, a cultural chronology spanning over 10,000 years has been established for the general area.

The most thorough investigations have occurred in the Clearwater River region in north central Idaho, which corresponds to the traditional center of Nez Perce country. Both of the earliest cultural phases found across the Columbia Plateau have been encountered here, and developments distinctive to the ancestors of the Nez Perce have been identified as beginning approximately 6,000 years ago.

The five-phase Clearwater River sequence (Sappington 1994) begins with the Windust phase (ca. 11,000–8,000 years ago), which is characterized by highly mobile foragers who made distinctive lanceolate Windust projectile points and hunted large and medium-size game; there is no evidence of the use of plants or fish or of residential structures during this time. The subsequent Cascade phase (ca. 8,000–4,000 years ago) is widely considered to be a direct successor, and it is associated with two hallmark tools: the leaf-shaped Cascade point and the edge-ground cobble. Edge-ground cobbles are generally assumed to represent the initiation of the use of plant resources.

Significant changes in settlement and subsistence occur across the Northwest following the Cascade phase, and in the Clearwater River region this development has been designated as the Hatwai phase (ca. 6,000–3,000 years ago). While aspects of the Cascade phase continued elsewhere, the middle prehistoric Hatwai phase represents the first house pit villages and the shift to resources characteristic of the ethnographic pattern—specifically, the focus on fishing and the use of mortars and pestles for processing root crops. The late prehistoric Ahsahka phase (ca. 3,000–500 years ago) represents the successful expansion of sedentary village life, and sites are relatively common during this period. The protohistoric Kooskia phase (ca. 500–200 years ago) represents a continuation of the late prehistoric lifeway and Euro-American material culture such as glass beads and metal items. With the adoption of horses around AD 1730, settlement shifted to shallower and more portable structures made of mats and hides, such as those described by the first Euro-Americans to visit the area, the members of the Lewis and Clark Corps of Discovery, in 1805.

IDAHO

The Spalding site is associated with the first missionary among the Nez Perce. Henry Harmon Spalding established his mission here in 1836, and the area later became the setting for the Indian Agency as well as the historic community of Spalding. Both historic and prehistoric archaeological investigations have been conducted here to facilitate development and interpretation of this site. The site was occupied as early as 11,000 years ago, with evidence of a Windust phase occupation followed by house pits from the Ahsahka phase. Historic archaeologists have located features from the mission as well as unique artifacts such as lead type used for the printing press that Spalding used to print documents, including translations of portions of the New Testament into the Nez Perce language. Artifacts from archaeological sites and ethnographic items of cultural significance are on exhibit at the park visitors' center. Historic archaeology has also been conducted at nearby U.S. Army Fort Lapwai, which was a cavalry post from the 1860s until the 1880s.

The multi-component Lenore site was occupied from the Windust phase into the historic period, when it was the location of a short-lived 1860s gold rush "tent city" known as Slaterville. Relatively extensive excavations conducted from 1967 to 1971

prior to development of the highway rest area focused on several partially excavated house pits dating to the Ahsahka and Kooskia phases. Several interpretive signs are on site.

Canoe Camp is another multi-component site best known for being the setting for the canoes constructed by the west-bound Lewis and Clark expedition in September–October 1805. Test excavations in the 1980s did not find any evidence of the expedition, but a 700-year-old house pit demonstrates that the ancestors of the Nez Perce were living here well prior to the historic period. Subsequent excavations have encountered additional house pits and moved the date of the late prehistoric occupation back to more than 2,000 years ago.

Hasotino Village, at Hells Gate State Park, is an ethnographic Nez Perce village associated with lamprey ("eel") fishing. Test excavations at this site on the lower Snake River encountered house pits associated with fishing and hunting tools as well as numerous faunal remains that were radiocarbon-dated at over 4,000 years old, which ties the site to the Tucannon phase on the lower Snake River and is contemporaneous with the Hatwai phase on the nearby Clearwater River. The adjacent *Wewukiyepuh* site had a Windust phase occupation, with lithic tools associated with the remains of grizzly bear and elk as well as two radiocarbon dates of around 10,200 years ago, which makes it one of the oldest known sites in the area (Sappington and Schuknecht 2001).

Buffalo Eddy is located on both sides of the Snake River in Hells Canyon, and this site has some of the best-known petroglyphs in the region. Boulders contain diverse images that represent at least three styles associated with the central Columbia Plateau, western Montana, and the Great Basin (Keyser 1992).

Tolo Lake, near Grangeville, was the setting of the last camp by the Wallowa band of the Nez Perce prior to the war of 1877. When the 30-acre natural lake was drained in 1994, mammoth remains were found. Extensive excavations in 1994–95 revealed evidence of six to eight mammoths as well as bison. Several lithic tools were found nearby in disturbed contexts and could not be associated with the megafauna.

The 1877 Clearwater Battlefield is located near the confluence of the middle and south forks of the Clearwater at Kamiah, and several significant archaeological sites have been examined in this vicinity. The Grove Mammoth site contained the remains of a mammoth radiocarbon-dated at around 13,000 years ago, but there was no direct association with humans. Excavations at Kooskia Bridge and Kooskia National Fish Hatchery documented villages at both locations, with occupations ranging from the late Cascade phase well into the twentieth century. Kooskia Hatchery includes the Looking Glass Campsite, where the Nez Perce leader was based in 1877, and artifacts associated with the conflict there were recovered by archaeologists in 1991. Numerous other cultural sites are located in the vicinity of Kooskia and Kamiah, such as the rock outcrop known as the Heart of the Monster, which is associated with the origin of the Nez Perce.

Weis Rockshelter was excavated in the early 1960s and provided the basis for the initial cultural chronology for the region, with occupations dated to the Cascade phase and later (Butler 1962). The nearby Grave Creek site on the lower Salmon River shows evidence of a possible pre–Windust phase occupation dated at over 11,000 years ago (Davis 2001).

The Nez Perce War began at the White Bird Battlefield in August 1877. Archaeological investigations have identified features such as rifle pits and recovered cartridges and other items from the conflict. Other park sites in Idaho are associated with historic figures and events—including fur traders, Protestant and Catholic missionaries and churches, skirmishes in the Nez Perce War, camas gathering, and rock formations—but they have not been evaluated by archaeologists.

WASHINGTON

In addition to Buffalo Eddy there are two other park sites in Washington. Most survivors of the Nez Perce War were not allowed to return to their traditional country, and many settled on the Colville Indian Reservation in 1885. Chief Joseph lived here until his death in 1904, and he is buried in the Nez Perce Cemetery at Nespelem. Historic Nez Perce Campsites are located nearby. Excavations in Lake Roosevelt, including the famous fishing and trading site at Kettle Falls on the Columbia River, have demonstrated that the general area has been inhabited for most of the past 10,000 years (Chance and Chance 1985a).

OREGON

Northeastern Oregon was the traditional homeland of the Wallowa band of the Nez Perce, and park sites here include the Joseph Canyon Viewpoint and the Grave of Old Chief Joseph, the father of young Chief Joseph, a Nez Perce leader during the 1877 war. Excavations have recently occurred at Dug Bar in Hells Canyon National Recreation Area, where the Nez Perce crossed the Snake River into Idaho prior to the conflict in 1877. There are eleven recorded archaeological sites here dating from 2,000 years ago into the recent period, with prehistoric settlement, ethnographic use, and rock art sites identified as well as historic mining and ranching sites.

MONTANA

All three park sites in Montana are associated with the Nez Perce War. Canyon Creek is the location where the Nez Perce left Yellowstone National Park and engaged in a rearguard action with the U.S. cavalry. Historical archaeology has documented features and recovered artifacts associated with the conflicts at the Big Hole National Battlefield in August 1877 and the Bear Paw Battlefield, where the nearly four-month war ended on October 5, 1877.

Further Reading: Butler, B. Robert, *Contributions to the Prehistory of the Columbia Plateau*, Occasional Paper No. 9 (Pocatello: Idaho State College Museum, 1962); Chance, David H., and Jennifer V. Chance, *Kettle Falls: 1978*, Anthropological Reports, No. 84 (Moscow: University of Idaho, 1985a); Chance, David H., and Jennifer V. Chance, *Archaeology at Spalding 1978 & 1979*, Anthropological Reports, No. 85 (Moscow: University of Idaho, 1985b); Davis, Loren, "The Coevolution of Early Hunter-Gatherer Culture and Riparian Ecosystems in the Southern Columbia River Plateau," Ph.D. diss. (Department of Anthropology, University of Alberta, and Bureau of Land Management, Cottonwood Field Office, 2001); Keyser, James. D., *Indian Rock Art of the Columbia Plateau* (Seattle: University of Washington Press, 1992); National Park Service, *Nez Perce Country*, Handbook 121 (Washington, DC: 1983); Nez Perce, National Park Service Web site, http://www.nps.gov/nepe/siteindex.htm; Sappington, Robert Lee, *The Prehistory of the Clearwater River Region, North Central Idaho*, Anthropological Reports, No. 95 (Moscow: University of Idaho, 1994); Sappington, Robert Lee, and Sarah Schucknecht-McDaniel, "Wewukiyepuh (10-NP-336): Contributions of an Early Holocene Windust Phase Site to Lower Snake River Prehistory," *North American Archaeologist* 22(4) (2001): 353–370; Scott, Douglas D., *A Sharp Little Affair: The Archaeology of the Big Hole Battlefield*, Reprints in Anthropology, Vol. 45 (Lincoln, NE: J & L Reprint Co., 1994).

Robert Lee Sappington

WHITMAN MISSION, FORT SPOKANE, SPOKANE HOUSE, ST. PAUL'S MISSION, AND OTHER SITES

Washington State

Historic Period Sites in the Plateau Region

The historic period begins with Lewis and Clark in eastern Washington and was a time of massive transformation of Native societies as Europeans and then Americans traversed, traded, settled, and gained military control of the region and ultimately dominated the landscape.

Although Lewis and Clark represented the first American presence in the area along the Snake and lower Columbia rivers in 1805–06, they were closely followed by Canadian fur traders such as David Thompson of the Northwest Company from Montreal, Quebec, who established Spokane House in 1810.

Spokane House, now part of the Washington River Side State Park, located east of the current city of Spokane, reflects the dynamic nature of the fur trade and the first European settlement in the eastern part of the state.

Established by the Northwest Company, it was taken over by the Hudson's Bay Company, which came to dominate the fur trade in Washington during the mid-1800s. Located along the confluence of the Spokane and Little Spokane rivers, this outpost reflected the evolution of a multicultural European, English, French, and Native American trader economy based on the trading needs of Native society and the expanding European capital markets for furs.

Archaeological excavations at Spokane House have revealed the changing configuration of the establishment, and archaeologists have recovered samples of fur trade artifacts that are now on display at the interpretive center, open to the public from Memorial Day through Labor Day.

An hour's drive north of the city of Spokane is the St. Paul's Mission in Kettle Falls. This Catholic mission, established by Father Peter de Smet of the Society of Jesuits in 1845, was rebuilt in the distinctive French Canadian style of post-and-log construction and exemplifies the mutually supportive relationship between the Hudson's Bay Company and the Catholic Church that served the French Canadian traders and the Native tribes who were increasingly participating in the fur trade.

Also part of the Washington state park system, and representing another fur trade establishment, is Fort Okanogan, established by Alexander Ross and David Stewart of the American Pacific Fur Company in 1811. This site represents the first American settlement and rival to the Canadian fur Traders. Located two hours east of the city of Spokane, the Fort Okanogan Interpretive Center is open from mid-May through August. Archaeological investigations by the National Park Service have yielded a large collection of fur trade artifacts and identified the structural elements of the establishment, its stockades, and its individual buildings. After the Hudson's Bay Company took over this fort in 1821, it became a way station and trans-shipment point in the movement of buffalo hides and products from the east to the north into Canada.

The decline of the fur trade and the increased migration of Americans over the Oregon Trail changed the nature of Native American, Canadian, and American interactions. The nature of the relationship between migrant Americans and the resident tribes and Canadian fur traders is perhaps best illustrated at Waiilatpu, also known as the Whitman Mission, located just west of the city of Walla Walla, Washington. The American Reverend Marcus Whitman and his wife established this mission in 1836 among the existing fur trader and Native American community referred to as Frenchtown. The

Canadian fur traders had settled in the area and formed relationships with local tribal communities. However, the establishment of the mission and its evolution into a major stop on the Oregon Trail precipitated a clash of cultures between the American settlers and the local tribal communities they were displacing. These communities experienced heavy rates of mortality from imported diseases associated with the migrants and the increasing trade, transportation, and communication with them.

The "clash of cultures" erupted into violence and slaughter on November 29, 1847, when the Whitmans and twelve others were killed and other people at the mission held hostage until being ransomed and brought to safety by Hudson Bay Company officials. The killings resulted in the formation of an Oregon volunteer militia, who initiated a string of killings that triggered the Indian Wars, which continued for a decade.

The immediate response to the killing of the Whitmans and the resulting militia actions against the local tribes led to the formation of the Oregon Territory and the expansion of military action against the Native American communities. Ultimately, this resulted in the negotiation of treaties by which tribes ceded the land and were forced to relocate on reservations. Today the Whitman Mission is part of the National Park Service and is open to the public. The most notable feature is the great grave containing the remains of those killed that November day.

The period that witnessed the establishment of the reservation system, mass relocations, and the forced assimilation of Native American communities is illustrated at the Fort Spokane Military Reserve, approximately one hour's travel northwest of the city of Spokane at the confluence of the Spokane and Columbia rivers. This fort, established in 1882, served a dual purpose as the U.S. Army's base for controlling local tribes on the newly formed reservations as well as a means of protecting them from American miners entering the region.

Initially established as a military outpost, Fort Spokane became an Indian Agency office in 1899 and served as an Indian boarding school. The opposition of Indian parents to their children's being sent away from home led to the school's closure. Today the complex is open to visitors, and a number of the buildings have been restored to reflect the period of military occupancy.

Further Reading: Newman, Peter C., *Empire of the Bay: The Company of Adventurers That Seized a Continent* (New York: Penguin, 2000); Thompson, Erwin N., *Whitman Mission: National Historic Site, Washington*, Historical Handbook Series, No. 37 (Washington, DC: National Park Service, 1964); Van Kirk, Sylvia, *Many Tender Ties: Women in Fur-Trade Society, 1670–1870* (Tulsa: University of Oklahoma Press, 1983).

Robert Whitlam

GLOSSARY

Accelerator Mass Spectrometric (AMS) Dating. A method of radiocarbon dating precise enough to count the proportion of carbon isotope (carbon 14) atoms directly and reducing the size of the sample of material required for accurate dating dramatically.

Anasazi (Ancestral Puebloan) Cultural Tradition. A well-known ancient cultural tradition that existed in the "Four Corners" area of the Colorado Plateau, around the common corners of Colorado, Utah, Arizona, and New Mexico, beginning about AD 900 and lasting until about AD 1300. Anasazi is the older and more traditional term used by archaeologists to refer to Ancestral Puebloan people. Many well-known sites are associated with this tradition, for example, the ancient architectural sites of Mesa Verde, Chaco Canyon, and Canyons of the Ancients National Monument (see the essays by Steve Lekson, Wirt Wills [on Shabik'eschee Village site], Paul Reed [Overview of Chaco Canyon], Jill Neitzel, Tom Windes, LouAnn Jacobson, John Kantner, Cathy Cameron, and Mark Varien in the Southwest section).

Archaic. A general term used to refer to a time period that encompasses the early Holocene from about 10,000 to 3,000 years ago, but varying in different regions. Developments during the Archaic included the manufacture of ground stone tools, the beginnings of food cultivation, and initial settled life. In some parts of North America this time period is divided into three sub-periods: the Early, Middle, and Late portions.

Assemblage. A group of artifacts recurring together at different places or times. Assemblages may be associated with particular activities or with a cultural tradition.

Atl atl. A spear-, arrow-, or dart-throwing tool. These are composite tools usually with several parts, including an antler or wood handle, a weight, and a hooked end. The atl atl works as a lever to propel the projectile for greater distance and with greater force.

Avocational archaeologist. Individuals with a serious interest in archaeology, but who do not engage in the discipline as their profession. Many avocational archaeologists have made important archaeological discoveries and contributions to our understanding of the ancient or historic pasts.

Basketmaker. A term used to refer to the early portion of the Ancestral Puebloan cultural tradition. Early Basketmaker people relied on hunting and gathering for much of their food, but during this period, domesticated plants, such as corn, beans, and squash, were added to the diet. During this period, ways of life became more settled and more permanent houses, called "pithouses" because they were dug partly below ground became common. Coiled and twined basketry also is common, and people began to make plain pottery for the first time.

Biface. A stone tool that has been chipped on both sides to shape and thin it.

Blade tool manufacture and technology. Blade manufacture is a quite different method of making flaked stone cutting and piercing tools than that employed in making chipped stone tools, such as a bifacial point or knife. The latter involves shaping, thinning, and sharpening a single piece of stone. In blade manufacture, a nodule of stone is carefully prepared to form a core so that multiple, long, narrow, parallel-sided flakes with very sharp edges can be struck. These "blades" then are used as knives for cutting, or snapped into segments that can be inserted into slots on the sides of antler or wooden points to form the cutting edges. Knives can also be made this way. One advantage of this technique over biface manufacture is that large cutting and piercing tools can be made using small pieces of stone when large pieces are not available.

Cation ratio dating. Cation ratio dating is used to date rocks that have a modified surface such as prehistoric rock carvings (petroglyphs). This is a relative dating technique that is not considered an accurate method of dating by some professional archaeologists.

Rocks are covered by a kind of varnish, a chemically-changed layer caused by weathering that builds up over time. The change in the rock varnish is due to calcium and potassium seeping out of the rock. The cation ratio is determined by scraping the varnish from the carved or petroglyph surface back to the original rock surface and making a comparison of the two. The technique relies on change due to weathering of the stone over long periods of time, so geographically distinctive patterns are needed to compare the original surfaces with the modern suface that show the results of weathering.

Chert. A type of very fine-grained stone rich in silica. It is often found in or weathered from limestone deposits. It was shaped into chipped stone tools, and sometimes for blade tools, using stone and bone or antler hammers.

Chipped Stone tools. Tools shaped and thinned by systematically flaking exterior portions off. Typically this manufacturing technique is used with very fine-grained stone (e.g., obsidian, chert, or flint) that can be flaked relatively easily because it fractures smoothly in a way that can be controlled manufacturing techniques skillfully applied.

Clovis. Clovis is a term used to name an archaeological culture, a time period, and a particular variety of fluted stone spear points or knives. The name derives from Clovis, New Mexico, near which is located the type site, Blackwater Draw. Clovis spear points have been found in direct association with extinct megafauna in ice age gravel deposits The Clovis culture is known to have occupied many parts of North America during the Paleoindian period. The distinctive Clovis spear point has a vertical flake scar or flute on both faces of the point that extends about 1/3 its length. Sites containing Clovis points have been dated across North America to between 13,500 and 10,800 years ago. In western North America Clovis points have been found with the killed and butchered remains of large animals like mammoth or mastodon. As a result, Clovis peoples are assumed to have targeted large game animals, although how much of their diet actually came from hunting, much less from large game, is unknown (see the essays by David Anderson in the Southeast section and Bonnie Pitblado and Dennis Stanford in the Great Plains and Rocky Mountain section).

Component. A culturally homogenous stratigraphic unit within an archaeological site.

Core. A lithic artifact used as the source from which other tools, flakes, or blades are struck.

CRM (Cultural Resource Management). This activity includes archaeological investigations done as part of public project planning required by federal or state laws to ensure that important archaeological sites are not wantonly destroyed by public undertakings. CRM also includes the long term management of archaeological resources that are on public lands and for which legal protections and preservation is required of the public agencies that administer these lands (see the general introduction for more details abut contemporary CRM in North America).

Dalton. Term used to refer to an archaeological culture dating to the end of the Paleoindian period and the beginning of the Archaic time period. Dalton artifacts and sites are recognized in the Midwest, Southeast, and Northeast of North America. The point distribution shows that there was a widespread Dalton lifeway oriented toward streams and deciduous forests. Dalton culture people were hunters and gatherers using a variety of wild animal and plant foods over the course of each year. Timber and nuts were important as raw materials and food. Like Paleoindians, Dalton groups probably consisted of families related by kinship and mutual dependence (see the essay by Dan Morse in the Southeast section).

Debitage. Stone debris from chipped-stone tool manufacturing or maintenance activities.

Desert Culture. Ancient cultural groups that occupied the present-day Great Basin and Plateau regions. They created a distinctive cultural adaptation to the dry, relatively impoverished environments of these regions. The Cochise or Desert Archaic culture began by about 7000 BC and persisted until about AD 500.

Earthfast foundation. Earthfast (also known as "post-in-the-ground") architecture was the most prevalent building tradition of 17th-century Virginia and Maryland. At its core, the typical "Virginia House" (as dwellings of this type were sometimes called) consisted of pairs of hewn wooden posts set into deep, regularly-spaced holes dug into the ground. Once set in the ground and backfilled, these posts were either pegged on nailed together with cross beams to form the sides and gables of a rectangular, A-framed structure. The exterior "skins" of such earthfast structures varied. Some were both roofed and sided with riven wooden clapboards. Others were sided in wattle-and-daub and roofed with thatch. Irrespective of their construction, earthfast structures tended to be rather impermanent, lasting no more than perhaps a decade or two at most in the hot, humid Chesapeake region.

Effigy pipes. A variation on the plain stone tube pipe carved in the likeness of an animal. A wide variety of animal images—birds, mammals, and reptiles—are used for these pipes which are frequently associated with the Adena and Hopewell cultures in the Midwest region.

Feature. Usually refers to types of archaeological deposits related to a particular focused activity or event. For example, hearths, garbage or trash pits, storage pits, and foundations or other architectural remnants are referred to generally as features.

Flotation. A technique for recovering very small organic remains, such as tiny pieces of charcoal, seeds, bone, wood, and other items. A soil sample is placed in a drum of water, sometimes mixed with other liquids. The liquid is agitated to loosen any soil from the organic material. This material, being lighter than water, floats to the surface and can be skimmed off using a fine mesh screen. The organic materials can be used in a variety of analyses, for example, to interpret diet, subsistence activities, for dating, and to determine use of wood for tools or structures.

Gorgets. Made of copper, shell or polished or smoothed stone these thin, often oval artifacts were often perforated by two or more holes and worn around the neck.

Hohokam Cultural Tradition. Hohokam refers to the Sonoran Desert region of Phoenix and Tucson in southern Arizona and further south. The Hohokam region witnessed remarkable cultural developments beginning about AD 900. In this general area, about 200 sites with large oval, earthen features (interpreted as local expressions of Mesoamerican ball courts) have been found. A distinctive cluster of large sites in the area of modern Phoenix clearly represent the Hohokam center. Hohokam had red-on-buff pottery, large towns composed of scores of courtyard groups (three to five single-room thatch houses facing inward into a small courtyard or patio), and ball courts. There were regular markets for the exchange of goods supported by canal-irrigated farming (see Steve Lekson's essay on the classic period ancient Southwest).

Holocene. The most recent geological epoch, which began about 10,000 years ago. The period after the last glaciation in North America.

Hopewell Cultural Traditon. An archaeological tradition of the Midwest dated to the Middle Woodland period (about 50 BC to AD 400). The Hopewell tradition is known for a distinctive burial patterns and a wide-ranging exchange among communities. Communities hundreds, even thousands, of miles from one another participated in this exchange system and raw materials, as well as finished products were exported and imported. The Hopewell tradition also is known for the mounds that they built for ceremonial and burial purposes. It is known to be one of the most considerable achievements of Native Americans throughout the ancient past. These mounds, especially in the Ohio River valley are large complexes incorporating a variety of geometric shapes and rise to impressive heights (see essays in the Midwest section by George Milner, Douglas Charles, N'omi Greber, William Dancey, and Bradley Lepper).

Horizon. A set of cultural characteristics or traits that has a brief time depth but is found across multiple areas or regions.

Kiva. Among modern Pueblo Indian communities in the Southwest, a kiva is a nonresidential structure or room that is owned and used by specific social groups, such as clans or religious societies. The activities that take place in kivas are different than the daily, domestic activities—such as food preparation and pottery manufacture—that occur in dwellings. Because of this historic affiliation of sociopolitical functions with kivas, archaeologists use this term to refer to large pit structures lacking evidence for domestic functions that may have been used as public buildings, rather than household dwellings.

Lithic. Stone.

Loess. Fine-grained windblown sediment deposited as soil layers on areas not ice-covered during the last glaciation.

Megafauna. Large mammal species, such as mammoth, mastodon, bison, giant beaver, giant ground sloth, and stag elk that lived in North America during the late glacial and early post-glacial time periods. Many megafauna species have become extinct.

Midden. The archaeological remains of a human settlement's garbage and trash deposits. Middens typically are an accumulation of decomposed organic refuse usually very dark colored that frequently also contains thousands of discarded pieces of stone artifacts and ceramics, animal bones, nutshells, and other remains.

Mimbres Cultural Tradition. The Mimbres cultural development occurred in the Mogollon region of western New Mexico between about AD 900 and 1150. It is most famous for its remarkable black-on-white pottery. While the majority of Mimbres bowls are painted with striking geometric designs, images include depictions of people and events using an artistic style that merits inclusion in the world's major art museums. Images also show Mimbres' wide interests: Pacific Ocean fish, tropical birds from western Mexico (and, perhaps, monkeys from the same area), and armadillos (see essays by Steve Lekson [Classic Period Cultural and Social Interaction], Karen Schollmeyer, Steve Swanson, and Margaret Nelson, and J. J. Brody in the Southwest section).

Mississippian Cultural Tradition. A widespread tradition centered on Midwestern and Southeastern North America beginning about AD 1000 and lasting in some places until AD 1600. Typically societies that were part of this cultural tradition had chiefdom level political organizations, had subsistence systems based on intensive agricultural production of corn, beans, squash, and other domesticated plants, and built settlements that incorporated earthen architecture, typically various kinds and sizes of mound architecture. Mississippian chiefdoms flourished across much of the Eastern Woodlands: as far north as Illinois and southern Wisconsin; as far west as eastern Oklahoma; as far east as the Carolinas and Georgia; and south to Florida and the Gulf Coast (see essays by Robin Beck in the Southeast section and Mary Beth Turbot in the Midwest section).

Mogollon Cultural Tradition. An ancient Southwestern cultural tradition dating between about A.D. 200 and 1450. The tradition is found in a vast, ecologically diverse geographic area in southwestern New Mexico, southeastern Arizona and northwestern Mexico. Mogollon takes its name from the mountain range and highlands that separate the Anasazi and Hohokam regions. The Mogollon area witnessed remarkable cultural development referred to as the Mimbres after the river in southwest New Mexico where this development was centered (see essays by Steve Lekson [Classic Period Cultural and Social Interaction] and Wirt Wills [the SU site] in the Southwest section).

Paleoindian (Paleoamerican) Cultural Tradition. The Paleoindian time frame extends from approximately 13,500 to 9,000 BC and is found in almost all parts of North America. It is the earliest widely recognized archaeological cultural tradition in North America. The Clovis culture is the earliest Paleoindian culture, but there are increasing numbers of investigations of sites that are purported to be older than the Clovis or Paleoindian tradition.

Pit. A hole in the earth constructed and used for cooking, storage, or garbage or trash disposal. Pits are a common kind of archaeological feature.

Pithouse. Pithouses typically are single room dwellings, although some have antechambers. Pithouses are semi-subterranean dwellings in which some portions of the walls consist of the sides of an excavated pit. They are constructed by excavating a large hole or pit, building a timber framework inside the pit, then covering the framework with the excavated dirt, resulting in a house that is very thermally efficient, but prone to rapid deterioration, depending on the climate, from the effects of moisture, as well as vermin infestation.

Pleistocene. The geological epoch dating from 1.8 million to 10,000 years ago. During the last part of the Pleistocene human populations began to migrate into North America. The end of this epoch is a period of repeated glaciations in North America. It is succeeded by the Holocene era.

Postmolds. The archaeological remains of timbers, posts, saplings, or other wood structural elements of former buildings or dwellings. Depending on the age and soil conditions, posts placed in the ground ultimately will decay into fragments or mere stains indicating where these portions of buildings once existed.

Prehistory, prehistoric. Regarded by some as a demeaning term indicating primitive, but, most often used simply to refer to the general period of time prior to written records. As such, the length of the prehistoric period for different parts of North America varies according to when written records are available, generally associated with the beginning of European contact with aboriginal cultures.

Radiocarbon Dating (also known as Carbon-14 [^{14}C] Dating). An absolute dating method that measures the decay of the radioactive isotope of carbon (^{14}C) in organic material.

Steatite (Soapstone). A metamorphic rock, composed largely of the mineral talc and relatively soft. Steatite has been used as a medium for carving for thousands of years. Steatite also was carved out in ancient times to create bowls, in particular in places and at times before pottery had begun to be produced.

Taphonomy. The study of the process of fossilization. Used in archaeology to examine the human and natural changes that produce the archaeological record. For example, changes to organic materials after the death of the organism, such as how bone is changed by chemical, mechanical or animal processes after burial.

Tradition. An archaeological concept indicating a consistent set of cultural characteristics and traits that has great time depth and covers a recognized area.

Wattle-and-daub construction. A building technique using poles placed vertically in the ground and then plastered over with mud to construct the walls. Usually structures of wattle and daub were topped with thatched roofs.

Woodland Time Period. A time period term used mainly in the eastern North America south of Canada between roughly 1000 BC and AD 1000. In the Midwest region the Woodland period is regarded as the centuries between Archaic times and the Mississippian period. During this long period, the technology of pottery developed and spread, social and political complexity increased, cultivated plants changed from a supplemental part of diet to dietary staples, and settlements grew from small groups of residences to some of the largest cities in the world at that time.

Younger Dryas. A cold climatic event that took place from 12,900–11,600 years ago. It was a rapid return to glacial conditions during the longer term transition from the last glacial maximum to modern climatic conditions.

Sources used for definitions: The definitions in this glossary are derived from a number of sources, including essays in this encyclopedia, and the following texts:

Renfrew, Colin and Paul Bahn (2000). *Archaeology: Theories, Methods, and Practice*, third edition. Thames and Hudson, London and New York.

Thomas, David Hurst (1991). *Archaeology: Down to Earth*. Harcourt Brace Jovanovich College Publishers, Fort Worth and New York.

INDEX

A page number followed by *i* indicates an illustration; *m* indicates a map; *t* indicates a table.